Y0-BHW-118

Ye Sylvan Archer
Volume VI
January 1940 - December 1941
Edited by J. E. Davis

Derrydale Press
1994

contents

Ye Sylvan Archer	January 1940	Vol. 11 No. 9
Ye Sylvan Archer	February 1940	Vol. 11 No. 10
Ye Sylvan Archer	March 1940	Vol. 11 No. 11
Ye Sylvan Archer	April 1940	Vol. 11 No. 12
Ye Sylvan Archer	May 1940	Vol. 12 No. 1
Ye Sylvan Archer	June 1940	Vol. 12 No. 2
Ye Sylvan Archer	July 1940	Vol. 12 No. 3
Ye Sylvan Archer	August 1940	Vol. 12 No. 4
Ye Sylvan Archer	September 1940	Vol. 12 No. 5
Ye Sylvan Archer	October 1940	Vol. 12 No. 6
Ye Sylvan Archer	November 1940	Vol. 12 No. 7
Ye Sylvan Archer	December 1940	Vol. 12 No. 8
Ye Sylvan Archer	January 1941	Vol. 12 No. 9
Ye Sylvan Archer	February 1941	Vol. 12 No. 10
Ye Sylvan Archer	March 1941	Vol. 12 No. 11
Ye Sylvan Archer	April 1941	Vol. 12 No. 12
Ye Sylvan Archer	May 1941	Vol. 13 No. 1
Ye Sylvan Archer	June 1941	Vol. 13 No. 2
Ye Sylvan Archer	July 1941	Vol. 13 No. 3
Ye Sylvan Archer	August 1941	Vol. 13 No. 4
Ye Sylvan Archer	September 1941	Vol. 13 No. 5
Ye Sylvan Archer	October 1941	Vol. 13 No. 6
Ye Sylvan Archer	November 1941	Vol. 13 No. 7
Ye Sylvan Archer	December 1941	Vol. 13 No. 8

Ye Sylvan Archer

January, 1940

Corvallis, Oregon

Vol. 11   No. 9

Ye Sylvan Archer

Vol. 11   January, 1940   No. 9

Published the fifteenth of each month
for archers by archers
505 North 11th Street, Corvallis, Oregon

J. E. DAVIS .... Editor
RUSSELL JONES .... Business Manager
Subscription Price .... $1.00 Per Year
Foreign Subscription .... $1.25 Per Year
Single Copies .... 10 Cents
Advertising Rates on Application

TABLE OF CONTENTS

	Page
PASSING THE BUCK By Erle Stanley Gardner	1
NATIONAL FIELD ARCHERY ASSOCIATION By John L. Yount	5
EDITORIAL	6
WITH OUR ADVERTISERS By Russell Jones	7
THE OLD TIMER	7
FIELD ARCHERS OF SOUTHERN CALIFORNIA By Elmer W. Bedwell	8
SOUTHERN CALIFORNIA ASSOCIATION	8
LOS ANGELES CLUB	8
LETTER BOX	9
DOGHOUSE SCIENCE By Dr. Paul Bunyan	10

Passing the Buck

By Erle Stanley Gardner

All of my life I have learned things the hard way. I got my legal training scrubbing floors and cleaning cuspidors in law offices. Gradually I worked up to briefing, and eventually passed the bar exams when I was twenty-two. I was the "innocent bystander" in a hectic political fight, tried to get fair play for the underdog and had a bunch of local polititions try to run me out of town.

When the smoke of battle cleared away, I found I'd built up a law practice—the hard way.

When I started writing, I waded knee-deep through a steady stream of rejection slips, to reach my goal. There's doubtless an easy way to drift through life—I've never found it.

Which means that I'm learning bow and arrow hunting the hard way. I've hunted from Mexico to Canada. I've been with Dusty Roberts when he killed one of the "small deer" on Cedros Island (one arrow at sixty-one yards after an all-day hunt). I've been with B. G. Thompson and the Catheys in British Columbia on their famous moose hunt. Mostly I've sort of held back on my own shooting, getting as much or more kick out of watching the other fellow's shots as from my own.

I'm just back from a hunting trip with Paul Klopsteg and Walther Buchen. It was the most unusual hunting trip I've ever taken in my life. I've hunted deer with a bow and arrow for going on fifteen years, and all the shots I've ever had until this last trip, could have been counted on the fingers of one hand. I didn't believe there was any place in the country where deer were so plentiful a man could literally see them by the hundred, and get shots by the dozen.

Well, there is.

I've been there. I've learned something about hunting deer with a bow and arrow. I've learned the hard way. I've missed about two dozen shots at distances under a hundred yards. I've seen Buchen and Klopsteg, who are much better shots than I, miss half a dozen or so shots each.

Lady Luck was against us. That much is certain.

But there are other elements which entered into the situation. In the first place, we weren't prepared for deer shooting. We hadn't taken the right course of training. I doubt if one archer in a thousand has taken the right course of training, or has even stopped to figure out what it is.

We like to hear stories of success. Hunters like to tell stories of success. We read too much about how "I drew the arrow back to the head and loosed. The shaft flew true and struck the deer just back of the shoulder." How many stories do we hear of misses? Virtually none.

I'm going to tell the story of a series of misses, and of why they were misses. Next year I'm going to write a story of success. I've learned a lot from my misses, and those of my companions. Because I think there's a lot of interesting conclusions to be drawn from what I've learned, I'm going to let my back hair down and tell the FACTS, plain, unvarnished facts.

All of my previous training in distance shooting has been at objects on the ground. I'm no great shakes as a bow and arrow shot, but give me a chance at a rabbit or a quail, and I'll connect once in a while.

Buchen and Klopsteg have shot mostly on target ranges.

Our preliminary training was all wrong.

A deer has his legs on the ground, but you can't get venison for dinner by shooting a deer in the leg. A bale of straw rests on the ground. Theoretically, a man can shoot at a bale of straw, pick a point three feet above the ground as his mark, and thereby learn how to shoot at deer. Actually, it just doesn't work out that way.

I don't know to just what extent the element of luck actually entered into our hunt. I doubt if anyone does.

It entered into it. That much is certain. The breaks were against us. Time after time my companions and I shot at deer around seventy yards, the arrows absolutely perfect so far as alignment was concerned, but with a difference of about two feet in elevation between the arrows. The body of the deer occupied that two feet.

That was luck—in a large measure.

I was inclined to figure the distance of the deer in terms of arrow trajectory (I seldom translate distance into yards) as being at the point where the deer stood on the ground. Once I clipped hair from a big buck. Several times I saw arrows from the bows of my companions come so close the feathers grazed the deer's back.

With one or two exceptions, the line of the shots was so accurate as to be, for all practical purposes, perfect. But where we fell down was in judging range in terms of arrow trajectory.

When Walther Buchen wrote that he had a ranch staked out where deer were so plentiful we could be certain of shots, I took the statement with a pinch of salt and a barrel of pepper. I knew there just wasn't any such place.

There are lots of places where you can be "guaranteed" shots. They're will-o'-the-wisps, hunting mirages which a hunter chases around the country. There's always some reason why the shots aren't there, at the time you get there.

I've hunted all over the country, going from state to state, place to place. I've seen a few deer missed, and a few killed, but the shots have been just the lucky breaks a hunter will see in years of hunting.

But, brothers, the HF Bar Ranch in Wyoming, a few miles out of Buffalo, has everything—even if I didn't believe it when I got off the plane.

I like to travel and I like adventure. Several times I've gone to "absolutely primitive" countries. Usually there's been someone along who took trinkets to "trade to the natives." That's been a laugh. The "natives" usually knew more of money, and rates of foreign exchange, than the members of my party ever thought of knowing. So, a few years ago, when I went off the beaten track into the South Sea Islands, and a couple of the gang took trinkets along, I laughed into my sleeve with a cynical and knowing chuckle. But this was the time that comes once in ten thousand blue moons. The natives had no particular use for money, but the stock of dime store trinkets purchased about ten thousand dollars worth of native curios. I, with my stock of francs (it was a French possession), was left stranded so far as purchasing power was concerned.

Now, the HF Bar Ranch is the ten thousandth blue moon in hunting —in fact, stalking was made difficult because the buck you were so carefully sneaking up on would be stampeded by a bunch of four or five deer you hadn't even seen. These would be deer standing within thirty or forty yards of you, invisible in the shade, and watching you with eagle-eyed curiosity. They'd start buck-jumping—and off would go the deer you had seen.

I sat perfectly still one day while a herd of thirty-two deer, including at least six fair sized, and two enormous, bucks, actually walked up to within fifteen paces of me. When it came time to jump up and shoot, there were so many does jumping and plunging that I had to wait several seconds to get one of the bucks sufficiently in the clear to risk a shot—but that's getting ahead of my story.

The HF Bar Ranch is a "guest" ranch, or a "dude" ranch, if you prefer to call it such. During the "season" for tourists, which is not the season for deer, there are a hundred or so "dudes" riding around the fifty thousand or so acres which comprise the ranch. When the tourist season ends, and the leaves on the trees start turning vivid yellows and browns, the ranch stays open for a select few of the hunters who straggle in.

Because one of the boys who run the place is an ardent archer, and another is rapidly going the same course, and because this year Wyoming has made the bow a legal weapon for deer shooting, there are thirty thousand acres of the BEST hunting set aside as an archery preserve.

In fact, that statement deserves a little amplification. Archers generally should doff their hats in tribute to "Jack" Horton, who quietly "sold" the state game authorities on bow and arrow shooting, and secured a change in the law.

He's a thorough sportsman, a quiet

spoken gentleman, who—Hell's bells, he's an ARCHER. 'Nuff said.

Anyhow, I've hunted a lot in places where you get taxed twenty to fifty dollars a day, including guides, grub and horses — and I haven't seen a heck of a lot of deer within bow and arrow range.

Out at the HF Bar Ranch you pay fifty-five bucks a week, and you get saddle horses—and if a day passes without adventure, spelled with a capital "A"—well, brother, I haven't seen that day yet, not at that ranch.

I'm mentioning this because within ten days I had more excitement, more experience, and learned more about hunting deer than I've had in fifteen years of batting around into the most primitive country I was able to find.

Bucks? Yes, we saw 'em. Shots? Yes, we got 'em.

I learned a lot of things some of you archers already know; but because they're things I haven't seen in print, I'm going to spill a few facts.

RANGE—A deer stands up from the ground. Don't make the mistake of shooting at the ground he's standing on—or of shooting under his tummy—belly to you.

TRAINING—Make a target consisting of a sack stuffed with straw. Stand it on stilts. Put a neck and head on it. Don't shoot several shots at it, but stick this target on a rise, or in a gully, come up on it, and shoot one shot. Then move the archer. After four tries, move the target.

ARROWS—There was a big difference of opinion as to whether the deer shooter should have a light, fast-flying arrow that would perhaps break with the first miss, or a heavy birch arrow with lots of spine that could be shot over and over. Use your own judgment. I'm not going to stick my neck out.

It all gets back to the question of judging range.

However, there's one thing I will tell you. Judging deer range is different from judging rabbit range, or quail range, or squirrel range, or animal-silhouette range. Examples? Proof? A rabbit jumped up on a rock, stood there for just a second before jumping into the little hole that was under the rock. Old man Gardner smacked an arrow straight into that rabbit's vitals. A squirrel ran up a tree. The old Gardner release got Mr. Squirrel right square in the bean. Ten minutes later, a deer jumped up, and old man Gardner shot just under his belly. I wasn't ac-

"The HF Bar Ranch Has Everything"

customed to shooting at deer marks at deer ranges.

I've stump-shot with Dr. Cathey off and on, and he's always picking a distant stump and saying, "Now, if that stump were a deer standing there—plunk!" I'm always picking little clumps of sage-brush a lot closer and saying, "Now, if that were a rabbit—etc."

I'm for the Cathey method now. But no stump on earth is going to give you deer practice—not unless you put it up on stilts.

ARROW RELEASE — Now, brother, you're getting right down to brass tacks. Some guys can release an arrow so there's just a whisper when the shaft leaves the bow. I can't. My arrows go pretty good—now (for years my half drawn arrows wobbled uncertainly toward their objective). But they sure do make a "slap" when they leave the bow.

Up in Wyoming, after I'd got most of the other things licked, I came up over a little rise and saw a pair of horns standing outlined against the skyline. I ducked and motioned for my companion to come up. By the time he got there, the deer had moved along about thirty yards. We both had shots that were at about sixty-five yards. My arrow was perfect. It was going right in a line for his heart. The range was judged correctly. The arrow was pulled clean back. It was going beautifully. BUT it slapped the bow.

The deer heard that sound. He didn't stop to see what made it or where it came from. Wild things live hair-trigger lives. They react instantly to any strange sound or scent. They move first and inquire afterwards. This deer swapped ends with neatness and dispatch. The arrow went where his heart had been. His tail was there when the arrow arrived. It clipped a few hairs from the end of his tail. Those hairs were still clinging to the serrated edges of the broadhead when I went to pick it up.

The deer? Oh yes, he was two hundred yards away.

But I hunt for adventure, for the thrill of the chase, for excitement which keys me to the highest pitch and makes me forget the problems of a mechanical and decadent civilization. I hunt for the companionship which comes to men who are gathered out in the wilds, away from the routine affairs of humdrum life.

I got what I went for.

I had a good time.

There isn't enough space available to tell half of the things we learned about deer shooting with a bow and arrow. It would take a book. And Buchen and Klopsteg have halfway promised to write that up completely in book form, or in the form of books.

The "s" meaning two or more. They took elaborate field notes, analyzed each shot, drew scientific conclusions.

Me? I had a good time.

I came back to the ranch house, to hot meals, pipes of fragrant tobacco, and the companionship of congenial friends, so emotionally exhausted from the exciting adventures of the day, that I was quivering all over. If a guy wants more than this from a hunting trip, he isn't an archer. He's a banker.

We'd spend the evenings in talk, discussions of the relative advantages of heavy vs. light arrows, of how to judge range, of how to get the does out of the way so there'd be a clear shot at the bucks, of the best places to go on the morrow—and then we'd just discuss.

Klopsteg has a ball-bearing mind of scientific precision. When he says seven, he doesn't mean six, point nine; or seven, point one. He means seven, naught, naught, naught. Buchen knows English language, logic and English literature as well as Brommers knows terms of opprobrium. His mind functions with the smooth acceleration of a sixteen cylinder motor in a ten thousand dollar car. Even his casual utterances have the polish of finished prose.

In the course of a legal career extending a quarter of a century, I've talked to a lot of juries, and listened to a lot of judges. But I learned more about putting one's adversary in a vocal encounter in the wrong in those ten evenings than I ever learned from my legal practice.

You see, a guy named Brommers had written them that Gardner was unbeatable in an argument. So I learned about the same way I learned about deer hunting—the hard way.

I'm hoping those two guys will will write some of the things we learned about deer habits and deer hunting, and will write more about

(Continued on page 11)

National Field Archery Ass'n
By John L. Yount

I am sorry that I haven't space in which to print all the fine letters that I have received in the last month showing the activities in field archery throughout the country, but I am going to take the liberty of quoting from a letter just received from Harry Glover, of Oakland, Calif.: "The boys can't seem to get enough tournaments up here and can hardly wait for the next one which is to be held on January 21. No one is so good that the tournaments are a walk-away, and most of the boys are right at that point where the competition is the toughest and there is a good chance for anyone to come out on top. Feathers, Peters, Spancel, and Poppy are all set for a terrific battle to get into the "Championship Class" and there is no telling how it will come out. We're going to have to start really shooting to stay in the class now, too. I have a lot of time to practice this winter and I can sure use it. I managed to shoot a 133 over fourteen targets the other day.

"We are putting up a nice new perpetual cup for the winner in the general division, and also starting a 'Championship Class' for the women at the next tournament, too. Do you have a 'Championship Class' for juniors down there?

"Just what do you fellows do about your targets during the winter? If past experience holds true all that we will have left on our courses after a few rains is a mass of mouldy straw."

After reading this letter, if there are any left who do not believe that field and instinctive archery can be made into a competitive sport complete within itself and of sufficient importance to occupy all the spare time any devotee has to give it I just wouldn't know how to go about convincing them.

In the same letter Harry mentions Herman Kinney and some of the boys as having returned from a bear hunt and that a number of the "White Company" of Oakland, his home club, are planning a pig hunt for this winter. This makes it quite evident that their organized and standard field shooting hasn't interfered with their hunting. Instead it has given them a real incentive to practice and a decent course to practice on. They agree with us that any group of field archers without a good permanent course is missing the grandest sport in archery. The temporary course set up for a single tournament is only a very poor substitute.

Now as to that hay in the winter time problem, this is what we do about it. To begin with we use the cheapest and not some extra fine, expensive kind. Then we make a wire stretcher. In case you don't know how to make one, get a piece of inch and a half pipe about 18 inches long, thread one end and put a T on. Then screw about 10 inches of one inch pipe into each side of the T for a handle. Now drill a quarter inch hole in the inch and a half pipe about one half inch from the open end, and that's all there is to it. For wire get some galvanized iron wire of whatever gauge you think best and put a small loop in one end, then run the wire around the bale to be repaired. Cut it off the proper length and run it through the loop. Then through the hole in the stretcher, grab the stretcher handles and begin to turn it. If everything balls up, you are turning it the wrong way, so try the other. From now on all you have to know is when to quit. It is possible to pull any wire in two. We think this simplifies the winter hay problem quite a bit. The rottener it gets the tighter we bale it. By spring the bales are about half size but are still holding arrows. We then throw them away and start over.

Some of you probably don't know what Harry was talking about when he mentions "Championship Class" so here is a short explanation. When the Northern California Association was formed they built up a separate class by making the winner of each of their first six tournaments a Champion. This group competes as a class at each tournament, but at each tournament the winner of the general division becomes a member of this exalted group while the low score in the "Championship Class"

(Continued on page 7)

Editorial

We were much disappointed in not being able to accept the invitation of the Detroit Archers to attend a "Rat Shoot and Roving Tournament" on December 17. The entry fee was 50c or five live rats. Not having the 50c or the five live rats we couldn't go.

Outdoor Life for January contains an article entitled "Bull Moose with a Bow" by Robert Scott Cathey. The story deals with his experiences in killing a bull moose in Canada while on the Gardner-Cathey-Thompson-Record expedition. Mr. Cathey also had an archery feature story in the January 7 issue of the Sunday Oregonian.

We are informed that Chester Seay of Los Angeles killed a seven hundred pound bear on a recent hunting trip. That sounds like a mighty big bear story to us but they say the bear didn't near go around when the boys started beating a track to Chester's front door clamoring for bear steak.

Kore Duryee says, "I. M. Stamps shot a dandy 4-point buck this year in 8-mile game preserve. He did a nice job of stalking. Took him 30 minutes to get from 100 yards to 65 yards. The arrow entered in front of the right hip and came out above the left shoulder. Never did find the arrow — it just kept going. Very dry, no rain or snow, though we camped at 4600 ft. elevation."

The leaders in the NFAA movement are encouraged by the attitude of the officers of the NAA. Mr. Cummings, chairman of the BG, NAA, in a letter to Mr. Yount, says in part: "I should like to congratulate you most heartily on having secured the requisite number of state associations so that you are now in a position to get organized on a national basis. I hope that the NAA will be able to assist you in securing the other associations in the Midwest and East so that the NFAA will be a truly national organization."

The Old Mission Field Archers of San Diego, Calif., "The Southland Gang," on the tenth anniversary of their first field shoot at Alisa Canyon on December 17, at the site of that "first of all" animal silhouette field shoots, spent the day in conquest of the several turkeys offered as prizes.

High scores for the fourteen target course were turned in by Clyde Day of Westminster, Calif., and Bob Hoover. In the shoot-off Clyde Day bested his opponent and claimed the coveted gobbler.

Three turkey shoots followed and were won by Bob Hoover, Clyde Day and Fred Tiffany. Clyde won the shoot-off following a tie with C. W. McNatt and Fred struggled through to win a tie shoot with Clyde Day and Bob Hoover.

Two chance turkeys were won by Don Lumley and Shorty Ashworth.

A vote of thanks goes to Harold Reed and George Birch, both from Laguna Beach, who were the prime movers of this shoot.

            Bob Hoover, Sec.,
      Old Mission Field Archers.

Kore Duryee tells us he has received over 40 entries for the Olympic Bowmen league tournament.

I. M. Stamps and four-point buck killed in 8-mile game preserve

With Our Advertisers
By Russell Jones, Business Manager

The first issue of "Tackle News," a mimeograph house organ publication by Russ Hoogerhyde, has just been received. It contains much of interest to archers, especially an article on backing bows with silk. Tackle News is to be published "occasionally." The first issue is dated December, 1939.

Willis Barnes reports that he has remodeled his archery shop, enlarging it and improving the working conditions. Mr. Barnes will have a new catalogue out soon. The December issue of Motor News contains an article about Mr. Barnes and his shop.

Notice the new ad of Alton's Specialty Shop. Looks like a real bargain in broadheads for small game.

The Old Timer

That's pretty good, Johnny, but it ain't the way I heered it. Now the way I heered it, that there bow just up an' busted right in the nock and I'll tell you why. I ain't much at drawin' but I'll make you a couple of pictures to show you what I mean, too. Now, I've noticed a lot of fellows put on a horn nock like the first picture and sometimes they hold. But, some other fellows put them on like the second picture and they never break at the nock. In the first place the bow looks better with the tip turned back a bit like No. 2, and then again the back grain or backing is not broken but runs all the way up to the tip making it a lot stronger. (I've noticed that a lot of fellows who don't use any nocks cut the groove all the way around the bow through the back grains and I figger that is a good way to break an otherwise good bow, too). Anyway, if you don't put your nocks on that way, try it and see if it isn't better. Leastwise that's the way the Old Timer sees it.

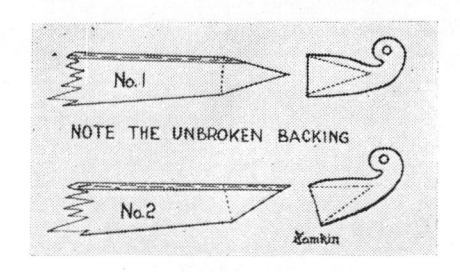

NFAA
(Continued from page 5)

goes back into the general division. This takes the six top shots out of circulation and greatly improves competition in the general division. To lend greater value to the Championship medal no man is allowed to win more than one. If a slump carries him back into the general division and he later fights his way back into the company of champions, he gets nothing more than a ribbon for doing it. As trophies in the "Champion Class," bars to be fastened to the medals are given. A gold bar for first place and a silver bar for second place. Naturally the man with the longest golden ladder leading up to his medal is the champion of champions.

After reading of all the Northern activities I am going to have to get patriotic and come to the defense of the South. The fall season opened with a tournament in Redlands October 22, followed by the Malibu club tournament October 29, the Redlands club tournament November 5. the Pasadena club tournament November 12, Redlands Turkey Shoot November 19, Malibu club tournament November 26, Redlands club tournament December 3, Pasadena Invitational Shoot and turkey dinner December 10, Southern California Association meet at Pasadena December 17, Red-
(Continued on page 11)

Southern California Field Archers

By Elmer W. Bedwell, Secretary

The Association's regular December tournament held at Pasadena, December 17, proved in every respect to be one of the most successful to date, in spite of the fact that it was only one week before Christmas. The attendance was good. The competition was close, and course in good order and the day perfect.

The "Championship Class" gold bar was won by Roland Quayle, and the silver bar by Wayne Stotler.

In the General Division M. D. Hathaway won and thereby received his championship medal. We are rid of him for a time at least. It is interesting to note that he has in a little over a year climbed from mighty close to the bottom until now he is counted among the best. Harry Stotler won second place, with brother Bob a close third. This with Wayne's second in the Championship Class gave the Stotler family three out of the five trophies awarded in the men's division.

In the ladies' division, first place was won by Eva Bedwell, second place by Naomi Baker, who is a comparative newcomer, and judging from her past performance should really go places in the game. Third place was taken by Glenn Curtis.

Bob King was the winner in the Junior Division and thereby got his name on the Bedwell trophy for the third time. Since this trophy is to become the permanent property of the boy winning it the most times during the year and the only other winner to date is Eddie Franklin, it is up to Eddie to win the next two tournaments and tie it up so we can all enjoy a good shoot-off. Otherwise it will be Bob's for keeps.

Our Association seems to be increasing its rate of growth. At this tournament there were 20 new members, a number of whom are members of the South-west Archery Club, a new organization insofar as our style of roving is concerned. We wish to take this opportunity to welcome them into our Association and promise them that we will be ready to shoot on their new course just as soon as it is finished. From the report of those who have seen this course it is going to be really fine.

Our next Association tournament is to be on the Malibu Mountain Archery club range. To reach this range, go up the beach past the town of Malibu about two and one half miles to the Latigo canyon road. Follow this road for three miles to the Malibu Mountain Inn and there you are.

It has been reported that regardless of the fact that this range was in first class condition when last shot on by the Association there have been a number of improvements made since that time.

Southern California Association

December 10 was the date of the second bi-monthly tournament of the Southern California archery association, held at Fullerton, with an attendance of seventy. Ted Mapes won first place in both target shooting and coffee drinking. His score at the targets was 1333 and his score at the coffee urn something less than a hundred cups. Bill Stoddard made the coffee.

The Izaac Walton club of Fullerton brings the cooperating membership in the SCAA to thirteen clubs. Charles Best and J. Block won in the B and C classes respectively.

Bee Hodgson, 1002, Cam Lambden, 773, and Dora Hill, 683, won, respectively, in the three women's divisions.

Dorothy Block was junior girl winner and Claude McCabe was high in the boys' division.

Los Angeles Club

About forty archers participated in the Los Angeles Archery club monthly tournament at Griffith park on December 3. The ladies shot a National and Columbia and the men a York and American round.

Gene Bacon scored 829 to win the ladies' trophy and Willard Bacon took the men's events with a score of 1124, as reported by H. G. Hall, secretary.

The National will be held at Amherst, Mass., on August 5 to 10, 1940,

Letter Box

From Dr. Klopsteg

Editor, Ye Sylvan Archer:

It seems advisable to comment on the article, "Some Notes on Scientific Bowyery," by J. M. Howard, in the November, 1939, issue of your magazine, since Mr. Howard seems to be misinformed about some of the points he discusses.

The first general comment to be made is that there have been numerous papers published on various aspects of scientific bow-making. Many of these are cited in the bibliography at the end of my monograph "Science Looks at Archery." A reading of the papers there listed, together with others which have appeared since that time, is very urgently recommended to those interested in the scientific aspects of bow design. All of the points mentioned by Mr. Howard have been fully covered in the publications mentioned.

The first part of Mr. Howard's article implies that the efficiency of a bow is found by ascertaining its force-draw curve. The implication is misleading, for two bows, one highly efficient, the other a "lug", may have identical force-draw curves. To find the efficiency of a bow when shooting an arrow of given mass, it is necessary to measure the velocity of the arrow when shot with that bow, then find its kinetic energy (one-half mass times velocity squared) and divide this numerical value by the potential energy in the drawn bow, found by plotting the force-draw curve.

It is also implied that the musical note of the string when plucked enables one to judge effecciency of the bow. That this is erroneous is easily understood when one considers what determines pitch of a stretched string. Under given tension, a thin, light string sounds a higher note than a heavy one; and, of course, the higher the tension, the higher the pitch. Thus an inefficient, strong bow equipped with a light string will cause the latter to emit a high-pitched note. An efficient, light bow will cause the same string to sound a low-pitched note. A short bow produces a higher pitch in a string of certain thickness than a long bow of the same weight. Although it is undoubtedly true that an experienced archer can pretty well judge whether or not a bow pleases him even before he has shot an arrow with it, and although the "feel" of the bow as he "works" it has a bearing on his judgment as does the note of the string when plucked, he is not able to do better than guess that its efficiency is fifty or seventy-five per cent.

Mr. Howard's independent research has unfortunately led him astray when he states that "the double midsection should be made as short as possible, since the limbs with the longer handle will be forced to describe a more extreme arc." The opposite is true. With limbs of specified length, the longer the rigid midsection, the less will the limbs have to bend for a given length of draw. (See "Getting the Most Out of the Bowstave," Archery Review, June, 1935). In line with this finding, I made a yew bow with 25-inch limbs and a 13-inch midsection, which, as regards cast and efficiency, is one of the best bows in my collection.

Mr. Howard's advocacy of the bending tip is sound, and is precisely what many of us have been writing about and doing for the past seven years. His remark, "the greater the safety achieved (in) stacking, the greater the cast" seems to advocate stacking the limbs within limits of safety. That this is a mistaken idea has been proved many times.

Making the limbs trapezoidal, with the narrow part the back, the wide part the belly, thus bringing the neutral axis of any section nearer the compression side, has been repeatedly suggested in previously published articles. It should be added that a constant ratio of the two bases of the trapezoidal sections should be maintained.

The enthusiasm for the application of physics to bow design which evidently inspired Mr. Howard's article, is commendable, and archery will stride ahead rapidly and more rapidly as more archers realize the importance of scientific design and acquire a thorough understanding of its fundamentals.

—Paul E. Klopsteg.

Doghouse Science

By Dr. Paul Bunyan, D.L., D.C.S.
As Told to the Doghouse Editor

I have been called many names in my life, some of them harsh ones. What loggers called me behind my back was more expressive than elegant, and what they called me when getting their time I blush to think of. So should they, but that's neither here nor there.

Naturally I am proud of being the first scientific logger in the country, if not in the world. In the old days we called it high-balling, a term that is still in use in some modern camps. That I should have been made an honorary member of the Lower Bracket Archers is as fair as it is complimentary—science and archery have always been my hobbies. The degree of Doctor of Logging is a well-earned one, and now to become a Doctor of Canine Science is a welcome distinction.

What gripes me, if you will pardon the expression, is the kind of company I am obliged to keep.

There is the Big Swede—pardon me again—I mean Dr. Brommers. I have nothing against him as a logger. He's got the round stuff, as we so quaintly called the logs in the old days. He was a useful enough foreman, but as a scientist—well, more about that later.

Now the big stiff — I mean Dr. Brommers—has gone into competition with me. At my urgent request—aided by my number fourteens—he betook himself to hell out of my camp. So he starts a camp of his own in the small sticks of Washington. He didn't set the world afire there, having nobody to furnish the brains for him, but he made enough to retire to Southern California with two shirts—both soiled—three pairs of socks—they stank — what was left of his pants and no coat or vest. In California he ran into some other ex-employees of mine, and here we are. Perforce I am dragged in as a consulting authority. It is either that or be misquoted and misrepresented again. By this time, you see, that ex-gang of mine has made its mark in science.

There is something about that gang that is vaguely familiar. The only display of brains that I ever knew the Big Swede to be guilty of was when he warned me against "them guys," as he expressed it. "They will take us for a coon hunt yet," he said.

Take Joe Cosner, now Dr. Cosner. As my camp clerk and timekeeper he was a complete washout, and I let him go. Joe was the one who thought of fitting ice skates to the Blue Ox in the winter and calks for the summer. I shoved some calk boots into Dr. Cosner's posterior with enough force to propel him down to Arizona, which is as good a place as any for him.

Will I ever forget the day when two hungry punks, Erle Gardner and Ted Carpenter, showed up. Today they are educators too.

What they wanted to learn was bull-whacking, of course. Erle said he didn't care so much about the pay or the future of the job; what he wanted to absorb was atmosphere and language. He gobbled up the language all right. The real future, said Dr. Gardner to be, was to be able to lie so convincingly that you were paid for it. Fiction writing, I think he called it. Ted Carpenter had the same ideas and I turned the pair over to Walt Wilhelm, the bull-whacker, who set them to greasing skids.

As skid greasers they were inventive little punks, I grant you that. Being too lazy to fill or carry the water buckets in the winter or the grease buckets in the summer, they used to catch wild hogs by the tail and lard the ice or the skid with them.

Dr. Wilhelm is another case I would just as soon forget. He was a fair enough bull-whacker, I do not deny that. The Blue Ox knew all there was any need to know about logging, but Walt came in handy for swatting the flies the ox couldn't reach with his tail.

There was Reed Williams — Dr. Williams today. At that time he was assistant flunky in the cookhouse. His work called for more skillful dodging of boots than it did for imagination. But I am telling you here and now that when it came to drawing cartoons and caricatures on the wall he was second to none. Cosner and Carpenter helped him, and the result was a nightmare. Was so bad, in fact, that none of the artists were allowed to sleep in the bunkhouse. Which shows what the loggers thought of them.

It didn't bother the outlaws so that you would notice it. They would bed down in the snow, and the hot air generated kept them steaming the coldest night. What a life I had! What a life!

In retrospect the matter of degrees makes a confusing picture. My foreman was working doggedly and hopelessly on his thesis for a master's degree in logging. It puzzled him—he had acquired his B.S. with such astounding ease. The other aspirants felt that neither would the B.S. degree offer any difficulties to any of them. As a matter of fact they were even then ready for final examinations.

But somehow I didn't see as many prospective doctors of science in the camp as there turned out to be. You never can tell, can you?

Passing the Buck

(Continued from page 4)

that ranch in Wyoming. I'm hoping to be there next deer season, and hope a lot of you archery fans will be there at the same time. If you want adventure—there it is. If you want an archery preserve that's fairly crawling with deer—there's the place.

The folks who run the ranch have a love of the out-of-doors, one of them is a bow and arrow hunter himself, all are fine sportsmen. They're admirable hosts and hostesses. The mountains are full of deer. The grub is marvelous, and the beds, when once you get into them, are soft as down. It's a hunter's paradise.

There's only one fly in the omelette—they have another section that's reserved to gun hunters. (A guy can kill a deer with a rifle within a few hours from the time he leaves the ranch house any old day.) The gun hunters don't clutter up the archery preserve any, but a couple did have the adjoining bedroom from Walther.

The first guy put his gun on "safety." Then he wanted to be certain it was on safety. He pulled the trigger—it wasn't on safety.

The second bird owned a gun that had the habit of not doing something or other right. He wanted to cure it. The gun took things into its own hands.

Neither hole in Walther's bedroom wall was very close to his head. But when I went in to call him the morning after that second shot, I found him sleeping with his red hat tied onto his head. He muttered sleepily, "Don't shoot again. I haven't any horns."

But Walther's a skeptical cuss.

We read a lot about the successful deer shot. We don't read so much about the shots that miss. There are reasons for those misses. Buchen and Klopsteg have catalogued every shot we made, paced off the distances, analyzed the causes. If enough of you chaps turn on the heat, they'll give you some of the real low-down on deer shooting.

And in the meantime, the HF Bar will still be there next year, in case you want to make some experiments on your own.

Any archer who goes up there and doesn't see more than fifty deer any day he hunts gets a free drink from the guy who lost all the bunkhouse discussions.

How about it, boys?

And don't let Klopsteg and Buchen put off that detailed analysis of deer shooting technique. There's a lot of meat in their conclusions. How do I know? I helped 'em reach 'em.

And as for Brommers—and his letters to hunting companions about Gardner, the unbeatable arguefier—Phooey! A guy should wait until he's shot at a deer head that wears deer horns before he sets himself up as an authority. What right has a fellow who goes around shooting at buck coons to talk about deer hunting, or deer hunters?

Two phooeys!!

NFAA

(Continued from page 7)

lands club tournament December 31, Yermo Invitational January 7, and the future reads just the same, except that there are two fine new ranges going in. With all these tournaments when do we practice? Why we just miss one once in a while and then if the worst come to the worst, we think up a good excuse to get off work a little early and shoot a 14 before dark. Do we ever shoot target? How can we? There isn't any time.

The Western Archery Association tournament will be held in San Diego, July 6-7, 1940.

CLASSIFIED ADVERTISING

RATES for Classified Advertising 5 cents per word per issue. Count initials and numbers as words. Minimum charge is 50 cents.

YEW BILLETS $2.50 and $3.50. Staves $3.50 and $5.00 postpaid. High elevation Yew, well seasoned. Fine dark ten-year-old Billets $5.00. Leon Chapin, Box 139, Albany, Ore.

BOWS, ARROWS, raw materials, Lowest prices. Lloyd Morrison, Waldport, Oregon.

RELICS AND CURIOS

INDIAN RELICS, Beadwork, Coins, Curios, Books, Minerals, Weapons. Old West Photos. Catalog, 5c. Genuine African Bow, $3.75. Ancient flint arrowheads, perfect, 6c each— Indian Museum, Osborne, Kansas.

BOOKS AND MAGAZINES

"ARCHERY TACKLE, HOW TO MAKE AND HOW TO USE IT." by Adolph Shane. Bound in cloth and illustrated with more than fifty drawings and photographs. Information for making archery tackle and instructions for shooting. Price is $1.75. Send orders to Ye Sylvan Archer, 505 North 11th street, Corvallis.

Arcadian Life Magazine
Tells the Story of the Ozarks
Nature, Health, Folklore, presented in a charming way. Published monthly in the backhills where the highway meets the by-ways. $1.00 pays for one year's subscription. Single copy, 25c. Try a classified ad in our Market Place. $1.00 pays for three insertions of your thirty word advertisement.
Short Pastoral Poems Wanted
O. E. RAYBURN, Editor
Caddo Gap, Arkansas

SUBSCRIBERS PLEASE NOTICE
A cross appearing in this space means that your subscription has expired and we would appreciate your prompt renewal so that your name may be kept on our mailing list.

Make Your Arrows
with a
Lampert Arrowmaker
parallel — tapered — barreled
3-8 to 1-4
$30.00—two models—$20.00
For Information Write
Claude Lampert
3527 N. Haight Ave.
Portland   Oregon

W. A. COCHRAN
Archery Equipment
High Elevation Yew Wood
Port Orford Cedar
Osage Orange
Air Seasoned
10,000 Billets and Staves in Stock
Route 2   Eugene, Ore.

Rose City Archery Co.
1149 NE 31st Avenue
Portland, Oregon

In 1940 competition, improve your scores with the tackle used by

Pat Chambers
National Champion
Catalogue on request

Alton's Archery Specialty
10c Buys Our "Baby"
BROADHEAD
Spring Steel Blades on Target Piles
25 Per Cent Discount to Dealers
These Are Real Hand-made Hunters!
210 N. Main   Washburn, Ill.

ULLRICH WOOD
The Choice of Champions

Mill run 11-32, 21-64, 5-16, and 9-32 in. Cedar Dowels. From split out, air seasoned (in the square) stock. Dowels from same source segregated. Should match up like hair on a dog's back.

1000	....	$30.00
500	....	$17.50
250	....	$10.00
100	....	$ 4.00

(Any combination permissable)

EARL ULLRICH
Roseburg, Oregon

(G)

"THE MARK OF DISTINCTION IN ARCHERY TACKLE

Fine Yew Target and Hunting Bows, Plain or Backed with Rawhide. Lemonwood Bows with Rawhide Backs.
College and School Equipment
Target, Hunting and Roving Arrows
Price List on Request
Wholesale — Retail

EARL GRUBBS
5518 W. Adams
Los Angeles, : California

Cassius Hayward Styles

BOWYER AND FLETCHER

—Tackle that has stood the test—

28 Vicente Place

BERKELEY, CALIFORNIA

YEW BOW TIMBER

High Altitude Air Seasoned Billets and Staves of Quality and Variety.

W. G. PRESCOTT
527 Chestnut   Ashland, Ore.

BROADHEADS

Blunts, and Broadhead Blades and Ferrules. Prices for one or a thousand. Circular on request.

ROY CASE   Racine, Wis.

WIN WITH BEN PEARSON ARROWS

Beautiful and accurate to the Nth degree but win their real laurels on the range. Arrows made as arrows should be—and at prices you can afford to pay. Send for catalogue.

BEN PEARSON, INC. — PINE BLUFF, ARK.

"The American Archer"

Complete your file with the 1st, 2nd and 3rd issues now out. Mail your subscriptions early. A subscription to a fellow archer makes a splendid gift.

THE AMERICAN ARCHER
521 Fifth Avenue
NEW YORK CITY, N. Y.

$1.00 Per Year   Published Quarterly

L. L. "Flight" DAILY
offers you
"Tackle That Talks"
Dry Cedar and Yew
Catalogue Free
245 Pearl, Eugene, Oregon

E. BUD PIERSON
Bowyer — Fletcher
Tournament Tackle, Sinew,
Glue, Raw Materials.
245 University Ave
CINCINNATI, OHIO
Custom Made Tackle

ARCHERY BOWS
*from the Heart of the
Yew Country*
**W. I. KING
Woodworking Shop**
1958½ Onyx St.   Eugene, Ore.

POTTER & MacQUARRIE

ROVING ARROWS

Split Birch or P. O. Cedar, 11-32 in. and 3-8 in., matched within 10 gr. in weight, and spined for heavy bows. Equipped with steel piles, 3 1-2 in. feathers and bright crest.

One Dozen $5.00

3400 Fruitvale Ave.
Oakland . . . . California

Beacon Hill Craftsmen
Beacon, N. Y.
Paul H. Gordon, Director

The Works   The McCoy
No Swanky Showrooms
We Put It Into the Product

Write for Complete Catalog

The Flat Bow—70 pages of Archery information for 50 cents, well illustrated. Ye Sylvan Archer, 505 N. 11th St., Corvallis, Oregon.

HUNTING ARROWS!

Every hunter has the right to expect careful workmanship and meticulous attention to detail in every arrow he buys. We, as fellow hunters, appreciate this fact.

The following arrows are made from milled and tapered birch shafts, they have long stiff feathers and are attractively crested.

Rabbit Arrows, 5-16 in. diameter, Case's Kiska head, per dozen $6.00

Deer Arrows, 11-32 in. diameter, Case's barbless Korrek head, per dozen $8.00

Boar Arrows, 3-8 in. diameter, these have a special blade with concave edges 3 in. long and 1 1-4 in. wide, mounted in a hard Duralumin ferrule, per dozen $10.00

**E & G ARROWSMITHS
3347 North Capitol
Indianapolis, Ind.**

Archery
Raw Materials

WM. A. JOY

9708 So. Hoover Street
LOS ANGELES, CALIF.

HANDBOOK—How to Make and Use Bows and Arrows—90 Pages well illustrated (with catalog) 35c.

CATALOG—100 pictures—color spread—Instruction Folder. 10c.

CATALOG alone 5c. Stamps or Coin.

L. E. STEMMLER · QUEENS VILLAGE · N·Y·

Please mention Ye Sylvan Archer when writing advertisers.

Ye Sylvan Archer

February, 1940

Corvallis, Oregon

Vol. 11 No. 10

Ye Sylvan Archer

Vol. 11   February, 1940   No. 10

Published the fifteenth of each month
for archers by archers
505 North 11th Street, Corvallis, Oregon

J. E. DAVIS .... Editor
RUSSELL JONES .... Business Manager
Subscription Price .... $1.00 Per Year
Foreign Subscription .... $1.25 Per Year
Single Copies .... 10 Cents

Advertising Rates on Application

TABLE OF CONTENTS

	Page
IN MEMORY'S STORE By W. B. Barksdale	1
NEW EXPERIMENTS IN MICHIGAN By Karl E. Palmatier	3
NATIONAL FIELD ARCHERY ASS'N. By John L. Yount	4
THE OLD TIMER	5
EDITORIAL	6
ARCHERY-GOLF TOURNAMENT IN OHIO By Dr. Paris B. Stockdale	7
FIELD ARCHERS OF SOUTHERN CALIFORNIA By Elmer W. Bedwell	7
LETTER BOX	8
DOGHOUSE SCIENCE Edited by George Brommers	10
OLD MISSION FIELD ARCHERS By Bob Hoover	11
OLYMPIC BOWMEN LEAGUE	11

In Memory's Store

By W. D. Barksdale

Between the icy blasts of winter and the balmy breezes of spring comes a time dear to the heart of every true archer—a time of tinkering, memories and anticipations.

A lot of archers get dreamy-eyed those days. And a lot of wives look forward with dread to the months to come. For at that season of the year, "shooting time" is not far away, and then the wives, unless they be archers too, will be "widows" until winter comes again.

Of course, the hunters have been in the field during the hunting season, but that is past, and so for them, too, the spring season has delights all its own.

You can tell your true archer as the days of spring draw nigh. There's an uneasiness about him, the which there's no mistaking. Early in the year, mayhap while the last belated snows still whiten the ground, he is afflicted with a restlessness. He is prone to wander about the room, often looking out the windows and never remaining still. He may pass remarks that it won't be long till spring.

Then he drifts toward the closet or racks where he keeps his tackle. From that, it's just a step to tinkering with his equipment.

You'll see him sitting with his bows across his knees, lovingly passing his hands along their polished surfaces and scrutinizing them carefully for possible flaws, marking the beginning of chrysals and frets.

Occasionally, he'll string one of them, fit an arrow to the string, and draw it full. Joy fills him as he feels the strong strain of the stout stave. Heart beats quicker and life pulses through his veins.

There's a joy in going over the arrows and in making new ones. Here a feather needs replacing; there another is somewhat ruffled and needs dressing again.

Quivers are to be re-laced and perhaps a new set of fingertips is needed. How comforting the feel of the stiff, smooth leather, perfect protection for tender digits. Wax and thread have an honest feel, dear to his heart.

And then, you'll see him gradually settle into inactivity, and for minutes he'll gaze into the fire without moving.

Perchance, the good wife, just now, makes some remark anent the affairs of friends or comments on the small happenings of the day and, receiving no reply, glances sharply at him—and shakes her head.

How little she understands—or does she?

He's not concerned with the gossip of the day. But in memory's fields, he's wandering afar, with a sturdy bow and the peace of all outdoors about him. The blare of the radio has faded, for him, into the sough of the night wind in the pines, and the chattering of the stream over its smooth-wasted stones. Shadows leap and dance against the wall of the surrounding forest, figures fanciful and strange create themselves before his eyes, and his ears are filled with the crackling sputter of the brilliant flames.

By his side rests a trusty stave and sharp broadheads lie in a nearby quiver.

In memory he is free!

Ah, me! That the toil of living should crowd out so many happy days afield! That pure, fresh air, and open sky, and rocks and hills cannot be one's constant lot.

Yet I should be thankful that, in memory, I can live those days again and thrill with anticipation of others equally delightful to come.

Many a happy hour I've spent in roaming the Ozarks region with quiver and bow, sometimes for single afternoons and at others with pack on my back and whole days at my disposal.

And the song of many an arrow, in those hills, has brought delight to my heart. How often the whistling shaft has just missed its mark! How often it has flown wide! But oh, those occasions on which it has sped true, causing the savage in me to leap with exultation!

The greatest joy that memory recalls for me has been in slow, easy-going trips, with small game as the quarry and no hurry anywhere.

Well do I remember an early spring afternoon, when I pushed through fields and meadows along a river bank, enjoying the beauty of the day, hardly expecting, but half-hoping that I might start game.

Suddenly from a tuft of grass at my very feet dashed a rabbit. He hopped across a little patch of corn, came out on the other side, and then sat up impudently upon a bank to see what it was all about.

It seemed a shame to shoot at him, but I drew my bow and released a shaft—the distance, about 40 yards. I was unable to see exectly what happened. The rabbit gave one leap backward over a little hump, and I walked forward to pick up the arrow, hardly regretting that I had missed.

But what was this? As I came over the bank, I saw. There lay the rabbit, dead, the arrow squarely through the forward portion of his body.

It works both ways. The shaft you thought went wild may have flown true, just as many a seeming hit is found to be a miss.

On another afternoon, a friend and I drifted slowly down a bayou in a light boat, hoping for a few shots at gars—scavengers of those murky waters. But the gars all seemed away. Not one appeared, and gradually, we dropped our alertness, I as I stood in the bow of the craft, and my friend sitting in the stern paddling. He slipped lazily into the "silent stroke", never removing the paddle from the water. We drifted along, just skirting the fringe of bushes along the heavily overgrown bank.

Suddenly a strange rustling caught my ear, and instantly I was alert. What was this? A long gray shape twisted and wound through the brush, crackling the leaves slightly. To my startled eye, it seemed a yard long. And then I realized! Moving soundlessly along, we had slipped up on a cotton-tail, feeding along the stream. Softly I raised my bow, slowly drew to the head and sped a shaft. It struck! The bush seemed to explode in dust and clatter. We hastily paddled to the bank and there lay—my arrow. Deeply imbedded in the soft soil, it had missed the rabbit a foot. And that at a distance of not more than 10 feet. Oh, well. What matter? We paddled on.

Quite often, on these lazy trips, the chance for a shot presents itself at the most unexpected moment. On one such occasion, I was standing in a heavy growth of pine and hardwood, resting after a strenuous hour of shooting at jaybirds. I have a standing grudge against them, and never miss a chance to shoot at one. But today the jays all, still were unscathed.

Softly, as I leaned against the tree, a huge owl floated through the forest and lit in a tree 35 or 40 yards away. I had a clear view. No limbs intervened. I don't like owls. They kill lots of things. So, easing into a firm position, I fitted an arrow to the string, drew and released. Straight as a taut cord the arrow flew, struck the huge bird in the breast and passed on through, flying far over the trees. The owl apparently sank his claws into the limb at the death blow, and he didn't fall. I sneaked a bit closer and shot another arrow. It also passed through. I did the same thing again, and still he didn't come down. I began to wonder if I would have to climb the tree to knock him out.

But the fourth arrow hit the limb under his feet, and he gave a convulsive leap into the air, and then tumbled to the ground. Another marauder less and three good shots for memory's store!

And so it goes. Good shots, bad shots, soft breezes, green grass and songs of birds are pictured in memory as the archer sits before the fire, caressing his tackle and dreaming of days past and to come.

Bob Morley and Bill Otto, well-known field archers of Los Angeles, made this community (Yermo) their headquarters while they conducted a search for Indian relics in a tour of the Mojave desert as guests of Walt Wilhelm, noted archer. Upon arrival here, the boys were joined by Jane Fuller, Gloria Connell and their host Walt Wilhelm on an interesting tour of the desert waste lands in the famous "Prowler," unique desert car owned by Wilhelm.—Pomona Valley Citizen.

Look for the Archery Column in the Christian Science Monitor.

New Experiments in Michigan
By Karl E. Palmatier

Each year the officers and members of the board of directors of the Michigan Archer's Association meet the first Sunday in February to make plans for the coming year. Each year we try out some new ideas. Last year we permitted local clubs to affiliate with the state association for five dollars and members of such affiliated clubs were permitted to join the state association for a dollar family membership. This one adjustment increased our membership of all kinds from 102 to 228 family memberships. Our family membership for 1938 was three dollars.

Field archery has been shot in one form or another in this state for 12 years. All activities are under the one organization. For many years there were very few archers who cared for field archery only but now that number is increasinig, due to our deer season. Over 475 hunters took out archery licenses last season. We have affiliated with the NFAA. and expect to be very active this year. Last year four field archery meets were scheduled and this year there will be six. The four last year had an average attendance of fifty-two.

Many of the field archers like to come to our target meets just to meet the other archers. They are not interested in the target event as such, so we have given them a few targets of their own. But that has not just filled the desire so this year it was suggested to them that we make up a special face for all the field archers who attend the target meets. The face is to have the regulation size target rings a quarter of an inch wide. There is to be a solid black three inch area in the center of the gold. This solid black area is really their target. It is understood that if they do make six golds in the gold area that they are not entitled to the NAA. six golds award. But it is understood that for all Michigan records their scores are to be considered the same as any other target archer's. This new style of target face has set the fellows up in spirits. It looks like a lot of fun for them now to come to a target meet.

Phil Palmer, C. Loveland, William Van Vorst and myself met at the little town of Evart, nearly centrally located in the lower peninsula of this state and from there went eight miles north to some hills covered with small poplar and birch. Here and there is a small clump of young fir trees and a few small swamps. The trip was made to locate a territory to have a "bunny hunt" such as Ohio and Indiana have. We waded in snow up to our knees and put up six snowshoes and saw the tracks of many gray rabbits which on that day were holed up. As a result of this exploration trip the MAA has on its schedule a bunny hunt for December 12, 1940.

We have been invited to hold our first target meet at the new field house at Michigan State College, Lansing. It is the largest in the United States. We can set up eighteen targets and will shoot a regulation double American round. There will still be fifty yards beyond the targets. This meet is expected to attract close to one hundred archers.

Fred Bear and his wife, Nelson Grumley, Carl Strang, and Jack Yaeger at the microphone, put on an archery demonstration between halves of the Wisconsin and Michigan State College basketball game. There were 7,500 present. The boys did an excellent job and have been invited back again for next year.

Michigan will hold its first field archery tournament on May 19. It will be a double round of twenty-eight targets. What other club would like to shoot against us?

Wm. E. Staff writes us that he has invented a double upper and double lower limb bow with adjustable poundage features. By moving the leather rings outward from the center one can graduate the increased poundage of the bow. Mr. Staff promises us a picture of the bow later.

Archery holds the "spot" position in the sports section of the Pomona Valley Citizen as edited by Walt Wilhelm. We very much enjoy reading Walt's weekly column.

National Field Archery Ass'n

By John L. Yount

We realize that in the past the NFAA. has been something of a mystery. We had no officers. We had no rounds. Nor had we done anything for the archer hunter. In plain words, we were to the average archer nothing but a name and one that he was probably getting pretty tired of hearing about.

It would have been a simple matter to have elected some officers and selected rounds and gone into active operation, but had we done so we would have been National in name only. Instead, we wanted this organization to be an organization of the field archers of America and felt that any delay would be justified, if it would ultimately lead to this end. Consequently we have spent quite a number of months in discussion with the NAA. and the various state associations, and have now reached an understanding. As a result, I can promise you that the letters N.F.A.A. will mean something in archery very shortly.

As a first step in this work, the following committees have been appointed, although at the time of going to press none of those appointed have received their notice of appointment, we sincerely hope all will be able to serve.

Constitution Committee—Kore T. Duryea, Paul Klopsteg, Wm. Folberth, John Yount and E. Hill Turnock. This committee shall elect its own chairman.

Rules Committee—Harry Glover, Northern California, Chairman; Fred Bear, Michigan; B. Ahman, Southern California; Leonard Erickson, Minnesota.

Tournament Committee—Karl Palmatier, Mich., Chairman; Dr. Hewitt, Oregon; Clayton B. Shenk, Pennsylvania; H. C. Mcquarrie, Northern California; Leyton E. Speer, New Jersey.

Game Conservation Committee—S. L. Michael, Washington, Chairman; Ed. Brock, Southern California; Forest Nagler, Canada; A. J. Cosner, Arizona; Fred J. Heckle, Pennsylvania; Dr. George A. Cathey, Oregon.

As to the duties of the various committees and the reason for the selection of the men named: in the case of the first, the name, Constitution Committee, pretty well defines its duties. As to the membership of this committee, four have been chosen not only for their leadership in field archery, but for their ability and experience in organization work as well.

The Rules Committee has the job of selecting or developing official rounds and making all the rules and regulations necessary if we are to shoot these rounds in official tournaments. For this committee I have tried to choose men of experience. Some of whom have had experience in broadhead events and Archery Golf as well as the usual type of roving round. As a result, this committee should be able to work intelligently with any type of field round.

The Tournament Committee has what is probably the toughest assignment of all. To begin with, it must be a publicity committee. What good is it to plan a tournament if you don't promote it, and promotion is publicity. Next, since for at least a year all our big tournaments will be intersectional mail tournaments, it is up to this committee to develop the proper procedure for the conduct of such tournaments and then finish off by attending to the tabulating of scores and awarding of trophies. Since the members of this comittee are all well known leaders, I don't believe there can be any question as to their qualifications. I might add that they had better like work, for with Karl Palmatier as their chairman they are going to have plenty to do and he will see that it is done.

Now comes the last and to many the most important committee, that of game conservation. It is our hope that this committee will be able to gather and make available to all who might need it, all information pertaining to archery hunting. Not just the laws of the various states, but every detail; the number hunting, the size of the kill, the number of wounded that were lost, how the

(Continued on page 9)

THE OLD TIMER

Well now Johnny, this is the way I he'ered it. One feller says to'ther feller, "Say," he says, "Them new-fangled thing-a-ma-gigs sure do beat a lot of the gadgets we uster use. Take that dingus you are a usin' to trim them feathers. Now that's what I calls a slick rig." "Yep," says to'ther feller, " Sure trims 'em slick as a pealed onion, just as easy as fallin' off a log. I figger that a lot of folks would like to be a usin' one of these if they knew how easy they are to make." Well, I listened in to what that feller said and I think it was about like this.

Take a board about eight inches wide and about a foot long. A porcelain light socket is screwed to one end of this and on the other end are fastened two porcelain posts about an inch and a half high. These are placed about six inches apart. The diagram shows how the fixtures are wired up in series. A common heater element is used for resistance, this is screwed into the light socket. A short piece of resistance wire just a bit heavier than the wire on the element is fastened between the posts and shaped according to the desired shape of the feather wanted. Various devices may be used to hold the arrow but a very simple arrangement may be made as illustrated from two short pieces of wire. Now plug it in and adjust the burner wire again as it will change somewhat as it is heated. Adjust the heat of the burner wire by removing some of the wire from the coil until the burner is a bright red but not too white hot, as this might cause the feathers to flame. Now place the arrow upon the arrow rest and turn slowly and see how easy it is to get perfectly trimmed feathers.

By cutting channels where the wires go, on the under side of the board, the wires may be hidden and the board set level. If one cares to, they may then be covered with sealing wax. If this is not clear enough, drop a line to the "old timer" for further explanation.

Have you sent in your membership to NFAA?

A—HEATER ELEMENT.   B—PORCELAIN POSTS.   C—BURNER.
D—ARROW SUPPORTS.   E—ELECTRIC CORD.   THE DOTTED LINES INDICATE LOCATION OF ELECTRIC HOOK-UP.

Editorial

"In Memory's Store" has been reprinted from the June, 1933, issue of Ye Sylvan Archer. In our estimation it is an archery classic and as the issue in which it was previously published is not available to most of our present subscribers we feel this is an opportune time to present it again. It may be a little early in the season for Southern California, Florida, and the rest of the country except the Pacific Northwest, from what we read in the papers, but here we feel that "spring has sprung."

Maj. C. L. Williams, the well-known archer and tackle maker who has been located at Plattsburg, N. Y., announces a change of address, 112 Hudson St., South Glens Falls, N. Y. He would like to have his archery correspondents take due notice. This is Maj. Williams' eleventh year in tackle making and instructing in archery.

A lot of good things have been crowded out this month on account of lack of space.

Give the Cartoon a Title

Kenneth Clayton, the artist who drew the cartoon on this page, wants a title for it and will give a dozen selected Port Orford cedar dowels for the best caption. Send your title to Ye Sylvan Archer at once. Contest closes April 1st.

Harold A. Titcomb, well-known English archer, member of the Surry Bowmen and Royal Toxophilites, has been visiting in California recently.

Archery-Golf Tournament in Ohio

By Dr. Paris B. Stockdale, Columbus, Ohio

Field archers in Ohio are looking forward to the sixth annual Ohio championship archery-golf tournament to be held at the University Country Club, in Columbus, March 30-31, under the sponsorship of the Ohio Archery-golf and Hunting Association in cooperation with the Ohio State University Physical Education Department. State winners will be determined from two 18-target round shoots. The 1939 defending champions are William Folberth, Cleveland, and Miss Frances Schweitzer, Lakewood. Any archer may participate, altho only residents of Ohio are eligible for championship awards.

A feature of the event will be the annual banquet and business meeting, which, this year, will be conducted at the club house on the golf course, immediately following completion of Saturday afternoon's play. Special prizes, for which all entrants are eligible, will be awarded at the banquet on the basis of the first day's results. Final championship awards will be made following tournament play on Sunday morning.

Because of the growing interest in archery-golf and field archery, and because of novel feature attractions which are being planned, an unusually large participation is expected this year. Special developments in matters of field archery should attract a large number of archery hunters and rovers.

Officers of the archery clubs who reside in Columbus comprise the local committee on arrangements as follows:

Paris B. Stockdale, president, Ohio Archery-golf and Hunting Association.

E. E. Kimberly, secretary, Ohio Archery-golf Association.

H. D. Anthony, president, Columbus Archery Club.

Clive Schneider, secretary, Columbus Archery Club.

R. M. Bruce, secretary, University Archery-golf Club.

Southern California Field Archers

By Elmer W. Bedwell, Secretary

Although the weather was not what one would call ideal, the January Desert Tournament was held at Yermo on schedule. It takes more than rain to keep field archers at home. (Although the "flu" in these parts did slow them down some). The shoot was unofficial for the S.C.F.A.A. This was done in order to give the Wilhelm boys a free hand to put on novel and interesting events, such as shooting at balloons 150 feet in the air and a broadhead event. Around 75 archers went home feeling glad that they had taken the chance with the weather. A grand barbecue dinner was served by the Circle 51 Rancho, and was ideal on a cool day. The desert at this time of year is something to write home about.

The next Southern California tournament will be held at Malibu, this month, so don't forget the date—February 25. The S.C.F.A.A. is forming a "Championship Division" for ladies, to work on the same order as the now existing "Men's Championship Division". A beautiful gold and ivory trophy has been donated by Henry Bitzenburger, to be perpetual for the high score entering each time.

To reach the Malibu Mts. Archery range drive north on Coast Route from Santa Monica about 16 miles to Latigo Canyon Road, turn right about 3 miles to Malibu Mts. Inn and Archery Club. See you there.

Hugh Slocum tells us that much interest in archery is in evidence at Lancaster on the edge of the Mojave desert. The Lancaster archers expect to take part in the parade at the next annual Lancaster fair.

Letter Box

From J. M. Howard

Editor, Ye Sylvan Archer:

I am happy to have received Dr. Klopsteg's corrections (Ye Sylvan Archer, January, 1940). Perhaps the fact that such dark issues exist to trouble us amateurs will call forth another of his authoritative treatises, in the course of which practical suggestions will be given to obviate the need for such doubtful contributions as mine.

I don't question that Dr. Klopsteg is a practical bowyer as well as a sound theorist in the field of bow dynamics, yet all of the statements made by me were the direct result of empirical convictions and I am unready to relinquish as many of them as Dr. Klopsteg thinks I should.

Perhaps Dr. Klopsteg could show me (though I am rather dense mathamatically), that a longer handle section for a stated length of working limb would put less strain upon the bow than a shorter. My experience, as well as diagrams I have made, indicate the contrary as true. To support this contention, Dr. Klopsteg cites a bow he made with 25-inch limbs and a 13-inch mid-section as being, in regard to cast and efficiency, one of his best bows. It certainly should have a sprightly cast, but I attribute its longevity to the skill which went into its manufacture, rather than the safety inherent in its design.

The musical note of the string must be a matter for every archer to ascertain for himself, using his own standard size of string on his own bows. I am glad Dr. Klopsteg clarified this minor point.

If I made claim to originality in any of my notes it was only to that sense of discovery and resulting urge to communicate the valuable to a fellow workman which every enthusiastic archer-craftsman is bound to feel now and then. The learned works quoted in Dr. Klopsteg's bibliography are only in part known to me; many of them are out of print, hence unavailable to general perusal; and finally it seemed to me that Dr. Klopsteg's own article in Ye Sylvan Archer for June, 1939, left certain critical points unelucidated. Such, for example, was the slender *bending* tip turned out to such perfection by Mr. Barton, of Wilmette. If Dr. Klopsteg and others have been making bows with these tips and writing about them "for the past seven years", why didn't Dr. Klopsteg incorporate an account of them in his Sylvan Archer article on bow design—the one place where it would have been vitally appropriate, I venture to say, indispensable?

I remain unconvinced that a graph of the "force-draw curve" of any bow will not be a fairly accurate indication of the bow's efficiency. The kind and quality of wood will of course condition performance to a large degree; therefore it is possible, as Dr. Klopsteg says, that of two bows with identical graph curves one may be highly efficient and the other a "lug". However, as Dr. Klopsteg will probably admit, a graph can with profit be made and studied by the craftsman who lacks his facilities for higher tests and computations.

It is my fervent hope that in the near future Dr. Klopsteg will give us more details for immediate application to bowyery problems in hand. Up to and including the present these have been scarce enough and lacking an organized comprehensive treatment. Of all men, Dr. Klopsteg is the one to perform this service.

—J. M. Howard

From Earl Hoyt Jr.

Earl Hoyt, Jr. writes: "Ken Wilhelm is engaged with the Southwest Sportsmen Show again this season for exhibition shooting. He has just completed a nine day run here in our city and will go with the show to Chicago for his next exhibition.

"The show is a very fine one from any outdoorsman's point of view, but from the archer's the Wilhelm attraction makes it doubly so. A very fine off-hand shot, that fellow. Not content with winning his laurels by his superb trick shooting on the scenes, he found it convenient to take a couple of the boys with the show to task behind the scenes. Someone suggested he could beat Ken two to one on the miniature skeet shooting range with the show. Ken, of course, put his reliance on his trusty bow, whereas the other fellow used a small caliber shot gun—and the result? Well, sir, Ken had six out of eight and his opponent five out of eight. Not bad wing shooting, I'd say, not bad.

"Yes, there are several of the so called field archers here in St. Louis as well as some out-state. Naturally it was quite a treat for us to meet first hand such an outstanding archer in this branch of the sport. Since we do considerable rabbit hunting hereabouts and the central and northern portions of Missouri affords some of the best bunny hunting to be had anywhere we have interested Ken in taking a little hunting trip with us. Not just at present, but we were able to extract from him his promise to return for this jamboree right after his present engagement with the sports show. So here's looking to the future.

"Having just read the very interesting article by Erle Stanley Gardner, "Passing the Buck", I feel moved to pass out a little advice which is the result of experience gained, as Mr. Gardner would put it, "the hard way". Mr. Gardner complains—not very demurely I'll admit—but then what archer, particularly those in the lower brackets, does take his shooting faults seriously—that when he releases the arrow 'slaps' the bow. Now I know exactly how he feels about this annoying 'slap'. It's just like the arrow giving the archer the 'bird' as its parting shout of gratitude for a poorly executed release. And the worst of it is there's nothing to get 'slap happy' about. Nevertheless, I have gone through a very strenuous period of hard knocks and bad slaps in my bow and arrow shooting and on this matter of arrow slapping I feel well qualified to give counsel.

"Usually, it seems, arrow slap grows by easy stages, like a disease that gradually becomes worse, until finally any archer that comes within 50 yards of you becomes unmistakably conscious of that 'slap' and even begins to flinch or blink his eyes in anticipation every time you draw up. That's when you've got it bad and that is the way I had it. But strangely enough, even though you have been fighting with arrow slap for a long time or even since you first began shooting the bow and arrow, the remedy is very, very simple. So simple that you will probably doubt it when I tell you. First of all, it is not one's release that causes the slap, it's the bow arm! And the bow arm will only cause the slap when it is held stiff and rigid. Perhaps you will say, 'But I don't hold my bow arm stiff; I most certainly flex it at the elbow but I get the slap just the same'. And you might be right, but flex it some more. In fact, flex it until you get that trio of harmony—no swat, no slap, no swear."

National Field Archery Ass'n.

(Continued from page 4)
fish and game commissions, the gun hunters, the forestry service, feel about the whole thing, and last but not least, the reaction of the Humane Society. I find that such information has in the past been very hard to get.

With this group of committees at work, and they have been appointed without regard to membership in the N.F.A.A., but wholly for their ability to do the job on hand, we should in the near future have some very definite information for those impatient souls who have been criticising our lack of activity.

We have this information from Mr. Harold A. Titcomb regarding Dr. Carl H. Bulcock, member of the Surrey Bowmen of England and known to many American archers: Last September he (Dr. Bulcock) gave up his medical practice, placed his wife and infant son in a zone safer from air raids and joined up with the British army once more, as lieutenant in the Royal army medical corps. Bulcock was in the Great War from 1914 to 1918 where he won the military cross. His reaction in joining the British forces is typical of all the many archers whom I knew personally in England. All of them who are at all fit physically are doing their bit for their country.

A splendid start has been made in the organization of the NFAA and the fine cooperation of NAA officials is very encouraging.

Doghouse Science

By Dr. Paul Bunyan, D.L., D.C.S.

THE ARROW THAT DIDN'T LEAVE THE GROUND

My brother doctors of canine science have often told you what happens when an arrow leaves the string. My part is to tell you of the arrow that never left the ground. It is a tragic tale.

All that science could do for that arrow had been done. It was the combined product of many master minds. We had given it every test that experience or ingenuity could devise.

We had special test tubes, thirty inches long, to hold the shafts. We had wind tunnels, weather vanes, our private glue factory; we had scales sensitive to the breath of a gnat. Outstanding scientists from all over the world cooperated.

It would have been far better, I thought, if we could have selected some leading physicists from outside our own circle. I tried it, but you know that Joe Cosner was there to short circuit the plan.

Joe, Dr. Cosner, I mean, admitted at once that he is as great a physicist as he is a prevaricator. Unfortunately, the only physics Joe knows is cathartics. So Dr. Einstein and the other outside lights went up in the air and withdrew after the first whiff of Joe.

I did get Dr. Gardner, the authority on Chinese whistling arrows. The sound, thought Erle, would enable us to locate an arrow in another state. By judicious crossing with meteors he raised the scale several octaves. It would have been a great boon to flight shooting, but the final product shrieked like a police siren, and instead of helping us to locate the shaft it only emptied the neighborhood. It shows what conscience can do, and we gave up the sound effect.

Resolutely we set about the preparatory work. Doghouse Counselors Lieuts. Latta and Sisler, U.S.N., worked out trajectories and other data, which I checked and verified.

To be sure, the counselors were used to small arms exclusively, but the fundamentals are the same.

We decided that our first major experiment was going to be a flight shoot from the Atlantic to the Pacific. Drs. Curt Hill, Homer Prouty, and Ken Wilhelm were to loose three arrows each. Drs. J. E. Davis and Chester Seay were made guards. The guards were stationed on top of Mt. Whitney, where our two bracketeers could lie and brag to each other about their trophies. Dr. Gardner, who lives at the foot of Palomar, stood at the 200 inch telescope to check stray arrows.

The flight shooters assembled in Dr. Henry Cumming's back yard. Drs. Teubner, Wetherill, and Shenk stood by to furnish language in case a string or bow should break. Master of Hounds Louis Smith checked the weapons and marked the arrows.

The bows were standardized, and no great matter. We had all agreed to use Oregon Onion wood on account of its strength. For strings we used ravelings of Dr. Brommer's socks. By using short limbs in our bows, with a long dead center, we found that we could get all the power we needed out of a 16 pound bow with four inch long limbs.

The arrow offered more difficulties. After trying several alloys and finding them unsatisfactory, we tested different woods. We finally chose the pussy willow. It's spine wasn't so outstanding, but the way it wrapped itself around the handle added all the impetus of centrifugal force. There—I hadn't intended to divulge the secret just yet.

The target was to be a wildcat in the Calico Mountains that Dr. Wilhelm would designate.

Somebody pulled a boner in the selection of our publicity committee. In the first place, we didn't need any. I flatter myself that anything sponsored by Dr. Bunyan gets enough publicity, anyway; too much if you ask me. Drs. Carpenter, Williams and Wilhelm don't know nothing in the first place, and in the second place, nobody would believe them under oath. I am just telling you these things so that you can discount any claims they make in thte future. If they as much as open their mouths, these fellows, or Joe Cosner, it will be just too bad for them. I have taken about all I intend to take from those guys.

To go on with the story, and ring down the curtain. How were we to know that the wildcat in the Calico Mountains should have a cousin mascoting in the Humane Society's pound in Barstow. The injunction against us was the last straw.

We aren't licked, of course, but to get all these scientific big-wigs together on foreign soil is going to take some doing. Their wives don't trust them enough.

Old Mission Field Archers

Ye Sylvan Archer:

Again we send news of the doings of the Old Mission Field Archers down here in San Diego.

On January 21 we celebrated our first birthday by staging one of our best field shoots up to this time. Silhouettes were the targets and many times were they punctured. Final scores found Bob Hoover high pointer, while in a vicious shootoff between Lafe Kemp, Don Lumley and C. W. McNatt, Lafe emerged winner of the handicap.

We tried something a little different in handicapping, using a third of the most hit target as basis for the handicapping for the balance of the shoot. It served its purpose quite well.

Following lunch the old officers, Lafe Kemp, president; Fred Tiffany, vice-president; Bob Hoover, secretary, were reelected.

A novelty shoot followed. A line was drawn some thirty yards from a big-horn silhouette where the archers were lined up. Each was supplied with a dowel, two feathers, a piece of thread and a piece of string.

At the word, a mad scramble toward brush or bamboo patch raised the dust as each archer lay about in search of bow wood. Then back to the starting line where bows were made, an arrow fashioned from the dowel (3 feathers required), and the shooting began. And such an exhibition! Arrows flew all over and only two entries managed to shoot even as far as the target. Archers rushed out under a cloud of floating arrows to retrieve their shafts for another shot.

After several exhausting minutes of this a hit was finally scored by Bob Hoover.

February 11 is the date for another go at the wily silhouettes.

Bob Hoover, Secretary,
Old Mission Field Archers.

Olympic Bowmen League

The third match of the thirteenth Olympic Bowmen league sees Detroit Archers leading with a 9254 total, Milwaukee second with 9226, Cleveland 9223, Soo Bowmen 9132 and Seattle Archers 9088. In the ladies' contest Detroit also leads with 8934; Seattle Archers, 8793; Milwaukee Archers, 8762; Detroit Archers No. 2, 8448; Cleveland Archers, 8411.

Individual high scorer is Jack Skanes of Detroit with an average of 786, Ernest Root of Soo Bowmen has 778.7, Fred Schweitzer of Cleveland 776, Leonard Carter of Seattle 775.3, Lawrence Belden also of Seattle and Bill Conger of Milwaukee are tied for fifth place with 772.7.

High average for ladies is 767.3 for Belvia Carter, Seattle, Shirley Richey of Detroit has 750.7, Paloma Kirkwood of Seattle has 750, Helen Marx of Milwaukee also 750, Marie Bear of Detroit 745.3.

In the third match Cleveland men were high with 3083 and the Detroit ladies team with 3016. Leonard Carter and Belvia Carter (no relation) both of Seattle, tied for high score of 794.

Many teams found weather conditions far from ideal for the third week's match. Atlanta, Georgia, had zero weather. Evansville, Indiana, shot with zero *inside*, Canton, Ohio, 10 degrees below.

SUBSCRIBERS PLEASE NOTICE
A cross appearing in this space means that your subscription has expired and we would appreciate your prompt renewal so that your name may be kept on our mailing list.

HANDBOOK—How to Make and Use Bows and Arrows—90 Pages well illustrated (with catalog) 35c.

CATALOG—100 pictures—color spread—Instruction Folder. 10c.

CATALOG alone 5c. Stamps or Coin.

L·E·STEMMLER· QUEENS VILLAGE·N·Y·

"KOOLER ARMGUARD"

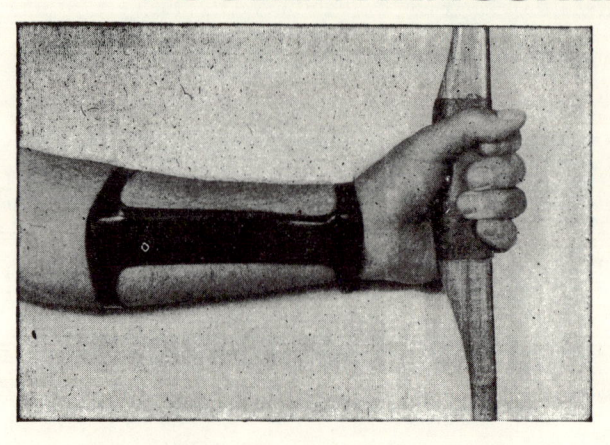

Cordovan leather
Lined with leather
Formed steel stay
Leather straps with buckles.

$1.25

Write for Catalog

A Complete Line of Archery Tackle
BEAR PRODUCTS CO.
4700 Burlingame
Detroit, Michigan

L. L. "Flight" DAILY
offers you
"Tackle That Talks"
Dry Cedar and Yew
Catalogue Free
245 Pearl, Eugene, Oregon

Paul H. Gordon, Director
Beacon Hill Craftsmen
Beacon, N. Y.
Where the serious archer's needs and desires are really consulted, and his orders exactly filled. Nothing too simple or too difficult.
Write for Complete Catalog

Alton's Archery Specialty
10c Buys Our "Baby" **BROADHEAD**
Spring Steel Blades on Target Piles
25 Per Cent Discount to Dealers
These Are Real Hand-made Hunters!
210 N. Main   Washburn, Ill.

Rose City Archery Co.
1149 NE 31st Avenue
Portland, Oregon

In 1940 competition, improve your scores with the tackle used by

Pat Chambers
National Champion
Catalogue on request

W. A. COCHRAN
Archery Equipment
High Elevation Yew Wood
Port Orford Cedar
Osage Orange
Air Seasoned
10,000 Billets and Staves in Stock
Route 2   Eugene, Ore.

The Flat Bow—70 pages of Archery information for 50 cents, well illustrated. Ye Sylvan Archer, 505 N. 11th St., Corvallis, Oregon.

Please mention Ye Sylvan Archer when writing advertisers.

INTRODUCING

The LAYTEX Bowstring!!

This is an outstanding improvement in bowstrings, both in treatment and construction. Special formulas of rubber latex such as are used in automobile tires, make possible the following:

Construction from start to finish under a high uniform tension.

The string will not fray or untwist. Waxing is never required.

Unaffected by heat, cold or moisture.

MOST IMPORTANT—This string is lighter in weight than the waxed string—and light weight means greater speed.

There is nothing experimental about this product. It has been thoroughly tested by more than 100 archers over a period of four years, and you may be assured that there is nothing better to be had, either in material or construction.

Single or Double Loop Strings 50c

E. AND G. ARROWSMITHS

3347 N. Capitol Ave.   Indianapolis, Ind.

Archery
Raw Materials

WM. A. JOY

9708 So. Hoover Street
LOS ANGELES, CALIF.

POTTER & MacQUARRIE
ROVING ARROWS

Split Birch or P. O. Cedar, 11-32 in. and 3-8 in., matched within 10 gr. in weight, and spined for heavy bows. Equipned with steel piles, 3 1-2 in. feathers and bright crest.

One Dozen $5.00

3400 Fruitvale Ave.
Oakland . . . . California

Arcadian Life Magazine
Tells the Story of the Ozarks
Nature, Health, Folklore, presented in a charming way. Published monthly in the backhills where the highway meets the by-ways. $1.00 pays for one year's subscription. Single copy, 25c. Try a classified ad in our Market Place. $1.00 pays for three insertions of your thirty word advertisement.
Short Pastoral Poems Wanted
O. E. RAYBURN, Editor
Caddo Gap, Arkansas

Ye Sylvan Archer—$1.00 per year.

ARCHERY BOWS
from the Heart of the Yew Country
W. I. KING
Woodworking Shop
1958½ Onyx St.   Eugene, Ore.

E. BUD PIERSON
Bowyer — Fletcher
Tournament Tackle, Sinew, Glue, Raw Materials.
245 University Ave
CINCINNATI, OHIO
Custom Made Tackle

ULLRICH WOOD
The Choice of Champions

Mill run 11-32, 21-64, 5-16, and 9-32 in. Cedar Dowels. From split out, air seasoned (in the square) stock. Dowels from same source segregated. Should match up like hair on a dog's back.

1000	$30.00
500	$17.40
250	$10.00
100	$ 4.00

(Any combination permissable)

EARL ULLRICH
Roseburg, Oregon

G

"THE MARK OF DISTINCTION IN ARCHERY TACKLE"

Fine Yew Target and Hunting Bows, Plain or Backed with Rawhide. Lemonwood Bows with Rawhide Backs.
College and School Equipment
Target, Hunting and Roving Arrows
Price List on Request
Wholesale — Retail

EARL GRUBBS
5518 W. Adams
Los Angeles, : California

Cassius Hayward Styles

BOWYER AND FLETCHER

—Tackle that has stood the test—

28 Vicente Place

BERKELEY, CALIFORNIA

YEW BOW TIMBER

High Altitude Air Seasoned Billets and Staves of Quality and Variety.

W. G. PRESCOTT
527 Chestnut   Ashland, Ore.

BROADHEADS

Blunts, and Broadhead Blades and Ferrules. Prices for one or a thousand. Circular on request.

ROY CASE   Racine, Wis.

WIN WITH BEN PEARSON ARROWS

Beautiful and accurate to the Nth degree but win their real laurels on the range. Arrows made as arrows should be—and at prices you can afford to pay. Send for catalogue.

BEN PEARSON, INC. — PINE BLUFF, ARK.

"The American Archer"

Complete your file with the 1st, 2nd and 3rd issues now out. Mail your subscriptions early. A subscription to a fellow archer makes a splendid gift.

THE AMERICAN ARCHER
521 Fifth Avenue
NEW YORK CITY, N. Y.

$1.00 Per Year   Published Quarterly

Ye Sylvan Archer

March, 1940

Corvallis, Oregon

Vol. 11   No. 11

Ye Sylvan Archer

Vol. 11 March, 1940 No. 11

Published the fifteenth of each month
for archers by archers
505 North 11th Street, Corvallis, Oregon

J. E. DAVIS .... Editor
RUSSELL JONES .... Business Manager
Subscription Price .... $1.00 Per Year
Foreign Subscription .... $1.25 Per Year
Single Copies .... 10 Cents

Advertising Rates on Application

TABLE OF CONTENTS

Page

IN THE EIGHT-MILE RESERVE
  By W. J. McFarlane 1
NATIONAL FIELD ARCHERY
ASSOCIATION
  By John L. Yount 2
SOUTHERN CALIFORNIA ARCHERS .. 4
GRAND AMERICAN TOURNAMENT 4
THE OLD TIMER 5
A MODERN ROBIN HOOD 5
LOS ANGELES CLUB 5
EDITORIAL 6
OLYMPIC BOWMEN LEAGUE 6
CHARLES G. NORTON 6
LETTER BOX 7
FIELD ARCHERS OF SOUTHERN
CALIFORNIA
  By Elmer W. Bedwell 8
AN ARCHERY GLOSSARY
  By Walt Wilhelm 9
DOGHOUSE SCIENCE
  By George Brommers 10

In the Eight-Mile Reserve

By W. J. McFarlane, Pasco, Washington

Bert Spurgeon and myself had been talking all summer about hunting in the 8-mile archery reserve but gave it up because we could get none of the archers to go with us. However, finding we could get a full week off, we finally decided to go.

We set up camp about 13 miles back in the reserve the evening of October 8. Early Monday morning we climbed the west slope of the mountain, seeing some deer but not getting close enough for a shot. After returning to camp we walked up the road about a mile and on returning saw several deer running toward us. "A bunch of does," we remarked, but soon saw one was a buck with branched antlers. We opened fire and arrows were flying all around the buck without effect.

Tuesday we went to the end of the road and saw many does and fawns. While Bert was eating his lunch in the car a buck came down the hill, right past the car. Bert assembled his weapons and was able to get in four close shots, close, but not close enough to mean meat in the pot.

Wednesday, on rounding a hill, I came upon a herd of does and fawns among the trees. Excitedly I observed that there was a buck among them. He ran away but stopped broadside at what I later found to be 66 steps. I missed with my first arrow, and he moved ahead a few feet. The second arrow passed under his belly. A doe entered the line of fire and I had to step to the left a few paces to put another shaft under the belly of the buck.

Nocking a fourth arrow, I aimed higher and the shot seemed to be going over him but, losing speed, it dropped to his back and he leaped away with lightning speed. I followed to the place he disappeared and sat down for twenty minutes, hoping the wounded deer would lie down if not followed too closely.

I followed what I thought were his tracks to the bottom of the hill and across a wide glade. This I did three times and then searched the forest around for two hours, with thoughts that can be better imagined than described.

About ready to give up, I started again at the place I had shot the deer and turned to the right about thirty yards away, where I had seen two startled fawns the first time. I noticed a fleck of blood on the ground and, raising my eyes, I saw my deer a few feet away, tumbled over a dead log.

I had hit him behind the shoulder above the middle. The arrow passed between the ribs on both sides and through the lungs. I had previously found the arrow near where I had shot him. About one-third of the feather end had broken off and did not enter the deer. The remainder of the arrow, which had passed through the buck, I found about fifty feet along the trail the deer had taken.

I was shooting a 55 lb. yew bow. The arrows were Port Orford cedar, 28 inches, with broadhead points one inch wide by 2¾ inches long made of band-saw blade inserted into 38 caliber bullet points.

The deer was a three and two point and weighed about 160 pounds.

There are hundreds of deer in the reserve and by the looks of the fawn crop there will be many more bucks to shoot at next year.

National Field Archery Ass'n

By John L. Yount

Harry Glover and his committee on rules, and the tournament committee headed by Karl Palmatier, have been very busy getting things in shape for the coming summer's shooting. They haven't had much time and for that reason haven't been able to do things as systematically as an organization of our type should, but I believe under the conditions they have done mighty well.

The rules committee has gotten together a pretty good set of rules which cover both the type of course and the rules for shooting it in very nice shape. At first glance, the program set forth by the tournament committee may seem rather ambitious, but after a little study I believe you will agree that it is not too much so. In the first place, it must be remembered that these five tournaments need not be extra tournaments. They may be combined with any local, club or association tournament. Also, since only the three best scores shot by any man are to be considered, the fact that you miss a tournament will not put you out of the running, neither will a windy day when good scores are impossible. If you only care to shoot in one there will be trophies for that tournament. Also to be considered are the isolated field clubs. They are completely removed from competition except among themselves. They have no strong local associations and their only chance of shooting in a major tournament is through some such arrangement of mail tournaments as here presented.

For lack of space the complete tournament rules will not be given. All interested clubs should write Karl Palmatier, 1317 Hillcrest Ave., Kalamazoo, Mich., for details and entry blanks.

Roving Round Rules

Targets

Four kinds of targets shall be used. (1) A 24 in. target with a 12 in. center and a 4 in. aiming center; (2) An 18 in. target with a 9 in. center and a 3 in. aiming center; (3) A 12 in. target with a 6 in. center and a 2 in. aiming center; (4) A 6 in. target with a 3 in. center and a 1 in. aiming center.

Targets shall be round. The centers may be either round or oval; if oval they must have an equivalent number of square inches and must be placed horizontal.

The outside ring shall be black, the center shall be white and the aiming center shall be black.

Ranges

A standard or official course shall consist of 28 targets containing 2 target shots at each of the following ranges.

15, 20, 25, and 30 yards at 12 in. target.

40, 45, and 50 yards at 18 in. target.

55, 60, and 65 yards at 24 in. target.

Position shots: each arrow to be shot from a different position or at a different target.

35 yards at 18 in. target.

(Each arrow from a different station or at a different target).

45, 40, 35, and 30 yards at 18 in. target.

80, 70, 60, and 50 yards at 24 in. target.

35, 30, 25, and 20 feet at 6 in. target.

A range to be official must be approved by the NFAA or by the affiliated state organization.

Official approval may be secured either from an individual authorized to give approval by the NFAA or by mailing a map of the range layout along with photographs and a description of the range to the NFAA.

Official approval shall depend upon the range answering the requirements previously listed and upon the SAFETY of the range.

Suggestions

Use straw butts.

Place targets in a figure eight so archers are always shooting out to eliminate danger and to speed up shooting as parties may be started off at targets one and fourteen.

Mix the targets up as much as possible, taking advantage of the terrain to make the course as tricky and interesting as possible.

Have no shooting position in any

place where there is any danger of anyone being hit by a stray arrow.

Wherever possible arrange targets so that shooting is into the hill to eliminate danger and reduce the time spent looking for lost arrows.

Scoring

A target captain and two score keepers shall be appointed by the field captain before starting.

All major tournaments shall use double scoring.

The target captain shall draw the arrows.

The target captain shall be the final judge of the value of all arrows.

Centers shall score 5.

The outside ring shall score 3.

Bounces out of the target shall be scored as 3.

Arrows passing through the target face but still in the butt may be pushed back and scored according to the hit.

Arrows passing completely through the target may be scored as 3.

Skids or glances into the target shall not be scored.

Shooting Procedure

The man with the highest score on the preceding target shall shoot first.

Archers shall shoot alone if they so desire—otherwise as many as there is room for shall shoot.

Four arrows shall be shot at each target or target group.

No sights or points of aim shall be used.

One minute only shall be allowed to shoot four arrows except on position shots.

Archers shall not approach the target until all have finished shooting.

Archers shall stand with both feet behind the shooting line.

Archers shall not hold up following parties while they look for arrows; enough arrows shall be carried so that the archer may continue his shooting and return later to find his lost arrows.

Tackle

Bows may not have any marks on them which can be used as sights.

Only arrows with blunt, roving, or target heads may be used.

Spectators

Spectators may not stand any farther than fifteen yards in front of the shooting line and then must be at least fifteen yards to each side of the shooting lane.

Spectators may not approach the target until the archers have finished shooting and then must not touch any of the arrows either in the ground or in the target.

Spectators interfering with the contestants shall be asked to leave the field.

Spectators shall not be permitted at any point where they interfere with the contestants.

Regulations for Competitive Mail Tournaments for 1940

There shall be five competitive mail tournaments.

Each tournament period shall consist of fifteen days.

The tournament dates are: first tournament any day from April 28 to May 12 inclusive; second tournament any day from June 9 to June 23 inclusive; third tournament any day from July 14 to July 28 inclusive; fourth tournament any day from August 11 to August 25 inclusive; fifth tournament any day from September 15 to September 29 inclusive.

The club must decide upon what date during the tournament period the club is to shoot in the mail tournament and then report only the scores made on that date. A date may be set ahead in case of rain.

The archers shall shoot a double Field Round.

Each entry shall be required to pay a 10c entry fee for each tournament to cover the expenses of reporting the meet and for purchasing medals.

The officers of the club must certify that the course has been properly laid out in accordance with the approved rules, and that the meet was conducted in accordance with the published rules of the game.

A report of the tournament shall be made and sent out to each club within ten days after the tournament period date.

Medals shall be awarded to the first, second, and third place high scoring archers in each mail tournament.

Awards shall be made to both men and ladies alike.

Championship medals shall be awarded to the first, second, and third places for both men and ladies based on the season's average.

To qualify for championship consideration an archer must have shot in at least three of the five tournaments.

The championships shall be determined by taking the average of the three highest scores each archer has shot during all the tournaments.

Mr. H. S. C. Cummings, chairman of the board of governors of the National Archery Association, has promised an award for the champion man.

The archers of the West have promised an award for the champion lady.

If scorecards are not available they may be had by writing to K. E. Palmatier, 1317 Hillcrest Ave., Kalamazoo, Mich., and inclosing five cents in money for each dozen.

MOST IMPORTANT — The registration fee must be mailed before the local club shoots in the tournament, and the date of the local tournament reported.

SOUTHERN CALIFORNIA ARCHERS ASSOCIATION

Of the twenty-eight teams registered in the 4th Bi-Monthly Team and Metropolitan Shoot, Long Beach, California, March 10, 1940, Long Beach furnished seven, Redondo three, Izaak Walton of Fullerton three, Huntington Park three. Fullerton three, San Pedro two, Los Angeles two, Elysian two, Santa Barbara one, San Diego one, and Pasadena one.

San Diego gave us a pleasant surprise by sending up a team that not only took the C class ribbons, but came near beating the "crack" Long Beach team, which won the B class honors.

Mr. Harold Titcomb, of Farmington, Maine, was a welcomed visitor and we hope he will turn in a favorable report of the shoot to his home folks.

Margaret Ogg shot another perfect end during the Metropolitan Round. Seems to be quite the usual thing for Margaret these days.

Mrs. L. Daley, a new member of the Long Beach Club, turned in a very favorable score for her first tournament experience.

Messrs. Brady, LaDow, Adams, and Tiffany, the surprise team from San Diego, have made the statement that they expect to capture the B ribbons at the next team shoot. What do you say, you fellows in the B division?

President Kelso and the members of the Long Beach Club are to be congratulated for the splendid arrangement of the field and facilities, and for the conduct of the shoot. Surely the Long Beach folks are a determined lot, for they have successfully built up a modern archery range, owned and operated by archers.

GRAND AMERICAN TOURNAMENT AT MILWAUKEE

The Golden Arrow that lured Robin Hood from the Green Forests of England eight centuries ago, will be the identical bait offered to entice modern American archers to Milwaukee this summer for the first annual Grand American Archery Tournament to be held at the Wisconsin State Fair Grounds, June 21, 22 and 23.

The 20th century bowmen will go their ancient rivals one better this year by tossing something like $5,000.00 into a pot for the feather-hatted sharpshooters to aim at.

This premier bow and arrow classic is being backed by the Archery Manufacturers association. Larry Whiffen, widely known Milwaukee archer, has been selected by the association as the Grand American tournament manager.

According to Whiffen, more than 1,000 of the country's greatest archery shots are expected to compete in the three day tournament.

Unlike former archery tournaments, this year's shoot will have none of the "hokus-pokus" that characterizes most meets. The ancient scoring systems, and meaningless rounds, handed down since the days of Richard the Lionhearted, will be abolished, thereby giving the American public an opportunity to understand thoroughly the thrilling archery sport.

Since the tournament was announced, only a few days ago, entries began pouring in, from Oregon to New York, and all indications point to one of the greatest gatherings the sport has ever known.

A pamphlet entitled "The Bow and Arrow for Big Game" will be published in the near future. It will consist of a collection of hunting stories by Forrest Nagler covering eight years experience after big game with bow and arrows. Further announcements will be made later.

The Old Timer

When you are on the trail, open canned milk by punching two small holes on opposite sides of the can, near the top. Then, in order to prevent the contents from spilling after using, place a small piece of paper over each hole and hold in place with a couple of turns of a rubber band.

For a short trip, try breaking the eggs you expect to take, into a jar which will hold about the required amount. It takes considerable shaking to break them and they may be poured out one at a time. I have found this saves much packing worry and is very convenient.

When hunting in brushy country, a small cork glued to the lower limb of the bow, 4 to 6 inches from the nock, with a notch cut a bit lower than the string to prevent it striking, will keep small twigs, etc, from catching under the string.

Let's hear from you with some of the little kinks which you have found convenient in your camping or hiking experience.

A Modern Robin Hood

A steel-tipped arrow sent winging through a window of Prime Minister Chamberlain's 10 Downing Street residence in the cause of "Social Credit" by a twentieth century would-be Robin Hood today, just missed one of the Cabinet members.

The arrow landed the green-jacket clad young man, Joseph Green, 22, by name, in court, where he said:

"A policeman told me the arrow just missed a Cabinet Minister standing in the anteroom."

However, because Green was to join the army tonight, he got off lightly, and was placed under a £2 ($8) peace bond for a year.

The arrow had a dangerous-looking steel head 2½ inches long. Attached to the shaft was a note four lines long, saying:

"End Hitlerism. The war demands a debt-free Britain. Social Credit is the only remedy. Social Credit is coming."

Green, who told reporters he could put an arrow through the throat of a man at fifty yards, used a yew bow of the legendary Robin Hood type. He said he shot through the window to avoid hitting the policeman in the door. He had intended to drive an arrow with his message attached into the Prime Minister's door in the best Robin Hood style.

As he entered Little Downing Street dressed in a green sports jacket and carrying his long bow he encountered the ever-present policeman, who remarked jovially: "Going shooting?"

"Yes, I am," replied Green.

The policeman laughed. Green laughed and let 10 Downing have it. (From newspaper clipping through courtesy of Forrest Nagler, Toronto, Canada.)

Los Angeles Club

The regular monthly tournament of the Los Angeles Archery club was held March 3. We were honored by having as our guest Mr. Harold Abbot Titcomb of Farmington, Maine, who is a member of The Royal Toxopholite Society, of London, England, and the Surrey Bowmen, Epsom Surrey, England. It was a wonderful day and as always when the Los Angeles Archers get together a good time was had by all. The winners were:

Ladies

Gean Bacon, Nat. 59-279; Col. 69-443; First Place.

Neenah Norton, Nat. 56-262; Col. 64-312; First H. C.

Men

1. Larry Hughes, York 134-782; Amer. 90-704.
2. Willard Bacon, York 120-620; Amer 90-602.
3. John Willard, York, 88-382; Amer. 86-472.

Handicap Division

1. P. K. Dugan.
2. W. Hibler.
3. Rex Bassett.

1st guest award went to H. A. Titcomb—York 100-422; Amer. 82-468.

Editorial

Friends of "Pop" Prouty, and all archers are his friends, will be sorry to learn that he recently met with an accident in which he received a broken hip. The hip is in a cast and it will be some weeks or even months before the cast can be removed. We hope that archers everywhere, whether they have known "Pop" personally or not, will send him a word of cheer by letter or card. Address "Pop" Prouty, 1604 N.E. 50 Ave., Portland, Oregon.

Mrs. Myrtle Miller of New York has accepted the archery chairmanship of the American Health and Physical Education and Recreation association. As chairman of the NAA junior archery committee Mrs. Miller hopes to conduct an inter-high school archery tournament early next fall.

We wish again to call attention to the regular weekly archery columns in the Pomona Valley Citizen, Pomona, California, by Walt Wilhelm; and the Antelope Valley Ledger-Gazette, Lancaster, California, by Hugh Slocum. Why not send a nickel to each of these papers for a sample copy and see what the boys have to say?

The sixth annual Ohio state championship archery-golf tournament will be held March 30-31, 1940, at the University Country Club of the Physical Education department of Ohio State University, Columbus, Ohio. Any archer is eligible to shoot, but only residents of Ohio are eligible for state championship awards.

Olympia Bowmen

At the end of the seventh match of the Olympic Bowmen League tournament, Belvia Carter still holds first place among the women shooters with an average of 781.4 points. Vivian Chambers is second with 757.1 and Shirley Richey is third with 755.4.

Jack Skanes is first in the men's division with 73.1 points, Fred Schweitzer second witth 782 and Larry Hughes third with 780.4.

The Detroit women's team still holds first place in total team points with Milwaukee second, Seattle third, Detroit No. 2 fourth, and Portland fifth.

For the men, Cleveland is again in first place, 51 points ahead of Detroit. Milwaukee is third, Elysian Archers fourth and Seattle fifth. Kore says, "the only secure spots seem to be the Detroit women's team and Belvia Carter's average." Three more matches to go and lots can happen to change the picture.

Charles G. Norton

Our genial and beloved member Charles G. Norton died from a heart attack on the subway Friday, February 23. His wife and friends were not aware of any heart trouble and it is reasonably certain that he did not know about it.

Charlie, as we all called him, had been interested in archery for many years. He was a member of the Mount Vernon, Scarsdale, Metropolitan and New York archery clubs. Like some of the rest of us he lived and breathed archery. He was an expert at flaking arrow heads from flint or glass.

It is believed that his last year was one of his happiest. For many years he had been an automobile salesman. Last year he became manager of the archery range at the Hunting Lodge concession at the New York World's Fair. His joy knew no bounds when he was at last able to spend all his time on the sport he loved so well.

Like many others, he had his "ups'" and "downs" with his scores. During the last month he had ascended the New York Archers Ladder to an enviable position. When he was "up" he was very happy but unlike many others, when he was "down" he was also happy. His happy-go-lucky disposition was envied by some of us who take life so seriously.

On at least one occasion he was known to have stayed at the New York Archers' Range shooting until three o'clock in the morning. Now he has gone where he can roam forever with his trusty bow. We shall miss him but we know he is happy.

NEW YORK ARCHERS
By C. N. Hickman.

Letter Box

Old Mission Archers

Ye Sylvan Archer:

Since last you heard from this locality two field shoots have passed into history. The first, which took place on February 11, 1940, was a dandy, bringing guest archers from the north and east besides an ever greater number of local archers.

Again silhouettes were the "game" and the greatest number of hits were credited to C. W. McNatt, our worthy "godfather." Succeeding honors went to Lafe Kemp and Bob Hoover. McNatt donated the prize of a half-dozen field arrows to the Club, and consolation prize went to John Grenfell, another of our members.

Following a hearty lunch a short business meeting ended with the conferring of an honorary membership on our friend from Imperial Valley, "Shorty" Clybern, who proceeded to prove his metal by winning the "William Tell" shoot which followed. This event wound up the affair for the day.

Then again on March 10, 1940, the Old Mission Field Archers gathered for a bit of "arching." But the turnout was poor, partly due to the absence of some of the gang who had left for a week-end hunt. However, a shoot of sorts was held and resulted in a tie for high score between Lafe Kemp and "Shorty" Ashworth. Lafe won the shootoff.

Another tie occurred between brothers Don and Russ Lunley, with Don taking the final lead.

In a drawing for the prize Tommy (Mrs. Bob) Evans was lucky and walked away with a dozen shafts, heads and nocks. Guess Bob will be heckled until he makes arrows for his "gal" but then she won the "makins"—that's fair! (Or is it?)

The archers who played "hooky" were Clyde Day, C. W. McNatt, Bill Horr, Gene Holston and Bob Hoover—and they've received plenty of comment therefor! But it seems fate evened things by bringing them home empty handed and mighty tired from their week-end. But it was fun, even though mighty disgruntling!

You see, the big "gripe" is this heartbreaking business of driving miles and miles to the tune of "No Hunting" signs, and most of them brand new from the quail season. I can't believe that all of those ranchers would object to archers prowling about in quest of rabbits and squirrels. Maybe we should inaugurate a new type of "No Hunting" sign—with a large broadhead in the background to indicate that the farmers' objections are only toward gun hunters, and that archers are recognized to be sportsmen and are welcome. How about this idea?

Yours truly,
Bob Hoover, Secy.
Old Mission Field Archers,
San Diego, Calif.

From Major Williams

Dear Editor:

Dr. Klopsteg's letter in the January Letter Box has induced me to break away from my bench and give attention to some of the so-called theoretical aspects of our craft and sport, of which he and Mr. Howard have written. After perusing both letters pretty carefully, the following thoughts are submitted to our readers, especially that large majority whose work and training has not involved a knowledge of scientific mechanics such as is employed in the writings of several of our well known contributors.

I have great admiration for the keen analytical ability and mathematical proficiency possessed by men of Dr. Klopsteg's type. I also stand in awe and reverence in the presence of a master of the violin; and I feel the same unbounded respect for the work of a master artist, whether he be of the brush-and-palette school, or a master of the pen, or crayon, or merely the lowly pencil. My respect for all these gifted people is largely due to my having made a slight start in each of the fields—sufficient to make me feel a keen appreciation of the sort of ability possessed by the masters. Having also been a teacher at one time and another during the past thirty-four years, I am inclined to read or listen to or view all products of the master minds, from a beginner's standpoint, and to see the points wherein a beginner is apt to be puzzled or confused. I therefore feel somewhat in the position of an interpreter, in my endeavor to make clear to non-scientifically trained readers, some of the matter contributed by the writers in question. If, as a result of my efforts, some readers will be able to say, "Oh! I begin to see what this is all about!" and to be able to follow through the details of a simple mechanical solution of scientific archery, I shall feel repaid for my time and effort. At the same time, I trust that the several authors of scientific archery contributions will understand and appreciate my effort to assist them in making their own writings of interest to a larger number of our readers.

To be able to form one's own opinion and think in scientific language, a clear understanding must be gained of a number of terms and expressions employed by our writers; these are: force; work; energy; velocity; acceleration; mass; weight; foot-pound; efficiency; elasticity; resilience; moment, or torque; stress; strain; tension; compression; and others that may perhaps have been overlooked by me at this time, but which I may have reason to use at a later time. Of the above list, the following are involved in Dr. Klopsteg's letter of January, and will be discussed in order, or incidentally in explaining other terms.

1. Force: That which produces, or TENDS to produce, motion; it is commonly measured in pounds or ounces, or grains, or tons, etc. Illustration: the pressure of one's fingers against the bow string; the pressure of one's feet on the ground; the pull exerted by the lifting cables of an elevator; the resistance encountered by an arrow when it strikes a target (this is a VARIABLE force, as is also the pull on the archer's fingers as he draws his bow; the latter, be it noted, starts with ZERO, nothing more; and ends with the final full-draw force commonly but inaptly and unfortunately termed the "weight" of a bow. This antiquated term is being gradually discarded, however, for the term "draw-force.') Note, also, that the force against the bow handle, from the bow hand, is, at every instant of the draw, EXACTLY EQUAL AND OPPOSITE IN DIRECTION, TO THE DRAWING FORCE. The old but correct expression, "Action and reaction are equal, and opposite in direction" is nicely illustrated in the drawing of a bow.

2. Work: A joke could readily be sprung here; but let us be serious, at least until my own "work" of getting my thoughts on paper, has been completed. In scientific mechanics, work means the product of FORCE and DISTANCE through which the force acts. It is expressed, commonly, in FOOT-POUNDS, or inch-pounds, or foot-tons, etc. Unless a force is able to produce MOTION in the thing against which it acts, no work is done. For example: a fifty pound weight is on the floor. My little grandson tries to lift it, but the force he exerts is insufficient, hence it, the force, does no work on the weight. (Yes, the boy "works hard," in the ordinary meaning of the term, but as far as

(Continued on page 11)

Field Archers Association of Southern California

The Malibu Mts. Archery Club played host to a large crowd of archers Sunday, February 25, but the weather was such that the event scheduled had to be postponed. At the Board of Governors meeting, held at the Club Honse, it was decided to have a return shoot at Malibu in June.

The next regular, which is the Annual Tournament, will be held at Redlands, April 28. It is hoped that all archers who entered this tournament will be able to attend the next, as their entry fees paid at Malibu are to be honored at the next tournament.

Several archers were down from Bakersfield, and they are getting a new permanent course for field shooting there, near the river with shade, and they are planning on holding a day's shoot soon, with special events and trophies. The date will be announced later.

Western Sportsman for March contains an article by Jim Browne on "Early Man the Hunter" that will be of interest to archers. The same issue contains an article entitled "Branding the Bums," describing the method by which a representative number of deer on each feed grounds were paint branded by means of bow and arrow by Forestry Service game specialists to check the drift of animals from one feed grounds to another.

An Archery Glossary

By Walt Wilhelm, Yermo, California

Like other exclusive groups, archers have their own names for every article of their shooting gear. They also have their own particular pet name for their tourneys and for the shooters that excell at the different archery games.

Shooting glove—A three-fingered affair, or a leather tab to protect the fingers on the hand that draws the bow. Without this device badly lacerated fingers would result if one indulged in much shooting, particularly if the bow was a heavy one.

Arm guard or bracer — A small leather covering strapped to the wrist of the arm that holds the bow. Most all archers wear this piece as it prevents the bow-string from whipping the forearm.

There is another sort of bracer, which is popular on cold mornings. Most of the boys use both kinds.

Nock—The groove on the ends of the bow that holds the string in place. The furrow that holds the arrow on the string is also called the nock. Placing the arrow on the string for shooting is nocking the arrow.

The loose—Is the most important step in archery. When you've let go the string and sent the feathered shaft towards its mark, you've loosed the arrow. A sloppy loose to an archer is like a slice to a golfer. You couldn't be a consistent high class marksman if you didn't have a steady, and even loose.

Broadhead—Doesn't mean that the archer's head is wide, or square. Heavy steel arrowheads used exclusively for killing big game are known as broadheads. Modern hunting points are three inches long and will cut a hole one and one half inches wide.

Blunt point—The archer's real pal, decidedly so for the bowmen that rove and do shooting on the ground. There are many kinds. Spent 38 caliber cartridge cases slipped over the business end of the shaft are the most common. Game up to the size of the coyote are easily taken with this master of arrows.

Shooteroo—Any major tournament for field archers.

Palorina—The guy who carries a bottle in his quiver.

Perfect end—Six consecutive bullseyes.

Bad end—To sit on some one's hunting arrow.

Stinkeroo—The lug that makes lousy tackle, yet persists in telling everyone what's wrong with the gear they've sweat blood to create. Here's the way they usually approach you: "Well, it's not so bad for the first bow, but if you'd cut two inches off each end, shorten up the handle, scrape a little off the belly of the lower limb and make a smaller string the thing would really shoot."

Stinkerina—The dame that sits down in front of the target to figure up her score when there's a foursome waiting to shoot at the mark she's obstructing.

Skunkeroo—The bird that insists on shooting first every time, and under pretense of getting his arrows broken, races to the target and pulls them out, calling bullseyes instead of three's.

A toughy—The guy that shoots a hunting bow without a shooting glove, and who doesn't remove his chewing tobacco when eating lunch.

Bruiser — The bird that shoots heavy blunts into a group of small target arrows, smashing the nocks.

Squaker—The illbred one who talks out loud when the ladies are shooting target.

Scallapants—The bird that shoots target tackle at a field archers' tournament.—Pomona Valley Citizen.

Doghouse Science

By George Brommers

EQUATIONS

I have what my friends call a phobia, I think of everything in mathematical terms. My scientific training and outlook causes me to refer to the most everyday matters by letter instead of by name.

Every married man knows what it means to get up in the morning and find his pants or some other conventional article of wear missing. The average male emits a rude bellow, inquiring in the name of Deity about the missing garment. I just meditate.

"S," I finally indicate, after hunting under the bed for a given length of time, "S should equal Socks in this house. Should do so in any normal household."

"In this case," corrects my better half, "S stands for Smell. Go out and wash your feet while I find you a clean pair." And so it goes.

Right now I am up against an equation that demands ingenuity and concentration. The fact of the matter is that I contemplate a Hunting Trip, H, very soon. The biggest unknown is the attitude of W, or Wife. Unknown, I say, unfortunately I know only too well.

"Hunting Trip," says W, "What should I wear?"

This is a poser. So far H minus W is as far as I have got. But how will it work out?

"It is a rough country," I begin.

"Yes," agrees W, "and a rough crowd."

"Now, now," I argue. "We aren't hunting coons this time, you know. Jack Willard, Chester Seay, George Miles, the Wilhelm Boys and Bill Joy are diamonds in the rough, but they can't corrupt me."

"Or vice versa," suggests W, "and what are you going to wear? What you need is a clean Khaki Suit, K. I suppose I will have to go out and buy you one again."

I wince. She will buy me one all right, and it will fit me like a tent. If I protest I will be urged to go along. I still flinch when I think of the last time we went shopping. It was just before the tournament in San Francisco, and the situation was about the same. What was I going to wear?

I had pointed out that my last suit was only four years old, and could stand one more cleaning and pressing. Did that get me anywhere, I ask you? Academic question, I know, but did it?

It ended, as such things have ended from time immemorial, in my being dragged downtown.

You know the rest. I picked out a dandy twelve dollar suit, just what I should have had. W saw one priced at $35. Why go on, you know what I got.

And now I am not allowed to use the suit for work clothes even, let alone for hunting trips. I had made the sacrifice for the sake of Domestic Happiness, D. So I gave in. W bought K. It fitted like I thought it would. The equation now stands:

D equals H plus K plus/minus W.

There were still P, Wife's Participation, and C, Wife's Clothes, to consider. Here was another poser.

"How about that black and white low-necked dress of yours," I ask. "The one you wear to parties. Cut off the trail or whatever you call it, the way a logger stags his pants. You will never get any more good out of it."

"My best dress," shrieks W. "Are you plumb off your base? Anybody would know that slacks are the only thing for the desert. I already have slacks. You do have the queerest notions!"

Again I gave in. What would you do? The equation now reads:

D equals H plus P plus W plus C.

"You will have a wonderful time." I tell W. "We will camp out in the open. We will be comfortable, too, with a rubber mattress. The rattlesnakes can't climb the sides of it, and the tarantulas can't sting through it. There aren't many hydrophobia skunks where we are going, either."

"Not where WE are going," agrees W. "You will have to learn to make some of your trips alone. I am going to make a quilt while you are gone."

It was up to me to make the most

of it. The equation now stands:

D equals H plus K minus W minus C. (Plus some unmitigated roughnecks who will probably try to get me soused).

And I have seen worse formulas.

P. S. Our old friend, Dr. Paul Bunyan blew in for a visit. Blew is right, too, he was laughing so hard that he blew down a ten foot fir tree right behind our cabin.

He was laughing at Joe Cosner, Reed Williams, Ted Carpenter and Walt Wilhelm, of course. He says they had better keep on taking it lying down or they will hear from him again.

Also, says Paul, we are to remember that that punk of a nephew of his, Paul Gordon, has nothing on the ball. Just thought I would let you know about it.

LETTER BOX

(Continued from page 8)

the weight is concerned, and the accomplishment of any USEFUL RESULT, it is as though he had spared himself all the useless effort; this must be clearly grasped if the reader is to "get" what follows, and understand the various articles on scientific archery.) Now, I come to his aid and lift the weight to a shelf, say two feet from the floor, thereby performing WORK, which is measured by the product of force by distance; 50 x 2, equals 100. 100 what? 100 FOOT-POUNDS. Now note this: had the weight been but 20 pounds, and the shelf 5 feet from the floor, the work would have been the same: 20 x 5, or 100 ft. lbs. Now use a pencil and paper yourself, for a simple example: What work is done when YOU walk upstairs, if your stairway is 12 feet, VERTICALLY, from floor to floor? (Your weight, times 12, equals what?) How would you put the result in FOOT-TONS? In inch-pounds?

Now, how about the work done in DRAWING your BOW to full draw? Here we have a VARIABLE FORCE, moving through a certain distance, which, for a 28-inch arrow, and a fistmele (bracing height) of seven inches from the bow's back, will be 21 inches. Force times distance moved equals work done; but what is the value of the force in this case? It starts with zero, and ends up with, say, 40 pounds. If you have ever measured the draw-force of a good bow or several good bows, reading the scales at every inch or so of the draw, you will have learned that the draw-force increases very nearly the SAME AMOUNT, PER INCH OF DRAW. This fact makes it possible to figure the work done, at any point of the draw, very easily; for the AVERAGE FORCE on the string from start to finish of the draw, is merely half of the final value; and if this average force be multiplied by the distance of the draw, the result is the number of foot-pounds of work done. Average value of force is 40/2, or 20; distance moved, in feet, is 20/12; work done is 20 x 1.75, or 35 ft. lbs. If this idea of average force is not quite clear, consider what a man is paid per month, if his daily pay varies; total up the month's pay, and divide it by the number of days worked; the AVERAGE PAY is the result. Multiply this by the number of days worked, and you have, of course, the total pay he received. Similarly, in the case of force and distance with the drawn bow; since the force increases practically uniformly from start to finish, the average is, in this case, JUST HALF THE FINAL AMOUNT. More of this later, when we come to the discussion of bow efficiency, and the graphs or curves referred to by Mr. Howard and Dr. Klopsteg. I shall hope to complete my contribution in subsequent issues, and to have inquiries sent you by any interested readers.

Sincerely yours
C. L. Williams,
(M. E., Cornell, 1905)

SUBSCRIBERS PLEASE NOTICE

A cross appearing in this space means that your subscription has expired and we would appreciate your prompt renewal so that your name may be kept on our mailing list.

HANDBOOK—How to Make and Use Bows and Arrows—90 Pages well illustrated (with catalog) 35c.

CATALOG—100 pictures—color spread—Instruction Folder. 10c.

CATALOG alone 5c. Stamps or Coin.

L·E·STEMMLER · QUEENS VILLAGE·N·Y·

CLASSIFIED ADVERTISING

RATES for Classified Advertising 5 cents per word per issue. Count initials and numbers as words. Minimum charge is 50 cents.

RELICS AND CURIOS

INDIAN RELICS, Beadwork, Coins, Curios, Books, Minerals, Weapons. Old West Photos. Catalog, 5c. Genuine African Bow, $3.75. Ancient flint arrowheads, perfect, 6c each—Indian Museum, Osborne, Kansas.

BOOKS AND MAGAZINES

"ARCHERY TACKLE, HOW TO MAKE AND HOW TO USE IT." by Adolph Shane. Bound in cloth and illustrated with more than fifty drawings and photographs. Information for making archery tackle and instructions for shooting. Price is $1.75. Send orders to Ye Sylvan Archer, 505 North 11th street, Corvallis.

"ARCHERY," by Robert P. Elmer M. D., revised edition, most complete book on archery published. 566 pages of valuable information for colleges, libraries, schools, camps archery clubs and individuals. Price $5.00 postpaid. orders to Ye Sylvan Archer, 505 North 11th street, Corvallis, Oregon.

BACK NUMBERS
YE SYLVAN ARCHER
Volumes I to V Inclusive
$1.00 Per Volume
B. G. THOMPSON
R. F. D. 1, Corvallis, Oregon

THE FLAT BOW
HUNT & METZ

70 pages of Archery information for 50 cents, well illustrated. Ye Sylvan Archer, 505 N. 11th St., Corvallis, Oregon.

Archery Raw Materials

WM. A. JOY

9708 So. Hoover Street
LOS ANGELES, CALIF.

Arcadian Life Magazine
Tells the Story of the Ozarks

Nature, Health, Folklore, presented in a charming way. Published monthly in the backhills where the highway meets the by-ways. $1.00 pays for one year's subscription. Single copy, 25c. Try a classified ad in our Market Place. $1.00 pays for three insertions of your thirty word advertisement.
Short Pastoral Poems Wanted
O. E. RAYBURN, Editor
Caddo Gap, Arkansas

POTTER & MacQUARRIE
ROVING ARROWS

Split Birch or P. O. Cedar, 11-32 in. and 3-8 in., matched within 10 gr. in weight, and spined for heavy bows. Equipped with steel piles, 3 1-2 in. feathers and bright crest.

One Dozen $5.00

3400 Fruitvale Ave.
Oakland . . . . California

ARCHERY BOWS
from the Heart of the Yew Country
W. I. KING
Woodworking Shop
1958½ Onyx St.   Eugene, Ore.

WIN WITH BEN PEARSON ARROWS

Beautiful and accurate to the Nth degree but win their real laurels on the range. Arrows made as arrows should be—and at prices you can afford to pay. Send for catalogue.

BEN PEARSON, INC. — PINE BLUFF, ARK.

Cassius Hayward Styles

BOWYER AND FLETCHER

—Tackle that has stood the test—

28 Vicente Place

BERKELEY, CALIFORNIA

Archery Raw Materials

WM. A. JOY

9708 So. Hoover Street
LOS ANGELES, CALIF.

POTTER & MacQUARRIE

ROVING ARROWS

Split Birch or P. O. Cedar, 11-32 in. and 3-8 in., matched within 10 gr. in weight, and spined for heavy bows. Equipped with steel piles, 3 1-2 in. feathers and bright crest.

One Dozen $5.00

3400 Fruitvale Ave.

Oakland . . . . California

(G)

"THE MARK OF DISTINCTION IN ARCHERY TACKLE"

Fine Yew Target and Hunting Bows, Plain or Backed with Rawhide. Lemonwood Bows with Rawhide Backs.

College and School Equipment Target, Hunting and Roving Arrows

Price List on Request

Wholesale — Retail

EARL GRUBBS
5518 W. Adams
Los Angeles, : California

ARCHERY BOWS
from the Heart of the Yew Country

W. I. KING
Woodworking Shop
1958½ Onyx St.   Eugene, Ore.

YEW BOW TIMBER

High Altitude Air Seasoned Billets and Staves of Quality and Variety.

W. G. PRESCOTT
527 Chestnut   Ashland, Ore.

E. BUD PIERSON
Bowyer — Fletcher
Tournament Tackle, Sinew, Glue, Raw Materials.
245 University Ave
CINCINNATI, OHIO
Custom Made Tackle

Write us for your needs in Archery books. Ye Sylvan Archer.

"KOOLER ARMGUARD"

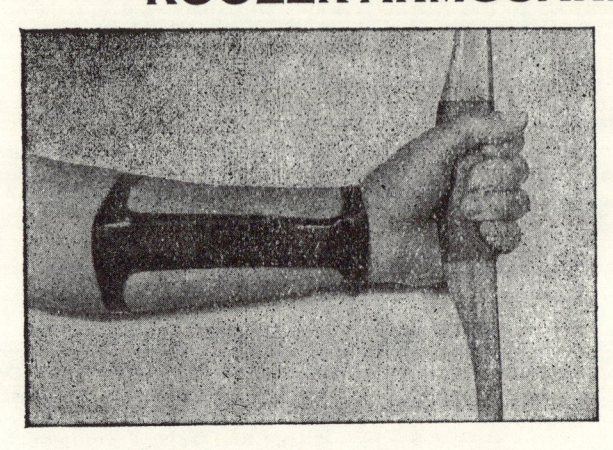

Cordovan leather
Lined with leather
Formed steel stay
Leather straps with buckles.

$1.25

Write for Catalog

A Complete Line of Archery Tackle
BEAR PRODUCTS CO.

4700 Burlingame
Detroit, Michigan

L. L. "Flight" DAILY
offers you
"Tackle That Talks"
Dry Cedar and Yew
Catalogue Free
245 Pearl, Eugene, Oregon

Paul H. Gordon, Director
Beacon Hill Craftsmen
Beacon, N. Y.
Where the serious archer's needs and desires are really consulted, and his orders exactly filled. Nothing too simple or too difficult.
Write for Complete Catalog

Alton's Archery Specialty
10c Buys Our "Baby"
BROADHEAD
Spring Steel Blades on Target Piles
25 Per Cent Discount to Dealers
These Are Real Hand-made Hunters!
210 N. Main   Washburn, Ill.

Rose City Archery Co.
1149 NE 31st Avenue
Portland, Oregon
In 1940 competition, improve your scores with the tackle used by
Pat Chambers
National Champion
Catalogue on request

W. A. COCHRAN
Archery Equipment
High Elevation Yew Wood
Port Orford Cedar
Osage Orange
Air Seasoned
10,000 Billets and Staves
in Stock
Route 2   Eugene, Ore.

The Flat Bow—70 pages of Archery information for 50 cents, well illustrated. *Ye Sylvan Archer*, 505 N. 11th St., Corvallis, Oregon.

Please mention Ye Sylvan Archer when writing advertisers.

Ye Sylvan Archer

April, 1940
Corvallis, Oregon

Vol. 11   No. 12

Ye
Sylvan Archer

"A magazine for the field archers"

Vol. 11　　　　April, 1940　　　　No. 12

Published the fifteenth of each month
for archers by archers
505 North 11th Street, Corvallis, Oregon

J. E. DAVIS .... Editor
RUSSELL JONES .... Business Manager
Subscription Price .... $1.00 Per Year
Foreign Subscription .... $1.25 Per Year
Single Copies .... 10 Cents
Advertising Rates on Application

TABLE OF CONTENTS

　　　　　　　　　　　　　　　　　　Page

HUNTING IN MOROLAND
　By Lieut. V. A. Sisler, Jr. 1

ARCHERY NOTES
　By "Uncle Hat" 5

A DYED-IN-THE-WOOL TARGET
　ARCHER BUILDS A TARGET
　COURSE
　By E. R. Teubner 6

EDITORIAL 7

OLYMPIC BOWMEN LEAGUE 7

NEWS SCOOPS OF FAASC
　By Elmer L. Bedwell 10

LETTER BOX 10

OHIO ARCHERY-GOLF CHAMPION-
　SHIP 14

THE OLD TIMER 15

Hunting in Moroland

By Lieut. V. A. Sisler, Jr., U.S.N.

The hot, high noonday sun beat down mercilessly on the small log-hewn banca which was lost in the wild labyrinth of the tropical swamp. For hours it had been hugging the protective shade of a clump of tall marsh grass. But now the sun was directly overhead and what little shade there had been was no more. One of the occupants moved — the one who was lying almost at full length in the inadequate bow of the canoe. The other occupant sat motionless, stirring only enough to remove the long black cigar from his mouth and exhale the smoke skyward. Bugs, flies, the intolerable heat — nothing animated him except the big homemade cigar. He was a small man, almost a pygmy, well muscled and exceedingly hard and tough. His skin that was dark brown with a coppery tinge glistened in the sun. Dark beady eyes peered out from sunken depths under shaggy brows and whenever he smiled or opened his mouth two rows of gleaming black teeth were revealed set in gums equally as black. This discoloration, it must be explained, was due to the fact that he was an addict of the habit-forming betel nut. Around his head of closely cropped hair was wound a turban, the original color of which had been pink, but now was almost black. The only other raiment was a dirty loin cloth of some ancient material held to his waist by a rope belt. Inserted in the belt was a wicked-looking dagger which was his only weapon.

The prostrate form in the bow of the craft was that of a white man who, from all appearances, was in the most excruciating stages of discomfort. His khaki clothes were wet with perspiration and the sun helmet pulled down over his face hid a red and blistered countenance. Every few minutes he would turn his body slightly to alleviate the strain of his position while the canoe tipped dangerously as he accomplished this feat.

The man was exhausted from the heat and at the present moment was torturing himself with thoughts of all the wonderful places there were to hunt except in the heart of a swamp on the Isle of Mindanao. The wilds of the Olympics, for instance, beside a cool mountain stream, deep in the shadows of spruce and pine; the wonderful hunting country of Oregon; the high mountain meadows of California, fragrant with pine and washed by the clean sweet wind; all of these places called to him and made his present location more detestable.

It seemed slightly idiotic to be on this wild goose chase with a wild man in a wild country. It occurred to him that perhaps only an archer, devoted to the bow, would be foolish enough to travel nearly half way across the southern portion of Mindanao to hunt game in what is reputed to be an extremely dangerous spot, though a veritable hunter's paradise.

He thought of the weary hot miles he had travelled from where the car

The Author practicing at corner of old Manila wall.

had deposited him and his belongings in the small hours of the morning. He could still feel the weight of the pack sack on his back as he trudged along, mile after weary mile. And how in the world he was to muster enough strength to tramp the long miles of the return trip he did not know — his imagination refused to carry him that far. The very idea of the narrow caribao trail through the steaming jungles, the only outlet to civilization, was at the present moment nauseating.

And now that the trip is over, and I am resting comfortably in my bunk, I find that I'm not such a fool for taking the journey as I thought at the time. Though the trip was a hard one, about the hardest I have ever taken, and left me weak and beaten for days, I can re-live again those experiences with a definite sensation of pleasure and deep satisfaction. True enough, if it had not been for my love of archery, I should never have attempted such a journey, but if the bow can lead me again to such a spot as that, I shall be well content to follow.

Ever since the ship put in at a small cove on the southern coast of Mindanao I had been casting about for information as to where one could hunt. After many excursions ashore one of the Mestiza natives told me of a place that he had heard was a paradise for game; namely, ducks, marsh-hens, herons, cranes, snipe, swamp-deer and wild hogs. I was eager to be off, so made immediate arrangements. I was to follow the crude map the native had drawn for me until I came to the end of the trail. Arriving there I might find a Moro who called himself Abdul. When (and if) I found him I was to present him with a letter written by my native informant.

And so it was that on a certain morning in late April I found myself walking down a narrow trail through the jungle. The faintest glimmering of dawn brightened the east and made the path visible.

A good number of miles had been covered by the time the sun was above the treetops. As the sun rose so did the noises of the jungle. Birds of brilliant plumage flew in and out of the green aisles, some squawking, some giving forth delightful song. I longed to shoot but resisted the temptation because every shot would mean a lost arrow and I wanted to save my supply of them for what was to come later. Monkeys scampered along the highway of trees above me, jeering and screeching. They made an easy target but I hadn't the heart to take a shot at one. I did keep an arrow on the string, however, for possible encounters with snakes. They are frequently found in that deep jungle country and I didn't want to miss an opportunity. However, I saw only two and they escaped unscathed. They were beautifully marked creatures closely resembling a King snake.

The sun had hardly topped the trees when I began to feel the heat. It seemed to rise in engulfing waves, all but suffocating me. Any physical effort in such a climate leaves one utterly exhausted and so it was that in fifteen minutes I was feeling the effects of it and my feet commenced to drag. The pack increased unbelievably in weight, and I looked at the crude map with some concern. The trail, if it could be called such, had degenerated until it was nothing but a jumble of twisted roots which, for the most part, were hidden under murky water, making the going extremely difficult.

The trail finally ended in a soggy mire on the edge of a great swamp which, from my vantage point, appeared impenetrable. Never have I seen a wilder and more forlorn looking spot. Looking about eagerly for evidences of life I saw only footprints in the mud on the banks of the sluggish stream which had barred my further progress. Nothing moved and only the faintest suggestion of a breeze whispered through the leaves. I dumped the pack from my shoulders and sat down to recuperate from the strenuous hike. For the moment I was totally disinterested in hunting — my only thought being to rest my weary, aching bones. Thus I sat for perhaps ten minutes. Then I straightened up to get a good breath and stretch my shoulders a bit — and was almost startled out of my wits. There, standing behind a log not twenty yards away, was my Moro with the pink turban and the dirty loin cloth. How long he had been there I had no way of knowing, but I suppose he had been standing there ever since my arrival.

"Are you Abdul?" I stammered.

He said nothing but hopped over the log and advanced toward me. Not knowing his intentions I pulled an arrow out of the quiver and commenced idly spinning it on my fingers with the greatest nonchalance I could muster, meanwhile thinking that it would serve as a weapon if necessary.

"What is your name?"

This time he stopped and ejaculated a jumble of words which were meaningless to me. However, when he finished speaking he smiled, the effect being quite startling, for he disclosed the blackest teeth I have ever seen. He pointed to the bow and came closer. This action, with the smile, somewhat relieved my fears and I permitted him to look at the weapon. He picked it up and scrutinized it closely and finally nodded his head in what semed to be approval. Next, he looked at the arrows and when he saw the steel broadheads his head waggled expressively and his face lit up in such a way that I knew he liked them. He probably told me so in his own language for he jabbered continuously and gestured wildly, making large sweeps with his arms and rolling his head to and fro. When he stopped I handed him the letter which he took, meanwhile mumbling to himself. After long and laborious examination, much turning of the letter and scanning of its contents, he looked at me in a way that made me quite sure he hadn't the vaguest notion of what it was all about.

"Abdul, if your name is Abdul," I said, "I want to go hunting in the swamp. Can you take me to the place where there are many birds?"

I made motions as I spoke, trying to show him that I wantd to shoot birds. Abdul, however, remained unimpressed. As a last resort, I finally loosed an arrow at an outline of a bird drawn in the mud. When he saw this he nodded and with a quick turn disappeared into the underbrush. Soon I heard him dragging something toward the small stream and in another moment the foliage parted and revealed that he had a log-hewn banca in tow. It was about fourteen feet long, with a beam of approximately eighteen inches at the widest point. With the greatest dexterity he had the banca in the water and had loaded my duffle amidships. He then motioned for me to sit in the bow. I accomplished that by barely managing to squeeze between the steep sides to sit on the wet bottom of the craft.

How Abdul could make that banca go! He seemed merely to will it to go in a certain direction and it would unerringly head that way. He was a one man marvel with the paddle. The route led down a winding narrow stream full of unexpected turns and floating logs and stumps. At its widest, the stream was only six feet across, yet my guide never allowed the boat to touch the banks.

At first I thought it impossible for that unbalanced banca to remain upright, for the slightest shift of weight would cause a near catastrophe. However, after ten minutes or so I got the feel of it and settled down to enjoy the experience. The banks on either side of the stream were overhung with rich and luxuriant growths which formed an archway overhead. Long trailers and vines hung down from the trees like a green curtain shutting out the sun so that we were travelling in a dusk-like solitude. We proceeded along this waterway, which was frequently crossed by others, for perhaps half an hour. On suddenly rounding a turn we shot forth into brilliant sunlight flooding a vast swamp which opened up before us, extending for miles as far as the eye could reach. Leaves and water lilies covered the surface of the coffee-colored water. Tiny islands of tall swamp grass interlaced in and out over the surface of the swamp. A slight breeze blew gently, rustling the tall grass and rippling the surface of the water, causing it to appear as if myriads of sparkling diamonds were sprinkled upon it. It was a marvelous sight, instilling in the soul a feeling of great beauty and vast loneliness. I forgot the aching toil of the long trek which had proceeded in wonderment at the existence of such a place in a far off Philippine jungle.

The canoe fairly skimmed over the surface of the water. The Moro seated in the stern was a master of the art without an equal. Skirmish lines of lazily flying herons and cranes preceded us. The smaller birds (more in evidence every minute) scattered half flying into the protective grass on either side of the channel. Birds of almost every description surrounded us — in the thickets, on the wing, in the water — screaming and calling, cackling and clucking. At intervals from far off we heard the long drawn-out wail of some unknown bird which added to the feeling of loneliness in the swampland.

I was eager to start shooting. By risky experimentation I found that it was possible to rise in the banca to shoot if the rising were done gradually. Once upright it was easy to maintain balance. The danger was in the getting up to a standing position.

Much to my disappointment no ducks, the game which I especially longed to shoot, were in sight so I tried my luck on a peculiar type of marsh-hen which inhabited the more open water thus allowing a chance for a fairly close shot. By shooting at these birds I got some much-needed practice and recovered more arrows than I might have otherwise. Abdul, for so I called him in spite of his doubtful identity, soon caught on and maneuvered so that I was of 'ered the best shots. The sport was easy and in an hour I had killed five of the marsh-hens. As yet I had seen no ducks and was beginning to believe that there might not be any. None-the-less there was plenty of sport without them for in addition to the peculiar birds at which I had been shooting there were fine white herons, cranes and fish-hawks in profusion, which always offer a good target for an archer's arrow.

About ten in the morning there occurred one of the strangest phenomena I have ever seen. The swamp, which was literally teeming with wild life, abruptly became as still as death. Where a minute before there had been thousands of noisy birds there were suddenly none. As the birds ceased their calls so the wind suddenly dropped. It was then that I became aware of the full force of the tropical sun. In short order I was soaked with perspiration. The sun pierced through my shirt in burning rays and the heat rose up in stifling waves around me making it a physical effort to breathe. I felt light-headed and dizzy. Trying to get comfortable and conquer the nausea that swept over me I stretched out in the bottom of the canoe. Abdul, apparently unmoved by the sudden change in our surroundings, paddled to a tall clump of grass and nosed the bow of the banca into the shadows, affording me a slight protection which he must have known I needed. Time seemed to stand still and for what seemed hours I squirmed, limp and bedraggled, in the bottom of the boat. I must have dozed off for when I opened my eyes the shade was gone and the coppery sun, which had just passed its zenith, shone with full force into our frail craft. Abdul remained motionless, except for the smoke he puffed out in great clouds from his long black cigar. I must have come very close to having a sun-stroke, because I vaguely remember that wierd and incoherent thoughts flashed through my mind. They were dispersed when I suddenly came to and found myself standing in water that was chest-deep. My clothes lying in the bottom of the canoe indicated that I must have undressed before plunging over the side. However, I have no recollection of so doing. At any rate the plunge brought me sharply to my senses, reviving me to the point where I was quite myself again. I relaxed and began to enjoy my swim in the cool water.

Abdul, however, was of a different opinion about this swim of mine. He was jabbering and gesticulating wildly, making clicking noises with his teeth as he did so. As soon as he had paddled close enough to me he grabbed my arm and attempted to haul me into the canoe, tilting the boat until it was precariously near the capsizing point. I did not know the reasons for his actions but did know that he was definitely emphatic, so without further delay or questioning I eased to the bow of the canoe and crawled in. Abdul immediately quieted and resorted to his smoking, while I busied myself with my clothes, trying to get them on before the sun had a chance to do its damaging work on my tender hide. I was at a loss to know what it was all about and gave up thinking about it when he picked up his paddle and started the craft moving ahead. Hoping there might be some shooting, and also feeling some relief, I reversed position so that I was facing the bow. Softly as night falling we glided down the narrow waterway which was bordered on either side by tall grass. In the distance, above the top of the grass, I

(Continued on page 11)

Archery Notes

By "Uncle Hat"—Harold A. Titcomb

Grass Valley, California
February 2, 1940

From Dr. Robert P. Elmer, of Wayne, Pennsylvania, I got the name of a California archer, Captain Cassius H. Styles, and spent a whole day with Captain Styles at Berkeley, California. He and his wife have a cheerful pleasant home in Berkeley, and he also has a shop where he manufactures high class bows and arrows, in the foothills several miles from his home.

Dr. Elmer told me that Styles had crashed, or had been shot down, three times during the great war when he was in the American Air Force. He was a prisoner in Germany and after the close of the war was in very poor health. He became acquainted with Dr. Saxton Pope, Art Young, and Stewart Edward White. Dr. Pope induced Styles to go up to the mountains, take up archery and learn to make his own tackle. By this kind of life Styles recovered his health and spirits.

It was a privilege to spend a day with him and I jotted down a few brief notes of his ideas about archery. He has hundreds of photographs of archers and letters from archers all over the world, including many from Saxton Pope written from 1920 to 1924. Pope's letters and directions gave Styles instructions about how to make a bow, and Pope made him a fine hunting bow of about 65 pounds weight.

Styles got acquainted with Indians and often goes hunting in the wilder regions of northern California with an Indian named Monte, and in Oklahoma was made a member of the Osage Indian tribe. He said that Monte is a very good shot with the bow and a wonderful hunter indeed. His skill in hunting and stalking is so great that he has often gone out with his bow and arrows and got his deer in less than an hour.

Both Styles and Mrs. Styles go hunting and camping together and Mrs. Styles has also shot her deer with bow and arrow. They regard a well made broad point arrow as more deadly than firearms and it causes less pain to the game shot. Styles has made high class bows and arrows for perhaps a hundred archers, including many in England. He and his wife are very fond of birds and have tamed them so that birds gather in numbers about their home and about the archery shop. In shooting game, Styles uses a point of aim, choosing a spot on the ground below the game if it is closer than 60 yards range. He corrects his second arrow by noting where the first arrow hit, and told me that the second arrow almost always hits the game. With a broad point arrow properly designed, the penetration is great, and he has shot an arrow clear through a bear's body and the arrow kept right on going up the hill for perhaps forty or fifty yards farther. He uses a rigid left arm and a light grip on the bow. He did not know whether Art Young used any point of aim or not. He regarded Art Young as probably the finest real archer of modern times.

Styles has made well over 700 at the single York Round and also six consecutive golds. He remarked. "That last sixth arrow seems difficult to place in the gold." In my pocket I had some recent letters from Weston Martyr and from Carl Bullock and I left those with Styles to read; he enjoyed them.

He hoped and expected that the allies would win the war against Germany, but said, "If I am needed I would want to join up and fight again and help them out."

Next week I hope to visit Southern California, and perhaps see other western archers there.

(Continued in next issue)

MISSOURI STATE TOURNAMENT AT SEDALIA

The Missouri State tournament will be held June 15 and 16 at Sedalia, Mo. The committee plans to make it the most interesting and enjoyable shoot ever held in the state of Missouri.

Anyone interested should get in touch with Mrs. Violette Henderson, 664 East 17th St., Sedalia, Mo.

A "Dyed-in-the-Wool" Target Archer Builds a Field Course

By E. R. Teubner, Horsham, Pennsylvania

I first shot the field archery course at the 1939 National Tournament at Minneapolis-St. Paul. So intrigued, was I at this combination of target shooting and hunting practice, that I determined to lay out a course on some wooded acreage in back of my place at Horsham, Pa. The layout was accomplished without great difficulty, and at a minimum of expense, and has provided keen enjoyment to the bowmen of my acquaintance in the east.

The map shows the general layout, which could be accomplished on any piece of ground of 6 or 7 acres or even less. The sketch also illustrates the construction of the bales of straw for the various target stations. We used a 3-bale stand for the 24 in. faces, 2 bales for the 18 in., and 1 bale for the 12 in. These bales were set on half logs, wired together with a heavy galvanized cable, and slate surface roofing nailed to half logs at the top. I might say that this scheme is inexpensive, and has provided adequate protection for the straw bales through a very heavy winter in this locality.

Rough benches were provided at all the stands, and direction arrows were cut out of sheet steel painted red and attached to rough cedar bean poles sunk in the ground. Pat Chambers provided the target faces painted on a light green sign painter's oilcloth, and, as you will note from the illustrations, speak for themselves.

Target No. 3 presented a problem in that this station could be most conveniently located practically on the lawn of the house. The straw

(Continued on page 7)

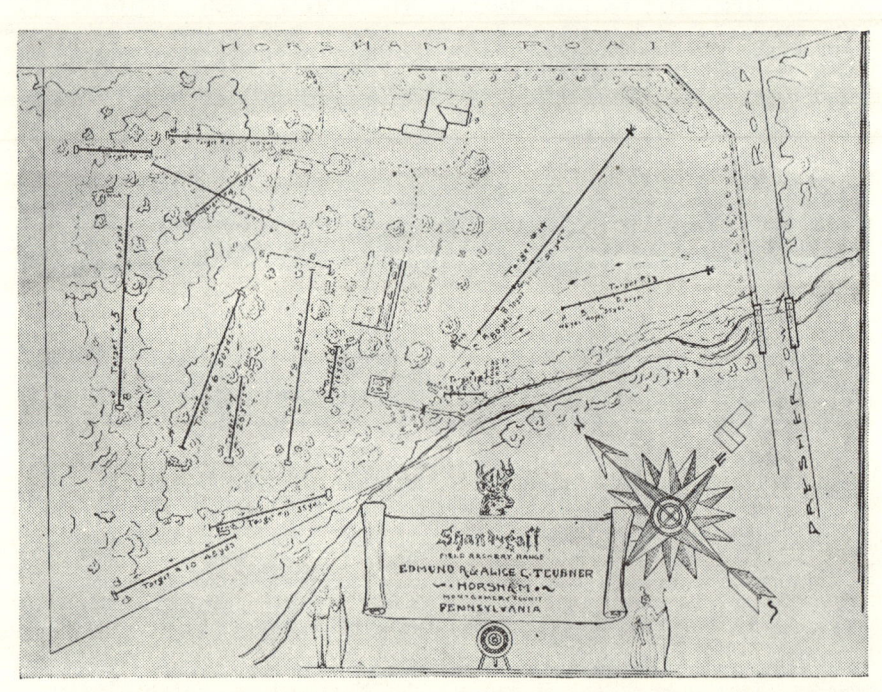

Editorial

We are mighty glad to report that "Pop" Prouty is getting along well and expects to be about again in four or five weeks.

Ben Pearson, of Pine Bluff, Arkansas, well known archery tackle manufacturer, was a Corvallis visitor recently.

Corvallis archers enjoyed a visit from Dr. Pfouts, of Payson, Utah, recently. Dr. Pfouts has many hobbies, and says his archery has been somewhat neglected lately. However, he expects to correct that.

First prize and a dozen dowels presented by Kenneth Clayton for the Caption Contest goes to Geo. F. Miles, Los Angeles, for, "So! There is another use for a shirt beside wearing it or betting it!" The dowels will be forwarded to George. We hope they are the three-eighths he wanted.

Archers are pleased to learn of the awarding of two additional honors to Dr. Paul E. Klopsteg. One is special recognition by the National Association of Manufacturers of Dr. Klopsteg as a "Modern Pioneer," to denote his initiative in pushing back the fronteers of a knowledge of applied science and in developing new products and methods out of which our standards of living are improved. The other new honor to Dr. Klopsteg is his election as Chairman of the Governing Board of the American Institute of Physics. At the 59th annual meeting of the NAA Dr. Klopsteg was presented the first J. Maurice Thompson Medal of Honor for outstanding service to archery.

Olympic Bowmen League

The Thirteenth Olympic Bowmen League was no hoodoo to the Detroit archers for in the final match they shot a record-breaking 3146, but Cleveland totalled 31004 to win the tournament. The Detroit women also broke records to win with a high match score of 3059 and 3018.8 average for a total of 30188 points.

Belvia Carter of Seattle was high individual in the women's division with an average score of 785.2. Shirley Richey was second, Vivian Chambers third, Paloma Kirkwood fourth and Helen Marx fifth. Leonard Carter lead the men with 784.2. Fred Schweitzer was second, Jack Skanes was third, Harry Gage was fourth and Bill Conyer fifth.

In team standings the east crowded out the west this time for high positions except that the Seattle women placed second. Milwaukee was third, Detroit No 2 fourth and Cleveland fifth. Milwaukee men were second, Detroit third, Soo Bowmen fourth and the Elysian archers of Los Angeles crowded Seattle out of fifth place.

This year's Olympic Bowmen League has been by far the most successfully conducted so far with teams entered from all parts of the country.

Field Course

(Continued from page 6)

bales were not very sightly in this prominent location. As you will see on illustration No. 2, we got around this by housing the bales in a rough wooden enclosure, making of the reverse side a bird sanctuary and a shrine to our good patron, St. Sebastian (photographs 2, 3, and 6). Photograph 5 is a close-up of "Old Debbil Moose," the 65-yd. baby. Note the sneer of utter complacence on his august countenance. Plate 4 shows stand No. 7, a short one, with bench and marker in the foreground. Plate 6, also a short one, shows the arrangement of standing posts, direction signs, and stands for targets 10 and 11 in the background. Plate 7 is another short one, the "four merry squirrels." This is the 12th stand.

For stands 13 and 14, as will be seen on the map, we utilize the American and York range in the meadow in front of the house, using the round target base. These two stations are the only ones on which we prohibit the use of broadheads.

(Photos are: No. 1, upper left; No. 2, center left; No. 3, lower left; No. 4, upper right; No. 5, center right; No. 6, lower right; No. 7, center. Bair Photo.—Ed.)

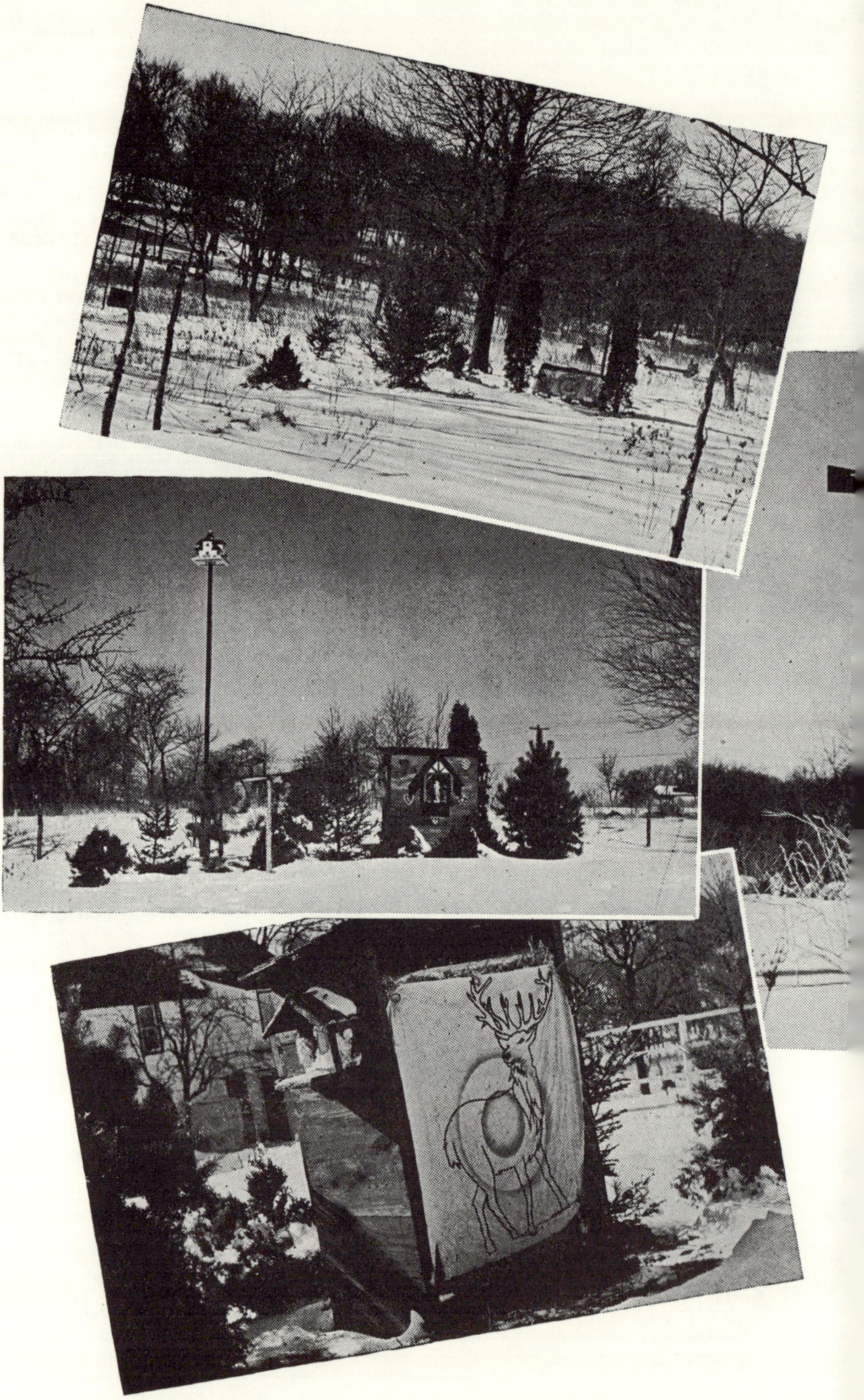

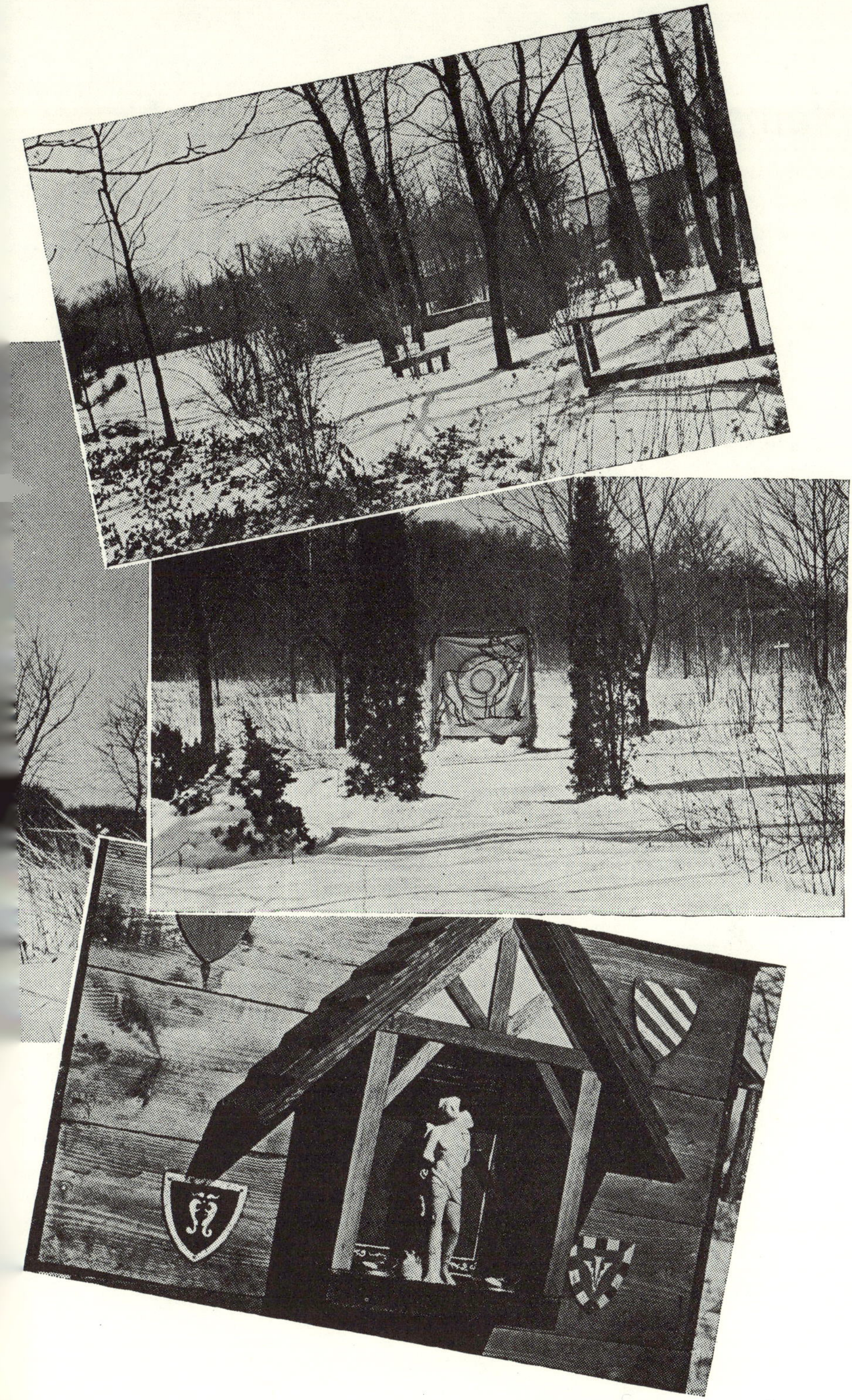

News Scoops of F. A. A. S. C.

By Elmer W. Bedwell, Secretary

We are pleased to report that our FAASC President, Edmund M. Brock, is able to be back on the job again after having had a major operation and being hospitalized several weeks. Sorry we didn't get to let the folks know sooner.

Southern California had the honor of a visit from Harold McQuarrie of Berkeley, vice-president of the SFAA. First trip down this far, he told us, and he seemed pleased with our shooting conditions and progress, and promised to come back again. The outstanding event of the month was the Field Tournament held by the Bakersfield Archery Club, and a nice job they did of it, too—nice grounds, and beautiful trophies. Everyone was happy, and we hope we can have more tournaments as successful

We hear the Southwestern Archery Club is doing some work on their trails, and are hoping to have a clubhouse one of these days. And we will wager that Heffner fixes that mud hole, too.

The other day we just happened to find out that there is a new Field Archers Club formed in Lancaster, and they are expecting to be represented at our next Southern California Tournament. It only goes to prove the field archers have something. The game sells itself once it is tried.

Redlands is doing some repair work on their course these days and are expecting to have it in A-1 shape for the next FAASC Tournament which is to be held April 28. They promise us new hay, and official targets, that pass the NFA approval. Also in conjunction with this tournament we will have a chance to enter the first NFA Tournament held sectionally by mail. You will be mailed more definite information about this before the tournament. This is also the annual, and election of officers are in order. We hope you will all be on hand to take part.

Letter Box

Dear Mr. Davis:

Yours of the 26th instant asking for a little story about game hunting with bow and arrow at hand. This is the third letter you have written so you must think I have something you want to know. Here is the whole secret.

When hunting game Indian fashion, get within bow range before you shoot. By this, I do not mean 100 yards, 75 yards or even 50, but close enough to place your broadhead in a vital spot, be it squirrel or deer. I once asked old Indian Joe of the Calipooys who had used a bow in his younger days, how close they figured to get to a deer before shooting. He said, "Just as close as the Lord will let us, brother." That is the system; use your skill in getting a close or short shot. The Indian did it and killed lots of game but Old Joe said that thirty feet was above the average distance that they had killed deer. I have spent years in study of these Indian methods with advice from Indian Joe and direct help and teaching from Don Chuck. Chuck is a younger man than Joe, but the hunting blood of his forefathers is sure in his veins. More about Chuck later. Lots of yew and cedar for our tackle and plenty of game if you do as Joe says, "get close."

I am perfectly willing to tell you of my experiences, but at this time would rather give you some exploits of Chet Stevenson who has hunted many times with Don and I. He has some of the finest hunting tackle I have seen and has been very successful in killing game that this country provides. I have his permission and with your consent, will send in a few stories of his hunts. I await your reply.

Sincerely,
—Tom O'Clayton.

(In the next issue of Ye Sylvan Archer we expect to have the first of a series of hunting stories by Tom O'Clayton.—Ed.)

Hunting in Moroland

(Continued from page 4)

could see thunder caps rolling up on the horizon and I wished fervently that there would be rain — the sudden deluging kind that leaves everything cool and fresh. Even as I wished for it I knew that it would not come — at least not when it was so sorely needed, for rain is a peculiarly contrary thing in these parts. The only way to conquer the heat was to sit as quietly as possible and attempt to forget it. However, I didn't have to attempt to forget— the birds came to my rescue.

Luck, or perhaps that odd zero hour of the day changed suddenly. Abdul started the ball rolling by doing a little hunting of his own. We were stopped in the narrow waterway with the banks only a foot from either side of the boat. A slight current was flowing and the water looked clear and fresh. I looked back at my guide to see why we had lingered there and saw that he was peering intently into the water. Then as quick as lightning his hand darted down and the next instant he was holding a wriggling, flapping silver fish. I was suddenly conscious that my mouth was hanging foolishly open. Never had I dreamed that such a feat was possible yet it had happened before my very eyes. As if he sensed my incredulity, Abdul repeated the trick. He did so six times until he was either sure that I was convinced or he figured that he had enough fish for his dinner.

Abdul went about his spectacular fishing in the following manner: the catfish (they more resembled that than anything) fed along the banks of the stream sticking their heads about three inches into the soft mud while doing so. The water was clear and only a few feet deep thus offering perfect visibility. My wily fisherman would merely glide up to them, a quick flash of a brown hand, kersplash! and there was a flopping fish in the boat.

Hardly had the last fish landed in the bottom of the banca when I heard the silken rustle of wings which caused my heart to leap. Looking up I observed a fine duck coming down over the grass about fifty yards ahead. The game had started! I carefully adjusted my arrows in the bow of the boat and shifted so that I could rise quickly. Abdul was a perfect guide, maneuvering so that only a small strip of grass was between us and the place where we had seen the bird come down. I gradually rose, so that I was in a crouching position, and peered over the intervening grass. What a marvelous sight!

Instead of the one duck we had seen, there, about twenty-five yards away, were twelve or fourteen grouped close together, bobbing their heads and feeding, completely oblivious to our presence. My heart was beating so furiously that I could scarcely raise the bow. In a way, I hated to shoot, so perfect was the picture. However, I yielded to the old primitive urge, took a bowman's privilege, and shot while they were siting on the water. The bow was firm in my grasp as the barb came against the back of it. It felt steady and powerful. For a moment every ounce of concentration was centered on the hold and aim — the nearest duck being the mark. Away flew the shaft in quick flight. A splash! A squawk! A flurry of wings! A quacking of ducks and then silence. I almost shouted. My bird lay still on the water and red was slowly spreading over the surface. The arrow floated a yard beyond, having gone completely through the handsome bird. A wild urge to yell swept over me as the boat approached and I felt that the trip was a huge success if not another thing was sighted. Such is the pleasure derived by an archer! It is not the killing power or the killing capacity but the feeling of closeness and companionship for the bow and a shot well made that makes for a successful trip.

The bird was a beautiful specimen —fat and in its prime. Undoubtedly the birds would all be good because the condition of this one proved that they were feeding on rice.

Abdul was maneuvering the boat again and a sharp hiss from him brought me out of my reverie. He pointed up ahead in the direction of the tall tulleries and suddenly there was a whir of wings and the same covey of ducks took flight heading directly away from the boat. Startled into action I fumbled an arrow on the string and loosed one at the fast disappearing birds. Of course I missed them a mile! The arrow fell with a faint chuck and buried itself in the bottom mud. It wasn't found, and to be frank, at least a dozen arrows were lost in this manner.

The wonderful sport lasted for hours. I shot till my arms ached. The swamp was the answer to an archer's prayer with game on all sides and ducks enough for even the most exacting huntsman. I had shots on the water and shots on the wing. At one spot I was able to shoot seven arrows into a group of ducks and they took flight only when I managed to hit one of them. On another occasion I made one of the best shots it has ever been my good fortune to make. It was Abdul who called my attention to the duck headed our way flying about ninety feet overhead. As a gesture, more than anything else, I loosed an arrow in its direction. With a hiss it left the bow and streaked skyward. For what seemed an interminable space of time we waited and suddenly a ring of feathers appeared and the bird plummeted to earth. The arrow that killed him was never found. He had been shot through the chest and killed instantly. Abdul must have been highly pleased because he gave a grunt that conveyed great tribute to me.

I wish I could describe all the shooting that took place in detail. It could have gone on indefinitely for there was never a moment, it seemed, when a mark was not in sight. The only limit to the shooting was the arrow supply and the physical endurance. The deer and the wild hogs which were reputed to exist in great numbers must have roamed into the forest, visible on the far horizon, for I saw no evidences of either. However, there was no lack of other game and I felt that I could forego the pleasure of a shot at the aforementioned animals in view of the abundance of other game.

Dusk was sifting down like a dark mist when I finally signed for Abdul to head back. I was completely lost in the maze of waterways and prairies but my companion in the stern did not hesitate. He headed back in the proper direction as unerringly as a homing pigeon.

It was while we were coursing through a channel in the prairies that the most exciting moment of the day occurred. With a sharp realization I understood why I had been scolded when I took that pleasurable swim earlier in the day.

As we entered the opening into the channel several ducks took flight and were almost out of sight before I had a chance to shoot. Peering through the dusk I observed one still on the water just getting ready to take off. I shot hastily and the arrow, directed by good fortune, caught the bird in the neck, killing him instantly. As the boat leisurely approached the kill Abdul gave his warning hiss and pointed toward a ruffle in the water, meanwhile indicating by excited speech and gestures that I shoot. I rose as quickly as possible and saw the corrugated back which was without doubt that of a crocodile. He was swimming toward the bird. Abdul was shaking the boat furiously and urging me to shoot without delay, and as I recollect, I was shaking just as furiously as that boat. I was so excited that I could hardly hold the bow steady as I drew up, yet I clearly remember how that "croc" looked over the tip of my arrow. That he was a crocodile, without a doubt, we later found. His head and body were moving from side to side and ripples "v'd" out where his snout cut the water. He was about thirty yards away and at the moment he appeared to be thirty yards long to me, though actually we found later that he was only a mere seven feet in length. I held low, for what seemed hours, hoping that the arrow would hit just behind where I thought the forelegs were. The shaft darted away and struck the water about a foot this side of him and with a sinking feeling I thought I had missed. But no! He was threshing around like a huge serpent, lunging and twisting, splashing the water high in the air and making a distinctive snorting noise. I could see the arrow protruding from his side as he turned over and over and it is a sight I shall never forget. I shot twice more but missed both times. Abdul, shouting like a mad man, paddled swiftly in the direction of all the commotion. The canoe came alongside the threshing creature and I could plainly see that my arrow was firmly affixed in the white portion, just below the foreleg, in the "croc's" body. My heart was in my mouth and I had a firm conviction that we were a little too close for comfort. In an instant, before I could grasp his intentions, Abdul had reached out and grabbed our small pet by the tail and was hanging on valiantly though it seemed that his arms were being pulled from their sockets. This time my heart did nipups. The crocodile's mouth opened horribly, disclosing a vicious looking set of teeth. The canoe was tipping dangerously and, in spite of my protests, Abdul clung to that snapping tail for dear life. I had another arrow on the string by this time and was looking for an opening—vainly, it seemed, for there was not a chance for a sure shot at that flashing body. The struggle went on until finally it seemed apparent that Abdul's strength was superior to that of the weakening beast and at length, with a supreme effort, my guide dragged the creature part way across the canoe. I saw my chance when the white portion of his body was exposed for an instant and plunged an arrow in up to the feathers. I could see the tip protruding from the thick hide of its back. Abdul was using his knife by this time and the air was rent with snorts and grunts and savage yells. To my consternation I realized that the canoe was rapidly filling with water and I knew that our minutes afloat were numbered. The stern went down first, depositing the two wrestlers in four feet of water. Abdul had a scissor grip around the beast with his legs, one arm around the throat, while the other arm wielded the dagger. I was breathing a prayed that the seconds of the animal be numbered for our only protection was Abdul's dagger and a broadhead that I had grabbed as the boat deserted me. Bow, arrows, pack, game, everything was somewhere on the bottom or floating near at hand. I could see nocks of arrows here and there bobbing on the surface. A small rubber life ring floated on the water, indicating the location of the pack. That was a precaution shown to me by Hugh Moffett while we were hunting in the Dismal Swamp of Virginia.

By the time I had waded to Abdul, with the intent of sinking the broadhead in at a vital spot, all struggling had stopped. The battle was over and the spoils to the victors, or victor, in this case, for Abdul alone had really fought the winning fight.

Thinking that there might be a mate to the beast that had been killed we made haste to empty the canoe and collect our belongings. It was only a matter of minutes before the canoe was lifted clear of the water, emptied, and flopped back right side up. We piled back in as soon as the equipment was dumped in the bottom. The boat was heavily laden, for in addition to the eight ducks and five marsh hens which had fallen to my arrows, there were six catfish and a crocodile. One might, with all honesty, call that a slightly mixed bag.

Abdul was quite obviously pleased with his crocodile. His grin stretched from one ear to the other. And for good reason, for I later learned that he could sell the skin, thereby obtaining enough money to provide for his simple needs for almost a year. I've no doubt that that thought motivated his actions concerning the animal and that it also explained his willingness to risk both our lives to obtain his end.

If only you archers who long for such opportunities could take advantage of what that remote swamp had to offer. Such experience could well prove to be the highlight in the life of a bowman. I am only a fair shot with the bow and the game shot that day was due solely to their great abundance and comparative tameness. However, my experience could be equalled and surpassed by anyone with the urge and energy to get there. That, I'm sorry to say, is not easy for most of us. And when all is said and done, I am glad in a way that this is so. If a place so alive with game were readily accessible it would soon cease to be the hunter's paradise that it is.

It was with just such thoughts as these in my mind that we glided through the dusk towards the entrance

(Continued on page 14)

Ohio Archery-Golf Championship

In the sixth annual state championship archery-golf tournament, conducted by the Ohio Archery-Golf and Hunting Association, March 30-31, at the University Country Club of the Athletic Association of the Ohio State University, Columbus archers wrested major laurels from players from Cleveland by winning first, second, and third places in the men's individual championship class, the club-team trophy, the inter-city cup, the light-weight flight shoot, and the lowest 18-target round. The new state champion is Paris B. Stockdale, of the Department of Geology of the Ohio State University, retiring president of the Ohio Archery-Golf and Hunting Association (just re-named "The Ohio Field-Archery Association"), whose score was 108 for the two-day, 18-target round. Dorothy Stanley, of Dayton, won the women's championship with a score of 143. Eighty participants registered in the tournament. Not a single winner of a year ago repeated this year.

The event was featured by a banquet, at which Karl Palmatier was guest speaker, and the annual business meeting. The organization went officially on record as endorsing the National Field Archery Association, with the condition that its attitude toward the style of archery-shooting be liberalized so as to allow any type of aiming, rather than to restrict shooting to the instinctive method. J. L. Heffernan, Dayton, was elected president to replace Paris B. Stockdale, who retired after five years of service. The new secretary-treasurer, Charles Rybolt, Middletown, succeeds E. E. Kimberly, of Columbus.

Following is a complete list of the tournament awards:

Championship Class—Men
1. Paris B. Stockdale, Columbus, 108; 2. J. P. Schweitzer, Jr., Columbus, 116; 3. Clive Schneider, Columbus, 119.

Championship Class—Women
1. Dorothy Stanley, Dayton, 143; 2. Doris Schenk, Newark, 152; 3. Patsy Schweitzer, Lakewood, 152.

Class B—Men
1. Fred Schenk, Newark, 131; 2. Charles Rybolt, Middletown, 137; 3. William Folberth, Cleveland, 137.

Lowest 18-target round, men— Paris B. Stockdale, Columbus, 52.

Lowest 18-target round, women— Dorothy Stanley, Dayton, 66.

Most bullseyes—Mike Humbert, Springboro, 29 bullseyes.

Club-team championship— Columbus, team composed of Paris B. Stockdale, J. P. Schweitzer, Jr., Clive Schneider, and J. S. Conner.

Inter-city cup—Columbus.

Longest flight shot, using archery-golf bow in regular archery-golf play—women's division, Frances Schweitzer, Lakewood, 252 yards; men's heavyweight, Curtis Hill, Dayton, 345 yards; men's lightweight, Paris B. Stockdale, Columbus, 288 yards.

"Columbus Bowbusters" Flight Arrow, awarded to the player entering the tournament for the first time, making the longest flight-shot on the first tee-off, won by Laurence A. Clark, Cleveland, 316 yards.

Hunting in Moroland

(Continued from page 13)

channel to the swamp. The setting sun over the far distant tree tops was closely followed by a rising moon that made the wild swamp take on an added beauty. Peace, tranquillity and an indescribable haunting sadness was the prevailing motif of the atmosphere. I slipped completely into the mood of the evening. The sun had dropped over the horizon and long fingers of dusk-dimmed light rose up into the sky. What had been an inferno earlier in the day was now a cool haven of peace and quiet and utter beauty. The moon, in its first quarter, cast its snowy light over the misty landscape as it crept up into the slowly deepening sky. Giant fruit bats swept and circled high overhead, lending an additional eerie wildness to the place.

The entrance to the swamp was suddenly upon us and as we shot through the opening I turned for a last look at this wonderful paradise. Far off, silhouetted against the dim twilight, I could see two slowly moving herons gracefully floating over the dark trees — a perfect last glimpse—a perfect ending to a hunter's day.

The Old Timer

That's pretty good, Johnny, but that ain't the way I heered it. Now, the way I heered it, the judge says t' the feller, "Say," he says, "Looks like you been guilty o' shootin' deer outa season. There's been everlastin' too much o' that goin' on around here. Think I better make a example o' you right here an' now, er ther won't be enny of us safe."

The best authorities on golf tell me that the main reason that I stand so close to the ball after I hit it is because I don't keep my eye on the ball. I have somewhat the same trouble with a rabbit or a squirrel when I am squinting out of one corner of my eye trying to find the cock feather on my arrow. For some time now I have been putting a very small gimp tack just ahead of the nocks on my hunting arrows back of the cock feather. I have found that it becomes a habit to pull the arrow from the quiver with the thumb on the tack head and the arrow may be nocked quickly with the cock feather in the correct position without having to glance at the arrow. This is especially convenient at night (now don't get me wrong) when it is impossible to see the cock feather anyway, and it has allowed me a chance for a shot numerous times while someone has been trying to get an arrow on his string. With some of the fellows with whom I hunt that is always a reason for gloating but far be it from me to mention it to them.

Speaking of cock feathers brings up another question to many. How am I going to dye a few feathers to be used for the cock feathers? Here is a method I have used with unusually good success. A few scraps of crepe paper of the selected color are soaked for a few minutes in a small amount of water. When most of the color has been taken out the paper is removed. A pinch of salt is added to the colored water and the feathers put in so that they are well covered. After they have been left in for a few hours (generally overnight) they are taken out and rinsed in cold water and spread out on old newspapers to dry. This will give them a very bright color and it is absolutely fast to rain or sun.

SUBSCRIBERS PLEASE NOTICE
A cross appearing in this space means that your subscription has expired and we would appreciate your prompt renewal so that your name may be kept on our mailing list.

Rose City Archery Co.
1149 NE 31st Avenue
Portland, Oregon

In 1940 competition, improve your scores with the tackle used by

Pat Chambers
National Champion
Catalogue on request

W. A. COCHRAN
Archery Equipment
High Elevation Yew Wood
Port Orford Cedar
Osage Orange
Air Seasoned
10,000 Billets and Staves in Stock
Route 2   Eugene, Ore.

Paul H. Gordon, Director
Beacon Hill Craftsmen
Beacon, N. Y.
Where the serious archer's needs and desires are really consulted, and his orders exactly filled. Nothing too simple or too difficult.
Write for Complete Catalog

CLASSIFIED ADVERTISING

RATES for Classified Advertising 5 cents per word per issue. Count initials and numbers as words. Minimum charge is 50 cents.

RELICS AND CURIOS

INDIAN RELICS, Beadwork, Coins, Curios, Books, Minerals, Weapons. Old West Photos. Catalog, 5c. Genuine African Bow, $3.75. Ancient flint arrowheads, perfect, 6c each—Indian Museum, Osborne, Kansas.

POTTER & MacQUARRIE

ROVING ARROWS

Split Birch or P. O. Cedar, 11-32 in. and 3-8 in., matched within 10 gr. in weight, and spined for heavy bows. Equipped with steel piles, 3 1-2 in. feathers and bright crest.

One Dozen $5.00

3400 Fruitvale Ave.

Oakland . . . . California

Arcadian Life Magazine
Tells the Story of the Ozarks
Nature, Health, Folklore, presented in a charming way. Published monthly in the backhills where the highway meets the by-ways. $1.00 pays for one year's subscription. Single copy, 25c. Try a classified ad in our Market Place. $1.00 pays for three insertions of your thirty word advertisement.
Short Pastoral Poems Wanted
O. E. RAYBURN, Editor
Caddo Gap, Arkansas

HANDBOOK—How to Make and Use Bows and Arrows—90 Pages well illustrated (with catalog) 35c.

CATALOG—100 pictures—color spread—Instruction Folder. 10c.

CATALOG alone 5c. Stamps or Coin.

L·E·STEMMLER· QUEENS VILLAGE·N·Y·

BOOKS AND MAGAZINES

"ARCHERY TACKLE, HOW TO MAKE AND HOW TO USE IT." by Adolph Shane. Bound in cloth and illustrated with more than fifty drawings and photographs. Information for making archery tackle and instructions for shooting. Price is $1.75. Send orders to Ye Sylvan Archer, 505 North 11th street, Corvallis.

"ARCHERY," by Robert P. Elmer M. D., revised edition, most complete book on archery published. 566 pages of valuable information for colleges, libraries, schools, camps archery clubs and individuals. Price $5.00 postpaid. orders to Ye Sylvan Archer, 505 North 11th street, Corvallis, Oregon.

THE FLAT BOW
HUNT & METZ

70 pages of Archery information for 50 cents, well illustrated. Ye Sylvan Archer, 505 N. 11th St., Corvallis, Oregon.

Archery Raw Materials

WM. A. JOY

9708 So. Hoover Street
LOS ANGELES, CALIF.

Please mention Ye Sylvan Archer when writing advertisers.

Folberth Needle Nock

DURALUM ARROWS HAVE BEEN PROVED

The Olympic Bowmen League has just announced the results of the ten-week tournament in which 57 teams from thirty-two cities competed. The results show that:

    The winning men's team for the entire ten weeks
    The winning men's team for the high single team match (new record)
    The winning man archer for the entire ten weeks
    The second-place man archer for the entire ten weeks
    The third-place man archer for the entire ten weeks
    The winner of an individual high single match
    ALL USED FOLBERTH NEEDLE NOCK ARROWS!

We believe that this remarkable showing was in part due to the new NEEDLE NOCK END that these arrows had which make possible a smoother release, and consequently result in more accurate shooting. All our arrows are tested for accuracy with a mechanical shooting bow. A paper pattern of their performance at 100 feet is included with each dozen arrows.

        Price—$10.00 to $15.00 per dozen

For additional information, write to—
    FOLBERTH ARROWS, 7821 Lake Ave., Cleveland, Ohio
        State arrow length and bow weight

BEAR
ALUMINUM ARROWS ARE MAKING RECORDS
BEAR PRODUCTS CO.
2611 W. Philadelphia Ave., Detroit, Michigan

Alton's Archery Specialty

10c Buys Our "Baby" **BROADHEAD**
Spring Steel Blades on Target Piles
25 Per Cent Discount to Dealers
These Are Real Hand-made Hunters!
210 N. Main   Washburn, Ill.

BACK NUMBERS
YE SYLVAN ARCHER
Volumes I to V Inclusive
$1.00 Per Volume
B. G. THOMPSON
R. F. D. 1, Corvallis, Oregon

L. L. "Flight" DAILY
offers you
"Tackle That Talks"
Dry Cedar and Yew
Catalogue Free
245 Pearl, Eugene, Oregon

The Flat Bow—70 pages of Archery information for 50 cents, well illustrated. *Ye Sylvan Archer,* 505 N. 11th St., Corvallis, Oregon.

WIN WITH BEN PEARSON ARROWS

Beautiful and accurate to the Nth degree but win their real laurels on the range. Arrows made as arrows should be—and at prices you can afford to pay. Send for catalogue.

BEN PEARSON, INC. — PINE BLUFF, ARK.

Cassius Hayward Styles

BOWYER AND FLETCHER

—Tackle that has stood the test—

28 Vicente Place

BERKELEY, CALIFORNIA

ULLRICH WOOD
The Choice of Champions

Mill run 11-32, 21-64, 5-16, and 9-32 in. Cedar Dowels. From split out, air seasoned (in the square) stock. Dowels from same source segregated. Should match up like hair on a dog's back.

1000	....	$30.00
500	....	$17.50
250	....	$10.00
100	....	$ 4.00

(Any combination permissable)

EARL ULLRICH
Roseburg, Oregon

Read
The AMERICAN ARCHER
"A National Quarterly"
J. C. Vives, Editor
521 Fifth Ave., New York, N. Y.
$1.00 per Year
First four issues now ready
Hunters enter A A National competition. Write for details.

Ye Sylvan Archer—$1.00 per year.

G

"THE MARK OF DISTINCTION IN ARCHERY TACKLE

Fine Yew Target and Hunting Bows, Plain or Backed with Rawhide. Lemonwood Bows with Rawhide Backs. College and School Equipment Target, Hunting and Roving Arrows
Price List on Request
Wholesale — Retail
EARL GRUBBS
5518 W. Adams
Los Angeles, : California

BROADHEADS

Blunts, and Broadhead Blades and Ferrules. Prices for one or a thousand. Circular on request.
ROY CASE   Racine, Wis.

YEW BOW TIMBER

High Altitude Air Seasoned Billets and Staves of Quality and Variety.
W. G. PRESCOTT
527 Chestnut   Ashland, Ore.

E. BUD PIERSON
Bowyer — Fletcher
Tournament Tackle, Sinew, Glue, Raw Materials.
245 University Ave
CINCINNATI, OHIO
Custom Made Tackle

Write us for your needs in Archery books. Ye Sylvan Archer.

Ye Sylvan Archer

May, 1940

Corvallis, Oregon

Vol. 12   No. 1

Ye Sylvan Archer

"A magazine for the field archers"

Vol. 12   May, 1940   No. 1

Published the fifteenth of each month
for archers by archers
505 North 11th Street, Corvallis, Oregon

J. E. DAVIS .... Editor
RUSSELL JONES .... Business Manager
Subscription Price .... $1.00 Per Year
Foreign Subscription .... $1.25 Per Year
Single Copies .... 10 Cents

Advertising Rates on Application

TABLE OF CONTENTS

	Page
JAVELINA! By A. J. Cosner	1
LOS ANGELES ARCHERY CLUB	2
NEW MEXICO FIELD ARCHERS	2
NATIONAL FIELD ARCHERY By John L. Yount	3
BROWN COUNTY OPEN	4
ARCHERY NOTES By "Uncle Hat"	5
EDITORIAL	6
WINTER INTERCOLLEGIATE MEET	6
INTERNATIONAL ARCHERY TOURNAMENT	6
OREGON STATE TOURNAMENT	7
WASHINGTON'S FIRST NFAA By George Brommers	8
SCFA NEWS NOTES	9
OLD MISSION FIELD ARCHERS	9
DOGHOUSE ARCHERY	10

Javelina!

By A. J. Cosner, Phoenix, Arizona

It is a euphonious name. It might be tacked onto a ravishing brunette of Latin persuasion or again it might be one of these Mexican dishes that can nourish a man equipped with a cast iron gullet, or burn him to ashes if he hasn't one.

This beautiful name that would do for a princess is wasted on a bristly, ornery, mean and contemptible little old hog. He isn't just these things, however. Although he only weighs forty pounds at the outside and sopping wet, he is fleet as a deer. He is lightning fast every move he makes. He can stop as quickly as he starts, which is instantly, and he can fight a buzz saw and bite out every other tooth if he wants to. He has vitality enough for two other animals. He may be dead, but you have to prove it to him.

From either side, the javelina looks like a lima bean with four tiny legs and a small triangular head pointed at the ground. His rear end is decorated with nothing.

The Arizona Game Department wanted to know how deadly a broadhead arrow might be and for the purpose of finding out, we were given a permit to hunt these worthless little wild pigs. They even wanted movies of the shindig so that there wouldn't be any faking. Added to that, a game warden went along so that he might testify as to whether an arrow was brutal or efficient. (After drinking two cups of coffee he made, I considered it immaterial. There are all kinds of brutality.)

The country selected was desert mountain. Javelinas eat cactus, roots, hunting dogs and people's legs, so they don't care where they live. This particular place was rolling desert with ocotilla about twelve feet apart all over it and that alone shows that they don't care. Ocotilla are branching bunches of bare sticks like buggy whips and are decked with thorns from ground to tip. Riding a horse through them is like using one of those Japanese bamboo combs, only on a larger scale.

Tom Imler and his brother Bud are used to horses and even own spurs to prove it, but twenty peaceful years have gone by since I had forked one. If they tell you that five hours of riding will darn near kill a greenhorn, they are right and it did. Little did that horse realize that he was carrying more driveling misery on his back than three men ought to have in a lifetime.

We rode for three miles (I rode six, counting up and down) at the heels of a skeptical rancher. Using my bow for a fender among the ocotillas, and kicking my horse in the belly with both heels, I came last. Bud Imler finally decided that such a spectacle as that needed an escort, so he rode behind and kept me company. We finally separated from the rest in combing a likely place, and in rounding a low hill we found hogs.

Imler, Klaus the warden, and Keith the rancher, had jumped a bunch of eight or ten. Klaus had the movie camera and was sighting through it while Keith was trying to maneuver a hog around so that Tom could get a shot recorded. Bud and I were above them doing the kibitzing. All of a sudden three of them separated from the bunch and came straight at us. We both strung our bows without dismounting. Bud didn't want to and I couldn't. Anyhow, try it sometime with a 75 pounder.

The hogs kept coming. They have poor eyesight and failed to see us until they were within thirty yards. At that time I got excited and tried a shot between my horse's ears. I missed him a good three feet, of course. All three of them went different directions and in a large hurry. The biggest one went down the hill and turned at about eighty yards so I decided to loose. The arrow caught him a little abaft the beam, as the sailors say, and with that he went into high gear. I still think that I distinctly heard his legs buzz, they went so fast. He went about fifty yards and started in dying. Bud and I helped him no little with another arrow through the heart.

In the meantime, Tom had gotten the setup he wanted. With the camera going and the hog at about thirty yards, Tom caught him at the point of the shoulder. The heavy birch arrow cut both shoulder points, the trachea and jugular. His wild pork simply fell over dead.

This hunt was of more interest to me on account of the fact that I have killed these animals before with a rifle. They can carry as much lead as a jaguar and if a man is afoot when they charge, he is in for trouble. The tusks are short but they are razor sharp and cut with a downward thrust. It is hard to imagine that he is dangerous, but his infernal speed gives him forty pounds of destructive fury. If a bullet is not instantly fatal, and it seldom is, trees are darned near a necessity. When it comes to a choice of weapons, for an animal of this kind, there is no choice. I have news that Bud went back to the same place and got his charging and right between the eyes and felled him like a shotgun would a rabbit.

We have the same old argument here that they have in every other state and will eventually surmount it, but it takes time and demonstrations and lobbying. Some time soon it will be legal to hunt here with the bow.

Los Angeles Archery Club

The sixteenth annual tournament of the Los Angeles Archery Club was held April 7, at Griffith Park.

The tournament got under way at 10:30 and inspired by the many trophies on display, every archer was in there doing his best. After shooting the York and National everyone was ready for lunch and a cup of that good coffee made by our excellent coffee maker, P. K. Dugan. While the boys were on the 60 yard line getting a little practice before the afternoon rounds, a big jack rabbit, who evidently had heard about point of aim archers, decided to run down the 80 yard line, which he did without a mishap. At 2 o'clock all were on the firing line and going strong. After the shoot a meeting was held at which time officers for the coming year were elected, as follows: Margaret Rand, President; P. K. Dugan, Vice President; and H. G. Hall, Secretary-Treasurer. A banquet was held in the evening and at that time the awards for the day were given.

The results of the tournament were: Ladies—1. Ilda Hanchett, Natl. 69-385 - Col. 72-502; 2. Gean Bacon, Natl. 61-276 - Col. 68-422; 3. Betty Bradstreet, Natl. 17-67 - Col. 46-208. Men—1. Larry Hughes, York, 139-812 - Amer. 90-636; 2. Willard Bacon, York 122-646 - Amer. 88-628; 3. Reed Williams, York 109-541 - Amer. 88-534.
H. C.—1. W. Hibler; 2. T. W. Brotherton; 3. Chester Seay.
—H. G. Hall, Secretary

New Mexico Field Archers

The New Mexico Field Archery Association was organized a month ago with ten charter members signing a petition to the NFAA to become the official representative body of that organization in this state. Officers were elected as follows: J. C. Trittin, President; Bud Rubins, Vice President; Joe Robb, Secretary-Treasurer; Dr. C. E. Buswell, Director of Junior Activities. Provisions were made in the constitution for any group of twenty or more individuals to be represented on the Governing Board by a director. Plans are rapidly being pushed to complete an official roving course so as to enter the five national tournaments.

An introductory Archery Golf tournament was sponsored to acquaint all archers with this sport. Two gold, two silver and two bronze arrows were donated by Mr. and Mrs. J. C. Trittin as trophies. Mr. Pard Wood, owner of the Sandra Golf Course graciously offered his facilities for this tournament. Even tho we competed with an eighty per cent eclipse of the sun, we had a lot of fun.

Our membership has more than doubled. The New Mexico F.A.A. will take an active part in the Coronado Cuarto Centennial Climax, the Entrala, the world premier of which will be held on the greatest open air stage of its kind in the Southwest, located at Albuquerque, New Mexico, May 29 to June 1, inclusive.

Strangely enough, in this land of the Redman, modern archery is still in its infant stage. We hope very shortly to have so many arrows flying around in New Mexico that people will instinctively duck as they go down the street.
—J. C. Trittin

National Field Archery

By John L. Yount

By the time you read this, if you do, the first of the national mail tournaments will be over, but don't let that discourage you. There will be four more. Each, we hope, bigger and better than the last. Since only the three best scores turned in by each archer are to be counted, you still have four chances to turn in three good scores. If you haven't a course, and you probably haven't or you would have been in the competition, you have plenty of time to put in a temporary course before the next tournament. You can build your permanent course later in the summer.

Having received more letters than I can possibly answer from people who want to know just how to go about laying out a good, official roving course, I am going to try to answer them collectively by describing the construction of our course here at Redlands.

Having had six previous courses, we had a pretty good idea of what we were looking for and what to avoid. We first wanted a place not too far out and on or near a good road. We expected to keep this course in good condition and fully equipped with targets for three hundred and sixty-five days in the year, and wanted to be able to get to it as easy as the average golfer gets to his course. It must be in a fairly wild state with scenery that wouldn't hurt your eyes and would have water available for drinking purposes. It took a surprisingly small amount of hunting to locate some hilly country that exactly answered every requirement.

Now for the course. As you know, the rules describe fourteen shots of which ten are single position shots and four are four position shots. While we expected to build a twenty-eight target course by putting in two of each so that we might shoot a full round without having to shoot any target twice, we also wanted each fourteen target course complete in itself, with each beginning and ending near our parking space. This makes it possible to start archers on both target number one and target number fifteen when conducting a large tournament and, even more important, it gives each fourteen the same par and thereby makes it possible for an archer with an hour to spare to shoot a fourteen and know just how he is doing. It may be true that this idea was lifted from golf, but having been a success there, we thought it might be popular in archery. It is.

We had learned from past experience that the way not to lay out a course was to take an hour off some afternoon and just hike over the proposed location with a friend and say, "Wouldn't that make a swell shot over there?" and then without further thought locate a target there and then rush on looking for another likely spot. Instead, we took a couple of weeks and a steel tape. We located each target only after considering the following: Would it make an interesting shot? How would the background be about finding arrows? What would the chances be of building a good trail to the target? Too much going into gullies and climbing out the other side will eventually take the joy out of any course. Was the target in line with any other target or trail? If so, it was too dangerous to be considered. If we were to place the target at that point where would our next shot be and would we be able to make the circuit in just the fourteen specified shots? Gentlemen, it is an engineering job but one well worth while.

After we had carefully measured and staked each shot we went to work on the trails. For a single tournament on a temporary course, any old trail or no trail at all will do; but for our purposes we must have good trails, not too steep and never running direct from the archer to the target, for such would spoil the nattural appearance of the shot. This meant, in our case, the spending of some $250, to which another $100 has since been added, but we now have trails that are wide, hard and smooth, and a pleasure to walk over. This hasn't made the course a bit easier to shoot a score on, but it has made it possible to shoot a round without looking like a ditch digger at the finish. These trails have made the round a shooting contest rather than a hiking and climbing contest, which fact is greatly appreciated by the ladies and older men who on some of our previous courses became so completely exhausted that good shooting was out of the question.

I have made no mention of the ranges. They are in the rules and you can probably have a copy, but here is how they are placed in our first fourteen.

Number 1 .... 60 yards
Number 2 .... 30 yards
Number 3 .... 25 yards
Number 4 .... 65 yards
Number 5 .... 40 yards
Number 6 .... 15 yards
Number 7 Four position,
    45, 40, 35 and 30 yards
Number 8 Four position,
    35, 30, 25 and 20 feet
Number 9 Four positions,
    all of them 35 yards
Number 10 .... 20 yards
Numbe 11 .... 45 yards
Number 12 .... 50 yards
Number 13 .... 55 yards
Number 14 Four positions,
    80, 70, 60 and 50 yards

You may not think they are very well mixed, but that is the way they fitted into the scenery, and to date no one has complained about their being easy to hit. We, of course, took advantage of light, shadows, scenery and angles to make the course "sporty." I use that word rather than "difficult," for we have found that while it is more fun to shoot on an apparently tricky course, there is very little, if any, difference in the score.

In laying out our four position shots we were careful to locate them at positions where it was possible to fan the shooting positions out in such a maner that the trail could be built to go from the longest to the shortest of the shots and then to the target without at any point being in line of fire. This saves a lot of time, for by the time the first archer has reached the fourth position the last of the foursome is already shooting from the first position.

Brown County Open

For the third year Brown County State Park will be the scene of the annual tournament of what was formerly the Missouri Valley Archery association, now called the Brown County Open association. The meet will be June 1 and 2 on the permanent archery range in south central Indiana, three miles from Nashville.

The park consists of 23 square miles of heavily timbered hilly country, and includes two lakes, 100 miles of trails and roads, and swimming, tennis and horseback riding facilities. Camping and trailer grounds, cottages and a hotel are available to accommodate the archers. Meals may be obtained at the Abe Martin lodge in the park, where an informal dinner meeting will be held Saturday night. Sandwiches and soft drinks are sold near the shooting field.

The men's championship will be based on the York score shot Saturday and the double American shot Sunday. Cups will be awarded to the men making the highest double American score, not counting the champion's scores.

A National and a Columbia will be shot by the women on Saturday and the same on Sunday. In the boys' and girls' junior division a single junior American will be shot Saturd v morning and a double junior American on Sunday. Clout events for all divisions will be shot Saturday afternoon. Flight events will be held on Sunday morning at the airport atop Weedpatch hill in the park. The hill is one of the highest in the state, with an elevation of 1152 feet above sea level.

W. B. Lincoln, Jr., 638 Berkley Rd., Indianapolis, Ind., is president of the association. Included on the board of governors are Fred Bear, of Detroit, Mich., E. S. Richter, of Chicago, Ill., and Charles Pierson, of Cincinnati, Ohio.

At the 1939 met it was decided that since the interest in the Missouri Valley meets had shifted farther east, the organization should be renamed the Brown County Open association, and all future meets should be held in the park on the week-end nearest May 30. An archery club from Michigan, Ohio, Illinois, Kentucky or Indiana will sponsor the meet each year. Bids for the 1941 meet must be presented to the board of governors before or at the 1940 meet.

Archery Notes

By "Uncle Hat"—Harold A. Titcomb

My last Notes to Oscar Lundberg, President of the Surrey Bowmen, were written at Grass Valley, Calif., and told of my first visit to Captain Cassius H. Styles at Berkeley, Calif., and of the delightful time I had there. These are further notes jotted down from time to time.

The Pacific Coast is a mecca for archers and during my limited stay in California I have been lucky in meeting many of them, but only a very small percentage of the total. These notes are therefore necessarily most incomplete and in the form of a diary. Time did not permit visiting the states of Washington and Orgeon where live many archers and where are published those splendid monthly journals, "American Bowman Review" and "Ye Sylvan Archer."

The climate of Southern California is especially adapted for archery all the year round, and interest in this splendid sport is increasing year by year. Many of these western archers also hunt wild game whenever they get the chance, and I have met in California probably a dozen men who have shot fair sized game including deer, bear, moose, wild boar, mountain lion, wild cats, etc.

I regret that I could not visit Walt Wilhelm who lives at Yermo in the Mojave Desert. His brother Ken is away giving exhibitions of his wonderful skill in archery; and Howard Hill, who lives in this Southern California district, was also away somewhere in the middle or eastern states, so I could not meet those renouned shots.

Arrived in Pasadena February 11. Heard of an archery range located in a beautiful arroyo or gulch at Pasadena and went there. Saw a chap shooting on the target range; he asked me if I was interested in archery and invited me to shoot, as he was a club member, Edmund Doty by name. Ed makes all his equipment in a neat shop adjoining his home. He makes beautiful tackle and showed me much about his favorite hobby. Through him I became a member of the Pasadena Roving Archers and met their secretary, Henry A. Bitzenburger of Los Angeles. Pasadena has two archery ranges in the arroyo, the first for target archery and the second for roving. With my helpful friend Ed Doty I have shot at both these ranges many times during the past month.

The field archery range is about 200 yards up the arroyo beyond the target range, and is most beautifully laid out by the Pasadena Roving Archers. There are benches and a large open-air fireplace used for barbecues or luncheons during a meet. The range occupies only about 300 yards in length along the valley and every advantage is taken of the steep irregular hillsides and trees to make shooting varied and exciting. One, two or three bales of straw form the butts on which are pinned the targets, which are of varying size. Wooden stakes, painted white, mark the shooting stations for each target, the stakes being numbered. There are 28 targets, cleverly designed to represent animals and birds, outlined on tough waterproof paper. The outlines are made with a template so they are always the same for the same animal. An outlined "vital" area is then colored red and counts 5 on the score; then a secondary area colored blue counts 3; then an outer area (which includes legs, tail, ears, etc.) counts 1. I shot over this range with Ed Doty, pacing most of the distances as best I could to give a rough idea of the range for each target.

Where possible, targets were placed so that an arrow would hit the hillside if it missed the target; this helps one find the missed arrow.

I bought a full set of these animal and bird targets and I hope to take these to England on my next visit.

Washington State Tournament

The Washington State Archery tournament will be held in Tacoma, June 15 and 16. S. L. Michael is secretary. It is expected that the shoot will be held on Jefferson Playfield.

Editorial

We regret that this issue of Ye Sylvan Archer is late but printing office difficulties made it impossible to get out on time. As this is an anniversary number we hoped to get out a special edition reviewing the progress of Archery since the publication of the first Sylvan Archer in 1927. Other duties prevented giving it the time necessary but our cover design denotes that we are launching out again. The prospect may be a little dim with conditions as they are in the world but we and Archery are on our way.

We seldom take space to publish "bouquets" but such as this from Mr. C. F. Schuster, Holyoke, Mass., makes us feel so good we cannot resist: "This little magazine rings true throughout with instructive information, story-telling wherein the song of the arrow is always there and a friendliness that brings closer together those of the feathered shaft clan."

One of George Brommers' California friends wants to know why the hero in all of Cosner's cartoons look so much like George. The answer is easy. Where, short of darkest Africa, could Joe find a more handsome or modest model?

Winter Intercollegiate Meet

Winners in Class A group, shooting a regulation Columbia round, of the annual winter intercollegiate archery meet were as follows:
1. Los Angeles City College 5553
2. Arizona State Teachers Col. 5017
3. San Jose State Teachers Col. 3086

Class B—60 Arrows at 30 Yds.
1. Oregon State College No. 1 5714
2. Oregon State College, No. 2 5367
3. Los Angeles City College 5324

Class C—60 arrows at 20 Yds.
1. Oregon College of Education 5385
2. Goucher College, Baltimore 5165
3. Willamette University 5087

Class D—60 arrows at 15 Yds. (2-foot target)
1. University of Nevada 3676
2. University of South Dakota 3563
3. Washington Univ., St. Louis 2610

Here we have some real news from Southern California not covered by other correspondents. Geo. Miles tells us "Bill Joy has a new summer suit, Chester Seay some mole-skin pants, P. K. Dugan wears new blue jeans when shooting a roving course so he will look dressed up as he does when he shoots target, John Yount is shooting a much better score as the NFAA gets in better shape, and Ben Pearson shot with us in Redlands. We like him."

International Tournament

I am pleased to advise that under the joint auspices of the Canadian National Exhibition and the Canadian Archery Association, the International Archery Tournament will be held again this year on the grounds of the Canadian National Exhibition, August 26, 27, 28, 29 and 30.

This will be the 8th annual tournament and it is expected that a larger number of archers will be taking part in the tournament.

The International Archery Tournament being held on the spacious archery ranges of the Canadian National Exhibition during the time the Fair is in progress makes this a very attractive and unique tournament. All archers who attend this tournament not only enjoy the visit to Canada, but will have the added pleasure of attending the world's largest annual exposition.

Although Canada is at war, there will be no handicap for visitors crossing the line. In this connection, the Hon. Mitchell F. Hepburn, Premier of Ontario, has stated "For United States citizens, entry and exit are just as free as formerly; no passport is required. An additional inducement to visitors is the fact that the United States dollar now commands a handsome premium in Canadian currency."

Yours very truly,
R. John Mitchele. Secretary.

Geo. Miles says, "It is a hard life; you want to shoot a good target score but can't so you take up field archery; and find out they check on you there too."

The Oregon State tournament is scheduled for July 4, 5 and 6 at Drain. The archery-golf event will be held at 1:30 p. m. on July 4 at the Cottage Grove golf club course, 17 miles north of Drain. Mr. C. W. Davis, president of the state association has just visited Drain and reports that the necessary preparations are well in hand. V. D. McCauley of Eugene is secretary.

The district target meet of the Michigan Archer's Association will be held at Baily Park, Battle Creek, on May 19. 1940.

They Won High Honors Competing With Nation's Best

Above are Oregon College of Education's two championship archery teams. Team at left won first in the national 20-yard event, and team at right won tenth in the 30-yard event. Left to right: Annabelle Furrow, Betty Sherman, Anne Drasdoff, Lillian Parker, Coach Stanbrough, Audrey Coyle, Melba Whitney, Edna Mae Russell, Annamae Holverstott, and Bernice Wilder.
—Courtesy The Oregonian.

Washington's First NFAA Tournament

By George Brommers

Hashimura Togo Duryee had a good idea, but it backfired.

Mrs. Duryee was home in bed, sick (we are glad to hear that she has now recovered), his daughter Pat couldn't be everywhere at once, and the many sided Mr. Duryee got busy.

First he went in cahoots with the weatherman, not a difficult feat in Washington, and the weatherman duly turned on his sprinklers.

As if this weren't enough handicap, Kore cunningly hid a few rocks where they would do the most good.

In any case, Pat Chambers looked somewhat doubtful by the time he had busted his third set of arrows. But in spite of all his industry, Kore was beaten both by Pat and by I. M. Stamps.

Chambers' high score, 489, wasn't up to his last year's high, but the season is young yet, and this was the first time he shot on this course. Stamps will bear a lot of watching, too. Even Kore isn't quite as innocent as he looks.

The course is a very tricky one, with plenty of natural hazards without Kore's help. For the first shoot the scores were surprisingly high. Washington will be heard from.

On account of the rain attendance was cut down, but there were several out of the state visitors, nevertheless.

John Garrett, the Canadian timberbeast, was there. Mr. Garrett took notes for a course the Canadians expect to install this year in order to give us some international competition.

From Portland came Pat and Vivian Chambers, Glendoline Vineyard, the Oregon Amazon, Gene Warnick, another flight shooter, and Mrs. Warnick. But we missed Pop Prouty, the grand old man who really put flight on the map to stay.

Belvia and Kay Carter (no relations), were there, and for the first time I had the pleasure of meeting their husbands. Leonard, that's Kay's incumbrance, is the well known dark horse, white hope, and eventual high score champion of this year's Olympic Bowmen League. Leonard, too, will take plenty of watching, once he warms up to the field round.

Glendoline took the ladies' first place handily, as had been expected, but my young friend, Jane Duncan, is warming up and, as I said before, the season is still young.

As this is written, no scores have come in from other sections. But if the other NFAA groups are as thoroughly sold on the new official round as Washington is by this time, that round is going to be hard to displace. Here are the scores:

MEN

		1st Round	2nd Round	Total
1.	Pat Chambers, Portland, Ore.	65-245	60-244	125-489
2.	I. M. Stamps, Seattle	61-233	58-212	119-445
3.	Kore T. Duryee, Seattle	48-177	60-230	108-407
4.	J. H. Strandwold, Tacoma	45-167	39-145	84-312
5.	Gene Warnick, Portland, Ore.	43-159	33-110	76-269
6.	Leonard J. Carter, Seattle	29-111	36-136	65-247
7.	Lawrence Belden, Seattle	30-108	36-134	66-242
8.	John Garrett, Vancouver, B. C.	34-122	31-117	65-239
9.	Harold Lusk, Seattle	30-106	34-126	64-232
10.	Fred Brockhoff, Port Orchard	31-107	29-105	60-212
11.	Elmer Erickson, Seattle	25- 91	28- 94	53-185
12.	Geo. B. Clark, Tacoma	22- 84	23- 89	46-173
13.	G. Meyer, Seattle	22- 82	22- 90	44-172
14.	M. Belden, Seattle	20- 66	29-105	49-171
15.	Glen W. Sutherland, Tacoma	18- 62	26- 98	44-160
16.	Herbert Halberg, Tacoma	15- 51	21- 69	36-120

17. Harold Strandwold, Shelton	11- 39	18- 66	29-105
18. Mike Errigo, Tacoma	11- 35	17- 61	28- 96
19. Jim McKinnell, Seattle	19- 63	....	19- 63
20. George Murry, Seattle	10- 30	....	10- 30
WOMEN			
1. Glendoline Vineyard, Portland	26- 98	29-101	55-199
2. Jane Duncan, Seattle	17- 63	21- 83	38-146
3. Ruth Boyle, Seattle	13- 43	14- 48	27- 91
4. Christine Stamps, Seattle	7- 27	10- 36	17- 63
5. Elsie Houle, Seattle	8- 30	8- 30	16- 60

S. C. F. A. News Notes

By Elmer W. Bedwell, Secretary

With over 100 archers and friends present at the Redlands Archery Course Sunday, April 28, the annual Southern California tournament and banquet was held. The goodfellowship of the archers, and the weather being pleasant, all summed up to a successful day.

Some of the scores were of special interest—Merle Hathaway, of Malibu, setting a new record for the new standard course in the morning, by making 291 points; and in the afternoon Larry Hughes beat the course record by making 314 points.

After the tournament, dinner was served at the Redlands Country Club, officers were elected and trophies were awarded. President Edmund M. Brock. Malibu. and Secretary-Treasurer Elmer W. Bedwell. Redlands. were re-elected. Ruth Hathaway, Malibu, succeeded George Miles as Vice President..

Awards were as follows for double rounds:

Men's Championship Class—Larry Hughes, gold bar, 585; Merle Hathaway, silver bar, 547.

General Division, Men — Richard Sands, Championship Medal, 433; Fred Woodley, red ribbon, 431; John Daulley, white ribbon, 427.

Ladies' Championship—Eva Bedwell, Redlands, gold bar, 311.

General Division, Ladies'— Glen Curtis, Redlands, Championship Medal, 249; June Franklin, Redlands, silver medal, 235; Margaret Quayle, Pasadena, bronze medal, 196.

Annual medals for high scores, men—Larry Hughes, Pasadena, gold, 585; Merle Hathaway, Malibu, silver, 547; Roland Quayle, Pasadena, bronze, 541.

Annual medals for high scores, women—Eva Bedwell, gold, 311; Glen Curtis, silver, 249; June Franklin, bronze, 235.

Juniors, for the Bedwell Trophy—Harold Robinson, Redlands, 298.

These scores were all entered in the National Archery Association mail tournament, the results of which will not be known for three or four weeks.

Ben Pierson, tackle maker, from Arkansas, and wife were guests of the day. We enjoyed having them.

The next regular S.C.F.A.A. tournament will be held at Malibu, June 23. This is a return tournament from the February 25 tournament, which was postponed on account of rain.

Old Mission Field Archers

April 15 found the Old Mission Field Archers assembled in the San Diego River bed, merrily slinging blunts in the general direction of various and sundry silhouette targets. We must admit the day was plenty warm; more of that "unusual weather" we have so frequently.

Anyway, the shoot wound up with Bob Hoover, C. W. McNatt and Lafe Kemp high scorers, and in that order. The prize was donated to the club for future use.

Following lunch the gang indulged in a bit of handicap shooting involving a silhouette and an apple, and called a "William Tell" shoot. In this event Lafe Kemp took the prize and is now wearing a new Bear Products "Kooler" arm guard.

Plans are going ahead for the field archers' part of the Western.

Doghouse Arching

You can buy meat at the butcher shop, so that isn't what you are after.

You can chase a golf ball, ride a bicycle, or dig in the garden. You won't, so exercise isn't what you are looking for.

You can hunt, or you can fish. You can camp out in the open, you can get filthily and unashamedly dirty. You can eat your own cooking, and somehow survive it. You can, and do, raise a prize crop of whiskers. Haven't they the most gratifying itch in the world?

You can hunt with the rifle, and it is fine sport. You don't get much game, and do you care. You fish—with worms—or eggs—or fly, all depending on how badly you want the fish. You have a grand old time.

Then you take up arching, more or less as a postgraduate fad. This time you know you aren't going to hit anything, but the way that rabbit, or deer, or rat, got out of the way delighted you hugely.

You have joined the game missers, and the rifle knows you no more.

Now there are archers who bring back game. I know quite a few of them myself. So they pack it out, and they clean it, and they brag and lie about it. Sometimes they even eat it. But somehow they haven't had nearly as good a time of it as the day they missed fifty ground squirrels in a row.

There is the game for you—ground squirrels. Any range is fair range, ten to a hundred yards. You do hit one occasionally, and you feel kind of ashamed of yourself. It is true that you aimed at it. It is true that you tried to hit it. It is also true that what you really wanted was to see how close you could get.

There is nothing wrong with the killing power of the long bow, but it is no weapon for grizzlies or lions, in spite of Art Young. Exceptions prove no rule. Every archer will freely admit that as a game getter the bow is far inferior to the rifle. The archer is no competitor of the rifle addict, has no wish to be.

I have known a number of successful archers, but they weren't the ones who brought home the biggest bags. They were the ones who utterly forgot themselves in the chase, the ones who came back tiredest, and dirtiest, and hungriest, and with the longest and scratchiest whiskers. The ones who got rained on, and snowed on, and who fell in the river. The ones who ate dough-gods of their own creation that a hungry dog would refuse.

We doghouse hunters rejoice mightily when one of our lower bracket brothers accidentally connects. We guy Chester Seay about that 700 pound bear he got, Joe Cosner about his javelina, J. E. Davis about his buck. We know they like to be razzed about it, just as Forrest Nagler is ribbed about the game he has missed—nothing is said about his hits—not by the doghouse or lower bracket gangs.

What we understand best is when Gardner, Klopsteg and Buchen spend ten days in a game paradise and come back without even an alibi. We don't rib them about it, though—we envy them. We think of the lugging, and the grief, and the expense hunters like the Catheys and B. G. Thompson had getting their moose out of Canada. We think of the aching backs of our more fortunate brothers in the chase—and laugh contentedly. That's arching for you—doghouse arching.

See that rabbit, sixty yards if it is an inch. Sitting there laughing at us. Fair game for a bow at that distance, sitting or running.

Why, damn your impudence, Bunny, smelling at that arrow right in front of you. I'll teach you. One more! Too high! All right, see how you like this one. Crouch, will you, I will straighten you. One right under the belly! Thought it was time to move, did you? Here's the chaser. What's that, a hit?

Good shot? No, poor Bunny! Doghouse arching, you said it!

P. S. All his old roughneck crew is quiet in the bunkhouse, testifies Dr. Paul Bunyan. Even the Oregon coon hunters know that the old Tom Cat is back on the job. Act accordingly. They had better take it lying down, says Paul.

We have a fine story by Erle Stanly Gardner for the next issue. Erle claims a new national record but we do not believe the palm should be conceded to him without a struggle as he has a host of hot competitors.

A. Y. Moore of Phoenix was high scorer in the Arizona State Association eighth annual tournament held March 9 and 10 at Tempe. His score for the York and American was 1125. A. J. Cosner was second with 949, and A. H. Caldwell, Jr. scored 894 for third. Tony Roomsburg led the ladies with 748 for National and Columbia rounds. Mrs. Cosner was second with 736 and Mary Rickel third with 700.

Jack Skanes of Highland Park was the winner of the annual indoor spring tournament of the Michigan Archer's Association, with a score of 180-1354 for the double American. Mrs. Lola Gaston was high in ladies' class A, score 179-1327. Class B, Mrs. Margaret Skanes, 169-979. Class C, Miss Marge Standacher, 149-743. Class B for men, George Sironko, 170-996, Class C, Carl Gill, 145-747. The tournament was held May 5.

CLASSIFIED ADVERTISING

RATES for Classified Advertising 5 cents per word per issue. Count initials and numbers as words. Minimum charge is 50 cents.

BOOKS AND MAGAZINES

"ARCHERY," by Robert P. Elmer M. D., revised edition, most complete book on archery published. 566 pages of valuable information for colleges, libraries, schools, camps archery clubs and individuals. Price $5.00 postpaid. orders to Ye Sylvan Archer, 505 North 11th street, Corvallis, Oregon.

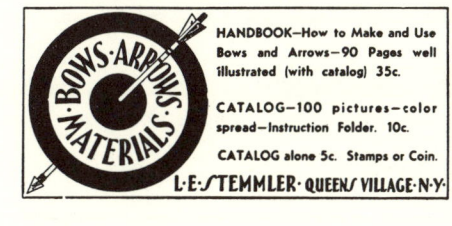

HANDBOOK—How to Make and Use Bows and Arrows—90 Pages well illustrated (with catalog) 35c.

CATALOG—100 pictures—color spread—Instruction Folder. 10c.

CATALOG alone 5c. Stamps or Coin.

L·E·STEMMLER· QUEENS VILLAGE·N·Y·

"ARCHERY TACKLE, HOW TO MAKE AND HOW TO USE IT." by Adolph Shane. Bound in cloth and illustrated with more than fifty drawings and photographs. Information for making archery tackle and instructions for shooting. Price is $1.75.

RELICS AND CURIOS

INDIAN RELICS, Beadwork, Coins, Curios, Books, Minerals, Weapons. Old West Photos. Catalog, 5c. Genuine African Bow, $3.75. Ancient flint arrowheads, perfect, 6c each—Indian Museum, Osborne, Kansas.

ULLRICH WOOD
The Choice of Champions

P. O. Cedar self air-seasoned SHAFTS, Roving-Target, fitted with parallel piles and pyroxalin nocks, matched for spine and weight. Made from same unit of stock and in the 19-64, 5-16, 21-64, and 11-32 in. sizes. Give over-all length in ordering.

$2.00 per DOZEN
Postpaid anywhere in U.S.A.

EARL ULLRICH
Roseburg, Oregon

Paul H. Gordon, Director
Beacon Hill Craftsmen
Beacon, N. Y.
Where the serious archer's needs and desires are really consulted, and his orders exactly filled. Nothing too simple or too difficult.
Write for Complete Catalog

SUBSCRIBERS PLEASE NOTICE
A cross appearing in this space means that your subscription has expired and we would appreciate your prompt renewal so that your name may be kept on our mailing list.

W. A. COCHRAN
Archery Equipment
High Elevation Yew Wood
Port Orford Cedar
Osage Orange
Air Seasoned
10,000 Billets and Staves in Stock
Route 2   Eugene, Ore.

DO YOU LIKE THE CHARM OF THE BACKHILLS?
If so — read ARCADIAN LIFE MAGAZINE. It tells the story of the Ozarks in a way that will captivate you.

$1.00 a year; 25c a copy. Classified advertising (for archers) 2c a word.

O. E. RAYBURN, Editor
Caddo Gap, Arkansas

FOLBERTH NEEDLE NOCK ARROWS
Stand Test of Keenest Competition

The Olympic Bowmen League has just announced the results of its annual ten-week tournament, with 57 teams entered from 33 cities of the U. S. and Canada. The results show that:

> The winning men's team for the entire ten weeks
> The winning men's team for high single team score (new record)
> The winning man archer for the entire ten weeks
> The second-place man archer for the entire ten weeks
> The winning man archer for high individual score

ALL USED FOLBERTH NEEDLE NOCK ARROWS!

We believe that this remarkable showing was in part due to the new stream-lined NEEDLE NOCK END, which makes possible a smoother release and results in more accurate shooting.

All our arrows are tested for accuracy with a mechanical shooting bow. A paper pattern of their performance at 100 feet is included with each dozen arrows.

Price—$10.00 to $15.00 per dozen

Write for complete details or order direct, giving bow weight and arrow length desired.

FOLBERTH ARROWS, 7821 Lake Ave., Cleveland, Ohio

BEAR
ALUMINUM ARROWS ARE MAKING RECORDS
BEAR PRODUCTS CO.
2611 W. Philadelphia Ave., Detroit, Michigan

Ye Sylvan Archer—$1.00 per year.

Read
The AMERICAN ARCHER
"A National Quarterly"
J. C. Vives, Editor
521 Fifth Ave., New York, N. Y.
$1.00 per Year
First four issues now ready
Hunters enter A A National competition. Write for details.

---

70 pages of Archery information for 50 cents, well illustrated. Ye Sylvan Archer, 505 N. 11th St., Corvallis, Oregon.

Rose City Archery Co.
1149 NE 31st Avenue
Portland, Oregon

In 1940 competition, improve your scores with the tackle used by
Pat Chambers
National Champion
Catalogue on request

Alton's Archery Specialty
10c Buys Our "Baby"
BROADHEAD
Spring Steel Blades on Target Piles
25 Per Cent Discount to Dealers
These Are Real Hand-made Hunters!
210 N. Main   Washburn, Ill.

AT LAST
all your archery needs on ONE shaft — with
CHANDLER
Interchangeable Arrow Points
Also Fish Heads, and many other Points
PAT. PEND. Target
Free Cat.
T.B. Chandler
11819 4th Ave
Compton,
California   Point

BROADHEAD

The Flat Bow—70 pages of Archery information for 50 cents, well illustrated. *Ye Sylvan Archer, 505 N. 11th St., Corvallis, Oregon.*

Ye Sylvan Archer—$1.00 per year.

BACK NUMBERS
YE SYLVAN ARCHER
Volumes I to V Inclusive
$1.00 Per Volume
B. G. THOMPSON
R. F. D. 1, Corvallis, Oregon

L. L. "Flight" DAILY
offers you
"Tackle That Talks"
Dry Cedar and Yew
Catalogue Free
245 Pearl, Eugene, Oregon

Please mention Ye Sylvan Archer when writing advertisers.

WIN WITH BEN PEARSON ARROWS

Beautiful and accurate to the Nth degree but win their real laurels on the range. Arrows made as arrows should be—and at prices you can afford to pay. Send for catalogue.

BEN PEARSON, INC. — PINE BLUFF, ARK.

Cassius Hayward Styles

BOWYER AND FLETCHER

—Tackle that has stood the test—

28 Vicente Place

BERKELEY, CALIFORNIA

(G)

"THE MARK OF DISTINCTION IN ARCHERY TACKLE

Fine Yew Target and Hunting Bows, Plain or Backed with Rawhide. Lemonwood Bows with Rawhide Backs.

College and School Equipment Target, Hunting and Roving Arrows

Price List on Request

Wholesale — Retail

EARL GRUBBS
5518 W. Adams
Los Angeles, : California

Archery Raw Materials

WM. A. JOY

9708 So. Hoover Street
LOS ANGELES, CALIF.

ARCHERY BOWS
from the Heart of the Yew Country

W. I. KING
Woodworking Shop
1958½ Onyx St.   Eugene, Ore.

YEW BOW TIMBER

High Altitude Air Seasoned Billets and Staves of Quality and Variety.

W. G. PRESCOTT
527 Chestnut   Ashland, Ore.

POTTER & MacQUARRIE
ROVING ARROWS

Split Birch or P. O. Cedar, 11-32 in. and 3-8 in., matched within 10 gr. in weight, and spined for heavy bows. Equipped with steel piles, 3 1-2 in. feathers and bright crest.

One Dozen $5.00

3400 Fruitvale Ave.
Oakland . . . . California

E. BUD PIERSON
Bowyer — Fletcher
Tournament Tackle, Sinew, Glue, Raw Materials.
245 University Ave
CINCINNATI, OHIO
Custom Made Tackle

Write us for your needs in Archery books. Ye Sylvan Archer.

Ye Sylvan Archer

June, 1940

Corvallis, Oregon

Vol. 12   No. 2

Ye
Sylvan Archer

"A magazine for the field archers"

Vol. 12   June, 1940   No. 2

Published the fifteenth of each month
for archers by archers
505 North 11th Street, Corvallis, Oregon

J. E. DAVIS .... Editor
RUSSELL JONES .... Business Manager
Subscription Price .... $1.00 Per Year
Foreign Subscription .... $1.25 Per Year
Single Copies .... 10 Cents
Advertising Rates on Application

TABLE OF CONTENTS

                                                                           Page

STICKING STUMPS ON STILTS
    By Erle Stanley Gardner 1
A DEER HUNT ON DEADWOOD
    By Tom O'Clayton 5
EDITORIAL 6
CLUB HOLDS ANCIENT SHOOT 6
NATIONAL FIELD ARCHERY
    By John L. Yount 7

Sticking Stumps on Stilts

By Erle Stanley Gardner

It was that delightful time of year when spring and summer take turns occupying the center of the stage. Also it was that part of the day when afternoon dissolves into long shadows, when little vagrant winds come up from nowhere, blow for a few seconds, and die down.

Ed Record was just ahead of me on the narrow trail which wound along the sagebrush slope about a hundred yards above the green live oaks and cool, deep shadows of the canyon.

Ed was swinging along with strong, steady strides, the long-legged pace of a good man in the mountains—his left leg started to swing up and over, and stopped midstep.

"What is it?" I asked.

He motioned me to silence, then squatted low, and beckoned for me to come up.

I crouched and came up to join him, looking in the direction of his fascinated eyes.

Eighty-five yards below us, standing in the trees, was a beautiful buck, unusually fat, standing there perfectly motionless as a deer stands when he's listening, that crucial moment when he sniffs the wind, twists his ears, freezes into immobility, and waits to see whether he goes on browsing or "clumpety-clumps" away through the trees.

Seventy of those eighty-five yards were sloping sagebrush, then the spreading branches of the big oaks twined their arms into a canopy. The deer was standing back of these first sentinel trees under a green arch of interlaced boughs. An arrow would need a flat trajectory to reach him.

We studied the lay of the land. There was not much chance to improve our position. At this point, the trail swung around the shoulder of the hill. We would have to go for at least thirty yards in plain sight before we could reach any cover. Of course, it was possible to shoot through the branches—if we were lucky.

That's the way with deer. They darn seldom stand out in the open. When you're stump hunting, you pick out a stump and say, "Now, if that stump over there happened to be a big four-point buck—" But the joker is, brother, that stump is only a stump after all. It stands out there in the open, and your arrows go "thunk" into it, and you say, "Well, I'm getting pretty good. This fall I certainly will smack a broadhead into a deer."

Then fall comes, and you hunt your heart out, and about the time you're ready to give up, look among the trees and see a deer standing just where a lot of branches will interfere with your arrows — No, they don't show any consideration whatever for a hunter.

"How about it, Ed?" I whispered.

Ed made a little motion with his right hand which indicated there was only one thing to do.

"Let's go," I said.

We jumped to an erect position. As with one motion, two arrows were drawn back to the head. (That shows how easy it is to get in a habit with

"Standing in the trees was a beautiful buck"

your writing and lie like hell. All deer hunters claim their arrows were drawn back to the head. — Well, as a matter of fact, Ed drew his arrow back to the head—myself, I always fudge a couple of inches. A twenty-eight inch arrow I pull twenty-six; a twenty-six, twenty-four; a twenty-five inch arrow gets drawn back twenty-three inches. — But to get back to our deer shooting.) For just the flicker of an eyelash we held the arrows, and then released them almost with a single motion. The shafts flashed out into the balmy air, outlined themselves against the blue sky. They climbed up out of the shadows to where the sunlight turned them to burnished gold; then, in a long, descending arc, they plunged down into the invisibility of the canyon shadows.

We waited.

There is no suspense on earth which can equal that of waiting after an arrow has disappeared into the shadows of late afternoon, watching the game stand unsuspecting, knowing that another second will bring the news.

Suddenly something went WHACK! The deer quivered from head to tail. One arrow had hit. We couldn't tell whose it was until after we'd rushed headlong down the slope into the shade of the trees. — (Since there were just the two of us, it should have been a fifty-fifty break that my arrow was the one that hit; but if you think I'm going to take you rushing down the slope with me to find out whether it's Ed's arrow or mine that's in the deer, you're nuts. I'll detour that very adroitly by changing the subject in the next paragraph.)

Of course, anyone except a Swedish logger knows that when spring and summer are playing tag, it's no legal time to be pursuing deer with a bow and arrow. And now that John Yount has gone around bestowing such liberal promises that we're all going to be good boys, I hate to put anything like this on paper, but facts are facts, and unless you belong to the school of article fiction writing in which the author socks an arrow into a cottontail rabbit, only to have it bare its teeth and come charging at him, while he desperately fumbles in his quiver for another arrow, you have to confine yourself to facts.

So before we go rushing down that sage-covered slope, we'll make a verbal detour to keep Yount from having kittens, and state two extenuating facts.

The first fact is that I never shoot without knowing exactly what I'm shooting at, which is a lot to say for a hunter. There are lots of hunters who shoot at anything which moves in the brush. Then there are rifle hunters who get bedroom fixations, like those two at the HF Bar Ranch, who used bullets to sprinkle powdered plaster all over Walther Buchen's bed. Then again there's the class of combination hunter who won't shoot at anything which is perfectly natural, but holds his fire for web-footed doves, or deer-horned coons. But *I* never shoot until I know *exactly* what I'm shooting at. That's one thing in my favor.

The other point is that this buck wasn't exactly out of season. I made him myself. He consisted of a nice gunny sack stuffed full of shavings with a *very* artistic job for the tail. A light bit of plywood stuck in at the proper angle formed the neck. This was wrapped with newspapers to build it up. The head consisted of a paper bag, stuffed with shredded paper, and given a semblance of the shape we wanted by careful tying. The horns were branches of dead sagebrush stuck into the top of the head. Occasionally, when we want a deer "in the velvet," we chop the tips from an oak bush. The legs are long and thin, about the dimensions of a lath, only taller. The idea is to get your deer pretty well up off the ground—and, brother, if you don't think these deer look natural when you see them sprinkled around the heads of canyons, under trees, or even against the skyline on a rocky outcropping, you have another guess coming. And don't kid yourself they aren't difficult to hit.

The idea germinated in a Klopsteg to Buchen to Gardner play on that trip to the HF Bar in Wyoming. Ordinarily, I don't particularly care about killing a deer. I like to hunt them, but if I can have an adventure or two, I'm satisfied. However, on this particular trip I wanted to impress Walther Buchen and Paul Klopsteg with the idea that I was really some shakes as a hunter. So I scattered various sacks around the ranch for a couple of months before the trip came off, and shot arrows into them from various ranges.

Believe me, I got pretty darn good, for me. Show me a deer lying on the ground at sixty or seventy yards, and I was pretty apt to put an arrow somewhere near him. The trouble with those HF Bar deer was that they wouldn't lie down. They stood up on four very long legs and stuck long, inquisitive necks up in the air. And I socked my arrows right where those deer would have been if they'd been lying down.

I'm darned if I know why, but it's a fact that an archer can learn to sock an object on the ground and get deadly at it. Then you put that object four feet above the ground, and he begins to pull alibis out of his repertoire faster than arrows out of his quiver. — "Certainly fooled me that time. The sun got right in my eyes." — "Gust of wind came down the canyon just as I let that arrow go." — "See that arrow jump to the left? That's one I've been carrying in my quiver ever since the day it rained. That one feather is all crushed down. I intended to steam it out but never got to it." —
"Say, I wonder what my bow's hitting? Oh, there it is! That little weed! I could tell the lower limb of the bow struck something from the way the arrow swung off to one side," etc, etc, etc.

I was like that up in Wyoming. I had about four dozen shots at deer, and I only went in there with a stock of thirty alibis. I lay awake nights and managed to think up twenty more. So I was fortunate enough to get out with two alibis to the good, but if I'd had three more shots, I wouldn't have had any alibi for the last one, and an archer caught in that position might just as well quit shooting for good.

I'm kidding on the square. You go out and train for deer season the way all the archers that I know train, and when you see the deer standing up looking at you, you're going to shoot right where they would be if they turned themselves into stumps.

I've demonstrated the same thing down here at the ranch since I've built these deer. I could take them off their legs, put them down on the ground, and sock 'em with every second or third arrow. I put them back on the legs and right away start using alibis. (I've thought of

"Yes, it's Ed Record's arrow that's sticking in the deer."

five new ones since the HF Bar, so the stock is now fifty-five.) I think I have about the best stock of alibis of any archer in the country—although I've been out with some chaps who had quite a few good ones. That moose hunt up in Canada taught me that some of the Oregon archers are pretty good, and those guys from Chicago aren't any slouches—but there's something about the Southern California climate which makes them bigger and better, and while I'm in the red-ribbon sub-basement class as an archer, I don't take back talk from anyone as an alibi manufacturer—although that one about the weed hitting the lower limb of the bow *is* imported. I got it from Dr. Cathey.

But you fellows who want to perfect yourself in deer hunting follow these simple rules: Manufacture your deer out of sacks and shavings, somewhat in accordance with the above specifications.

DON'T plant your deer in the places that you dream of finding deer—out in an open grassy glade standing broadside on—because when you get out in the woods this fall, you're going to find most of your deer wondering what's been making that crackling noise in the brush, and they'll be standing facing you with their necks way up in the air, looking directly at you; or they'll have satisfied their curiosity as to what did make that noise, and, as you come out facing north, you'll find the deer also facing north and going at a very rapid speed. All you'll have to shoot at will be the part which is facing directly south.

Which brings up the subject of tails.

Making a good deer's tail out of a gunny sack is quite a job. There's an opportunity for some real artistry. You stuff in a few shavings at the extreme end of the sack right up at the top of the seam. Then you catch it about three inches down with some twine and wrap it around until you have it nice and tight. Then take some newspaper which will show up well in the dusk, and tie that on, and shred the ends so it will wriggle back and forth in the breeze.

It's probably human nature to shoot where you look, and it's certainly human nature to look at the thing which is the most prominent, so when a deer goes streaking out of the forest with a patch of white tail receding in the distance at the rate of twenty feet to the jump, five jumps to the second, you naturally tend to concentrate on the tail. So if you're going to practice stern shots, be sure to have an artistic tail to make it look natural.

And don't put your deer in the nice places where you won't lose your arrows after you've missed them, or make it a practice to stand and empty your quiver, counting your hits. That's not the way you do things in the hunting country. Put your deer up where you have to hit them—or else. Never shoot at a distance of under forty-five yards and never shoot more than two arrows at any one deer from any one position. That helps, in the same way that it helps to use a pencil which has no eraser on it. When you know you *have* to make good, you're more apt to pay a little closer attention to what you're doing.

But I'm almost overlooking one thing. This deer hunting started out simply as a training. It's turned out to be more fun than I've had since my brother had the mumps and I sneaked up behind him and socked him on the side of the jaw. There's something about these deer which is so natural that it just about gives you buck fever, and you'll find that by changing the location around from place to place every week or so and then walking around the hills so you come on them from unexpected angles, you get the thrill of actually encountering game. And if you have a companion, always shoot together from the same position and count the number of deer each one brings into camp. It gives a real thrill, and . . . . . What's that? — Oh, *all* right. . . . . The customer always has to be right. Come on, brother, let's go down that slope.

Yes, damn it, it's Ed Record's arrow that's sticking in the deer. Now I hope you're satisfied.

We have been informed that Pat Chambers has accepted a position as field man for Ben Pearson, Inc., of Pine Bluff, Arkansas. Pat left recently for the East, and expects to shoot in the coming Milwaukee Open shoot.

A Deer Hunt on Deadwood

By Tom O'Clayton

Steve, Don and I were on our way. Our headquarters for this vacation and hunt were to be at Don's secret cabin a few miles above the mouth of Deadwood. To appreciate this camp you would have to know Don. I can only lightly describe it. To get to it you leave the road, never twice in the same place, through the brush to the creek and cross, again, never twice in the same place, then up the steep mountain side guided by certain land marks. The final approach was made around the rugged roots of a huge Douglas fir which had fallen up the mountain side, then up the trunk of this tree to the cabin itself. The camp was walled on three sides, the open side facing the mountain against which was built a rock fireplace. A dandy place to cook and loaf. A few yards away was a small ice cold spring. A perfect place but we could have camped a lot handier down by the road. But again you don't know Don. He is right, too, for being in a place like that does something to a fellow and somehow goes with bow hunting. It had only been necessary to carry up our bows, arrows, blankets and food; camp equipment was all there. A fir snag had fallen across the rocks, breaking up and giving us an abundance of fuel for the fire. Steve and I made ourselves right at home. Don insisted we have fish for supper, and taking his pole, which, by the way, was a casting rod made of yew wood, and disappeared down the mountain. In a few hours he was back with a dozen fine trout all cleaned and ready for the pan, and did he fix us up a good meal! After shaping things up for the night we sat before the fire and Don gave us the works. "It's like this," he said. "You birds want to get a deer and there are plenty within a mile of us; they will be hard to see and harder to shoot, but I will fix that if you will pay attention. We have several days before the opening and I am going to give you the works, so be ready tomorrow morning to follow me."

A good night's rest and early the next morning found us down at the creek, a heavy yew bow each and a quiver of arrows, mostly heavy blunts which exactly matched our broadheads. This was to be a day of practice and education with Steve and I on the learning end. Don was equipped with a heavy bow of Steve's, his arrows are short and he only pulled about twenty-two inches, he drew to his belly Indian fashion and could shoot very fast. He put up several targets, mostly pieces of bark, then led us to them and pointed them out as deer. In the brush a deer is seldom seen as a whole unless he is running. You usually see a pair of antlers or large ears which appear to be part of the bush or landscape, or a nose and one eye sticking out from behind a tree with his rump protruding on the other side; sometimes he is lying down with part of his head and back showing. You have to know what you are looking for. A deer seems to know he is hard to see and will frequently stand and let you walk by in a few feet of him. If he catches your eye or you stop and then step towards him he is gone like a flash, usually keeping a tree or something between you and him and making a difficult shot. All this and much more Don told us in our lessons. He showed us a piece of bark which he said was a deer. It was lying beyond a large over-hanging limb and between us was fern and huckleberry several feet high. It was impossible to get an arrow through from where we were. Don said to me, "Tom, that deer is in his bed and knows we can not approach him. You stand here and continue to look to the right. Steve and I will duck out of his vision and go to the left and try to get an arrow to him." They sneaked around to within fourteen or fifteen yards and made a perfect hit on that piece of bark. Don said, "That is the way it is done and Wednesday morning we will get a shot at a real one."

He next showed us the hind end of a buck which was a piece of bark sticking out on the side of a tree, impossible to place an arrow in a vital

(Continued on page 10)

Editorial

We are glad to announce that "Pop" Prouty is recovering rapidly from the results of his accident. We learn that the cast on his hip was removed weeks ahead of schedule, and "Pop" can't be kept away from the shop.

The publication of Archery News, English archery magazine, in spite of the terrible conditions in Europe, should be an inspiration to all. While most archery meetings are not being held, some are carrying on as usual. The Royal Richmond Club announces: "The Club opens on Friday, April 19, shooting 3 P. M. No Prize Meetings will be held. There will be tea and biscuits provided each Friday until September 27."

Through the generosity of Harold A. Titcomb, subscriptions to English archers will be continued and several more names added to the list. We extend our congratulations to our English friends on their great fortitude. We thrill to the fact that English archers are carrying on for the rights of man as they did at Crecy and Agincourt.

We enjoyed a visit with T. B. Chandler of Compton, California, maker of the Chandler interchangeable points, while he was on a business trip into Oregon and Washington. Mr. Chandler will announce soon the rules for an archery hunting contest. We do not have the complete rules for the contest at this time, but the fact that a dozen Chandler points will be given for the first of each of a dozen or more kinds of game to be killed with these points should put archery hunters on their toes for this season's hunts, and have them practicing on "stilts" and otherwise.

Club Holds Ancient Shoot

The Ancient Silver Arrow archery tournament dating from 1672 and originating in the village of Scorton, England, was won by Arnold Wyttenbach on the grounds of the Toronto Archery Club. Mr. Wyttenbach hails from the land of William Tell, and has the proud distinction of winning the Silver Arrow for a second time.

The Scorton Ancient Silver Arrow is the oldest, regularly held archery tournament in the world, having originated over two hundred and sixty-eight years ago. The tournament is unique in many respects. All shooting is done at one hundred yards range. The archers shoot two arrows each and draw lots for the order of shooting. Although there is an award for high score, the main object of the tournament is to win the Silver Arrow. This is achieved by the archer who first sinks an arrow into the gold or bullseye of the target. In recent years, accommodation was made for women archers, and they shoot an eighty yard range for a smaller silver arrow.

Mrs. R. John Mitchele, with unerring accuracy, scored a direct hit in the gold with her first arrow and won the lady's award. Miss Rita Williams, who won the lady's silver arrow last year, won the silver bugle this year by scoring the first hit in the red circle. Mr. Forrest Nagler, veteran archer and big game hunter with the bow, and holder of the Canadian Championship, won the high score medal, but on his own suggestion took advantage of the tournament rules and graciously passed it to the next in line, Alfred Long, and accepted instead the Great Horn Spoon, which he also won by having the arrow nearest to the outside rim in the last end. Mr. Allen Baggs was then in line for the men's Silver Bugle.

Following the tournament, the archers gathered for afternoon tea on the veranda of the Toronto Cricket Club, where they received awards.

A one hundred and eighty yard and a one hendred and twenty yard clout shoot for the men and women, respectively, was held in the evening. The honors for the men went to Mr. Wyttenbach, first; Mr. Jack Luck, of Montreal, second; and Mr. Nagler, third. Mrs. A. R. B. Knight, Mrs. Nagler and Mrs. Clayton won first, second and third places in the ladies' event.

National Field Archery

By John L. Yount

E. Hill Turnock again proves his field shooting ability by winning the first NFAA national mail tournament. The first ten finished as follows:

Men

E. Hill Turnock	314	355	669
Larry Hughes	271	314	585
Merle Hathaway	291	256	585
Harry Glover	274	273	547
Roland Quayle	253	288	541
Jess Quayle	246	265	511
Volus Jones	269	221	490
Pat Chambers	245	244	489
Jack Peters	223	239	462
Bill Holmes	204	255	459

Ladies

Eva Bedwell	159	152	311
Glenn Curtis	146	103	249
June Franklin	118	117	235
Glendolene Vineyard	98	101	199
Margaret Quayle	108	88	196
Babe Bitzenberger	97	96	193
Babe Dauley	99	92	191
Mrs. W. D. Perry	120	60	180
Dorothy Ahman	101	64	165
Margaret King	77	79	156

E. H. Turnock high in Field Meet

The interesting feature of this tournament is the proof that field archers are made and not born. Eight out of the first ten men and eight out of the first ten ladies have competed regularly for at least a year on permanent roving courses, but not on the course on which these scores were shot.

We want to call your attention to the winning ladies' score. It shows that they can compete with the men on this round, but they must first learn field shooting. They can't just step from a target to a roving course and expect to get results.

Controlled Handicap

While our game is new and the archers are shooting it for the novelty and thrill of trying something a little different is the time to take stock and see what we are going to be able to offer to keep this interest when the novelty is gone.

When the average shot finds that he is paying most of the cost and doing most of the work, while the five per cent at the top win all the prizes, it is our opinion that we can expect a rather sudden letdown in interest. Why not prepare for that time by copying some of the ideas that have been used to make certain other sports outstanding, and doing it now before we are forced to it by lack of interest? The first of these is a good handicap system.

We realize that handicapping has never been very popular in archery, but you must remember that we are now speaking of field archery, a game more comparable to golf than to other forms of archery and for that reason a game especially suited to handicapping. Even so, the success of handicapping in any sport lies, first, in the system used. It must be one designated to promote interesting matches between players, and the ideal sought is to make it possible for any two players in the association to meet with equal chances of winning. Friendly matches at the home club should by far constitute the greater number of rounds shot.

The sociability of such matches promotes the existence of your local clubs, and the handicap must be liberal enough to give the player a feeling of confidence that if all the participants in such rounds shoot approximately to their real capabilities, the match will be a close one. At the same time, in club competition, inter-club tournaments and invitational and sectional meets, the system must be strict enough to ensure that players must approach their top form to win.

A system could fulfill all the requirements listed above and yet fail as an answer to our problems. We must realize that the finest of handicapping can be of no value if not properly used. The events in which it is used must be made the very life of the game and not just left as an excuse to pass out a few more ribbons. We believe that all club tournaments, with the possible exception of an annual championship, should be strictly handicap events. Many inter-club and some association tournaments could be included in this these should there be high score trophies. Such trophies would only detract from the honor due the handicap winner.

We should keep in mind that in these tournaments we are honoring the man who has bettered his past performance the most and are not in the least interested in the natural shot, who even though he may have a far better score, is still many points below his real capabilities.

We have worked out the following system of handicapping. We do not believe it perfect, but do think it is an improvement over those considered in the past. As in all worthwhile handicaps, it is based on averages. In this case the averages are controlled by fixing for each handicap bracket a limit score on each round and requiring that every score be reported, whether made on tournament or practice. Scores below the limit are counted at the limit score for that particular bracket and affect the total used for obtaining averages on that basis.

The purpose of fixing a limit score for each handicap bracket is to prevent a player from acquiring an average which he can better with ease when sufficient inducement exists. Otherwise unduly high averages could be acquired by careless and indifferent archery or from rounds shot during abnormal weather conditions. When players' scores are below their limits they may well feel that their game that day was not representative of their ability, and such scores should not have too much influence on handicaps. The limits for each bracket serve the additional purpose of stabilizing handicaps and restricting to a reasonable extent the raise in handicap which a player may receive when his handicap is revised.

The difference between a player's average score, as controlled, and the 275 score, which we have set as par for our round of 28 targets, is represented by a handicap which is approximately 90% of this difference.

This sounds rather complicated, but really isn't, for by handicapping only in multiples of 5 and by insisting on 10 complete scores before issuing a handicap, it is possible to use the enclosed table. This reduces the actual work to addition of the 10 scores.

In the case of archers who are being handicapped for the first time and so have no limit score, we list their ten scores in numerical order, then use the sixth for a limit score, adding it five times and discarding the four poorest scores.

After adding the archer's last ten scores as corrected by the limit score, the only additional work to be done is to check with Column 4. The archer's handicap is then shown on the corresponding line in Column 1. His limit score is in Column 2. The club can rehandicap as often as desired, but always on the basis of the last ten scores. If a club wishes to use the handicap system quicker than the ten scores will allow, it may use whatever number it desires, find the archer's average, locate it in Column 3 and use the corresponding handicap in Column 1. We highly recommend that such a handicap be considered only as a tentative one to be used for match play, etc, and that it never be allowed in official tournaments.

It is our opinion that this matter of handicapping is one that must be handled in a hard boiled manner. All must be treated fair and all must be treated alike. If a club is charging a fair sized target fee and has offered some valuable trophies, it must insist that only those who have acquired an official handicap are eligible. Club members who are not sufficiently interested to earn a handicap are of no particular value, anyway. Worthwhile new members will see the justice of this and turn in the necessary number of scores just as soon as possible.

It is highly desirable that each club set a maximum handicap to avoid that feeling on the part of the better shots that they are shooting against a handicap rather than another archer. This maximum handicap should be set high enough that any archer with practice can make it, yet low enough that it can be considered something of an honor to be handicapped. In clubs where field shooting is new, this figure could be considerably higher than in clubs where most members are more or less expert at the game.

To handicap match play, give one target for each ten points difference in handicap. This is true whether the shooting is between two archers or the two teams of a foursome. For example, if the aggregate handicap of Team A is 40 points less than that of Team B, it must give Team B four targets, such gift to be in excess of the 28 to be shot for, making in this case a total of 32 targets in all.

Controlled Handicap System as Adapted to Field Archery

Col. 1 Handicap	Col. 2 Limit Score	Col. 3 Average for Tentative Handicaps	Col. 4 Adjusted Total of 10 Scores
0	263	273 and over	2725 and over
5	257	267 to 272	2665 to 2724
10	251	261 to 266	2605 to 2664
15	246	256 to 260	2555 to 2604
20	240	250 to 255	2495 to 2554
25	235	245 to 249	2445 to 2494
30	229	239 to 244	2385 to 2444
35	224	234 to 238	2335 to 2384
40	218	228 to 233	2275 to 2334
45	212	222 to 227	2215 to 2274
50	207	217 to 221	2165 to 2214
55	201	211 to 216	2105 to 2164
60	196	206 to 210	2055 to 2104
65	190	200 to 205	2995 to 2054
70	185	195 to 199	1945 to 1994
75	179	189 to 194	1885 to 1944
80	174	184 to 188	1835 to 1884
85	168	178 to 183	1775 to 1834
90	162	172 to 177	1715 to 1774
95	157	167 to 171	1665 to 1714
100	151	161 to 166	1605 to 1664
105	146	156 to 160	1555 to 1604
110	140	150 to 155	1495 to 1554
115	135	145 to 149	1445 to 1494
120	129	139 to 144	1385 to 1444
125	124	134 to 138	1335 to 1384
130	118	128 to 133	1275 to 1334
135	112	122 to 127	1215 to 1274
140	107	117 to 121	1165 to 1214
145	101	111 to 116	1105 to 1164
150	96	106 to 110	1055 to 1104
155	90	100 to 105	995 to 1054
160	85	95 to 99	945 to 994
165	79	89 to 94	885 to 944
170	none	89 & under	884 & under

DEER HUNT ON DEADWOOD

(Continued from page 5)

spot. Then a pair of antlers showing above a stubby hazel—that deer was perfectly safe. Don said all these conditions and many others were possible and tomorrow we would go up higher and locate where the deer were using.

During the day we had not gone far from the creek and noon found us several miles up stream. We ate lunch which we had carried with us. After a smoke and some more advice about hunting from Don, we started toward the camp. Along the creek were several small meadows surrounded by wild blackberry bushes. Sizing one of these places up, Don said, "This is a dandy place for brush rabbits and about dusk we could get some good shooting. Maybe we can get one or two anyway for supper. Tom, you and Steve go to the other side of this clump and I will try and stir them up. Get close to the ground and if you see one move, shoot him in the head with a blunt." Don threw some rocks over in the bush which was about thirty feet across, then he poked around with a pole, and pretty soon we saw some movement. We began to shoot and soon we had four bunnies, which was enough for our needs. Oh, yes. I forgot to tell you we made some misses and had six or eight arrows deep in that tangle; we finally got them all after plenty of scratches. Don told us the proper way to get these rabbits was to sit quietly near by just before dusk and shoot them as they came out to feed. In the clear that way the arrows would not glance and you could make every shot count.

Don had left his fishing pole at the creek below camp and when we arrived there I told him he could have my share of the rabbits if he would catch me a trout for supper. "O. K.," he said, "I'll show you how it is done. You roll one of those rocks over in the water and catch me a couple of craw dads." We did, and he broke off the tail, took the meat from the shell and baited his hook with it. "Now watch," he said, as he cast the bait just below a large rock near the further shore. There was a splash and in a few minutes he had landed a beauty of eleven inches. After a few more casts he brought in a mate to the first. This was all we needed so we made for camp and a good supper.

Does this sound like a deer hunt? We had made a start and had a good day of fun. In camp that night, Don showed us another stunt; he took a piece of broken opal glass from an old jar lid and with the aid of my brass car key, fashioned a beautiful Indian arrow head. It looked simple and took only a short time, but was quite a trick at that. Don knows every foot of these mountains and in planning for the next day, said he would take us up where the deer were using and show us a buck, and if we had time would go over on to the head waters of Indian Creek where he would treat us to a surprise.

While stopping for a rest going up the mountain Tuesday morning, Don said, "Now for the next three hours I am going to show you fellows how to really hunt; you speak only when spoken to, and quiet is the word. I will do the talking," which we later found consisted mostly of signs and motions. We were in heavy timber and brush. After a few hundred yards we came to a pocket of several acres on a mountain side. It was covered with dense vine maple, near the center was a small rise a hundred feet across, and on this little knoll were small firs and a couple of large yew trees. Don pointed and whispered, "There will be deer bedded under those evergreens and when aroused will slide into the vine maple. Tom, you go a third of the way around to the right; Steve, the same to the left. In fifteen minutes we will start in. You will have to go slow as it is almost impossible to get through, but be as quiet as you can and don't hurry. The deer have ways of getting through and you may see one at any time and it will be close. We will all meet on the knoll later." That sure was a thrill crawling through that vine maple. How could one get his bow in position to shoot? A doe almost bumped into me, then later, a couple more. The others had the same experiences. There were a dozen beds on the knoll and as far as we know none of the deer had run out—they were all still in the vine maple. This looked easy for the morrow, but Don said not to count our chickens. You have to see horns and get your bow in position and when you shoot the arrow has to go clear without a glance.

Near the top of the divide Don said, "Now, here, if conditions are right, I will really show you something. There have been deer going up ahead of us and several are probably hiding in that canyon. You fellows circle to the right and left, go to the top and hide in one of the passes there, find a trail if you can, and in thirty minutes I will play dog up through the brush." A few minutes after we were set, three nice bucks sneaked up ahead of Don and through a little pass between Steve and me. We both saw them about fifty yards away, but it would have taken much luck to have placed a fatal arrow through the brush at that distance. When Don came up he said, "There are more in that canyon," and to prove it he circled and came back through again, this time he made more noise. Sure enough, there was another and he was a dandy. I had taken the center trail where the first had gone through. This big fellow, a four or five point buck, came up to where he could see me, then made a dash toward the other gap and ran within five yards of Steve. That would have been a real Indian bow shot but unfortunately the season was tomorrow and our quivers contained nothing but big blunts. Don had insisted. "No broadheads," he said one day, "makes quite a difference in the taste of venison."

Our day was about over now and we would not have time for the surprise trip to Indian Creek. Don told us the secret was a herd of elk, the finest he had ever seen, and if the season was ever opened on elk in that country he would sure get one.

He was in hopes he could show them to us, although they are difficult to see on that range. We would get back to camp and prepare for morning. Nothing much to do, though, as extra strings were made and broadheads sharpened to the last degree. This day there would be no blunts in our quivers.

Daylight Wednesday morning found us up in the deer country. Don had us pretty well trained by this time and was most anxious for one of us to get a buck. I had nineteen broadheads in my quiver and think Steve and Don had as many. Seventy pounds of yew bow and any one of these arrows should make a kill with a fair shot. What confidence at this time of the morning when you know you are in good hunting country.

After the first two hours I couldn't say nineteen arrows any more—my quiver was much lighter. On the first drive I shot and missed five times. Don saw me shoot once at a deer forty yards or more away. The arrow struck a limb ten feet from the ground half way to the mark. He sure gave me the devil. "Don't do that; wait for a closer or more open shot. You have to hit your deer in a vital spot to get him. Shoot him in the neck or chest cavity." Don himself had missed a shot or two, Steve had missed several. He had shot at a buck about seven yards and the arrow broke in a vine maple limb almost against the deer. He said he did not see the limb until the arrow struck. Don says you have to see everything. In the morning Steve and I expected to have at least one buck each by this time and be back in camp. Here it was noon and all we had was experience and a lot of fun. Don said after lunch, "Now, you Jaspers get down to business and do some straight shooting. The deer will be bedded down now and we will try to slip up on one." Don was serious and wanted to see blood on an arrow. He said, "The first one of you fellows who kills a deer, I will make a coon skin cap like mine." Of course, we both wanted the cap and expected to get it but it didn't really take the offer to make us want to get a buck.

An hour later we were following around the mountain side, Don was below in the middle and Steve above. Don said this was a good bedding ground and we should get a shot. I was sure on the alert and thought I had the advantage in the center position. There was a slight noise in the brush above me and shortly I heard Steve yell. I thought, "The damn lucky cuss, there goes my coon skin cap." Don came dashing by and we made our way up the hill. We found the grinning Steve standing over a beautiful forked horn buck. When he first saw the deer it was lying in its bed looking down the hill to where I was. It did not see him at all. His first arrow went diagonally through the chest cavity. It arose, and standing in its bed, turned around and around slowly. It turned four or five times in ten or twelve seconds when Steve's second arrow struck it in the neck. It saw Steve then and started to run and fell the second jump. It was the noise of this jump that I heard. There was no other noise during the whole affair that could have been heard forty yards, until Steve busted loose with his war whoop, which could have been heard two miles.

Don said we had spoiled the hunting close by, but we tried it for a while anyway, but without success. We carried Steve's deer down to the road where we found it weighed 122 pounds. Steve was all puffed up. I didn't begrudge him the game but still think he will look like h—— in a coon skin cap!

SUBSCRIBERS PLEASE NOTICE

A cross appearing in this space means that your subscription has expired and we would appreciate your prompt renewal so that your name may be kept on our mailing list.

CLASSIFIED ADVERTISING

RATES for Classified Advertising 5 cents per word per issue. Count initials and numbers as words. Minimum charge is 50 cents.

BOOKS AND MAGAZINES

The AMERICAN ARCHER, a national quarterly, $1.00 per year, 521 Fifth Ave., New York City.

The Flat Bow—70 pages of Archery information for 50 cents, well illustrated. *Ye Sylvan Archer*, 505 N. 11th St., Corvallis, Oregon.

"ARCHERY," by Robert P. Elmer M. D., revised edition, most complete book on archery published. 566 pages of valuable information for colleges, libraries, schools, camps archery clubs and individuals. Price $5.00 postpaid. orders to Ye Sylvan Archer, 505 North 11th street, Corvallis, Oregon.

"ARCHERY TACKLE, HOW TO MAKE AND HOW TO USE IT." by Adolph Shane. Bound in cloth and illustrated with more than fifty drawings and photographs. Information for making archery tackle and instructions for shooting. Price is $1.75.

RELICS AND CURIOS

INDIAN RELICS, Beadwork, Coins, Curios, Books, Minerals, Weapons. Old West Photos. Catalog, 5c. Genuine African Bow, $3.75. Ancient flint arrowheads, perfect, 6c each—Indian Museum, Osborne, Kansas.

Ye Sylvan Archer—$1.00 per year.

```
BACK NUMBERS
YE SYLVAN ARCHER
Volumes I to V Inclusive
$1.00 Per Volume
B. G. THOMPSON
R. F. D. 1, Corvallis, Oregon
```

WESTERN ANTIQUES COLLECTOR

Corvallis, Oregon

P. O. Box 403

A monthly illustrated magazine devoted to items of interest to the collector of antiques.

$1.50 per year.

BOWS·ARROWS·MATERIALS

HANDBOOK—How to Make and Use Bows and Arrows—90 Pages well illustrated (with catalog) 35c.

CATALOG—100 pictures—color spread—Instruction Folder. 10c.

CATALOG alone 5c. Stamps or Coin.

L·E·STEMMLER· QUEENS VILLAGE·N·Y·

WIN WITH BEN PEARSON ARROWS

Beautiful and accurate to the Nth degree but win their real laurels on the range. Arrows made as arrows should be—and at prices you can afford to pay. Send for catalogue.

BEN PEARSON, INC. — PINE BLUFF, ARK.

Cassius Hayward Styles

BOWYER AND FLETCHER

—Tackle that has stood the test—

28 Vicente Place

BERKELEY, CALIFORNIA

Archery Raw Materials

WM. A. JOY

9708 So. Hoover Street
LOS ANGELES, CALIF.

POTTER & MacQUARRIE
ROVING ARROWS

Split Birch or P. O. Cedar, 11-32 in. and 3-8 in., matched within 10 gr. in weight, and spined for heavy bows. Equipned with steel piles, 3 1-2 in. feathers and bright crest.

One Dozen $5.00

3400 Fruitvale Ave.
Oakland . . . . California

Ⓖ

"THE MARK OF DISTINCTION IN ARCHERY TACKLE

Fine Yew Target and Hunting Bows, Plain or Backed with Rawhide. Lemonwood Bows with Rawhide Backs.
College and School Equipment
Target, Hunting and Roving Arrows
Price List on Request

Wholesale — Retail
EARL GRUBBS
5518 W. Adams
Los Angeles, : California

ARCHERY BOWS
from the Heart of the Yew Country
W. I. KING
Woodworking Shop
1958½ Onyx St.   Eugene, Ore.

YEW BOW TIMBER

High Altitude Air Seasoned Billets and Staves of Quality and Variety.
W. G. PRESCOTT
527 Chestnut   Ashland, Ore.

E. BUD PIERSON
Bowyer — Fletcher
Tournament Tackle, Sinew, Glue, Raw Materials.
245 University Ave
CINCINNATI, OHIO
Custom Made Tackle

Write us for your needs in Archery books. Ye Sylvan Archer.

BEAR
ALUMINUM ARROWS ARE MAKING RECORDS
BEAR PRODUCTS CO.
2611 W. Philadelphia Ave., Detroit, Michigan

Rose City Archery Co.
1149 NE 31st Avenue
Portland, Oregon

In 1940 competition, improve your scores with the tackle used by

Pat Chambers
National Champion
Catalogue on request

Ye Sylvan Archer—$1.00 per year.

70 pages of Archery information for 50 cents, well illustrated. Ye Sylvan Archer, 505 N. 11th St., Corvallis, Oregon.

AT LAST
all your archery needs on ONE shaft — with
CHANDLER
Interchangeable Arrow Points
Also Fish Heads, and many other Points
PAT. PEND.
Free Cat.
T.B. Chandler
11819 4th Ave
Compton, California

BROADHEAD   Targe   Point

Paul H. Gordon, Director
Beacon Hill Craftsmen
Beacon, N. Y.
Where the serious archer's needs and desires are really consulted, and his orders exactly filled. Nothing too simple or too difficult.
Write for Complete Catalog

L. L. "Flight" DAILY
offers you
"Tackle That Talks"
Dry Cedar and Yew
Catalogue Free
245 Pearl, Eugene, Oregon

DO YOU LIKE THE CHARM OF THE BACKHILLS?

If so — read ARCADIAN LIFE MAGAZINE. It tells the story of the Ozarks in a way that will captivate you.

$1.00 a year; 25c a copy. Classified advertising (for archers) 2c a word.

O. E. RAYBURN, Editor
Caddo Gap, Arkansas

W. A. COCHRAN
Archery Equipment
High Elevation Yew Wood
Port Orford Cedar
Osage Orange
Air Seasoned
10,000 Billets and Staves in Stock
Route 2   Eugene, Ore.

Please mention Ye Sylvan Archer when writing advertisers.

Ye Sylvan Archer

July, 1940

Corvallis, Oregon

Vol. 12   No. 3

Ye
Sylvan Archer

"A magazine for the field archers"

Vol. 12   July, 1940   No. 3

Published the fifteenth of each month
for archers by archers
505 North 11th Street, Corvallis, Oregon

J. E. DAVIS .... Editor
RUSSELL JONES .... Business Manager
Subscription Price .... $1.00 Per Year
Foreign Subscription .... $1.25 Per Year
Single Copies .... 10 Cents

Advertising Rates on Application

TABLE OF CONTENTS

Page

WALT AND THE BIG JACK
  By Walt Wilhelm 1
OREGON STATE TOURNAMENT 3
FIELD ARCHERY ASSOCIATION
  OF SOUTHERN CALIFORNIA 4
BROWN COUNTY OPEN
  TOURNAMENT 4
THIS AND THAT ABOUT THOSE
  By George Brommers 5
EDITORIAL 6
TROUBLE FOR RABBITS AND
  RATTLESNAKES
  By Hugh Slocum 6
CANADIAN MAIL TOURNAMENT 6
NAGLER WINS SIX GOLDS PIN 8
FIELD ARCHERY CONTEST 9
ARCHERS DEFEAT GOLFERS 10
FIELD ARCHERS IN N.A.A.
  PROGRAM 10
PACIFIC NORTHWEST ASS'N. 11
FROM N.A.A. PRESIDENT 11

Walt and the Big Jack

By Walt Wilhelm, in Pomona Citizen

Here on the desert it gets pretty hot during the summer months. Most of the desert folks just lay around in the shade if they can find any, through the heat of the day.

You wouldn't do any night hunting for sport, but if the jack rabbits were eating the crops you'd get 'em any way you could. A bunch of us decided to help the farmers, so we took one of our hunting cars and went jackrabbiting. It was a warm night and rabbits were plentiful.

Of course, we used bows and arrows. We agreed from the start of the hunt for each man to take ten shots, no more, no less. If we got a rabbit every shot, fine, if not, it was a bargain, and we all shook hands on the deal. The farmers were urging us to stay out all night and try to kill a thousand, but archers are sportsmen and always give the game a chance, even though they're hunting predators.

It's nobody's business how many we got with our ten shots each, and besides, that's not what I'm trying to tell. My brother Ken had his wife and two small children, Ed Hill from Barstow and his wife, and my family were also in the party.

Five miles out of town we got into the rabbit country—and what rabbit country. There were thousands of them. We hunted five hours, that is, we hunted thirty minutes and spent four and one-half hours looking for arrows.

We had powerful spotlights, and more than once some long ear would get confused and dive against the car. Suddenly we jumped a different rabbit; he was the mangiest, longest eared, bob tailed critter I've ever seen. The beast was the largest on the desert and measured six hands high at the withers.

Evidently the old boy had never seen a light before. He'd just crouch around when the rays played on him. When he did run, which was just for a short distance, he kicked up more dust than a wild mustang.

We almost wrecked the car trying not to run him down. We couldn't shoot because the women and kids were in back of him. Blunts wouldn't have done the radiator any good, either, if we'd missed.

Ken's young son, Denny, aged four, was looking over the wind shield trying to scare the bunny off the car. Ed Hill claimed the jack was near the radiator just to get warm. I tossed my hat at the rabbit and away he went, straight up in the air and back, all at the same time. Smack into little Denny's face he landed, knocking the lad down and nearly breaking his neck.

The long ear jumped from the car, then back in, out on the hood he went, then to the ground. Now, a rabbit or anything else can't abuse my favorite nephew and get away with it. I threw down my bow and made a dive for the black tail. I put everything into that leap, and was proud of such a jump; but I'm ashamed of the outcome of the tussle.

I landed square on Mr. Rabbit and tried to pin him down. When I'd get his front end down his other end would rare up. I thought for a few minutes I'd have to have help to turn him loose. He had claws like a wild cat and the strength of a mule. In just a few seconds he tore my shirt to ribbons. My belly was bleeding like I'd run into a wire fence. Just as I thought I had the brute, he cut loose with a double and landed both hind feet square on my chin, then with his front feet in my eyes, he made a jump that put him into the darkness and freedom.

Two deep scratches in my chin told the story. You all know what the rest of the party were doing. They still do. I guess I'll never live that one down. But, believe you me, I've tackled my last he jack rabbit with my bare hands.

Here and There with N. F. A. A.

By John L. Yount

At the time of going to press the only mail tournament results available were those from Southern California. This meet occurred on the Malibu roving course, June 23, and was featured by some real upsets. To begin with, Roland Quayle, who finished fifth in the first mail shoot with a nice 541, really went wild, and shot a 630, the second highest score of which we so far have records.

On the other hand, Merle Hathaway, who finished third in the last National, with 547, hit the skids and finished 100 points down. Larry Hughes, runner-up to Turnock in the first meet, did not compete.

Neither Hughes' failure to compete, nor Hathaway's low score will affect their chances to win the National Championship, as that is based on the best three out of five scores. The championship can be won by some archer who has not yet entered, for there are three more tournaments.

In the Women's Division, Eva Bedwell remained in something of a slump, shooting 309, and being beaten by Naomi Baker, whose score of 328 quite definitely shows that here is one lady who is going places in this game. Another one to be considered in the future is Margaret Quayle. Her score of 267 would have been good for second place in the last National.

Hunters' Field Round

With hunting season just around the corner in some of the states, it is time this association gave some thought to that subject.

We are going to begin by publishing the rules for a broadhead round, as submitted by Fred Bear, of the Rules Committee. This round uses the standard roving course and targets, and, consequently, is no trouble to lay out. It is designed distinctly as a hunting round with all emphasis on the archer's ability to hit the target with the fewest number of arrows, rather than on his ability to shoot a score with a definite number of arrows. As you will see, the archer who must use the first two arrows as range finders hasn't a chance in the world. It also keeps the number of arrows that must be removed from the butt at a minimum. At the same time, it gives the archer who isn't too good a chance for a bit of practice.

Rules—Use broadhead arrows only. They must weigh 425 grains, or more, and have a head not less than 7/8" wide. Each archer is allowed to shoot four arrows at each target unless a hit is made with one of the first three. After a hit is made the archer is finished on that target. A bullseye with the first arrow counts 8, a hit 6; a bullseye with the second arrow counts 6, a hit 4; a bullseye with third arrow counts 4, a hit 2; a bullseye with the fourth arrow counts 2, a hit 1. Since each archer stops when he scores a hit, at the most he removes only one arrow from the target.

Battle Clout

Another event that will help put muscles on the boys with the heavy bows is the Battle Clout. This is, also, a pretty good test of that aforementioned heavy tackle. It had better be good, as well as heavy, or you will have a score of zero, with all arrows about thirty yards short.

Distance, 200 yards. Target, 12 ft. diameter center, and 4 rings, each 6 ft. wide. Thirty-six arrows shot in ends of 6. Arrows must weigh 425 grains, or more, and have broadheads not less than 7-8" wide. Score as is usual on ringed targets, i.e., 9 for a bullseye, 7 for next ring, then 5, 3, and 1.

N.F.A.A. Stickers

Bill Folberth has presented the association with 5,000 stickers designed primarily to seal the sights on bows before tournament competition. They are one and a half inches in diameter and bear no printing, except the emblem, or seal, of our organization. We find they look swell when pasted to your bow or quiver. If you would like to see for yourself, just send a self-addressed envelope to John L. Yount, P.O. Box 383, Redlands, California. We shall soon have felt emblems for your hunting jacket or shirt. We hope all members in the field will wear one.

Big Game Pin

The N.F.A.A. feels that the king of all archers is the big game hunter. For this reason, it has been decided to give special distinction to this group. It has been felt that this could best be done by awarding an appropriately designed gold pin to be worn in the lapel, for the envy of others.

The rules for winning this pin are few and simple. First, you must be a member of the N.F.A.A. Then you must present affidavits to the effect that you have succeeded in bagging, legally, of course, a specimen of any of the recognized big game animals, such as deer, bear, moose, elk, lion, etc. We suspect that while the rules may be simple, they will be the only simple thing about winning one of these pins. It's hats off to the men who succeed.

We do not believe that any trophy this organization might present in the future for any other purpose can ever quite equal this pin in the eyes of the archers.

N.F.A.A. SECOND FIELD ARCHERY TOURNAMENT

Men	First Round	Second Round	56 Targ. Total
1—Roland Quayle, Long Beach, Calif.	74-298	84-332	158-630
2—Nelson Grumley, Detroit, Mich.	64-254	68-264	132-518
3—Carlos Barfield, Detroit, Mich.	61-245	57-233	116-478
4—Merle Hathaway, Los Angeles, Calif.	61-217	60-226	121-443
5—Emery Watts, Los Angeles, Calif.	58-218	56-208	114-426
6—J. G. Daulley, Long Beach, Calif.	55-213	55-213	110-426
7—Stanley Baker, Inglewood, Calif.	49-181	64-242	113-423
8—Earl Grubbs, Los Angeles, Calif.	52-198	58-224	110-422
9—Andy Wilson, Detroit, Mich.	54-210	43-209	107-419
10—Willard Bacon, Redondo Beach, Calif.	48-179	60-232	108-410

Women			
1—Naomi Baker, Inglewood, Calif.	49-181	43-147	92-328
2—Eva Bedwell, San Bernardino, Calif.	41-161	40-148	81-309
3—Margaret Quayle, Long Beach, Calif.	34-122	39-145	73-267
4—Kay Ratcliffe, Highland Park, Mich.	36-130	36-130	72-260
5—Lulu Stalker, Flint, Mich.	36-132	32-122	68-254
6—Mary Calvert, Flint, Mich.	34-124	26-104	60-228
7—Babe Daulley, Long Beach, Calif.	23-87	33-119	56-206
8—June Franklin, San Bernardino, Calif.	21-89	30-108	51-197
9—Jessie Doyle, South Gate, Calif.	21-81	26-90	47-171
10—Dorothy Ahman, San Bernardino, Calif.	22-81	26-90	46-166

Oregon State Tournament

DeWitt Hawkins and Mrs. Vivian Chambers of Portland won the men's and women's state shampionships at the Oregon State tournament at Drain on July 5. 6 and 7. Mrs. Chambers raised the state records in both National and Columbia rounds. Muriel Reichart of Corvallis won the junior girls' championship with a new state record. L. L. "Flight" Dailey won the men's flight and Glen Vineyard the women's flight. Mr. and Mrs. Gene Warneke of Portland carried away the clout trophies. Glen Vineyard won the archery-golf event and the field round for women, while Gene Warneke added the archery-golf cup to his collection. J. B. Whitmore of Portland. was high in the men's field round. Dean Gibson won the junior boys championship.

Ted Hunter qualified for the six golds club at 40 yards.

Next year's tournament will be held at Cottage Grove on July 4, 5 and 6, 1941. Officers elected were: President, J. E. Davis, Corvallis; Vice-Presidents, Bill Collins, Cottage Grove; Dick Thomas, Newport; Mel Barnes, Portland; and V. D. McCauley, Eugene, secretary.

The fifth annual international open archery tournament will be held August 26, 27, 28, 29 and 30, at the Canadian National Exhibition in Toronto, Ontario, Canada.

FIELD ARCHERY ASSOCIATION OF SO. CALIFORNIA
By Elmer W. Bedwell, Secretary

At the Arroyo Seco roving course, the Pasadena Field Archers sponsored an invitational tournament on May 5, which was held in honor of the past year's officers of the Southern California Field Archery Association, and the State and National Archery Association. Edmund M. Brock is president, George Miles, vice-president, and Elmer W. Bedwell secretary-treasurer of the Southern California organization. John L. Yount is president of both the State and National associations.

This meet was held to show appreciation for the efforts of these officers in doing their bit for the advancement of Field Archery. The officers were presented with gold ash trays, with a gold figure of an archer mounted in the center—very beautiful, and practical, too. (But to date, have not known anyone who has dared to drop an ash in one of them.)

The regular S.C.F.A.A. June tournament was held in Malibu on the 23rd, with sixty-nine registered archers participating, a few under par, but quite a few had gone to try their hand at the G.A.O. Archery Tournament in Milwaukee. The day being ideal shooting weather, the scores were as follows: championship class, men—Roland Quayle, gold bar, score 630; Merle Hathaway, silver bar, score 443. General division— Volus Jones, blue ribbon, score 472; Fred Woodley, red ribbon, score 448; Emery Watts, white ribbon, score 426.

Championship class, ladies— Eva Bedwell, gold bar, score 309. Glenn Curtis did not shoot. General division—Naomi Baker, championship medal, score 328; Margaret Quayle, silver medal, score 267; Ruth Hathaway, bronze medal, score 214. Juniors, Bedwell trophy — Harold Robinson, score 357; Bob King, second, score 294; Angus Bruce, third, score 235. These scores and more also were entered in the second National Mail Tournament.

The Beacon Craftsmen of Beacon, N. Y., have moved into a new extension on their shop which has more than doubled their facilities.

BROWN COUNTY ANNUAL OPEN TOURNAMENT

Amid the twenty-five square miles of picturesque rugged hill country in Brown County State Park, Indiana, seventy-three archers competed for awards at the Brown County Open Tournament, June 1 and 2.

Grand weather both days, and a chicken dinner in the Abe Martin Lodge helped make the meet a pleasant and unique experience for those attending.

The tournament was held on the permanent archery field constructed by the conservation department.

Mrs. Lola Gaston set a new world's record for the Columbia round—72 hits for a score of 590. She will receive her six golds pin for a perfect shot at 40 yards while shooting her record breaking score.

The trophy winners were as follows: men's championship trophy— Arnold Gebler; most golds cup—G. Anderson; men's flight cup — Curt Hill; men's clout trophy—A. Lincoln; men's team cup—A. Gebler, F. George, J. Pinkard, F. Strain; York trophy—K. Hazeldine; double American cup/J. Thompson; high 100 yds. score—A. Gebler; good sports award —P. Earl.

The women's awards follow: women's champ cup—L. Gaston; National cup — M. Lanzer; women's flight cup—M. Hill; women's clout trophy— E. Radtke; team cup— L. Gaston, E. Radtke, T. Eble, F. Martin; National trophy—W. Druckmiller; Columbia trophy—M. Lanzer; good sports award—L. Ashcroft.

The girls' championship cup was won by M. Bramblett, and the boys' flight trophy by R. Lamping.

Next Year's Tournament

E. S. Richter is president of the 1941 tournament, which will be sponsored by the Chicago Park District Archers. The place will be, of course, the Brown County State Park, Indiana, and the dates, May 31 and June 1. The permanent board of control for this annual tournament is composed of W. B. Lincoln, Jr., M. Anthony, and G. F. Martin. The permanent secretary-treasurer is Mrs. G. F. Martin.

60th National at Amherst, Massachusetts, August 5-10, 1940.

This and That About Those
By George Brommers

(This article was crowded out of last issue.—Ed.)

There is one city in these United States where archery is treated as a major sport, and that city is San Diego. The man who brought it about is this year's president of the Western A.A., Lieut. Col. F. E. Pierce, U.S.M.C., Ret.

Col. Pierce, in spite of steady hospitalization and operations resulting from a foot shattered by a machine gun slug in Nicaragua, has found a lot of time to give to archery. He is also president of both the San Diego and the Coronado Archery Clubs this year, as well as head of the Western.

One reason for the growth of archery in the Southern city is the attitude of the San Diego Union, and its sports writers. These writers know what it is all about and they give archery equal publicity to that accorded golf, baseball or polo, for instance.

Yes, archery has come into its own! The sports goods dealers of San Diego have contributed a perpetual field archery trophy, and named it in honor of an outstanding sports feature writer and columnist, Tom F. Drummond. This trophy will be shot for the first time at the Western AA tournament in San Diego, July 6-7.

Mr. Drummond knows the sport. He was an intimate friend of Dr. Pope, of Art Young and of "Chief" Compton. He is eminintly competent to write, and to write authoritatively. Fortunately he is willing. His circulation does the rest.

Speaking of sports columnists, we are very fortunate here in the West. Archery magazines and archery writers do the best they can, but what is needed is big league circulation and big league talent. Our metropolitan dailies have nothing else but.

Mr. Drummond is not alone in helping us. Both the Oregonian and the Oregon Journal in Portland carry exceptionally authentic copy. Of course they have Pop Prouty and Dr. Cathey to fall back on for data, and these writers know how to use the data supplied them.

They also know how to exploit exceptional opportunities. When John Davis, the Oregon basement champion, hit a deer by accident last fall, they recognized it as the front page story it undoubtedly was. Personally I would say that it was more of a miracle than it was news.

I have just read Royal Brougham's "The Morning After," in the Seattle P. I. In the May 29th issue he says:

"Consider Belvia Carter, the national women's archery champion. An orphan from early girlhood, for many years she has toiled as waitress to help support a sister with tuberculosis. She is happily married, but hasn't forgotten her obligation to Sis in Colorado. For two or three hours a day she practices on the archery range to maintain the skill which made her the best woman archer in America, and then works a full shift at the Gowman Hotel Coffee Shop. The other day doctors told her that her eyes were cracking under the strain, and that she may have to choose between her job and archery, in which case she will give up her bows and arrows and relinquish her title. The red badge of courage to Billie Carter." A tribute well deserved!

We all know that we have outstanding examples of this same kind of courage in archery. I am thinking of Bill Palmer, and his terrible handicap, as well as his indomitable courage.

I am thinking of Ilda Hanchett, who has been under the same kind of strain as Billie Carter. She, too, has worked hard—at times at very uncongenial jobs—to support herself and her son Hollis. Was it worth it? Ask Ilda. Ask Hollis. Hollis has had a wonderful scholastic record, and is now offered a Caltech scholarship. He has also been selected for an Annapolis appointment, and should by this time have taken his entrance examination. Fortunately for Ilda, she is now engaged in work that she loves. Let us hope that Billie Carter's ship, too, will come in soon.

Then consider Beatrice Hodgson, Audrey Grubbs, Genevieve Johnson

(Continued on page 8)

Editorial

Paul H. Gordon of the Beacon Hill Craftsmen is author of the lead article in the July-August issue of The Home Craftsman magazine, on the making of simple bows and arrows. The article is designed not only for the individual craftsman but for archery counsellors and teachers of manual and industrial arts as well. It is illustrated with both technical drawings and cartoons.

Portland, Oregon, is bidding for the 1941 National tournament. The Portland Chamber of Commerce has offered to guarantee the expenses of the tournament and the invitation committee, under the leadership of W. G. Williams, has already collected 60 target fees, mostly from Oregon archers. A beautiful site has been provided for the events of the tournament and Portland archers are planning many special attractions if the National sees fit to visit Oregon for the first time.

We are in receipt of a copy of a very interesting letter written by Major Carl H. Bulcock, of Surrey, England, to Mr. Harold A. Titcomb. Major Bulcock was a practising physician when the war began but he gave up his practice, rejoined the British forces, and is now in charge of an ambulance train. Major Bulcock is a member of the Royal Toxophilite Society and of the Surrey Bowmen. He says, in part, "I'm really rather proud of being British at a time like this, much as I hate war; and as a peace-loving individual I feel very annoyed at having to take part in two wars in one lifetime.........Cheer up, old man. Things might be a lot worse. I don't think we shall let you down and we are not downhearted yet. No, Sir."

TROUBLE FOR RABBITS AND RATTLESNAKES

By Hugh Slocum

The small game around here surely is getting acquainted with us archers by leaps and bounds—especially if they (don't) leap and bound. Two of our staunch archers who are really there with the bow, Bill Towne and Dick Carr, went ahunting recently, and Bill bowled four chipmunks over in a row, then topped off with a rabbit. Dick did his bit by killing a large snake, species unknown, that he had found—which reminds me of my first fight with a huge desert rattler recently. It was found coiled up on the shady side of David Lesh's target hay. We were plucking arrows out of the hay when an earsplitting rattle caused us to spring back. With my hand on my hip, pardon me, quiver, I began circling the hay looking for the snake when David grabbed me and pointed it out. There just three feet away lay this king of the desert all coiled and ready to strike; but I quickly fitted an arrow to the string and waited for that weaving head to pause so I could be sure of 'hitting the mark'. At last I had an opportunity to let fly at the chosen spot, but, alas, the arrow missed his head, penetrating the body about four inches back. My next idea was to run, whereupon I discovered that the arrow had pinned him to the ground.

If it were not for this trusty bow and quiver of arrows on my back, someone else would be writing this story. I probably would have been at the mercy of this Goliath of the desert—a nine inch rattlesnake. Anyway, they do come smaller, and little snakes into big snakes grow.

—Antelope Valley Gazette.

Canadian Mail Tournament

Two championship silver cups, owned by the Canadian Archery Association, are to be shot for in a mail match tournament to be held on Saturday, August 3, 1940, without participation by any Toronto club. These championships will be determined on the shooting of a double American round for men and a double Columbia round for women. The tournament is open to all Canadian clubs outside Toronto which have paid registration fees of $1.50 to the Canadian Archery Association. Write for rules and particulars to R. J. Mitchele, 69 Grenville St., Toronto, Ont.

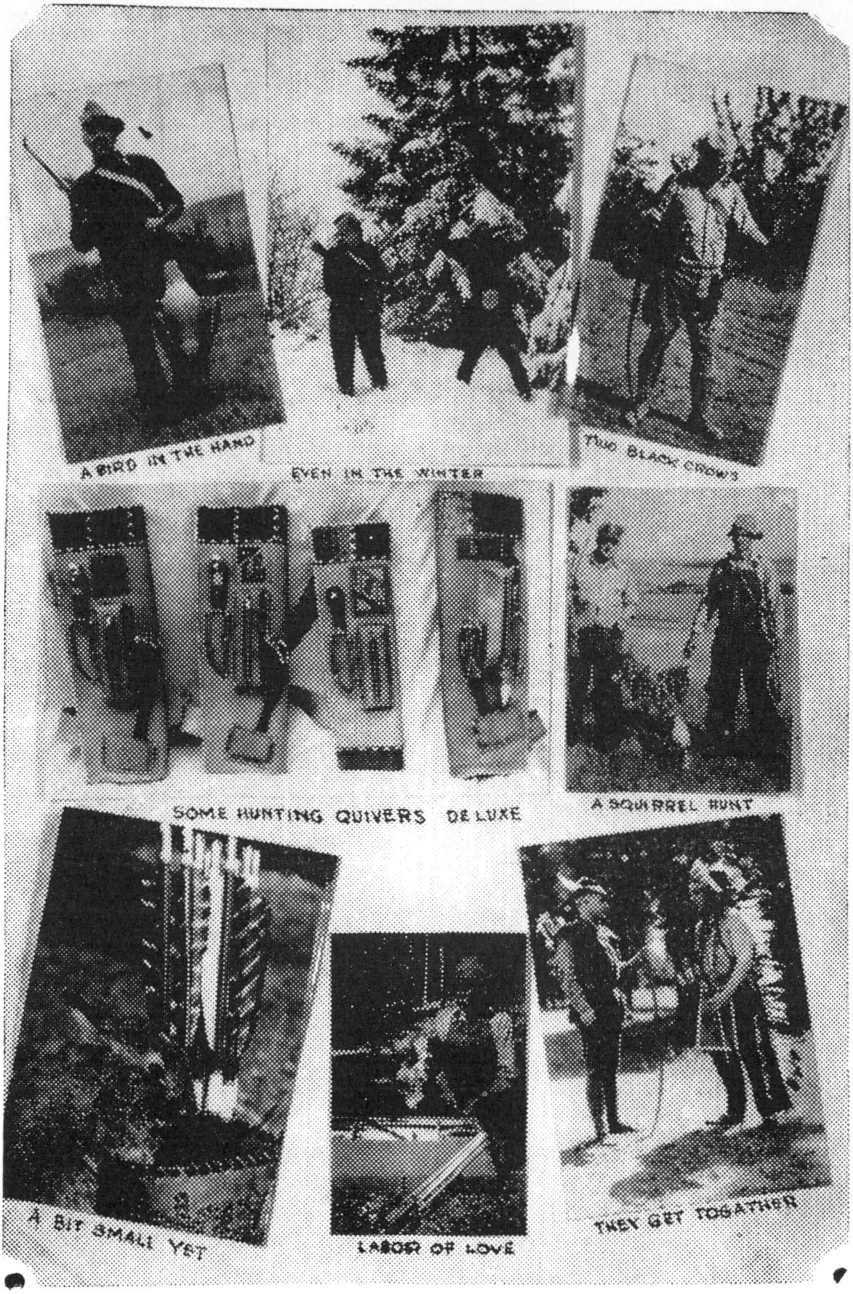

A BIRD IN THE HAND

EVEN IN THE WINTER

TWO BLACK CROWS

SOME HUNTING QUIVERS DE LUXE

A SQUIRREL HUNT

A BIT SMALL YET

LABOR OF LOVE

THEY GET TOGATHER

THIS AND THAT

(Continued from page 5)

and Gladys Hammer. These women have had responsible, even strenuous positions to fill, but each has made some worthwhile contribution to archery by her excellence in the sport. Long may they wave!

I think of our Army friends. Col. Pierce and his shattered foot, C. H. Styles and his punctured hip, John Willard and his broken nose. There are Monte Hammer and Joe Cosner, both gassed. (Joe, unfortunately, is now gas proof). I think of all our other disabled soldiers, who in archery have found a new interest.

I recall Dr. Butts and Dr. Bradfield, both of whom have now passed on. Every issue of the archery magazines has some examples. Archery has just been fortunate in bringing these people together; the qualities that we respect in them were there before.

Speaking of writers again I do not know when I have liked a hunting story as well as I did Sisler's in the April issue. It just had everything. Literarily it had more than a touch of Maurice Thompson (this is as high a compliment as I can think of). It had the ease and fluency of a professional writer—Gardner and Willard will, I think, attest to that. It had action and it had excitement, as well as quiet humor. Some story!

Now you can see how I would like to see archery's best hunter-writers get together and collaborate on a book of hunting stories, similar to the one Forrest Nagler will bring out within a month or so.

There is another Navy man who could make some valuable contributions to such a book, and that is Frank Latta, another submarine officer. These fellows get around, and they know how to tell about it factually and interestingly.

Now don't forget that the Western tournament at San Diego this year will feature field archery as well as target events. The field course, if I understand John Yount right, will be official, and count for NFAA sectional awards and records.

Don't, whatever you do, forget the National at Amherst, the main event of the season.

Nagler Wins Six Golds Pin

The June tournament of the Toronto Archery Club witnessed a sight equal to any of the mythical feats of Robin Hood when Forrest Nagler, president of the club, shot a "perfect end" at 50 yards. Mr. Nagler emptied his quiver of six arrows into the center of the target, and thus won for himself the distinction of being the first Canadian archer to shoot a "possible" at this distance during a tournament, and is one of not more than a score to have done it. His accomplishment wins for him the most coveted award in archery, a "Six Gold" pin.

The tournament, which commenced at three P.M., consisted of shooting the club's favorite round, an American plus an added 30 arrows at 80 yards for the men, and a women's Metropolitan for the ladies. Winners of the men's event were Mr. Nagler, first, with 745 points and making a new club record of 638 for an American Round. Mr. Alex Macdonald was second, with 722 points.

The ladies' event was captured by Mrs. A. R. B. Knight, holder of the ladies' Canadian Championship title, with a score of 716. Mrs. R. John Mitchele placed second, with 676 points. The new prizes in the form of sterling silver teaspoons bearing the club's emblem and which were originated by Mrs. Nagler, wife of the president, to whom considerable credit is due for hitting upon this most welcomed form of award, were presented by the Lady Paramount, Mrs. Frank Hill. In addition to the above winners who received spoons was Mr. Alan Baggs, Handicap winner. Miss Rita Williams and Mr. Alex Macdonald won the Novelty Balloon Shoot, and received decks of cards with archery designs on the backs.

—R. J. Mitchele,
Sec. Canadian
Archery Ass'n.

The Palisades Interstate Park Commission is sponsoring an exhibition double American tournament on July 21 at the Bear Mountain Inn, N. Y. There is no target fee and free parking in the park will be provided for the archers. Waldo C. Wood is sports director for the commission.

Field Archery Contest

Sponsored by T. B. Chandler Co. and Ye Sylvan Archer

This contest is sponsored for the purpose of creating greater interest in archery in such a way as to entice people to want to get out in the open, not only to see America, but to see it as the archer sees it, as Nature herself intended you to see it. The contest is also to interest people in vacationing in America, by inviting all vacationists to add archery to their list of sports while on their vacations.

The contest is open to all archers in North and South America, and all American possessions, starting September 1, 1940, and ending when all awards are claimed.

The first person to make a perfect end in any of the distances of the American Round and the Columbia Round will receive one prize for each perfect end in each distance.

The first person to kill any of the following animals, fish or birds will receive one prize for each one killed:

Badger; bear, black; bear, brown; bear, grizzly; bear, polar; bob cat; caribou; coon; coyote; elk; fox; lion; lynx cat; moose; mountain sheep; possum; skunk; tiger; wolf; wild boar; wild goat; rattlesnake (over 5 feet long with 8 or more rattles); rabbits (12 or over in one day's hunt; squirrels (12 or over in one day's hunt).

Deer, 50 prizes (one for each state in U.S.A., one for Canada, and one for Old Mexico, Panama Canal Zone and South America).

Fish, first 6 different varieties that are over 3 feet long.

Birds, duck, pheasant, quail, hawk, owl, and crow.

Eighteen (18) other prizes for unlisted animals, fish and birds that are, in the opinion of the judges, worthy of prize awards.

Each winner of the archery target division will receive one dozen target sets of Chandler Interchangeable Arrow Points, consisting of: 1 dozen ferrules, No. A-14; one dozen target points, No. A-21; one dozen blunt points, No. A-26.

Each winner of the fishing group will receive three Chandler Fish Heads, catalog No. A-80.

Each winner of the hunting division will receive one dozen Chandler Interchangeable Arrow Points of the kind used in making the kill.

To insure that the public is fairly treated, all claims of award will be submitted to three judges, and their decision is final. The judges are Larry Hughes, Roland Quayle, and Chester Seay.

All applicants must comply with the following rules:

1—All contestants must use Chandler Interchangeable Arrow Points.

2—A picture must be sent with the claim of award. For claims of target awards the picture must show the person, with the equipment used, standing by the side of the target with arrows all in bullseyes as they were shot. For all claims of hunting and fishing awards, the picture must show the person, with the equipment used, and the kill, or catch, showing arrow in contact or point of entrance.

3—All pictures sent must have the name, age, and address of the person claiming the award on the top of the back of the picture, and giving the approximate distance, hour, day, and place, stating the weight of bow, weight and length of arrow, (depth of penetration, for hunters), kind of point used, and the dealer from whom the points were purchased, (with any other information deemed necessary), and signed by two witnesses who were or were not present.

4—All animals, fish, and birds must be killed in season and lawfully taken. All target awards are good only at official target shoots.

5—45 days will be given from date of receipt of first claim of any award for other claims to arrive.

6—All pictures, stories and information sent become the property of T. B. Chandler to be used for publication or as desired.

7—In all claims of awards the decision of the judges will be final, and immediately after the decision is rendered the winner will be sent, free and postpaid, the prize for said award.

8—The names of all winners of

awards will be published in Ye Splvan Archer. (A story will be appreciated of your hunting experience in making any kill, such as hardships endured, pleasure of trip, excitements, thrills, dangers in close contact, methods used, place, time of trip, or any other information you feel would be of interest to archers. For the betterment of archery, your story will be appreciated, and all stories or accounts that are of public reading interest will be published in Ye Sylvan Archer.)

9—No limit on the number of awards received by any one person. No officials or employees of T. B. Chandler Co. are eligible to compete for prizes.

10—Archery is a game of sport, and your sporting ethics will be taken as authentic and official.

Archers Defeat Golfers

Arnold Wyttenbach and Forrest Nagler, prominent Toronto archers, scored a two-up victory over Don Carrick and Phil Farley in an unusual golf-archery match over the Mississauga Golf Club course. The match was an added feature in connection with the International Alumni Association golf tournament. Wyttenbach and Nagler used bow and arrow and got tremendous distance off the tees, frequently well over the 350-yard mark. To hole out, they were required to hit toy balloons or small pyramid markers the size of a regulation golf cup.

Wyttenbach had a medal score of 57, out of 28 and back in 29. Nagler scored a 65. Carrick carded a 78, and Farley 73.

The archers spotted their golfing opponents a stroke a hole.

Competition against archery exponents was no new experience for Phil Farley. He was introduced to it in an exhibition match at Banff back in 1931. And according to his own confession. "I haven't been hit by an arrow yet."

At the time of going to press we do not have the complete returns of the big Milwaukee open championship tournament but we are informed that Russ Hoogerhyde won the target championship and Howard Hill the field events.

FIELD ARCHERS TO HAVE PART IN N.A.A. PROGRAM

There will be one day of field shooting at the 60th annual tournament of the NAA at Amherst, Mass. As the official NFAA round will be shot, it will give many who have been competing in the NFAA mail tournaments a chance to fight it out on the same field.

Archers will be glad to know that "Pop" Prouty was able to get to the shooting line and shoot a few flight arrows. Pop's broken hip has healed nicely but his knee is still a little stiff.

Some months ago we told of the long hours Chester Stevenson, of Eugene, Oregon, was putting in making a bow from one of Fred Bear's first class osage staves. Well, here it is, but the cut doesn't show the beautifully carved nocks by Bill King, a rattlesnake head on one end and rattles on the other. Chet still has a kink in his neck from trying to sight down the bow, in the process of construction.

Ye Sylvan Archer—$1.00 per year.

PACIFIC NORTHWEST ASSOCIATION MEETING

According to Secretary Duryee, the 1940 Pacific Northwest annual tournament, with 78 paid entries, was the largest, finest and most enjoyable tournament ever held by the association.

New association records were established by Mrs. Vivian Chambers, as follows: single Columbia, 72-544; double Columbia, 143-1071; 50 yard score in Columbia, 24-176; 30 yard score, 24-204.

Perfect ends were shot by Leonard Carter at 50 yards, DeWitt Hawkins at 50 yards and 40 yards, and Sonny Johns at 30 yards.

At the business meeting of PNAA, the following officers were elected: President, J. H. Adams, Seattle; Vice-presidents, Dr. Henry Hewitt, of Portland, Oregon and Damon Howatt, of Yakima, Washington; Secretary-treasurer, Kore T. Duryee, of Seattle, Washington. The 1941 tournament will be held in Seattle.

Grand championships were won by DeWitt Hawkins and Mrs. Vivian Chambers, both of Portland. Wm. Haynes, of Spokane, was second in men's totals and Gene Warnick of Portland, third. Mrs. Belvia Carter and Paloma Kirkwood, both of Seattle, were second and third in women's events, respectively.

Sonny Johns, of Tacoma, was first, Billy Boak, of Bordeaux, Washington, second, and Dean Gibson, of Vancouver, Washington, was third in junior boys' target events.

Muriel Reichart, of Corvallis, and Dorothy Axtelle were, respectively, first and second in the junior girls' contest.

Stanley Stevens shot 455 yards, 1 foot, 6 inches, to defeat L. L Dailey and Dr. Henry Hewitt in the men's flight shoot. Glendoline Vineyard was first with 394 yards, 1 foot, 6 inches, and Mrs. Donna Hewitt was second in the women's flight. Dick Williams shot 370 yards, 2½ inches in the junior flight. Sonny Johns was second.

Men's clout event was won by Gene Warnick. Bob Schmid was second, and Jim Saling, third. Miss Mary Marquis, Miss Glen Vineyard, and Miss Natalie Reichart placed in the order named in the women's clout. Dick Williams, Billy Boak, and Dean Gibson were first, second and third in the junior clout.

Dr. Henry Hewitt had low score of 57 in the archery-golf round, and Glen Vineyard was low woman with a 68.

The field archery round consisted of 14 small animal targets, nearly all partially hidden. The archers shot around this course twice. In the men's division, Stanley Stevens, of Portland, was first, I. M. Stamps, of Seattle, second and A. W. Galloway of Portland, third. In the women's division, Glen Vineyard was first, Mrs. Mabel Tatro, second, and Katherine Wheeler third. Dick Williams lead the junior boys with Bill Boak, second, and Dean Gibson, third.

From N.A.A. President

Friends of Archery:

It is my privilege and pleasure, as president, to extend to you a most cordial invitation to participate in the sixtieth National Archery Tournament to be held at the Massachusetts State College, Amherst, Massachusetts. The dates—August 5, 6, 7, 8, 9 and 10, 1940.

I can assure you that the sponsoring group (the Massachusetts State Archery Association) and your host institution (the Massachusetts State College) desire to make your stay here at the National Tournament a most interesting and enjoyable one. I assure you that those in charge of the events have worked hard at their many and varied assignments to make details go smoothly and to give you a week of maximum enjoyment. It has often appealed to me that one of the outstanding features of archery groups is that they are family affairs and we would like to have the sixtieth National Tournament an archery festival, an archery "old home week," as it were, which will bring to you once again a renewal of genuine archery friendships. Make it a real vacation full of fun and enjoyment. It's your opportunity to shoot with the nation's best, as well as a chance to shoot with those in your own class. There are a large number of prizes and awards which offer many opportunities for the novice and average archer as well as the expert.

On behalf of the housing committee, your hosts, we would recommend that if feasible you bring your own blankets, sheets and pillow cases, face cloths and towels. On this basis, rooming accommodations will be only fifty cents per person each night. This way you can save one half the rooming fee. Each occupant to take care of his or her own room. For a fifty year period, the weather records show the average temperature to be 70 degrees F.; the highest has been 100, and the lowest 41. This is for your information so you may plan bedding accordingly.

We have been very fortunate in being able to make one fee cover all expenses including meals, banquet, rooms, tips, etc., (exclusive of registration fee). If you bring your own bedding, $11.50 for the week. If it is furnished, $15.00 for the week. This fee is available only to those who register for the entire week, and is inclusive except for a Field Archery event fee.

So in closing, may we once more extend to you a most cordial invitation to come and spend the week of August 5-10 at the National Archery Tournament at the Massachusetts State College, Amherst, Mass. Looking forward to your visit with us at that time, I am,

Sincerely yours,
Larry Briggs,
President.

SUBSCRIBERS PLEASE NOTICE

A cross appearing in this space means that your subscription has expired and we would appreciate your prompt renewal so that your name may be kept on our mailing list.

CLASSIFIED ADVERTISING

RATES for Classified Advertising 5 cents per word per issue. Count initials and numbers as words. Minimum charge is 50 cents.

RELICS AND CURIOS

INDIAN RELICS, Beadwork, Coins, Curios, Books, Minerals, Weapons. Old West Photos. Catalog, 5c. Genuine African Bow, $3.75. Ancient flint arrowheads, perfect, 6c each—Indian Museum, Osborne, Kansas.

BOOKS AND MAGAZINES

The AMERICAN ARCHER, a national quarterly, $1.00 per year, 521 Fifth Ave., New York City.

The Flat Bow—70 pages of Archery information for 50 cents, well illustrated. *Ye Sylvan Archer*, 505 N. 11th St., *Corvallis, Oregon.*

BACK NUMBERS
YE SYLVAN ARCHER
Volumes I to V Inclusive
$1.00 Per Volume
B. G. THOMPSON
R. F. D. 1, Corvallis, Oregon

E. BUD PIERSON
Bowyer — Fletcher
Tournament Tackle, Sinew, Glue, Raw Materials.
245 University Ave
CINCINNATI, OHIO
Custom Made Tackle

WESTERN
ANTIQUES
COLLECTOR

Corvallis, Oregon
P. O. Box 403

A monthly illustrated magazine devoted to items of interest to the collector of antiques.

$1.50 per year.

HANDBOOK—How to Make and Use Bows and Arrows—90 Pages well illustrated (with catalog) 35c.
CATALOG—100 pictures—color spread—Instruction Folder. 10c.
CATALOG alone 5c. Stamps or Coin.
L·E·STEMMLER· QUEENS VILLAGE·N·Y·

WIN WITH BEN PEARSON ARROWS

Beautiful and accurate to the Nth degree but win their real laurels on the range. Arrows made as arrows should be—and at prices you can afford to pay. Send for catalogue.

BEN PEARSON, INC. — PINE BLUFF, ARK.

Cassius Hayward Styles

BOWYER AND FLETCHER

—Tackle that has stood the test—

28 Vicente Place

BERKELEY, CALIFORNIA

(G)

"THE MARK OF DISTINCTION IN ARCHERY TACKLE

Fine Yew Target and Hunting Bows, Plain or Backed with Rawhide. Lemonwood Bows with Rawhide Backs.
College and School Equipment
Target, Hunting and Roving Arrows
Price List on Request

Wholesale — Retail

EARL GRUBBS
5518 W. Adams
Los Angeles, : California

Archery Raw Materials

WM. A. JOY

9708 So. Hoover Street
LOS ANGELES, CALIF.

Hunters and Field Archers

It is time to begin thinking about a new hunting bow for this fall. Write for that new big catalog, which explains everything. By America's oldest tackle maker.

WILLIS H. BARNES
Sturgis — — Michigan

THE FLAT BOW
HUNT & METZ

70 pages of Archery information for 50 cents, well illustrated. Ye Sylvan Archer, 505 N. 11th St., Corvallis, Oregon.

Special Introductory Offer

Yew Wood Target Bow and 6 matched Port Orford Cedar Arrows, ladies' or men's weight $7.75
Matched P.O. Cedar Target Arrows, tapered or plain, per doz. $4.50
12 Cedar or Fir dowels, any type or size .... $ .75

Postpaid

Umpqua Archery Shop
UMPQUA, OREGON

CHANDLER
Interchangeable Arrow Points

Attention all Archery clubs, Dealers and Archers. Write for rules of a Nation-wide hunting and target shooting contest — 110 prizes. Proper equipment is the success of any sport. For catalogue write—

T. B. CHANDLER
11819 - 4th Ave. Compton, Calif.

TARGET SET BALANCED
SMALL HUNTING SET BALANCED
FISH HEAD

BEAR
ALUMINUM ARROWS ARE MAKING RECORDS
BEAR PRODUCTS CO.
2611 W. Philadelphia Ave., Detroit, Michigan

Rose City Archery Co.
1149 NE 31st Avenue
Portland, Oregon

In 1940 competition, improve your scores with the tackle used by

Pat Chambers
National Champion

Catalogue on request

W. A. COCHRAN
Archery Equipment
High Elevation Yew Wood
Port Orford Cedar
Osage Orange
Air Seasoned
10,000 Billets and Staves in Stock
Route 2   Eugene, Ore.

DO YOU LIKE THE CHARM OF THE BACKHILLS?

If so — read ARCADIAN LIFE MAGAZINE. It tells the story of the Ozarks in a way that will captivate you.

$1.00 a year; 25c a copy. Classified advertising (for archers) 2c a word.

O. E. RAYBURN, Editor
Caddo Gap, Arkansas

Paul H. Gordon, Director
Beacon Hill Craftsmen
Beacon, N. Y.

Where the serious archer's needs and desires are really consulted, and his orders exactly filled. Nothing too simple or too difficult.
Write for Complete Catalog

YEW BOW TIMBER
High Altitude Air Seasoned Billets and Staves of Quality and Variety.
W. G. PRESCOTT
527 Chestnut   Ashland, Ore.

Ye Sylvan Archer—$1.00 per year.

Ye Sylvan Archer

August, 1940

Corvallis, Oregon

Vol. 12   No. 4

Ye Sylvan Archer

"A magazine for the field archers"

Vol. 12 August, 1940 No. 4

Published the fifteenth of each month
for archers by archers
505 North 11th Street, Corvallis, Oregon

J. E. DAVIS .... Editor
RUSSELL JONES .... Business Manager
Subscription Price .... $1.00 Per Year
Foreign Subscription .... $1.25 Per Year
Single Copies .... 10 Cents
Advertising Rates on Application

TABLE OF CONTENTS

	Page
A-BOWING THEY WOULD GO	1
FIELD ARCHERS OF SOUTHERN CALIFORNIA By Elmer Bedwell	2
NFAA NEWS By John L. Yount	3
EDITORIAL	4
THE SIXTIETH NATIONAL	4
AHWAHNEE TOURNAMENT	4
STANLEY F. SPENCER	5
BOOK ON OZARKS	5
WHO'LL GET BIG GAME THIS YEAR	6
BAY CITY, MICHIGAN, FIELD TOURNAMENT	10
OREGON ANNUAL FIELD SHOOT	10
HOWLS FROM THE DOG HOUSE By the Basement Champion	11

A-Bowing They Would Go

The joy is great of him who strays
In shady woods on summer days,
With eyes alert and muscles steady,
His long-bow strung, his arrows
  ready.

At morn he hears the wood-thrush
  sing;
He sees the wild rose blossoming,
And on his senses soft and low
He feels the brook song ebb and flow.
 —From the Witchery of Archery.

And so it was that five archers strayed forth into the dawn of a summer morn, out into the vast expanse of the Eastern Oregon desert country. The morning sun was lazily rearing a golden arc over the ridge of rocky pinnacles that mark the old shore line of what once was a great inland sea. The sun seemed far away and so unlike the business-like orb that bursts above the horizon near our home, urging us to action each work day.

In our sleepy-eyed condition we wondered if it could be the "soft moon" of the old song. But the sting of the sage in our nostrils helped to wake us to the realities of a desert morning, to the songs of the birds; to the changing colors of sand and bush and rocky crags as the sun erased the last dull shadows of the night; to the more prosaic toot of a logging donkey, borne on the clear and rare air. We even became aware of our immediate surroundings when Charley took a bump in the road at sixty.

Five archers were out for a day with the bow—with eyes alert and muscles steady, bows strung and arrows ready.

The two cars entered the four thousand acre hay field of the Bell A ranch for a try for coyotes. Young coyotes often can be found out foraging early in the morning and can be overtaken and shot. The cars swung in and out, up and down and around those four thousand acres of level meadow with the occupants straining their eyes for a glimpse of a wary prairie predator. Too wary they were, and an hour's tour netted no coyotes shot or seen.

Ravens and magpies were there by the dozens and numerous hawks and owls were busily searching for breakfasts. But coyote hunters could not be bothered with such game, especially as the birds winged rapidly away whenever a car stopped. Ducks by the hundreds flushed along the irrigation ditches but they were "no sale", as it was closed duck season, except as they contributed to the feeling of nearness to Nature of those who stray with taut bow string.

A try for rabbits followed and four rabbits, two cotton tails and two jacks, were the score for many times that number of shots. Doc accounted for a cotton tail that tried to play pom-pom- pull-away with the whole group of archers. Ben wouldn't be bothered with large targets and proved his marksmanship on a small rabbit. Doc and Ben also each dispatched a rattlesnake. Charley broke two of his broadheads getting his jack among the rocks. A jack chose to "freeze" right beside John rather than try running past the other archers. John ungallantly poked an arrow in his ribs and pulled the trigger. Clarence didn't have the luck of the other archers and, unfortunately, hasn't been an archer long enough to alibi. He is respectfully referred to Gardner, Cathey and others for lessons.

The jacks were "afeard fur their ears," as a native said, because of banging twenty-two's and a five cent county bounty on each pair of jack ears. The cottontails did not run so hard nor so long when disturbed, as did the jacks, but had effective ways of protecting themselves from prowling archers.

Even the promise of one of Charley's wife's famous breakfasts didn't prevent a stop at the ghost town of Harney City. Harney City lost the county seat in the early days by three votes but it took an armed delegation from the rival town, Burns, to move the county records.

An old SALOON sign still adorns the front of a windowless, doorless building. The bar and its footrail still are in place. The old pool table is badly weathered and its felt is gone. The card table is turned over in the corner. If we could only catch the whispering echoes from those old walls, what stories we would have!

The sign on the old post office is aslant; gaping holes replace the doors and windows; a pile of old home-made brick in a corner is all that is left of the chimney. Parts of the walls still are covered with newspapers dated 1890, and the Oregonian and San Francisco Examiner still cry out in headlines to the few who come and read of the desperate cattle thieves caught in Nevada, the hanging of a murderer in San Quentin and the poor prices offered for wheat and cattle.

The village smithy evidently expected to be back as he had boarded up the windows and placed huge padlocks upon the doors. He probably said, "Just wait till next election and we'll show Burns whose cows ate the cabbage." A peek through the cracks showed the forge and tools still there, a buggy waiting to be repaired, and a plow with the share removed for sharpening.

A short distance above Harney City was old Fort Harney, established by the United States government in 1867 to protect the settlers from the Indians. The fort was abandoned in 1889. The buildings of the fort are all gone but on the hill above the site are the pathetic remains of the old fort cemetery. Dozens of sunken places among the sage and a few rotten pickets that once marked graves are all that is left to tell us of brave men who gave their lives for the settlement of the West. Is this the way our government honors her soldier dead?

All this before that breakfast prepared by Charley's wife, a breakfast of bacon and eggs, hot cakes and syrup, coffee and all the trimmings.

And then the revived archers were off to a rim-rock ridge sixteen miles to the southeast of Burns where a new bed of geodes had recently been discovered. A geode, if you happen not to know, is formed in an old volcanic bubble. Water seeping into the bubble deposits minerals. The disintegration of the lava leaves round, rough-looking rocks which, when cut, are found to contain beautifully colored agate formations.

The cars had to be left about a half mile from the geode bed. The sun by that time was not the softly indulgent mother of the early morning, but a blazing tyrant beating down unmercifully upon the perspiring archers as they lugged load after load of the heavy geodes to the cars. The geodes are just dull-looking rocks when picked up and it is impossible to tell whether they are valuable agates or worthless rocks until they are sawed in two, but according to reports this bed has produced some beautiful stones.

A leisurely return landed the group in Burns in time for dinner at Charley's, a dinner long to be remembered for its big juicy T-bone steaks.

"And," you may ask, "what have ghost towns, cemeteries and geodes to do with archery?" The answer is that archery is tradition and legend and romance. Archery is far more than a game or a sport; it is man's most delicate touch with the infinite wonders of Nature. The bended bow is emblematic of the magic of a living world.

THE FIELD ARCHERS OF SOUTHERN CALIFORNIA

By Elmer Bedwell

Of interest this month is the Southwest Archery Club, whose members have been busy getting their course in shape for official shooting. They are planning on having an invitational opening shoot and barbecue on the second Sunday in September, and a great deal of time and thought is being given a junior division by Mr. and Mrs. Wm. Joy. They want to try out some entirely new ideas in this line, and would welcome other clubs having juniors to contact them in an effort to establish shoots for the younger set that will be interesting. We wish their club much success, and hope to be able to be at the opening.

The Malibu Mts. Archery Club and the Redlands Archery Club held a regulation N.A.A. mail tournament shot Sunday, July 28. This was the last day of the third mail tournament, and the weather was exceptionally nice.

The next regular Southern California tournament will be held at Malibu Mts. Archery Club on August 25. This will also be the fourth shoot of the N.A.A. mail tournament.

N. F. A. A. News

By John L. Yount

The Redlands club is already hard at work preparing for the California State Field Archery Tournament, to be held November 9 and 10. The first and biggest job is the construction of an entirely new 28 target course. We believe this will make the local club the only one in America with two complete courses. When this course is completed we expect to be able to handle any sized tournament without the delays sometimes caused by a jammed course, and one can have a full day's shooting without shooting the same target twice.

Foursomes can be started on targets 1 and 15 of each course, making it possible to start 16 men at a time. This will eliminate any delays in getting the fellows started, and as the actual shooting for either course should not take two hours, we have a maximum of four hours roving for the day. This will leave plenty of time for novelty, flight, and clout shooting.

This tournament is planned principally as a handicap meet, with first consideration for those archers who are tired of the second-hand glory of having shot in the same tournament where so and so did such and such, and had just about as soon stay home as spend their time and money at a tournament where they didn't have a chance.

Yes, it will also be the State Championship Tournament. and we shall award some mighty fine medals and a proper amount of applause to our champions, BUT we are going to give all the big prizes—yes, prizes, not trophies—to the handicap winners. By using target fees and our powers of persuasion with right-minded philanthropists we hope to have several hundred dollars worth of prizes by tournament time.

Our first state tournament can be a success only through your cooperation. We expect to use the handicap system described in the June issue of this magazine. It calls for ten consecutive scores shot on a regulation course for every field archer in California. If there are some who, for lack of courses, cannot turn in the required number of scores they are no worse off than in any other tournament. They can shoot but not in the handicap division. Wouldn't it be worthwhile to build at least a temporary regulation 14 target course on which to shoot the required 10 scores and for once have a chance to be in the money at a big meet?

You will find the handicap system is fair and does not work a hardship on either the poor or the good shot. To win you will have to show improvement over your past performance, and the man who can shoot over his head in a big tournament is entitled to win.

The following are the present tentative handicaps of some of the Southern California archers. In the coming tournament they will be divided into two divisions, with those having a handicap of 120 or more in one division, and those with less than 120 in the other, because of consideration to the higher scoring archers, who in many cases might feel they were shooting against a handicap rather than an individual, if all were put into one group. We believe this arrangement combines the best features of both classifying and handicapping.

Men—Bob King, 110; B. Wallace, 115; Bill Joy, 100; H. Robinson, 100; F. B. Chandler, 95; John Dauley, 55; E. Watts, 65; B. Ahman, 115; H. Franklin, 90; E. Grubbs, 75; W. Bacon, 70; R. Sands, 55; F. Woodley, 45; R. Quayle, -22; V. Jones, 30; M. Hathaway, 5; J. Yount, 70; B. Gandy, 140; E. Franklin, 145; G. Miles, 150; Percy High, 125; J. Willard, 125; E. Brock, 125; B. Sells, 120; P. Ludwig, 135; E. G. Opper, 145; Elmer Bedwell, 125; A. Bruce, 140.

Ladies—M. Quayle, 140; M. King, 165; B. Dauley, 155; F. Watts, 150; R. Hathaway, 135; D. Ahman, 150; J. Franklin, 145; M. Gandy, 165; E. Bedwell, 100; Glenn Curtis, 135.

It must be remembered that these handicaps are only tentative, and in many cases are based on an insufficient number of scores, but they
(Continued on page 5)

Editorial

The editor of Ye Sylvan Archer is deeply grieved to learn of the death of Stanley Spencer, a personal friend and a great name in archery. In a feature article on archery written last winter for the Oregon Sunday Journal, we said, "The spark of enthusiasm that set off the present revival in archery was supplied by Stanley Spencer, who was trained by the beloved old 'Chief' Compton." We hope that the name of Stanley Spencer will long be revered in archery annals.

We learn that Dr. E. K. (Dusty) Roberts of Ventura, California, has installed a private roving range. It is also reported that Jack Willard, of Hollywood, and George Miles and Bill Joy of Los Angeles, recent visitors to the range, took a handsome—if not unexpected—trimming.

We are taking it upon ourselves to look into the matter of a suitable design for a leather medal for G. B. Our artist is working on one that should put the "champion bull thrower" in the "Doghouse."

The Sixtieth National

Our reports from the National are meager at this time but we do know that Russ Hoogerhyde made a notable comeback to win the national championship for the sixth time. Miss Ann Weber of Bloomfield, New Jersey, won the crown in the women's events, breaking records in every event.

Mary C. Thompson of Phoenix, Arizona, won the girl's championship, with Nancy Loss of Skaneateles, New York, second. Fred Folberth lead in the boy's events.

Mr. and Mrs. Curtis Hill of Dayton, Ohio, won in most of the flight shoot classes but Glendolene Vinyard of Canby, Oregon, shattered the mark for the regular style with a distance of 394.1 yards.

Marvin T. Schmidt of Chicago, won the clout shoot and led in the first York round.

Next year's National will be held at Portland, Oregon, with W. G. Williams as president.

Ahwahnee Tournament

A. Mericourt won the Ahwahnee open tournament held at Golden Gate Park, San Francisco, on July 14. M. E. Spansel was second, and L. Berg third.

Alice Mericourt was high in the women's events, with Verrel Weber second and Margaret Thompson third. Wayne Thompson won the men's clout and Margaret Thompson the women's.

HOW COME?

It seems to me that a couple of paragraphs in Walt Wilhelm's archery column in the Pomona Citizen needs some explanation or qualification. Here they are:

"You take guys like Gilman Keasey of Corvallis, Captain Styles of Berkeley, Pat Chambers of Portland, Doc Kelso of Long Beach, Fred Bear of Detroit, Ken Jones of Bakersfield, and hundreds of others.

"Most of the good boys are tops at any kind of archery. The men mentioned above use the best tackle for big game hunting, but they could kill their deer any time with target arrows because they wouldn't shoot unless they could see the whites of a deer's eyes, and *any of them could place twenty-four arrows out of that many shots between a deer's eyes at fifty yards.*" (The italics are ours.)

That's some shooting, Walt. A recent NAA bulletin lists a total of fourteen men who have been able to score *six* successive bullseyes at 50 yards, and a bullseye is nine and three-fifths inches across, and that at a known distance with point of aim or sights. My deer was only three and one-half inches between the eyes. Though I'm admitting it wasn't a very broadminded deer, I still insist that one nine and three-fifths inches between the eyes would be related to Paul Bunyan's blue ox.

Walt's next paragraph is one we have no quarrel with. It follows:

"Then there's a logger up at Index, Washington, that could get his deer with a double-bladed axe—providing the deer was tied and his wife wielded the axe."

STANLEY F. SPENCER

Stanley F. Spencer passed away at the age of 52 at the home of his brother at Day's Creek, Oregon, July 24, 1940.

Fifteen years ago, when modern archery (target) was practically unheard of on the Pacific Coast, Spencer, through his association with Will Compton, Art Young and others, took up archery in serious way and made good.

I remember how, day after day, Stan would come to our home after working hours to try out his new ideas in the technique of shooting. Before he wrote his book, "The Spencer System of Shooting the Bow," he had won the national championship at Philadelphia in 1926. He had won most local contests and was instrumental in organizing archery clubs throughout Southern California, being a charter member of the San Pedro Club and the Southern California Archery Association.

He taught his sister, Bee Hodgson, the fundamentals of the art of good shooting with the bow, and many of the top-notch archers throughout the United States have used the "Spencer System" in making new records.

Stanley Spencer

During the last few years of his life, he had been mining with conditions such that it was impossible to carry on with his archery practice. He has for the past year been living with his brother. He suffered a paralytic stroke about a year ago and had not been well since.

Stanley's many friends will be shocked at the news of his death but will carry on the practice of good marksmanship and good sportsmanship just as Stan would have them do. Stan's motto was, "When you meet an archer, you meet a friend."

—Ray W. Hodgson

NFAA NOTES

(Continued from page 3)

will bear watching. I think you will be surprised at how well they will function. Most of these people will shoot at our next Southern California field tournament to be held at Malibu, August 25. Try adding their handicap to the score they shoot at that time.

For further details write John L. Yount, P. O. Box 383, Redlands, California.

Book on Ozarks

Otto Ernest Rayburn, who publishes Arcadian Life Magazine in a cove of the Ozarks at Caddo Gap, Arkansas, has been selected by a New York publisher to write the book on the Ozarks for the American Folkways Series to be published in 1941. Erskine Caldwell, of "Tobacco Road" fame, is editing the series. Rayburn, a native of Iowa, has spent the past quarter of a century following folklore trails in the Ozarks and is considered an authority upon the subject. His book will be a 100,000 word study of the customs and culture of the Ozark people as expressed in their folkways.

"The Jungle Garden Archers of Buchanan, Michigan, held their annual Robin Hood wand shoot and bow-arrow vs. pistol competition at Sherwood Forest in southwestern Michigan on July 28. High honors in archery went to Col. C. H. Hayden, Gary, Indiana, and in pistol vs. bow and arrow to Herman Hess, Buchanan, Michigan," reports L. B. Spafford, Buchanan, Michigan.

Who'll Get Big Game this Year,

Chas. W. Trachsel hit this wild cat right between the eyes, in 1929.

S. L. Michael of Tacoma, Wash., and "Old Monarch," killed in 1934.

Major H. D. Cranston bagged this big black bear with bow and arrow in New Mexico last year.

Kore T. Duryee, Seattle, Wash., proved the effectiveness of bow and arrow for big game in 1928.

August, 1940 YE SYLVAN ARCHER 7

And Win NFAA Big Game Pins?

Chester Seay with shark and ray killed with bow and arrow in 1935.

Rev. Karl Thompson of Indiana shot this 6-lb. carp in 1929.

Bob Hodgson got his wild boar on Santa Cruz Island in 1937.

Dr. Klopsteg's game may be a trifle small, but what a marksman he must be!

John E. Cooter, of Salem, Oregon, got his first buck with bow and arrow, in 1937. He is still after the second.

August, 1940　　　　YE SYLVAN ARCHER　　　　9

Capt. C. H. Styles of Berkeley, Calif., with hides of bear, wild cat and cougar, victims of his bow in 1927-28. Capt. Styles has also killed his deer.

Stef Ludvicson of Headquarters, Idaho, killed this bear with a broadhead in 1938.

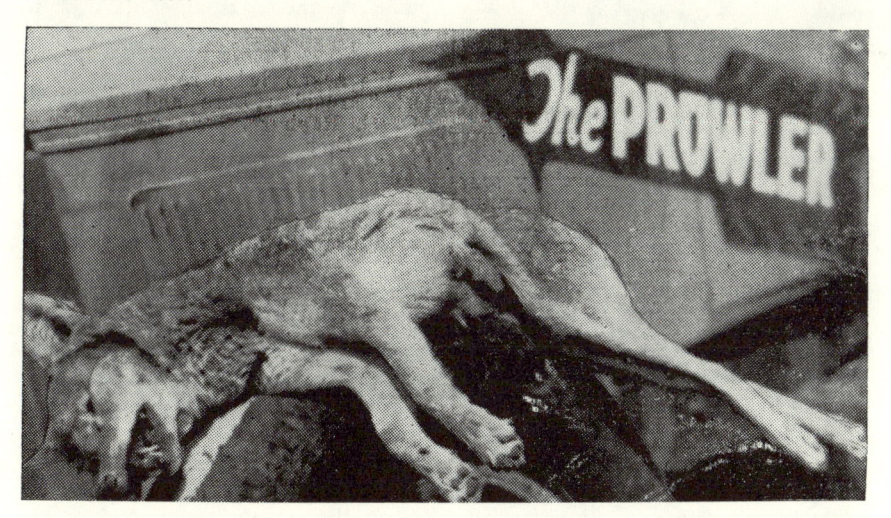

An arrow killed this desert coyote in 1938, but, according to Walt Wilhelm, the argument still goes on between Ken Wilhelm and Charlie Diehr as to whose arrow actually did the business.

A. G. Mortensen's eagle certainly is big game. Killed in Idaho in 1938.

The city of South Haven, Michigan, is this year holding an archery tournament in connection with its annual Peach Festival on August 30. Russ Hoogerhyde, national champion, will be present and give a demonstration after the tournament.

BAY CITY, MICHIGAN, FIELD TOURNAMENT

Forty-nine archers entered the Bay City, Michigan, field archery meet on July 21. Nelson Grumley of Detroit, won the "instinctive" class with a 56-target total of 120-454. J. Vaughan Blanchard of Howell, was high in the "free-style" class with 96-360. Mrs. Lulu Stalker of Flint, led the ladies with a score of 77-297.

Albert Rosenwald of Utah has a right to smile. He got his deer in 1938.

We acknowledge receipt of a copy of "Arcadian Lore and Logic," by O. E. Rayburn. We just don't see why that man Rayburn isn't an archer.

It has been ruled that it is illegal to hunt with the cross bow in Michigan.

Oregon Annual Field Shoot

The fifth annual tournament of the Pope-Young Field Archers of Oregon will be held at Alsea on September 1 and 2. The NFAA round will be shot Sunday afternoon. The feature event of Sunday evening is a barbeque with the business meeting following. Monday the championship events, the battle clout, wand and Pope-Young round, will be shot.

An archery entertainment for the public is planned for Saturday night.

Howls From the Doghouse

The NFAA is coming out with a new big game pin, and I am strong for it. Was for it, rather, until I applied for my own.

Here I am, the foremost middle weight bull slayer in archery. I say middle weight advisedly, I realize that there are some exalted heavy weights, whose volume is somewhat dimmed by static, but they can, and do, speak for themselves.

I also know that there are certain light weight contenders, who are entitled to recognition in their class. But their feeble best is not for a moment to be compared with mine.

Erle Stanley Gardner, Jack Willard, Walt Wilhelm, Ted Carpenter, Joe Cosner, Reed Williams, and Paul Gordon, they all throw a mean enough bull. This I freely concede, all I say is that they are not in my class. If they were, you may be sure that they would dare to meet me on this page, I have given them every opportunity. Q.E.D.

Now, just because John Yount couldn't hit a skunk without raising a stink—let alone a deer or a bear—just because John is jealous of me because I can do both if I choose to do so; just because I saved the honor of Oregon by stopping a charging coon in his tracks; because of all these things the aforementioned John Yount has ruled that a bull is not big game, and that I am entitled to no pin. We will see about that. John shouldn't forget that I fought for years for recognition of my national basement title before I had official recognition. This fight will be no exception, I am going to have that pin.

It would, says John, take amendment of the constitution and the by-laws. Well, go ahead and amend both, just so I get my rights.

So here is my challenge to the NFAA. If your first distinction is going to mean an injustice to an accomplished toreador, there is going to be trouble, and plenty of it.

What's that, why don't I go out and shoot my deer, bear, cougar, or what have you? Why should I, I am not that fond of labor, and what would happen if I missed? Anybody can get that kind of vermin, and usually does. Look at John Davis and his deer. He gets a pin, doesn't he, on account of a lucky accident. There is no accident about my bull. Do I, or don't I, get that pin?

I realize that toreadors are not what they used to be in archery. If you doubt it, read Forrest Nagler's new books, "Archery — An Engineering View," and "The Bow and Arrow for Big Game." Both debunk archery with a vengeance.

There is only one perfect end registered in these two books, and the less said about that, the better. Innocent bystanders can check up by reading the chapter on, "The English Long Bow—Fallacy or Fad?" Shame on you, Forrest, can't you leave us some illusions?

The hunting stories and the technical data are factual and authentic, but nevertheless, hold your unfailing interest. Archery has graduated into long pants, and Mr. Nagler's books are some of the late milestones on the path of progress. We haven't had anything like it since Dr. Pope. No archer can afford to miss these books. Published by Frank Taylor & Son, Albany, Oregon. Price, one dollar each.

Just to Keep the Records Straight

G. B. has submitted no proof of ever having bagged a bull, or any other game larger than a ground squirrel, although he did send me a pair of pants with a long rip in the southeast corner and claimed that it was made by a bull. That man must have a brain with reverse English.

To keep peace I offered to compromise. If he would send me the bull's name and address, I would recognize his evidence and forward the pin even though there still was some question as to whether or not a long, lean Swede could be considered as big game for a bull.

Fair as this was he isn't satisfied, and since without further evidence we can't present the pin, will you back me in offering him a leather medal for the tree climbing, fence jumping championship of the universe? If we handle this matter diplomatically and use the proper build-up, we may be able to get him to put on an exhibition at one of our tournaments.

Such an exhibition of bull baiting by the country's foremost bull thrower should be worth going a long way to see. It would have to be held in the West where the trees are highest, otherwise he might go right on out the top. —J.L.Y.

This big black bear fell to the bow of Ely Miller, Duluth, Minn., in 1936.

CLASSIFIED ADVERTISING

RATES for Classified Advertising 5 cents per word per issue. Count initials and numbers as words. Minimum charge is 50 cents.

RELICS AND CURIOS

INDIAN RELICS, Beadwork, Coins, Curios, Books, Minerals, Weapons. Old West Photos. Catalog, 5c. Genuine African Bow, $3.75. Ancient flint arrowheads, perfect, 6c each—Indian Museum, Osborne, Kansas.

BOOKS AND MAGAZINES

The AMERICAN ARCHER, a national quarterly, $1.00 per year, 521 Fifth Ave., New York City.

The Flat Bow—70 pages of Archery information for 50 cents, well illustrated. *Ye Sylvan Archer*, 505 N. 11*th* St., Corvallis, Oregon.

SUBSCRIBERS PLEASE NOTICE

A cross appearing in this space means that your subscription has expired and we would appreciate your prompt renewal so that your name may be kept on our mailing list.

**BACK NUMBERS
YE SYLVAN ARCHER
Volumes I to V Inclusive
$1.00 Per Volume
B. G. THOMPSON
R. F. D. 1, Corvallis, Oregon**

WESTERN
ANTIQUES
COLLECTOR

Corvallis, Oregon

P. O. Box 403

A monthly illustrated magazine devoted to items of interest to the collector of antiques.

$1.50 per year.

HANDBOOK—How to Make and Use Bows and Arrows—90 Pages well illustrated (with catalog) 35c.

CATALOG—100 pictures—color spread—Instruction Folder. 10c.

CATALOG alone 5c. Stamps or Coin.

L·E·STEMMLER· QUEENS VILLAGE·N·Y·

WIN WITH BEN PEARSON ARROWS

Beautiful and accurate to the Nth degree but win their real laurels on the range. Arrows made as arrows should be—and at prices you can afford to pay. Send for catalogue.

BEN PEARSON, INC. — PINE BLUFF, ARK.

Cassius Hayward Styles

BOWYER AND FLETCHER

—Tackle that has stood the test—

28 Vicente Place

BERKELEY, CALIFORNIA

G

"THE MARK OF DISTINCTION IN ARCHERY TACKLE

Fine Yew Target and Hunting Bows, Plain or Backed with Rawhide. Lemonwood Bows with Rawhide Backs. College and School Equipment Target, Hunting and Roving Arrows
Price List on Request
Wholesale — Retail
EARL GRUBBS
5518 W. Adams
Los Angeles, : California

Archery Raw Materials

WM. A. JOY

9708 So. Hoover Street
LOS ANGELES, CALIF.

Hunters and Field Archers

It is time to begin thinking about a new hunting bow for this fall. Write for that new big catalog, which explains everything. By America's oldest tackle maker.

WILLIS H. BARNES
Sturgis — — Michigan

---

70 pages of Archery information for 50 cents, well illustrated. Ye Sylvan Archer, 505 N. 11th St., Corvallis, Oregon.

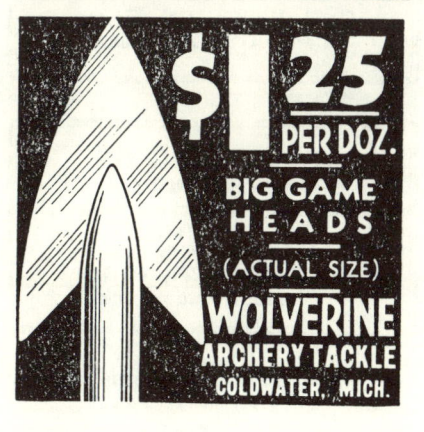

$1.25 PER DOZ.

BIG GAME HEADS

(ACTUAL SIZE)

WOLVERINE ARCHERY TACKLE
COLDWATER, MICH.

CHANDLER
Interchangeable Arrow Points

PAT. PEND.

Attention all Archery clubs, Dealers and Archers. Write for rules of a Nation-wide hunting and target shooting contest — 110 prizes. Proper equipment is the success of any sport. For catalogue write—

T. B. CHANDLER
11819 - 4th Ave. Compton, Calif.

FISH HEAD A-80
TARGET SET BALANCED
SMALL HUNTING SET BALANCED

BEAR
ALUMINUM ARROWS ARE MAKING RECORDS
BEAR PRODUCTS CO.
2611 W. Philadelphia Ave., Detroit, Michigan

Ye Sylvan Archer—$1.00 per year.

DO YOU LIKE THE CHARM OF THE BACKHILLS?
If so — read ARCADIAN LIFE MAGAZINE. It tells the story of the Ozarks in a way that will captivate you.

$1.00 a year; 25c a copy. Classified advertising (for archers) 2c a word.

O. E. RAYBURN, Editor
Caddo Gap, Arkansas

W. A. COCHRAN
Archery Equipment
High Elevation Yew Wood
Port Orford Cedar
Osage Orange
Air Seasoned
10,000 Billets and Staves in Stock
Route 2   Eugene, Ore.

Paul H. Gordon, Director
Beacon Hill Craftsmen
Beacon, N. Y.
Where the serious archer's needs and desires are really consulted, and his orders exactly filled. Nothing too simple or too difficult.
Write for Complete Catalog

E. BUD PIERSON
Bowyer — Fletcher
Tournament Tackle, Sinew, Glue, Raw Materials.
245 University Ave
CINCINNATI, OHIO
Custom Made Tackle

YEW BOW TIMBER
High Altitude Air Seasoned Billets and Staves of Quality and Variety.
W. G. PRESCOTT
527 Chestnut   Ashland, Ore.

Write us for your needs in Archery books. Ye Sylvan Archer.

Ye Sylvan Archer

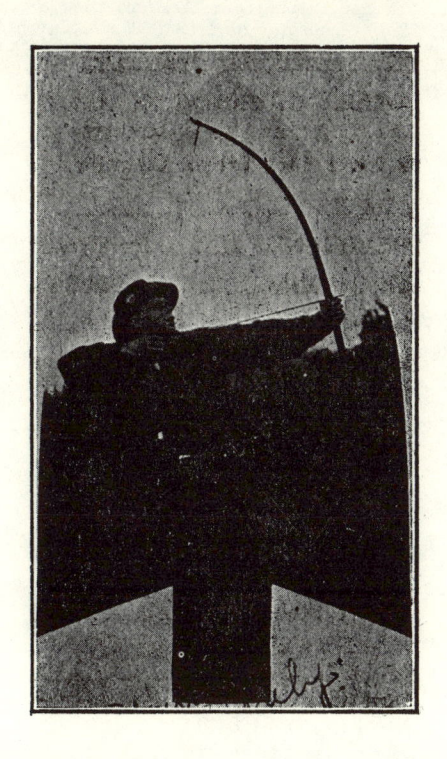

September, 1940

Corvallis, Oregon

Vol. 12　　　　　　　　　　　　　　　　No. 5

Ye Sylvan Archer

"A magazine for the field archers"

Vol. 12   September, 1940   Number 5

Published the fifteenth of each month
for archers by archers
505 North 11th Street, Corvallis, Oregon

J. E. DAVIS .... Editor
RUSSELL JONES .... Business Manager
Subscription Price .... $1.00 Per Year
Foreign Subscription .... $1.25 Per Year
Single Copies .... 10 Cents
Advertising Rates on Application

TABLE OF CONTENTS

	Page
ARCHERY IN AUSTRALIA By Perce Stokan	1
N.F.A.A. NEWS By John L. Yount	2
EDITORIAL	4
COMING FIELD SHOOTS	4
OREGON'S FIELD TOURNAMENT	5
FIELD ARCHERS OF SOUTHERN CALIFORNIA By Elmer Bedwell	5
WILL HISTORY REPEAT IN 1940?	6
THIRD NFAA MAIL TOURNAMENT	8
NEW RESERVE IN WASHINGTON By Kore T. Duryee	9
PORTLAND AND THE NEXT NATIONAL By George Brommers	10
FIELD ROUND AT NAA TOURNAMENT	11
LOS ANGELES ARCHERY CLUB	11

Archery in Australia

By Perce Stokan, Sydney, Australia, in Archery News—London, England

Archery is a very new sport in this country, although we have a number of people who have been practising privately for many years. I had been a One-man Club for about five years before I discovered a small club. During this time I was entirely self-taught, developing my technique by a system of trial and error. At first I tried to use the pinch draw, naturally without success, although I was using a thirty pound lancewood bow. I discovered first the assisted pinch draw, thinking I was cheating, and later becoming bold, saying, "In for a penny, in for a pound," as it were, and using the two finger draw which I later changed to three fingers. I did in fact go through the whole development of the past centuries in a couple of years. Still more remarkable is the fact that before I had ever met an archer or had read a single word on the subject, I discovered the point of aim, feeling guilty of a most unethical action and when I finally joined a club I tried hard to eradicate this evil until after some months I was surprised to see the president instructing a young lady in the use of a point of aim. The other members were surprised when my score took a sudden jump of over a hundred points in the very next American Round we shot.

I was one of the founders of the New South Wales Archery Society which first met on December 12, 1937. Since that time we have been instrumental in spreading the gospel of archery among the heathen and now there are five clubs in New South Wales, three in Queensland, one in Victoria and one in Western Australia. I think we can claim credit for the formation of all these clubs with the exception of two by reason of the reams of paper we used in answering enquiries and giving advice and information. These letters became such a problem that I set out to write a small book designed expressly for such enquirers and dealing with the unique difficulties confronting the enthusiast in this country. I have completed the manuscript, complete with sketches and diagrams and today we made the necessary photographs. I hope to go to press within the next few weeks and I have already received fifty orders. I do not expect to make a fortune out of it, I will be satisfied if I clear expenses and if this book furthers our sport it will be recompense enough. The book is named "Archery in Australia" and will be dressed in an archers green jacket with gold lettering and a Boomerang and Arrow as its motif.

Our shooting is not yet of as high a standard as that in England or the U.S.A. and that is perhaps the reason that I have the honour to be Champion. I will have to defend my Championship on the 21st of this month and although I consider myself to be fortunate to return to Sydney in time to compete I am afraid that they have caught me bending this time as I have had only five days of shooting in eleven months. I am practising diligently, but am stiff and sore from my first day out. Luckily it is decided on a Double American Round, which is not nearly as arduous as a York and I may be able to pick up in time. Today I shot a 451 American, but will need to put at least another hundred on to that to have anything like a chance.

We have no first class bow timbers in Australia, although we are for ever experimenting and have not yet exhausted the possibilities of our forest wealth. If the war continues for a number of years, as I believe it will, we may be reduced to using Australian timbers, suitable or not. One of my clubmates has found a timber named Ivory wood of which he has great hopes. To give it as severe a test as possible he made a 5 ft. 3 ins. flat bow and drew 28 inch arrows and after several hundred shots the tips have come back only two inches. He says that it shoots as sweetly as lemonwood and if only it will stand the gaff, it may prove the answer to an Australian Archer's prayer. The same man discovered a small quantity of Osage Orange and has a stave or two seasoning, but

(Continued on page 8)

N. F. A. A. News

By John L. Yount

As a politician would say, the crying need of field archery is for more and better courses. The roughly laid out temporary 14 target course should not be considered as anything but a means of introducing the game to your locality.

The ideal course that every field club should strive for is one that will appeal to your more elderly members by being reasonably easy to walk around, to your lady members by having trails wide and smooth enough that they can shoot in ordinary sports clothes and not finish looking like something the cat drug in, and, finally, to your husky young hot-shots by being sporty enough to satisfy anybody. Yes, fellows, such a course can be built, but not in a couple of hours.

We, here at Redlands, are now building our second course in preparation for the California State Field Tournament to be held November 9 and 10, and here is how we are going about it.

Today was the fourth day of work on this course, and we haven't cleared a foot of trail, or even considered where we are going to put the shots on the second 14, except that we know that there is room for a good course and that the terrain is suitable. This is how we wasted all that time. First, we picked a likely looking place, one where we knew it would be possible to lay out two 14 target courses and have each one start and finish close to headquarters.

As a starter we stood at one side of this central spot and decided that we could put a tricky 50 yard shot over the first knoll at a target on the next hill. The fact that most of the foreground was hidden by the knoll should make it deceptive and the target being against a hill would take care of the lost arrow problem. All very simple, but we learned some six courses ago that it would save a lot of time and work to just guess at the distance and mark the shot by tying rags to bushes. Next was a nice 80 yard down hill shot where an easy trail could be built. Let me once more repeat that a hard trail does not make a tricky course, but it will keep a large number of archers from doing much shooting. Number 3 was up a long, narrow ravine with the target under a tree, measured 60 yards but looked 80. This long inclined shot gave us a short, sharply down shot, again with an easy trail.

After selecting three or four more nice shots we suddenly found we were far, far from home and without a Chinaman's chance of getting back. If we went over the hill, it would take a dozen shots to make it. If we tried to get back down the same ravine somebody would get hit in the first tournament. Now, three days later, all shots are located, measured and staked, and they are all in that one ravine with plenty of safety and even trickier shots than those first marked. Number 1 is in the original location but shortened from 50 to 40 yards, and number 14 is a rather sharply uphill shot, but a four position one to ease the climb, with the target just as close to headquarters as safety will permit. All it took was a lot of planning.

Now for a double check we are going to have the test squad shoot over the course using rags tied to bushes for targets and if there are any that don't make interesting shooting we shall change them. Ladies are never allowed near the course during the testing, for the desirability of a shot is best measured by the quality and volume of profanity. Any shot that doesn't get a good cussing has something wrong with it and needs changing. When we are sure everything is O.K. we will start building trails and not before. In the past we have built miles of trails to nowhere, but even an archer will learn if given enough time.

When this 14 is finished we will start the other 14 and expect to have things in order in time for the state tournament. With this course to supplement our present 28 target course we should be able to handle a large tournament without any of the usual delays. All we need is a little help from old man weather in the form of some rain to settle the dust of our activities. Otherwise, ladies, we apologize, and if we do not have rain it might be possible to talk us into letting you shoot both rounds on the old course which is in fine shape, and free from dust.

More About California State Shoot

We want you, wherever you live, to come to this tournament. If you cannot attend we want you to watch the results. Not because it will be the world's greatest tournament, but because we are making a sincere effort to overcome the big tournament's weakest point, which is the fact that the average contestant pays his target fees, knowing that all he is going to get in return is the privilege of being on the same field with some of the country's finest shots. We want you to judge the result, and believe you can best do so by first sending in your last ten scores and then coming to this tournament and taking an active part.

If you will dig out your last issue of this magazine you will find under the NFAA news the names of a number of Southern California archers and their tentative handicaps. You will find that we really stuck our neck out by asking you to check those handicaps with the results of the Southern California Association shoot to be held at Malibu the twenty-fifth of last month. We certainly would not have done so if we hadn't had faith in the system used in arriving at our handicaps and, believe me, fellows, satisfactory results cannot be obtained without a sound system. Two scores and a guess will not do it.

How the System Worked at Malibu

Ninety-five was the average handicap and the results showed that in the first ten there were five with larger handicaps and five with smaller. Also, in the first ten there were 4 with handicaps of 70 or less and 6 over 70. Of the total number of archers shooting, four out of ten had handicaps of 70 or less. Such results are almost too exact to be true. In the morning the first four had handicaps of 70, 120, 45, and 30, respectively, and finished with only 11 points between first and fourth place. In the afternoon the winners were handicapped at 125, 100, 70 and minus 22, with 24 points between first and fourth place. For the day the four winners were handicapped at 70, 100, 125, and minus 22, and there were only 20 points between first and fourth.

Another interesting feature is that the first, second, and third place men in the morning round were out of the running in the afternoon. Naturally, the first three in the afternoon were men listed as also rans in the morning, but who really got in and shot in the second round.

These are exactly the results we had hoped for. Everybody had a chance, nobody ran away with the tournament. Those who placed had to really strut their stuff to do it and, for that reason, can feel just as proud as they would have had it been any other kind of tournament.

Jones Wins Pin

A toast, gentlemen, to Mr. Russell B. Jones. He has won big game pin NUMBER ONE by bagging a bear while on a hunting trip in his home state, Oregon.

His witnesses are a couple of other archers, Perry Wright and Ben Thompson. It seems very appropriate that this first pin should be given in recognition of a successful bear hunt. There is just something about
(Continued on page 8)

Editorial

Col. Pierce, of Long Beach, Calif., has been visiting Oregon archers recently.

The Pope-Young Field Archers of Oregon has been incorporated under the laws of the state of Oregon.

We are glad to report that Mrs. Geo. Brommers, who has been ill, is recovering and hopes to get the check rein on George again soon.

Friends of W. I. King, the bowmaker of Eugene, Oregon, will be sorry to learn that Bill has been quite ill for the last two weeks but Bill, being a "good man," can't be kept down and expects to be out and around again soon. He had just finished making a set of crooked arrows, when he took sick, out of the same piece of wood from which he made his famous crooked bow, a job that would make anyone dizzy.

We have to admire the spirit of the English archers. The June-July issue of Archery News arrived only a little late. Many of the English clubs are still carrying on although some have ceased to hold meetings for the duration of the war.

We have recently had a communication from Ernesto Revira de Hostas, Mayaguez, Porto Rico. We are sure our readers would like information on the status of archery in Porto Rico.

Now is the time to take the National Field Archery association seriously and make a concerted drive for membership. A permanent constitution is being considered by the directors and will, no doubt, soon be adopted. Several states have organized and the many field tournaments advertised throughout the country attest the popularity of this phase of archery.

The Antelope Valley Archers recently opened a new range known as The Archers' Rendezvous.

Coming Field Shoots

Some of the field archery tournaments to be held during the next two months are as follows:

Pittsburgh Archery club field shoot at Pittsburgh, Pa., Sept. 29. Tom Mansell, 115 Jones St., Aliquippa, Pa., secretary.

Cleveland Archery club field shoot at Metropolitan Park, Cleveland, Ohio, Sept. 29. Millie Chetister, 17401 Miburn Ave., Cleveland, secretary.

Hoosier State Archery association archery-golf championship shoot at Pokagon State Park, Ind., Sept. 29. H. Shields, P. O. Box 5, Indianapolis, Ind, secretary.

Detroit Archers field archery championship shoot at Detroit, Oct. 6. Bob Sale, 16031 Ellsworth Ave., Detroit, Mich., secretary.

West Michigan Bowmen field meet at Newaygo, Oct. 6. H. J. Neinhuis, 1316 8th St., Muskegon Heights, Mich., secretary.

Waltham Archers turkey shoot, at Waltham, Oct. 6. C. K. Peeling, 55 Boynton St., Waltham, Mass, secretary.

New York Archers Pope-Young round at Alley Pond Park, Queens, L. I., Oct. 20. Dr. W. E. Utterback, 494 Hudson St, New York, secretary.

Swampscott Archers turkey shoot at Swampscott, Mass., Oct. 20. Edward B. Pollard, 64 Atlantic St., Lynn, Mass., secretary.

Morris Archers field shoot at Hait farm, Hanover, N. J., Oct. 27. Roswell Hait, Whippany, N. J., secretary.

Hoosier State Archery association cottontail festival at Brown County State Park, Ind., Oct. 27. H. Shields, P. O. Box 5, Indianapolis, Ind., secretary.

Pennsylvania State field archery championship meet at Lancaster, Nov. 10. Clayton B. Shenk, Rt. 3, Lancaster, Pa., secretary.

California State field archery tournament at Redlands, Nov. 9 and 10. John L. Yount, Redlands, Calif., secretary.

Will the secretaries of the above meets please send us reports of their tournaments for publication?

Oregon's Field Tournament

Seventy-five archers registered for the fifth annual field archery tournament of the Pope-Young Archers of Oregon, held at Alsea, Oregon, September 1 and 2.

Two Portland archers, Stanley Stevens and Vic Adcook, tied for championship honors in the men's events and will share the trophy and honors for the coming year. Bond Whitmore of Portland was third man and L. L. "Flight" Daily fourth. Howard Dixon of Eugene was the winner of the Pope-Young round, consisting of 36 shots at animal targets covering a course through the woods, up hill and down, with only one shot at a target. Dixon had 17 hits. DeWitt Hawkins had the same number of hits but was ineligible for a prize as he did not shoot in all the events. Vic Adcook had 15 hits, and Bond Whitmore 14. Vic Adcook won the battle clout, scoring 175. Stanley Stevens was second with 172 and Bond Whitmore third with 166. Five hits were made in the hundred yard wand shoot. Stanley Stevens registered two hits, and H. L Knight of Portland, L. L. Dailey of Eugene, and Bill Collins of Cottage Grove one each. Ned Myers of Corvalllis won the NFAA round of fourteen targets with a 96 score, Bond Whitmore taking second with 90 and Stanley Stevens third with 79.

Mrs. Mabel Tatro of Portland won the women's championship, winning first place or tying for first in all events. Mrs. Daisy Hamlin of Eugene took second place and Mrs. Gene Warnick of Portland third.

Chester Stevenson Jr. of Eugene won the boy's championship and Shirley Duer of Portland took the honors in the junior girls' events.

Saturday night a pageant was presented under the direction of Clare and Daisy Hamlin showing the development of archery from cave man to modern times. This entertainment was free to the public and a large crowd enjoyed the performance.

A barbecue supper, prepared by Charles Schroeder of Burns, was a feature event of Sunday evening. At the annual business meeting of the organization the Bar L ranch in the heart of Oregon's archery reserve was selected as the location for the 1941 annual tournament and the following officers were elected: Dr. Geo. A. Cathey, Portland, president; Larry Williams, Canyon City, Dr. L. E. Hibbard, Burns, and Russell Jones, Eugene, vice presidents; and J. E. Davis, Corvallis, secretary-treasurer. Ye Sylvan Archer was designated as the official publication of the organization.

FIELD ARCHERS OF SOUTHERN CALIFORNIA

By Elmer Bedwell, Secretary

Competing around the Malibu Mts. Archery Club range on August 25, were sixty archers from Southern California, including from the border on the south to Bakersfield on the north. The sea breeze was a welcome factor for a warm August day, and the shoot was of special interest as it was the Fourth National Mail Tournament, in addition to being the regular Southern California bi-monthly tournament.

The scores of the day were: Men's Championship Class, the Gold Bar—Roland Quayle with 612 points; Silver Bar—Larry Hughes, 511. In the General Division, the Championship Medal—Earl Mace, 576; the Red Ribbon—Dr. Erwin Pletcher, 560; White Ribbon—John Daulley, 464. Ladies Championship Class, Gold Bar—Naomi Baker, 419; Silver Bar—Eva Bedwell, 301. General Division, the Championship Medal—Ruth Hathaway, 312; Red Ribbon—Babe Bitzenburger, 311, White Ribbon—Margaret Quayle, 300. Juniors, Bedwell Trophy — Harold Robinson with 380 points wins the new trophy for the first time, which will be a two out of three times winner. Second place, Angus Bruce, 153. Bob King won the last year's junior trophy, which he will now keep.

The next regular tournament will be held at the new South West Archery Club. They have put in money and hard work to get the new range in order. Their opening will be Sunday, September 8. I hope that most all the archers will be able to get down for the opening shoot.

Will History Repeat in 1940?

Howard Hill has killed all kinds of big game with bow and arrow.

Ohio archers *after* wild boar in Tennessee, according to Ohio Conservation Commission Bulletin, but they got boars, just the same.

Geo. Brommers favorite hunting pose.

Ivan L. Smith killed a deer in Southern Oregon in 1936.

See rules in July issue for hunting contest sponsored by T. B. Chandler Company and Ye Sylvan Archer.

September, 1940　　YE SYLVAN ARCHER　　7

Who Will Win Hunting Contests?

Just like shooting fish! Victor Burke in Washington in 1927.

Dr. B. G. Thompson killed a moose in Canada in 1938.

Third NFAA Mail Tournament

Men

	First Round	Second Round	56 Targ. Total
1—E. Hill Turnock, Wilkinsburg, Pa.	80-326	90-364	170-690
2—Merle Hathaway, Malibu Mts., Calif.	62-262	73-281	135-543
3—Darrow Olson, Oakland, Calif.	61-233	58-236	119-469
4—Jack Peters, Oakland, Calif.	55-211	68-254	123-465
5—I. M. Stamps, Seattle, Wash.	70-252	49-181	119-433
6—Emery Watts, Malibu Mts., Calif.	50-186	59-221	109-407
7—Joe Brooks, Oakland, Calif.	44-174	59-223	103-397
8—E. J. Woodward, Redlands, Calif.	53-205	45-191	97-396
9—Earl Grubbs, Malibu Mts., Calif.	47-181	53-201	100-382
10—Kaiser Wilhelm, Irwin, Penn.	45-163	56-200	101-363
11—John Yount, Redlands, Calif.	46-178	46-178	92-356
12—Russ Olson, Oakland, Calif.	41-157	53-197	94-354
13—LeRoy Smith, Oakland, Calif.	48-178	46-168	94-346
14—E. A. Melzer, Ellwood City, Penn.	42-162	48-170	90-332
15—George Hamaker, Flint, Mich.	47-171	42-156	89-327
16—Kore T. Duryee, Seattle, Wash.	45-173	41-151	86-324
17—J. R. O'Rourke, Pittsburgh, Penn.	34-132	43-163	77-295
18—Leo Hoffmeyer, Flint, Mich.	40-150	37-137	77-287
19—Elmer Bedwell, San Bernardino, Calif.	29-106	47-181	76-287
20—Tom Mansell, Aliquippa, Penn.		74-284	74-284

Ladies

	First Round	Second Round	56 Targ. Total
1—Eva Bedwell, San Bernardino, Calif.	43-157	48-176	91-331
2—Ruth Hathaway, Malibu Mts., Calif.	44-162	35-127	79-289
3—Lulu Stalker, Flint, Mich.	32-112	34-130	66-242
4—Mary Calvert, Flint, Mich.	33-119	30-112	63-231
5—Ruth Davis, Bryn Mawr, Calif.	36-134	26-96	62-230
6—Margaret King, Redlands, Calif.	26-102	31-111	57-213
7—Ann Melzer, Ellwood City, Penn.	23-83	37-129	60-212
8—Minerva Gandy, Malibu Mts., Calif.	24-90	30-108	54-198
9—Marcilla Kunz, Pittsburgh, Penn.	15-51	23-91	38-142
10—Mrs. H. Strandwold, Tacoma, Wash.	21-75	15-51	36-126
11—Mrs. Leo Hoffmeyer, Flint, Mich.	23-79	12-42	35-121
12—Helen Berry, Malibu Mts., Calif.	16-54	12-46	28-100
13—Mrs. G. Diehl, Flint, Mich.	10-34	18-62	28-96
14—Christine Stamps, Seattle, Wash.	15-55	11-41	26-96
15—Jean Tritton, Albuquerque, N. Mex.	9-31	18-62	27-93

AUSTRALIAN ARCHERY
(Continued from page 1)

there is not sufficient to meet the needs of our club alone.

I am experimenting with Rami fibre for bowstrings. Rami is being grown experimentally in the vicinity of Sydney and it is claimed that it is considerably stronger than linen or flax. I have made up test pieces of Rami and two different varieties of linen and next week I intend taking them to a firm of which I know where I will test the three pieces to destruction. If this shows that Rami possesses a greater tensile strength than linen, I will make up a number of strings and try out the shooting quality.

NFAA NEWS
(Continued from page 3)

a bear that puts him right close to the top of the big game. That something may be the fact that you can't depend on him taking it like a gentleman, and when he is mad he can outrun, outfight and outclimb any archer.

Who will win the next pin and what will the game be? If you are going hunting you had better join the NFAA first, and not miss your chance for a pin if your hunt is successful.

New Reserve in Washington

To all hunting archers:

At last we have succeeded in obtaining the hunting territory for archers only that we have always wanted—THE MAD LAKE COUNTRY. Stamps, Partee and I hunted there in 1936 and 1937. The area is about 30 square miles. Little and big meadows, yet plenty of cover, but little underbrush. The main valley is from 5000 to 6000 feet elevation with ridges on the east and west sides rising from 1000 to 1500 feet higher. You can hunt all you want and do very little climbing or you can get just as tough climbing as you may want. There are three little lakes with good fishing. Mad River Ranch is in the very heart and horses will be there at all times to pack out your deer. Also there is a telephone at the ranch if needed. There is nothing in the country that can beat this for scenery and good hunting.

In driving from Seattle, go over Stevens Pass to Coles Corner where you turn left for Lake Wenatchee. Just before you reach the lake turn right. After crossing the Wenatchee River turn left on the Chiwawa River road to Deep Creek, then right till you come to the top of the ridge. Here, where the road makes a sharp reverse curve, is Maverick Peak and the beginning of the Archers Hunting Reserve. This is an elevation of 4300 feet. You can start hunting from here, going north. Less than a quarter of a mile from here on the Mad River trail there are good camp sites along Mad River. Six miles in is Mad River Ranch over a beautiful trail up Mad River and on this six miles of trail you only climb 1200 feet. There are beautiful campsites all over the whole valley. We are packing in about two miles north of Mad Lake or in about 11 miles.

For those wishing to go up the Entiat River road there is a good forest camp near Three Creek and there are two trails from there going up into the Reserve. One trail goes to Klone Peak and the other is Three Creek trail which is the north boundary of the Reserve. They are steep.

If you come over Stevens Pass you can get information from Cole's Store and Service Station where you leave the highway for Lake Wenatchee. They also have food supplies and serve meals.

If enough archers send in reservations Al Constans will open up Mad River Ranch for the hunting season at the following rates: per week, including meals, bedding and bringing in your duffel, $25.00; per day, including meals and bedding, $4.00. This rate means that you can hunt in from the car, stay overnight, have three meals and bedding furnished you and hunt back to your car for only $4.00.

Mad River Ranch will only accommodate about 15 people so get your reservation in by the 15th of September. After October 1st, Al Constans' address will be: Mad River Ranch, Leavenworth, Wn. You can phone Mad River Ranch through Stiliko Ranger Station by Antiat, Wn. Al packed us into the Mad Lake country in 1936 and 1937 and you can depend on anything he tells you. Riding horses will be available at the ranch for an additional charge of $1.50 per day.

Remember, this is about 6000 feet elevation so bring plenty of wool clothes. You may have a foot of snow and the temperature may go down to 20 degrees above at night. Hunting season is October 6 to 27, inclusive. Grouse is October 6 and 7 only. License for Washington citizen is $3.00, plus 50c for Big Game Seal. Out of state, $25.00.

Sincerely yours,
Washington State Field
Archers Association,
Kore T. Duryee, Pres.

Portland and the Next National

By George Brommers

The National at Amherst is history, a wonderful success in every way, breaking all records for attendance. The next one will be held in Portland, Oregon.

For geographical reasons alone it is inevitable that a tournament on the Pacific Coast will be fortunate if it draws even half the attendance that the Eastern tournament did. The Coast has some outstanding target archers, but the majority go in for field archery of some form.

Here is both a challenge and an opportunity. Thanks to the cordiality that has developed between the two groups this year, the relations are the best they have ever been. The NAA and the NFAA know how to cooperate, and do.

Field archers feel rather friendly towards the NAA for another reason—the character of the honorary members added to the NAA roster at Amherst. Styles, of Berkeley, is one of our oldest and best known bow and arrow hunters, Nagler, of Canada, is another one. Both stand for the highest degree of sportsmanship, for what is best and cleanest in the game.

Dr. Klopsteg may qualify as a field archer mostly by courtesy and inference. Certainly his bag has not been impressive (see photo in the August Archer). But as one who has had the highest degree of enjoyment out of his hunts, he rates very high. It isn't what you get, it is how you get it, that counts. As gifted writers of technical articles and true-to-life hunting stories, all three have done more than their share to advance the sport. These are excellent selections.

Also, in awarding this year's Maurice Thmopson medal of honor to Louis C. Smith, the NAA has finally recognized the unselfish services of its oldest—in the point of years—organizer and official. It was a plain act of justice, if the medal in question is going to mean anything. It is thanks to services like those of Mr. Smith's that archery today is riding on an even keel, instead of going boom and then bust. There is no substitute for work and for experience. Once more I repeat, the organizer is the forgotten man in archery today.

Portland, and Major "Bill" Williams, the new NAA president, are going to need all the support we can give them. If we will try to arrange our vacations to take in the tournament week next year, we can be of the greatest aid. Certainly this applies to the field archer as well as the target archer. We can better afford to miss a few bucks next year than we can afford to miss meeting these friends of ours from all sections of the country.

It is going to be Oregon's first National. Let us make it one that we will remember with pleasure as long as we live.

P. S.—Those lightweight bull throwers mentioned in the last issue know who is boss, don't they? Never a peep out of one of them.

P.S., P.S.—Don't try to get funny with me, John Yount. You dig up that pin, or else—

At a dinner given August 21, 1940, by L. B. Spafford, Buchanan, Michigan, entertaining the city officials and local Lions club, Mr. Spafford offered to donate to the city for a public park, the grounds on which the Jungle Gardens field and target ranges are located, reserving for the archers all previous privileges enjoyed by them. Following the dinner the group inspected the ranges and had their first close-up view of archers in action.

Field Round at NAA Tournament

The sixtieth National Archery Tournament was held the week of August 5, 1940, at the Massachusetts State College, Amherst, Massachusetts.

About seventy-five archers shot the National field round. The grounds were on the campus near the buildings. They were rolling, which gave up hill, down hill, over knolls, across hollows and across water, and through light and shadow. Old timers said that it was a dandy. One group started at two o'clock. The second started at about four-thirty, and a number of the last group did not finish because of the banquet at six-thirty. Both Hill Turnock and Pat Chambers were in the last group but they finished in a hurry. However, their scores indicate that a high score can be made, and had they had plenty of time their scores would no doubt have been higher.

The first ten men and the first five women scored as follows:

Men

1—Pat Chambers	Pine Bluff, Ark.	78-308
2—E. Hill Turnock	Wilkinsburg, Penn.	68-278
3—Ralph Hulbert	Brookline, Mass.	60-219
4—William Folberth	Cleveland, Ohio	54-214
5—Bob Goldich	Newtonville, Mass.	51-211
6—Carl Oelschleger	Cleveland, Ohio	50-200
7—Harold Hill	Red Bank, N. J.	47-197
8—Fritz Schenk	Newark, Ohio	50-186
9—Howard Hicks	Lakewood, Ohio	46-172
10—C. A. McCandliss	Balston Lake, N. Y.	44-172

Ladies

1—Glendoline Vineyard	Canby, Ore.	31-113
2—Doris Schenk	Newark, Ohio	20-78
3—Ethel Madlin	Covington, Ky.	21-75
4—Millie Hill	Dayton, Ohio	16-62
5—Alice Lacker	Cincinnati, Ohio	15-59

Los Angeles Archery Club

We had a very nice turn out for the monthly tournament of August 4. There were 22 men and 8 ladies vying for the honors of the day. Bob Lanborn, a newcomer to our club, won the men's Improvement Cup by improving his score 342 points over his last tournament score. Betty Bradstreet is staging a comeback, after being out of archery for some time, as is evidenced by her winning of the ladies' Improvement Cup twice in succession. The results of the shoot were:

Ladies—	Natl.	Col.
1—Gean Bacon	68-382	72-532
2—Ilda Hanchett	67-379	72-468
3—Lillian Bordan	60-302	68-420

1. H. C.—Betty Bradstreet.
2. H. C.—Margaret Rand

Men—		York	Amer.
1—Willard Bacon		125-635	90-672
2—E B Gibson		107-481	88-610
3—J. R. Austin		98-492	89-545

1. H. C.—Bob Lanborn.
2. H. C.—Rex Bassett.
3. H. C.—W. Hibler.

H. G. Hall, Secy.

Oregon archers were greatly pleased to see Homer Prouty sufficiently recovered from his hip injury to be able to attend the Pope-Young tournament and compete in some of the events.

The Oregon deer season opens Sept. 20 and many Oregon archers will be found at the Williams Bar L ranch in the heart of the archery reserve on the opening day.

CLASSIFIED ADVERTISING

RATES for Classified Advertising 5 cents per word per issue. Count initials and numbers as words. Minimum charge is 50 cents.

RELICS AND CURIOS

INDIAN RELICS, Beadwork, Coins, Curios, Books, Minerals, Weapons. Old West Photos. Catalog, 5c. Genuine African Bow, $3.75. Ancient flint arrowheads, perfect, 6c each—Indian Museum, Osborne, Kansas.

"ARCHERY TACKLE, HOW TO MAKE AND HOW TO USE IT." by Adolph Shane. Bound in cloth and illustrated with more than fifty drawings and photographs. Information for making archery tackle and instructions for shooting. Price is $1.75. Send orders to Ye Sylvan Archer, 505 North 11th street, Corvallis.

BOOKS AND MAGAZINES

The AMERICAN ARCHER, a national quarterly, $1.00 per year, 521 Fifth Ave., New York City.

The Flat Bow—70 pages of Archery information for 50 cents, well illustrated. Ye Sylvan Archer, 505 N. 11th St., Corvallis, Oregon.

SUBSCRIBERS PLEASE NOTICE

A cross appearing in this space means that your subscription has expired and we would appreciate your prompt renewal so that your name may be kept on our mailing list.

BACK NUMBERS
YE SYLVAN ARCHER
Volumes I to V Inclusive
$1.00 Per Volume
B. G. THOMPSON
R. F. D. 1, Corvallis, Oregon

A Solid Book for the Serious Archer

THE NEW ARCHERY
By Paul H. Gordon

The most comprehensive treatment of archery available. A professional maker "comes clean" on the best methods of his craft in this unusual book for serious archer, novice and general reader.

CONTENTS:
Target Making. All wooden bow types. Hunting Tackle. Fitted and Footed Arrows. Accessories. Special Equipment. Easy craft approach for the novice. Advanced projects for the highly skilled. Illustrated. $3.50.

At All Booksellers

D. Appleton - Century Co.
35 W. 32nd St.   New York

WESTERN ANTIQUES COLLECTOR

Corvallis, Oregon
P. O. Box 403

A monthly illustrated magazine devoted to items of interest to the collector of antiques.

$1.50 per year.

HANDBOOK—How to Make and Use Bows and Arrows—90 Pages well illustrated (with catalog) 35c.

CATALOG—100 pictures—color spread—Instruction Folder. 10c.

CATALOG alone 5c. Stamps or Coin.

L·E·STEMMLER · QUEENS VILLAGE · N·Y·

Please mention Ye Sylvan Archer when writing advertisers.

WIN WITH BEN PEARSON ARROWS

Beautiful and accurate to the Nth degree but win their real laurels on the range. Arrows made as arrows should be—and at prices you can afford to pay. Send for catalogue.

BEN PEARSON, INC. — PINE BLUFF, ARK.

Cassius Hayward Styles

BOWYER AND FLETCHER

—Tackle that has stood the test—

28 Vicente Place

BERKELEY, CALIFORNIA

G

"THE MARK OF DISTINCTION IN ARCHERY TACKLE

Fine Yew Target and Hunting Bows, Plain or Backed with Rawhide. Lemonwood Bows with Rawhide Backs.

College and School Equipment Target, Hunting and Roving Arrows

Price List on Request

Wholesale — Retail

EARL GRUBBS
5518 W. Adams
Los Angeles, : California

Archery Raw Materials

WM. A. JOY

9708 So. Hoover Street
LOS ANGELES, CALIF.

Hunters and Field Archers

It is time to begin thinking about a new hunting bow for this fall. Write for that new big catalog, which explains everything. By America's oldest tackle maker.

WILLIS H. BARNES
Sturgis — — *Michigan*

THE FLAT BOW
HUNT & METZ

70 pages of Archery information for 50 cents, well illustrated. Ye Sylvan Archer, 505 N. 11th St., Corvallis, Oregon.

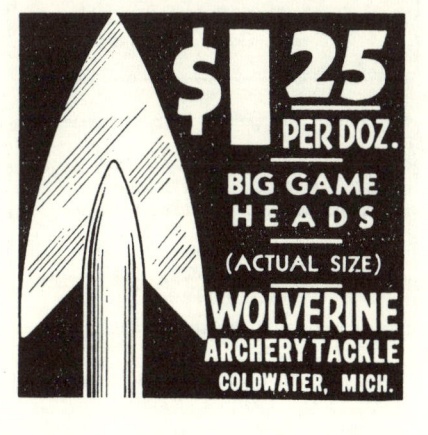

$1.25 PER DOZ.

BIG GAME HEADS
(ACTUAL SIZE)

WOLVERINE ARCHERY TACKLE
COLDWATER, MICH.

CHANDLER
PAT. PEND.
Interchangeable Arrow Points

TARGET SET BALANCED
FISH HEAD
A-80
SMALL HUNTING SET BALANCED

Attention all Archery clubs, Dealers and Archers. Write for rules of a Nation-wide hunting and target shooting contest — 110 prizes. Proper equipment is the success of any sport. For catalogue write—
T. B. CHANDLER
11819 - 4th Ave. Compton, Calif.

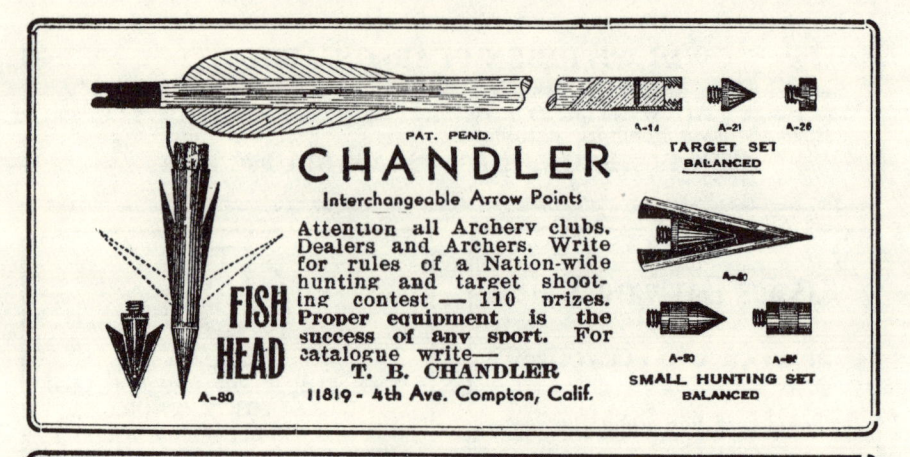

BEAR
ALUMINUM ARROWS ARE MAKING RECORDS
BEAR PRODUCTS CO.
2611 W. Philadelphia Ave., Detroit, Michigan

Ye Sylvan Archer—$1.00 per year.

DO YOU LIKE THE CHARM OF THE BACKHILLS?
If so — read ARCADIAN LIFE MAGAZINE. It tells the story of the Ozarks in a way that will captivate you.

$1.00 a year; 25c a copy. Classified advertising (for archers) 2c a word.

O. E. RAYBURN, Editor
Caddo Gap, Arkansas

E. BUD PIERSON
Bowyer — Fletcher
Tournament Tackle, Sinew, Glue, Raw Materials.
245 University Ave
CINCINNATI, OHIO
Custom Made Tackle

Write us for your needs in Archery books. Ye Sylvan Archer.

W. A. COCHRAN
Archery Equipment
High Elevation Yew Wood
Port Orford Cedar
Osage Orange
Air Seasoned
10,000 Billets and Staves in Stock
Route 2   Eugene, Ore.

Paul H. Gordon, Director
Beacon Hill Craftsmen
Beacon, N. Y.
Where the serious archer's needs and desires are really consulted, and his orders exactly filled. Nothing too simple or too difficult.
Write for Complete Catalog

YEW BOW TIMBER
High Altitude Air Seasoned Billets and Staves of Quality and Variety.
W. G. PRESCOTT
527 Chestnut   Ashland, Ore.

Ye Sylvan Archer

October, 1940

Corvallis, Oregon

Vol. 12   No. 6

Ye Sylvan Archer

"A magazine for the field archers"

Vol. 12   October, 1940   No. 6

Published the fifteenth of each month
for archers by archers
505 North 11th Street, Corvallis, Oregon

J. E. DAVIS .... Editor
RUSSELL JONES .... Business Manager
Subscription Price .... $1.00 Per Year
Foreign Subscription .... $1.25 Per Year
Single Copies .... 10 Cents
Advertising Rates on Application

TABLE OF CONTENTS

	Page
THE SECRET OF GUT SHOT GAP By Walt Wilhelm	1
CALIFORNIA STATE TOURNAMENT By Ilda Hanchett	4
WHIFFEN JOINS BEN PEARSON, INC.	4
BROMMERS LOCATES NEAR SEATTLE	5
HISTORY REPEATS FOR KORE	5
FROM THE OLD ARCHERY ALBUM	6
EDITORIAL	8
NFAA NEWS By John L. Yount	9
NORTHERN CALIFORNIA TOURNAMENT By Dawson Feathers	10
INTERNATIONAL ARCHERY TOURNAMENT	11
GRAND RAPIDS CLUB ENTERTAINS	11

The Secret of Gut Shot Gap

By Walt Wilhelm, Yermo, California

If unusual things didn't happen on hunting trips, who'd wanna go hunting. If the guys that make the long jaunts to the back country wasn't different they wouldn't be out on a hunting trip. If no one went hunting we'd be in a fix for stories. Jevver hear of a right good yarn that wasn't originated by some hunter?

Now I hate towns. I've got to be clean out of some thing that I can't get anywhere else before I'll venture into one. I was walking down a street of a big Southern California city one Saturday afternoon. Like some farmer, I was trying to get the roof of my mouth sunburned by gawking around and not looking where I was going.

As I rounded a corner I smacked belly to belly into another out-of-towner that was also gawking around. I stepped back and got ready to swing on the guy. He was just about ready to lower the boom on me. We recognized each other before any harm had been done. The guy was Ralph "Snuffy" Walters, here and after to be known as Snuffy.

Snuffy is one of those archers you rarely hear anything about. He lives in a small cabin in one of the wildest sections of the Coast Range of mountains; makes his own tackle the way he wants it and shoots it the same way. He's short and chunky, has curly hair and will weigh about 175 pounds when everything is going to suit him.

Spends all his change on hunting trips that takes him all over the West, does his hunting with bow and arrow and knows more tricks about fooling game than a politician does about fooling the people.

"What the heck you doin' in town?" Snuffy asked.

"Looking for some flax for bow strings," I answered.

"Well, I'm a son-of-a-gun," said he, "that's what I'm huntin'."

We looked the town over before we found what we wanted, but finally purchased a pound ball each. Snuffy's choice was six strands; I always buy the four strand.

"Whatcha doin' for the next couple days." he asked.

"Nothing in particular. Why?" I said.

He motioned me close to him and kept looking around to make sure no one would hear what he had to say.

"Listen," he began, "I've got the swellest bait for squirrels you ever

Curtiss (left) and Snuffy on the spot where we got our best shooting.

saw. They can smell it a mile and when they get to chewing on it you can't run 'em away."

"Yeah, what is it?"

"Never mind what it is. If you wanna come up to my shack I'll guarantee you the swellest shootin' yever had in your life; darn good chance to get a pop at a cat, too."

A couple big policemen came walking past us. Snuffy nudged me with his elbow and put his finger to his lips. I was thinking the guy was nuts. I've been hunting with the bird many times and never knew him to violate the game laws, or do anything out of the way, but that day he was nervous and acted like he had stolen something.

"What ails you?" I asked him. "It's not against the law to shoot squirrels, or put out bait for 'em either, is it?"

"That's not it," he said. "This new bait of mine is so good that I don't want anyone to get wise to it. I'm not going to tell you or anyone else. If a copper got wise he'd tell the other bulls and pretty soon all the cops in the country would be shootin' squirrels with their six-guns. With this new dope of mine all you have to do is put it out and go some place and sit down and the squirrels will come right up to you."

"Well, how do you use this dope?" I asked.

"Just smear it around on the logs and rocks."

"Smear what around on logs and rocks?"

"Wouldn't you like to know? Come on up to my cabin tonight and I'll show you. I'll wager that you can shoot your arm off tomorrow."

"How'd you get hold of the stuff anyway?"

"I discovered it by mistake."

"You mean you discovered it by accident."

"I mean just what I said. I discovered it by mistake."

"How in thunder could anyone discover something by making a mistake?"

"I did and how. You see, one day when I was cutting wood over in Gut Shot Gap I took my lunch along in a paper sack. After I'd worked a while pretty hard I sat down on a log to roll a smoke. I glanced over at my lunch and there was a whole flock of squirrels messing around. Them brown devils didn't do a thing but ruin my eats. One of them liked the stuff so well that he was sitting on his haunches rubbing it all over his face."

"Well, that was just luck that the squirrels found your lunch," I said.

"Luck me eye! I went hungry that day and just because I made the mistake of not carrying my lunch in a tin pail."

"So the stuff is good food for humans too, eh?"

"I sure eat plenty of it."

"Do you buy it in cans, glass jars, or does it come in paper sacks?"

"Ain't goin' to do you no good to ask questions 'cause I won't let this one out to anybody."

My curiosity was aroused as never before, so I agreed to meet the guy at his cabin that night. We hadn't more than clinched the trip when up walked Big Glenn Curtiss. Glenn is one of the best known archers in the country, and one of the largest.

"What you birds doing in town?" he asked.

"Buying a little bowstring and planning a hunt," we told him.

"About what I expected. Where you aim to go hunting?"

"Over in Gut Shot Gap," I told Glenn. "Better join in because Snuffy has a new system for luring the squirrels out of the rocks."

"None of that Gut Shot Gap country in mine. One guy can break more arrows up there than sixteen men can pay for."

"No more bustin' arrows," Snuffy said. "I have a dope now that squirrels can smell a mile, and when you smear it on the bark and rocks they'll come right to it and all you have to do is shoot at 'em while they're eating."

"What do you do, soak grain in whiskey and shoot the diggers when they get too drunk to walk?"

Snuffy went all over the conversation again. Glenn couldn't figure his system either, but said he couldn't go hunting because he had an ice box to repair. I kept urging Glenn to go with me.

"Come with me while I make a phone call," Glenn asked us. We followed the big guy to a service station. He grabbed the telephone and dialed a number.

Said he, "Curtiss talking, how's the machine working? Is that so? Did you open the drain cock that I told you about? What! Gets hotter. You don't think it'll run all night. That pounding sound is just the compressor, won't hurt anything. Yeah. No. I think so. Well, I guess I could, but don't you think it will be okay until Monday? I have a hurry up job in the mountains that's got to be taken care of right away, very important and the guys can't wait. Swell, see you Monday."

We jumped in Glenn's car and went to his home to get some tools for the mountain job. The tools happened to be a couple bows and a quiver full of arrows.

Gut Shot Gap is a land mark in the Coast Range and was named by the Mormans when they came through in the early days. It's the highest pass in the range and can be seen for miles by travelers approaching from the desert. Snuffy and Curtiss drove through the mountains; I went in from the desert side.

Just before I turned off the main hi-way for the hills I met my brother Ken. He was headed for a field tournament that was scheduled for the next day.

I explained the deal to him. "Nothing doin'," Ken said. "I can shoot squirrels anywhere along the road. I'm going to make the shoot and mix with the gang for a day."

I knew that Ken's weakness was to get out with a few good sports and just spend the day shooting the daylights out of everything from a jay bird to a dried cow chip. So I told him that most all his friends would be up to watch Snuffy lure the diggers away from the rocks.

"Whataya mean, all my friends," he said, "all my friends will be at the tournament tomorrow."

"That's what you think," I told him. "I just called Jack Willard, and he said he'd be there if the old lizzie held together. Ted Carpenter, Erle Gardner, Jack Low, and several more should be there."

I didn't lie when I said they should be there. And the guys I mentioned are the guys that would have been there if I'd had time to get word to 'em. Ken knew it too.

"Do you suppose Snuffy has something new?" Ken asked, "or is the guy having a pipe dream?"

"Well," I told him, "you know how he fooled the geese, don't you, by sticking arrows in the ground and tying hunks of canvas to them so the geese flying above could see the shadows. And you remember how he caught the coon by putting a dollar watch down in the water?"

"That guy is always trying to outfigure something, ain't he?"

When Ken said that I knew I had him sold. We pulled up to Snuffy's cabin just after dark.

Curtiss was busy filing his broadheads; Snuffy was stretched out on his bunk smoking a cigarette.

"Where's the rest of the gang?" Ken asked.

I winked at Curtiss and he replied, "Should be in any minute now." Ken gave me a look that was colder than a mother-in-law's kiss. We sat down and started chewing the rag.

If a guy ever got the third degree Snuffy got it that night. We used everything at our command to make the bird open up and tell us how he could coax the squirrels out of the rocks so we could get plenty shooting without breaking every arrow we had. Snuffy was as silent as the big pines that towered above his cabin.

Next morning we walked over to the gap. Towering cliffs of granite were all around us. In between was a few trees and open country. Snuffy stationed us at the foot of a ridge in some tall ferns.

"You guys stay here," he said. "I'm going up and put out my magic dope. When the shootin' starts, everybody has got to stay right where you are; no slipping up closer; we'll shoot about forty yards."

We just stood and watched the guy. He went up the hillside and reached down in his quiver. We could see that he was taking something out of a can and smearing it on the rocks and limbs. We followed him around a big bunch of boulders and he did the same thing again. The whole procedure didn't take but a few minutes. But Snuffy wouldn't let us look in his quiver.

The goofy guy lighted a cigarette. He took a deep drag and as the smoke poured from his nostrils he gave the final orders.

"We'll slip back to the first place now. If you don't see a squirrel as soon as you get around the rocks I'm a locoed coyote. Shoot at 'em sittin', runnin', or eatin', and when you've shot all your arrows we'll get 'em and then come back here. They'll be a bunch here by that time."

We nocked arrows and stalked back to the spot. Our bows were half drawn as we rounded the boulders. Nothin' happened. There wasn't a rodent in sight. We looked at Snuffy reproachfully.

"Too early," he apologized, "they'll be here as soon as the sun gets a little higher."

We answered with taunting remarks. Snuffy led us back to the second place. There wasn't a time that he didn't have complete confidence in his system, which made us more eager to play along with him.

Just as we rounded the rock heap on the way to the second baiting spot big business picked up—and what I mean, picked up! There was at least six fuzzy tails sniffing along the trail left by Snuffy. It's tough shooting up hill, and a squirrel is a small target at forty yards when he's moving around through the pine cones.

Just as Snuffy had told us, the rodents would dart back and forth but were hard to frighten away from the magic lure. We emptied our quivers in short order. It was the finest sport we'd ever had. Ken and Snuffy both got a big one. Curtiss and I got a boot out of just watching Ken and Snuffy smoke 'em.

It was Snuffy's turn to razz us, and he didn't overlook any bets. When we went to retrieve our arrows we tried to locate some of the lure. Snuffy got wise and hurried us up. "Come on, you birds," he said, "we gotta get back to the other place and let this one rest for a second."

At the first place we found squirrels stepping all over each other; they were even scrapping over the choice morsels that Snuffy had left on the hillside.

We started to throw arrows like mad men. I broke a bow string right when shooting was best. In my haste to replace the string I let the short osage slip twice and smack me on the kisser.

None of us collected, although we emptied our quivers. Did you ever try to do good shooting when four guys were trying to outshoot each other? It can't be done, but the thrill and the sport is there just the same.

While we were getting that bunch of arrows Curtiss gave me a jab with his bow. He also gave me a big wink as he patted his hip pocket.

(To be continued)

Next month—how we made the big discovery!

California State Tournament

The California Archery Association held its seventh annual tournament at Griffith Park in Los Angeles on August 31 and September 1, and it turned out to be the finest state shoot ever held by this association. Ninety-seven archers all report having a fine time.

Larry Hughes proved to be the iron man of the shoot by winning both the target events and the field archers round, and setting a new record in the American round (728).

Gene Bacon came through for the ladies in record breaking fashion with the best score ever shot in a state tournament. She also made six golds for the first time and thus gained entry to the National six golds club.

Colleen Zirbel also shot six golds, and won the ladies' flight event.

A very successful banquet was held on Saturday evening at the Hollywood Plaza Hotel and the following officers were elected for the following year: Mr. C. W. Moore of Santa Barbara, president; Mr. Art. Fisk of Santa Barbara, vice-president; and Mr. C. L. Batkin of Lompoc, secretary-treasurer. Jim Hendrix, H. Macquarrie, L. A. Hodgert, J. W. Canfield, Ray Hodgson, and Willard Bacon are the new board of directors.

The tournament is to be held in Santa Barbara next year. Let's all start saving our nickels and dimes and make the meet next year bigger and better than ever before.

—Ilda Hanchett, secretary.

Whiffen Joins Ben Pearson, Inc.

Larry Whiffen who has been exceptionally busy the last few years gathering the tackle manufacturers together, running tournaments in the rain, and pumping newspaper editors for unprecedented space, has turned over the operation of his company in Milwaukee to his local organization while he has gone to Pine Bluff to take over the general sales management of the Ben Pearson company.

When Whiffen arrives he will be greeted by quite a collection of nationally known archery celebrities who preceded him. During the past year Pine Bluff, Arkansas, has greeted in turn Harris Stafford of Dallas, Texas; Henry A. McCune of Fairmount, Minnesota; Nat Lay of Indianapolis; and Pat and Vivian Chambers of Portland, Oregon; and now Larry Whiffen of Milwaukee.

Brommers Locates Near Seattle

George Brommers writes that he is settled permanently in Bellevue, on the east side of Lake Washington, near Seattle. Mrs. Brommers is better, but needs rest and quiet. George, however, is thoroughly down in the dumps because he can't get any results from his insults to Gardner, Cosner, Walt Wilhelm and others. He thinks they are getting weak-kneed. Maybe they feel that it would be impossible to do it in a nice way that would get through the mails.

A field tournament was scheduled for October 13 at Germain Park, Toledo, Ohio, as a competitive shoot between the Ohio field archers and the Michigan archers.

Kore proudly displays his buck.

History Repeats for Kore

One of the most persistent and enthusiastic bow and arrow hunters is Kore T. Duryee of Seattle, the genial and efficient secretary of the Pacific Northwest Archery Association, and a member of the Board of Governors of the National Archery Association. In November, 1928, Kore killed a buck deer with the bow in British Columbia. He has been after them each season since that time, and has been active in the promotion of special preserves for archery hunting, at last securing a highly desirable preserve in Washington.

However, Kore couldn't wait for the Washington season to open. He again went to British Columbia and killed a forked horn dressing 170 pounds. John A. Garrett of Vancouver, B. C., with whom Kore was hunting, joined that famous "Society of Moose Missers" by nearly getting one at 80 yards. Kore saw his first moose in the woods (250 yards), and heard his first moose grunt.

T. B. Chandler informs us that New Mexico has granted the archers of that state a special range for antelope hunting this year, and that Dr. C. E. Buswell of Albuquerque, is going after one. Chandler thinks that killing an antelope with a bow and arrow on the open plains of New Mexico, or anywhere else, would be something to crow about. Well, our Russell Jones almost did it, as he parted the hair on the back of a big antelope buck in Eastern Oregon.

The Editor's family enjoyed the enclosures accompanying the annual remittance from Mr. Van Allen Lyman, Balboa, Panama Canal, such as a price list of many kinds of food and a cap from a bottle of "pura leche fresca." His "I enjoy your magazine" is appreciated.

From the Old Archery Album

This genial gentlemen was the president of an archery club in New York State in 1931.

Publication of old pictures in recent issues of Ye Sylvan Archer has aroused considerable interest, so we are giving our readers a little guessing contest this month. These pictures are from old issues of Ye Sylvan Archer. How many can you recognize? In the next issue we shall give details regarding each picture.

Can you recognize any of these Central Illinois archers who met in 1931?

The archer shooting is a former National Champion. The archer next in line lived in Buffalo, New York in 1926.

Noted Archers of a Decade Ago

Archery instructor at White Sulphur Springs, West Virginia, in 1931.

Who are these two prominent Wisconsin archers pulling arrows in 1929?

Editorial

WELL, WE MISSED 'EM!

A year ago there was considerable jubilation in the office of Ye Sylvan Archer as we were announcing the fact that the editor had really killed a deer with bow and arrow after thirteen years of deer hunting with the feathered shafts.

This year it is different. The story got out that we had repeated, and a great deal of explaining has been in order. But let it be understood here and now that the editor of Ye Sylvan Archer hasn't killed a deer this season, but the season has a few days to go yet, and there is still hope.

We went to Canyon Creek again this year. Our only alibi is that we couldn't hit them. What more could a fellow want than seven shots at one buck? If you haven't had the experience you are missing something by not taking membership in the great "Society of Buck Missers." Klopsteg, Garrett, and a few others can be rather snooty with their Society of Moose Missers. Thompson, Cathey, Nagler and a very few others can put on lordly airs with their exclusive Society of Moose Killers. But think of the great fraternity of Red Ribboners belonging to the S-B-M. Even George Brommers could qualify for that honor if there were no coons around to distract his attention.

Well, if we had really needed alibis, we had plenty thought up; and besides, B. G. Thompson was along and, in the genial mood he was in, we could have borrowed an unlimited number from him.

ECHOES FROM CANYON CREEK

Coyotes howl,
 Wildcats prowl,
  Arrows hiss,
   Archers miss!

Cudd breaking his bow when shooting at a deer.......Those superfine meals served by Mrs. Williams....... Cooter, the deerslayer, getting such a case of buck fever he couldn't get his arrow nocked when a deer walked up to within fifteen feet of him....... Another case of buck fever when Dr. Laird tried to nock the wrong end of the arrow, cut his bow string and threw the bow at the buck....... The helpful spirit shown by Lee Williams in making a better story out of a good one.......Major Williams blowing up a 6-foot by 6-foot air mattress.......Bill Williams (Bill of the L-Bar-L Williamses) playing hooky from school to go deer hunting, and waiting for the buck to stop before he shot. It stopped behind a tree....... The Clark boys' climb into and out of East Fork Canyon.......Chuck's saddle, the envy of any cowboy....... To be frank about it—Davis forgetting his arrows and Dr. Cathey being good enough to drive back after them.......Larry Williams laying his bow down to take a picture and a big buck nearly running over him....... B. G. Thompson gamely hobbling along on blistered feet.......B. G. wasn't the only sore-footed one in the crowd, either.......John Hubler still trying.........Stanley Stevens' flight shooting........Dr. Baker thinking it worth while coming, even for one day.......Larry's fine collection of broadhead arrows (by the way, if you are a bow and arrow hunter one of your arrows should be on display at the L-Bar-L Ranch in Larry's display case. The address is: Larry Williams, Canyon City, Oregon, and Larry would be tickled to get one from you).......And above all the tang of the pure, clear air of that four-hundred-acre mountain meadow.

PEARSON BUYS TARGET CO.

It was announced recently that the Ben Pearson, Inc., of Pine Bluff, Arkansas, has taken over the complete factory facilities and contracts of the National Target Company of Independence, Missouri. According to Mr. L. E. Piper, who organized and has operated the business since its inception two years ago, he and part of the personnel will move to Pine Bluff, Arkansas, shortly, where the production of the targets will be continued.

New manufacturing facilities will allow for about three times the volume that Piper had at Independence, Missouri. According to J. T. Haun, Purchasing Agent of Ben Pearson, Inc., they have recently contracted
(Continued on page 11)

N. F. A. A. News

By John L. Yount

Although the results of our fifth and last mail tournament are not yet in, I feel fairly safe in predicting the following results.

First place for the year's shooting will be won by E. Hill Turnock of Pennsylvania. That is, providing he has shot in the last tournament and has come anywhere close to his two former scores. Second place will go to Roland Quayle, Southern California; third to Larry Hughes, S. C.; and fourth to Merle Hathaway, S. C. These last three are definite and can only be changed by Turnock failing to shoot up to expectations.

These mail tournaments were decidedly an experiment. We didn't know whether the archers would be interested, but we had to have some kind of National tournament and no other kind was practical at this stage of our development.

Now that we know that there is a place in Archery for these mail tournaments, and with this year's experience and better courses, they should be even more popular next year.

Through the courtesy of Mr. Shenk, I have just had a preview of the medals to be given the winners. I don't believe any organization offers anything finer. They must be seen to be appreciated, so there is no use trying to describe them except to say that they are designed from the NFAA emblem.

Big Game Pin to be Known as the Art Young Award

Some time ago Mr. Klopsteg wrote me, enclosing a check for $40, from the Art Young foundation, and asking that we use it to purchase trophies for some field event that would properly commemorate the memory of Art Young.

Since he was the greatest of modern archer hunters—the man who through his deeds and sportsmanship did more to popularize the bow as a hunting weapon than any other man—what could be more appropriate than to honor him by naming our big game pin the "Art Young Award."

This pin is to be a small silver NFAA emblem mounted on a gold replica of an Indian arrowhead, with the words, "Art Young Award" at the top and the year in the point.

The sort of letters we sometimes get. These are from Joe Cosner, Phoenix, Arizona.

"Dear John:

"When your note came I was busy at perfecting a deer call. I was not having an easy time of it, either. Nobody here seems to know what kind of a noise a deer makes. I have already tried waiting for deer to call me and none of them ever did. I have decided not to be so egotistical about it and to call them instead. To be honest about it, I have never been able to come upon a deer at suitable range. However, I have found lots of spoor, if you know what I mean, and rather fancy myself as an expert on them. It is a study in itself if one goes in for that sort of thing............."

We didn't want him to feel too bad about this and so admitted to the same kind of success as a hunter. We even broke down and admitted to being something of an expert along the lines mentioned in his letter, and now see what we received by return mail:

"Dear John:

"It is a source of gratification to me to find that we have a common interest in our hunting and that we have carried it to such lengths as we have. We should adopt a common emblem such as a handful of olive seeds on a grassy background and surmounted by crossed arrows. I am all agog over the coming deer season on October 16, when I shall once more carry my strung bow through the carpeted aisles of the forest and peer intently through my bifocals at the scattered treasures of the hunt that are our reward............"

Archery has proved so popular among the co-eds at Oregon State College that several more classes than those originally scheduled were necessary. Archery classes are also provided for the men.

Northern California Tournament

By Dawson Feathers, Secretary

One of the most enjoyable shoots in the history of the Northern California Field Archers' Association was experienced by Association members and guests, September 9. Some of the highlights were: a real "feed" after the morning round, an exciting balloon shoot, a hectic battle clout lasting into the evening dusk, another sensational score (286 on 28 N.F.A.A targets) by our local star, Harry Glover and, of course, "perfect California weather."

The dinner, a testimonial to the skill of some of the members' wives, had been planned for twice the number of diners but, owing to the great gusto of the group, was nevertheless almost annihilated before the end of the day. As most of the scores attested, however, it did not militate against accuracy during the afternoon round. Which just goes to show that field archers can take—or give it? A rather low attendance was ascribed to the imminent closing of the deer season in these parts; many stout archers being off in the greenwood in quest of the elusive buck.

Jack Peters, long an ardent runner-up, came into his own and the NCFAA Championship Class Gold medal and gold trophy. In the battle clout, Jess Stanisich took a fine first place and the gold cup from a valiant field, headed by Edgar Mullens. Harry Glover easily cinched the Championship class gold bar, and your scribe sneaked in to cop the silver one. The choice of some fine prizes of appropriate merchandise became the privilege of some of the other men and ladies with ranking scores.

In the Ladies Division, Mrs. Helen Brooks, shooting a bit below normal, still romped in ahead of the rest of the girls and won the coveted Gold Medal. The Gold Bar, reserved for Championship Class competition, was won by Mrs. Zelda Haskell.

Some of the scores:

Men—General Division

Jack Peters	218
Jess Stanisich	213
Ray Poppe	211
Darrow Olsen	206
Dave Peters	191
Boyd Hammond	181
Russell Olsen	175
Joe Brooks	171
Peter Ting	158

Men—Championship Class

Harry Glover	286
Dawson Feathers	181
Edgar Mullens	169
LeRoy Smith	162

Ladies—General Division

Helen Brooks	86
Agnes Hammond	72

Ladies—Championship Class

Zelda Haskell	32

On October 27, when this past tournament has become a pleasant memory, the Northern California Field Archers' Association will hold its eighth bi-monthly tournament at the roving range of the San Francisco Archers in Sutro Forest, San Francisco.

Michigan Field Tournament

Eighty-nine archers attended the thirteenth annual field tournament of the Micigan Archers Association held at Detroit on September 29, 1940.

Nelson Grumley of Detroit was the winner in the "Instinctive Division," Class A, with a 56-target score of 116-440. Stanley Sokolowski of Detroit scored 116-434, and Carlos Barfield, also of Detroit, shot 108-410 for third. In Class B, William Scheffler and R. L. Findlay of Detroit and K. E. Palmatier of Kalamazoo tied for first with scores of 59-205. In the "Free Style Division," Class A, J. Vaughan Blanchard of Howell was high with 122-474, and in Class B, Gordon Ash was first with 71-261.

Mrs. Lulu Stalker of Flint led the ladies shooting in Class A, with a score of 68-254. Mrs. Mary Calvert and Mrs. Bertha Hoffmeyer, both of Flint, were second and third, respectively, with scores of 59-213 and 61-209. The ladies who placed in Class B were Mrs. Ardis Hayes, Wyandotte, 37-131; Mrs. Marie Bear, Detroit, 30-102; and Mrs. Irene Stork, Flint, 26-84.

International Archery Tournament

The old English slogan "Business as usual" adopted by the Canadian National Exhibition authorities carried through to the International Archery Tournament for 1940. There were more Canadian archers entered but fewer competitors came from the United States. This was accounted for by the war conditions and the National Tournament being held in the East. Scoring was very close and first places changed from time to time, keeping up a keen competition right up to the last arrow. For the first time Canadians won the International Cup. Six new Canadian records were set up. A word of praise should be said for the good sportsmanship of those archers who, despite sore hands, fingers and temperatures said nothing and stuck to the shooting line throughout the tournament. Such really makes archery.

This tournament, held in Toronto, Canada, was the fifth annual International Championship Tournament and was held in connection with the eighth annual Canadian Archery Tournament on August 26-30.

Miss Alice Schafer of Dunkirk, New York, won the women's championship with a total score for the double National and double Columbia of 284-1812. Mrs. A. R. Knight of Toronto was second with 273-1635, and Mrs. Marie Graeber of Kenmore, New York, third with 275-1631.

Margaret Beedham of Leaside, Ontario, won the junior girls' championship, her score being 247-1207.

The men, shooting a double York and double American, conceded the the championship to Alex MacDonald of Toronto, who scored 405-2253. Forrest Nagler of Toronto was second with 402-2118, and Alfred Long, Toronto, third with 379-2049.

The junior championship went to Phillip Ratcliff, Jr. of Toronto who scored 348-2102 in the double junior American and double senior American rounds; Peter Clayton, Toronto, second, 218-1002; Donald Shaw, Mimico, Ontario, third, 213-989.

Mrs. R. J. Mitchele won the women's clout and Forrest Nagler the men's.

On account of the difference in exchange it is considerably easier for Americans to visit Canada than for Canadians to visit the United States. The International Tournament will be held next year, and a special effort will be made to encourage archers from across the line to participate. R. John Mitchele is secretary of Canadian National, and Forrest Nagler Chairman of the Advisory Board.

PEARSON BUYS TARGET CO.

(Continued from page 9)

for 100 tons of unthreshed rye straw.

The new owners also announce that there will be no change in the price schedule of targets for the time being and that all contracts will be carried out. They did, however, announce that improvements will be made in the manufacture of targets which should give them longer life and durability. The targets will not be made in the present plant of the Pearson Company in Pine Bluff, but in an additional building which has recently been acquired. Ben Pearson announces that the present facilities are taxed to their capacity and there is no chance nor room for making targets in that building.

Grand Rapids Club Entertains

The Grand Rapids archers entertained the Michigan Archers Association at a field tournament on September 22, 1940.

Winners were as follows:
Instinctive Division, Class A—
1. Stanley Sokolowski, Detroit — 91-349.
2. Elisha Gray, Benton Harbor — 90-324.
3. Richard King, Grand Rapids — 83-319.

Class B—
1. Fred Hall, Buchanan —48-184.
2. Wm. Stocking, Jackson—47-177.
3. Earl Riggleman, Grand Rapids—47-167.

Free Style Division, Class A—
1. William Loomis, Newaygo — 88-328.

Class B—
1. Wm. Thompson, Buchanan — 79-299.
Ladies Division, Class A—
1. Edith Hastings, Muskegon — 31-113.
2. Ellen Reed, Grand Rapids—25-87.
Class B—
1. Gertrude Mainone, Muskegon—22-74.
2. Elsie Mache, Muskegon—20-74.
3. Mrs. F. D. Pace, Grand Rapids—16-56.

CLASSIFIED ADVERTISING

RATES for Classified Advertising 5 cents per word per issue. Count initials and numbers as words. Minimum charge is 50 cents.

BOOKS AND MAGAZINES

The AMERICAN ARCHER, a national quarterly, $1.00 per year, 521 Fifth Ave., New York City.

"ARCHERY TACKLE, HOW TO MAKE AND HOW TO USE IT." by Adolph Shane. Bound in cloth and illustrated with more than fifty drawings and photographs. Information for making archery tackle and instructions for shooting. Price is $1.75. Send orders to Ye Sylvan Archer, 505 North 11th street, Corvallis.

"ARCHERY," by Robert P. Elmer M. D., revised edition, most complete book on archery published. 566 pages of valuable information for colleges, libraries, schools, camps archery clubs and individuals. Price $5.00 postpaid. orders to Ye Sylvan Archer, 505 North 11th street, Corvallis, Oregon.

RELICS AND CURIOS

INDIAN RELICS, Beadwork, Coins, Curios, Books, Minerals, Weapons. Old West Photos. Catalog, 5c. Genuine African Bow, $3.75. Ancient flint arrowheads, perfect, 6c each—Indian Museum, Osborne, Kansas.

SUBSCRIBERS PLEASE NOTICE

A cross appearing in this space means that your subscription has expired and we would appreciate your prompt renewal so that your name may be kept on our mailing list.

A Solid Book for the Serious Archer

THE NEW ARCHERY
By Paul H. Gordon

The most comprehensive treatment of archery available. A professional maker "comes clean" on the best methods of his craft in this unusual book for serious archer, novice and general reader.

CONTENTS:
Target Making. All wooden bow types. Hunting Tackle. Fitted and Footed Arrows. Accessories. Special Equipment. Easy craft approach for the novice. Advanced projects for the highly skilled. Illustrated. $3.50

At All Booksellers

D. Appleton - Century Co.
35 W. 32nd St.   New York

Please mention Ye Sylvan Archer when writing advertisers.

BACK NUMBERS
YE SYLVAN ARCHER
Volumes I to V Inclusive
$1.00 Per Volume
B. G. THOMPSON
R. F. D. 1, Corvallis, Oregon

HANDBOOK—How to Make and Use Bows and Arrows—90 Pages well illustrated (with catalog) 35c.

CATALOG—100 pictures—color spread—Instruction Folder. 10c.

CATALOG alone 5c. Stamps or Coin.

L. E. STEMMLER · QUEENS VILLAGE · N·Y·

CHANDLER

PAT. PEND

TARGET SET BALANCED

Interchangeable Arrow Points

PRICES CUT NEARLY 50%

The prices now are cut so low,
Yet the quality is so great,
Every archer now should know,
That he cannot afford to wait.
see the dealer nearest ye,
Or mail your order in to me.

Free Catalogue.

T. B. CHANDLER
11819 - 4th Ave. Compton, Calif.

FISH HEAD A-80

SMALL HUNTING SET BALANCED

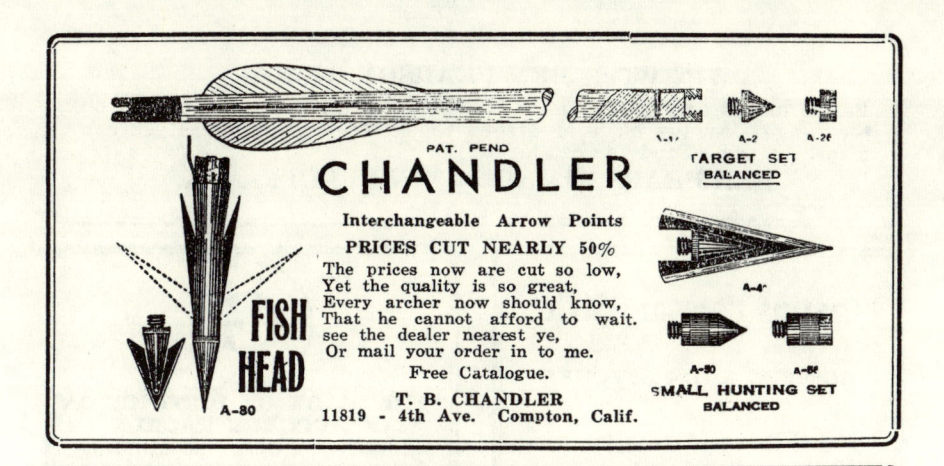

BEAR
ALUMINUM ARROWS ARE MAKING RECORDS
BEAR PRODUCTS CO.
2611 W. Philadelphia Ave., Detroit, Michigan

Ye Sylvan Archer—$1.00 per year.

DO YOU LIKE THE CHARM OF THE BACKHILLS?

If so — read ARCADIAN LIFE MAGAZINE. It tells the story of the Ozarks in a way that will captivate you.

$1.00 a year; 25c a copy. Classified advertising (for archers) 2c a word.

O. E. RAYBURN, Editor
Caddo Gap, Arkansas

YEW BOW TIMBER
High Altitude Air Seasoned Billets and Staves of Quality and Variety.

W. G. PRESCOTT
527 Chestnut   Ashland, Ore.

WESTERN ANTIQUES COLLECTOR

Corvallis, Oregon
P. O. Box 403

A monthly illustrated magazine devoted to items of interest to the collector of antiques.

$1.50 per year.

E. BUD PIERSON
Bowyer — Fletcher
Tournament Tackle, Sinew, Glue, Raw Materials.
245 University Ave
CINCINNATI, OHIO
Custom Made Tackle

Write us for your needs in Archery books. Ye Sylvan Archer.

The Flat Bow—70 pages of Archery information for 50 cents, well illustrated. Ye Sylvan Archer, 505 N. 11th St., Corvallis, Oregon.

WIN WITH BEN PEARSON ARROWS

Beautiful and accurate to the Nth degree but win their real laurels on the range. Arrows made as arrows should be—and at prices you can afford to pay. Send for catalogue.

BEN PEARSON, INC. — PINE BLUFF, ARK.

Cassius Hayward Styles

BOWYER AND FLETCHER

—Tackle that has stood the test—

28 Vicente Place

BERKELEY, CALIFORNIA

G

"THE MARK OF DISTINCTION IN ARCHERY TACKLE"

Fine Yew Target and Hunting Bows, Plain or Backed with Rawhide. Lemonwood Bows with Rawhide Backs. College and School Equipment Target, Hunting and Roving Arrows

Price List on Request

Wholesale — Retail

EARL GRUBBS
5518 W. Adams
Los Angeles, : California

Archery Raw Materials

WM. A. JOY

9708 So. Hoover Street
LOS ANGELES, CALIF.

Hunters and Field Archers

It is time to begin thinking about a new hunting bow for this fall. Write for that new big catalog, which explains everything. By America's oldest tackle maker.

WILLIS H. BARNES
Sturgis — — Michigan

THE FLAT BOW
HUNT & METZ

70 pages of Archery information for 50 cents, well illustrated. Ye Sylvan Archer, 505 N. 11th St., Corvallis, Oregon.

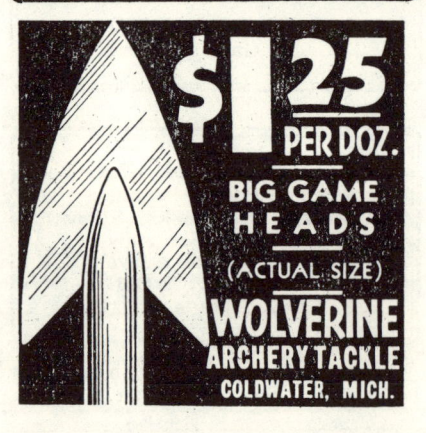

$1.25 PER DOZ.

BIG GAME HEADS

(ACTUAL SIZE)

WOLVERINE ARCHERY TACKLE
COLDWATER, MICH.

Ye Sylvan Archer

Thanksgiving

November, 1940

Corvallis, Oregon

Vol. 12　　　　　　　　　　　　　　No. 7

Ye Sylvan Archer

"A magazine for the field archers"

Vol. 12　　　November, 1940　　　No. 7

Published the fifteenth of each month
for archers by archers
505 North 11th Street, Corvallis, Oregon

J. E. DAVIS	Editor
RUSSELL JONES	Business Manager
Subscription Price	$1.00 Per Year
Foreign Subscription	$1.25 Per Year
Single Copies	10 Cents

Advertising Rates on Application

TABLE OF CONTENTS

　　　　　　　　　　　　　　　　Page

ADD ANOTHER NAME
　By Erle Stanley Gardner 1

THE SECRET OF GUT SHOT GAP
　By Walt Wilhelm 5

EDITORIAL 6

OLYMPIC BOWMEN LEAGUE 6

LAST MONTH'S WHO'S WHO 6

FROM JOE COSNER 9

DOGHOUSE DOINGS
　By Geo. Brommers 10

FROM THE UTAH HILLS
　By F. H. Zimbeaux 11

PARACHUTISTS MAY SIT ON
　ARROWS 12

Add Another Name

By Erle Stanley Gardner

Just about half of the pleasure of a hunting trip lies in sitting in a big half circle the night before, and laying plans. Each man has his bottle of beer and his pipe.

Well, it was one of those nights.

We talked about past hunting trips and laid tentative plans for a deer hunt this fall. This year we were all going to be pretty busy, and couldn't get away for as long as we'd like, but next year it was going to be different. We were going to take a real trip next year. Life was too short to put in all of our time money-grabbing. (I've talked the same way for the last twenty years now. It's always been next year that is going to bring the real trip.)

We discussed broadheads and bowstrings, silk-backing, sinew-backing, hickory-backing, and rawhide-backing. I told a couple of stories about former hunting trips, then we dragged a lot of exciting hunting adventures out of the limbo of the past.

There was an interval of smoke-filled silence. The eyes of the others were dreamy with contemplation.

Jack Roripaugh, the newest addition to the archery group—a mere neophyte whose experience with the bow was less than forty-eight hours, but a natural shot if ever I saw one—stirred in his chair. "I've got quite a day ahead of me tomorrow," he said.

No one said anything. We knew what was going to follow.

"But," Roripaugh went on, "I don't know as it would make so much difference if I didn't get started until ten o'clock. We could be back by ten o'clock."

Now Jack Roripaugh has a ranch on which there is real hunting. And when you talk hunting in this section of the country, you mean hunting just the way it used to be fifty years ago: Quail running around in huge coveys; rabbits without number, doves flapping lazily upward from sand bars with their peculiar "koo-koo-koo"—a short, high-pitched note of plaintive protest, apparently synchronized with each beat of their wings; quite a sprinkling of bobcats and coyotes.

"Well," Nienke said positively, "I can't go."

Buck said, "I won't be here. I'll have to be in Los Angeles tomorrow morning."

Ed Record's face was wistful. "Gosh, I'd like to go, but—"

Walt Wilhelm had driven down from Yermo. He had his trailer parked out under a shade tree back of the cabins. "I'll go," he said. "I ain't got no business doing it—but I'm going."

They looked at me. "I'm sorry, boys. I simply can't make it. I had some work to do over the week-end, and I'd postponed it. It has to go out—beating a deadline. What time would we get back? All right, count me in."

We looked at Nienke.

Under the silent accusation of our eyes, his moral resistance melted like ice in the sun.

The smile of triumph!

We shifted our eyes to Buck. He fidgeted. "I have an appointment, and—Oh, hell, I'll go."

"Start at five o'clock?" Nienke asked.

I doped it all out for them. I'd bring the pick-up, meet at Jack Roripaugh's at five o'clock. That would mean Nienke's place at quarter to five, leaving my place at four-thirty, breakfast at four. That would mean I'd have to get up at three-forty-five, fifteen minutes to get the others up, half an hour to get breakfast cooked, the bows loaded into the car. I decided to set the alarm for three-fifteen.

We sat and talked for a while. A note of excitement crept into the conversation. We began to build air castles. Walt Wilhelm had never seen the property. We told him stories about it which sounded simply incredible to him. He knew we were liars. There wasn't that kind of hunting left anywhere in the United States.

Buck (short for H. R. Buckerfield) of the Western Mechanical Works—another newcomer to archery—also hadn't been out there. He was a little more credulous than Walt, but both of them knew we were liars. It kept getting later, and I decided on three-thirty as time for the alarm.

The party broke up about eleven o'clock. I came down to get my hunting things together, put films in my camera, get my arrows assorted, put some service on a bowstring. I set the alarm at quarter to four. Then I had a lot of odds and ends to attend to.

I finally got to bed at midnight.

At quarter past four the alarm went off.

A mad scramble, coffee pot on the stove, rushing around pitching things into the automobile in the dark, hurrying around to the guest cabins getting people up, opening cans of tomato juice and pineapple juice—coffee boiling over—looking at the watch every few minutes.

Then the blow.

Walt's wife had been feeling badly. She'd suffered all night with nervous indigestion, and Walt felt that he simply couldn't leave her. Shucks, half of the kick in the whole business had been anticipating how Walt's eyes were going to bulge when he saw that country. We discussed it over a sketchy breakfast. There was nothing to be done. The others were going to be strung out along the road, waiting for the pickup. Walt decided he'd have to get his wife back to San Bernardino. We rode out and left him standing there watching us. I saw his eyes. It was as though we were all going to a funeral somewhere.

Gradually the depression wore off. There was light in the east, a bank of low-flung clouds over the desert which meant it was going to be a hot day. The clouds were a dark silhouette against the steely blue. Then a little trace of color appeared around the upper edge. The lower borders began to assume golden tints. The tang of dawn was in the air.

We left the smooth roads, started rattling along over washboarded ranch roads, down across sandy washes, stopping now and again for gates. (About fifty per cent of the gates were locked due to the influx of a whole smear of city hunters—the sort of scatter-gun enthusiasts who shoot at everything in sight, trample crops, leave all gates open, and toss burning cigarette butts into dry sagebrush. The farmers used to be glad to see an occasional hunter. Now, to get to hunt on one of these ranches is so difficult that you have to wait ten years after you know a man well enough to ask him to endorse your note at the bank before you dare suggest the possibility of hunting on his ranch—even with a bow and arrow.)

I don't know exactly when I started shooting a bow and arrow—that is, I can remember the occasion clearly, but I don't know the date. It was either nineteen-twenty-two or nineteen-twenty-three, and I've been shooting ever since. But to me, each hunting trip is still a major adventure. I get so interested that the happenings become an overlapping blur, and this trip was no exception.

Starting out in the glow of dawn—strange how loud your feet sound—this stubble is so dry it explodes when you walk on it—how archery has straightened Nienke's shoulders, and put supple life into his back muscles. Notice the way he walks. There's Buck getting a shot. Hurry up, Buck, get that right elbow back inside the line of the arrow—full draw now. That's it. Can't see the arrow, but can tell from the way Buck's standing that it's a good shot. Now he's running. Nope, slowing down to a walk. Too bad. He missed.

Ed record whirls and shoots, all with one graceful, breath-taking motion. Strange how game can realize when the day's going to be a veritable scorcher. Jump them once, they head into the deep shade of the big cactus patches, and they're gone for the day. This place is midway between ocean and desert. The desert influence is predominating now. We'll have desert weather for three days, then it'll turn cold. We'll be having frost in another week or two. Right now it's hot and dry. Gosh, it's dry! Mouth is filled with shreds of blotting paper. Try to spit, and nothing comes out except dust.

I decide I'll drift over to see how Jack Roripaugh is coming. He may need a little coaching on distances.

There he is. He's getting a shot. That's the boy. Look at the way that arm comes back, that smooth, steady spread. And look at that arrow leap from the bow, going straight and with hardly a sound. Look at the expression on his face. That keen, deadly concentration, the expression of a natural hunter. You can tell he isn't thinking of anything else when he is on the trail of game. No wonder they say he's one of the best trackers in this part of the state. "Hello, Jack, what did you shoot at?"

"Rabbit."

"Close?"

"So-so."

We go down and pick up the arrow. I see the tracks of the rabbit. The shot was about forty yards. The arrow missed by about two inches.

"I'll learn," Roripaugh says. Give me just a little time."

We fool around a bit, getting an occasional snap shot. It's getting frightfully hot—one of those freak September days when hunting is over almost before it starts.

"Going to be a lot of quail here this fall," Roripaugh says. "We'll get some good shooting. Bet we can have a lot of fun with bow and arrow."

"And how," I tell him.

We start looking over the country. "There's a road goes up here," Rori-

Congratulations! Left to right—Ed Record, Jack Roripaugh, Al Nienke.

paugh says, "in case you want to get up to the head of this canyon where the walls come together. You can nearly always find coyotes coming back through this pass into the mountains if you get up there early enough."

I'm disappointed and trying not to show it. I did want Roripaugh to really connect with something. He's an old-time hunter from away back, a man who more or less instinctively knows the habits of game, knows—well, it's too late now. Everything's bedded down for the day. We're just trudging along because we hate to go back. There's something over there. Where? To the right, over there behind that sagebrush. Something moved. It's a jack rabbit. It's a long shot, but: "Let him have it, Jack."

He pulls back his arrow, and makes a perfect release. The arrow went right where he wanted it to, but he has a lot to learn yet about measuring distance in terms of arrow trajectory. The arrow falls far short. The jack rabbit stands up to look.

Jack pulls another arrow out of his quiver. That's one way you can tell a real hunter. He manages to get out his next arrow with a minimum of fumbling. Looking at him, you'd think he's a veteran archer. This one is as much too high as the other one was too low. It went over the rabbit and down into a barranca thick with brush, one of those little washes with steeply precipitous banks.

The jack rabbit goes away.

Jack and I walk over in that direction. I look at him to see if he's feeling a little disgusted. His lips are just tight with grim determination. "I'll get it," he says. "Give me another week, and I'll surprise you. I'm getting the hang of it now."

I explain to him that his release is all right, that when he was shooting yesterday at fixed distances, he was doing some marvelous shooting, that the shot he made at the cottontail rabbit in the wash was at just about the distance he'd been familiar with so he made a good shot. But this jack rabbit was a hundred and twenty-five yards away, and it's darn hard to drop an arrow on him.

That's the way things go. There we were crashing along through the brush, me handing out a line of condolences, Jack feeling just a little sore at himself despite the fact that he knew he shouldn't, both of us thinking the hunt was over, and here adventure was just around the corner.

Jack picked up his short arrow. We walked over to the edge of the barranca. It was a ten-foot drop down into a thick patch of tall sagebrush and greasewood. We stood and looked it over. I saw a little ledge about five feet below to which I could jump. I put my bow down on the ground, sat down, slid one hip over the edge of the bank, dropped to the ledge, and sent a clatter of dry earth and an occasional rock rolling into the sagebrush below me.

Something moved.

I glanced up the barranca. A tawny, yellow streak came out of the deep shade as though it had been shot with a catapult.

"Coyote!" I yelled.

I looked up at Jack.

The edge of the barranca hid everything from me except the upper part of his bow and the top of his hat. I saw the bowstring coming back, saw the bow tip bend to a full arc.

The coyote was going like a streak of light, but he couldn't get up the bank that way. Yes, he could, too. At any rate, he was going to try it.

And I heard the twang of the bowstring.

Jack's arrow went pretty close to where the coyote should have been, but the coyote was scrambling up that steep bank, and he'd turned a bit to one side.

I'm so disgusted I could put cream and sugar on a dish of tenpenny nails and chew them easily.

"You can't shoot with a bow and arrow the way you do with a rifle," I yell. "Couldn't you see that coyote was going to have to scramble up that bank? Why the devil did you shoot when he was going full tilt? Why didn't you—" Oh well, what was the use? The guy just had to learn a lot about shooting with bow and arrow, and what the hell.

The coyote was over the top of the bank but there was still a good steep slope. He came into sight from where I was standing, going up that slope with long, springy bounds.

I stood there, clinging precariously to a narrow ledge, wishing I had my bow, estimating range, not over forty

(Continued on page 7)

The Secret of Gut Shot Gap

By Walt Wilhelm, Yermo, California

(Continued from last issue)

After Curtiss gave me the big wink I knew there was something in the wind so I worked over close to him.

"I think I have some of the stuff," he whispered. "One of the squirrels dropped a hunk of bark when he hitailed it for the rocks and I believe I got the right piece."

Each man had picked up every arrow he came to and we'd sort 'em out at our shooting position. While we were doing the sorting I whispered to Ken, "Curtiss has some of the dope."

Ken looked over at Glenn and Curtiss nodded in the affirmative. We were just a few minutes getting the arrows sorted—some were broken and many of them were dulled or rolled up on the ends after connecting with the loose rocks that were scattered around on the hillside.

"Hey, Snuffy," Curtiss asked, "where does a guy get a drink around here?"

"Down in the bottom of the draw," Snuffy told him, "swell little stream running through those willows."

"I'm headin' for water," Glenn said, "be back pronto."

We all sat down and had a smoke. Ken and I couldn't hardly wait for the big guy to return for we knew he went down the draw for but one purpose, and that was to inspect the hunk of bark.

It had only been a matter of seconds since we left the hillside but the squirrels were beginning to gather again. Among the group was a big gray. There's no open season on the grays and we were wondering how we'd manage to shoot around the pretty fellow.

It was a stiff climb from the stream to where we were, but Curtiss came bounding up like a young deer. To Snuffy, who wasn't wise to Glenn's jaunt, the big boy looked just like a guy that had gone and had a drink for himself. To Ken and me he seemed to have something up his sleeve.

He buckled on his quiver and braced his big yew bow. As he thumped the string a few times, he said, "two bits I get a digger before I shoot six arrows."

"I'm takin' it," said Snuffy, "and bettin' 'nother two bits that you don't get any with the quiver full."

"I'll call that, and bet you ham and eggs tonight that I get more than you do with the first arrow," the big guy answered.

"It's a deal; roll the dice."

Zing, zing went the bow strings. Arrows were flying and squirrels were jumping. Ken dropped one just back of the big gray. The bushy tail couldn't take it and scrammed up a big pine. Ken socked a broadhead fully two inches into the tree just ahead of him.

"Hold everything there, Ken," Snuffy snorted, "lay off the monkey foot."

"Whataya mean monkey foot?" Ken snapped, as he smacked another broadhead into the pine tree.

"We call the grays monkey feet," Snuffy told him, "because their feet look just like a monkey's. If you killed one I'd shore as h--- get the blame, for some of the mountain guys have accused me of eating gray squirrels already."

"And of course you wouldn't do a thing like that," Curtiss said sarcastically.

For better shooting positions we kept working back and forth along the dead line that Snuffy had arranged for us. As soon as I got close to Curtiss I whispered, "what'd you find?"

"Bacon grease," he hissed, "just common old bacon grease."

Well, I knew the stuff was good, all right, but was skeptical if Snuffy was using it. When Ken got in range I whispered to him, "The guy's using bacon grease." Ken just batted his eyes and shook his head; he didn't believe it, either.

But what shooting we had. There wasn't a million squirrels, of course, but they kept coming and as we stayed in one place we had the time of our lives. That guy Snuffy put us on the spot when he made us shoot so far but, after all, it was his idea.

(Continued on page 7)

Editorial

We usually do not make excuses when we are late but this month we have not an excuse but a reason for our tardiness. Everything seemed to be going fine and we were congratulating ourselves that for once we would be out on time, but while the compositor was setting Geo. Brommers' dog house article the linotype just couldn't take it and the heating unit burned out. Well, we can't blame the machine much; it has stood a lot.

The Scholastic Archery Bulletin, a mimeographed publication edited by Miss Natalie Reichart of Corvallis, Oregon, began with the October issue. It will contain archery news and information of interest to students and teachers.

Lieutenant Clarence G. Thompson, son of Dr. B. G. Thompson, has been appointed archery instructor for his regiment at Fort Bragg, N. C. He found little equipment on hand with which to start practice but found plenty of enthusiasm for the sport.

Kore Duryee has great ambitions, now that he has killed his second buck with bow and arrow and deer are too tame for him, to break into the exclusive Order of Moose Slayers. He was to leave Seattle on the 14th of November for Vancouver, B. C., for another moose hunt with Garrett and De Wolf.

The veteran bowmaker, W. I. King, of Eugene, Oregon, suffered a $200 loss when thieves broke into his workshop and stole bows, quivers, arrows, and carving tools. Mr. King is an excellent wood carver, having won prizes in National exhibitions, and he had a set of very fine carving tools. Mr. King's many archery friends throughout the country will be glad to learn that he is recovering from his recent illness and is able to be about his shop for a few hours each day. On a recent visit we found him just tuning up a violin he had just finished and we were privileged to sit in on the maiden performance of the new instrument.

The members of the Sherwood Archery Club have a novel sticker to advertise their club. It seems to be made by photographic process and bears the picture of members.

The only buck killed in the Washington state archery reserve was the trophy of Donald McKay of Seattle. We are promised more information about this buck later.

Olympic Bowmen League

The Seattle Archers are sponsoring the 14th Olympic Bowmen League mail tournament starting January 12, 1941, and lasting ten weeks.

Entries should be in by January 1, the acceptance of any entries after that date being optional with the committee. The entries will be limited to 50 teams. Entry fee is $5.00 per team.

The League round is 90 arrows at 30 yards at a standard 48 inch target face, shooting 6 arrows at each end, and it may be shot either indoors or out. Further information and entry blanks may be secured from Kore Duryee, Secretary, 301 White Bldg., Seattle, Wash.

Last Month's Who's Who

Upper left—R. L. Rimer of Silver Springs, N. Y., who was president of the Genesee County Archers, host club for the New York State Archery Tournament in 1932.

Upper center — Central Illinois archers at the annual fall invitational shoot of the Blackhawk Archery club at Decatur, Illinois, on September 27, 1931.

Lower center—The shooting lines at the National tournament, August 17-20, 1926, Polo Field, Bryn Mawr, Pa.; Dr. P. W. Crouch shooting and G. A. Mang of Buffalo, N. Y., with bow in hand.

Upper right—Miss Helen Thompson, archery instructor at the Greenbrier Golf and Tennis club, White Sulphur Springs, West Virginia, in 1931.

Lower right—Yes, of course, you know. It was Roy Case, senior and junior, at Racine, Wisconsin.

ADD ANOTHER NAME

(Continued from page 4)

yards—forty-five—fifty.

Twang.

It was Jack's bowstring. I'd forgotten about how smoothly he could get another arrow out of the quiver.

I glanced up at the coyote again, and there was that sight which thrills an archer to the very marrow of his bones—an arrow winging its way against the blue of the sky in a perfect arc, headed toward running game—and you only need one look to know it was going to be close.

I held my breath. It seemed as though time and eternity halted to watch. The coyote kept going. The arrow swung across the top of its flight and started down. Gosh, I knew it was going to be close. Gee whiz, what a shot. IT'S A HIT!

I let out a war whoop when I heard the thunk of that arrow.

It's only a forty-five pound bow, and it was sixty-five yards to the hit, but the blade of the broadhead was keen as a razor. It was one of those Ken Wilhelm broadheads which are built for penetration, and I'd sharpened them the night before, showing Jack how to sharpen broadheads for deer. The arrow isn't in very far, but it's far enough. The coyote's throwing his head back trying to snap at it. He's staggering—now he's turning, coming back downhill. Now he's down. I don't know when I picked my path across that barranca or up the other side, but I'm tearing up there, my face scratched with brush, the smell of sage dust bitterly acrid in the back of my nostrils. I'm running—Jack's already across. How the devil did he do it? I'm yelling, "Finish him! Shoot him! Put another arrow on!"

Jack's outwardly cool as a cucumber, but it needs only one look at his eyes to tell the story. And what a whale of a story it is. A neophyte out on his first actual hunting trip, bagging a running coyote as his first game. He socks an arrow right in the coyote's head. The blade penetrates the skull, and the coyote goes down and stays down.

It isn't just accident back of that shot. There have been hours of faithful practice. I started him out with a thirty-pound bow, had him shooting for nearly an hour into a hay bale, not more than fifteen feet away, paying no attention to where his arrow hit, simply building up his pull and release. Then we did some shooting at marks. Then he "graduated" to a heavier bow. He deserves every bit of it. But what a break! From neophyte to veteran coyote killer in three days.

And did I get a kick out of Jack. As I've said, he's an old-time hunter. He tried to be just a little above getting excited. But, boy oh boy, all the way home, all he could talk about was that kill, reconstructing every move he'd made—and every time, as we picked up one of the members of the party, and Jack had an opportunity to tell it all over again, you could see that it wasn't the most unpleasant chore he'd ever had to do in his life

So add another name to the list of archers.

SECRET OF GUT SHOT GAP

(Continued from page 5)

We'd kick dirt on them and actually turn some of them over but never killed or wounded a single one that round. When we retrieved the arrows I gathered several pieces of bark and pine cones but couldn't smell any bacon grease.

Ken was scraping something off a limb with a broadhead. Curtiss and I kept our eyes on the bird. Snuffy was so interested in getting his arrows and shooting again that he didn't suspect we were trying to check on him.

We headed for the other spot around the boulders, the three of us purposely lagging behind so Snuffy would take the lead. Ken turned around and whispered, "It's candle grease; look on the back of my quiver."

He'd wiped his broadhead on his quiver and left the stuff sticking there. He'd also scraped so much wood and dirt with it that we couldn't tell much about what it was.

If Snuffy would have been looking, he'd of seen first one, then the other of us dipping our finger in the stuff and not only sniffing it, but tasting it. I couldn't smell anything, but it did taste kind of greasy. Curtiss swore it was bacon grease. Ken said he knew it was from a candle.

We done some more shooting. The

sun was getting pretty hot and we gave up trying to find any more of the lure.

"What say, you guys, that we scram over to the shack and put on the nose bag, lay around a couple of hours and come back and smoke 'em some more later," Snuffy asked us.

He had to ask but once. We'd shot hundreds of times, our muscles ached worse than if we'd shot a double York with the hunting bows. Like the real host that he was, Snuffy rolled up his sleeves and was making sandwiches like a master chef. He'd brought in a chunk of roast meat as big as my hat and was neatly slicing it.

Did we go for that food! "Snuffy," I said, "did you ever try bacon grease or tallow candles as a lure for squirrels?"

"Are you having a good time or ain't yuh," he answered.

I had to admit it was the best time I'd ever had, and the most mysterious.

"Well," he said, "that's what I want you guys to do, but don't ask me any questions because I ain't puttin' out any information, savvy?"

We were sitting around a big table made from rough planks. As we went into the cabin we unloaded all our outfit on a wood pile out in the yard. We'd just about finished a sandwich when Snuffy made a dive for the coffee pot that had started to boil over.

For a hurry up job he'd removed a stove lid and placed the pot on the live coals. Cuss words were flying and Snuffy had his finger in his mouth.

"It would have to be the right finger," he said, "now it'll spoil my shootin'."

"Can't take it, eh?" Ken said, "making all that fuss over a little burn. Calm down, pal, you'll forget all about it when you get back shooting at squirrels."

Glenn Curtiss had ripped open his sandwich and was sniffing at the meat.

"Hey, Snuffy," he said.

"Yeah."

"You wouldn't eat a gray squirrel, would you?"

" 'Course not. Why?"

"Well, how many points did this roast have?"

"Ah, you're crazy, that's beef. Mom Hamrick over at Running Springs cooked it up for me only yesterday."

"Oh, yeah! Well, they don't call it beef where I came from."

Snuffy poured four cups of good smelling coffee and said to Ken, "Scram out to the cooler and grab a can of milk. You'll find it down under them wet sacks."

Ken made a dive to do as he'd been told. Snuffy had placed a few small sticks in the stove and was replacing the lid. The slab door of the cabin was standing half open, and was between Ken and Snuffy. Ken stopped in his tracks and leaned close to the door. He didn't say anything but kept pointing towards the wood pile.

Curtiss and I were all eyes and craned our necks to get a look. Prior to that moment we'd all just about forgotten the magic lure and was having a good time in general. What we seen on the wood pile quickly revived old thoughts and our curiosity was aroused stronger than ever.

The wood pile wasn't over three bow lengths from the door and there was a big bushy tail very much interested in Snuffy's quiver. He was the most handsome fellow I'd ever seen, as he stood there with his tail straight up in the air. Snuffy had the deer skin so full of arrows the squirrel couldn't get his head inside, but he was trying to.

Curtiss and I sat there in bewilderment. Ken headed straight for the quiver. We watched him from the corner of our eyes as he snatched it up and darted for the cooler. We'd seen Snuffy take a can from his quiver and smear something on the bark, yet it had never occurred to us to get our hands on that quiver.

Ken came in and set the can of milk on the table. He sat down and started munching his sandwich. As he was eating he kept shaking his head, and we could see that he had a hard time to keep from laughing out loud. I know Ken; I knew the guy had found out something, and was plenty surprised.

He kept snickering to himself. Snuffy sensed something wrong and asked Ken what was up. Ken caught Snuffy off guard and pulled a can from the inside of his shirt. He put it on the table with the label aimed at Glenn and I.

When we read that label we bust-
(Continued on page 9)

Letter Box

From Joe Cosner

Dear Davis:

You will, of course, excuse me for not contributing more freely during the last few months. Of course, it could be that it was the only real relief you have had since you took the SA to run. Be that as it may, George has been a terrible trial to me since he went to Washington. I have tried to remould his character and, as you know, I have had a job on my hands.

George responds to character remoulding much as a brush hut would to a tin roof. It can be done, but after it is done you find out that you have done a lot of hard work and wasted a lot of tin, and that you have a brush hut with a tin roof. So it is with George. I have him now where he is so cowed that he hardly dares do anything but yip once in a while. He tries to make out that the rest of us are losing our spine or following the string or something. On the contrary, he hardly dares talk. I can't get a letter from him once a month. He is deathly afraid he might say something that would bring me down on him again. Of course, I like the feeling of power that it gives me, but with all that, I am sorry now that I did it. I am considering the thing now, and may let him out again. He was better the way he was.

Maybe the strip I am sending (Look for this in next issue—Ed.) will cause Erle Gardner to cock his leg and wind up and throw an oration at someone. Here's hoping. He feels like Hitler would on confronting infantry armed with pea-shooters, but still he ought to let us shoot just one teeny weeny little pea at him before he lets the boom down. We would like to see the eruption.

John Yount violated a confidence of mine. He had allowed me to think that we had a beautiful friendship built up and based on a solid foundation of deer spore. He let me down by exposing the whole thing in the SA with the idea that he might have been kidding. At least, he was somewhat patronizing. I am beginnin to doubt that he is the expert that he said he was at first. I wish now that I had never sent him my diary of my recent hunt.

The Sylvan Archer is the one publication that I will always feel at home with. It is the first archery periodical that I ever saw, way back yonder, and to my mind is the homiest and nicest of them all. It features writers who can't write, and cartoonists who can't draw, and photographers who would make a good one groan, and out of all that you never fail to get out a copy that has something we can't put our finger on but are pleased to call homey. We like it as archers because, after all, it is "us guys." It is all of us. Not just a few good writers.

Please accept my kindest and best wishes. Thank you for being so tolerant with myself, as well as other oddities with which you deal from time to time. I mention no names.

Sincerely,
Joe Cosner.

SECRET OF GUT SHOT GAP
(Continued from page 8)

ed out laughing. Who wouldn't? The simplest little thing in the world, and something that's found in every household.

Snuffy was irked to think we had a joke and didn't let him in on it, but he soon got in on it, all right. When his wandering eyes got sight of that can, you should of seen the blue flame spurting through the cracks in the cabin.

"Why, you dirty double crossin' sons of he jackasses," he snarled. "Who in h--- got into my quiver? Might of known with you three mugs around that you'd get wise."

Since that time I've used the stuff several times. I found that the little desert squirrels will come right into the house for it. Rabbits like it, and other animals. Archers shouldn't be without it when they're in the woods. Any one who hasn't tried it before will think of Snuffy Walters if they ever use it.

Perhaps we wouldn't know a thing about it if Snuffy hadn't of gone in the timber to cut wood, and took his lunch in a paper sack. Folks, that label read, "PEANUT BUTTER."

Doghouse Doings

By George Brommers

Today I understand, there is a spirit of premature rejoicing in the State of Oregon. Our Webfoot friends seem to take it for granted that, just because your doghouse editor finally settled in Washington, the day of reckoning is over.

Have no such illusions, brother coon hunters. Do not think, Dr. Cathey, Major Williams, Dr. Hewett, Professor Thompson, J. E. Davis, and Frank Taylor, that you are going to be allowed to run wild from now on. I will see that proper measures are taken.

And let me warn you, you Californians, that I still have your number. Thanks to a visit of Colonel Pierce, and letters from George Miles and Ray Hodgson, I have enough dirt on you to make any outbreak a matter for prayerful consideration.

It is just because Washington has been allowed to run wild for fifteen years that the time has come for a showdown. Take Kore Duryee—

It hurts me to give the sordid details. It would have been a mighty lonesome winter for us up in the mountains if we hadn't been cheered by the visits of Louise and Pat Duryee. Kore, being excess baggage, had to be assimilated in the process, but what the heck? How did a charming lady like Louise pick such a lemon?

A few weeks ago I had business in Seattle. I knew that Kore needed a little uplift, so I called.

Not that day he didn't, brothers, not that day. He was talking over the telephone to Dr. Hoffman.

"A friend of mine," he said, "is looking for some wild life photos for a magazine article. I have given him one of a deer I just shot in British Columbia, but he wants more."

"What's that, you didn't know. Say, now that was some deer now. All of 300 pounds. I shot it at 400 yards. How many prongs? Oh, just two; they grow big up in that country, you know."

And so on, and so on. Dick and Billie Carter, Stamps, Partee, Sergeant Shaughnessy of Seattle's Finest, Leonard and Kay Carter, and about two dozen other victims before he stopped for breath. You will get the general idea, and admire the sound technique.

Miss Howard, that's Kore's secretary, looked unhappy. She could see where she would have to begin to train her boss all over again. I got Mrs. Duryee on the phone.

"Please," wailed Louise, "take that spouse of mine out for lunch, won't you. I just can't stand any more of him today. He and his deer. . . ."

I promised.

Just then Jane Duncan came into the office. Kore had promised her some venison, so that he would have a chance to impress her.

Jane looked properly impressed, the more so as the package was by this time strong enough to impress anybody. If Jane ever cooks it, she will have to use a nose clip, and the cats will stage a convention under her window. But never mind that.

We went out to lunch. Kore collared, in due order, the waitress, the proprietor, an insurance adjuster, two cops, a barber and a bootblack, gently breaking the news to them and modestly accepting their congratulations.

I suggested that he call the Associated Press and the news photographers, but Kore is, as I told you, a modest man. I suspect that he will accidently run into Royal Brougham of the P. I., and I more than suspect that Mr. Brougham will do his duty. Which is as it should be. Kore's deer has a real news value, second only to that of John Davis last year. What more can I say?

As this is written I do not know whether Mr. Roosevelt or Mr. Willkie will guide the destinies of the nation for the next four years. I do, however, know who is going to be the boss of the doghouse, and it will be a very smelly place to live in unless some of you fellows reform. A word to the wise. . . . .

There are two new impoundments to announce this month. E. Hill Turnock shot a score of 404 in the fifth sectional NFAA meet, and Larry Hughes shot 348 at Santa

Barbara. For what these gentlemen have done to advance interest in archery they are going to have honorary quarters in the penthouse, and cushions to sleep on if I have to take them off my own bunk.

The first national inter-scholastic archery tournament was held from October 21 to November 1, 1940, sponsored by the National Archery Association. The NAA also sponsors an inter-collegiate telegraphic match in April and May. Mrs. Myrtle Miller is chairman of the tournamet committee.

FIELD ARCHERS OF SOUTHERN CALIFORNIA
By Elmer Bedwell, Secretary

The first field meet of the fall was held on the roving range in the Arroyo Seco at Pasadena. The settling of the dust by the recent rains and the autumn colors on the trees and shrubs made the day for the tournamen perfect.

The following emerged as victors: Men's championship class — Roland Quavle, gold bar; Larry Hughes, silver bar. Men's general division— Dr. Erwin Pletcher, championship medal; D. K. Olson, red ribbon; Philip Conrad, white ribbon.

Ladies' championship division—Naomi Baker, gold bar; Ruth Hathaway, silver bar. Ladies' general division—Eva Bedwell, blue ribbon; Gene Bacon, red ribbon; Babe Bitzenburger, white ribbon.

In the junior division Bob King won the Bedwell Trophy for that division, but owing to the fact that he was the only junior competing, he refused to take the trophy, preferring to wait until the next tournament and have competition with the winning.

Our President, Edmund M. Brock, has just spent four days this last month in the north representing our organization, and doing some hard work toward helping our cause in getting a reserve for the archers.

Southern California archers are all looking forward to the next major event in California archery this fall, the State Field Archery Tournament, to be held at Redlands. We hope to greet many Central and Northern California archers as well as some from out of state.

The next S.C.F.A.A. tournament will be held at the Redlands roving range, December 22, with a turkey shoot included.

From the Utah Hills
"Deer Hunt, '39"

There's a camp fire a-waiting,
  And a stew pot a-boiling;
A glad cry of welcoming
  After a hard day of toiling.

The sun has just set,
  And the coyotes are calling;
The breeze has come up,
  And dry leaves start falling.

And Archers come striding down
  From the hills.

Welcome to the camp fire,
  Unstrap your arrows,
Unstring your good bow,
  And warm to the marrow.

Fill up with stew
  And tell us your story
Of the deer you had seen
  (And those you had missed;)
It will all be unfolded as Archers glory.

And Hunters came striding down
  from the Hills.

Oh! There is nothing so fine
  As a camp fire's bright glow,
With the coffee pot boiling,
  And lighted up faces of Archers you know.

There's a heaven full of stars,
  An owl in the hollow,
Sleepy Archers pile in,
  All dream of the morrow.

And Archers striding down with their kills.
        —F. H. Zimbeaux.

Parachutists May Sit on Arrows

It is learnt from the newspapers that Mr. J. H. Davey, Platoon Leader, Home Guard, bears his trusty bow and arrows (points sharpened) as well as his revolver when out on duty. The parachutists may not like it!

Moreover Messrs. Jaques of Hatton Garden tells us that some people in the country are ordering high-class bows of yew, and arrows with hardened barbed steel points for possible use against parachutists.

Soldiers in lonely places have taken up archery in their spare time.

—Archery News (England).

SUBSCRIBERS PLEASE NOTICE
A cross appearing in this space means that your subscription has expired and we would appreciate your prompt renewal so that your name may be kept on our mailing list.

CLASSIFIED ADVERTISING

RATES for Classified Advertising 5 cents per word per issue. Count initials and numbers as words. Minimum charge is 50 cents.

BOOKS AND MAGAZINES

The AMERICAN ARCHER, a national quarterly, $1.00 per year, 521 Fifth Ave., New York City.

"ARCHERY TACKLE, HOW TO MAKE AND HOW TO USE IT." by Adolph Shane. Bound in cloth and illustrated with more than fifty drawings and photographs. Information for making archery tackle and instructions for shooting. Price is $1.75. Send orders to Ye Sylvan Archer, 505 North 11th street, Corvallis.

"ARCHERY," by Robert P. Elmer M. D., revised edition, most complete book on archery published. 566 pages of valuable information for colleges, libraries, schools, camps archery clubs and individuals. Price $5.00 postpaid. orders to Ye Sylvan Archer, 505 North 11th street, Corvallis, Oregon.

RELICS AND CURIOS

INDIAN RELICS, Beadwork, Coins, Curios, Books, Minerals, Weapons. Old West Photos. Catalog, 5c. Genuine African Bow, $3.75. Ancient flint arrowheads, perfect, 6c each—Indian Museum, Osborne, Kansas.

THE FLAT BOW
HUNT & METZ

70 pages of Archery information for 50 cents, well illustrated. Ye Sylvan Archer, 505 N. 11th St., Corvallis, Oregon.

A Solid Book for the Serious Archer

THE NEW ARCHERY
By Paul H. Gordon

The most comprehensive treatment of archery available. A professional maker "comes clean" on the best methods of his craft in this unusual book for serious archer, novice and general reader.

CONTENTS:

Target Making. All wooden bow types. Hunting Tackle. Fitted and Footed Arrows. Accessories. Special Equipment. Easy craft approach for the novice. Advanced projects for the highly skilled. Illustrated. $3.50.

At All Booksellers

D. Appleton - Century Co.
35 W. 32nd St.   New York

Please mention Ye Sylvan Archer when writing advertisers.

CHANDLER
PAT. PEND

TARGET SET BALANCED

Interchangeable Arrow Points
PRICES CUT NEARLY 50%
The prices now are cut so low,
Yet the quality is so great,
Every archer now should know,
That he cannot afford to wait.
See the dealer nearest ye,
Or mail your order in to me.
Free Catalogue.
T. B. CHANDLER
11819 - 4th Ave.   Compton, Calif.

FISH HEAD A-80

SMALL HUNTING SET BALANCED

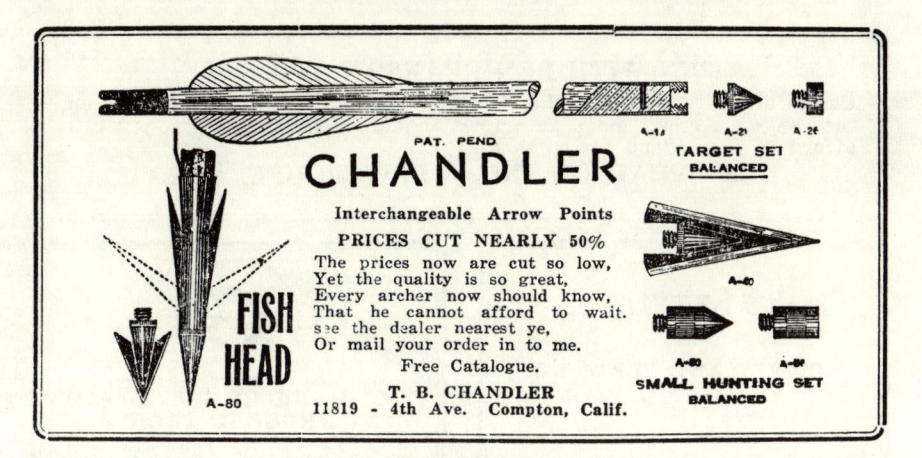

BEAR
ALUMINUM ARROWS ARE MAKING RECORDS
BEAR PRODUCTS CO.
2611 W. Philadelphia Ave., Detroit, Michigan

Ye Sylvan Archer—$1.00 per year.

DO YOU LIKE THE CHARM OF THE BACKHILLS?
If so — read ARCADIAN LIFE MAGAZINE. It tells the story of the Ozarks in a way that will captivate you.

$1.00 a year; 25c a copy. Classified advertising (for archers) 2c a word.

O. E. RAYBURN, Editor
Caddo Gap, Arkansas

E. BUD PIERSON
Bowyer — Fletcher
Tournament Tackle, Sinew, Glue, Raw Materials.
245 University Ave
CINCINNATI, OHIO
Custom Made Tackle

Write us for your needs in Archery books.   Ye Sylvan Archer.

YEW BOW TIMBER
High Altitude Air Seasoned Billets and Staves of Quality and Variety.
W. G. PRESCOTT
527 Chestnut   Ashland, Ore.

WESTERN ANTIQUES COLLECTOR

Corvallis, Oregon
P. O. Box 403

A monthly illustrated magazine devoted to items of interest to the collector of antiques.

$1.50 per year.

The Flat Bow—70 pages of Archery information for 50 cents, well illustrated. *Ye Sylvan Archer, 505 N. 11th St., Corvallis, Oregon.*

WIN WITH BEN PEARSON ARROWS

Beautiful and accurate to the Nth degree but win their real laurels on the range. Arrows made as arrows should be—and at prices you can afford to pay. Send for catalogue.

BEN PEARSON, INC. — PINE BLUFF, ARK.

Cassius Hayward Styles

BOWYER AND FLETCHER

—Tackle that has stood the test—

28 Vicente Place

BERKELEY, CALIFORNIA

**BACK NUMBERS
YE SYLVAN ARCHER**
Volumes I to V Inclusive
$1.00 Per Volume
B. G. THOMPSON
R. F. D. 1, Corvallis, Oregon

THE FLAT BOW
HUNT & METZ

70 pages of Archery information for 50 cents, well illustrated. Ye Sylvan Archer, 505 N. 11th St., Corvallis, Oregon.

BOWS · ARROWS · MATERIALS

HANDBOOK—How to Make and Use Bows and Arrows—90 Pages well illustrated (with catalog) 35c.

CATALOG—100 pictures—color spread—Instruction Folder. 10c.

CATALOG alone 5c. Stamps or Coin.

L·E·STEMMLER · QUEENS VILLAGE · N·Y·

G

"THE MARK OF DISTINCTION IN ARCHERY TACKLE"
Fine Yew Target and Hunting Bows, Plain or Backed with Rawhide. Lemonwood Bows with Rawhide Backs.
College and School Equipment
Target, Hunting and Roving Arrows
Price List on Request
Wholesale — Retail
EARL GRUBBS
5518 W. Adams
Los Angeles, : California

Paul H. Gordon, Director
Beacon Hill Craftsmen
Beacon, N. Y.

Where the serious archer's needs and desires are really consulted, and his orders exactly filled. Nothing too simple or too difficult.

Write for Complete Catalog

**$1.25 PER DOZ.
BIG GAME HEADS
(ACTUAL SIZE)
WOLVERINE ARCHERY TACKLE
COLDWATER, MICH.**

Ye Sylvan Archer

A Merry Christmas
and
A Happy New Year

December, 1940

Corvallis, Oregon

Vol. 12   No. 8

Ye Sylvan Archer

"A magazine for the field archers"

Vol. 12   December, 1940   No. 8

Published the fifteenth of each month
for archers by archers
505 North 11th Street, Corvallis, Oregon

J. E. DAVIS .... Editor
RUSSELL JONES .... Business Manager
Subscription Price .... $1.00 Per Year
Foreign Subscription .... $1.25 Per Year
Single Copies .... 10 Cents
Advertising Rates on Application

TABLE OF CONTENTS

                                                                Page

THE BOND OF THE BOW
    By Capt. Cassius H. Styles 1

KIT-CHEE-WAH-BOOS
    By B. G. Thompson 3

EDITORIAL 4

CALIFORNIA STATE TOURNAMENT
    By John L. Yount 5

INTERSCHOLASTIC TOURNAMENT 6

MICHIGAN REPORTS
    By Lulu Stalker 7

NFAA NEWS NOTES
    By John L. Yount 7

NAA COMMITTEES 8

The Bond of the Bow

ARTHUR YOUNG IN EARLY FIELD ARCHERY

By Capt. Cassius H. Styles

Friendship, real and very deep, has always been the lifeblood of archery in its heroic chapters. The devotion of the Thompson brothers, Will and Maurice, we know, brought forth the adventures so happily told in the "Witchery of Archery." Next, it was the friendship of the hearty California trio, Will Compton, Saxton Pope and Arthur Young, that made their broadhead a recognized big game weapon. I never heard one of the three cronies speak of any of the others but that he was lighted up by beaming happiness. Compton's first words to me, of Arthur Young, I shall never forget. Their tenderness surprised me, for Will Compton was indeed a hardy, flint-framed pioneer if I ever saw one; his voice became gentle and low as he said, "Now, there's a lovable fellow." Indeed, everyone loved this stately bowman.

Compton taught Arthur the Sioux four-finger draw, and was with him when they got their first bow-killed deer. The young man had hunted much in the mountains during his boyhood, and was a really competent woodsman before he thought of the bow. The bow-carrying trio proved themselves as deer slayers before they tried panther and black bear. This period, spent in the baffling study of close stalks upon blacktail bucks, was a far more difficult one than we ordinarily realize, for then they had everything to learn—shooting technique; making of tackle when there was no field archer whose gear they could look over; and they had to manage to undergo scornful ridicule from all sides. That they did not master all, we now well know, though no one today is made the butt of so much scorn as they were. As we hunt each year we respect their findings with more and more comprehension and deep gratitude. And I, for one, envy the long hunting friendship that held them together, and carried them onward.

Arthur Young was the best shot of the trio. He was one of the very few men I have seen who was really master of an 80 pound hunting bow. This was not because he was gifted with enormous strength; he commanded that bow because he was not too lazy to practice with simple persistence. He was a violinist with enough real talent to give finished recitals with the same hand that gripped his heavy shooting gear. His shooting was as artistic as a recital, and almost as thrilling. When you watched his broadheads chop up a wad of paper the size of your hand, arrow after arrow pounding it, at a

"They did master all, we now well know."

distance of 20 yards, then you understood how so much game fell before him.

He studied shooting as one would who was not only an artist but a scientist. For instance, he told me never to waste any strength at full draw in getting a line—that I should have my arrow always in line, from the very first part of the draw. Thus I could drive all my attention into the loose, wasting no energy or attention when under the full load of holding. His work on dangerous game proved that he studied well.

Arthur was always in dead earnest about the bow. To go on one hunt with his comrades, Pope and Compton, he was obliged to give up his position; he gave it up right off, the doctor told me. I've heard of no one else who ever did this.

The three great strokes he made, bagging a Montana grizzly, next a Kadiak bear, and finally a magnificent black-maned African lion—each of these with a single arrow, not backed by any fire arms—these three acts I say were decisive victories for future sportsmen, comparable in the history of conservation to those victories in American warfare, Yorktown and Gettysburg. They were against high odds; the grizzly has strength such that he can with an indifferent cuff of the paw send an 80-pound pack of camp grub sailing 60 feet through the air. Such force we can hardly believe to be inherent to any muscle or animal tissue. It is like the ripping power of a high-explosive shell, except that a grizzly repeats, and the H. E. can blow up but once. You may be sure that Arthur knew this well when he stood in the high grass of that Alaskan meadow near the salmon riffles, with four great Kadiaks just about to play croquet with him, and only his strung bow with which to protect himself and the camera man. Even as he shot, one of them, a female, started to charge from his right. Very fortunately it changed its mind when it saw Arthur's arrow lay low its enormous comrade, and veered off to disappear in the brush. If this sow grizzly hadn't veered off we never would have seen the movie of this item of unbelievable coolness and skill.

Arthur's bow was not backed up by a gun at any time on the Alaskan trip, nor was it when he shot the Montana *Ursus horribilis*, or on the occasion next to be referred to, an incident of the African Odessey. This anecdote really closed the story of Pope, Compton and Young, and their years with the bow.

How many people know what a "boma" is like? Few, I'm sure. It is just a brush heap, over which, or into which any lion could leap, if he forgot his etiquette. It is a briar structure that would collapse if any heavy person leaned against it, yet Simba will not even strike such a heap of sticks, due to some very strict code of veldt conduct, and a similar regard for his hide. So, fancy yourself in such a twig igloo with a lion 20 feet from you, eating kongoni. You shoot him with an arrow. He knows instantly from what angle came the assault, as alert wild animals can do, and with a roar bounds to the door of the boma. Pope said that if he had dipped the upper nock of his bow downward a foot he could have touched the animal's yellow jaw! Lions aren't supposed to enter bomas. This is a pretty well accepted precedent. (Likewise, they knew when they came to Africa that lions couldn't climb trees—and the very first one the archers met climbed a tree.)

It was a moment of mental strain. Fate had it that the lion's mental poise snapped first. As the Doctor said, "fear clutched the great beast," and he turned away, and ran. He left his slayer, Arthur Young, a victory so thrilling and inspiring that scores, even hundreds of men are now hunting with the bow and the broad arrow.

Now I shall copy the sentence with which Dr. Pope closed his account of this African incident: "In such moments as this, grasping the hand of Arthur Young over the body of that fallen monarch, the triumph is not only that of the hunter over the beast, but one of enduring friendship."

Kit-Chee-Wah-Boos

By B. G. Thompson, Corvallis, Oregon

Some ten years ago, while driving through a high mountain valley in Grant County, Oregon, I first met *Kit-chee-wah-boos* (White-tailed jack rabbit to you.). I had heard a lot about the beauty of this largest of American rabbits, but the grace and beauty of the magnificent specimen which crossed the road in front of me surpassed all expectations. It was the largest rabbit I had ever seen. It was a light silvery-gray in color with snow-white tail which it held, not down like a black-tailed jack, nor up like a cotton-tail, but straight out behind like the flag of a white-tailed deer.

What a trophy for an archer!

As it crossed the road in front of me and bounded up the hillside in rod-long leaps, it switched its tail from side to side; in fact, its every movement suggested a deer rather than a rabbit. What a trophy he would make for an archer!

The white-tailed jack, *Lepus townsendii*, has many names. Prairie hare, Rocky Mountain hare, Townsend hare and white jack rabbit are a few. The Indians called it Kit-chee-wah-boos (big white rabbit) and that, we think, is a very good name.

The literature states that this rabbit is the largest and fastest rabbit found in temperate North America. The weight of an adult as given is from seven to twelve pounds. It is silvery-gray in summer and nearly all white in winter. The tail, which is three to four inches long, is white, even in summer. It has long hind legs and when crowded moves in long leaps. Leaps of over twenty feet have been recorded. It is not gregarious; seldom are more than two adult rabbits found in a given locality.

My second contact with Kit-chee-wah-boos was in 1937 when I discovered him in the archery hunting reserve on Canyon Creek. Since then, each hunting season, I have hunted more and more for the white jack.

When the 1940 deer season rolled around, my main objective was Kit-chee-wah-boos. Deer were of secondary consideration. But the results were the same as before. I saw rabbits. I shot at rabbits — standing shots at 30 yards — but no hits. I began to despair of ever connecting with one of these wily creatures.

Finally, on November 21, came word from the Williams' that four large whitetailed rabbits were working on their garden and something should be done about it.

It took considerable talking to convince friend wife of the necessity of making a 600 mile trip just to hunt a rabbit. If it was a white rabbit I wanted, one of the neighbor boys had one which he would sell for 50 cents, etc., etc. Finally, son Ted decided he wanted to go, too. With

(Continued on page 6)

Editorial

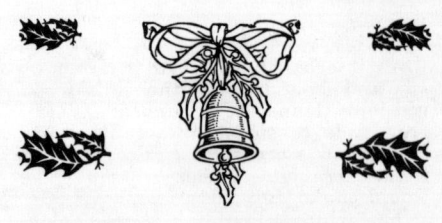

A Merry Christmas and A Happy New Year

Archers in Massachusetts are agitated over the laws which exist in that state which prevent Sunday shooting on public property. They are planning to devise legislation to permit the holding of tournaments on Sundays where grounds are distant from churches. Shooting on private ranges is permitted but the law controls public properties where competition is involved.

We are pleased that someone in the editorial family has at last accomplished something in archery. Marion, the editor's younger daughter, who is a freshman at Oregon State College, has won the Keasey Arrow tournament. This tournament is held each year for the girls in the beginners' classes in archery at O.SC. The trophy was presented by Gilman Keasey, and is an arrow used by him in a National championship tournament. Names and scores of winners of each shoot are inscribed on small round tags which are attached to the arrow. First score to win was 507, that of Lorraine Bewley in 1935; highest score to date, 90-726, that of Doris Brown in 1939; highest score in 1940, Marion Davis, 90-654.

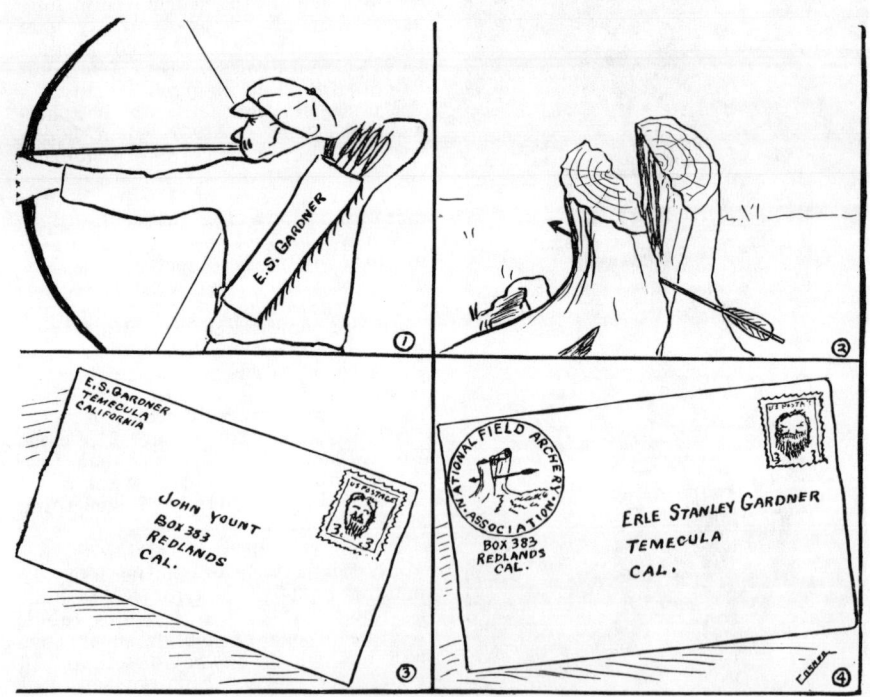

Does Cosner Expose a Conspiracy?

California State Tournament

By John L. Yount

It may sound egotistical for me to say that I believe the first annual California State Field Tournament was a success, when it was held in my home town, and the Redlands club managed to work in a number of our pet ideas, but I still think it was a good shoot.

The weather on Saturday, November 9, was not what we expected as it was somewhat more than chilly and put up a first class threat of rain. This was enough to keep a few of the Southern California archers at home. Some of the boys down this way are a bunch of pansies when it comes to weather. Sunday was perfect. A real made-to-order day.

We had two full twenty-eight target courses. One is in as near perfect condition as any course I have seen. The other, while new, is in reasonably good shape.

The most noticeable thing about this meet was that it was one of the first big Western tournaments to live up to its name. This was really a state tournament, with every part of the state well represented. To get an idea of what this means, one must remember that there is room for about four Eastern states between Los Angeles and the San Francisco Bay region, and our state keeps on going both ways.

The California State Championship was won by Larry Hughes with 1263 points for the two days. Second place medal went to Willard Bacon, 1101 points, and the bronze medal to Merle Hathaway with 1069. The following archers, who were kept out of Saturday's competition by work and not weather, might have had something to say about the results had they been on hand both days: Roland Quayle, 641 for one day's score; Thomas Farnsworth, 525; Nate Rogan, 518; and Erwin Pletcher, 511. Anywhere near double those scores would have given the winners something to worry about— not that they didn't have their troubles as it was. Truman Farnsworth and Dawson Feathers, with 1025 and 992, respectively, were right on their heels.

In the ladies' division, it was Gene Bacon, first, with 834, an average of better than 208 points for each 28 targets. Eva Bedwell, second, with 788, and Babe Bitzenberger third, scoring 608. Gentlemen, I have seen many a wild-talking, hairy-chested, he-man field archer who couldn't even come close to this kind of shooting.

The Battle Clout

The battle clout was what might be termed an "upset." Here we had the pick of the state's broadhead experts, each with the tackle he had carried on his last hunting trip. Their arrows were balanced to the bow and both made to fit the man. This perfect combination naturally made for some mighty fine shooting. The only fly in the ointment was that a certain P. K. Dugan, who had never before shot a broadhead, borrowed a set of them and, I believe, a bow, and won for himself the finest trophy offered in the tournament.

Field Tackle Flight

This event was put into the novelty class by being shot under a special set of rules. In the first place, a field resembling an elongated football field was laid out. The side lines were 100 feet apart with the first cross line at 180 yards. Cross lines were then placed every 20 yards. The tackle used had to be the same as was used in the roving round that morning. All contestants shot six arrows and the event was scored as follows:

Only the arrows between the side-lines counted. An arrow that fell between the 180 and 200 yard line counted one point; between the 200 and 220 yard lines, 2 points, etc. All six arrows were scored and the archer with the highest score won. It made no difference whose single arrow flew the longest distance. We paid off not only for distance but for consistency and accuracy. One thing can be said for this event, it saved the officials a lot of headaches, and here is one who has never found much of anything else in a flight shoot.

First place was won by Walt Wilhelm with a score of 31. Second place, Jack Willard, 30, and third place went to Ken Wilhelm with 26 points.

In the ladies' flight shoot, the shooting line was moved forward 30 yards, since 180 yards is quite a shot with a roving arrow and a light bow. The winner was Babe Bitzenberger, scoring 16 points. Second, Ruth Mace with 12, and third place, Ruth Hathaway, with 11 points.

New Officers

The business meeting was held Saturday night, which left Sunday free for a swell chicken dinner and nothing but fun to end a big two-day tournament. Edmund Brock, of Los Angeles, was elected the new state president; H. C. Macquarrie, Oakland, succeeds himself as Vice-President, and John L. Yount, Redlands, was elected secretary-treasurer.

KIT-CHEE-WAH-BOOS

(Continued from page 3)

two against one we succeeded in convincing the girl friend, and at 3:30 A. M. the next morning we were on our way.

In spite of ice and snow we reached the Williams ranch by noon and immediately set out after rabbits. The ground was covered with snow and we felt sure that this time we would get our rabbit.

We finally jumped one but he was as wild as a deer. The last we saw of him he was going away from there over a ridge a half mile away, still making fifteen feet at a bound.

We continued on down the ridge and into a thicket of jack pines. Ted spied a rabbit under a bush about ten feet away. It was so close he missed. The rabbit ran about fifty yards and sat up in plain view. Suddenly he flattened out on his belly in the snow, crawled about six feet and "froze." If I had not had my eye on him at the time, I surely would have lost sight of him; and when once lost they are hard to spot, being just the color of the snow. They will lie quietly in the snow and allow you to pass within a few feet of them without moving.

I sneaked up until I could see his head and shoulders between two small pines. I looked first at the rabbit and then at the trees, and wondered if I could get an arrow between them. I must have been looking at the tree on the left—anyhow, that is what I hit.

The rabbit bounded off for a hundred yards, stopped, and again went through the crawling and freezing process. I got up to within forty yards and missed again. The rabbit headed back into the pines.

We located him again and this time I managed to put an arrow through his heart. He was a beauty, snow-white except for the black tips of his ears and a little gray on the shoulders and legs. He only weighed nine and a half pounds, but looked as big to me as J. E. Davis' buck deer. Ted was as excited as if we had killed a deer. I was pretty much elated myself. Carefully we carried him to the house and posed for pictures.

The next morning we headed for home by way of Burns. As we came down into Bear Valley, Ted spied a rabbit under a sage bush. He quickly strung a bow and stood on the running board as I backed up. His first arrow was cleanly through the shoulders. Ted's rabbit was almost a "dead ringer" for mine, except it had considerably more gray on the shoulders and back.

Interscholastic Tournaments

The first Interscholastic Archery tournament, sponsored by the NAA and directed by Mrs. Myrtle Miller, chairman, has just been completed. About twenty-five teams took part. Bloomfield High School of Bloomfield, N. J., took first place among the girls' teams with a score of 428-2888. There were six girls on each team, and they shot a junior Columbia round.

In second and third place were the first and second teams of Salinas Union High School of Salinas, California, with scores of 410-2474 and 362-2024, respectively. The boys shot a junior American round. In first place was the Will Rogers High School of Tulsa, Oklahoma. There were entries from more than ten states.

Michigan Reports

By Lulu Stalker

Deer hunting in Michigan with bow and arrow was probably a lot like deer hunting in any other state—a grand vacation among congenial friends in God's "Great Out-of-doors," with about as much chance of getting a buck as of winning the jackpot on a nickel machine. But—jackpots are now won and bucks are shot and there's no law against hoping!

As far as we can determine, only six or seven deer were bagged with over six hundred archers in the wood throughout the state. The concentation of Flint and Detroit archers was around St. Helen, near the Ogemaw deer reserve; the concentration of legal bucks was elsewhere. While many bowmen preferred cabins or sportsman clubs, our immediate camp consisted of a little village of trailers and tents in the heart of the State Forest. Five women were included in our group and all agree that if you have never tried winter camping, you've missed something.

The writer counted fifty-seven doe and fawn in one day's ride along the trails but only two bucks; one of which provided her with admission into the famed Society of Buck Missers recently described by Ye Editor. Many archers reported one or more shots at reasonable distances but the big ones still got away. One "Honest Abe" confessed to loosing five arrows at a bewildered spikehorn before the "target" decided to travel for his health. State records released after the bowmen had reached camp, show more than four thousand bucks taken out of this county alone last year by the gunmen, which might explain their scarcity this season.

An archer in a neighboring camp decided, with apparently no shooting available, he would record the movements of some of the deer population with his movie camera. A proof of his whereabouts, perhaps? As he ground away, out stepped a spikehorn and wonderingly watched the proceedings. The archer element in him quickly submerging the photographer, he put down his camera, picked up his bow and bagged his quarry.

The first buck obtained in our camp has heretofore provided a barbecue or banquet for all the archers in the vicinity but as no meat was forthcoming this year, we had a feed anyway at Luke's Place, a food dispensary near St. Helen, sort of an unofficial headquarters for archers. Following this, two prominent attorneys, A. J. Michelson of Flint, president of the Michigan Archery association, and his former partner, Leo Lange, now of Detroit, provided frolicking entertainment by staging an impromptu mock trial, charging one Bob Cooper, Detroit, with trespassing on the "preserves" of "His Majesty, Franklyn the Third."

For the past two years all Michigan has had a special archery deer season two weeks in advance of the regular season. There is much talk of a further concession to be made: that is, allowing archers to take does. This is due to the excessive doe count in the state, far exceeding the natural food supply. The subject is still in a controversial stage, however, as most bowmen have no desire to shoot does.

After interviewing scores of archers, the concensus of opinion seems to be that taking inventory of the exercise, fresh air, clean fun and fellowship enjoyed, the State owes us nothing on our unfilled licenses. Besides, we learned some things and maybe next year—who knows?

NFAA News Notes
By John L. Yount

NFAA FIELD OFFICERS

The honor of being the first elected officers of the National Field Archers Association goes to the following, who have just been elected to the Executive Committee: T. C. Davidson, Springfield, N. J., is Eastern representative; Fred Bear, Detroit, Michigan, Midwestern member, and H. C. Macquarrie, Oakland, California, from the West.

We expect to be able in the next issue of Ye Sylvan Archer to give not only the names of the new chairman and secretary-treasurer, but also the new committees. This should give time to really plan next summer's activities. In that connection, if you have any suggestions to make, please put them in order and be ready to send them to the proper committee.

Big Game Pin

We have just received the first of the Art Young Award pins and find them more handsome than expected, so if you have an idea that you might possibly be entitled to one send in all information and a photo, if possible, and let the Association be the judge.

NAA Committees

The personnel of the several committees of the National Archery Association are as follows:

Legal—Duryee, chairman, Folberth and Kloss.

Membership—Turnock, chairman, Palmatier and Hodgson.

Rules—Hodgson, chairman, Dorsey and Shenk.

Publicity—Folberth, chairman, Dorsey and Turnock.

Field archery—Palmatier, chairman, Duryee and Shenk.

Classification — Shenk, chairman, Dorsey and Kloss.

Affiliated clubs—Kloss, chairman, Duryee and Turnock.

Medal of Honor—Louis C. Smith, chairman, Klopsteg and Styles.

Ladies—Mrs. Frances Styles, chairman, Mrs. Carl Oelschlager and Miss Ann Weber.

International — Dr. Elmer, chairman, Nagler and Titcomb.

Scholastic — Mrs. Myrtle Miller, chairman, Mrs. Jackson, Miss Natalie Reichart and Mr. F. D. Stern.

CLASSIFIED ADVERTISING

RATES for Classified Advertising 5 cents per word per issue. Count initials and numbers as words. Minimum charge is 50 cents.

BOOKS AND MAGAZINES

"ARCHERY TACKLE, HOW TO MAKE AND HOW TO USE IT." by Adolph Shane. Bound in cloth and illustrated with more than fifty drawings and photographs. Information for making archery tackle and instructions for shooting. Price is $1.75. Send orders to Ye Sylvan Archer, 505 North 11th street, Corvallis.

The AMERICAN ARCHER, a national quarterly, $1.00 per year, 521 Fifth Ave., New York City.

"ARCHERY," by Robert P. Elmer M. D., revised edition, most complete book on archery published. 566 pages of valuable information for colleges, libraries, schools, camps archery clubs and individuals. Price $5.00 postpaid. orders to Ye Sylvan Archer, 505 North 11th street, Corvallis, Oregon.

RELICS AND CURIOS

INDIAN RELICS, Beadwork, Coins, Curios, Books, Minerals, Weapons. Old West Photos. Catalog, 5c. Genuine African Bow, $3.75. Ancient flint arrowheads, perfect, 6c each—Indian Museum. Osborne, Kansas.

SUBSCRIBERS PLEASE NOTICE

A cross appearing in this space means that your subscription has expired and we would appreciate your prompt renewal so that your name may be kept on our mailing list.

BACK NUMBERS
YE SYLVAN ARCHER
Volumes I to V Inclusive
$1.00 Per Volume
B. G. THOMPSON
R. F. D. 1, Corvallis, Oregon

WIN WITH BEN PEARSON ARROWS

Beautiful and accurate to the Nth degree but win their real laurels on the range. Arrows made as arrows should be—and at prices you can afford to pay. Send for catalogue.

BEN PEARSON, INC. — PINE BLUFF, ARK.

Cassius Hayward Styles

BOWYER AND FLETCHER

—Tackle that has stood the test—

28 Vicente Place

BERKELEY, CALIFORNIA

G

"THE MARK OF DISTINCTION IN ARCHERY TACKLE"
Fine Yew Target and Hunting Bows, Plain or Backed with Rawhide. Lemonwood Bows with Rawhide Backs.
College and School Equipment
Target, Hunting and Roving Arrows
Price List on Request
Wholesale — Retail
EARL GRUBBS
5518 W. Adams
Los Angeles, : California

---

70 pages of Archery information for 50 cents, well illustrated. Ye Sylvan Archer, 505 N. 11th St., Corvallis, Oregon.

YEW BOW TIMBER
High Altitude Air Seasoned Billets and Staves of Quality and Variety.
W. G. PRESCOTT
527 Chestnut   Ashland, Ore.

HANDBOOK—How to Make and Use Bows and Arrows—90 Pages well illustrated (with catalog) 35c.

CATALOG—100 pictures—color spread—Instruction Folder. 10c.

CATALOG alone 5c. Stamps or Coin.

L·E·STEMMLER· QUEENS VILLAGE·N·Y·

A Solid Book for the Serious Archer

THE NEW ARCHERY
By Paul H. Gordon

The most comprehensive treatment of archery available. A professional maker "comes clean" on the best methods of his craft in this unusual book for serious archer, novice and general reader.

CONTENTS:
Target Making. All wooden bow types. Hunting Tackle. Fitted and Footed Arrows. Accessories. Special Equipment. Easy craft approach for the novice. Advanced projects for the highly skilled. Illustrated. $3.50.

At All Booksellers

D. Appleton - Century Co.
35 W. 32nd St.   New York

CHANDLER
PAT. PEND

Interchangeable Arrow Points

PRICES CUT NEARLY 50%

The prices now are cut so low,
Yet the quality is so great,
Every archer now should know,
That he cannot afford to wait.
see the dealer nearest ye,
Or mail your order in to me.

Free Catalogue.

T. B. CHANDLER
11819 - 4th Ave.   Compton, Calif.

FISH HEAD A-80

TARGET SET BALANCED

SMALL HUNTING SET BALANCED

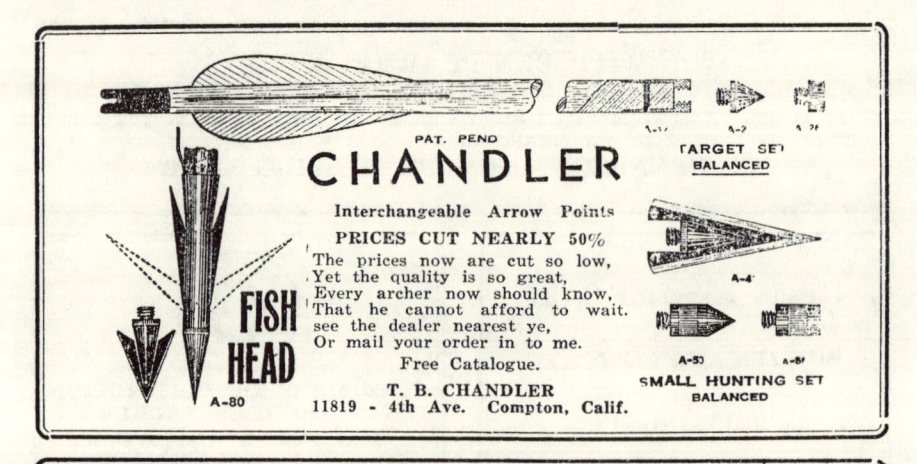

BEAR
ALUMINUM ARROWS ARE MAKING RECORDS
BEAR PRODUCTS CO.
2611 W. Philadelphia Ave., Detroit, Michigan

Ye Sylvan Archer—$1.00 per year.

DO YOU LIKE THE CHARM OF THE BACKHILLS?

If so — read ARCADIAN LIFE MAGAZINE. It tells the story of the Ozarks in a way that will captivate you.

$1.00 a year; 25c a copy. Classified advertising (for archers) 2c a word.

O. E. RAYBURN, Editor
Caddo Gap, Arkansas

YEW BOW TIMBER
High Altitude Air Seasoned Billets and Staves of Quality and Variety.

W. G. PRESCOTT
527 Chestnut   Ashland, Ore.

WESTERN ANTIQUES COLLECTOR

Corvallis, Oregon
P. O. Box 403

A monthly illustrated magazine devoted to items of interest to the collector of antiques.

$1.50 per year.

E. BUD PIERSON
Bowyer — Fletcher
Tournament Tackle, Sinew, Glue, Raw Materials.
245 University Ave
CINCINNATI, OHIO
Custom Made Tackle

Write us for your needs in Archery books. Ye Sylvan Archer.

The Flat Bow—70 pages of Archery information for 50 cents, well illustrated. Ye Sylvan Archer, 505 N. 11*th* St., Corvallis, Oregon.

Ye Sylvan Archer

January, 1941

Corvallis, Oregon

Vol. 12   No. 9

Ye Sylvan Archer

"A magazine for the field archers"

Vol. 12   January, 1941   No. 9

Published the fifteenth of each month
for archers by archers
505 North 11th Street, Corvallis, Oregon

J. E. DAVIS .... Editor
RUSSELL JONES .... Business Manager
Subscription Price .... $1.00 Per Year
Foreign Subscription .... $1.25 Per Year
Single Copies .... 10 Cents
Advertising Rates on Application

TABLE OF CONTENTS

	Page
THE CASE OF THE MISSING BUCK By Dr. Paul E. Klopsteg	1
EDITORIAL	6
APPEAL FOR BOWS AND ARROWS	6
THE ROYAL TOXOPHILITE SOCIETY	6
THE BUCK I LEFT BEHIND ME By Dawson Feathers	7
FIELD ARCHERS ASSOCIATION OF SOUTHERN CALIFORNIA By Elmer W. Bedwell	8
DOGHOUSE LITERATURE By George Brommers	10
NATIONAL FIELD ARCHERS By Karl E. Palmatier	11
BRONZE AGE FIND IN WALES	12

The Case of the Missing Buck *

By Dr. Paul E. Klopsteg

Twice—in the autumn of 1939 and again in 1940—the gods of the chase have granted me a few days of bow-and-arrow hunting for deer on the slopes of the Big Horns, at the HF Bar Ranch in Wyoming. Both times they granted the same high privilege to Erle Gardner, at the same time and place, and the first year to Walther Buchen, also.

I am aware that bow hunters expect others of the tribe to share their experiences with them. Last year I didn't do it. This year I have hesitated a long time. You see, when a fellow hunts with a guy like Gard-

---
*With apologies to Erle Stanley Gardner, for snitching the composition and rhythm of the titles of his Perry Mason stories. The significance of the title is merely that the buck is missing because we missed him. There's no mystery about it.— P. E. K.

ner, whose ideas come tumbling from his mind like a swollen mountain torrent, and whose flow of language is such that he dictates a whole book of mystery fiction in ten days, well, said fellow naturally shrinks from exposing his own trickle of puny observations and parading his meager dribble of words before the public gaze. He waits for Erle to tell the story, for he can do it with so much greater facility and felicity.

Ordinarily I'd have let it go at that. Last year my expectation was rewarded—Erle's story came forth in the January, 1940, Sylvan Archer, immeasurably better than I could have done it. I have a feeling that he will repeat this year. Why then, you ask, do I venture to paint the lily? Why do I rush in, and stick my neck out? Let me explain.

For a week I've been supine—horizontal—with an undiagnosed ailment which didn't prevent my cogitating

Looking into the Red Canyon. Left to right—Teague, guide; Gardner; Marie Klopsteg; Bill Horton

about many things. Among them were the Wyoming hunting trips. On due and sufficient reflection, I have come to the unassailable conclusion that despite his great gift of expression, Erle will tell only part of the story, and that there's another part that should be told but won't be unless I do it. Erle is so retiring by nature that he would blush to think of telling anything that might reflect favorably on himself or seem in any way boastful. I see no way out— there isn't a thing I can do about it. I must let my fingers pick their way about the keyboard and let the story spread itself before my eyes. I sense that it will not be smooth-flowing. There is no diary, nor notes to tie it together. It comes out of unassisted memory. There will be only reflections off the peaks, only highlights. The lower elevations have already become immersed in shadow, and are difficult to perceive.

¤ ¤ ¤ ¤ ¤

If the urge should ever come over you to write the specifications of a companion with whom you'd like to go bow-hunting, all you need to do is write the description of Nagler, or Case, or Buchen, or Gardner. And if you are so fortunate as to find a man who fits the description, your hunt will be a great success, whether or not you bring down your bull moose or buck deer. My most recent experiences having been with Gardner, I shall write about him. What I shall say will not be duplicated by him, for reasons mentioned.

Gardner's ranch in California, in the general vicinity of Mt. Palomar, where the 200-inch telescope is being erected, is almost the same distance from HF Bar as is Evanston, Illinois, where I live — about thirteen hundred miles. Train service, with changes, delays and other inconveniences, isn't attractive. We could, either of us, have come via Union Pacific to Rawlins, but that would have meant an all-day drive of more than 500 miles for Bill or Bob Horton to get us to the ranch. So we decide to travel by auto, and meet each other half way.

My daughter Marie is my traveling companion, which greatly reduces the boredom of distance and time. Erle drives his Buick Super by himself, with a dictaphone for his traveling companion. Among other items, he brings sixteen pairs of wool socks, three sweaters, six leather coats, one hundred and sixty-three blunts and broadheads, seven bows, four pairs of hunting boots, six pairs of trousers and breeches, a sleeping bag, a pair of seven-by-fifty binoculars, three quivers, miscellaneous gloves and armguards, one pair of BVD's and one of denim overalls for purposes of poetry on cold mornings, means for libations to adventure, and fifty dictaphone cylinders. The idea of the dictaphone is that he can talk to it continuously without backtalk.

Erle arrived at the ranch the evening before we did. Next morning Bill suggested that he practice on some of his wild creek-bottom chickens and eventually Erle shot one through the neck. It made a superfine lunch. I thereupon sent a wire to Walter Buchen, third member of the Society of Buck Missers, who was detained in Chicago by an impending wedding. It read: "ERLE MADE PERFECT NECK SHOT AT SIXTY YARDS AND PROVIDED FINE CAMP MEAT STOP BILL WRANGLED THE CHICKEN FOR HIM STOP PLACE IS LOUSY WITH DEER STOP MISS YOU EVEN MORE THAN THE BUCKS STOP YOU CAN GET HERE BY PLANE IN EIGHT HOURS (Sgd.) PAUL." Neither my salesmanship nor the telegram could budge Walther. He wanted to come, but circumstances ruled otherwise. Next fall, maybe? We live in hope.

¤ ¤ ¤ ¤ ¤

Considering his a d v a n c e d age, Grampa Gardner is well preserved, and ever so spry. He is six weeks younger than I am, but I never did see six weeks anywhere that made so much difference. He climbs the mountains like a goat, with me dragging behind, at ever-increasing distance, gasping for oxygen. Of this indispensable atmospheric constituent there is a deficiency at 6000 feet. I think he must live in a rarefied atmosphere, and be used to it.

¤ ¤ ¤ ¤ ¤

Nor have you ever seen anyone so uniformly cheerful under all circumstances and conditions. Neither rain, nor snow, nor hail, nor any other kind of precipitation, if any, can dampen his spirits. He talks to the horses, and they nod understanding; any dog is immediately his friend; he utters words to the jackass rabbit, and that wary creature senses kinship. Even the coyote imagines himself a dog under his reassuring if not soporific conversation. I doubt greatly that he could ever shoot a deer. The does and fawns crowd around him as if seeking his autograph. The bucks take the cue and approach with only slight misgivings.

In fact, in one of our hunts, one buck came wandering across the top of a mesa, four hundred yards or more, to find out for himself and report back to his brotherhood, whether Erle would really shoot an arrow at him, given the opportunity. Erle was 200 hundred yards to my right, both of us below the rim of the mesa. The buck walked straight towards Erle, stopped, and kept looking in his direction. It was snowing, and I could see only his head and the top of his back, without the benefit of intervening territory to help judge distance. The buck found out that Erle wouldn't shoot, and was somewhat surprised when arrows began spattering around him from another direction. On the seventh arrow I had the range and heard the "thunk," but it was only a glancing hit. He winced, and wheeled, and trotted away. I could see that his high opinion of Erle, supposedly his friend, who had permitted a sneakin' hunter to shoot arrows at him, had suffered severely. We found the arrows and the tracks where he had suddenly jumped, also a spoor of blood on the snow, which was soon lost in his trail. From where I shot to where the buck stood, looking at Erle, was 109 yards.

※ ※ ※ ※

Erle's kindness to, and considerateness of his fellow man, are as great as his friendliness towards animals. Time and again he failed to take a shot because he wanted to be sure that I shot first. If there were two places to hunt which we planned to explore separately, he would insist on my going where he thought the chance of finding deer was best. I realize, of course, that his friendship for deer and his knowledge of my inferior marksmanship may have been the reason, but I don't think so. I believe it is pure generosity and goodness of heart.

It is amazing how completely silent Erle can be—and I do mean silent—when hunting deer. And motionless, like a statue. When the wind is right, he can stand in the open, and the deer will come and graze in such proximity to him that he could touch 'em with the end of his bow. . . . . . I mentioned earlier his flow of language—when he isn't hunting, I mean. He must be quite devout, for many of the words he uses are commonly used by clergymen also. I am sure that with an assortment of them, well selected, he could blister a buck at seventy yards. He should try it sometime and see if it isn't as effective as a broadhead . . . . . There's no doubt about it—if you want a hunting partner so delightful that it makes little difference whether you bring down a trophy, the specifications of Erle Stanley Gardner should fetch him.

※ ※ ※ ※

Gardner is an excellent marksman. He shoots a sixty-five pound bow and twenty-six inch arrows which he draws twenty-three. He is the best arrow-slapper I have ever heard, but his accuracy at any distance within the shooting range of his bow is remarkable. I suspect that the arrow slap may be intentional, to give the deer two seconds warning of what's coming, and a chance to buckjump out of line. At small game, and at magpies on the wing, he is good. At cattle chips he is perfect. He is a true lover of the bow. He has found in it that complete relaxation which a man of his strenuous and nervous activity needs.

※ ※ ※ ※

The Gardner quiver for hunting arrows is, to date, the best I've seen, and I shall use one on my next hunt; he had one of them custom-made for me. It has three compartments, for blunts and for different kinds of broadheads. It hangs obliquely from the belt, with the opening towards the front or back, as preferred. Any desired arrow can be easily and quickly located and withdawn, and in going through brush and climbing fences it is all one could wish. The back-of-the-shoulder quiver I've been using gives me a hunter-like appearance, but getting an arrow out of it reminds me of the fellow in "Hellzapoppin" who was struggling most of the evening, trying to get out of a

Erle Gardner is a most active person... This picture is unusual because he is resting

straight-jacket. In the accompanying picture of Erle, taken near the head of Red Canyon after one of our morning hunts, you can see how conveniently the quiver adapts itself to the situation when you sit down for a rest.

※ ※ ※ ※ ※

The hunting area at HF Bar is a territory of magnificent distances in three dimensions, practically treeless except along the creek bottoms and on the highest ridges. With good binoculars you can see deer several miles away, almost anywhere you look, and you are deceived into an impression that you could easily go there and stalk some particular deer or herd. But if you try you find that it takes you an hour to get there, and the deer have gone elsewhere. It can't be done, and certainly not in the open. The best chance of getting a shot is to come upon them over a rise, or over the edge of a mesa, up wind. Another possibility is to select a pass at the head of some draw or canyon and wait for the deer to come up from the meadows on their way to bed in the timber. If you wait at the head of Red Canyon and have one of the cowboys ride his horse into the lower end of the canyon, deer will almost certainly pass you within bow range. Whether a buck will be among them can't be predicted. In any case, you have to be up there early, because some of the wise old fellows head for the high timber at daybreak, or before.

※ ※ ※ ※ ※

Although the Ranch had closed much of its area to rifle hunting, there seemed to be plenty of poachers, judged by the rifle fire we heard and by the wariness of the deer. One morning I came upon a buck, some hundreds of yards distant, apparently walking with difficulty. Putting my glasses on him, I saw that his left hind leg had been shattered above the knee, leaving it dangling. A bad shot with a rifle, no doubt... On one occasion, Bill Horton came upon two rifle hunters sitting in a tree, with Bill's bull downstairs, pawing dirt and bellowing protests.

When Bill had driven Duke away, he suggested to the poachers that they were poachers, and asked what it was they were hunting up there. They climbed down, grateful, red-faced, contrite and humble, and promised never to do it again. . . . The rifle hunters I have seen are relatively no more accurate with their rifles than the bow hunter with his bow; their sole advantage is the distance at which they can shoot. It takes no skill to get within 300 yards of a deer—anyone con do that. The great adventure in hunting is the stalk. The rifle takes most of the fun out of it.

✗ ✗ ✗ ✗ ✗

Two seasons of experience with the Big Horn mule deer, totalling sixteen days of hunting for me and twenty for Erle, have given us reliable, first-hand information about their habits under varied conditions. Amply and repeatedly have we paid our dues in the Society of Buck Missers by missing numerous long shots —between 100 and 130 yards—and a few short ones of fifty or sixty. Each time we go we know that our prospect of getting a buck improves. Next year we should collect on our investment. . . . . Bill Horton, who knows every foot of the ranch, has taken to the bow and arrow. He also knows his deer, many of them by their first names. He can spot a deer in the landscape farther with normal vision than I can with binoculars. If Bill goes with us next year, we'll have some close shots.

✗ ✗ ✗ ✗ ✗

Among the mementos of our recent sojourn, and of last year's hunt, is a comprehensive diary, all neatly typed from Erle's careful notes and dictation, giving every detail of every move we made in every hunt. The pages are filed in a loose-leaf notebook, together with a collection of photographs to help bring back the memories. And the memories they bring! The companionship in roving and hunting, the early morning prowl, the chattering of Gardner's teeth through which improvised poetry is emerging concerning frogs in ice-bound pools and the lack of warmth in denim overalls and BVD'S,

(Continued on page 9)

" . . . I am satisfied we could have worked the irrigation ditch and had some close shooting." Note—The ditch which runs uphill to the left, is seen below the sloping table land in the middle of the picture.

Editorial

L. B. Spofford Loses Leg

L. B. Spofford, Jungle Garden Archers, Buchanan, Michigan, had the misfortune to have to have his right leg amputated. He had planned to go deer hunting with seven other members of his local club, but with only one leg he had to give it up. One of the seven shot a deer and another a fox.

Fred Hall of Buchanan shot the deer. He used a 55-pound osage bow and broadhead arrows of 340 grains. At a distance of 32 yards the penetration was 26 inches. The deer was killed instantly, never moving after it was hit. Mr. Hall used a sight, which is popular among the Buchanan archers for hunting.

Mr. Spofford expects to be back on his FEET again by the first of March with a new leg.

George Brommers, Columnist

George Brommers has been engaged to write a weekly column for the Bellevue (Wash.) American, in spite of the fact that the editor seems to have his number in advance.

Seems queer that the Bellevue editor would stick his neck out when he includes the following in his announcement regarding the new column: "There seems to be nothing sacred to the gent. He belabors his friends with insulting personals. If they come back in the same vein he chuckles fiendishly—and uses it for his next copy. If they fail to come back—well, there is nothing like trying again. If that is his idea of friendship we are far from sure we want to keep on good terms with him."

Appeal for Bows and Arrows

The following item in "Archery News," London, speaks for itself. With the "all out for Britain" campaign in full cry, archers should not neglect to heed this appeal:

"The Medical Superintendent of the Wharnecliffe Emergency Hospital, Wadsley, Sheffield 6, appeals for old bows and arrows for men in the special Neurosis Centre of this Hospital.

"Archery affords remedial exercises and has been found of great help in these cases.

"The N.C.O.'s and soldiers will make their own targets, but cannot manage bows and arrows.

"Any gifts should be sent straight to the Hospital."

The Royal Toxophilite Society

It may interest archers to hear something of the vicissitudes through which the Club has been passing lately. In September a bomb fell on the shooting ground, doing much damage to a row of new houses at the far end and leaving a large crater. At the same time debris from a bomb dropped on the flats near the Club House, sent chunks of masonry falling through the roof and breaking all the windows.

Some weeks later an incendiary bomb fell into the Committee Room and almost completely burned it out, falling through the floor into the garage below and destroying three Aschams under the staircase by the doors. The rest of the house is intact, but a second bomb has made a crater in the middle of the 60 yard range.

Much valuable work has been done by Dr. Mackay and Mr. Nelson who have gone to the Club whenever their own duties permitted, and removed pictures, medals, etc., from the walls to the cellar and kept the Hon. Secretary and Members of the Committee au fait with events. I have been up once or twice to help and discuss plans for removing everything to the country. Many of the old prints and photo albums have been scorched and spoilt by water, but none wholly destroyed. By now everything except the books have been taken away by different members for safe storage.

Mr. Melville Foster, the Hon. Secretary, has arranged for temporary repairs and we can only hope that no further damage will be done and be thankful that there was no loss of life. The caretakers had only previously left the house. Any member who has anything in their lockers would be well advised to remove them at once.—Archery News, London.

The Buck I Left Behind Me

By Dawson Feathers

As you may guess by the somewhat lugubrious title, this is a story of failure. But a pleasantly memorable one, withal. It was in southern Trinity County, two thousand acres of deer were ours for a few days, and the weather was perfect.

Mother Nature sounded the alarm before the crack of dawn. I shot the flash on my wrist watch and zipped out of the sleeping bag with an exclamation. Roy continued trying to snooze a three-pointer to earth. I soon had the gas stove roaring dutifully, got the coffee pot on and sliced some bacon. Then it wasn't long until the rattle of pots and dishes brought Roy back from that far away realm.

"Whatimzit?" from the tent.

"I dunno, but pile out!" from the stove.

It didn't take any more urging. Boy, the smell of that coffee! Yeah, I know, it makes me nervous, too, but what's the use. If we were perfectly rational people, we wouldn't hunt deer with a bow, either.

Bacon and eggs, toast and jam were sunk by wave after wave of the good old steaming hot. We slopped off the dishes, dunked the perishables into the car and took a look around. Our quivers were soon full, bows strung and all the rest of the war harness accounted for.

We ducked through the fence (no worry about a BOW going off here), and commenced easing along, toes down first. I sucked in a couple of big lungfuls. Man! You could practically taste the sweetness of the damp white-oak leaves. The aromatic scent of laurel was there, too. Everything underfoot was soaked from the misty rain the previous day, while the grass bent low with the weight of a very heavy dew. This and low hanging, misty clouds, which held back the dawn, made our progress a silent, shadowy phantasy.

As we approach a hog-tight fence, my eye catches something out of tune with the inanimate vegetation. I hiss and freeze; Roy right with me. No, it's only a big jack-rabbit. But what a shot! On his haunches, forty yards across a little draw. But the high, hog-tight fence! I jockey around to get a square of the coarse mesh lined up right, draw and loose. Chonk!

"I got him!" I blurt out. But no, he's runing up the hill, with no arrow a-trail. He staggers, falls and slides back nearly where he started from. We dash over. The sharp broadhead is buried in the earth and gravel as though it had missed. The red stripe down the shaft and the dead jack attest otherwise, however. Both shoulder blades sliced in two without even slowing it up. And from a forty-five pound bow. How much do we need to worry about penetration? Well, I'd better not start in on that one.

Yes, this DID start out to be a deer hunt, and it WAS only a jack, but with the bow it's different. Nearly everything is big game, then.

The rabbit is cleaned and stowed at camp, and Roy and I are easing slowly down through the tall, wet grass, along the edge of some white-oaks, fringing a draw, when he asks, "What's that down there?"

I strain my eyes through the mist, then suddenly declare, "Deer, boy, nothin' else." They are about a quarter mile down, at the lower edge of the steeply tumbling glade, and within fifty yards of the white-oak fringe. As there is no cover for us but the broken terrain of our open ridgetop, we decide to split and make a try at them through the trees, from opposite sides of the ridge. There are six or seven of them. A buck? Maybe.

We "mitt" each other, call for luck of the right kind and separate. I have just dropped down to one of the bumps on the ridge, figuring on my route through the oaks when, as I round the bump—BUMP! There, down in the cup of the hill below me, stand a beautiful three-pointer and a doe. Sure, looking right at me. Well, I look right back, you can bet on that. My eyes say seventy yards, but my thumping heart squawks an overcautious "fifty." As soon as the arrow leaves the string, I know I'm

(Continued on page 8)

Field Archers Association of Southern California

By Elmer W. Bedwell, Secretary

Southern California archers gathered under difficulties for the last shoot of 1940, with the barometer insisting on staying on the falling side, and the "Flu" epidemic doing its part in keeping a large number of people home, the president and assistant secretary being among those absent, a number having to work. Also, there were only two more shopping days before Christmas.

Nevertheless, those attending did have a grand day to shoot. As the regular November Turkey shoot that Redlands has always held was postponed this year because of the State Shoot, it was decided to hold one in conjunction with the regular bi-monthly tournament of the F.A.A.S.C., having only one official round of Rovers in the morning, and devoting the afternoon to the Turkey Shoot, consisting of trick targets, balloons, etc.

The scores for the official round of 28 targets were as follows:

Men Championship Class Gold Bar—Volus Jones, score 246.

General division Championship Medal—Irving Davis, score 241.

Red Ribbon—C. Conrad, 234.

White Ribbon—N. Rogan, 232.

Ladies' Championship Class, Gold Bar—Eva Bedwell, score 231.

Silver Bar—Naomi Baker, 159.

General division, Championship Medal—Ruth Davis, 162.

Red Ribbon—Little Glenn Curtis, score 103.

White Ribbon—Helene Rosen, 99.

Junior division, Bedwell Trophy—Harold Robinson, score 199, with second place honors going to Angus Bruce, score 103.

A general meeting was called and it was decided to enlarge the Ladies' Championship Class to six, making it the same as the Men's Championship Class. Heretofore, there have been only three, making it necessary for second place lady to drop out in case the third was absent, as they are held over in case of absence.

The Redlands club invited the F.A.A.S.C. to Redlands for the February 23 tournament, which was accepted. The trails are well packed and will take quite a bit of rain without damage, so here's hoping the weather and the archers will be able to get together on a pleasant day of shooting, February 23, 1941.

The Buck I Left Behind Me

(Continued from page 7)

crazy. It slogs into the grass beneath his feet; he and his doe trot around the shoulder of my knoll and I go tumbling after—on the other side, above them. My "Injin" craft comes to my rescue, and I slow down. While I slip another broadhead down to the nocking point, I'm easing forward like a cat.

The buck has stopped just where I had anticipated, and his eyes are on the retreating doe, who disappears into the oaks at my left. As I draw, he swings his beautiful head toward me and freezes, taut as my bowstring. Broadside at forty. The string twangs, the buck twangs and the shaft speeds true—true to where he had been before he shot backward, propelled as if by some gigantic invisible bow.

You know how it is, when the shot is right. You can almost feel it hit. Well, that's the way it is—straight for his shoulder. But he beats it, God bless him! Still I don't quit, as I tear back around my knoll to intercept him. I nock the arrow on the fly, slide to a stop and let drive without conscious effort, as he flashes by below me. As my heart goes with the shaft, it looks like a meeting is due, but something is out of time and he sails on with strong, sure leaps into the trees.

I stepped off that buck's jumps, and he was in the air fully twenty feet between each time he touched the ground. He was jumping slightly down hill from me at forty to fifty yards and I led him at least twenty feet. As I said, it seemed the lead was about right, but I later found the arrow, so I know I missed him.

When I later met Roy, he had had a heartbreaking episode to relate, wherein a buck had caught him stretched out on the ground watching a doe and fawn, his arrows meanwhile all reposing blissfully in his quiver. When, in desperation, he attempted to disturb this all too blissful repose of his shafts, the buck, apparently liking not the look of all this squirming and suppressed hell-fire and damnation, took lustily to his heels— showed 'em to Roy, too, I understand, despite a valiantly sped shaft.

We had more days of hunting— three, to be exact—and more experiences I might go into, but I'll just say that we're goin' back again, to slip through the white-oaks, laugh at the grey squirrels, thrill at the whirring wing beat of the sooty grouse, and wax mellow at the call of the mountain and valley quail, just as soon as the Lord will let us. And who knows, maybe the next time he won't jump. And maybe the other next time, there'll be one arrow—the right one—which isn't blissfully reposing in the quiver.

Case of Missing Buck

(Continued from page 5)

the stalk with its infinite possibilities and attending excitement, perhaps a shot or two, the return to the ranch house for a sumptuous lunch, the discussions about the merits of bows, broadheads, quivers, footwear and clothing, the story telling, the jokes and the banter—all these things together make this the best outing of the year.

The Gardner diary is not copyrighted, but I wouldn't think of presuming on friendship by reproducing extensively from its pages. I find, among his general observations gathered in October, 1940, passages which reveal some sides of the true Gardner better than any word picture I can draw. The reader who has come with me through hell and high water up to this point has realized that the hunting flavor in this story is camouflage. It is rather an attempt to sketch, in words clumsily assembled, a truly remarkable bow hunter—remarkable not for the number of his kills but for the qualities that make him the ideal hunting partner. Without his knowledge or consent, I am letting him put in the really artistic touches, by gleaning from the observations he has recorded. The first sentence quoted relates to his hunt the day after my departure — he stayed on for five more days:

" . . . . I am satisfied we could have worked this irrigation ditch and had some close shooting. Think I could have worked it by myself, but wasn't getting any kick out of it, as most of the pleasure with me is sharing in adventures and recounting them afterwards . . . . . Deer are more frightened of the scent than of the sight of man . . . . . After a deer has seen you, he will apparently become confused if you remain absolutely motionless. It is as if he can't see you clearly and he, or, as is usually the case, she, will do everything to make you betray yoursef. One little doe lowered her head and pretended to be grazing, but I was close enough to see that she wasn't moving her jaws, but was merely moving her nose in the grass . . . . . They lower their heads, toss them, stamp their feet. If you stamp your heel on the ground without their seeing the motion, it makes them all the more curious. They will keep approaching, at times throwing up their heads as if to say, 'Oh, THERE you are! I see you clearly now!' But if you keep completely still, they keep working closer. Finally they either spook, or give you a clean bill of health . . . . . The bucks came out of the timber and joined the does as the snows came in the mountains and the rutting season started. By the time I left, there were lots of BIG bucks down with the does . . . . . The Red Canyon drive can surely get us deer next year, and if the weather is right, will get us some BIG BUCKS."

Okay, Boy, I'll be seeing you, *Deo volente*, at the head of Red Canyon next October!

Every year archery is becoming more and more popular in Ohio.. It is especially popular among young people. Hunting with bow and arrow, while not as deadly as the shotgun, gets results if practiced by experts. Witness the fifty-two members of the Future Farmers of America of Xenia, who bagged two rabbits each with bow and arrow while hunting.—The Ohio Conservation Bulletin.

Doghouse Literature

By George Brommers

In the Nov. issue of this magazine Joe Cosner offered a handsome apology for his failure to stand up and fight. Joe knows when he is licked, and I am glad to restore him to full doghouse privileges. I will be the judge of just what these privileges are.

But what particularly drew my attention, and restored my faith in his courage, was his reference to writers who can't write. I do not fully share his opinion of Gardner, Willard, Klopsteg and Nagler, though. I feel that they are not wholly and irredeemably hopeless; they just haven't associated with Joe and the doghouse gang long enough to absorb the needed technique.

I think they realize it, too, and are anxious to improve. I just had a letter from Mr. Willard, who told me that he missed me. In the next breath he tells me that he is engaged on a new play, so I knew that his sentiments were not just white lies, but that he really needed my advice.

Mr. Gardner, too, felt disheartened over Joe's rash dictum. So disheartened that he and Dr. Klopsteg betook themselves to Wyoming for a hunt. Results, well, the same as last year, if you must know, but must you?

Never mind, Joe, I know what you mean all right, but don't give me this kind of an opening again. It just wouldn't have been human to resist it, and if your face is red, who parked it too close to the radiator?

In all seriousness, Joe, I agree with you on the main issues. No magazine of this size is ever going to get very far with nationally and internationally famous professional writers such as Gardner and Willard. They give freely, more freely than they should, perhaps, but they have a living to make and a reputation to sustain. No archery magazine will ever have the financial rating that allows it to pay for that kind of talent, and writers can give just so much to their hobby gratis.

No, that kind of writing is lagniappe. The ones who make a field archery magazine a success are the writers of hunting stroies, and the organizers who run our field archery tournaments. Also the hunters who do not write themselves, but who know spontaneous writing when they read it.

As far as these amateur writers are concerned, technique is far less important than the angle the writer uses. Do they deal with the quest, the chase, the human element, the intangibles that make archery a sport, or are they solely interested in results and trophies. If the latter, all the technique in the world will not make the story worth reading.

I am thinking, and so are you, of fellows such as Klopsteg, Buchen, Nagler, Case, Lieuts. Sisler and Latta of the Navy, Walt Wilhelm, Sasha Siemel, Styles, Dr. Thompson, Dr. Cathey, Russel Jones and Chester Stevenson. As long as we have hunters of their type we will have stories that ring true because they are true in all essentials. The readers will gobble them up because they sense the lack of artificiality and striving for literary effect.

But you are thinking of our doghouse gang. Our products are about as imperishable as Fido's breakfast, but ain't we got fun? We have a real mission in life—we furnish the Halloween spirit. If, in the process, we upset some literary back houses or unstarch some stuffed shirts, well, what business did they have in our rowdy way?

Think of our advantages, the bliss of our profound ignorance. Do we know our moods and tenses? Not we, we can't even spell them. Do we recognize this phrase as stuffy, that sequence as dragging, that the skeleton structure is unsound and the whole thing out of balance? Is our treatment mangy, and our plots antique? A real writer would know about these things, and have to do something about it.

Believe me, Joe, when these writers tell us that they miss us and envy us, they really mean it. There was a time when they, too, could get some fun out of life. Not no more they do, their public expects, and is entitled to, a finished job.

We doghouse writers are saved all the griefs and worries of authorship. We know that our literary output is both lousy and a crime against humanity, but we don't know why, and we care less, and as far as our influence goes towards making or breaking even a field archery magazine, forget it. We don't count either way. We are just strutting across the stage make-believing we are actors. What's a mere audience or a sordid subscription list to us? What we are after is a good time, and we are having it.

You mourn about cartoonists who can't draw. Personally I hope they will never learn. I am no more of a judge of art than I am a literary critic, but I have laughed myself sick over some of the cartoons you, Williams, Carpenter, Shaw and Turner have drawn. To make us laugh was the object of it, wasn't it, or did you plan an exhibit at the Louvre?

I do share your grievance against the photographers, though. Why, the last photo I had taken made me look sixty years old, and far from handsome. No halo of romance was apparent, no S.A., no oomph, no nothing. What kind of an art do you call that?

A word to you readers. I can't promise you a cessation of atrocities in the future—my associates are an untrustworthy lot—but I can, in radio language, thank you for listening, and I wish you most sincerely

A HAPPY NEW YEAR

National Field Archers

Championship Standing for 1940

MEN

	Fifty-six Targets			Total
E. Hill Turnock, Wilkinsburg, Pa.	168-669	170-690	194-776	177-712
Roland Quayle, Long Beach, Calif.	139-541	168-630	158-612	155-594
Larry Hughes, Burbank, Calif.	145-585	131-511	160-624	145-573
Merle Hathaway, Los Angeles, Calif.	141-547	135-543	153-597	143-562
J. G. Daulley, Long Beach, Calif.	110-428	110-426	118-464	113-439
Willard Bacon, Redondo Beach, Calif.	108-410	122-448	119-433	116-434
I. M. Stamp, Seattle, Wash.	119-445	119-433	103-389	114-422
Emery Watts, Los Angeles, Calif.	114-426	109-407	109-401	111-411
E A. Melzer, Ellwood City, Pa.	108-406	90-332	130-492	109-410
Stanley Baker, Inglewood, Calif.	113-423	112-422	94-366	106-404
E. J. Woodward, Redlands, Calif.	107-407	108-408	97-396	104-404
John Yount, Redlands, Calif.	99-381	92-356	106-390	99-376
Earl Grubbs, Los Angeles, Calif.	103-424	100-382	84-302	96-369
George Hamaker, Flint, Mich.	103-385	89-327	101-379	98-364
Kore T. Duryee, Seattle, Wash.	108-407	90-326	86-324	95-352
T. B. Chandler, Compton, Calif.	92-356	96-368	83-311	90-345
Harvey Franklin, San Bernardino, Calif.	92-344	82-310	86-312	87-322
Harold Robinson, Redlands, Calif.	82-298	95-357	81-307	86-321
W. J. MacIntyre, Royal Oak, Mich.	86-326	69-249	84-316	80-297
Bernie Ahman, San Bernardino, Calif.	75-249	77-289	70-256	74-276
George Calvert, Flint, Mich.	67-229	65-239	85-325	72-268
R. W. Carmichael, Los Angeles, Calif.	56-204	72-254	88-314	72-257
Paul Ludwig, Los Angeles, Calif.	73-267	65-251	67-245	68-254
Robert King, Redlands, Calif.	74-272	76-294	40-150	67-239
Jack Willard, Hollywood, Calif.	64-238	88-328	40-154	64-239
Glen Ebert, Flint, Mich.	68-252	61-219	62-234	64-235
E. G. Opper, Los Angeles, Calif.	66-236	56-246	61-213	61-232
Bennett Gandy, Los Angeles, Calif.	61-221	68-248	60-214	63-228
Tracy Stalker, Flint, Mich.	59-213	66-238	59-225	61-225
Angus Bruce, Redlands, Calif.	46-162	59-235	62-240	56-212
Edmund Brock, Los Angeles, Calif.	62-238	58-208	44-166	55-204
George F. Miles, Los Angeles, Calif.	52-184	65-241	47-177	55-201
Harold Strandwold, Shelton, Wash.	29-105	40-146	41-139	37-130
Henry Bitzenburger, Los Angeles, Calif.	16-60	23-91	58-214	32-122

Howard Mudgett, Albuquerque, N. Mex.	29-109	15-53	29-101	24-88
Joe Robb, Albuquerque, N. Mex.	24-80	25-93	16-60	22-78

WOMEN

Naomi Baker, Inglewood, Calif.	92-328	111-419	117-439	107-395
Eva Bedwell, San Bernardino, Calif.	83-311	91-333	92-340	89-328
Ruth Hathaway, Los Angeles, Calif.	79-289	86-312	71-249	79-283
Lulu Stalker, Flint, Mich.	68-242	85-325	66-254	73-274
Margaret Quayle, Long Beach, Calif.	52-156	73-267	78-300	68-241
June Franklin, San Bernardino, Calif.	61-235	65-241	64-226	63-234
Mary Calvert, Flint, Mich.	60-228	63-231	69-241	64-233
Minerva Gandy, Los Angeles, Calif.	54-198	63-241	55-201	57-213
Margaret King, Redlands, Calif.	45-157	57-213	50-190	53-187
Helen Dauley, Long Beach, Calif.	53-191	56-206	43-151	51-183
Dorothy Ahman, San Bernardino, Calif.	55-165	46-166	48-182	50-171
Jane Duncan, Seattle, Wash.	38-146	28-102	28-96	31-115
Helen Berry, Los Angeles, Calif.	29-101	18-53	28-100	24-85

The championship standing is determined by the average of the three highest scores shot in five mail tournaments.

Mr. H. S. Cummings, Chairman of the NAA, has personally given a trophy for the national men's champion. This goes to E. H. Turnock. Mr. MacQuarrie accepted the responsibility for having a trophy for the ladies' champion. This will be sent to Naoni Baker.

Karl E. Palmatier,
Tournament Secretary.

All fishermen are liars but — all liars are not fishermen! (No, some may be archers—Ed.) Once a fisherman always a liar! —The Ohio Conservation Bulletin.

Dr. Jess Baker of Ontario, Oregon, reports they have an island in that locality which is infested with the big white rabbits (Kit-chee-wahboos). Dr. Baker and his archer friend, J. W. Cudd, expect to make a bow and arrow raid on them soon.

Bronze Age Find in Wales

During an air raid "alert" in London lately, Sir Cyril Fox, director of the National Museum of Wales, talked to the Society of Antiquaries about his excavations of a Bronze Age barrow in Glamorgan. In it an archer was found buried about three thousand years ago.

The Editor wrote to ask why he thought it was an archer, and Sir Cyril kindly replied: "The evidence on which I base my description of the Early Bronze Age burial near Sutton Farm, Llandow, Glamorgan, as that of an archer is that seven arrow heads were found with the skeleton; he was what is known as a 'Beaker' man, and the bow is well recognized as one of the weapons of these people in Britian."—Archery News, London.

CLASSIFIED ADVERTISING

RATES for Classified Advertising 5 cents per word per issue. Count initials and numbers as words. Minimum charge is 50 cents.

BOOKS AND MAGAZINES

The AMERICAN ARCHER, a national quarterly, $1.00 per year, 521 Fifth Ave., New York City.

The Flat Bow—70 pages of Archery information for 50 cents, well illustrated. *Ye Sylvan Archer*, 505 N. 11th St., Corvallis, Oregon.

RELICS AND CURIOS

INDIAN RELICS, Beadwork, Coins, Curios, Books, Minerals, Weapons. Old West Photos. Catalog, 5c. Genuine African Bow, $3.75. Ancient flint arrowheads, perfect, 6c each—Indian Museum, Osborne, Kansas.

SUBSCRIBERS PLEASE NOTICE

A cross appearing in this space means that your subscription has expired and we would appreciate your prompt renewal so that your name may be kept on our mailing list.

WIN WITH BEN PEARSON ARROWS

Beautiful and accurate to the Nth degree but win their real laurels on the range. Arrows made as arrows should be—and at prices you can afford to pay. Send for catalogue.

BEN PEARSON, INC. — PINE BLUFF, ARK.

Cassius Hayward Styles

BOWYER AND FLETCHER

—Tackle that has stood the test—

28 Vicente Place

BERKELEY, CALIFORNIA

Ⓖ

"THE MARK OF DISTINCTION IN ARCHERY TACKLE

Fine Yew Target and Hunting Bows, Plain or Backed with Rawhide. Lemonwood Bows with Rawhide Backs. College and School Equipment Target, Hunting and Roving Arrows

Price List on Request

Wholesale — Retail

EARL GRUBBS
5518 W. Adams
Los Angeles, : California

---

70 pages of Archery information for 50 cents, well illustrated. Ye Sylvan Archer, 505 N. 11th St., Corvallis, Oregon.

**BACK NUMBERS
YE SYLVAN ARCHER**
Volumes I to V Inclusive
$1.00 Per Volume
B. G. THOMPSON
R. F. D. 1, Corvallis, Oregon

YEW BOW TIMBER

High Altitude Air Seasoned Billets and Staves of Quality and Variety.

W. G. PRESCOTT
527 Chestnut   Ashland, Ore.

HANDBOOK—How to Make and Use Bows and Arrows—90 Pages well illustrated (with catalog) 35c.

CATALOG—100 pictures—color spread—Instruction Folder. 10c.

CATALOG alone 5c. Stamps or Coin.

L·E·STEMMLER·QUEENS VILLAGE·N·Y

"ARCHERY," by Robert P. Elmer M. D., revised edition, most complete book on archery published. 566 pages of valuable information for colleges, libraries, schools, camps archery clubs and individuals. Price $5.00 postpaid. orders to Ye Sylvan Archer, 505 North 11th street, Corvallis, Oregon.

"ARCHERY TACKLE, HOW TO MAKE AND HOW TO USE IT." by Adolph Shane. Bound in cloth and illustrated with more than fifty drawings and photographs. Information for making archery tackle and instructions for shooting. Price is $1.75. Send orders to Ye Sylvan Archer, 505 North 11th street, Corvallis,

Write us for your needs in Archery books. Ye Sylvan Archer.

CHANDLER
PAT. PEND

Interchangeable Arrow Points
PRICES CUT NEARLY 50%

The prices now are cut so low,
Yet the quality is so great,
Every archer now should know,
That he cannot afford to wait.
see the dealer nearest ye,
Or mail your order in to me.

Free Catalogue.

T. B. CHANDLER
11819 - 4th Ave.   Compton, Calif.

FISH HEAD   A-80

TARGET SET BALANCED

SMALL HUNTING SET BALANCED

BEAR
ALUMINUM ARROWS ARE MAKING RECORDS
BEAR PRODUCTS CO.
2611 W. Philadelphia Ave., Detroit, Michigan

Ye Sylvan Archer—$1.00 per year.

Arcadian Life Magazine
Stories of the Ozarks

Pioneer History - Folklore

Pastoral Living

$1.00 a Year; 25c a Copy

Display Adv. $1.50 per inch Classified, 3c a word. Three insertions for the price of two.

O. E. RAYBURN, Editor

616 S. Benton St
Cape Girardeau, Mo.

P. O. Box 200
Caddo Gap, Arkansas

E. BUD PIERSON
Bowyer — Fletcher
Tournament Tackle, Sinew, Glue, Raw Materials.
245 University Ave
CINCINNATI, OHIO
Custom Made Tackle

Paul H. Gordon, Director
Beacon Hill Craftsmen
Beacon, N. Y.

Where the serious archer's needs and desires are really consulted, and his orders exactly filled. Nothing too simple or too difficult.
Write for Complete Catalog

WESTERN
ANTIQUES
COLLECTOR

Corvallis, Oregon
P. O. Box 403

A monthly illustrated magazine devoted to items of interest to the collector of antiques.

$1.50 per year.

Please mention Ye Sylvan Archer when writing advertisers.

Ye Sylvan Archer

February, 1941

Corvallis, Oregon

Vol. 12   No. 10

Ye
Sylvan Archer

"A magazine for the field archers"

Vol. 12   February, 1941   No. 10

Published the fifteenth of each month
for archers by archers
505 North 11th Street, Corvallis, Oregon

J. E. DAVIS	Editor
RUSSELL JONES	Business Manager
Subscription Price	$1.00 Per Year
Foreign Subscription	$1.25 Per Year
Single Copies	10 Cents

Advertising Rates on Application

TABLE OF CONTENTS

Page

NFAA EMBLEM AND THE MEN RESPONSIBLE
  By John L. Yount 1

THE ART YOUNG AWARD OF THE NATIONAL FIELD ARCHERY ASSOCIATION 2

GREENWOOD TOURNAMENT 2

BIG GAME WINNERS FOR 1940
  By John L. Yount 3

NFAA NEWLY ELECTED OFFICERS 4

OLYMPIC BOWMEN LEAGUE 5

FROM PRESIDENT MICHELSON 6

NFAA NEWS AND VIEWS
  By John L. Yount 7

EDITORIAL 8

BEEF, MOSTLY!
  By Bill Van Vorst 9

DOGHOUSE TABOOS
  By George Brommers 11

ANCIENT ARCHERY BUTTS 13

ALL IN THE LIFE OF A SECRETARY
  By Karl E. Palmatier 14

YEWS IN CHURCHYARDS 15

NFAA Emblem and the Men Responsible

By John L. Yount

Last spring following a discussion of the desirability of an emblem for our organization, Bill Folberth volunteered to have artists of Ohio submit some designs and if we decided that one of the designs was suitable he would supply the association with 5000 stickers bearing the emblem to be used on letters and to seal adjustable sights during tournaments. (See cut of emblem on cover.)

Naturally there was no time lost in taking up Bill's proposition even though we did have misgivings as to what some romantic-souled artist might do when given a free hand. We could picture everything from Cupid to a glorified Robin Hood and had a strong feeling that we should have given the artist a little advice.

When the designs arrived they were all good, but the stump and arrow was the work of a genius, an unknown genius. You see Bill sent no names along. He wanted to be sure the emblem was favorably received by the archers first. Now, since it has received nothing but favorable comment, he reports that the artist was Dick Schroeder, of the Cleveland Archery Club. A sportsman, a photographer and an artist, and good at all of them. Here is what he has to say of Dick and the "Missus."

"Dick Schroeder, an artist of National fame, is one of the most honored and respected members of the Cleveland Archery Association. Mrs. Schroeder, Helen, recently won the Cleveland Archery Club's championship shoot. As so often is the case, Dick was an outstanding hunter and has to his credit many successful big game hunts extending as far away as the Canadian Rockies where he bagged everything that Jasper Park can offer. He not only brings back the horns, but his artistic sense makes him an expert movie operator. In combination with another hunter named Wagner, they have taken such wonderful movies of the game country that the Canadian Government has purchased the film to be used for tourist information.

"For the past five or six years he has given up the high powered rifle in favor of the 65 pound bow. He shoots 700 grain arrows instinctively and is the only Ohioan ever to have brought his deer out of the State of Pennsylvania with this equipment. He loves and talks his favorite sport and is a tireless worker in anything connected with it."

All we have to add is that the artist certainly knows field archers. Some are hunters and care little for competitive games. Others love their tournaments and seldom hunt, but all are outdoors men and women and none could resist breaking an arrow on such a stump as he pictures. Thanks, Dick, for a good job.

Brought down a Pennsylvania deer with bow and arrow

The Art Young Award of the National Field Archery Association

When Art Young passed away in February, 1935, a small group of his friends, headed by Dr. Paul E. Klopsteg, decided to do something to honor his memory. They established an informal organization which they called "The Art Young Foundation" to carry out the idea. Through it they hoped to build up a small fund out of which, at an appropriate time, they might finance some worthy project, preferably in archery and particularly in field archery.

The organization of the National Field Archery Association gave the cue for suitable action. When it appeared that the association was a going concern, Dr. Klopsteg corresponded with the secretary to see in what manner the Art Young Foundation might cooperate with NFAA and, in so doing, achieve its purpose. After some discussion, it was decided to establish the Art Young Award, to be awarded by NFAA to its members who were successful in bringing down big game with bow and arrow. The award is in the form of an attractively designed emblem. The halftone herewith is enlarged about four times.

In putting its fund at the disposal of NFAA for establishing the Art Young Award, the Foundation has achieved its aim in a way which honors the memory of Art Young in that field with which he was so closely identified. This award to field archers corresponds closely to the Six Golds Award of the NAA.

With the establishment of the Art Young Award, the Foundation has closed its books and given up its existence.

According to the NAA reporter, the NAA now has a colored movie film showing the 1940 NAA tournament at Amherst, Massachusetts, which may be rented by any affiliated archery club by request to the NAA secretary, Louis C. Smith, 77 Franklin Street, Boston. There will be a charge of $2.00, plus postage, to obtain this film, which is 400 feet in length (16 mm). The film shows the shooting field, the flight, the clout, and field archery events; it pictures the leading archers, and gives a very comprehensive glimpse of what happened last August at Amherst.

Greenwood Tournament

The Greenwood Archers of Oakland, California, announce their fifth annual Open Tournament to be held at Bushrod Park on Sunday, April 20, 1941.

We hope to see all our old friends on the line, as well as a large number of new faces.

This will be a "Six Gold" tournament, and there will be a prize for every target.

E. D. George, Secretary.

The Sixty-first National Tournament will be held at Portland, Oregon, starting August 4, and continuing through that week to August 10.

Big Game Winners for 1940

By John L. Yount

This list may not be complete. There are a couple of applications yet to be passed on by the committee.

The first was won by Russell B. Jones, of Eugene, Ore. His trophy was a full grown black bear taken at the head waters of the Umpqua River in his home state. This is real game and we are mighty glad to see the first Art Young Award go to Mr. Jones.

The Jones Boy

Number two pin went to Kore Duryea, Seattle, Wash., for a fine buck killed in the Caribou District of British Columbia. This is his second deer in two years and was brought down at good range by an excellent shot made through a small opening in the brush.

The third was won by Fred Campbell, of Bernalilla, N. M. His bear was taken in the James Mountains about seventy-five miles north of Albuquerque, N. M. The bear was shot from a tree at sixty-five yards.

We will let the winner of the fourth pin tell his own story: "What is that old saw, 'If at first you don't succeed, try—etc.'? After trying for seven years without success, the old 57 pound osage and broadhead finally hit pay dirt, the heart of an eight-point buck. Along with several other archers I spent the first week of December hunting on the archery preserve in Forest County, Pa. I must have been a good boy this year, or else the field archery practice de-

(Continued on page 13)

Kore

E. H. Turnock is both a target and a hunting archer

NFAA Newly Elected Officers

President—A. J. Michelson

Known to his friends as "Mike."

Occupation—Attorney, with offices at 610 Flint P. Smith Bldg., Flint, Michigan.

Experience—President of the Michigan Archery Association. Owing to his modesty I had to get this from a letterhead. For hunting experience he has put in twelve years after big game with the bow, but fails to mention the kills—modesty, or else.

Mr. Michelson has been a member of the Flint Archery Club for the past twelve years. This club has sponsored field tournaments all that time, and has had a standard course for two years. It has also been instrumental in obtaining special legislation for archers. We understand from reliable sources that it was our new president who was largely responsible for the advance hunting season enjoyed by the archers of his state.

Vice-President—Paris B. Stockdale

Known to his friends as (?), but we'll bet they don't bother with "Mr." even if he is a professor—not if we know our archers. They might unbend to the extent of calling him "Prof.," but I doubt it.

Occupation—Dept. of Geology, Ohio State University, Columbus, Ohio.

Experience—Past president of the Ohio Field Archery Association, and has a long record of leadership in both field and target archery.

Executive Committee Members

Western—H. C. MacQuarrie, 3400 Fruitvale Ave., Oakland, California.

Mid-western—Fred Bear, 2611 W. Philadelphia Ave., Detroit, Michigan.

Eastern—T. C. Davidson, 53 Mountain Ave., Springfield, N. J.

All are experienced archers and well qualified to represent their sections of the country.

A. J. Michelson, new president of the NFAA.

Secretary-Treas.— John L. Yount

Signs his letters "John." What he is called varies but, of course, is always quite complimentary ? ? ?

Occupation—Rancher and Zanjero. We are going to put Zanjero on a quiz program sometime. Address: P. O. Box 383, Redlands, California.

Experience—Twelve years of shooting the bow, and still entitled to a lower bracket ribbon. Was for two years president of the Southern California Archery Association, a strictly target organization, and field captain of the NAA tournament in 1935. He has worked for organized field archery since 1934, and held offices in both sectional and state organizations.

John L. Yount, secretary of NFAA, and his constant companion, which John says is a necessary part of the picture.

Olympic Bowmen League

As Ye Sylvan Archer goes to press the latest report we have is that of the third match. The Cleveland men's team was first, Albany (California) second, Carlisle (Pennsylvania) third, Chicago fourth, and Pittsburgh fifth. The Umpqua (Oregon) Archers jumped from twelfth to sixth place, and the Simon Paint Store (Madison, Wisconsin) team from twentieth to eleventh.

For the women the Chicago team maintains its lead, Milwaukee jumped from fifth to second, Cleveland held third, while Cincinnati came from sixth to fourth place.

Individually, E. H. Turnock of Pittsburgh is still leading with a 796.7 average. Harry Bear of Carlisle jumped from sixth to second, Truman Farnworth of Albany from eighth to third, and Jack Skanes of Highland Park, Michigan, kept his fourth place. Edith Radtke of Chicago kept her first place in the women's division, while her teammate, Rennette Yanke, came up from eleventh to second, Ethel Gates of North Shore Archers (Long Island, N. Y.) from seventh to third, while Belvia Carter of Tacoma, Washington, dropped from second to fourth.

Sixty-four teams are entered in the tournament, from Victoria, B. C., to

(Continued on page 10)

From President Michelson

To archers everywhere the National Field Archery Association sends its greetings:

The NFAA is no experiment. It has been adopted by archers in twenty-four states. It is a live, national organization, serving, promoting and expanding the interests of field archers everywhere.

The NFAA is not of mushroom growth. More than two years have been spent in intensive and careful organization work; contacting field archers from coast to coast, learning their views and reconciling their differences; eliminating friction with, and securing the endorsement of the NAA; committees working on the constitution, rules, tournaments and conservation; experiments with various types of field rounds to develop and standardize the various field games.

The NFAA is now ready and proceeding with its permanent organization work. Its constitution and by-laws are being drafted in final form and will be submitted to the various states for adoption. The various committees for the coming year are being selected with care and with a view of fair representation and efficiency. Few changes will be made in the constitution and the rules, and only those that are shown by experience to be advisable to best promote the interests of field archery.

The NFAA was organized to serve not only that group of dyed-in-the-wool, exclusive, field archers and hunters, but also to serve that vast unorganized group of independent back yard and stump shooters, who shoot just because they love the bow. This latter group will find in the NFAA the opportunity to meet fellows like themseves, join with or organize field groups, and find greater recreation, enjoyment and competition, if they desire, in playing the various association field games. The novice and beginner will receive a welcome hand and encouragement and instruction. The most loyal supporters of, and workers in the NFAA, is that large group of experienced archers who are both target and field enthusiasts, and find time for both.

To the target archer who has never tried field shooting the NFAA extends an earnest invitation to try our field round, and he will find new thrills and joys in archery.

Field archery has a strong appeal to women, too. Field archery can be made a part of the activities of every archery club without conflicting in any way with target activities. This added activity will increase the pleasure and enthusiasm of its members, as well as expand the club's membership.

To Henry Cummings and the Board of Governors of the NAA the NFAA gratefully acknowledges its appreciation of their unselfish endorsement and support. Both organizations are primarily interested in the advancement of the sport of archery, and there is no reason why they cannot both work side by side in harmony and without friction.

The Executive Board of the NFAA will need the sincere support of every member of the Association in working out the many new problems that face a rapidly expanding Association. The officers alone cannot assure the Association's progress and success. They need the active response of every field archer.

We must express our admiration and appreciation for the persistent efforts of the California archers in initiating a national organization of field archers, and in originating and developing a field round for archers. This also goes for the various committees in other states who have worked during the experimental and organization period.

Last, but not least, the NFAA expresses its warmest and deepest gratitude to the moving spirit that conceived the NFAA, to the hand that filled the lamps that kept its flame alive—to the determined and untiring energy that pushes it forward — John Yount, of Redlands, Calif., the secretary and treasurer of the National Field Archery Association. There is no one to whom could be better trusted the guardianship of the soul of field archery. John Yount is the "Louis Smith" of

(Continued on page 13)

NFAA News and Views

By John L. Yount

It will be appreciated if you people who have written me sometime in the past three months and haven't received an answer would write in again. It is a long, long story. Two bouts with the flu, I think I must have lost the first and won the second, and a bunch of accumulated, unanswered mail mixed with the answered but not filed mail. Result, some letters answered twice and some not at all.

We owe a vote of thanks to Karl Palmatier. He took hold of a mighty tough job and put it over. Field tournaments by mail had never been tried before and we didn't even have a finished organization to try them out on, but the fact remains that practically single-handed he put them over.

Another good job well done was the designing of the NFAA medals by Clayton B. Shenk. Most people would have tried to dress our emblem up with a lot of fancy frills and made a medal of the result. He didn't. Instead, he had the good judgment to have a die made of the emblem just as it is. It is one of the most striking medals I have seen.

Mail Tournament Winners Attention

Medals have been sent to the victors in the first three tournaments. The winners of the fourth and fifth and the year's champions will be taken care of very shortly. This delay is the result of lack of organization and the experimental nature of the tournaments. We promise you it won't occur again.

California and Arizona each have a bill before their state legislatures asking for archery reserves. We are keeping our fingers crossed and everything.

Two years ago the California bill was passed only to be vetoed by the Governor at the request of the Humane Society, the people who should be our best friends. I guess they never heard that you have to hit a deer before you can be cruel to it. The California bill calls for five reserves of an average of 25 square miles each, all located in game preserves of long standing.

The Arizona bill was also presented two years ago, but was, I believe, snowed under by a deluge of bills and was never reached.

When a golfer wants to tee off and there is some one loitering on the fairway he just sings out, "Fore!" and the loiterer moves on. Here is what a field archer says under similar circumstances, "Hey, you get the ——— away from that target if you don't want to get shot." Now, I am going to suggest as a cure for this condition that we adopt the golfer's idea, but a far more appropriate call and one that will do honor to one of the organizers, the old timberman, George Brommers. What could be more appropriate than the woodsman's call of "Timber!"—the call used to warn of falling trees. The timber shot from bows may be a bit small, but the danger is just about as great.

National Field Champions

For the benefit of any who have missed previous announcements we wish again to report that the winner of the Henry Cummings championship trophy was E. Hill Turnock of Pennsylvania. His average score of 356 for the 28 target round is really something to shoot for in the years to come. Runners-up were Roland Quayle and Larry Hughes, both of Southern California.

In the ladies' division, the championship, and the Potter and MacQuarrie trophy that goes with it was won by Naomi Baker. Second and third places went to Eva Bedwell and Ruth Hathaway. All are of Southern California.

Mrs. Baker's average score was 197, enough, if competing with the men, to have put her in twelfth place.

Editorial

John L. Yount recently underwent a "major but not serious" operation. According to latest reports we have from Mrs. Yount, John had recovered fully from the anesthetic and "hadn't an ache or a pain."

We were pleased to see the picture of Russell Jones on the left hand side of the front page of a recent issue of the Eugene Daily News. A picture of the Governor of Oregon appeared on the right hand side of the same page and balanced the page fairly well. The occasion for the picture and accompanying write-up was a sort of "home town boy makes good" idea. It told of the mention of the Jones boy in the Dean Collins column of the Oregon Journal, Portland daily, as the killer of a big black bear with bow and arrow—a feat that brought our Russell the first big game pin to be awarded by the National Field Archery Association.

The editor always enjoys the annual letter we receive from Miss Stella Ives with her subscription remittance. Miss Ives says, in part: "I went to my first National meet in Jersey City in 1916—just 25 years ago—and had been shooting before that with our Newton Archers, so I've seen archery grow—since that first meet when Mr. Duff, as president of the National, gave us such a royal welcome to his city. When you meet in Portland, Oregon, in August, I shall be with you all in spirit and wish that it might have been in person."

Through Earl Hoyt, Jr. of St. Louis, Missouri, we have the following information on field archery in his city: "The St. Louis Archery Club has set up a fourteen target range on our present field in Forrest Park and it has been decided to leave this range up permanently, even through the summer target season. Furthermore, it has been voted on and passed that the club sponsor an invitational open field tournament just after the close of the '41 target season, along around the latter part of October."

We feel that this issue of Ye Sylvan Archer proves rather conclusively that The National Field Archery Association is fully organized and under the leadership of men who will see that the organization goes forward for the betterment of field archery. With such men behind it NFAA will push on but it depends upon the individual members whether the task of the officers will be hard and thankless or result in pleasant memories of a job well done. We especially wish to appeal to that great group of true lovers of the bow who do not care for organized competition. There is much that NFAA can do for these archers and much that they can do for NFAA and field archery. There are barriers to our full enjoyment of archery caused by prejudice which can be broken down only by organized effort, can be broken down only by education and publicity, and this campaign can be carried on by the NFAA. The first way to help is by sending in your membership to John L. Yount, Box 383, Redlands, Calif.

We have often wondered why O. E. Rayburn, editor of Arcadian Life magazine, isn't an archer. His love of the outdoors and his interest in traditional and legendary lore should qualify him as a true disciple of Roger Ascham. Either he hasn't been exposed or else he has lived the arcadian life so long he is too darned lazy to pull a bow string. How come, Mr. Rayburn?

T. B. Chandler has designed a hunting broadhead that he believes combines serviceability and cheapness. He believes that the cheapness of the new head will make it unnecessary to spend time hunting arrows and more time can be spent in hunting game.

G. Wayne Thompson, president of the Western Archery Association, announces the dates for the WAA tournament have been set for Saturday and Sunday, May 31 and June 1, in San Francisco. Mr. Thompson promises more information for later issues.

Beef, Mostly!

By Bill Van Vorst, Lowell, Michigan

"O. K., you'd better send over that quarter of beef, since I didn't even get a shot!" That's the usual line that we hear from the bow hunters of Michigan.

The archers of Michigan are very fortunate in having the Michigan Archers Association. They worked for a long time on a special bow season on deer and in 1937 we were given our first chance; then it was two counties. That year there were one hundred eighty-seven licenses sold and three bucks killed. I was one of the lucky boys. There was a steady increase in the number of licenses sold until this year they list five hundred sixty-one to date with the records incomplete. However, the kill has remained low, even in view of the fact that the state gave us all the territory open to gun hunters in 1939. This year we know of six bucks killed and there are rumors of two more.

We should have been ahead of the average in that the Michigan Conservation Department estimates, and they usually can back up their statements, that there are between 800,000 and a million white tails in this state. Anyway there were over 45,000 bucks killed legally by gun hunters in 1939.

Michigan has all kinds of cover. When the glacier passed over this country it left a variety of surfaces, hills, valleys, plains and even some small mountains. There are oak ridges, poplar thickets, jack pine plains, and deep cedar swamps for winter cover. The cedar is becoming over-broused and is causing alarm as to the future of our deer.

The question is so often asked by non-bowmen, "Why, with such good territory to hunt, is there such a small kill with bow and arrow?" I feel that the element of luck enters into about ninety per cent, with a very small percentage of skill.

I have hunted all four years since we have had the special bow season, and have killed only one buck, a spike horn, and I thought I was a successful rifle hunter before. Nevertheless, I've had the time of my life even if I've frozen by degrees, soaked up the rain and caught many a cold. I can truly say I'll never go back to the rifle. I've talked with many field archers, who never killed a deer or had a shot, that feel the same as I do.

In our state there are many archers who never shoot at a target and others who like both ends of the game. The kill seems to be about evenly divided. They seem to favor Osage for bows while a variety of woods are used for arrows — fir, cedar, pine and birch—even a few basswood shafts. It seems that most of us have our own ideas regarding broadpoints as every known brand and invention is used. The Detroit Club makes a big event of the season and all live in a big camp with their

Left: A group of Michigan hunters with meat, even if not what they were after. Center: The author goes up after a porcupine. These take a lot of strain off the deer. Right: Loring Pangborn of Hemlock, Michigan, with a nice buck taken in 1940.

individual tents and trailers.

We have a real bowman in western Michigan who has accounted for a buck each year for three years in a stretch. He is Charles Paine of Walkerville, an excellent shot who shoots a bow from ninety to a hundred pounds and really pulls it back. He never shoots target. Nelson Grumley of Detroit is another successful archer with three deer to his credit, but he missed out this year. He is one of our best field shots and makes bows for a living.

I couldn't wait for the season to open this fall, so two days before time I cast my office work aside and by noon was pitching my tent in Ogemaw county in the jack pine plains. In spite of a drizzling rain, my wife, two small daughters and myself were eating supper in a comfortable structure that would be home for two weeks. Previously I had thought Newaygo county the tops but after hunting last year in Ogemaw I couldn't resist returning. Here you get a variety of cover with but a short walk or drive from our camp. Also there is a large acreage of wild land owned by the state and which is always open to hunting, due to the fact that it was purchased with part of our $2.25 license fee.

The next morning was spent helping a lone archer get his tent up and he in turn helped get our wood supply. We also visited the State Refuge and after seeing the tame herd felt our memory was refreshed as to horns. My wife spent the first week hunting birds but that doesn't mean we had partridge.

The first morning found me sitting on a good runway in the small pine. I was seized with a coughing spell, so took a short walk and on returning found a deer, a bear and two cubs had crossed my stand. The idea of shooting a bear, which had been running in my mind for weeks, got the better of me. After locating a den, I wasted most of a week watching at the entrance but after the log I was sitting on wore through I gave up and decided on bucks instead.

My family left to spend the remainder of the time visiting so I felt I could really get down to business. By the middle of the week I was beginning to think we'd eat beef when Loring Pangborn of Hemlock, with whom I hunted part of the time, connected. He made a perfect shot at nineteen paces and it was an eight point buck. It runs in my mind that most of the deer killed other years have been found a hundred yards or less but this one was different. The yell of delight from Pangborn must have given the deer wings as he ran about three quarters of a mile. It took us over three hours to locate him as there was no snow. The arrow had cut through the top of the heart but the bleeding was nearly all internal. He presented me with the heart, which I ate for supper, thinking this would bring me luck; but have been told since it should have been eaten raw to be effective.

The bucks were still sticking close to the thick cover and I saw most of them in the poplar where it was impossible to get an arrow through. I got within fifty yards of bucks several times. In eleven days of roaming I saw 269 deer of which 22 were known bucks. It seems unbelievable that I failed to get a shot. I passed up a small spike horn at fifteen yards one evening because I believed his horns were too short. As he turned to run I could see they would have passed, but it was too late. However, the record of Michigan archers was maintained; that is, no record of a doe or illegal deer killed by them in their four years.

There is something about breaking deer camp that always brings a lump in my throat but duties called me back and nineteen forty is history. Now bring on the beef until forty-one.

OLYMPIC BOWMEN
(Continued from page 5)

Hialeah, Florida, and from Tulare, California, to Rochester, N. Y. Fourteen states and British Columbia are represented.

We want to put Alan E. Miles of Everett, Washington, on record as having invited us on a hunt next fall in "some swell hunting country." If we do not get there, Mr. Miles, it will not be because we do not want to go.

The "Bow and Broadhead Club," a hunting club, claims the largest membership of any archery club in Oklahoma City. W. B. "Curley" Parsons is secretary.

Doghouse Taboos

By George Brommers

Four or five years ago I had occasion to consult the literary criminal who edits and publishes this outstanding field archery organ. Them was the days before John had accidentally shot a buck. He could still manage two consecutive sentences without switching the subject, and when he switched it was to bugs and I must confess a wholesouled indifference to bugs of any kind. All I ask of them is to be let alone.

We were discussing a column that would bring all archers to their feet—most of them in admiration, and the rest to gasp for air. In other words, the doghouse column.

We had agreed that my mission in life was to stir up the lower forms of literary life to where they would rush out to defend themselves in print. I couldn't know at that time that they would stand in such awe of me that they wouldn't dare to call their souls their own. I thought I knew how to provoke a come-back.

"Take Cosner," I illustrated. "Joe draws like a leaky flue, but he has a certain low cunning that could pass for wit with the indiscriminating. He is hard to get started, though. Now, if I call him a hyena, he can't stand for that, can he?"

"He shouldn't," agreed John, "but on the other hand he might think you flattered him. Aside from that it is a good term, hyenas don't vote, and neither do they subscribe to magazines. It is worth trying."

So I went ahead, to the vast and enthusiastic unconcern of every archer whose tail wasn't pinched, and most of the injured considered the source and let it go at that. My trouble came from an unexpected source, from John Davis, in fact.

First, it should be understood that I am a tolerant and broadminded guy. But as the only doghouse editor in captivity I can't help but know my value.

It isn't that I try to snub or patronize the common or garden variety of editor. He has his functions, I have mine. He furnishes the medium and pays the printer's bill. That should be privilege enough for him.

The well trained garden variety does not talk back. In the first place he don't know nothing, and in the second place he has had ample opportunity to see lightning strike in deserving corners and has no wish to stick out his own neck. But John is an exception. He registered a howl.

"The cash customers are objecting to your profanity," he says. "From now on you are limited to one single damn and one solitary hell. I am getting tired of apologizing for your logger's vocabulary."

I yawned without interest. Just how the aitch were you going to emphasize if you had no emphasis.

The next time I read my column I was shocked, to put it mildly. I had my allowance, no more. The rest was aitches, asterisks and da-a-a-rns. He had butchered my literary gem. Something has to be done about it.

Maybe I have been too hard on John, I don't know. Maybe I should allow him a little self expression, if he can muster the courage for it.

Go on and have your say, John. Don't get self conscious now, this is a country of equal opportunity. If you do your stunt well I may even appoint you associate doghouse editor. The devil knows that the yes-men I have need a shaking up.

No holds are barred, except that you can tell me nothing about bugs. I forgot more about them in Alaska than you ever learned. And if you as much as mention bucks again I will trow a fit.

"Aitches and da-a-a-rns," he says. My gosh!

From the Editor

We just can't take all that lying down. Our readers know that George

Brommers prides himself on being a modest man; in fact, he brags and boasts about it. But we just have to let the cat out of the bag. Really, he isn't modest at all but is most conceited. He claims to be a logger of the old school with all the earmarks. However, the truth must be told:

In the first place, George has anything but a logger's physique. You think of a logger as a big handsome he-man with muscles of cement and the chest expansion of a bellowing bull. As a matter of fact, George is a skinny little guy with legs like those of a target stand, and, except by his mother and his wife, never has been called handsome by less a liar than Joe Cosner or Jack Willard. Even knowing Joe and Jack as he does, he puffs out his chest to his full three-quarters of an inch expansion whenever either of those scoundrels refers to him as an Adonis. Physically, his only claim to logger-like proportions are his bellowing voice and his big flat feet. The voice, I understand, comes from no deeper than his throat and the hoarseness was acquired when our George was a professional clam digger on the mud flats of Puget Sound. The big feet are a natural heritage, but served well a scow-like purpose in the bivalve hunting work.

Socially, Brommers acquired his claimed membership in the fraternity of the Descendants of Paul Bunyan by listening to the Loggers Quart-ette over the radio. In truth, if a logger caught our pseudo-timberbeast in a bunkhouse, he'd probably dust him off with a hearty fog of buhach powder.

Educationally, Mr. Brommers is an offensively gross imposter. In his endeavors to substantiate his assertions that he is a famous harvester of our forests, he employs language that is highly obnoxious to sensitive ears. In sooth, Mr. Brommers is a collegiate gentleman, a master of the faculty of verbal expression that would put to blush a Bostonian such as Louis Smith. In other words, Mr. Brommers normally speaks a language that would be considered a foreign tongue by one of those crude personages commonly designated as loggers.

Commercially, George ranks as a logger only on the basis of his purchase on several occasions of knotty, twisty yew logs which he sold as very raw material. He once saw a growing, low-altitude yew tree from a train window.

But poor old G. B. really thinks he makes his principal bid to fame as a timberbeast on what might be called a spiritual plane—his profanity. He prides himself on the fact that he has taken lessons from Erle Stanley Gardner. As a matter of fact, it wouldn't mean anything if George had taught Erle all Erle knows of profanity. Erle, of course, did offend the tender sensibilities of Dr. Klopsteg and Walther Buchen, but Dr. Cathey and Dr. Thompson report Erle a perfect gentleman, with a fluent but mild flow of language. George, we admit, has listened many times to the language of Los Angeles policemen, he has hobnobbed with Howard Hill and Chester Seay, he has even ridden in the Wilhelm Brothers' Prowler. The Prowler, we are told, is a considerable stimulus to mental profanity, but very discouraging to any kind of oral expression. George thought he learned something from the Eugene archers while he associated with them for a month or so a few summers ago, but he didn't get the cream of the crop from the Oregon gang. He didn't hear Howard Richards when Howard shot a blunt *against* a big buck; he didn't hear the imprecations voiced by Major Williams as Bill tore down a hillside from an equally scared black bear; he didn't hear Bert Cowling, honest-to-goodness logger, when someone sat on and broke Bert's best target arrows. By kinking his bow arm, Bert can get by with a thirty-one inch arrow and Earl Ullrich charges a lot for enough wood to make Bert a set of arrows. And George never heard John Hubler when Chet Stevenson used John's highly prized Port Orford cedar bolts for kindling; he never heard Dr. Cathey when the doctor broke his flight bow; he never heard Grover Gouthier, another real logger, when Grover missed that big buck at a distance at which he'd have potted a squirrel nine times out of ten. He has never even heard, and seen, Dr. Thompson when the good doctor paused over a hornets' nest to take a shot at a porcupine. Dr. Thompson made no sound, but employed what we have heard called wooden swearing, such as slamming doors and making faces—behind their backs—at policemen. Of course, these examples are just "darns" and "hells" as compared with the plastic profanity induced by the hornets. Yes, George might learn something in Oregon that he never acquired in effete California, and never will get in the urban regions of Washington in which he has chosen to settle.

So we ask our readers, are we going to use a couple of "hells" and a handful of "darns" when we have to pass up such masterpieces as those we have mentioned? And, of course, we couldn't afford the asbestos to print those on, even if Uncle Sam would let them pass through the mails. Hell, no!

BIG GAME WINNERS

(Continued from page 3)

clared a dividend, because at eleven o'clock on opening day the old boy came over the hill 'carrying the mail" right toward me. At eighty yards I came to full draw and swung with him for a running shot. He must have seen my motion or become cautious as he approached the path near me, because he obligingly slowed down to a walk, turned nearly broadside as he looked right at me, then even advanced his left foreleg to completely expose his heart to the broadhead. I let drive before he changed his mind. He departed at full speed and traveled 275 yards before dropping. The shot was at 20 yards. Subsequent examination showed that the arrow entered at an angle, sheared completely through a rib on the entering side, through half a rib on the far side, and stopped with the broadhead about four inches beyond the far side. To me it was a very convincing demonstration of killing power.

"To say the least, I was elated. The most satisfaction comes from the fact that I shot with confidence for the heart (since the range was short) rather than the whole chest cavity— and actually hit it. I repeat that I must have been a good boy this year to deserve all that luck, because my experience these past several years convinces me that an archer has to have about fifteen or twenty factors all add up PLUS at the same time lady luck smiles on him in order to get his buck. Experienced archers around here estimate the odds at from 50 to 100 to one against the archer as compared to the rifle hunter. Do you Westerners agree with the estimate?"

E. Hill Turnock,
Wilkensburg, Pa.

Yes, we do agree.

Some men have all the luck. There is this fellow Turnock, after taking all the tournament honors he goes hunting and has a deer walk right up to him. It may be that we don't live right, but nothing like that ever happens to us.

FROM THE PRESIDENT

(Continued from page 6)

field archery. National chairmen and executive committees will come and go, but as long as John, as secretary, continues to plot the course, the old ship will carry the NFAA to greater service and achievement.

To John, I assure my whole-hearted cooperation; and to the NFAA, I pledge my best efforts in advancing its interests.

Sincerely,
A. J. "Mike" Michelson,
Chairman.

ANCIENT ARCHERY BUTTS

The English archer only obtained his skill by regular practice, and this was enforced by Statute and Royal Command. Henry VIII ordered all his male subjects under 60 years of age, except the clergy and the judges, to practice archery, etc., and butts were ordered to be set up in every township. This Statute was made perpetual by further, and later, enactments. The butts probably consisted of mounds of sod and earth placed at each end of a large space set apart for the purpose, and the shooting would be done from one butt to another, turn and turn about, and the arrows would be sharpened, when necessary, on some handy stone, or one that had been specially erected for the purpose. Many of my readers will know Newington Butts, London, and there are other similar place names, obviously archery practice grounds, of the days gone by.

—A. W. in Archery News (London)

All in the Life of a Secretary

By Karl E. Palmatier

I pick up the NAA Reporter to find out what the official business of the NAA has been during the last month and to get an idea of what is being worked on now. What do I find? An assignment to write this. It is one more thing to do in the life of a secretary.

Spelling is one of the troubles of a secretary. Last spring I reported that our state champion flight archer, Mr. Yaeger, would give a demonstration of fright shooting! For another meet I announced a tournament of the Michigan Yield Archers. After all, the field archers have yielded a long time.

Did you ever ask the secretary to assign you to target number so and so because it is just the same as target so and so upon which you have been practicing for the last two hours? Or complain that the face of this target shines in your eyes when you look at it and the secretary explained that gold is the official color but glare is on your mind (and eyes)?

And the little things that I am told would cause as much trouble as a physician who loved to gossip. Mr. A stands too close to me, I am left handed and if I face another archer it annoys me. Jack takes so much time I have to shoot alone and I can do that at home. Why not provide a special place for relatives somewhere besides where we want to place our tackle? I know I am late but who ever thought a meet would start on time? I am going to send in my membership just as soon as I get home and call a meeting of the officers and have them send in the affiliation fee. Why don't you put those instinctive archers on a target by themselves somewhere? So and so gives all the best tackle he makes to his wife and we get the rest. Why let her shoot as an amateur? What we should have is more publicity! Why let the newspapermen hold up our meets and spoil our scores for pictures?

I open my mail about a month before the national tuornament and find a friendly request to please send me some of the things that happen at the national tournament so the writer may use them for his column. I obligingly help my friend out with a few items of fun and then find in the next magazine a title "What Mr. Secretary Saw at the National." I am on the spot again because of telling tales out of school.

There should be a meeting of club and association secretaries at the time of the national tournament for an exchange of ideas that will build up enthusiasm. As the secretary is the one who stays on year after year the archers expect him to have a well of new ideas. He is supposed to have a last minute bit of fun held back to make up for what the local club did not have time to do.

Every secretary should be warned that if he wants to be happy from now on he must know how to pass the buck. So he will encourage the archers to elect a board of directors whose business it is to be responsible for everything, finances included. Then if an archer comes to the secretary with a complaint he simply says, "Sure, there are enough members of the board here to make a quorum and I shall tell them about it right now. Won't you come with me?" So you leave it with the board and watch them squirm. It is fun, isn't it?

The secretary is often in charge of seeing that the field is in proper shape before the tournament and if it is not it is up to him to get it so. He will arrive at least the day before the tournament. Archers will ask him to come to their home for the night because he stayed with So and So last year. Then Mrs. N reminds him that his wife wrote her that he would stay with them but his wife did not tell him about it. He had written James and accepted his invitation to stay with him. If they want him to stay with them they should write at least a week before he is expected to arrive. Michigan archers please note! If no invitations are received he had better register at the hotel just to have an excuse that will satisfy everybody. And by the way, no invitations is a good sign that he will have very little help.

And have you ever been asked to remember that I have a bow made of —— that pulls —— and is —— long and I have only used it —— times and will sell it for —— dollars and it was made by —— over in —— who is the best bowyer in that section of the ——?

Have you met the archer who came from the place where archery tournaments were run as they should be run? As a secretary you must be a good bluffer and to be a good bluffer requires that you have a very well worked out set of regulations provided you by your board. Then have the latest copy of the NAA tournament rules plus a telegram from the chairman of the NAA rules committee with the latest up-to-date new regulations. Then there is one more help—let him know you have been away from home yourself. Do you take in the larger tournaments? Soon the grouch will lose standing among the archers.

If you have a classification system, and are new at the game, you have another thorn in the flesh. Soon somebody will come in and report that so and so is deliberately throwing away his arrows so that he may remain top in a lower class. This makes them all mad because too many of them are after the same trophy while still shooting in the proper class. Do not be concerned. Such sportsmanship is false and the person who does it will feel worse about it than anybody else. Give them time to develop. Sportsmanship in our schools teaches the youngsters too much about winning and not enough about sportsmanship. That lesson comes from being snubbed. It is much easier to learn if learned from sportsmen.

"And say, Mr. Secretary, would you tell me a place where I can go and get a deer without having to wait too long? I only have two days and if I go and don't bring one back the guys at the shop will sure kid the life out of me." Or perhaps the wife will simply say, "I told you so!"

I could relate more that causes the day of the secretary to be full. I have not mentioned scoring, flight shooting, the way so and so dresses, taking groups to meets, etc. To do so would stir up plenty of argument that any gentleman should know is not necessary.

Then some day the mail brings a letter from George Brommers. It says, among other things, that the Archers of Michigan have made more constructive suggestions to field archery than any other group. That we have given in for the sake of harmony and have given time a little chance to help work things out. Such a letter of appreciation and congratulation from an old timer in a distant place makes you take heart and accept another year's work.

By the way, have you mailed the secretary your 1941 dues? If not, upon what do you expect him to run that archery club, anyway?

YEWS IN CHURCHYARDS

One often sees it stated that yew trees were ordered, by Act of Parliament, to be planted in churchyards by the church authorities in order to provide material for making bows and arrows, yew being the hardest, most compact, and elastic wood for the purpose. But this was not so. The real reason for planting them in churchyards, or near by, was in order to have supplies of this evergreen to decorate the church at Eastertide, as the special emblem of immortality, a custom which was widely prevalent, particularly in country districts. Indeed, this significant custom prevailed up to the middle of the 19th century, and, even if every churchyard in the country had a yew tree planted in it this would not provide material for the enormous number of bows and arrows which would be required for the army in days gone by.

We know that an enormous number of bow staves and arrows were imported through Danzig, the wood coming from the vast Carpathian forests. In various port records mention is made of wood for these implements, and so we lose another illusion, for, to a certain extent, the bows and arrows used at Agincourt and Crecy would seem to have been "made in Germany."

In a collection of very important and most interesting official letters and papers relating to the business of the Ordnance Office, 1626 to 1685, known to the writer, there is a document which shows that bows and arrows were used in the Navy in 1627.

Yew is poisonous to horses and cattle, although cases have occurred where they have eaten it without ill effects but as a rule it is poisonous. The partially dried twigs and leaves are even more poisonous than fresh ones. (With acknowledgments to the Preston Guardian.)
—A. W. in Archery News (London)

"ARCHERY," by Robert P. Elmer M. D., revised edition, most complete book on archery published. 566 pages of valuable information for colleges, libraries, schools, camps archery clubs and individuals. Price $5.00 postpaid. orders to Ye Sylvan Archer, 505 North 11th street, Corvallis, Oregon.

"ARCHERY TACKLE, HOW TO MAKE AND HOW TO USE IT." by Adolph Shane. Bound in cloth and illustrated with more than fifty drawings and photographs. Information for making archery tackle and instructions for shooting. Price is $1.75. Send orders to Ye Sylvan Archer,

---

SUBSCRIBERS PLEASE NOTICE
A cross appearing in this space means that your subscription has expired and we would appreciate your prompt renewal so that your name may be kept on our mailing list.

CLASSIFIED ADVERTISING

RATES for Classified Advertising 5 cents per word per issue. Count initials and numbers as words. Minimum charge is 50 cents.

BOOKS AND MAGAZINES

The AMERICAN ARCHER, a national quarterly, $1.00 per year, 521 Fifth Ave., New York City.

The Flat Bow—70 pages of Archery information for 50 cents, well illustrated. *Ye Sylvan Archer, 505 N. 11th St., Corvallis, Oregon.*

RELICS AND CURIOS

INDIAN RELICS, Beadwork, Coins, Curios, Books, Minerals, Weapons. Old West Photos. Catalog, 5c. Genuine African Bow, $3.75. Ancient flint arrowheads, perfect, 6c each—Indian Museum, Osborne, Kansas.

BACK NUMBERS
YE SYLVAN ARCHER
Volumes I to V Inclusive
$1.00 Per Volume
B. G. THOMPSON
R. F. D. 1, Corvallis, Oregon

Hunters and Field Archers

It is time to begin thinking about a new hunting bow for this fall. Write for that new big catalog, which explains everything. By America's oldest tackle maker.

WILLIS H. BARNES
Sturgis — — Michigan

Archery
Raw Materials

WM. A. JOY

9708 So. Hoover Street
LOS ANGELES, CALIF.

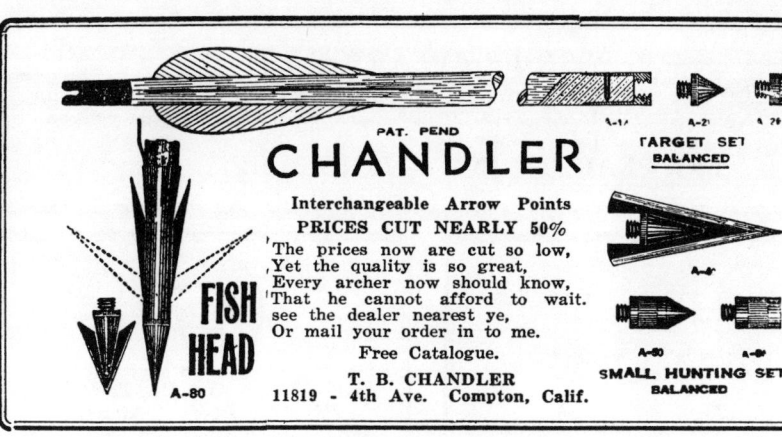

CHANDLER

PAT. PEND

TARGET SET BALANCED

Interchangeable Arrow Points
PRICES CUT NEARLY 50%
The prices now are cut so low,
Yet the quality is so great,
Every archer now should know,
That he cannot afford to wait.
see the dealer nearest ye,
Or mail your order in to me.
Free Catalogue.

T. B. CHANDLER
11819 - 4th Ave. Compton, Calif.

FISH HEAD A-80

SMALL HUNTING SET BALANCED

BEAR
ALUMINUM ARROWS ARE MAKING RECORDS
BEAR PRODUCTS CO.
2611 W. Philadelphia Ave., Detroit, Michigan

Ye Sylvan Archer—$1.00 per year.

Arcadian Life Magazine
Stories of the Ozarks

Pioneer History - Folklore

Pastoral Living

$1.00 a Year; 25c a Copy

Display Adv. $1.50 per inch
Classified, 3c a word. Three insertions for the price of two.

O. E. RAYBURN, Editor

616 S. Benton St
Cape Girardeau, Mo.

P. O. Box 200
Caddo Gap, Arkansas

E. BUD PIERSON
Bowyer — Fletcher
Tournament Tackle, Sinew, Glue, Raw Materials.
245 University Ave
CINCINNATI, OHIO
Custom Made Tackle

Paul H. Gordon, Director
Beacon Hill Craftsmen
Beacon, N. Y.
Where the serious archer's needs and desires are really consulted, and his orders exactly filled. Nothing too simple or too difficult.
Write for Complete Catalog

WESTERN
ANTIQUES
COLLECTOR

Corvallis, Oregon
P. O. Box 403

A monthly illustrated magazine devoted to items of interest to the collector of antiques.

$1.50 per year.

Please mention Ye Sylvan Archer when writing advertisers.

WIN WITH BEN PEARSON ARROWS

Beautiful and accurate to the Nth degree but win their real laurels on the range. Arrows made as arrows should be—and at prices you can afford to pay. Send for catalogue.

BEN PEARSON, INC. — PINE BLUFF, ARK.

Cassius Hayward Styles

BOWYER AND FLETCHER

—Tackle that has stood the test—

28 Vicente Place

BERKELEY, CALIFORNIA

G

"THE MARK OF DISTINCTION IN ARCHERY TACKLE"

Fine Yew Target and Hunting Bows, Plain or Backed with Rawhide. Lemonwood Bows with Rawhide Backs.
College and School Equipment
Target, Hunting and Roving Arrows
Price List on Request
Wholesale — Retail

EARL GRUBBS
5518 W. Adams
Los Angeles, : California

THE FLAT BOW
HUNT & METZ

70 pages of Archery information for 50 cents, well illustrated. Ye Sylvan Archer, 505 N. 11th St., Corvallis, Oregon.

IMPORTANT!

MIDDLETON'S IMPROVED REPLACEABLE NOCKS

are available to all dealers after
APRIL 1st

Ad in next issue of this magazine will outline complete new merchandising set-up with new low retail prices and complete list of dealers and addresses.

DEALERS please make immediate application for new price lists and information for obtaining this free listing.

Arrangements for stock must be completed by March 10, to assure listing in next issue.

Carl W. Middleton
160 West 2nd Street
POMONA, CALIFORNIA

YEW BOW TIMBER
High Altitude Air Seasoned Billets and Staves of Quality and Variety.
W. G. PRESCOTT
527 Chestnut   Ashland, Ore.

BOWS · ARROWS · MATERIALS

HANDBOOK—How to Make and Use Bows and Arrows—90 Pages well illustrated (with catalog) 35c.

CATALOG—100 pictures—color spread—Instruction Folder. 10c.

CATALOG alone 5c. Stamps or Coin.

L. E. STEMMLER · QUEENS VILLAGE · N·Y·

Ye Sylvan Archer

March, 1941

Corvallis, Oregon

Vol. 12　　　　　　　　　　　　　　　　　　　　No. 11

Ye
Sylvan Archer

*Official Publication of the
National Field Archery Association*

Vol. 12   March, 1941   No. 11

Published the fifteenth of each month
for archers by archers
505 North 11th Street, Corvallis, Oregon

J. E. DAVIS .... Editor
RUSSELL JONES .... Business Manager
Subscription Price .... $1.00 Per Year
Foreign Subscription .... $1.25 Per Year
Single Copies .... 10 Cents

Advertising Rates on Application

TABLE OF CONTENTS

                                                                   Page

IN THE MAD LAKE RESERVE
  By Kore T. Duryee 1
NFAA BULLETIN
  By John L. Yount, Secretary 3
EDITORIAL 7
POPE-YOUNG FIELD ARCHERS OF
  OREGON 7
THE WESTERN TOURNAMENT 7
AN ARCHERY BROADCAST 7
BLUNTS FROM THE OLD STUMP 10
MIDWEST ASSOCIATION 11
1941 NFAA MAIL TOURNAMENT
  REGULATIONS
  By Karl E. Palmatier 13
MORE FOR THE RECORD 13
WILLIAM B. ALLEN 15

In the Mad Lake Reserve

By Kore T. Duryee

This Reserve is just one hundred and twenty-five miles from Seattle, over Stevens Pass. It is between Lake Wenatchee and Chelan Lake. You leave the Chiwawa River road at Deep Creek, which is about 2,000 feet elevation, and in the next five miles you climb 2,300 feet over a good mountain road. This brings you to the top of the ridge near Maverick Peak and the beginning of the Reserve. Those who have only a day or two to hunt may camp beside their car. The nearest water is about a quarter of a mile away.

The Reserve runs in a northwesterly direction, with the Mad River valley in the middle, and is about thirteen miles long and three wide. For the first two or three miles the valley is rather narrow and rugged, and then it opens into a big meadow for nearly ten miles. The McDonald Ridge on the west is about 1,000 feet higher, and the trail at the top is the west boundary.

Just six miles in is the Mad River Dude ranch owned and operated by Al Constans of Seattle. This is opened during the hunting season, and this year the charge was only $25.00 per week including the use of a horse at all times. This also means that the pack horses are kept in the middle of the Reserve.

On our trip in this year Irl M. Stamps and Art Partee were in my tent. Dr. H. W. Smiley and wife of Indio, California, occupied another.

We packed in ten miles, which was nearly two miles above Mad Lake. We had the prettiest camp site a person could ever want—a big meadow nearly a mile wide, with small groups of trees on knolls all over. We pitched our tent on one side of such a group and the Smiley's camped on the other side, windward of another smaller grove. We were about one hundred yards apart, and still entirely out of sight of each other. Our water supply was about one hundred yards away in a small stream about three feet deep, and much to our surprise, Mrs. Smiley caught several messes of small trout in the deep holes. Mad Lake was her favorite place and we all enjoyed good meals from her prowess as a fisherman.

This was our third time to hunt in this territory. The first time we camped at Mad Lake in 1936. The next year we were about a half-mile beyond this year's campsite. This was the year that Stamps shot his first deer with the bow and arrow.

When staying for a couple of weeks and packing in, it is foolish not to take in everything needed. We even took in a new cookstove weighing over ninety pounds, with a polished cast iron top. For the previous trips we had used one with a sheet iron top which soon warped out of shape, and pots heated slowly on the uneven surface. This one was a revelation to us—hotcakes cooked right on top of the stove—and the time we saved.

We always make a good camp, and it pays. It is 12x14 with five-foot side walls, with an eighteen-inch sod cloth and a special three-foot overlap at the entrance. Then, there is a fly over this, twenty-two feet long, giving us an eight-foot roof beyond the front of the tent. We always put up a framework around the inside of our tent, drive in plenty of nails, and have a place to keep our clothes out of the way. It only takes a few hours more work to make a real camp. After everything was fixed as usual, Art turned to Stamps and said, "Wouldn't it be pretty nice to have beds about two feet off the ground?" "By gosh, Art, you got something there," said Irl, "and we could make them, too, out of that small dead Sitka spruce tree over there." Personally, I thought they were a little crazier than I was, but three beds were made in a couple of hours, and I must admit they were fine. A few bows over the split slats and ground cloth to protect the air mattresses and we were just as comfortable as could be. Yes, we have been using air mattresses for several years, and there is nothing like it. The Smiley's and I had gone in late Friday and Art and Irl arrived about 2:00 P. M. Saturday. I had the tent up and fire in the stove, but that was all. By the same time the next day, camp was complete with wood cut for several days, a hole for garbage, and the "Specialist" as only Irl can construct. "Without a plan or blueprint of any kind," said Irl, proudly. Had two plywood boxes with a shelf in the middle and two doors. They are thirty inches wide, eighteen inches high, and eight inches deep. These have now been on four field trips and the field mice and squirrels have failed to get into them to date. From all this you see that we were comfortable, and why not? We had an unusual amount of rain this year but it did not bother us any. One year it was down to zero because the season was a month late that year, but it was warm in the tent. We always take in all the food we will need, not depending on getting game, and yet our two weeks' trip has never cost over $18.50 each.

The season opened Sunday so, after finishing camp that afternoon, we all took a short hunting trip in different directions. Monday, I was at the top of the ridge above Mad Lake, and jumped a grouse. As the season was open, I quickly took off my broadhead and put on a blunt. A few seconds later I heard some rocks rolling down a slide about 200 feet to my left. Curious as to whether it was a doe or buck I dropped down about one hundred feet and quietly followed a game trail. Soon, at the edge of some cover, I spotted a big three point (we count only one side out here, so it would be a six point back east) buck, standing broadside to me and a good 95 yards away. Felt sure it would be impossible to get any closer so I shot, the arrow going a good two feet over the middle of his back. It was the blunt arrow I had put on for the grouse. Would a broadhead have gone any lower? The line was perfect. We all came home with grouse.

The next day I was walking up a steep trail when I heard a noise behind me and, on turning around, saw a big two point just about 45 yards away. He was facing me and my arrow went a half foot under his chest. He ran about ten yards and stopped behind a small tree. I had to shoot through the branches or shoot for his neck and head. I chose the latter, and as I had just undershot and he was now 55 yards away I decided to be more careful and not go under. I didn't. The arrow hit the top of his head, passing through the skin, and glancing off his antlers. He turned and ran out of sight. The arrow had blood on it but tracked the buck for some distance and saw no signs of blood. As I had seen exactly where the arrow hit, and even heard it strike the antlers, I knew it was only a surface wound.

Underwood and Davis of Olympia were camped just a quarter of a mile from us. Wallace Burr and Imes of Seattle, came in a few days later and camped next to us and stayed for several days. When they left Burr hunted all the way out, following the McDonald Ridge trail, and wound up some ten miles from his car, having taken a wrong turn on the ridge. Imes had tired of waiting for him and had gone to sleep in his sleeping bag. We hated to see Partee leave at the end of the week, but he only has one week of vacation. The next day the Smileys broke camp, and as Underwood and Davis had also gone, Irl and I were left to try to get a buck.

Tuesday night Irl reported that he had seen his first buck and made a good down hill shot. However, the buck jumped as Irl released and the arrow missed. Irl said he was glad as it turned out to be a spike, and the law here requires a forked antler. We had missed several chances the last two years by waiting to make sure he was a two pointer. None of us had ever seen a spike, and had it confirmed by several game wardens, that it was a rare thing to find one in the hunting season. This year we had determined not to wait, as long as we could see horns. This buck, Irl said, was very small for a mule deer, so was probably born very late in the preceding year.

As the hunting was not very good we decided to break camp Thursday morning. Irl wanted to get back so he could go pheasant hunting at the season opening two days later.

We decided to take one last hunt, going to the top of the McDonald ridge where Irl had seen the spike. As we left camp Irl said, "Now, let us be as smart as the deer. We are not going across any open meadow spots, but will go around them, keeping in the timber. It will take longer but we have plenty of time, and we

(Continued on page 14)

NFAA Bulletin

OFFICERS

President—A. J. Michelson
610 F. P. Flint Bldg., Flint, Mich.

Vice-President—Paris B. Stockdale,
Geology Dept., OSU, Columbus, Ohio.

Secretary-Treasurer—John L. Yount,
Box 383, Redlands. California.

EXECUTIVE COMMITTEE

Western—H. C. MacQuarrie.
3400 Fruitvale Ave., Oakland, Calif.

Mid-Western—Fred Bear,
2611 W. Philadelphia, Detroit, Mich.

Eastern—T. C. Davidson,
53 Mountain Ave., Springfield, N. J.

NFAA OFFICIAL COURSE
By John L. Yount

As you probably know, our round is based on a 14-target unit. This unit includes all the required ranges, which are from 20 feet to 80 yards.

A regulation course consists of two such units, or 28 targets, although it is official to have only one unit and shoot it twice. The latter is not recommended for large clubs or associations. Fifty-six archers will jam the course and make it practically impossible to conduct a full 56-target tournament in one day. Also, a single 14-target unit is apt to become monotonous, a thing fatal to a field round. We field archers demand variety in large doses, and 14 targets is hardly large enough. Twice is just about as many times as we can stand the sight of any target in a single day.

Now, for the course itself. The ranges and target sizes may be found at the end of this article, purposefully put there that we may study some of the other equally important requirements of a good course. The ranges and target sizes may make a course official, but they will not make it interesting. That job is up to the men who lay it out. I believe we can best study the matter by planning a course and facing the problems as we meet them, rather than listing a lot of do's and don'ts.

The first job is to locate a field of at least 20 acres. If no such field is available or you are confident, and I am sure your confidence is unfounded, that you will never need or want more than the 14-target unit, a 10 acre field will do.

The fact that hilly, eroded, brushy, forested or practically any waste land is better for roving than open fields somewhat simplifies the problem. The chosen field should be within a reasonable distance and located on a good road. Otherwise it will only be used for an occasional tournament, and you will have missed the opportunity for regular practice and play that is the life of any sport.

Suppose, for the sake of this article, that we have leased a good field less than 10 miles from town and decided on the location for our headquarters. We have chosen a spot on a fairly good road with plenty of parking space and a good water supply. Hiking over the course will build up a real thirst and it will not be the kind that a bottle hidden in the bottom of the quiver will satisfy.

Headquarters is centrally located so that it is possible to have both 14-target units start and finish nearby. This has many advantages. The archer, whose time is limited, can shoot 14 targets and be on his way, or if the western style tournament is used where the contestants are started as in golf, and not assigned to targets, numbers one and fifteen are available, and eight archers can be started at a time. Another big advantage is that after 14 targets you are back where you can get a cool drink and a little rest before tackling the last 14.

With this off our minds, we fill our pockets with white rags, take a handful of dowels and begin work on the course. We will not do any measuring yet. It takes too much time and for the present a guess is just as good. Our first job is to plan the course, which calls for some real engineering, plenty of time, and work. The shots must be authentic appearing hunting shots. At the same time, we must remember that we are going to have to build a good trail to each target., one that we will enjoy hiking over, not once, but many, many times. So we cannot put in any long shot straight up a mountain or any shot across a deep ravine unless we can build a contour trail around the end. A short, high shot is O.K. We can build a switch-back trail that will reach it without walking too far or climbing too hard.

We also have to consider the matter of lost arrows, so will try to place our targets in such a manner as to keep the number of unfound arrows at the minimum. In hilly country this is easy. Place each target against a hill. In the flat field it is a real problem, and can probably best be solved by dirt banks some 20 or 30 feet behind the targets. It may even be necessary to stretch a wire and hang a curtain of heavy sacks above the dirt bank. When we do this we will try to hide the curtain behind shrubbery for the sake of appearance.

The purpose of the rags and dowels is to mark the shots as we plan them. We are getting along in great shape and have eight targets marked when we wake up to the fact that we have only six to go on the first 14 and cannot get back to headquarters, so back we go for a fresh start. After doing this about four times everything comes out fine and we are ready to measure the shots and build our trails.

A straight line may be the shortest distance between two points, but this is field shooting and we want the scenery left as is, so the trails go the long way round and never direct from shooting position to target. We are even going to keep the target clearing as small as practical, but it must be large enough to enable us to collect our scattered arrows without coming too much in contact with dirt and brush. We are saving those old clothes for hunting and don't want to have to put them on every time we go roving.

Knowing how much hard work is connected with this trail building business, we will just draw a curtain over the whole thing until the job is finished, which brings us face to face with the club treasury and the target problem. If there is no treasury and the ground is firm, we may even have to use piled dirt for target butts. If we have just a little money or a good stand-in with a junk dealer, burlap bags filled with dirt are somewhat better. While they are not very long lived, they will hold the targets upright and give the archer the full face to shoot at, something the piled dirt will not do.

We consider straw best for a permanent course. One bale for the smaller targets and two bales for the larger ones. It is not too expensive, usually fifty or sixty cents per bale, and can be made to last for a full summer's shooting, even in the wettest of weather, if the wires are replaced or tightened occasionally. This can easily be done with the aid of a simple wire stretcher which will be described in the next issue of this magazine.

Of course, the ultra, ultra in targets is the small round bass, a younger brother of those used on target ranges. Naturally, these are quite expensive, but are very convenient when a course is to be set up for tournament purposes only. If left out they probably would be ruined by the weather, or stolen.

For target faces on permanent courses, we are all for the round ones cut from corrugated cardboard cartons. Such targets will stand a surprising amount of both use and weather and will give forth a very satisfying "whack" when hit.

If, for tournaments, you would like to use animal silhouettes, official ones may be purchased from the Bear Products Company, Detroit, Michigan.

For those who are just experimenting with the field idea, we say, forget most of the foregoing. With a 100 foot tape and a shovel you can build a shootable course in a few hours. A few rounds on that and you will probably want a real course, so save this article and read it again at that time.

The official rules follow:

ROVING ROUND RULES

Targets

Four target sizes shall be used:
1. A 24-inch target with a 12-inch center and a 4-inch aiming center.
2. An 18-inch target with a 9-inch center and a 3-inch aiming center.
3. A 12-inch target with a 6-inch center and a 2-inch aiming center.
4. A 6-inch target with a 2-inch center and a 1-inch aiming center.

(Aiming centers are for the sole purpose of giving the archer a fine mark to concentrate on, and do not have any additional scoring value).

Targets shall be round. The centers may be either round or oval. If oval they must have an equivalent number of square inches and must be placed horizontally on the butt.

The outside ring shall be black, the center shall be white, and the aiming center shall be black.

Animal targets with circles on them may be used. Only hits within the circles shall be scored. Such circles need not be painted, only outlined, but aiming center must be plainly visible.

Targets must be placed in such a manner that the full face of target is exposed to the shooter.

Ranges

A standard or official course shall consist of 28 targets, or two of the following 14-target units:

15, 20, 25, and 30 yards at 12-inch target.

40, 45, and 50 yards at 18-inch target.

55, 60, and 65 yards at 24-inch target.

Four position shots; each arrow to be shot from a different position or at a different target, as follows:

35 yards at 18-inch target.

(Each arrow from a different station or at a different target).

45, 40, 35, and 30 yards at 18-inch target.

80, 70, 60, and 50 yards at 24-inch target.

35, 30, 25, and 20 feet at 6-inch target.

A range to be official must be approved by the NFAA. If otherwise satisfactory, a 14-target unit will be approved for all NFAA shoots.

Official approval may be secured either from an individual authorized to give approval by the NFAA or by mailing a map of the range, along with photographs and a description of the range, to the NFAA.

Official approval shall depend upon the range answering the requirements previously listed, and upon the safety of the range.

Range Lay-out Suggestions

Place targets over a figure 8 shaped course in order to eliminate danger by having the archers always shoot "out" and to speed up shooting at tournaments, as parties may be started out at targets No. 1 and 15.

Mix the target ranges up as much as possible in order to take advantage of the terrain to make the course as tricky and as interesting as possible.

Scoring

No group of less than 3 may turn in an official score. All major tournaments shall use double scoring.

The status of doubtful arrows shall be determined before drawing any arrows from the target.

The target captain shall be the judge of all disputed arrows. The target captain shall draw the arrows.

An arrow cutting two rings shall be scored as being in the ring of greater value.

Skids or glances into the target shall not be scored.

Arrows passing through the target face, but still in the butt, may be pushed back and scored as a hit in the circle through which it went.

Centers (including aiming centers) shall score 5 points. The outside ring shall score 3 points.

Witnessed bounces or arrows passing through the target may be scored as 3 points.

Field Captain's Duties

The Field Captain shall appoint a target captain and two score keepers for each foursome.

He shall start the groups in both rounds.

He shall settle any question which arises.

He shall give out and collect all score cards and turn them in to the secretary.

Shooting Procedure

Archers shall shoot in groups of 4. After the first 28 targets have been shot, archers shall be placed in groups according to their scores.

Four arrows shall be shot at each target, or group of targets. No sights or points of aim shall be used, except as outlined below.

In major tournaments, archers shall shoot alone in each foursome. At minor tournaments as many may shoot at one time as there is room for. The order of shooting shall be that the man having the highest score on the preceding target shall shoot first. In case of a tie, the target captain may state the order of shooting.

Archers shall stand with both feet behind the shooting line. No one shall approach the target until all have finished shooting.

One group shall not hold up the following groups while looking for lost arrows. Enough arrows shall be carried so that each archer may continue shooting and return later to find his missing arrows.

An archer who has to stop shooting because of a broken string or similar cause, must take witnesses along when he finishes the round.

Tackle

Bows may have one mark on them which may be used as a sight. Only arrows with blunt, roving, or target heads may be used.

Spectators

Spectators may not stand any further than 15 yards in front of the shooting line and then must stand at least 15 yards to each side of the shooting lane. They must not approach the target until all archers have finished. They must not touch arrows, either in the target or on the ground, nor shall they be permitted at any point where they interfere with the archers. They shall be asked to leave the field if they annoy the contestants.

FIELD ARCHERS—ATTENTION!

In the future, NFAA membership dues shall be $1.00, and include a subscription to Ye Sylvan Archer, our newly adopted official organ.

The magazine will contain all notices, reports, and news of the NFAA, as well as stories and articles of interest to field archers.

In the case of husband and wife the dues shall be $1.50 for both, but shall include only one subscription to the magazine. This offer does not apply when they become members on different dates.

Those who have only recently paid the former 50c NFAA dues may obtain the magazine for the unexpired life of their membership upon payment of an additional 50c.

Others whose membership has not yet expired may receive it by paying a full year's dues of $1.00. Such members will receive cards dated for one year plus one half of the unexpired life of the present membership.

Members who do not wish to pay the additional dues need not do so. Their membership will be fully honored and they may participate in any activity of the organization, but they will not receive the magazine, and so will remain quite largely in the dark as regards NFAA activities.

In the past we have been unable to keep proper contact with our membership. It just couldn't be done on 50c dues. It couldn't be done for twice that if we had to depend on mimeographed letters. Under our present arrangement we have all the space we need for notices, results, plans, or any other news of the NFAA, and we will have a good hunting story or two as well. These stories will mostly relate the experiences of our own members.

John Yount, Secretary NFAA
Box 383, Redlands, California

Editorial

The Corvallis archers were pleased to have a visit from Pat Chambers on their regular shooting night, February 27. With two national champions present, Pat Chambers and Gilman Keasey, it was suggested that they stage a contest, and that the other archers take to the gallery. Pat and Gil modestly declined, however.

Dr. H. S. Hedges of Charlottesville, Virginia, has a preference for osage bows. He has a number of bows by famous bowmakers, including bows by Dr. Saxton Pope, and by Ayres and Philip Highfield of London.

One of our Oregon field archers, Bond Whitmore of Portland, is with the Air Training Corps at Santa Maria, California, taking pilot training. He would like to contact archers in that locality, as he has his hunting tackle with him and would like to try out the California jackrabbits. Bond placed third in the Oregon field archery state tournament last fall so, you see, he flicks out a mean broadhead.

POPE-YOUNG FIELD ARCHERS OF OREGON

By the Secretary

EMBLEMS

The emblem committee appointed at the last meeting has done a fine job, and felt emblems may be secured from the secretary at 25c each. It is a three-color emblem that any archer would be proud to wear.

ARCHERY RESERVE

The changes regarding the Canyon Creek archery reserve, as discussed at the Labor Day meeting, have been enacted into law by the recent session of the Oregon legislature. John E. Cooter, chairman, and the other members of the legislation committee, B. G. Thompson and N. E. Tyrrell, and President George Cathey had the full cooperation of the State Game Commission. The bill passed both houses of the legislature without a dissenting vote or voice, and several members had nice things to say about the archers, their observance of game laws, and good sportsmanship. The new law limits the reserve to that part of the old reserve north and east of Canyon Creek, and closes it to gun hunting for the entire season.

ANNUAL TOURNAMENT

Remember that the next annual tournament will be held at the Williams ranch, on the Reserve, just before the hunting season opens, probably on September 18 and 19, 1941.

The Western Tournament

Are you coming to the Western on May 31 and June 1? We like crowds in San Francisco. We are especially fond of them when they come to archery tournaments. We have a field that will accommodate all of you. It is large enough for flight shooting, with plenty of space left over for the clout. You'll have a chance to shoot both of these events, too. We think that we have some pretty good clout shooters around here, but as for flight—well, we shall expect the visitors to show us how it is done.

Don't get the idea that you are coming to Golden Gate Park just to shoot flight and clout. We're going to throw in a couple of Yorks, some Americans, and if you'd like to shoot with the ladies, practice up on your Nationals and Columbias.

The weather is sure to be good for the tournament. It's too late for rain and too early for fog. Just remember the dates, May 31 and June 1. Plan on coming to the Western Archery Association tournament in San Francisco. We'll be expecting you.

An Archery Broadcast

Joseph F. Wright, director of WILL radio station, has announced that archery will be the subject of a series of broadcasts beginning April 7. WILL is the station operated from the University of Illinois on a frequency of 580 kilocycles with a power of 5,000 watts. Dr. M. J. Dorsey, an authority on archery and bow woods, will be one of the speakers. Others

(Continued on page 15)

Upper—Duryee looking into Mad Lake. Lower—Stamps at Duryee's tent.

Upper—In the reserve. White spot near center is Duryee's tent. Center—Art Partee, I. M. Stamps, Kore Duryee, and L. D. Hunter. Lower—Entering Mad Lake Bow and Arrow Reserve at Maverick Peak.

Upper—Art Partee takes a look. Lower—Mad Lake and beyond.

Blunts from the Old Stump

The Executive Committee of the NFAA is proud to announce the selection of "Ye Sylvan Archer" as the official magazine of the National Field Archery Association. With an experienced field archer and a capable editor in the person of J. E. Davis in charge, this magazine is really going places. With an increased circulation and plenty of archery material to draw from we'll gamble our four-bits you will get many times your money's worth for your subscription.

If this issue of the Archer is a little late, don't blame the editor. The Executive Committee is responsible. With new officers coming on the job in January, they have been busier than the proverbial one-armed paper hanger, getting the summer program in shape for this issue. We even had John, while in the hospital getting his appendix "lifted," writing for the NFAA. Between giving John pills and taking dictation, he had the nurses so groggy that one of them gave him a spoonful of Carter's ink by mistake. This ought to keep his inkwell from running dry for a while. Which reminds us that the officers should be elected in the fall, so that the year's program can be planned and studied well in advance.

This issue carries the announcements of the mail tournaments. There isn't a better man in the country to run them than Karl Palmatier. If you don't get in on these tournaments you are going to miss a lot of fun. With archers divided into three classes there is a basis for fair competition, and an opportunity to win. Who wouldn't be proud of a medal or ribbon won in a national match? We Class "C" archers have something to work for, to get into Class "B," and Class "A" is within the reach of every Class "B" archer. When you get into Class "A" you don't have to unstring your bow. To make competition fairer between Class "A" archers, we have a handicap system. After all, why shouldn't an archer who really works hard and improves his shooting be entitled to win an award over a top-notcher who shoots indifferently and below his average? The handicap will force the top-ranking archers to shoot their best in order to win. It gives the lower ranking archer, by working hard, an opportunity to win. Let us know how you Class "A's" like the handicap system. Even if you are not interested in competition, why don't you get into the shooting anyway, just for the fun of it and to meet the other archers?

Some clubs shoot target and field at different seasons of the year. In Michigan, and other states, field and target meets are alternated during the month. We notice that a large percentage of the archers attend both; and the good target shots are usually the good field shots. Fred Bear of Michigan uses a 75 pound hunting bow in his field shooting, and we notice that it hasn't cramped his target style any—he still shoots well over 600 Yorks and Americans. Mixed field and target shooting apparently didn't hurt Turnock, either. He shot seventh place in the 1940 NAA National Tournament, and first place in the 1940 NFAA Mail Tournament. His field shooting must have done him some good, as his broadhead brought down an 8-point buck—and this after seven fruitless years.

In this issue archery clubs will find full instructions for building a field course. If you want to use burlap bags filled with dirt and sand, and corrugated cardboard faces for targets, you can build your own field course at the price of some perspiration and callouses. If you buy straw bales you can build a 14-target field course for the cost of one standard woven target. In the outskirts of every city and village you will find farmers who will be tickled to death to rent you a part of their pasture or woods for a field course, for next to nothing. What the field archers of the flat central states wouldn't give for some of those beautiful hills, ravines and woods that are available to you lucky Easterners and also lucky Westerners!

No organization ever started out with more good wishes and offers of cooperation than the NFAA. The American Bowman Review of Albany, Oregon, writes, "The American Bowman Review will cooperate in any way that we can in giving any extra publicity that is needed, and any material that you wish to send in will be handled in the best manner that is possible." The Northern Sportsman of Detroit, Michigan, with a splendid archery department edited by Walt Wilhelm, writes as follows, "We need all the magazines to cooperate. A selfish motive on our part or anyone else might not be for the best. Let's all work to one end— the increase in membership of the NFAA." We are deeply appreciative of the generous offers of these magazines to make their columns available to us. In reciprocation, we can only suggest that these magazines are also worthy of your support.

No more suitable memorial to Art Young, one of America's foremost field archers, could be devised than the Art Young Award Pin, created by the Art Young Foundation to be awarded to our members who are successful in bringing down big game with the bow and arrow. To be eligible for this award you must be a member of the NFAA at the time your big game is shot.

Roy Case tells us that 1170 bow and arrow deer hunting licenses were issued in Wisconsin during the 1940 deer season. Plans are being made for organizing these bow and arrow hunters. They asked for the services of Palmatier to help organize them and explain our field games. The Michigan Archers Association are sending Palmatier over with our portable field course to show them how we practice for our hunting. If a day with Palmatier on a real field course doesn't sell field archery to the Wisconsin archers, we'll give our bows and arrows back to the Indians.

That guy—George Brommers—has been poking in again. Even though the editor had him floored for the count of eight in the last issue, George is back on his feet again. But, you have to admit "he's got ideas." In all that chaff you will find many a golden kernel. Wish we had a lot more like him. If you have ideas, why don't you shoot a few blunts at the old stump? The address is 610 F. P. Smith Building, Flint, Michigan. We will welcome your broadheads of criticism, too, if you will only throw in a few blunts with them. We will acknowledge through this column, or personally, as time will permit, but you can rest assured that your suggestions will be appreciated and utilized wherever possible.

Requests are flocking in for information on field and roving ranges. Information has been sent to: Tamaque, Pennsylvania; Milwaukee Archery Association; Chicago, Illinois; Black Hawk Rovers, Waterloo, Iowa; Eustis, Florida. Eagle River Archers' Club, Wisconsin; Kimberly, British Columbia; Fellowship Archers of Visalia, California. This issue contains further information on the subject. New members are flocking in by the scores.

A tackle manufacturer has inserted a brief description of the field round and the NFAA in his catalogue, and where to contact the secretary for information. If tackle makers generally adopt this idea, they will be rendering a splendid service to field archery, and establish contacts for their customers that will insure future orders for them.

John and I discovered that we were running out of stamps, so we went down to the Government to see if we could borrow some, but we found out our credit was no good—which reminds us that it is time for you to send your "buck" to the secretary of the NFAA. He is John Yount, P. O. Box 383, Redlands, California. This pays your 50c NFAA membership fee for one year, and takes care of your year's subscription to "Ye Sylvan Archer." If you are already a subscriber it will be applied on your renewal. And don't forget to send a "half for your better-half." Better still, let your club secretary send in the dues of your club members. Why not make your club a 100 per cent NFAA club?

Midwestern Association

The 1941 Midwestern Archery Association tournament is to be held in Cincinnati, Ohio, on Saturday and Sunday, July 5 and 6. The scene of the tournament will be the Lunken Airport range, and arrangements are being made by Charles Pierson and J. M. Finnegan, president and vice-president of the association for the current year. Fred Kibbe, Coldwater, Michigan, is the secretary-treasurer of the organization.

The Midwestern has been growing
(Continued on page 16)

1941 NFAA Mail Tournament Regulations

There will be one tournament each month, starting with April and continuing through December. This should not conflict with any club or association program.

The tournaments shall be based on fifty-six targets.

A tournament need not be shot in one day.

The dates for shooting any part, or all, of a tournament must be set in advance and only the scores from those dates reported.

The tournament may be held any time during the month.

Scores not reported by the seventh of the following month shall not be considered in the official report.

Scores not reported on time shall be considered in the championship averages for the year.

The national champion shall be the archer who has the highest average score.

The average score for championship computation shall be the average of the highest actual scores made in any mail tournaments.

For a score to be considered in the championship computation the score must have been made after the archer paid his full dues for 1941 membership in the NFAA.

The target fee for each mail tournament shall be 25c per archer.

Reports of each meet shall be mailed directly to each archer.

Score cards may be had upon request, from the mail tournament secretary.

Double scoring must be used and carefully checked.

The accuracy of the scores reported must be verified by the secretary of the tournament.

The secretary of the tournament shall retain one complete set of score cards and send the other to the mail tournament secretary.

The secretary of the tournament shall make sure that the name and address of the archer can be easily read.

Score cards requested but not used shall be paid for at the rate of ten cents per dozen.

The archers are to be divided into three classes for both men and women.

MEN

Class "A" — Actual score of 321 or more.

Class "B" — Actual score of 201 to 320, inclusive.

Class "C" — Actual score of 200 or less.

WOMEN

Class "A" — Actual score of 201 or more.

Class "B" — Actual score of 101 to 200, inclusive.

Class "C" — Actual score of 100 or less.

The first tournament score shall place the archer in the class in which his score falls.

After the first tournament an archer participates in he shall shoot in the class that his score at the last tournament placed him. To illustrate: Jack shoots a score of 175 at his first tournament. He is classed as a Class "C" archer. At his second tournament he shoots a score of 270 for fifty-six targets. This is a Class "B" score but he is a Class "C" archer determined by his score of 175 for fifty-six targets at the last tournament. At his next tournament he must shoot as a Class "B" archer. So, you see, no matter how high a score is shot you cannot shoot out of your class at the tournament you are shooting in. Do your best at every tournament.

The archers in Class "A" are to be handicapped. The variation in scores in this class is great. The medal winners last year felt that too many medals went to too few archers. Because of this fine spirit it was thought some scheme should be devised to make the best archers shoot their best at all times. As the championship is determined on the actual scores and not on the handicap score the championship standing will not be affected by the handicap. The handicap will determine the winners in each mail tournament for the Class "A" division.

A medal, not the official NFAA championship medal, shall be awarded to the winner of each class.

Ribbons shall be awarded to the 2nd 3rd, 4th, and 5th places in each class.

Medals and ribbons shall be awarded as long as the income from the tournaments is sufficient to buy them.

If the income is not sufficient the tournaments shall be conducted without medals or ribbons, as the income warrants.

Regardless of income, the championship medals shall be awarded.

The secretary of each club shall certify that the tournament was held in accordance with the NFAA regulations and rules.

If an archer is quite certain that his score for the fifty-six targets is 221, or more, or very near, he should shoot four twenty-eight target rounds and report the scores. These are necessary to determine his handicap for the first tournament. If he has four such scores shot recently he may use them.

If an archer does shoot a Class "A" score in his first meet and does not have the four twenty-eight target rounds upon which to base his handicap, his score cannot be used in the mail tournament, but will be used in the championship consideration.

Secretaries of tournaments are to indicate on each score card sent in whether or not the archer is a member for 1941 with full dues paid.

Instructions for figuring the handicap will be sent to club secretaries soon. They will appear in the next issue of Ye Sylvan Archer, the official NFAA magazine.

Because the time is too short to inform the archers on the handicap system worked out by the NFAA officials, based on experience in California, the mail tournament secretary will take care of all figuring of handicaps.

In general, the handicap will be figured on the basis of a twenty-eight target score.

275 will be the top score to handicap from for the men — 175 for the women.

The handicap will be 90 per cent.

The handicaps are to be kept at even multiples of 5.

The handicap will be figured on the basis of an average score.

Use will be made of a limit score, a score that prevents the archer who shoots high at one meet and low at the next meet from getting too high a handicap. The limit score is lower than his average but takes the place of all actual scores lower than it is.

The organization of the NFAA was finally announced about two weeks ago. Since that time everybody has been in a rush to get things under way. There must be many things done to get a program under way and so some of them will just have to wait until we can get to them. A complete explanation of the whole handicap system will be worked out and reported in an early issue of the magazine. It is expected that the mail tournament secretary do all he can to educate the archers. He must first educate the secretaries so that there will be a working-informed few to conduct the meets. He must correct and explain. Will you be patient and help us along this year? We are new at this. We are doing our best to promote a game the archers want. Help us smooth out the wrinkles this year.

Tournament Secretary:
Karl E. Palmatier,
1317 Hillcrest Avenue,
Kalamazoo, Michigan.

More for the Record

Dear Mr. Davis:

Thank you, my friend, for the editorial mention you gave me in February "Ye Sylvan Archer." I *am* an archer but not an expert. I own a good bow and am teaching my 11-year-old boy to handle it. I hope each of us get good enough to do some hunting with the bow and arrow in the future.

Come and see me if you visit Arkansas. We will get Ben Pearson and try bagging a few ducks in the rice fields if the season is right. I'll let you and Ben do the shooting and I'll carry the ducks.

Sincerely,
O. E. Rayburn.

(We intend to make a point of publishing these invitations to hunt. Some day we may have an opportunity to take advantage of some of them, and we then may need to have the invitations down in black and white where we can find them. Ed.)

IN MAD LAKE RESERVE
(Continued from page 2)

are not going to let any of those bucks see us coming toward them."

I have hunted with Irl for five years now, and he has one of the best pair of eyes to spot any wild life in the woods I have ever seen. Nothing escapes him, and he is by far our best shot. Never gets excited—just as cool a man as you ever saw.

Finally we arrived at the Marble Creek canyon where we had plenty of cover, and would start to climb. We separated, agreeing to meet at the top in about fifteen minutes. After waiting for thirty minutes and no Irl, I started on. Saw no game, and as it was getting dark and I was in new country to me, I started for camp. I arrived about ten seconds after Irl. He was very quiet. He wasn't much good in helping get dinner, which was very unusual, as he always does more than his share. After dinner was over and dishes washed, we sat down near the stove for our usual chin, chin. After I finished my account of what happened after we separated I waited for Irl to tell his story. I would give anything if I had a record of it. There is no better hunter or better sport than Irl. If he should miss a buck at 15 yards he would tell us about it, and *it would still be fifteen yards*. Do you get me? He is another Nagler. Here is Irl's story as near as I can tell it:

"Gosh, Kore, I wish you had stayed with me this afternoon. You hadn't been gone five minutes when I spotted a big doe feeding about 60 yards away. I knelt behind a log hoping for a buck to show up. I must have knelt there for all of ten minutes, and she wasn't over 40 yards away. I said to myself, 'If that was only a buck, now, I'd put an arrow right through her heart.' She evidently had gotten wind of me as all of a sudden she raised her head straight up high and there was a two point buck. I got weak as a cat. Had a good four feet in height to hit, and only forty yards away. I couldn't pull my bow back. My left hand shook, and my right arm trembled, and the arrow rattled against the bow. The arrow flew two feet over the top of his head. Away he went. Fifteen minutes later I scared up a three point buck, and missed again. In the next forty-five minutes I located my three point three more times, shot and missed, and all of the shots were from 40 to 60 yards. I am still weak. Well, I had my opportunity."

I have never had buck fever, so I have something to look forward to. Have had a good many experienced hunters tell about getting it, and usually it is caused by some surprise or unusual occurrence.

The next morning as we were breaking camp, Irl stopped and said, "I wonder if that buck is waiting for me to come and play with him some more."

Blackmore of Marysville, was hunting near the entrance each week end. The last week McKay, a new archer of Seattle, and a member of the police department, shot his first buck, which ran a short distance and died in the brush not over fifty feet from Blackmore's tent. I am reliably informed that the latter was fit to be tied.

S. L. Michael of Tacoma, wrote me the following about the archers from his city:

"Bob Schmid, Mike Errigo, and myself spent a very enjoyable week end in the Reserve the first Sunday. Saw several doe and I jumped a big buck but did not see it. Mike got one shot at it at 20 yards, but being his first attempt at hunting in any form, he was so excited he missed it by several feet. He said he had plenty of time for two or three more shots but all he could do was to get an arrow on the string. Did not have the strength to pull the bow. It was worth the trip just to hear Mike tell about it. Then after the buck left Errigo, it ran straight into Schmid, who was sound asleep and didn't have an arrow on the string. He would have had plenty of time for several fine shots at 20 to 25 yards, had he been prepared. He was plenty sore over the incident. We had a lot of fun getting a couple of grouse, and in general, had a fine time."

The following week-end Harvey Strandwold and his family spent three days in the Reserve, camping at the car. He got several shots but failed to connect. He was very enthusiastic about the Reserve, and he is already planning on a real stay there next year.

Franklin Jones of Everett, had a good shot but missed.

The Howatt and Stewart families and Harvey Wilson, all of Yakima; Schiller of Walla Walla; J. W. McFarlane of Pasco; Stangle and a friend of Bellingham, and McDonnoe of Marysville, all hunted in the Reserve this year. Understand most of them had shots.

Harry Johns of Tacoma, spent a few days at the Ranch but had such a headache (due to the altitude, I understand) that he could not stay the full week he had planned.

There were a number of other archers whose names I did not get and do not know how they came out. The deer seemed to be much lower this year and those that hunted lower had the most shots.

There are a number of new members on the Game Commission this year. However, we are hoping that they will make this a permanent Reserve for the archers. If they do, the hunting will get better each year. This year the Reserve was obtained at the last meeting of the Commission and the game wardens did not have time to post the Reserve properly. The first game laws came out without any mention of it. Therefore, rifle hunters could not be blamed so much if they got into our Reserve, as quite a number did.

Nearly all the archers that were there this year are going again, and are planning a longer stay, when possible. There is plenty of cover, but very little underbrush. You can find as rough country as you want, or you can take it easy and do very little climbing. There are three lakes in the middle and all are good fishing.

Doesn't that sound like an "Archer' Paradise?" It is.

An Archery Broadcast

(Continued from page 7)

will include Harold E. Kenney, assistant professor of physical education; Miss Marion Marshall, active in archery for women, and Dr. A. M. Buswell, profesor of chemistry and chief of the Illinois water survey. Dr. Dorsey is head of the department of horticulture at the university.

Mr. Wright has been making arrangements for these broadcasts since Christmas. The discussions he has arranged will include early and recent history of archery, bows, arrows, techniques, competitive and recreational archery. The broadcasts will be heard at 5:30 each Monday evening, immediately following a 30-minute concert by the University of Illinois concert band.

So far as known, this is the first time a university has devoted so much time to archery. The series will continue for eight weeks.

WILLIAM B. ALLEN

We are grieved to report the death of William Belknap Allen, 73, of Louisville, Kentucky, in the Presbyterian Hospital, Chicago, on Sunday, January 26. Archers of this country will remember this gracious Southern gentleman, and those knowing him will realize what his death has taken from their sport.

Mr. Allen, a native of Louisville, was graduated from Yale University in 1881, and at the time of his death was making his home in the Blue Grass section of his native state.

In addition to his archery activities, Mr. Allen was a sailing enthusiast,

Col. W. B. Allen

having won several races with his sailing yachts. He was a member of the Biscayne Yacht Club of Miami, Florida.

Disdaining sights and points of aim, Mr. Allen was one of the finest "off-hand" archers in the country, posting American Round scores of over 600 consistently. His last appearance at a national tournament was at St. Paul in 1939, when he was the oldest archer, in point of years, on the line. At that tournament, Mr. and Mrs. Allen donated a perpetual trophy to the NAA, to be awarded the lady competitor over 60 years of age posting the highest total at the national tournaments. The trophy, known as the Frances G. Allen Trophy, was won in 1940 by Mrs. C. H. Warner.

Midwestern Association

(Continued from page 11)

in importance the past few years and it is expected that the 1941 gathering will be one of the largest in its history. Its territory embraces the states of North Dakota, South Dakota, Nebraska, Kansas, Oklahoma, Iowa, Minnesota, Missouri, Michigan, Wisconsin, Illinois, Indiana, Ohio, Tennessee, and Kentucky.

In addition to the target competition, the Midwestern program will contain championship events in flight, clout, and field shooting.

Details as to headquarters, and other facts pertaining to the tournament, will be announced in an early issue.

SUBSCRIBERS PLEASE NOTICE
A cross appearing in this space means that your subscription has expired and we would appreciate your prompt renewal so that your name may be kept on our mailing list.

CLASSIFIED ADVERTISING

RATES for Classified Advertising 5 cents per word per issue. Count initials and numbers as words. Minimum charge is 50 cents.

BOOKS AND MAGAZINES

The AMERICAN ARCHER, a national quarterly, $1.00 per year, 521 Fifth Ave., New York City.

RELICS AND CURIOS

INDIAN RELICS, Beadwork, Coins, Curios, Books, Minerals, Weapons. Old West Photos. Catalog, 5c. Genuine African Bow, $3.75. Ancient flint arrowheads, perfect, 6c each— Indian Museum. Osborne, Kansas.

"ARCHERY TACKLE, HOW TO MAKE AND HOW TO USE IT." by Adolph Shane. Bound in cloth and illustrated with more than fifty drawings and photographs. Information for making archery tackle and instructions for shooting. Price is $1.75. Send orders to Ye Sylvan Archer,

"ARCHERY," by Robert P. Elmer M. D., revised edition, most complete book on archery published. 566 pages of valuable information for colleges, libraries, schools, camps archery clubs and individuals. Price $5.00 postpaid. orders to Ye Sylvan Archer, 505 North 11th street, Corvallis, Oregon.

Archery Raw Materials

WM. A. JOY

9708 So. Hoover Street
LOS ANGELES, CALIF.

THE FLAT BOW
HUNT & METZ

70 pages of Archery information for 50 cents, well illustrated. Ye Sylvan Archer, 505 N. 11th St., Corvallis, Oregon.

CHANDLER
Universal Broadheads

The Broadhead that costs less than a big rifle bullet, from 5c to 8-1/3c each. The inexpensive Broadhead for hunting.

Also Universal Broadhead Kits, with complete material for making one doz., good Broadhead Arrows.

Also Hunting, Fishing and roving Points.
FREE CATALOGUE
T. B. CHANDLER
11819 4th Ave., Compton, Calif.

FISH HEAD
B-80   B-1

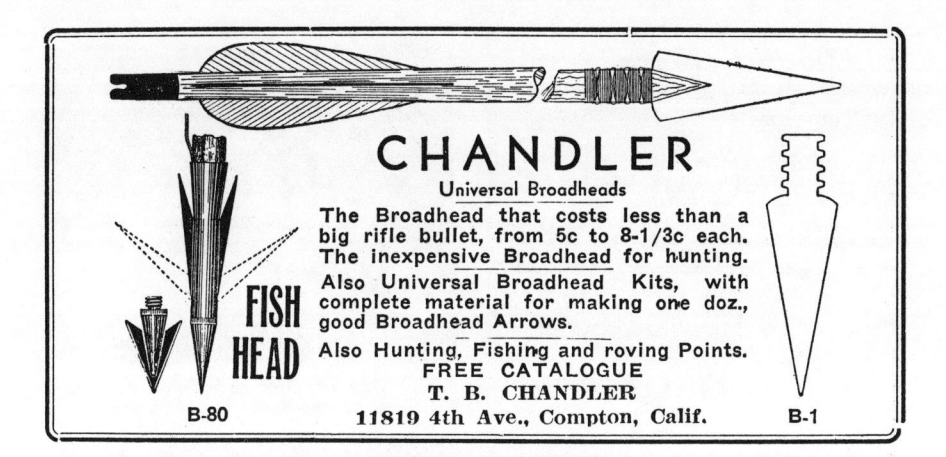

BEAR

Has a new catalog ready. It contains only field and hunting equipment. Your copy is ready. Just drop us a card.

BEAR PRODUCTS CO.
2611 W. Philadelphia Ave., Detroit, Michigan

WIN WITH BEN PEARSON ARROWS

Beautiful and accurate to the Nth degree but win their real laurels on the range. Arrows made as arrows should be—and at prices you can afford to pay. Send for catalogue.

BEN PEARSON, INC. — PINE BLUFF, ARK.

Ⓖ

"THE MARK OF DISTINCTION IN ARCHERY TACKLE
Fine Yew Target and Hunting Bows, Plain or Backed with Rawhide. Lemonwood Bows with Rawhide Backs.
College and School Equipment
Target, Hunting and Roving Arrows
Price List on Request
Wholesale — Retail
EARL GRUBBS
5518 W. Adams
Los Angeles, : California

Arcadian Life Magazine
Stories of the Ozarks

Pioneer History - Folklore
Pastoral Living

$1.00 a Year; 25c a Copy

Display Adv. $1.50 per inch
Classified, 3c a word. Three insertions for the price of two.

O. E. RAYBURN, Editor
Dept. 15
616 S. Benton St
Cape Girardeau, Mo.
P. O. Box 200
Caddo Gap, Arkansas

Please mention Ye Sylvan Archer when writing advertisers.

Ye Sylvan Archer—$1.00 per year.

E. BUD PIERSON
Bowyer — Fletcher
Tournament Tackle, Sinew, Glue, Raw Materials.
245 University Ave
CINCINNATI, OHIO
Custom Made Tackle

Cassius Hayward Styles

BOWYER AND FLETCHER

—Tackle that has stood the test—

28 Vicente Place

BERKELEY, CALIFORNIA

Paul H. Gordon
Author of "The New Archery"
Producing
Tackle — Materials
Latest and Finest for Field or Range
Write for Free Catalog
Beacon Hill Craftsmen
Beacon, N. Y.

Hunters and Field Archers

It is time to begin thinking about a new hunting bow for this fall. Write for that new big catalog, which explains everything. By America's oldest tackle maker.

WILLIS H. BARNES
Sturgis — — Michigan

HANDBOOK—How to Make and Use Bows and Arrows—90 Pages well illustrated (with catalog) 35c.

CATALOG—100 pictures—color spread—Instruction Folder. 10c.

CATALOG alone 5c. Stamps or Coin.

L·E·STEMMLER· QUEENS VILLAGE·N·Y·

MID-NOX

PRECISION ✓
STRENGTH ✓
ECONOMY ✓
BEAUTY ✓

now **MID-NOX**

Formerly Sold as Middleton's Improved Replaceable Nocks

ARE AVAILABLE AT NEW LOWER PRICES
AND IN SUFFICIENT QUANTITIES TO SUPPLY ALL DEMANDS

MADE IN THE FOLLOWING DIAMETERS
3/16" and 7/32" 30c per Doz. $2.25 per 100.
1/4", 9/32" and 5/16" 35c per Doz. $2.50 per 100.
11/32" Diameter 50c per Doz. $3.00 per 100.

All Made in the Following Colors:
WHITE, YELLOW, PEACH, ORANGE, LIGHT GREEN, LIGHT BLUE, MEDIUM BLUE, BRIGHT BLUE, BLUE MOTTLE, ORCHID, JADE MOTTLE, RED AND BLACK

◄ MID-NOX ► the original replaceable nocks are not new—or an untried product—they have been very thoroughly tried out and improved from time to time during a period of ten years, through such trials, until today they can be placed upon the market with justified pride.

My apologies to the many customers who have wanted ◄ MID-NOX ► during this experimental period at a time when I was unprepared to meet demand.

The material used in ◄ MID-NOX ► is ideal from the Archer's standpoint but is very hard to control during the manufacturing process. There are many other materials and processes which will produce a similar looking nock in only a fraction of the time but the saving of only a few cents per hundred could not induce me to use either materials or processes which would produce an inferior nock.

◄ MID-NOX ► are precision made, they are extremely tough, they burn off easily to facilitate replacement, every care has gone into their production to give the individual user ultimate satisfaction.
Place your faith in the dealers who recognize the superiority of ◄ MID-NOX ►

Watch this space next issue for list of dealers who carry complete stocks in all sizes and colors.

DEALERS—WRITE FOR NEW PRICE LIST.

CARL W. MIDDLETON
160 West 2nd Street
Pomona, California

MID-NOX
For Archers who Prefer the Best

Ye Sylvan Archer

April, 1941

Corvallis, Oregon

Vol. 12   No. 12

Ye Sylvan Archer

Official Publication of the National Field Archery Association

Vol. 12   April, 1941   No. 12

Published the fifteenth of each month
for archers by archers
505 North 11th Street, Corvallis, Oregon

J. E. DAVIS .... Editor
RUSSELL JONES .... Business Manager
Subscription Price .... $1.00 Per Year
Foreign Subscription .... $1.25 Per Year
Single Copies .... 10 Cents

Advertising Rates on Application

TABLE OF CONTENTS

Page

ARCHERY-GOLF—A FIELD ARCHER'S GAME
By Paris B. Stockdale 1

AIMS AND ASPIRATIONS OF THE NATIONAL FIELD ARCHERY ASSOCIATION
By A. J. Michelson 3

OLYMPIC BOWMEN LEAGUE 5

THE LOWER BRACKET BOYS 5

EDITORIAL 6

ATTENTION—ROVING ARCHERS 6

NFAA BULLETIN
By John L. Yount, Secretary 7

BLUNTS FROM THE OLD STUMP 9

FROM COSNER 11

BROWN COUNTY OPEN 12

Archery-Golf --- a Field Archer's Game

By Paris B. Stockdale

The field archer is a fellow who craves the out-of-doors; one who enjoys a tramp across the country-side. With it all he loves his bow and arrow. He is a down-to-earth chap who likes variety in his shooting. Because of these things, he is intrigued by such archery-games as hunting, the several kinds of roving rounds, stump shooting, flight shooting, and last, but not least, archery-golf. There is no intent, here, to infer that the target shooters are tabooed in these activities, since many of them, too, (especially here in Ohio and adjoining states) are strong boosters of the field games.

Recognizing the need for organization, the Ohio leaders in field archery set up a formal organization on May 4, 1935, called the "Ohio Archery-Golf and Hunting Association." J. Harlan Metcalf of the Physical Education Department of the Ohio State University, was elected the first president. One hundred paid-up members were quickly obtained. The objectives of the organization were so sound and appealing that growth and greater strength came year by year. A year ago the name was changed to "The Ohio Field Archery Association." Although all varieties of field archery are encouraged by the organization, greatest emphasis has been placed upon archery-golf and archery-hunting. (Even tho we have no game bigger than cottontails and ring-pheasants.) Popularity in these activities is measured by participation, of course. At one of the hunting parties, conducted on the central Ohio archery game preserve set up by the State Division of Conservation, there were 150 archery-hunters in one day; at a recent rovers shoot sponsored by the Dayton Archery club there were over 300 shooters; and at the annual state championship archery-golf tournaments the registration reaches nearly 100.

Archery-golf offers a variety of styles that requires a combination of techniques found in no other archery game. First, there is the flight shooting which challenges one for distance and direction accuracy with his pet flight arrow. Then there is the approach shot from an unknown distance which challenges one's estimating ability. And finally, there is the putt requiring refined accuracy in marksmanship. And, at the end of the game, the archer has had perhaps a five mile or more envigorating hike across mother nature's open air course.

In Ohio much thought has been given to the ever-lurking problem of rules and scoring. One of the functions of the state organization was to study the problems of the game and to formulate some standard plan for play. Out of this came the adoption of a set of "official" archery-golf rules. Practically all clubs in Ohio abide by these rules. Some organizations outside the state have adopted them. The rules allow considerable flexibility in the lay-out of the course. Generally, a golf course is selected for the layout. For this reason, most play is confined to the winter season when regular golf play is at a minimum. (There are, however, two all-year courses in Ohio; one at the Ohio State University Country Club in Columbus, and the other at the Sharon Woods Park near Cincinnati.) The course generally has nine or eighteen "holes" (targets). Distances from tee to target range anywhere from 80 yards to 650, with an average somewhere around 350. The target, under the Ohio rules, is a fixed one suspended from some sort of a standard on each "green." It is three feet in diameter, with a 4½ inch bull's-eye surrounded by a 12-inch red band. The remainder is white. On the final putt at each target, which must not be taken closer than 10 yards, if the gold is hit, one shot is added to the number of flight and approach shots already made; two shots for one in the red; three shots for one in the white; and four shots for a rarely missed target.

As in golf, the winner is the one with the lowest score after completing play around the entire course. The player is allowed any weight bow up to 60 pounds, but is restricted to one bow. He may use sights or he may shoot instinctively. He is not permitted to pace-off distances.

During the past winter more than a dozen club, district, and state archery-golf tournaments have been held in Ohio. With its challenge for so many types of shooting, its variety, its liberal rules for play, its opportunity for fellowship, and its appeal to the out-door field lover, is there any wonder at the increasing popularity of archery-golf? The future will see interstate and nationwide archery-golf competition.

The following is a complete list of awards in the seventh annual Ohio championship archery-golf tournament, 36-target round, held at Columbus, Ohio, April 5-6, 1941, sponsored by the Ohio Field Archery Association:

State Championship Class—Men
1. Paris B. Stockdale, Columbus, 102.
2. Fred Schweitzer, Cleveland, 114.
3. Fred Schenk, Newark, 114.

State Championship Class—Women
1. Peggy Donaldson, Cleveland, 128.
2. Doris Schenk, Newark, 135.
3. Helen Rybolt, Middleton, 145.

Class B—Men
1. Clive Schneider, Columbus, 131.
2. W. A. Rhoton, Columbus, 135.
3. E. Bud Pierson, Cincinnati, 135.

Class B—Women
1. Mrs. W. T. Lewis, Columbus, 162.
2. Myrda Nusserderfer, Columbus, 172.
3. Kate Smith, Cleveland, 173.

Trophy for most bullseyes—Paris B. Stockdale, 31 bullseyes.

Men's club team championship—Columbus Archery Club team, composed of Paris B. Stockdale, J. S. Conner, Richard E. Stultz, H. C. Ramsower; total 466.

Women's club team championship—Columbus Archery Club team, composed of Mildred Cozad, Evelyn Stultz, Jean Sceurman, Ruth Hook; total score 603.

Inter-city cup—won by Columbus.

Lowest score for one-day 18-target round, men—Paris B. Stockdale, Columbus, 50; women—Doris Schenk, Newark, 64.

Gold-in-one—Charles Pierson, Cincinnati.

Longest flight shot, using archery-golf bow in regular archery-golf play: Men's heavyweight division—Charles Pierson, Cincinnati, 372 yds.; men's lightweight division — Bud Pierson, Cincinnati, 346 yds.; women's division — Irene Hartman, Cincinnati, 240 yds.

Novice flight award—Richard E. Stultz, Columbus, 305 yds.

Noon Time Group of Ohio Archery Hunters

Aims and Aspirations of the National Field Archery Ass'n

A. J. Michelson, National Chairman

These questions have been asked about the National Field Archery Association: Why was it organized? What has it to offer archers that cannot be found in other organizations? What are its future plans?

First of all, the National Field Archery Association is not a rival organization nor competitive with the National Archery Association. Nor is it interested merely in membership expansion. An archer can belong to both organizations without conflict in interest or loyalty. The finest friendship, understanding and cooperation exists between these two organizations. Five of the six members of the executive committee of the NFAA are active members of the NAA.

If all this is so, why are two national archery associations necessary? To answer this question you must look a long way back into history. Although the NAA is less than one hundred years old, yet its traditions go back a thousand years into English history. Its rules, tournaments, organization, rounds, etc., are so founded upon precedent, that change is slow and almost a heresy. You would no more think of changing the York round from 100, 80, and 60 yards to 90, 70 and 50 yards, or shooting four arrows at an end instead of six, than cutting off your right arm. We are proud to belong to such an organization as the NAA, whose origin is so steeped in tradition and antiquity; whose policies are conservative; and whose mission is to perpetuate the traditions of the Woodmen of Arden.

But through the years, a group of archers have developed who belonged to no archery associations. They shot no targets or tournaments as we know them in the NAA. They shot a bow, just because they loved it. They shot in the back yard or in the fields and woods; at tin cans or stumps, just for the fun of shooting. Others took up the bow in the sport of hunting for large and small game. Still others shot at "rovers," archery-golf and field rounds, and tournaments, entirely different from the traditional target tournament.

This group grew, began organizing locally and soon its voice was heard. They were demanding National recognition. Could and should the NAA take care of this group of unorganized archers, field archers, we call them? Many of us thought it could. But the rules, tournaments and organization of this century-old target association were not drafted to adequately provide for this new (and yet very old) type of archery. Should radical changes be made in its constitution and by-laws to accommodate this new-born babe? Should a governing body of target archers direct the activities of field archers? This might cause dissention. Organized field archery was new. Much experiment, many head aches, trial and error, lay before any organization which undertook the organization of field archers. Wouldn't it be better that the field archers should have their own organization, make their own mistakes, and work out their own salvation, instead of asking the NAA to undertake to raise and educate this obstreperous youngster? The best minds of American Archery came to that conclusion, and the National Field Archery Association was born with the blessing and good wishes of the National Archery Association.

Webster's New International Dictionary defines the word "archer" as follows: "A bowman; one skilled in the use of the bow and arrow."

The words "target archer" and "field archer" are not defined. We will attempt our own definition. A "target archer" is a person who shoots arrows from a bow at inanimate objects placed at predetermined, and announced or known distances. A "field archer" is a person who shoots arrows from a bow at animate or inanimate objects at unknown, unannounced and not predetermined distances. The definition of "field archer" allows of no narrower or hair-splitting distinctions. If you are a target archer you should support the NAA. If you are a field archer you belong to the NFAA. If you shoot both target and field, you should support both associations. Both associations are promoting archery in their respective fields, in harmony, and without conflict or friction. There is no reason why state and local associations cannot do the same.

For whom was the NFAA organized? If you are a so-called dyed-in-the-wool field archer, not interested in regulation target tournaments, this is your organization. If you don't belong to any archery club, but just shoot for the fun of it—at stumps, tin cans, or nothing in particular— you belong in this organization. If you are a beginner or a novice, we are glad to welcome you and instruct you. If you enjoy both target and field shooting, we want you in our association, too. If you are an archery-golfer or a roving archer, or want competitive field games, your place is with us. If you are a target archer, we urge you to try our various field games and you will find a renewed and increased interest and joy in archery. Field archery has an appeal to women too. Every target club should have field archery as a part of its active program. This will increase the pleasures of its members as well as the club membership. If you hunt with the bow, you need a national organization to establish and improve your hunting privileges, and keep you in touch with hunting conditions everywhere.

While the NFAA will promote and provide competition and tournaments in various field games for those interested in competitive field shooting, yet tournaments are by no means a major part of its program. Primarily we are interested in providing for those thousands of archers, who are not interested in target archery, an organization which they can feel is their own, whether they ever shot or shoot an arrow in a field tournament. The NFAA is interested more in the social side of field archery — the health, recreation and pleasure that comes from loosing a well-spent shaft, when a group of archers (perhaps just you and your pal) get together to spend an hour in the woods and fields, or on your own rover or field course. The NFAA will bring to you information on all that is new and old in field shooting — equipment, shooting technique, hunting conditions, interesting bow hunting experiences, of all of which there has been too little available in the past. The bow and arrow hunter can be proud to belong to the NFAA, whether he hunts woodchucks in New Jersey, rabbits in Ohio, javalina boar in Texas, or deer in Wisconsin. Bow and arrow hunters need a strong national organization to protect and promote their interests, in providing more and better hunting conditions, areas and seasons of them, nationally as well as in the several states. They need a national clearing house for an exchange of ideas and information on hunting conditions and methods. This the NFAA will provide.

While the NFAA is not interested in membership drives simply to get people who are not archers to join, we believe that every archer is potentially eligible for membership in our organization. There are only two qualifications for membership in the NFAA—good sportsmanship and an interest in field archery. Field archery will be given the right kind of publicity, and methods will be provided to make it available to those of the general public who are interested. We repudiate the dogma that archery belongs to the grown-ups. Any tackle dealer will certify to the enormous demand for inexpensive bows and arrows by the younger group. They have the interest—where is the organization to lead them along the right path? The NFAA should and will provide for this junior group.

Field archery is as old as the first bow, drawn tens of thousands of years ago, in defense or in the hunt by our primitive ancestors. But organized field archery is very young. We have much pioneering to do. We will try many experiments and make many mistakes. But all of these will be but to one end—to make the NFAA a finer and better organization—to make it more enjoyable and beneficial to you. In organized numbers there is strength. Field Archers of America! This is your organization! Let's get together!

Olympic Bowmen League

The fourteenth annual tournament of the Olympic Bowmen League has ended with the Chicago Grant Park Archers clamping down the lid on the team championship with nine points to spare over the Cleveland Archery Club.

The ten high teams are as follows:

Chicago Grant Park—No. 1	31361
Cleveland Archers—No. 1	31352
Albany Archery Club	31106
Carlisle Archers	31104
Highland Park Archers	30789
Spokane Archery Club	30727
Pittsburgh Archers	30671
Milwaukee Archers	30616
Chicago Grant Park—No. 2	30531
Cleveland Archers—No. 2	30307

The ten high women's teams:

Chicago Grant Park	29806
Cleveland Archers	28792
Cincinnati Indoor Archers	28266
Highland Park Archers	28156
Goodyear Archery Club	28020
Milwaukee Archers	27767
Seattle Archers	27245
Umpqua Archers	26902
New York Archers	26809
Spokane Archery Club	26382

Individual high scores — men — 10 matches:

Harry Bear	85	818	792.8
E. Hill Turnock	83	805	791.
Fred Schweitzer	77	790	788.
Stanley Gajewski	59	778	785.6
Bill Haynes	62	769	782.6
Henry Evers	54	763	782.2
Jack Skanes	51	758	781.
Forrest Lemly	58	767	780.6
Lewis Whitmarsh	45	764	780.2
Glen Lightner	48	742	778.4

Individual high scores — women — 10 matches:

Ethel Gates	50	759	778.4
Kathleen Wheeler	26	689	765.5
Edith Fraser	32	686	758.
Alyce Clayton	20	638	755.6
Mildred Miller	21	643	755.4
Belvia Carter	16	633	754.1
Alta Benedict	13	550	733.9
Edna Howatt	9	542	731.2
Pat Costello	8	522	726.4
Peggy Donaldson	7	514	720.3

Tom Farnsworth of Albany, California, tied Gilman Keasey's 1938 individual single score record of 808. Ethel Gates set a new individual single score record for women with 802.

In the future the National Archery Association will sponsor the Olympic Bowmen League tournament, and the winners will be recognized as the National Indoor Archery Champions of the United States. Kore Duryee has done a wonderful job for archery in his management of the Olympic Bowmen League for the last fourteen years.

The Lower Bracket Boys
By the President

I am pleased to see that our low down body is due for some belated recognition. The National Archery Association proposes a Good Sportsmanship Trophy, to be awarded to some lucky fellow shooting 'way at the bottom at a national tournament.

The sponsorship isn't wholly, to be sure, above suspicion in some respects. If there are more logical candidates for the honor than Erle Stanley Gardner, Jack Willard, Col. F. E. Pierce, John Yount, Kore Duryee and Erma Haberle, you will have to go far to find them. Of course — there is always John Davis.

Can't say that I make out the game of the other two initial sponsors, E. Hill Turnock and Bill Folberth, unless they are beginning to feel Father Time creeping up on them, and are making suitable provisions. However, this is no time to throw asparagus on the gents, seeing that in this case we are fellow travelers.

Your president hereby waives any future speculations, no matter how pertinent to the case. On behalf of my fellow bracketeers, I wish to heartily endorse the plan. Furthermore, I will at once send in one buck, cash money, myself. That I will feel not just a little honored to have the opportunity to associate myself with the project is something I won't stress right now.

Seriously, I think that this trophy is going to mean much more to the recipient on account of its multiple sponsorship, than if it were due solely to the generosity of one individual. It is the participation of our lower brackets that make our tournaments feasible from an economic standpoint. Another feature that I like is the dollar ceiling placed on contributions.

Therefore, if you, my fellow bracketeers, feel as I do about it, please send one dollar or less to Mr. Henry Cummings, 33 Oak Hill Street, Newton Center, Massachusetts.

Editorial

We very much appreciate the confidence in Ye Sylvan Archer that has been shown by the board of directors in naming this magazine the official publication of the National Field Archery Association. We wish to thank all those who have helped to bring this endorsement to us. We recognize the responsibility that the endorsement places upon us, and will do all in our power to prove worthy. NFAA has as fine a set of officers as could be hoped for, and with the cooperation of individual field archers, there is no doubt regarding the success of the new organization.

"Susquehannock Shots" is the name of the three-page, mimeographed monthly publication of the Susquehannock Archers. We thank Bertha K. Drebelbis, the corresponding secretary and editor, for a copy of the March issue. Mrs. Drebelbis would be glad to see copies of other archery club publications. The address is 2534 Canby Street, Penbrook, Harrisburg, Pennsylvania.

WILHELMINA BROMMERS

Archers everywhere will be saddened to learn of the passing of Wilhelmina Brommers, wife of George Brommers, on March 24, 1941, at Bellevue, Washington. Mrs. Brommers had been ill for some months but she had been thought to be much improved in health, and her death was a sudden and unexpected blow to her husband and friends.

Mrs. Brommers had taught school many years. The writer once asked her what she taught, and her answer was, "Children." Her life work will carry on the principles of industry, integrity and honor which she instilled in the hearts of her "Children."

Atttntion—Roving Archers

It has been suggested that many feet of film, taken on roving courses all over the country, could be used to promote this fascinating phase of our sport.

If archers, or clubs, in possession of such film (16 m.m. black and white or color) would be willing to donate it for the purpose of publicity, a movie of five or six hundred feet could be made up and sent around to various clubs when requested. To further this worthy cause, have a reel taken at your next roving meet.

Forward all film, along with a few pertinent comments regarding it, to H. C. McQuarrie, 3400 Fruitvale Avenue, Oakland, California, so that it may be coordinated and edited with other film. Mr. McQuarrie is film editor for the National Field Archery Association project.

It is understood that the film will become the property of the NFAA, and can be requisitioned from John Yount, Secretary, Box 383, Redlands, California.

Don't forget the National Tournament in August at Portland, Oregon.

"Pop" and "Ma" Prouty do a little blowing.

NFAA Bulletin

OFFICERS

President—A. J. Michelson
 610 F. P. Flint Bldg., Flint, Mich.

Vice-President—Paris B. Stockdale,
 Geology Dept., OSU, Columbus, Ohio.

Secretary-Treasurer—John L. Yount,
 Box 383, Redlands, California.

EXECUTIVE COMMITTEE

Western—H. C. MacQuarrie.
 3400 Fruitvale Ave., Oakland, Calif.

Mid-Western—Fred Bear,
 2611 W. Philadelphia, Detroit, Mich.

Eastern—T. C. Davidson,
 53 Mountain Ave., Springfield, N. J.

By John L. Yount

CORRECTION IN ROVING RULES

Please note that the six-inch target should have a *three-inch center*, instead of a two-inch center as stated on page 5 of the March issue of Ye Sylvan Archer.

TEAM TOURNAMENT

The officers of the NFAA have worked out rules and plans for a series of team matches to begin in May, in addition to our regular program of mail tournaments as announced in the last issue.

We plan two leagues—a Class A and a Class B with a limit of 8 teams each. If enough more register in either class a second league will be organized and a playoff arranged.

All we need now are the teams, so how about signing your club up right away so we can work out the schedule and get things started on time. The cost will be $2.00 a team, and since the league is so arranged that there will be little secretarial expense, this money will be used to purchase trophies to be the permanent property of the winning teams.

In place of the usual archery system where high score wins and every team is matched against the field, this is to be a round robin team league in which each team meets each other team at some time during the season, but is never matched against more than one club at a time. This gives a personal contact between clubs that should lead to some real inter-club rivalry, and believe you me, that is what it takes to make a strong home club. When you were a kid it was school spirit—now let's call it club spirit—whatever it is, it takes team to team matches to bring it out. Just a high total score is too d——d impersonal. We also hope and believe that these matches will better acquaint the archers of the various parts of the country.

A club doesn't live and prosper by the glory of its stars, so to deflate those chesty individuals and make these matches club affairs, they are to play under the following rules:

Each club team shall consist of four two-man teams. These teams shall be numbered from one to four with the highest ranking archers in the first team, next best in the second team, etc.

The match shall consist of two full 28-target rounds in which each two-man team will be matched against the corresponding team of the opposing club, team No. 1 against opposing team No. 1, etc.

The scoring will be by the Nassua system with the teams of each foresome, these are foresomes, even though the teams may be hundreds of miles apart, competing for the three possible points, one for the first round, one for the second and a third for the highest total score for both rounds. Under this scoring system no two-man team can win or lose over three points. Even though your No. 1 team may be hopelessly outclassed, your 4th team may make it up by shooting just a little better than their opponents. So don't worry about the Turnocks, Hughes or Quayles. This makes it possible for a club whose four teams win all rounds to make 12 points. Naturally any club winning 7 points in any match wins the match.

The standing of the clubs in each league will be decided on a percentage basis as in baseball or football.

Tie matches will not be shot off. Each club will receive 50 per cent for the match.

If the league finishes with the winners tied, the championship shall go to the club whose team shot the highest total score in the final match.

Each club must mail a lineup of its teams to the NFAA secretary and to the secretary of the opposing club before shooting any rounds of the match. Team lineups may be changed between matches but not during a match.

If any club has reason to believe that an opposing club has purposely wrongly ranked its teams it may appeal to the NFAA for an investigation. If the charges are found to be true the match shall be declared to be forfeited.

Any team which does not complete its match in the prescribed time shall forfeit the match.

If a club enters teams in more than one class the 8 highest ranking shots must be entered in the higher ranking class.

Any team may be entered in Class A.

A team may be entered in Class B, if it does not have over three Class A men on it, i.e., men shooting scores of 160 or over as covered in the NFAA rules for the summer's tournaments.

Beginning with May there will be one match a month until October when the season will end with two matches, making a total of seven.

To save having too many tournaments the scores shot in any competitive round. three or more in the squad, may be used. providing the contestant declares in advance his intention of shooting his match round at that time. Once this is done the score must be turned in and no other can be considered.

The two rounds of these matches need not be shot on the same day.

All scores must be mailed to the secretary of the NFAA and to the secretary of the opposing club not later than three days after the closing date for the match.

More About NFAA Movies

If you haven't read Macquarrie's request in this issue, hunt it up and read it. Then if yau have a good course, get busy and send in some film, but don't be sore if Mac doesn't use it all. We want this film to show as many courses and tournaments as possible and so naturally cannot give too much time to one course.

This film should make an interesting evening's entertainment for any field club and we want them all to see and enjoy it; but we think this picture will have a more useful purpose than mere entertainment. Our sport is new and very little is known about laying out good courses, consequently this picture, by showing the good features of a number, should be of considerable help to clubs planning new courses or improvements to old ones.

It will also have a real publicity value for where there are archers there are groups, Elks, Legion, Rotarv, etc., looking for entertainment. Here will be a chance for the archer to furnish the entertainment and at the same time demonstrate that Field Archery can be a worthwhile game, one that should appeal to any average sportsman.

To the Tackle Makers

If you think this effort being made by the NFAA to interest new archers is a worthy one, get in touch with Mac. You know pictures cost money and while we realize that you are already spending all you think you can afford for advertising, we don't believe you have put out so very much toward getting new archers. Here is your chance.

Stanley Stevens, field co-champion archer of Oregon, had the misfortune to lose most of his fingers on both hands. Stanley finds he is still able to shoot the bow, however.

Blunts from the Old Stump

Last summer, in a conversation with Dr. Elmer, we stated that it was regrettable that the archers did not have a simple word to express "shooting with the bow and arrow." We suggested the word "arching." Dr. Elmer, in a very dignified manner, said the archers had coined a word which had been in use for thousands of years, and that verb is "shooting." "Shooting" means "shooting with a bow and arrow"—and nothing else. So, the next time you invite your friend to go "shooting" with you, you mean shooting with a bow and arrow, and not with firearms or other weapons. "Shooting" belongs to the archers. Let the firearms sportsmen coin their own word.

The archery golfers were among the first organized field archers. Archery golf is one of the NFAA field games. It is very popular throughout the East, and in many central states, and some western states. Dr. Paris B. Stockdale, of Ohio, is submitting an interesting and instructive article on "Archery Golf" for our archers who have access to golf courses, for the play of this game.

A uniform archers' emblem—button for men and pin for women—has been devised. It does not represent any archery association, and may be worn by all archers, organized as well as unorganized. It is a modification of the 150-year old Woodsmen of Arden emblem, showing a target arrow and broadhead crossed, symbolic of the two great branches of archery, target and field. This emblem may be obtained in groups of ten for 50c each for the men's and 60c each for the women's, from Edward Frenz, 76 Cottage Street, Melrose, Massachusetts.

Tom Imler, Joe Cosner, and Russ Mulholland of Phoenix, Arizona, on Washington's birthday, each bagged a javelina boar. In Texas, the javelina boar is classed as big game, and undoubtedly is dangerous game. The Art Young Award Committee is preparing its report on what shall be considered big game to be eligible for the Art Young big game award. Full requirements for this award will be published shortly.

Who is the oldest living field archer? We nominate George R. Robinson of Frankfort, Michigan, who was a field archer in 1879, when Charlotte, Michigan, had an active archery club. George R. Robinson has a sixty-five acre roving course, as well as standard target ranges, with overnight cabin accommodations, on beautiful Crystal Lake. If you vacation in Michigan it will be well worth your while to visit with a real old-time field archer.

Round Robin Team Shoots between clubs in an eight-club league are being formed. This is an interesting type of shooting. It gets the clubs acquainted, and the lowest score man on your team may win points for your club, when your best shots may lose points. Your team scores and mail match scores may be shot at the same time and counted for both, if so announced before the shoot.

By this time you have shot your first NFAA mail matches and are ready to send in your first scores to the Tournament Secretary. We wish each club Secretary would advise the Tournament Secretary how many archers your club has who are not shooting, but would shoot in the mail matches if a "free-style" class were provided. "Free-style" means with or without sights or other aiming devices, and any type bow and roving or target arrows would be permissible in this class. If there is a sufficient demand for a "free-style" class in the mail tournaments we will provide it for about the June or July matches. Announcements will be made later. You still have plenty of time to start shooting in the mail matches.

Tom Imler, Jr., took some fine colored action films of their javelina boar hunt, which will be available for club use. Will field archers who have good, interesting films of bow and arrow hunting advise the Secretary, giving a description of the films? We would like to have this information and films available for other archers and clubs for entertainment and educational purposes. It would be a fine gesture if tackle dealers and manufacturers would sponsor some educational films on field archery, to be prepared and used under the direction of the NFAA, the films to give proper credit to the sponsors.

Field archers in Iowa, Wisconsin, New Hampshire, and other states, are active in organizing state field archery associations. Let us know what the field archers of your state are doing to organize. The NFAA will be glad to advise and assist you in your organization work. Instructions on committee work have been sent out to the various district committees. If your committee has not sent in its recommendations for appointments to zone committees, please do this at once. We need your help for a smoothly, efficiently functioning organization.

We have received a copy of the New Mexico Field Archery Association Constitution, which is splendidly drafted. All members of the New Mexico FAA are required to hold membership in the NFAA. Joe Robb, their president, 322 Harvard Ave., Albuquerque, New Mexico, tells us they are looking for a new location for their field course because their former grounds, located near the city reservoir, have been taken over and fenced in by the military authorities as part of the national defense program.

We are pleased to see that the field archers in Bakersfield, Calif., have organized and will participate in the mail matches. Kenneth L. Jones, 913 33rd St., Bakersfield, is their live-wire secretary. We are sure that field archery will be well represented in that part of the state.

The Saint Louis Archery Club, Emmet B. Johnson, president, 917 Clarendon Ave., Saint Louis, Mo., is very actively sponsoring field archery in that state. Field archers in Missouri interested in helping organize a state field association should contact them.

Many field archers have inquired whether it is necessary to have their field courses approved by the NFAA before they shoot in the mail matches. It will be OK for you to shoot your matches on your courses laid out in accordance with your understanding of the rules. Then, when you report your mail scores to Palmatier, tournament secretary, also send a penciled sketch of your field course, giving shooting direction, distance and description of each target, to John Yount, NFAA secretary, for official approval.

We wish folks, when writing of their hunting experiences, would identify themselves with their addresses, as well as their names, and instead of saying they hunted in "Wild Gulch," etc., tell the name of the state, and the location with more exactness. The whole value of your experience will be lost, if you don't tell us when and where it occurred.

California field archers are busy endeavoring to secure from their legislature special hunting areas for their bow and arrow hunters. Bow and arrow hunting isn't even legal in Arizona. Michigan archers are now requesting their legislature to change their licensing statutes to permit rifle men to try the bow during the bow and arrow deer season without compelling them to sacrifice their rifle privileges during the rifle season. Many other states do not recognize the bow and arrow hunter, nor give him those privileges to which his particular type of hunting is entitled. In many states bow and arrow hunting is not even considered humane. It is for this reason that bow and arrow hunters need a strong, national organization to protect and advance their special interests. Right now the Conservation Committee of the NFAA and its various sub-committees, are gathering information from every state on the following questions:

1. Is bow and arrow hunting for game legal?
2. Restrictions, if any, on use of the bow in hunting?
3. Kind of game hunted?
4. Special seasons for archers and periods?
5. Special areas for archers and size?
6. License fees for residents and non-residents?
7. Experience and reaction of game commissions to archery hunting?
8. Are season and areas controlled by game commissions or legislatures?
9. Hunting conditions generally, and where to hunt?
10. The manner in which archers in the various states obtained special privileges for their bow and arrow hunters?

It is impossible for the NFAA to

personally contact all unorganized field archers, but if you appoint yourself a committee-of-one and tell archers you know, about the NFAA, and why they should belong to it, you will be doing them a good turn, as well as doing your bit for organized field archery.

Letter Box

FROM COSNER

Dear Davis:

For two days I rode a horse in groaning misery trying to bring back enough hog meat to feed my starving wife. I sat upon the palpitating and mangled result for two hundred miles in order to bring it back. When I did get it back, a buzzard would have been ill at even flying over it, let alone pecking himself out a mess of it. With stiff and painful gait I went to bed. All I had left to hope for was that the pig wouldn't stink as bad or that my condition (new name for it) would permit sitting. I had practically no hope that my wife would call me other than a dam fool. I was justified.

The next morning the pig stunk worse and looked like an enraged police dog with no tail. He was ably assisted by the other two we killed. Not having been drawn, all three of them needed testing with a tire gauge in case of leaks. My wife had thought it over during the night but was unable to arrive at anything better than the prevailing prefix for "fool." She unwillingly used it but in a hopeful fashion as though there was still time to work out a better way to say it. And then to top it all, I could scarcely move except in a peculiar sidling shuffle like one of those toy men that you wind up and that hardly ever work.

Moving through the house in this fashion, my eye fell upon a copy of the Sylvan Archer that had arrived while I was gone. I grabbed it eagerly. Here I would find word of my friends. I would laugh at good old George and his "Doghouse." I would read the notes by the editor in an appreciative fashion. All this I would read first as a sort of main body of my literary meal. John Yount and a possible story by one of the less apt like Willard or Gardner would be the dessert. So far, so good. Off I started.

As I got through about half of Brommers' literary wet wash, the hair on my neck began to rise. None above that point rose, due to absence. I managed to finish his attempt to work out something in the nature of humor and then started in on two or three columns of some stuff that I couldn't identify. I read through a paragraph or two and as my mad at old George let off a little I began to wonder who the hell had enough pull with Davis to get that sort of bilge printed. I turned back a page in order to see. It said, "From the Editor."

At first I stood transfixed like a startled fawn. Then I grabbed at the next page and read on. I was not startled then. Cold and implacable rage mounted up my limbs, got as far as the sore part, jumped over it and went on up. There was my name in cold print. There also was the name of Jack Willard, as truthful and fine a gentlemen as ever poured dead rabbits out of a gunny sack. After both these names was that word that has caused so many men to start beating people across the knuckles with their chins, that word, "liar."

With a quavering squeal of rage I bared my two fingers and made for the typewriter. In silent fury I wrote for two minutes before I hit anything but the back-spacer and the dollar sign. I became aware that there also was no paper in the thing. By the time I had hunted up a sheet and squared off to lay two guys out like two leaves of boarding house lettuce, I began to see things in a better light.

A belief in a creator is a great thing. Just to show you. Davis had indicated in his dribble that he was an entomologist and needed bugs in order to carry on. Brommers is a logger and needs an entomologist to carry off, so to speak. There is no need for them to run around the country looking for each other. It is far better not to disturb that balance that exists among all creatures. How much better it is for me to calmly sit and squirt the tobacco juice of contempt upon these two toiling scarabs as they roll their balls of literary fertilizer toward my feet.

While thinking these lofty and noble thoughts, I remain,

Sincerely,
Joe Cosner.

Brown County Open Tournament

The Brown County Open Tournament will be held in beautiful Brown County State Park, 45 miles south of Indianapolis, Indiana, May 31-June 1. E. S. Richter of Chicago, 1941 president of B.C.O., and a number of fellow-Chicagoans are to conduct the meet. Over and above two days of Yorks, Nationals, etc., this year's committees plan to provide a lot of fun for the archers who think that is a legitimate part of our sport.

Abe Martin Lodge will be headquarters there, and twenty cabins nearby will provide room for those who get their reservations in early. Write the Lodge for living quarters. For information, contact E. S. Richter, 11th Street and Indiana Avenue, Chicago, or Paul E. Baldwin, 6054 Harper Avenue, Chicago.

Yours truly,
P. E. Baldwin,
Chmn. Pub. Com.

SUBSCRIBERS PLEASE NOTICE

A cross appearing in this space means that your subscription has expired and we would appreciate your prompt renewal so that your name may be kept on our mailing list.

CLASSIFIED ADVERTISING

RATES for Classified Advertising 5 cents per word per issue. Count initials and numbers as words. Minimum charge is 50 cents.

BOOKS AND MAGAZINES

The AMERICAN ARCHER, a national quarterly, $1.00 per year, 521 Fifth Ave., New York City.

The Flat Bow—70 pages of Archery information for 50 cents, well illustrated. *Ye Sylvan Archer*, 505 N. 11th St., Corvallis, Oregon.

RELICS AND CURIOS

INDIAN RELICS, Beadwork, Coins, Curios, Books, Minerals, Weapons. Old West Photos. Catalog, 5c. Genuine African Bow, $3.75. Ancient flint arrowheads, perfect, 6c each—Indian Museum, Osborne, Kansas.

ARCHERY SUPPLIES
at prices everyone can afford to pay.
YEW WOOD STAVES
at .... $2.00 and $3.00
P. O. CEDAR DOWELS
per 100 .... $2.75
FINE YEW WOOD BOWS
any weight and length
to 6 feet .... $6.50 to $12.50
Send money with order.
Monte Vista Archery Co.
Rt. 1, Box 149, Tacoma, Wash.

---

70 pages of Archery information for 50 cents, well illustrated. Ye Sylvan Archer, 505 N. 11th St., Corvallis, Oregon.

Archery Raw Materials

WM. A. JOY

9708 So. Hoover Street
LOS ANGELES, CALIF.

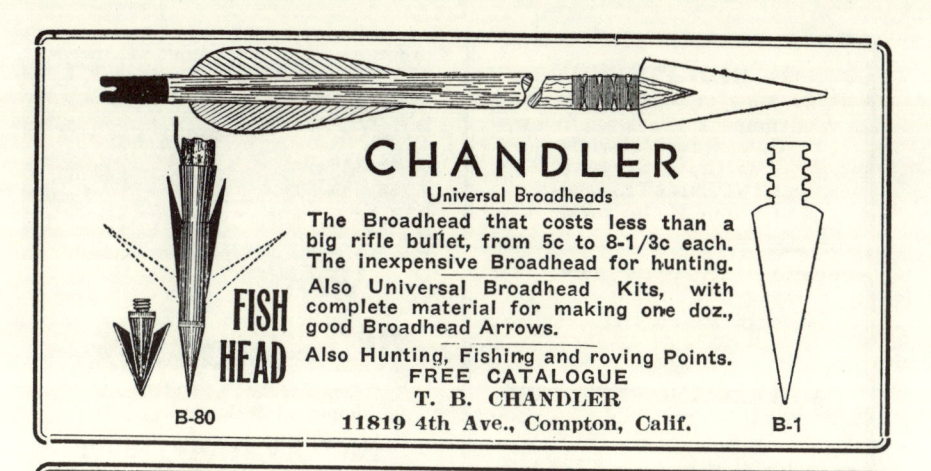

CHANDLER
Universal Broadheads

The Broadhead that costs less than a big rifle bullet, from 5c to 8-1/3c each. The inexpensive Broadhead for hunting. Also Universal Broadhead Kits, with complete material for making one doz., good Broadhead Arrows.

Also Hunting, Fishing and roving Points.
FREE CATALOGUE
T. B. CHANDLER
11819 4th Ave., Compton, Calif.

FISH HEAD
B-80   B-1

BEAR ARCHERY CO.
Specializing in
FIELD AND HUNTING EQUIPMENT
A Catalog for a Post Card
2611 W. Philadelphia Ave., Detroit, Michigan

WIN WITH BEN PEARSON ARROWS

Beautiful and accurate to the Nth degree but win their real laurels on the range. Arrows made as arrows should be—and at prices you can afford to pay. Send for catalogue.

BEN PEARSON, INC. — PINE BLUFF, ARK.

G

"THE MARK OF DISTINCTION IN ARCHERY TACKLE
Fine Yew Target and Hunting Bows, Plain or Backed with Rawhide. Lemonwood Bows with Rawhide Backs.
College and School Equipment
Target, Hunting and Roving Arrows
Price List on Request
Wholesale — Retail
EARL GRUBBS
5518 W. Adams
Los Angeles, : California

Arcadian Life Magazine
Stories of the Ozarks

Pioneer History - Folklore
Pastoral Living

$1.00 a Year; 25c a Copy

Display Adv. $1.50 per inch Classified, 3c a word. Three insertions for the price of two.

O. E. RAYBURN, Editor
Dept. 15

616 S. Benton St
Cape Girardeau, Mo.
P. O. Box 200
Caddo Gap, Arkansas

Please mention Ye Sylvan Archer when writing advertisers.

Ye Sylvan Archer—$1.00 per year.

E. BUD PIERSON
Bowyer — Fletcher
Tournament Tackle, Sinew, Glue, Raw Materials.
245 University Ave
CINCINNATI, OHIO
Custom Made Tackle

Cassius Hayward Styles

BOWYER AND FLETCHER

—Tackle that has stood the test—

28 Vicente Place

BERKELEY, CALIFORNIA

Paul H. Gordon
Author of "The New Archery"
Producing
Tackle — Materials
Latest and Finest for Field or Range
Write for Free Catalog
Beacon Hill Craftsmen
Beacon, N. Y.

Hunters and Field Archers

It is time to begin thinking about a new hunting bow for this fall. Write for that new big catalog, which explains everything. By America's oldest tackle maker.

WILLIS H. BARNES
Sturgis — — Michigan

HANDBOOK—How to Make and Use Bows and Arrows—90 Pages well illustrated (with catalog) 35c.

CATALOG—100 pictures—color spread—Instruction Folder. 10c.

CATALOG alone 5c. Stamps or Coin.

L·E·STEMMLER· QUEENS VILLAGE ·N·Y·

PRECISION ✓ STRENGTH ✓ ECONOMY ✓ BEAUTY ✓

now MID-NOX

Formerly Sold as Middleton's Improved Replaceable Nocks

ARE AVAILABLE AT NEW LOWER PRICES
AND IN SUFFICIENT QUANTITIES TO SUPPLY ALL DEMANDS

MADE IN THE FOLLOWING DIAMETERS
3/16" and 7/32" 30c per Doz. $2.25 per 100.
1/4", 9/32" and 5/16" 35c per Doz. $2.50 per 100.
11/32" Diameter 50c per Doz. $3.00 per 100.

All Made in the Following Colors:
WHITE, YELLOW, PEACH, ORANGE, LIGHT GREEN, LIGHT BLUE, MEDIUM BLUE, BRIGHT BLUE, BLUE MOTTLE, ORCHID, JADE MOTTLE, RED AND BLACK

← MID-NOX → the original replaceable nocks are not new—or an untried product—they have been very thoroughly tried out and improved from time to time during a period of ten years, through such trials, until today they can be placed upon the market with justified pride.

My apologies to the many customers who have wanted ← MID-NOX → during this experimental period at a time when I was unprepared to meet demand.

The material used in ← MID-NOX → is ideal from the Archer's standpoint but is very hard to control during the manufacturing process. There are many other materials and processes which will produce a similar looking nock in only a fraction of the time but the saving of only a few cents per hundred could not induce me to use either materials or processes which would produce an inferior nock.

← MID-NOX → are precision made, they are extremely tough, they burn off easily to facilitate replacement, every care has gone into their production to give the individual user ultimate satisfaction.
Place your faith in the dealers who recognize the superiority of ← MID-NOX →

Watch this space next issue for list of dealers who carry complete stocks in all sizes and colors.

DEALERS—WRITE FOR NEW PRICE LIST.

CARL W. MIDDLETON
160 West 2nd Street
Pomona, California

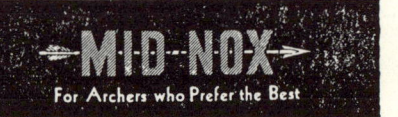

← MID-NOX →
For Archers who Prefer the Best

Ye Sylvan Archer

May, 1941

Corvallis, Oregon

Vol. 13   No. 1

Ye Sylvan Archer

Official Publication of the National Field Archery Association

Vol. 13   May, 1941   No. 1

Published the fifteenth of each month
for archers by archers
505 North 11th Street, Corvallis, Oregon

J. E. DAVIS .... Editor
RUSSELL JONES .... Business Manager
Subscription Price .... $1.00 Per Year
Foreign Subscription .... $1.25 Per Year
Single Copies .... 10 Cents

Advertising Rates on Application

TABLE OF CONTENTS

	Page
THE PROOF OF THE PUDDING By Donald M. Cole	1
BLUNTS FROM THE OLD STUMP	3
ARCHER ON ADVISORY BOARD	4
NFAA BULLETIN By John L. Yount	5
EDITORIAL	6
FIELD ARCHERY AT NATIONAL	6
FIELD ARCHERY FOR WOMEN By Lulu Stalker	7
OHIO FIELD ARCHERS IN PICTURES	8 and 9
HOW TO FIGURE HANDICAPS By Karl E. Palmatier	10
FIELD ARCHERS OF SO. CALIF. By Elmer Bedwell, Secretary	12
MID-WEST ADDS FIELD ARCHERY	13
NFAA MAIL TOURNAMENT FOR 1941	14

The Proof of the Pudding

By Donald M. Cole, Redfield, S. Dak.

Every man's conclusions are pretty largely the result of his measuring matters by the yardstick of his own experience. The following, therefore, is merely an account of such archery practice as I have found good in the pursuit and taking of big game.

My first error was in yielding to the very common desire for a bow beyond my strength, and harboring the erroneous idea that great killing power, or penetration, could be had only with heavy bows. Equipped with an 80 pounder of tremendous cast I entered British Columbia, wrestled mightily but futilely with my master, and drove arrows at blinding speed all over the place. None of them, however, connected with game. It was a discouraging experience, and left me convinced that control of one's weapons should be the archer's first concern.

My return to sanity was prompt and I next carried a 60 pound yew, a weight I could control and which as a hunting weapon is within the strength of the average man. This, however, also proved a disappointment, failing to drive shafts completely through the chest cavity of a large animal, although a moose was laid low.

Pondering upon my dilemma while sitting before the campfire and whittling a pine stick with a dull knife, I began to view penetration not from a poundage basis, but from the standpoint of a cutting edge. True, I had always kept my broadheads keen, but perhaps they could be made much keener. This seemed most doubtful, but was, in fact, a field which I had not widely explored.

The following morning experiments were under way. The moose hide was folded double and, taking three broadheads, I sharpened number 1 in the usual manner, number 2 with a different cant to the file, and number 3 in a wholly unorthodox manner. A criminal appearing companion, Dr. Rastall, was then called in and asked to press each through the double moose hide and select the one which penetrated with the least effort. He promptly chose number 3. All arrows were retouched, the hide quadrupled and the test repeated. Number 3 was again selected. The hide was now folded to six thicknesses, the heads again retouched, and to our amazement number 3 sliced through easily and cleanly.

On returning home, archer friends were contacted by mail and asked to forward a broadhead, sharpened in their best manner, for purposes of comparison. A basement laboratory was set up wherein these heads were pressed through various materials whose resistance approached that of hair, hide and muscle. The poundage necessary for complete penetration was registered on a weight scale. The number 3 method of sharpening proved superior to all others, and in many instances was vastly superior. To a cautiously applied thumb its edge did not feel much different than the edges I had always given my hunting arrows, but there was no denying the evidence of the scales; yet for ab-

Ready for the field test

solute proof there remained the need of a field test, performance on big game, and the following season I again entered British Columbia, armed with a 60 pound yew of very ordinary cast but with my arrows bearing the supposed super edge.

The first shot at big game occurred when a mule deer stepped from behind a thicket at about 40 yards. The ancient yew bent like a twig and in that moment felt foolishly weak in my hands. My eagerness to drive a hard, swift shaft was such that the brief interval of flight seemed endless, yet I distinctly saw the feathers vanish through the buck's side. With a bound the animal was gone and I followed slowly to find him in less than 50 yards, standing quartering away and apparently in great distress. No second shaft seemed necessary but I moved forward to within 25 yards of the animal, drew and loosed. The arrow entered the left flank, ranged full through the body forward, cut through the thin upper portion of the right shoulder blade and emerged to sail several yards before coming to earth. The buck gave three or four spasmodic leaps and dropped stone dead.

A few days later a bull moose revealed his presence on a mountain side by giving two hoarse coughs. The stalk was without difficulty but the denseness of the jackpines and limbs guaranteed the deflection of an arrow, even at close range. I decided to approach within touching distance if that were necessary or possible, but a vagrant air current must have given warning and with a snort and tremendous crashing he was off, running down grade and quartering away. Automatically I drew and in that moment saw ahead a single opening perhaps ten feet wide, a hole in the crisscross of trunks and limbs. Holding the 60 pound yew easily at full draw where a heavier weapon would have been beyond my strength, I waited until the bull's head appeared in the opening, then loosed. The distance was fully 40 yards and, while I watched, the arrow whispered, dove down the tunnel and struck the animal full through the lungs with that faint chukking sound all archers know. While running forward there was no opportunity for a second shot for the bull quickly slowed, wobbled, staggered and crashed. The arrow had sunk to the feathers, severing every vein and artery it touched, and slicing through both lungs.

Here then, I thought, was proof that no man needs a bow of more than 60 pounds, providing his arrows are of a proper keenness to assure deep penetration. Thus armed, he commands the bow, and accuracy is his servant.

This super-edge is accomplished by what is known as draw filing. At the start employ the usual steps. For solidity secure the blade in a vise and with an 8-inch double cut file prepare the edges in a wide smooth bevel. This type of file is of no advantage except that it cuts the steel with evenness and unusual rapidity and is a time saver. Now remove the head and change to a 6-inch flat single cut file with fine teeth. The best is none too good, for upon this tool depends the excellence of the completed product. Mark this well, hold the file stationary and draw the head against its cutting surface, nearly parallel with the tool, and in this backhanded manner "filing" the head from barb to point. Let the pressure be light but even. The motion might be described as wiping, and when properly executed will give the workman the feel of making a light, clean, continuous cut. All four bevels should be treated in this manner, and the finished job should appear without any trace of a wire edge.

Thus sharpened, a broadhead cuts through tissue with surprisingly little force. It remains, however, like all cutting tools which possess a fine edge. That edge is easily affected by rough treatment. Therefore, carry a "new file" in a pocket of the quiver, and promptly restore the super-cutting edge of any broadhead the moment its keenness has been impaired.

NOTICE TO ADVERTISERS

President W. G. Williams of the NAA wishes to notify all archery tackle makers or others who may wish to advertise in the NAA tournament program to send in copy at once, as the programs will be printed soon. Advertising rates will be the same as last year. Write to W. G. Williams, 6635 NE Alameda, Portland, Oregon.

Blunts from the Old Stump

The results of the April mail tournaments are reported in this issue. Congratulations to the winners! Competition is pretty keen, and you top-notchers in order to win will have to shoot just a little better next time. We want all our field archers interested in competition to participate.

Some archers think that because there is a mail tournament monthly, it is necessary to shoot in all nine mail matches in order to be eligible for the National Mail Trophy. This is to correct this erroneous impression. Nine monthly shoots were provided to enable archers in all parts of the United States to participate. Archers in some Southern states do not shoot during the summer months, and archers in some Northern states do not shoot in the early spring or late fall. You can shoot in all nine monthly tournaments if you wish, but you can be eligible for the mail championship if you only shoot in three. Your three best scores will be counted in determining your national total and national standing for the year's shoot. So, you still have plenty of time to enter into the monthly mail tournaments.

Several tackle manufacturers are preparing target faces, plain and animal, for the field round, as well as portable backstops and other accessories for the NFAA field round. These will be advertised shortly in Ye Sylvan Archer.

We congratulate the Arkansas archers in their success in having their Legislature pass a bill establishing two special bow and arrow seasons for deer hunting each fall — each season being seven days before the regular rifle season. It looks as if California will also be successful in their quest for special areas for their bow and arrow deer hunters.

The Wisconsin Bow Hunters Association was formed on March 30. Wisconsin has more bow and arrow hunters than any other state. We are glad to welcome Roy Case of Racine, Wisconsin, and Clarence Rhubesky of Wauwatosa, Wisconsin, editor of the Wisconsin Archer, as members of the National Field Archery Association. The NFAA will be assured of active support from the Wisconsin bow and arrow hunters.

Many sportsmen's clubs are showing an active interest in field archery. The Ventura County Rod and Gun Club is making provision for field archery as one of its club activities. Field archers are sportsmen of the first water, and we can look for many more sportsmen's clubs to provide field activities for their archer members, as well as encourage gun hunters to try the bow in field games and in hunting.

We didn't know there were any deer in Utah — but along comes a letter from F. H. Zimbeaux of 124 South 6th Street, East, Salt Lake City, in which he says: "We here in Utah have quite a few field archers. Many more than target. We have been fortunate in having for several years now, an archery reserve for deer hunting and lots of deer in it, with license fees dropped to a dollar and a half for buck, doe or fawn. During the 1939 season eight deer were killed by archers in this state." Glad to hear from you, Utah. Utah archers can contact Zimbeaux and start your state field organization.

We were under the impression that there were many more target archers than field archers in the East. This is probably because the target archers in the East are better organized. It is, therefore, a distinct surprise and pleasure to hear from an old time field archer like C. F. Schuster, 577 Pleasant Street, Holyoke, Massachusetts. The Holyoke archers are inquiring about the field round. We have given them the dope and we are sure that if they add field archery to their club activities, they will not only sustain, but increase, club interest.

We are pleased to learn of the development of organized field archery in many new states. We are in receipt of letters from C. E. Morrill, 6104 Hickery Street, Omaha, Nebraska; George Needhams, 4057 Tejon, Denver, Colorado; Roy Storlie, 615 Chestnut Street, Anaconda, Montana. Archers in these states interested in forming local and state field associations can contact them. The NFAA will be glad to help you organize.

We suggest that you Eastern archers, who are curious but perhaps skeptical as to whether the NFAA field round is worth while, ask E. R. Teubner Jr. of Horsham, Pennsylvania. Teubner writes: "I am sympathetic to this field archery, as you know. I have built a field archery course in the back of my home and have enjoyed this phase of archery as much as target archery." — And to be sure his membership in the NFAA does not lapse, he sent his check to cover a five-year membership.

Hall Burris of Detroit, Michigan, has returned from a six weeks bow hunting trip in Mexico. While there he bagged two deer and a javelina boar. He has a film record of his hunt, which we hope can be made available to interested clubs.

Sasha Siemel is back in the states for a two months lecture tour. Sasha, you know, is a field archer who shoots jaguar in South America with the bow, and also hunts them with a spear. He has created a tremendous amount of good publicity for field archery, and if he should be in your neighborhood, don't miss attending his interesting lecture and pictures.

Recommendations for zone committee appointments are coming in fast. We will appreciate it if those who have not already done so would send in their committee recommendations at once. The good workers in field archery are not as well known as those in organized target archery. So, if you know of some real live wire field archers who are good organizers and willing to work won't you please send us their names? We need them and can use them in promoting field archery.

It has been suggested that the NFAA should incorporate. There are many benefits to be derived from being an incorporation, but there are also certain disadvantages. For instance, the requirement of most states that foreign corporations cannot operate in their states without becoming domesticated. The Legal Committee is making a study of this question and will report soon.

Ye Sylvan Archer can use your good hunting stories and pictures, as well as your field club news. Why not let the rest of us know about your hunting experiences and your club activities? If you have something to contribute to the knowledge of hunting technique, or equipment, write Ye Sylvan Archer about it. If you want information on bow and arrow hunting conditions, equipment, or technique, ask about it in Ye Sylvan Archer, and our experienced field archers will advise you. Ye Sylvan Archer is the magazine of the field archers of America. Let's all contribute our bit to increase its interest and value.

Archer on Advisory Board

Paul H. Gordon, archery authority, craftsman, author, and lecturer, director of the Beacon Hill Craftsmen, at Beacon, New York, has been appointed to the Advisory Board of The Hobby Guild of America, it was announced by Albert O. Bassuk, president of the Guild, from the organization's headquarters, 34 W. 33rd Street, New York City.

Mr. Gordon, a maker of bows and arrows whom one well-known archer has called "a clever craftsman, a great student of archery, and an artist in his chosen profession," has a background of unusual fitness for

(Continued on page 6)

NFAA Bulletin

OFFICERS

President—A. J. Michelson
610 F. P. Flint Bldg., Flint, Mich.

Vice-President—Paris B. Stockdale,
Geology Dept., OSU, Columbus, Ohio.

Secretary-Treasurer—John L. Yount,
Box 383, Redlands. California.

EXECUTIVE COMMITTEE

Western—H. C. MacQuarrie.
3400 Fruitvale Ave., Oakland, Calif.

Mid-Western—Fred Bear,
2611 W. Philadelphia, Detroit, Mich.

Eastern—T. C. Davidson,
53 Mountain Ave., Springfield, N. J.

CHISELERS AND CHEATS

By John L. Yount

In a strictly amateur sport such as archery, it seems a shame that we must sooner or later expect to find a thin sprinkling of these undesirable gentry, but they are found in every sport, and we can be thankful for having gotten this far without them.

So, now while our records are still clean, let's plan to keep them that way by using an ounce of prevention. I think we will find this much better than being forced to use a pound of cure later. This can only be done by the clubs themselves who must strictly enforce all NFAA rules and at the same time keep a close watch for crooked play, which can take a number of forms in our sport, the chief of which would probably be illegal sights and crooked scoring.

In keeping our sport honest there is no need of hurting the feelings of anyone. Don't single out an individual, but treat all club members alike. If you think that some archer is using a flock of sights see to it that all bows shot in the tournament are inspected and any possible sights covered with masking tape. If the suspected is innocent, nobody will be hurt; if he is guilty, his score will soon prove it.

If you want to avoid suspicion and at the same time make the cheat's actions the more noticeable, don't carry a list of target distances in your pocket. They will not help you if you do not have sights. By the same rule, if you see someone using such a list or any kind of range finding gadget, look for sights. Names, trademarks, or any number of things properly placed on a bow will make a nice string of sights, one for each yardage.

Don't run to the target and start pulling arrows until the rest of the foursome gets there, and don't let anybody else do it.

Follow the rules. If they call for double scoring, double score, and check at each target. Don't just copy the other fellow's card at the end of the round. If the NFAA finds that any rule is undesirable it will be removed, but while it remains a rule abide by it and insist that the other fellow does likewise. The rigid enforcement of rules may make an occasional enemy, but a lack of respect for the rules of any game will wreck the game.

A last word to those who may be planning to cheat. Don't do it! You will eventually be caught, greatly to your embarrassment. I know it looks exceptionally easy to chisel in our game, but believe me it isn't, and when you are caught it will be hard to laugh it off.

Editorial

This issue is the initial number of volume thirteen of Ye Sylvan Archer. The number thirteen has no superstitious fears for us, especially since killing our first deer during our thirteenth season of archery hunting. We believe this will be an auspicious year for archery and Ye Sylvan Archer in spite of the topsy-turvy condition of the world in general.

President Williams of the NAA has announced the appointment of Dr. Geo. A. Cathey of Portland as field captain, and Natalie Reichart of Corvallis as lady paramount at the National meet.

Fred B. Bear announces that he has acquired the interest of the Bear Products Co., engaged in the archery and sporting goods business at 2611 Philadelphia Avenue, Detroit, Michigan. Mr. Bear will continue the business as sole owner at the above address under the name of Bear Archery Company.

From Ingo Simon

Scotland Hall,
Suffolk, England.
Dear Sir:
In your issue for February, just arrived, someone asks what to call to warn a person getting into danger from his arrows. The old English call for that was FAST. I believe, having called this, that the archer was held blameless if there was an accident to anyone between him and his mark.

Yours truly,
Ingo Simon.

Field Archery at National

President W. G. Williams of the NAA has announced the appointment of Dr. H. H. Hewitt as chairman of the committee on field archery for the NAA tournament in Portland.

Dr. Hewitt announces that the field archery events will be a round of archery-golf played under the rules of the Portland Archery-Golf Club, the NFAA round of 56 targets and the Pope-Young field round as shot by the Pope-Young Field Archers of Oregon. The round consists of 36 animal silhouette targets, one shot at a target, at unknown distances. Oregon rules require the use of broadhead arrows weighing at least an ounce, but at the National target arrows will be used. However, archers are invited to bring their heavy bows and heavy arrows, with 35 calibre points. The targets can take it.

Archer on Advisory Board

(Continued from page 4)

service to the Guild. An Eagle Scout, scout and camp leader for many years, he brings to his work a knowledge of other hobbies and craft skills. He has lectured extensively before audiences ranging from young children to business clubs and university social study groups. His "The New Archery: Hobby, Sport, and Craft," published by Appleton-Century in 1939, is already by way of being a classic. "Making Bows and Arrows" and "The Archery Workshop" were also materially assisted by his pen. Articles by Mr. Gordon have appeared in Leisure Magazine, The Journal of Health and Physical Education, Ye Sylvan Archer, and American Bowman Review.

As advisor in the field of archery, Mr. Gordon will be called upon to answer questions on his subject posed by Guild members; also to act as the Guild's representative in his neighborhood. He already serves as archery merit badge counselor in his local Boy Scout Council, and is called in from time to time to assist in the training of camp staffs, and to plan camp archery programs.

The new Board member's interest in archery is many sided, touching other hobbies besides his own specialty. Among other things, he has created what is perhaps the finest and most extensive collection of old and rare archery books in the world.

Mr. Gordon, who joins a distinguished body of experts, was born in Newport News, Virginia, in 1902, and educated at Morris High School and Columbia University in New York City.

Field Archery for Women

By Lulu Stalker, Flint, Michigan

"So long as the new moon returns in heaven, a bent, beautiful bow, so long will the fascination of Archery keep hold of the hearts of MEN." Too long has Maurice Thompson's immortal tribute to the fascination of this ancient sport been taken literally and the generic term "men" interpreted as applying exclusively to the stronger sex. With the advent of Field Archery, in many clubs this impression has deepened, but listen a while to the effervescence of any woman who has really given the roving game a fair trial, and the illusion will be readily dispelled.

The point I would like to make is that if you enjoy target archery, you have a chance now to double your pleasure by adding a new "game" to your recreational repertoire, and the resulting enjoyment will make you wonder why you ever left field archery so long to the men.

Do you shoot for relaxation? Field archery seems to supply this in full measure, with its everchanging distances for each shot, the proportionately varied sizes of target faces, and the evershifting landscape as you follow the trails up-hill, down-hill, across ravines and around this and that group of underbrush. Just try to take your worries with you!

Do you shoot for exercise? You can find exercise to delight the hardiest on most roving courses if you rush madly about the course, jumping creeks, and ignoring the stairs like many of our younger members enjoy doing. On the other hand, a milder, equally healthful, form of exercise is provided if you avail yourself of the steps on the steeper grades and go a bit farther up the ravine till you come to the foot bridge. You eventually cover all the targets, and your score isn't a speed record, anyway.

Do you shoot for accuracy and precision, with its resultant high scores? This is attainable, as well, if you put enough time and practice into your game. Many converted target shots are of this type, and some of the scores they turn in are surprising.

Or — do you just shoot for F U N? In this group you will find a large majority of our Field Archers — both women and men. Classes B and C in the tournaments, Field Meets they are called, have been cleverly devised to keep us interested in making some improvement in our scores but never to make shooting a strain.

Much has been said and written covering the benefits to be derived physically from the use of the bow and arrow, even in indoor shooting, but when you add to this the zest of competition and the thrill of a day out-of-doors, "lady, you've got something!"

Maj. Chas. L. Williams and grandson, Jackie, aged, respectively, 59 and 3.

Upper left—Perhaps another rabbit after this loose. Lower left—Who wouldn't smile? Three bunnies and one pheasant with bow and arrow. Upper center—Teeing off a flight shot in archery-golf. Lower center—In the thicket, after another pheasant, at the Central Ohio archery-hunting preserve.

Upper right—Winners 1941 Ohio Championship Archery-Golf Tournament, Columbus, Ohio, April 5 and 6. Left to right: lightweight flight champion, Bud Pierson, Cincinnati; heavyweight flight, Charles Pierson, Cincinnati; women's flight champion, Irene Hartman, Cincinnati; women's champion, Peggy Donaldson, Cleveland; tournament champion, Paris B. Stockdale, Columbus. Center right—Holing-out in the championship tournament. Lower right—Drawing the arrow after a putt.—All Ohio photos.

How to Figure Handicaps

By Karl E. Palmatier

MEN

Handicap	Limit Score	Actual Average
-120	396	406
-115	390	400-405
-110	385	395-399
-105	379	389-394
-100	374	384-388
-95	368	378-383
-90	363	373-377
-85	357	367-372
-80	351	361-366
-75	346	356-360
-70	340	350-355
-65	335	345-349
-60	329	339-344
-55	324	334-338
-50	318	328-333
-45	313	323-327
-40	307	317-322
-35	301	311-316
-30	296	306-310
-25	290	300-305
-20	285	295-299
-15	279	289-294
-10	274	284-288
-5	268	278-283
0	263	273-277
5	257	267-272
10	251	261-266
15	246	256-260
20	240	250-255
25	235	245-249
30	229	239-244
35	224	234-238
40	218	228-233
45	212	222-227
50	207	217-221
55	201	211-216
60	196	206-210
65	190	200-205
70	185	195-199
75	179	189-194
80	174	184-188
85	168	178-183
90	162	172-177
95	157	167-171
100	151	161-166

WOMEN

Handicap	Limit Score	Actual Average
-70	240	250-255
-65	235	245-249
-60	229	239-244
-55	224	234-238
-50	218	228-233
-45	212	222-227
-40	207	217-221
-35	201	211-216
-30	196	206-210
-25	190	200-205
-20	185	195-199
-15	179	189-194
-10	174	184-188
-5	168	178-183
0	163	172-177
5	157	167-171
10	151	161-166
15	146	156-160
20	140	150-155
25	135	145-149
30	129	139-144
35	124	134-138
40	118	128-133
45	112	122-127
50	107	117-121
55	101	111-116
60	96	106-110
65	90	100-105

The score from which the handicap for men is figured is 275 for 28 targets.

The score from which the handicap for women is figured is 100 for 28 targets.

The limit score is 10 points below the left hand number in the actual average score.

The limit score is to be used in place of any 28 target score less than the limit score.

The purpose of the limit score is to prevent giving a large and unfair handicap when an archer has a bad round.

How to Figure the Handicap and Limit Score for the First Tournament

Suppose an archer expects that his score for 28 targets will be 161 or more. In this case he will be in class "A" and subject to the handicap system. If he does not have the score for four 28 target rounds he should shoot four before shooting his first tournament score.

Suppose his four practice scores are 189, 135, 215, and 170. For his first tournament the method used to determine his handicap must be worked out. Since 135 is the lowest score we throw it out and in place of it take the next lowest score, 170, the limit score. The first tournament is the ONLY time the limit score is determined in this manner. After the first tournament the limit score can be determined from the chart.

Add the actual scores of 189, 215, and 170, and the limit score of 170, and get 744 for the total. Divide 744 by 4 and get 186, the actual average. Look on the table under actual average and notice that 186 has a handicap of 80. So 80 is the handicap for his first tournament. Also note that the actual average of 186 shows a limit score of 174, which is to be used when the handicap is figured for the second tournament.

How to Figure the Handicap Score for the First Tournament

The archer turns in a score of 190 for the first 28 targets and 210 for the second 28 targets. We note that the handicap was 80 points. Add 190 and 80 and get 270 as the handicap score for the first 28 targets. Add 210 and 80 and get 290 as the handicap score for the second 28 targets. Add the two handicap scores, 270 and 290, and get the total handicap score for the tournament, 560.

How to Figure the Handicap and Limit Score for the Second Tournament

As both actual scores turned in in the first tournament are above the limit score it will NOT be necessary to make use of the limit score to figure the handicap. Note the following very carefully — use only the average of the past two tournaments plus the two 28 target scores of the last tournament to determine the new average which tell us, from the table, the new handicap and the new limit score.

As there is but one past tournament we use that average twice for this time. The average is 186. We add 186, 186, and the last two actual scores of 190 and 210 for a total of 772. Divide 772 by 4 and get the new average of 193. Find where the actual average of 193 is on the table, and you will note that it shows a handicap of 75 points and a limit score of 179. The handicap of 75 points will be used to figure his handicap score for the second tournament. The limit score of 179 will be used to figure the average score for his third tournament if the limit score is necessary.

How to Figure the Handicap Score for the Second Tournament

Suppose the scores for the second tournament were 166 and 154. The handicap for the second tournament is 75 points. Then 166 and 75 give a total of 241 for the first 28 targets. Add 154 and 75 and get 229 for the second 28 targets. Then add 241 and 229 for a total handicap score of 470 for the second tournament.

How to Figure the Handicap and Limit Score for the Third Tournament

As mentioned before, we use the averages of the last two tournaments plus the two 28 target scores of the last tournament. The first average was 186. The second average was 193. The last two scores were 166 and 154. Because the scores turned in are below the limit score, the limit score will be used in place of them. Add 186, 193, 179 and 179 for a total of 737. Divide 737 by 4 and get 184. Find the actual average of 184 on the table and note that it gives a handicap of 80 points and a limit score of 174.

How to Figure the Handicap Score for the Third Tournament

The scores for the third tournament were 215 and 224. To the 215 add the 80 point handicap and get 295. To the 224 add 80 and get 304. Add the two 28 target handicap scores of 295 and 304 for a total handicap score of 599.

How to Figure the Handicap and Limit Score for the Fourth Tournament

Starting with the fourth tournament the real method of determining the average is under way. All future averages will be figured in the same manner. The averages to be used are 193 (from the first tournament) and 184 (from the second tournament). The two last scores would be those from the third tournament. Add 193, 184, 215 and 224 for a total of 816. Divide 816 by 4 and you get a new average of 204. It will be noted that the scores for the third tournament were both above the limit score and, therefore, no use was made of it. Look on the table for the average score of 204 and note that it shows a handicap of 65 and a new limit score of 190.

How to Figure the Handicap Score for the Fourth Tournament

The scores sent in were 208 and 176. Add 65 points to each and get 283 and 241. Add these two handicap scores for a total handicap score of 524.

How to Figure the Handicap and Limit Score for the Fifth Tournament

To figure the new average, add the averages of the last two tournaments plus the two scores of the last tournament. The averages are 184 and 204. The last two scores were 208 and 176. But 176 is below the limit score of 190, so 190 must be used in its place. Add 184, 204, 208, and 190, for a total of 786. Divide 786 by 4 and get 196. Look on the table for the actual average of 196 and note that it shows a handicap of 70 points and a new limit score of 185.

How to Figure the Handicap Score for the Fifth Tournament

Add 70 points to the two scores turned in and add these two totals for the total handicap score.

Only the archers in class "A" come under this system. This system has been experimented with in California and has been found to be very efficient.

Not every archer is expected to know how to figure the handicap score. But every club secretary and the secretary of every state organization should know how. The scores will all be figured by the mail tournament secretary. The local secretaries should also figure them for practice and to check the mail tournament secretary. A major part of the mail tournament secretary's work is to educate the local secretaries, and thus build up an informed leader in each club. Please feel free to ask any questions you care to.

Karl E. Palmatier,
1317 Hillcrest Avenue,
Kalamazoo, Michigan.

Field Archers of Southern California

Although it may seem that your secretary has been a bit lax in sending in the reports of the Southern California Field Archers' activity, it isn't quite that way — the "unusual" weather that we have been having has been in a large measure to blame. (Ed. note: The quotes with the word "unusual" furnished without charge by an Oregonian.)

The regular Southern California field tournament of February 23 was held on schedule, but the weather the preceding week was so unsettled that no one could plan ahead on going, and the tournament was consequently small, but those that were there had a nice day for shooting; the threatening rain waited until the shooting was over. The scores were as follows:

Men's Championship Division — Gold Bar - Volus Jones, score, 445; Silver Bar - Irving Davis, score, 375. General Division — Championship Medal - Harold Robinson, score, 479; Red Ribbon - E. J. Woodward, score, 466; White Ribbon - Bernie Ahman, score, 398.

Ladies' Championship Division — Gold Bar - Ruth Davis, score, 332. General Division — Championship Medal - June Franklin, score, 255; Red Ribbon - Viola Maull, score, 228; White Ribbon - Helene Rosen, score, 143.

Bedwell Trophy — Angus Bruce, score, 214. Harold Robinson, being a Junior, made his choice of the Championship Medal, therefore forfeiting his rights on the Junior Trophy, which was taken home by Angus Bruce.

The annual tournament and banquet was held at Malibu on April 27, with seventy-five registered archers and families attending. If we had ordered the weather for the day, we could not have improved upon it, and after roving around 56 targets for the day, the banquet was really appreciated, and I didn't hear of anyone going home hungry. Most of the "Oh's" and "Ah's" were from trying to eat all the serving.

The election of officers for the new year followed, and are: Roy Hoff of Malibu, as President, succeeding Edmund Brock; Henry Bitzenburger of Pasadena, Vice-President, succeeding Ruth Hathaway; Elmer Bedwell, Secretary-Treasurer, succeeding himself.

The new president was immediately put into action by taking over after the election and presenting the awards, which were:

Men's Championship Class — Gold Bar - Merle Hathaway, score, 584; Silver Bar - Dr. Erwin Pletcher, score, 579.

General Division — Championship Medal - Willard Bacon, score, 553; Red Ribbon - Earl Mace, score, 549; White Ribbon - Dr. Delmar Pletcher, score, 538.

Ladies' Championship Class — Gold Bar - Ruth Davis, score, 361; Silver Bar - Eva Bedwell, score, 333.

General Division — Championship Medal - Gene Bacon, score, 485; Red Ribbon - Ruth Mace, score, 343; White Ribbon - Babe Bitzenburger, score, 274.

Annual Medals, Men — Gold - Merle Hathaway; Silver - Dr. Erwin Pletcher; Bronze - Willard Bacon. Ladies — Gold - Gene Bacon; Silver - Ruth Davis; Bronze - Ruth Mace. The Bedwell Trophy for Juniors was again taken home by Angus Bruce, score, 226.

A special guest of the day was Pat Chambers, who with friends spent the day with us. He scored a 570, which will give a start in the National, as this tournament was also the first of the 1941 National Mail Tournament, for those wishing to assert themselves.

Bob Hoover was present from San Diego, and extended an invitation in behalf of the San Diego club, to come to that city for the next association tournament. The invitation was accepted, the date being June 22. More details of the tournament will be announced in the next issue.

MID-WEST ADDS FIELD ARCHERY TO PROGRAM

Due to the widespread interest in field archery in the Middle West, the Mid-West Archery Association has decided to add an extra day of activity to its annual tournament to be held in Cincinnati this summer. Originally scheduled for Saturday and Sunday, July 5 and 6, the revised set-up calls for the target competition on Friday and Saturday, July 4 and 5, with the field round to be shot Sunday, July 6.

Last year, the field rounds and target shooting were held simultaneously, but inasmuch as there are so many archers participating in both phases of the sport, it was decided to arrange the schedule so as to permit the competitors the opportunity of testing their skill in both.

The program, as it now stands, will be as follows:

Friday, July 4 — First day's target rounds, and clout shoot.

Saturday, July 5 — Second day's target rounds, and flight competition, with the annual banquet to be held Saturday night, at which time the target winners will receive their awards.

Sunday, July 6 — Field round to be contested over a course composed of 28 targets. A total of 56 targets will be shot at to complete the field round, or twice around the course. Awards will be made on the field.

The Alms Hotel has been selected as headquarters for the 1941 tournament. This hostelry is situated in one of the residential districts of Cincinnati, far from the downtown noises found in large cities. It is within a few miles of the shooting grounds, Lunken Airport, and will meet with the favor of visiting archers. The hotel has made attractive rates for the tournament visitors, the details of which will be communicated to the various archers with the program of the tournament. This is expected to be in the mail shortly.

Due to Cincinnati's central location, the Mid-Western this year will afford the archers of Tennessee, Arkansas, Kentucky, Missouri, Oklahoma, and other southern states taken in by the association, the opportunity of testing their arrows against their fellow archers in the more northern section of the association's boundaries.

Don't forget the dates — July 4, 5 and 6; and the place — Cincinnati, Ohio, the Queen City of the Mid-West.

Archers, Everywhere

We received a letter a few days ago from Oliver Willington, Johnston Island, Pacific Ocean. Mr. Willington is planning a long archery hunting trip when his work on Johnston Island is finished, and wishes to know where the ideal archery hunting spots are in North and South America. Some more of us might be able to take hunting trips if we lived in a spot where there is no chance to spend money, as is the case on Johnston Island.

NFAA Mail Tournament for 1941

	Actual 28 Target Score	Actual 28 Target Score	Actual 56 Target Score	Handicap Score
CLASS "A"				
Alfonso Gonzales, Bakersfield, Calif.	54-204	65-257	119-461	591
Delmer F. Pletcher, Bakersfield, Calif.	77-285	72-284	149-569	589
Merle Hathaway, Los Angeles, Calif.	77-303	71-281	148-584	584
Emery Watts, Los Angeles, Calif.	58-214	60-238	118-452	582
Earl Grubbs, Los Angeles, Calif.	45-177	46-174	91-351	571
Roy Hoff, Los Angeles, Calif.	54-188	53-203	107-391	571
Robert Hoover, San Diego, Calif.	59-215	54-204	113-419	559
Fred Gadberry, Bakersfield, Calif.	59-239	53-225	112-464	554
K. L. Jones, Bakersfield, Calif.	61-229	61-237	122-466	550
Bernie Ahman, Bryn Mawr, Calif.	42-162	57-207	99-369	519
John Yount, Redlands, Calif.	45-155	55-201	96-356	496
Roland Quayle, Long Beach, Calif.	71-267	73-273	144-540	490
E. J. Underwood, Redlands, Calif.	52-194	54-206	106-400	470
George Calvert, Flint, Mich.	50-184	42-157	92-341	451
Willard Bacon, Redondo Beach, Calif.	72-278	69-275	141-553	
Dr. Delmer Pletcher, Bakersfield, Calif.	69-283	69-255	138-538	
Phil Conrad, Long Beach, Calif.	56-228	68-260	124-488	
Volus Jones, Los Angeles, Calif.	64-240	52-210	116-450	
Perzy High, Los Angeles, Calif.	55-209	62-238	117-447	
Pat Chambers, Portland, Oregon	60-236	57-209	117-445	
Irl Stamps, Seattle, Wash.	58-210	61-225	119-435	
L. J. Carter, Seattle, Wash.	54-200	51-193	105-393	
Robert King, Los Angeles, Calif.	52-200	47-181	99-381	
Leo Hoffmeyer, Flint, Mich.	48-168	47-181	95-349	
C. W. Seastrom, West Hollywood, Calif.	47-179	42-154	89-333	
Kore Duryee, Seattle, Wash.	37-145	48-180	85-325	
J. F. Murphy, Bakersfield, Calif.	55-197			
LADIES—CLASS "A"				
Gene Bacon, Redondo Beach, Calif.	66-250	61-235	127-485	425
Ruth Davis, Bryn Mawr, Calif.	53-205	42-156	95-361	401
Mary Calvert, Flint, Mich.	41-158	26-130	77-288	348
Bessie Stephenson, Flint, Mich.	36-134	27-123	73-257	327
Babe Bitzenburger, Los Angeles, Calif.	38-132	38-142	76-270	314
Eva Bedwell, San Bernardino, Calif.	49-179	40-154	89-333	293
Margaret Quayle, Long Beach, Calif.	33-117	29-205	66-322	272
June Franklin, San Bernardino, Calif.	25-93	33-113	58-206	266
Mrs. Glenn Curtis, San Bernardino, Calif.	34-114	37-147	71-261	
Bertha Hoffmeyer, Flint,, Mich.	32-120	38-134	70-254	

Those listed in Class "A" but not in the handicap score column did not send in the four twenty-eight target rounds upon which to figure a handicap. This eliminates them from from winning this mail tournament. Their scores will be figured in the championship standing.

	28 Target Score	28 Target Score	Total
CLASS "B"			
T. B. Chandler, Compton, Calif.	38-134	49-179	87-313
Ken Moore, Los Angeles, Calif.	29-113	42-156	71-269
George Walkey, Burbank, Calif.	31-125	39-143	70-268
Meryl Graham, Flint, Mich.	40-134	36-134	76-268
Tracy Stalker, Flint, Mich.	31-127	33-125	64-252
Carl Seastrom, West Hollywood, Calif.	35-127	31-117	66-244
S. Leo Sipe, Los Angeles, Calif.	40-152	18-76	58-228

	28 Target Score	28 Target Score	Total
LeRoy Stephenson, Flint, Mich.	33-117	31-109	64-226
Angus Bruce, Redlands, Calif.	28-96	34-130	62-226
Bill Wallis, Seattle, Wash.	32-110	31-109	63-219
Fred Brockhoff, Seattle, Wash.	26-96	32-110	58-206
John Tinsley, Bakersfield, Calif.	42-144		

CLASS "C"

Sam Hobbs, Flint, Mich.	35-87	30-110	55-197
Paul Ludwig, Los Angeles, Calif.	24-86	32-110	56-196
Joe Monroe, Redlands, Calif.	23-83	23-83	46-166
Bert Wallis, Seattle, Wash.	18-72	24-92	42-164
W. B. Blackmore, Marysville, Wash.	15-51	27-95	42-146
Con. Cadwell, Seattle, Wash.	18-62	16-60	34-122
Harold Lusk, Seattle, Wash.	23-81		
Lawrence McDonough, Marysville, Wash.	19-77		
Perry McAllister, Everett, Wash.	13-47		
Chester Babcock, Seattle, Wash.	11-41		
Clare Babcock, Seattle, Wash.	6-22		

LADIES—CLASS "B"

Donna Diehl, Flint, Mich.	29-99	25-95	54-194
Lulu Stalker, Flint, Mich.	26-98	25-95	51-193
Phyllis Diehl, Flint, Mich.	27-89	21-79	58-168
Ruth Hathaway, Los Angeles, Calif.	28-90	20-74	48-164
Kathleen Carter, Seattle, Wash.	17-57	22-82	39-139
Blanche Wallis, Seattle, Wash.	12-44	19-71	31-115
Freda Hoff, Los Angeles, Calif.	24-96	8-26	32-122

LADIES—CLASS "C"

Maie de Gallier, Seattle, Wash.	7-23	14-56	21-79

Secretaries:

You are to deduct any postage or express expense from the income of any tournament.

The medals are being selected by John Yount, and will be mailed to the winners by him.

The ribbons will be mailed to the winners in the same mail as the report.

Copies of the handicap system have been sent to all Class "A" archers in this report.

The score cards should include total hits for each round and for the total score.

In cases where the names of Babe, Cleo, Clare, etc., are used will you indicate whether or not it is man or woman.

The tournament in April was expected to be small. Before this report was started results for May were coming in and we may expect a very much larger report next month.

The mail tournament secretary will appreciate it very much if the secretaries will make suggestions that will add interest to the reports.

A. J. Michelson,
3800 Mason Street,
Flint, Mich.
Chairman.

John Yount,
P. O. Box 383,
Redlands, Calif.
Secretary

Karl E. Palmatier,
1317 Hillcrest Avenue,
Kalamazoo, Michigan.
Mail Tourn. Sec'y.

SUBSCRIBERS PLEASE NOTICE

A cross appearing in this space means that your subscription has expired and we would appreciate your prompt renewal so that your name may be kept on our mailing list.

ARCHERY TOOL SPECIALTIES
Tapering and Tenoning Tools for fitting Nocks and Points
— *Send for Pamphlet* —
RICARDS TOOL & MACHINE CO.
17 Dumont Ave.   Plainfield, N. J.

Cassius Hayward Styles

BOWYER AND FLETCHER

—Tackle that has stood the test—

28 Vicente Place

BERKELEY, CALIFORNIA

Archery Raw Materials

WM. A. JOY

9708 So. Hoover Street
LOS ANGELES, CALIF.

Paul H. Gordon
Author of "The New Archery"
Producing
Tackle — Materials
Latest and Finest for Field or Range
Write for Free Catalog
Beacon Hill Craftsmen
Beacon, N. Y.

E. BUD PIERSON
Bowyer — Fletcher
Tournament Tackle, Sinew, Glue, Raw Materials.
245 University Ave
CINCINNATI, OHIO
Custom Made Tackle

BACK NUMBERS
YE SYLVAN ARCHER
Volumes I to V Inclusive
$1.00 Per Volume
B. G. THOMPSON
R. F. D. 1, Corvallis, Oregon

HANDBOOK—How to Make and Use Bows and Arrows—90 Pages well illustrated (with catalog) 35c.

CATALOG—100 pictures—color spread—Instruction Folder. 10c.

CATALOG alone 5c. Stamps or Coin.

L·E·STEMMLER· QUEENS VILLAGE·N·Y·

---

70 pages of Archery information for 50 cents, well illustrated. Ye Sylvan Archer, 505 N. 11th St., Corvallis, Oregon.

ARCHERY SUPPLIES
at prices everyone can afford to pay.
YEW WOOD STAVES
at .... $2.00 and $3.00
P. O. CEDAR DOWELS
per 100 .... $2.75
FINE YEW WOOD BOWS
any weight and length
to 6 feet .... $6.50 to $12.50
Send money with order.
Monte Vista Archery Co.
Rt. 1, Box 149, Tacoma, Wash.

The AMERICAN ARCHER, a national quarterly, $1.00 per year, 521 Fifth Ave., New York City.

The Flat Bow—70 pages of Archery information for 50 cents, well illustrated. *Ye Sylvan Archer*, 505 N. 11th St., *Corvallis, Oregon.*

CHANDLER
Universal Broadheads

The Broadhead that costs less than a big rifle bullet, from 5c to 8-1/3c each. The inexpensive Broadhead for hunting.

Also Universal Broadhead Kits, with complete material for making one doz., good Broadhead Arrows.

FISH HEAD

Also Hunting, Fishing and roving Points.
FREE CATALOGUE
T. B. CHANDLER
11819 4th Ave., Compton, Calif.

B-80   B-1

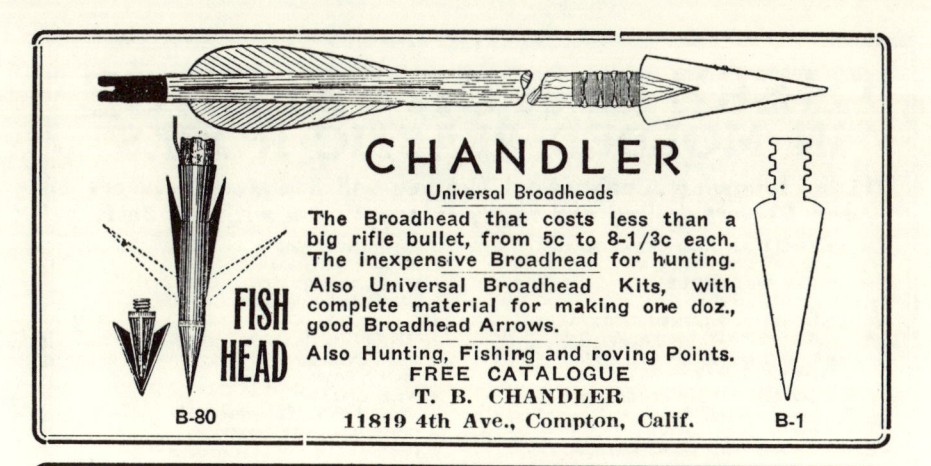

BEAR ARCHERY CO.
Specializing in
FIELD AND HUNTING EQUIPMENT
A Catalog for a Post Card
2611 W. Philadelphia Ave., Detroit, Michigan

WIN WITH BEN PEARSON ARROWS

Beautiful and accurate to the Nth degree but win their real laurels on the range. Arrows made as arrows should be—and at prices you can afford to pay. Send for catalogue.

BEN PEARSON, INC. — PINE BLUFF, ARK.

G

"THE MARK OF DISTINCTION IN ARCHERY TACKLE"
Fine Yew Target and Hunting Bows, Plain or Backed with Rawhide. Lemonwood Bows with Rawhide Backs.
College and School Equipment
Target, Hunting and Roving Arrows
Price List on Request
Wholesale — Retail
EARL GRUBBS
5518 W. Adams
Los Angeles, : California

Arcadian Life Magazine
Stories of the Ozarks

Pioneer History - Folklore
Pastoral Living

$1.00 a Year; 25c a Copy

Display Adv. $1.50 per inch
Classified, 3c a word. Three insertions for the price of two.

O. E. RAYBURN, Editor
Dept. 15
616 S. Benton St
Cape Girardeau, Mo.
P. O. Box 200
Caddo Gap, Arkansas

Please mention Ye Sylvan Archer when writing advertisers.

Ye Sylvan Archer—$1.00 per year.

THERE IS A DIFFERENCE
IN MOLDED PLASTIC NOCKS

In the following Alphabetical List you will find Manufacturers and Dealers willing and ready to supply you with the Best.

‖* AMERICAN ARCHERY COMPANY
30 Burlington Ave., Clarendon Hills, Ill.

* TOM W. ARMOUR
Potlatch, Idaho

‖* HENRY A. BITZENBURGER
800 East 4th St., Los Angeles, Calif.

‖* T. B. CHANDLER COMPANY
11819 4th Ave., Compton, Calif.

* COVELL'S ARCHERY SERVICE
Turnpike Road, Hornell, N. Y.

† CHAS. A. CUDAHY
159 Winchester St., Rochester, N. Y.

‖* JIM DEEDS
803 57th St., Oakland, Calif.

* THE FARMER'S UNION
151 W. Santa Clara St., San Jose, Calif.

‖* EARL GRUBBS
5518 W. Adams St., Los Angeles, Calif.

* FREDERICK DUSTIN HESS
1094 Meldrum Ave., Detroit, Mich.

* HOYT ARCHERY PRODUCTS COMPANY
6906 Edison, St. Louis, Mo.

* INDIAN ARCHERY & TOY CORP.
16 Clark St., Evansville, Ind

* KNOBLOCK HARDWARE COMPANY
2118 Lewis St., Detroit, Mich.

* DAVID MASON
91 Sagamore St., Manchester, N. H.

* L. H. MORSE
820 Parker St., Springfield, Mass.

* CARL OELSCHLEGER
8407 Madison Ave., Cleveland, Ohio

‖* OUTDOOR SPORTS MFG. COMPANY
Forestville, Conn.

‡‖ POTTER & MACQUARRIE
3400 Fruitvale Ave., Oakland, Calif.

‡ ROBIN HOOD ARCHERY COMPANY
971 Broad St., Newark, N. J.

‖* CHESTER SEAY
6219 Alviso St., Los Angeles, Calif.

* SPORTLAND, INCORPORATED
Green at Oakland, Pasadena, Calif.

* GEO. V. STEADMAN
2131 E. Broadway, Long Beach, Calif.

* SUPERIOR SPORTS MFG. COMPANY
Birch St., Forestville, Conn.

* TRUEMAN'S ARCHERY SHOP
1231 Solano Ave., Albany, Calif.

‖* VIKING ARCHERY COMPANY
1847 Market St., San Francisco, Calif.

* V. H. ANDERSON
106 Blain St., Syracuse, N. Y.

* BEAR ARCHERY COMPANY
2611 W. Philadelphia, Detroit, Mich.

* L. E. BRADY
4933 Voltaire St., Ocean Beach, Calif.

* W. A. COCHRAN
Route 2, Eugene, Oregon

* W. P. COZAD
270 N. High St., Columbus, Ohio

‖* CUPID ARCHERY COMPANY
1168 Glendale Blvd., Los Angeles

§‖ JAS. D. EASTON
1919½ 5th Ave., Los Angeles, Calif.

‡ FLEETWOOD ARCHERY COMPANY
4430 East 8th Ave., Denver, Colo.

* RAYMOND J. HEBERT
408 Maple St., Holyoke, Mass.

‖* HOWARD HILL ARCHERY COMPANY
11523 Chandler Blvd., N. Hollywood, Calif.

* RUSS HOOGERHYDE, INC.
1865 Shermer Ave., Northbrook, Ill.

‖* GILMAN KEASEY
700 N. 3rd St., Corvallis, Ore.

* ORVILLE E. LEE
4214 Orleans Ave., Sioux City, Iowa

‡‖ MONO ARCHERY COMPANY
Route 1, Box 349, Fresno, Calif.

* LESTER K. MORSE
108 Manheim Pike, Lancaster, Pa.

* EDGAR OSWALD
Nazareth, Pa.

‡‖ E. BUD PIERSON
245 University Ave., Cincinnati, Ohio

‖* HOMER PROUTY
1604 N. E. 50th Ave., Portland, Ore.

* ROUNSEVELLE-ROEM, INC.
Box 3A, Hazel Crest, Ill.

* SHERWOOD LANE COMPANY
Pawtucket, R. I.

* SPRINGBORO ARCHERY COMPANY
Springboro, Ohio

* CASSIUS HAYWARD STYLES
28 Vicente Pl., Berkeley, Calif.

* TEEPEE ARCHERY TACKLE COMPANY
415 Lexington St., Auburndale, Mass.

* EARL L. ULLRICH
Roseburg, Oregon

* UTE ARCHERY TACKLE COMPANY
128 1st Ave., Salt Lake City, Utah

§ Carrying complete stock of all colors in both dozen and 100 size boxes.
‡ Dozen and 100 size boxes in White, Yellow, Orange, Bright Blue, Red, Black.
† Dozen size boxes only in all colors.
‖ Manufacturers using MID-NOX exclusively on their arrows.
* Carrying only sizes and colors popular in their locality.

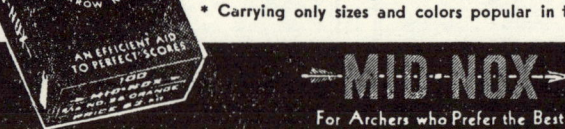

MID-NOX
For Archers who Prefer the Best

Ye Sylvan Archer

June, 1941

Vol. 13, No. 2

Ye Sylvan Archer

Official Publication of the National Field Archery Association

Vol. 13　　　　June, 1941　　　　No. 2

Published the fifteenth of each month
for archers by archers
505 North 11th Street, Corvallis, Oregon

J. E. DAVIS .... Editor
RUSSELL JONES .... Business Manager
Subscription Price .... $1.00 Per Year
Foreign Subscription .... $1.25 Per Year
Single Copies .... 10 Cents

Advertising Rates on Application

TABLE OF CONTENTS

　　　　　　　　　　　　　　　　　　　　　　Page

PLENTY HITS, PLENTY MISSES
　By Dave Cartwright 1
BLUNTS FROM THE OLD STUMP 2
A BEARLY MISS
　By Kore T. Duryee 4
THE OLD TIMER 5
EDITORIAL 6
SOLDIERS TRAINED IN BOW AND
　ARROW ART 6
THE ILLUMINATING POINT-OF-AIM
　By V. D. McCauley 6
THE NATIONAL AT PORTLAND
　By George Brommers 7
AN OPEN LETTER 7
BEAR MOUNTAIN MEET IN
　PICTURES 8, 9
NFAA BULLETIN
　By John L. Yount 10
FIRST OHIO NFAA TOURNAMENT 12
MAY NFAA TOURNAMENT REPORT
　By Karl E. Palmatier 13
LETTER BOX 15

Plenty Hits, Plenty Misses

By Dave Cartwright

At our last roving meet, which by the way was the only one that was rained out in spite of what a certain Wenatchee archer would like to believe, Damon Howatt and his wife from Yakima suggested that we come over and try their jack-rabbit hunting. We field archers here in Seattle had been looking for just such a place and this seemed perfect. So Kore Duryee organized a party consisting of Earl Stamps, Art Partee, Dave Cartwright and himself. But, alas, poor Art; his boss called him at the last minute to fill a rush order, so he missed the trip.

As soon as we crossed the mountains we left the California dew that had settled on Seattle and, although it was pretty windy, we thought that it would be fine for rabbits. We stopped in Yakima and picked up the Damon and the George Howatts and their friend, Harvey Wilson. Damon led the way up the valley to Hanford, crossed the Columbia there, and followed the road about ten miles up the river to our camp site.

We were all anxious to start hunting so without wasting much time we organized a party and started to comb the side of a dune. Well, the Howatts had said there were plenty of rabbits, but we were a bit skeptical, that is, until we hit this dune, when it seemed as if all hell had turned bushels of the jacks out at us.

We were all, as you can guess, extremely busy the rest of the afternoon. There were plenty of rabbits, but there were also plenty of misses. However, all of us except Kore, Mrs. George and Mrs. Damon Howatt had at least one by the end of the first day. Well, Kore and the girls took quite a lot of ribbing until they organized the "Pure and Innocent" club. That made them feel better. After supper and some of the Howatt's welcome black coffee, we sat around the fire and told tall archery tales until some friends of the Howatts, Lloyd Dopps and Fred Anderson, arrived.

As soon as it was dark we decided to try some spot-light hunting. By now the wind had really whipped up and it was pretty cold, so most of the party turned in. A few of us, however, were anxious to try this spot-light hunting, so we bundled up and set out over the old dirt roads with the car and an old headlight rigged to the battery for a spot. We hunters would all ride on the running board and when the spotter would catch a jack in his light we would jump off and start shooting. Maybe this sounds easy. Well, it isn't, 'specially the part where you look for your lost arrows. Anyway, we all had a swell hunt, and by early morning we had helped the annual roundup of these pests by the score of thirty-five or forty.

I guess Kore was irked quite some by his ill luck the day before, because he got up about four-thirty and actually killed a rabbit. Later in the day the rest of the "Pure and Innocent" club were disqualified. Mrs. Damon Howatt made a beautiful running shot at about forty-five yards, and Mrs. George Howatt a hard-to-get sitting shot. Damon Howatt, who was the high man the first day with a score of five, gave way to Kore the second day, who finally also nailed five.

About noon of the second day four more Yakima archers came out to join us. I'm sorry that we couldn't stay longer and get to know them. They were Ed Carrick, Roy Crewdon, Marie Miller and Ted Donaldson.

Most of the fellows agreed that a fairly heavy bow and concave blunts were the "cool ticket," although, as one fellow put it, "It doesn't make much difference what you hit them with as long as you hit 'um."

As is invariably the case, we archers had a grand weekend — in fact, everyone was so enthusiastic that Damon plans to make this hunt an annual affair. How would you like to join us next year?

Blunts from the Old Stump

After reading the instructions on how "Class A" is to figure its handicaps, you probably think that you will need a couple of Philadelphia lawyers and a dozen government experts to figure it out, but it really is simple if you work out the illustrations. Anyway, let your club secretary do the worrying about the handicaps, and if he has difficulty Palmatier will help him work it out.

When field archers shoot scores over 500, like Willard Bacon, 553; Delmer F. Pletcher, 569; Merle Hathaway, 584; Roland Quayle, 540; and Dr. Delmer Pletcher, 538; you can't tell us that a high degree of accuracy cannot be developed in field shooting. Congratulations to these archers, and we are looking for many more to join their ranks soon. Those Bakersfield, California, boys really can shoot. But don't forget the ladies who are shooting "Class A" men's scores, with Gene Bacon shooting a remarkable score of 485.

Pat Chambers of Oregon—a target and field champ—made this observation on target and field shooting. He said, "A target archer counts his misses and a field archer counts his hits." Perhaps that explains why some target archers suffer a nervous breakdown when they miss the target, and why the average field archer gets a big kick out of making a hit on a long, difficult shot.

For those who think field archery isn't really taking hold in all parts of the country, note this: On May 18 at Redlands, California, the Redlands Club held its annual field tournament with an attendance of 80. On the same day the Michigan Archers Association held its opening field meet at Fenton, Michigan, with an attendance of 99. 97 archers shot in the instinctive class, and only 2 in the free style class. The free style class, however, will be continued in Michigan to take care of new archers who prefer that type of shooting. On the same date, the Columbus Archery Club put on a field tournament for the Ohio Field Archery Association at Columbus with an attendance of 75, and with instinctive and free style archers pretty well divided. To the surprise of all, the instinctive archers outshot the free style archers. The Columbus shoot was well publicized and representative field archers from all over the state attended. The Columbus Archery Club is to be congratulated for its efforts in staging such a successful shoot.

On the same date, May 18, the Pittsburgh Archery Club held a field tournament for the Pennsylvania archers in the North Park range. We do not have the report on the attendance or the scores. The Pittsburgh Archery Club is sponsoring the NFAA field tournaments at their North Park range on June 8, July 20, August 10 and September 28. Pennsylvania archers and those in nearby states who have not tried the NFAA field round will be welcome in these tournaments.

Franklin L. Davis of Forham Park, New Jersey, Chairman of the New Jersey Field Archery Committee, has designed a practice field course which covers all the standard NFAA distances and targets for use where only a limited field is available. This is not intended to take the place of the standard NFAA course, and cannot be used in the monthly mail tournaments. Details of the layout of this practice course will be published in Ye Sylvan Archer.

Some archers have commented that a 56 target tournament in one day is too strenuous, and takes too long to shoot. If the tournament is well planned, and conducted smoothly with no bottle necks this should not be so. 28 targets should be shot in not more than two to two and one-half hours. This can be accomplished, if: (1) Targets are so placed as to have a natural back stop, free from tall grass or weeds, so that a minimum of time is used in hunting for arrows: (2) Not too great a distance between targets: (3) If archers are assigned in groups to different targets and shooting starts simultaneously on time: (4) If shooting positions are so arranged that two archers can shoot at the same time. We, personally, find a 56 target NFAA tournament shot with a 60 pound bow less fatiguing than the York round shot with a 45 pound bow—perhaps because less concentration and tension is involved in shooting the field round.

We regret to learn that the California archers were not successful in getting special reservations for bow and arrow hunting. This was largely due to the opposition of well-meaning, but grossly misinformed members of various humane societies. The public needs to be educated to know that the bow is as humane as a shot gun or rifle, and under reasonable regulations is suitable for hunting of all game on the American continents. The NFAA is sponsoring this much needed educational program, and will soon be in a position to render valuable assistance to archers in all states interested in archery legislation.

The NFAA 56 target course and an archery-golf course will be available at the National Archery Association national tournament at Portland, under the direction of Dr. H. H. Hewitt. Field archers who are planning to attend the NAA tournament should bring their field equipment along, and show the target archers the degree of accuracy that can be developed in field shooting.

You have all heard of "buck fever" among rifle hunters — where the hunter stands and looks at a fine specimen with mouth wide open and forgets to shoot — or stands and pumps the shells out of his gun without firing a shot — or closes his eyes and shoots all his shots in the air. What are the archer's reactions in a case of "buck fever." Here is one from a novice archer who used to be a rifle hunter. A group of archers were driving to their hunting grounds when a nice buck was spied near the road. The car was stopped and this archer was the first to tumble out. He strung his bow, drew a full arrow, and then froze. His companions kept urging him to shoot, but he couldn't. He advanced slowly, his drawing fingers twitching on the string as if trying to pull the trigger on a gun. The buck, unafraid, watched the performance with curiosity, and then leisurely loped off. The arrow was never released.

Paul L. Henderson of Houston, Texas, P. O. Box 3128, is chairman of a committee to revitalize the Texas State Archery Association. If a state association is to really represent all the archers, an adequate program for field archery must be provided. If this is done the state association provides a diversified program which not only promotes harmony and good will among the archers, but increases archery interest as well as membership. The NFAA extends to Texas its best wishes, and offers it all assistance needed.

Some archers have expressed the opinion that there are too many long shots in the NFAA field round. The field round was devised to provide not only recreation and fun, but to give the bow hunters something to practice on. The round expresses as nearly as possible the wishes of all the field archers from the gulf to the Great Lakes, and from the Atlantic to the Pacific.. The big game hunters need the long shots, and there are plenty of shots under 30 yards for the small game hunters. Statistics in Michigan show that in deer hunting one-third of the shots are under thirty yards, and one-half of the shots are over fifty yards. We ask you to be patient and give the field round a fair trial. If experience shows that the field round needs changes, these can be easily made.

The Sequoia Club of Berkeley, California, writes: "Our first shoot of the year held at the beautiful new Sequoia range had an attendance of 82, which is the best we have had as yet. *** The Mill Valley archers have got a course going in connection with the country club over there, and everyone is looking forward to shooting over it in a couple of weeks."

How many thousands of archers in the United States are there like J. C. Franklin, 164 Robie Street, St. Paul, Minnesota, who writes, "For quite a while we have been trying to find out about field archery clubs, their aims and purposes. In the Twin Cities we have many archers that would like to join an archery club that is not governed by traditions and custom. Your definition of the NFAA seems to be just what we wanted. *** After talking your article over with several of the regular archers we feel that your organization is the kind of club we want to belong to." The NFAA is helping the Twin Cities field archers to organize. Let us hear from other unorganized field archers. The NFAA is for you, too.

(Continued on page 15)

A Bearly Miss

By Kore T. Duryee

"Now, kiddies, I will tell you a "bear" story."

On my recent bear hunting trip I left Seattle Thursday morning, arriving in Vancouver about 2:30 P. M., where I met John Garrett and we drove to Harrison Lake, a distance of about ninety miles. A speedboat was waiting for us at 7 o'clock, taking us thirty miles up the lake to a logging camp. This lake is about forty miles long, and while ninety miles from Vancouver, is only thirty feet above sea level. It is believed to be the largest glacial lake in the world. The steep hillsides come straight down to the water's edge. Mountains border the lake, and I would say that they are four or five thousand feet high. Snow covers the tops of them. Most of the time we were there the weather was not good for photography, but one day cleared up and I was able to get a few fair pictures.

Arriving at the camp we were put up in the guest rooms adjacent to the office. The logging is all done by logging trucks and they have constructed very fine graveled roads, with very few places where the grade is higher than ten per cent. They use big Mack trucks and haul from eighty to ninety thousand pounds at a load, and also haul logs as long as one hundred and two feet. After they have delivered their logs in the lake they unhook the four wheel trailer, lift it by crane, and set it on top of the truck with the long tongue resting on top of the cab, and sticking out in front about fifteen feet. This is modern logging, entirely different to what experience I had thirty years ago.

Friday morning we climbed to about two thousand feet elevation but saw no signs of bear or deer. Of course, bear was the only game that was in season. One of the truck drivers said he had seen a black bear two days before near the garbage dump, which was along the road a half mile up the mountain from the camp. We hunted all around there several times in the morning and afternoon but failed to see any signs of bear. We had planned on leaving this logging camp Friday afternoon and going ten miles further north to the head of the lake. The same company has a new camp there and, we understood, much better prospects for bear. However, the owner did not arrive until Saturday morning, and he wanted to stay over until Sunday. We spent another day scouting around without any luck. That evening after supper Mr. Rogers, one of the partners, wanted to go up to the end of the road and look at some timber. John Garrett was going along, so I decided to go, and took my B. & A., of course. None of us expected to see any bear along the garbage dump, but as we were passing it, a big black bear ran down the steep ravine and out of sight. They stopped the truck at once. I told them they could go on, that I was sticking around, and I took a position about fifty feet above, where I had a log to sit on and was hidden by some brush. I sat there very patiently for about forty-five minutes but no bear came back. Thought I heard the truck returning down the mountain, so dropped down the mountain about fifty yards to where I was about fifty feet below the dump. The ravine was still steep and very brushy, and there was a clump of small trees blown down about fifteen feet from me and about ten feet below me. I had my back to this, facing the dump and standing behind a bush. It was rather cold, so I had my right hand in my pocket to keep the fingers warm, holding the B. A. in my left hand. I had only been there about five minutes when I thought I heard a sound nearly behind me. I turned my head to the left just as this big black bear jumped on top of two logs. Holding himself there with his front paws, his rear feet off the ground, and the upper half of his body clearly exposed to me. He held this position, as he was just as surprised to see me as I was to see him. He was just fifteen feet away. As quickly as possible I got my right hand out of my pocket and onto the bow string, turned and started to draw the arrow back. Before I could get it drawn back, the bear dropped back on the ground and turned and ran down the steep ravine. So much brush was between that I could not shoot. He had the blackest and shiniest coat you ever saw, and would weigh between three and four hundred pounds. This estimate was also made by the others in the truck when we first saw him. I think that I have learned one little lesson. That is, if you hear a noise in back of you, get all ready to shoot before turning and looking. I don't believe it would have been possible for me to have missed this shot. I was at about a forty-five degree angle and could see the full upper half of his body. The shot ranged from the right shoulder towards the hips. It was as close as I had ever been to a bear in the woods, and I sure got a kick out of it.

The next morning we went in a speedboat to the other camp, and the owner had lunches packed for the three of us. We hopped a logging truck and went up to the end of the road. The driver of the bulldozer remarked that one hundred feet further up he had seen a good sized grizzly the day before. Grizzly wasn't anything I was hunting for, but John said he would shoot if he had a chance. Whether I would, I do not know; conditions would have to be very favorable. We spent four or five hours with the owner looking through some of the finest timber I have ever seen. Eighty per cent fir, ran three

(Continued on page 12)

The Old Timer

There have been a number of inquiries as to how the stripes are applied to arrow crests. There are many kinds of jigs with which this can easily be accomplished, but I have attempted to illustrate a very simple arrangement with which I have done a great many very satisfactory jobs. The old skate wheel in the right end centers the nock nicely and allows it to be turned very easily and evenly with the left hand as the brush is held in the right. A ruler attached to the base underneath the arrow is convenient to duplicate the stripes.

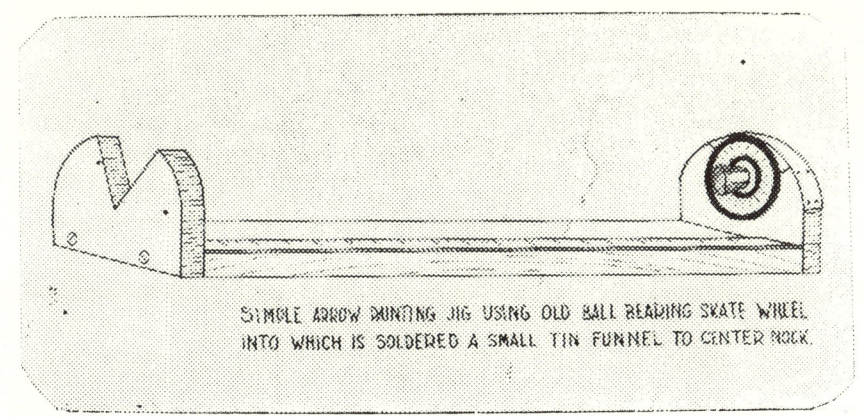

SIMPLE ARROW PAINTING JIG USING OLD BALL BEARING SKATE WHEEL INTO WHICH IS SOLDERED A SMALL TIN FUNNEL TO CENTER NOCK.

Editorial

The Editor of Ye Sylvan Archer is looking forward to the pleasure of meeting many friends at the National tournament, many of whom we have met in former years but still more of whom we have known only through correspondence. With the President of the NFAA in attendance it seems a good time to get the members present together for a meeting to talk over plans and to hold a general gabfest.

We recently learned that Capt. Styles has been in the hospital but we heard from him a few days ago and he is out and rapidly improving in health.

While the NFAA Mail Tournament is in progress, Ye Sylvan Archer will be issued a little late each month in order that the results of the previous month's shooting may be published. We shall appreciate your getting in your scores as promptly as possible so that Mr. Palmatier may be able to get his copy to us promptly.

The Southern Oregon Archery Association tournament will be held at Umpqua Park, Roseburg, June 22. Earl Ullrich says all archers are invited to go and shoot but only Southern Oregon archers are eligible for prizes.

The Editor was reminded a day or two ago that it might be a good plan for him to get his arrows ready for the Pope-Young tournament right away and not wait, as he usually does, until a day or two before the tournament and then hope to get a friend to paint them the morning of the shoot. Of course, few archers are so dilatory (?) but it might be well to pass the information on to others who intend to be at Canyon Creek this fall. The Eastern Oregon boys are promising us the biggest tournament ever. Each year has seen a larger registration, and you will miss something if you are not there. Remember September 18 and 19 at the Williams Ranch, in the Archery Reserve.

The 15th Annual Oregon State Archery Association tournament will be held at Cottage Grove on July 4, 5, and 6. The NFAA field round will be shot the morning of July 4 and archery-golf will be the event of the afternoon of the 4th. The morning of the 5th (Saturday) the clout event will be held. The York and American rounds and National and Columbia, the championship events, will be on the program Saturday afternoon and Sunday morning. At 7:00 A. M. the flight shoot will be held. A souvenir program, giving a resume of the activities of the association from 1927 to date, will be issued.

SOLDIERS TRAINED IN BOW AND ARROW ART

Any soldier at the Everett air base who waxes poetic and quotes he shot an arow into the air and it came to earth he knows not where, has a good opportunity to find out, or at least to exercise some control over the flight of the arrow. The men are to receive instruction in the arts of the bow and arrow through the cooperation of the WPA recreation program.

Franklin Jones, WPA senior recreation leader, inaugurated instruction at Forest park to a group of men from the base on Tuesday evening. As the class develops, it was stated, the men will be taught the skill of making their own equipment under the direction of Mr. Jones.

There is no indication, however, that the bow and arrow will supplant the rifle as regular equipment in the army. —Press Dispatch.

The Illuminating Point-of-Aim

By V. D. McCauley

I have read about a lot of archery gadgets, so will add my own to the list in the hope that it will help some "Lower Bracketeer" to increase his target score as it has me.

I read in a mechanical magazine one time that a very nice table favor could be made by building an artificial flower around a flashlight battery with a globe attached by means

(Continued on page 12)

The National at Portland

By George Brommers

The field archers of the Northwest face an unusual opportunity this year. For the first time in NAA history, a national tournament will be held at Portland.

It goes without saying that Portland and the NAA will need all the support we can give. The attendance from the East will be cut down by curtailed vacations and the national emergency. However, if we can bring out the field archers, who do not normally take in any target tournaments, we will go a long way towards offsetting geographical and other disadvantages.

Dr. Hewitt has already announced the field events which will take place, so I will not go into that phase of it, though these events alone will give you your money's worth.

To my mind there is an equally, if not more important angle, the social side of any tournament, let alone a national. Only a very small percentage attend because they expect to place or win prizes, the majority go to have a good time.

The average field archer may—and usually does—shoot a poor American, and a worse York. Does it really matter? Most of us go to meet old friends and to make new ones; I know I do. Is there anything in life that is more worth-while in the long run, anything that can give more lasting satisfaction? I, for one, ought to know — friends have meant a great deal to me lately.

But, you say, you won't know anybody there. Don't let that bother you, it will be your own fault if you do not get acquainted. Walk up to Major Williams, the president, Mr. Smith, the secretary, or Mr. Michelson, the Chairman of the NFAA, who will be there to represent the field archers. Introduce yourself, tell them that it is your first tournament. They will find somebody to take you around, you may be sure. I, for one, will certainly volunteer for this kind of service. I will point out to you the champions, the big game hunters, the old timers and the lower bracketeers, and, when they are not shooting, I will be glad to introduce you to anybody you want to meet. It will be my idea of having a good time, too. We have gone a long way towards humanizing tournaments, lately.

I hope you can come, even if only for a few hours. Shoot, if you possibly can, even for a single day or half day, your target fee will help a lot this year. But whether you shoot or not, remember that national tournaments are few and far between in our sparsely populated section. Every archer who has ever attended one of them has stored up some treasured memories for life.

See you in Portland, I hope.

AN OPEN LETTER

Mrs. Target Archer,
Anywhere, World.
Dear Friend:

If I were a poet, I'd love to describe the joy of a trek through the trees on a beautiful morn, of a day newly born, with wild flowers scenting the breeze. In fancy I'd take you a bit out of town, to a wood we might dub "Archer's Trail;" and here we would find well-worn paths as they wind 'cross bridged creek and o'er hill and dale.

As you stand at the top of a brush covered hill and view its undisciplined beauty, you're just glad you were born, petty troubles you scorn, and life promises Fun 'long with Duty! And there at the end of each newly-found path, a target is waiting to greet you. Up comes your bow — maybe hit? — maybe no? Takes more than a miss to defeat you.

If you find it a joy to loose arrows, yet never have shot in the field, just try it some day and I'll bet you will say: "Why has this fun so long been concealed?"

Yes, were I but a poet, I'd write and I'd write of the sport, of the thrills, of the view; and, between you and me, try it — EARLY — and see if you don't try to write poetry, too.

Sincerely yours,
A. Devotee.

At the Field Archery Meet at the Bear Mountain Park, N. Y., May 4th. Photos by Leon Dunn, courtesy of Paul H. Gordon. Upper left—General view of field, Pope-Young round, taken from top of Bear Mountain Inn. Center left—Shooting line, Pope-Young round. Lower left—Officers of field archery meet, left to right, William Carr, Director of Trailside Museum, Bear Mountain Park; Waldo Wood, Park Director of Recreation; Jule F. Marshall, Past President Metropolitan AA; A. Vanderkogel, President of MAA; J. J. Tamsen, Superintendent of Buildings, Interstate Park.

Upper center—Geo. F. Crouch, Pope-Young round. Lower center—Franklin L. Davis, Pope-Young round. Upper right—Mrs. Crawford and Paul Gordon, NFAA round. Center right—Pretty good work, NFAA round. Lower right—A. Vanderkogel, Pope-Young round. Right corner—Ready for target No. 1, NFAA round.

NFAA Bulletin

OFFICERS

President—A. J. Michelson
610 F. P. Flint Bldg., Flint, Mich.

Vice-President—Paris B. Stockdale,
Geology Dept., OSU, Columbus, Ohio.

Secretary-Treasurer—John L. Yount,
Box 383, Redlands, California.

EXECUTIVE COMMITTEE

Western—H. C. MacQuarrie,
3400 Fruitvale Ave., Oakland, Calif.

Mid-Western—Fred Bear,
2611 W. Philadelphia, Detroit, Mich.

Eastern—T. C. Davidson,
53 Mountain Ave., Springfield, N. J.

By John L. Yount

The NFAA is rapidly becoming a power in archery. Our membership has now passed the five hundred mark and the speed of its growth is increasing each month. Best of all, our events are no longer looked on simply as the lighter side of archery. Some excellent archers have had to admit that while their ability to shoot a 700 American wasn't exactly a handicap, it still didn't make them a field champion and that possibly there was something to this field shooting business, after all.

This admission usually comes after some archer, who couldn't shoot a 500 American if his life depended on it, has pinned their ears back in nice shape on a field course, and usually leads to some serious practice on the part of the expert target man. For this practice there are a steadily increasing number of permanent roving courses scattered from coast to coast.

Now for a little of the darker side. Some of our most important committees are doing a fine job of thumb twirling while there is so very much that needs doing. For example, we need every item of archery hunting news, favorable or otherwise, also a record of every game law that affects the archer wherever he may be.

We also need some planned publicity. What we usually get is worse than nothing. That we need this publicity has just been demonstrated here in California, where the humane society has once again convinced the legislature that the bow is not a fit weapon for deer hunting. The archers in a number of other states are faring just as badly.

Won't you get behind your president in his plans to make field archery a major sport and to educate the public to the bow's value as a humane hunting weapon. He has taken great care to plan his committees so as to get the job done without working a hardship on anyone. All that is necessary is that each of us remember that this is our association, and be willing to do our small share. If the game is worth playing it is worth just a little time and work, so if you are on a committee or have any information that might be of value, won't you write the chairman of the proper committee and thereby help start the ball rolling. If you happen to be a chairman and are a little in doubt as to your duties, please write President Michelson at once.

FROM FLINT BOWMEN

As secretary-treasurer of the first and only archery club I ever belonged to, I wonder if you would bear with me if I do a bit of boasting about the Flint Bowmen. In common with many archery clubs throughout the nation, Flint archers suddenly deserted the traditional target forms of archery, American, Columbia, and York, and went in for roving in a big way. While many of us hated to see the precision and form of target shooting give place entirely to the more instinctive type, our policy is—let the majority rule. Consequently, our permanent target butts stand practically abandoned while the thud of roving arrows makes merry the area about the twenty-eight field targets.

Rather as an experiment, our first fourteen targets were laid out in the fall of '39, as practice for the deer season coming up. So popular did this type of archery prove that the club voted to maintain a permanent field course in connection with our regular range, making field shooting available throughout the entire summer. Last spring when the range was again put into shape for use, many improvements were made, but still fourteen targets seemed adequate.

Then along came the National Field Archery Association's series of mail tournaments. Our members were urged to get into this, and twelve were finally persuaded to enter a score for the second tournament. When the results were received, interest was greatly increased, comparative scores showing that our archers were not so bad!

With the increasing popularity, more targets seemed called for, so a "working weekend" was designated, providing us with fourteen more targets. This required considerable hard labor, mowing, brushing out, building bridges, etc., but the membership turned out fine (was it due to the potluck the ladies provided?) and soon we had a regulation twenty-eight target range with many natural "hazards" to maintain interest.

For the second NFAA match, we put on an invitational tournament, sending cards to every small archery club or unaffiliated archer we could locate in adjoining towns. Ribbons and medals were presented in two classes, both men and ladies, and even the Juniors were not forgotten. Fifty-one archers turned out for this meet, thirty-one outsiders, and shot twenty-eight targets in a steady rain despite slippery clay hill steps, all hoping for a break in the weather. Since noon brought no promise of sunshine, we called it a day and presented the medals. Those competing for NFAA scores completed them the following day.

Somehow, a meet with outsiders appealed to our membership—and our budget—so a repeat performance was requested for the following month. This time sixty-six archers enjoyed a perfect fall day, shooting fifty-six targets, stopping at the halfway mark for picnic dinners. A number of incidental prizes, many made by one of our members, contributed to the interest of the awards.

The social side of our club has not been neglected and this, too, has helped to swell our attendance. A roast of some kind, or a potluck, has been planned at least monthly, with each time a different committee providing, at club expense, coffee and fixings at the close of the evening's shoot.

An indoor range for the winter months was secured and not only served to hold the club together until spring, but greatly increased our membership. Here many novelty shoots for instinctive archers not only proved highly entertaining, but the early outdoor scores showed the benefit of the winter's practice.

In less than three years the Flint Bowmen membership has increased from thirteen families to eighty-three, with additional recruits constantly being added. Monthly meets are planned for this year which, as heretofore, are treated as local tournaments, medals and ribbons being awarded. The scores of the NFAA members, who request it before the shooting, are then entered in the monthly mail meets where additional honors may or may not be acquired.

We do feel that the progress of the National Field Archery Association has been surprisingly reflected in the growth of our club, which now boasts thirty-five NFAA memberships. The popularity of competing nationally is stimulating our archers to more concerted efforts toward score improvement as well as promoting a more discernible club spirit. Keep the good work up!

George Calvert,
Sec.-Treas. Flint Bowmen.

First Ohio NFAA Tournament

The first NFAA roving round tournament of the 1941 season in Ohio was conducted by the Columbus Archery Club, on an especially-laid 28-target course at Camp Mary Orton, on Sunday, May 18. A majority of the 75 participants came from well-scattered archery centers from throughout the state. Other archery clubs in Ohio plan similar roving round tournaments during the summer months to follow.

A feature of the Columbus tournament was the dual classification of the registrants: (a) one group adhering to the official shooting style of the National Field Archery Association; (b) the others shooting "free style" with the use of any sort of sights. The two highest tournament scores were made by NFAA style shooters. Awards were made in both classes, as follows:

NFAA Regulation Style—Men
1. Paris B. Stockdale, Columbus.
2. Phil Cozad, Columbus.
3. Sam Cureton, Mt. Vernon.

NFAA Regulation Style—Women
1. Frances Wallingford, Chillicothe.
2. Pauline Benner, Newark.
3. Adelade Neil, Columbus.

"Free Style"—Men
1. M. L. McCammon, Ashland.
2. Norman Isabel, Columbus.
3. Tom Lewis, Columbus.

"Free Style"—Women
1. Helen Isabel, Columbus.
2. Merda Nussdorfer, Columbus.
3. Irene Shea, Chillicothe.

Juniors
1. Ted Sharenberg, Columbus.
2. Alan Kilbourn, Columbus.

A BEARLY MISS

(Continued from page 5)

to four feet in diameter, and reached a height of one hundred feet before there were any branches. In fact, no underbrush and exceptionally level country, moss all over, and small creeks every hundred yards or so. We had lunch beside one of these little streams. There were plenty of broken, rotten stumps to shoot at, and we spent four or five hours in roving, but saw no sign of game. We had planned on coming home Sunday but the owner wished to stay over until Monday afternoon. He had a special speedboat coming up from the other end of the lake to take us back, so we spent most of Monday roving around near the camp. Tried a little fishing without any luck, as it wes too early.

It is always interesting to me to see new country, and archers always have a good time whether they get any was too early.

The Illuminating Point-of-Aim

(Continued from page 6)

of a wire wrapped a couple of turns around the globe and slid down the side of the battery inside the paper covering so as to make contact.

Somehow I have never forgotten the idea and I now have a good use for the principle. I tried many points of aim in our indoor range; a golf ball on a spike, a black spot on a white background, a section of broom handle painted with alternate rings of black and white, small reflectors of the type used for fastening car licenses to their brackets, a nail run at right angles to the black cap of a wine bottle, etc. They were all hard to see, the range not being very well lighted between the shooting line and the target, and they did not present a small enough spot for me to concentrate on, especially after I drank the wine in order to get the cap. (Me being a Scotchman.)

The reflector idea brought to mind the battery and globe. I tried that but there was too much light, so I bored a block of wood to hold the battery and fitted a piece of plywood to one end and bored a small hole in it opposite the globe. It still gave off too many rays of light, so I rigged up the globe in the reflector of an old flashlight and covered the hole in the plyboard with black paper, then punched a small hole in it, arranging the reflector back of the hole. I painted the whole thing black and by adjusting it properly I have a very fine spot to hold on, and one I can see. With a little patience anyone who shoots on a range lighted in such a way as to make a point of aim hard to see can make shooting more enjoyable by rigging up a similar outfit. There is only one handicap and that is you have to keep an eye on the "Blunt Boys" for they delight in taking potshots at such strange gadgets if left unprotected.

June, 1941   YE SYLVAN ARCHER   13

May NFAA Tournament Report

By Karl E. Palmatier

	Actual 28 Target Score	Actual 28 Target Score	Actual 56 Target Score	Handicap Score
CLASS "A"—MEN				
Robert Hoover, San Diego, Calif.	57-215	65-241	122-456	586
Elmer Bedwell, San Bernardino, Calif.	48-182	43-159	91-341	581
Delmer Pletcher, Bakersfield, Calif.	70-275	79-305	149-580	580
K. L. Jones, Bakersfield, Calif.	54-204	73-275	127-479	559
Alfonso Gonzales, Bakersfield, Calif.	57-221	59-226	116-447	547
Jim Murphy, Bakersfield, Calif.	52-187	52-194	104-381	541
Fred Gadberry, Bakersfield, Calif.	61-230	57-230	118-460	540
William Horr, San Diego, Calif.	47-175	45-171	97-346	536
Bernie Ahman, Bryn Mawr, Calif.	46-174	49-191	95-365	515
E. J. Woodward, Redlands, Calif.	25-229	48-184	103-413	493
George Calvert, Flint, Mich.	49-169	49-177	98-346	466
Irving Davis, Bryn Mawr, Calif.	44-170	46-168	90-338	458
John Yount, Redlands, Calif.	48-168	35-133	83-301	441
John Scott, Detroit, Mich.	57-217	69-259	126-476	
Jack Peters, Oakland, Calif.	62-236	58-224	120-460	
Irl Stamps, Seattle, Wash.	50-196	61-241	111-437	
Leo Cornell, Oakland, Calif.	59-214	57-213	116-427	
M. E. Spansell, Oakland, Calif.	50-182	55-218	105-401	
Kore Duryee, Seattle, Wash.	52-203	46-180	98-383	
Jack Young, Oakland, Calif.	59-232	39-149	98-381	
Paris B. Stockdale, Columbus, Ohio			91-368	
Phil Cozad, Columbus, Ohio			92-358	
Charles Ratcliff, Highland Park, Mich.	41-161	47-173	88-334	
Leo Hoffmeyer, Flint, Mich.	33-131	40-140	73-271	
CLASS "A"—LADIES				
Bessie Stephenson, Flint, Mich.	38-130	39-147	77-277	357
Mary Calvert, Flint, Mich.	42-140	43-145	85-283	333
Eva Bedwell, San Bernardino, Calif.	40-140	51-199	91-339	309
June Franklin, San Bernardino, Calif.	31-117	32-120	63-237	307
Ruth Davis, Bryn Mawr, Calif,	37-139	25-85	62-227	254
Bertha Hoffmeyer, Flint, Mich.	40-146	22-82	62-228	
Margaret King, Redlands, Calif.	20-85	33-117	53-202	

	28 Target Score	28 Target Score	Total
CLASS "B"—MEN			
Franklin Jones, Everett, Wash.	47-185	35-131	82-316
Tracy Stalker, Flint, Mich.	37-149	40-154	77-303
William Smith, Flint, Mich.	39-133	45-167	84-300
Jim Hendrickson, Detroit, Mich.	44-164	37-133	81-297
Harvey Franklin, No City, Calif.	40-152	32-144	72-292
C. M. McGillivray, Flint, Mich.	35-129	41-149	76-278
George Hamaker, Flint, Mich.	38-138	36-136	74-274
Russell DeForest, Flint, Mich.	40-148	29-109	69-257
George Overfield, Columbus, Ohio			71-249
J. H. Strandwold, Tacoma, Wash.	31-117	36-132	67-249
Meryl Graham, Flint, Mich.	39-137	30-112	69-249
L. J. Markham, Durand, Mich.	35-135	31-107	66-242
Angus Bruce, Redlands, Calif.	32-120	28-104	60-224
Fred Brockway, Tacoma, Wash.	29-99	31-123	60-222
Walter Knoblock, Flint, Mich.	28-93	35-127	63-220

	28 Target Score	28 Target Score	Total
H. Strandwold, Shelton, Wash.	29-103	31-105	60-208
Bill Wallis, Seattle, Wash.	21-71	21-103	50-174

CLASS "C"—MEN

Bert Wallis, Seattle, Wash.	31-123	30-108	61-231
Sam Hobbs, Flint, Mich.	33-133	28-94	61-227
Fred Brockhoff, Seattle, Wash.	21-71	35-127	56-198
Kilbourne Anderson, Trenton, Mich.	30-110	24-88	54-198
D. S. Cartwright, Seattle, Wash.	24-92	27-105	51-197
W. C. Woolnough, Trenton, Mich.	28-94	25-97	53-191
Harold Lusk, Seattle, Wash.	23-89	29-93	52-182
Jimmy Ratcliff, Detroit, Mich.	22-80	27-99	49-179
Herbert Halberg, Tacoma, Wash.	24-86	26-92	50-178
A. J. Michelson, Flint, Mich.	23-93	23-83	46-176
Robert Green, Springfield, Ohio			45-171
W. Harmon, Langley, Wash.	19-65	24-86	43-150
Joe Monroe, Redlands, Calif.	21-71	17-77	38-148
Karl Palmatier, Kalamazoo, Mich.	21-83	19-63	40-146
Robert Kumpula, Detroit, Mich.	19-71	19-71	38-142
R. G. Smith, Newark, Ohio			39-137
William Irvin, Seattle, Wash.	18-64	11-41	29-105

CLASS "B"—LADIES

Lulu Stalker, Flint, Mich.	29-107	41-153	70-260
Kay Ratcliff, Highland Park, Mich.	22-82	25-93	47-175
Donna Diehl, Flint, Mich.	22-74	26-98	48-172
Phyllis Diehl, Flint, Mich.	23-79	23-89	46-168
Irene Wierzbicki, Flint, Mich.	19-69	22-84	41-153
Blanche Wallis, Seattle, Wash.	17-59	19-65	26-124
Ina Woolnough, Trenton, Mich.	14-52	19-67	33-119

CLASS "C"—LADIES

Vira Anderson, Trenton, Mich.	11-43	10-34	21-77
Val Irvin, Seattle, Wash.	5-17	8-30	13-47
Bessalee Jones, Everett, Wash.	8-26	5-19	13-45

The Ohio archers did not report the scores for each 28 targets so only the total could be reported.

The first score you send in classifies you. After that you remain in your class until after the next tournament has been shot. If your score at the last tournament is large enough to place you in a higher class you are classified in the higher class for the NEXT tournament.

Bert Wallis and Sam Hobbs shot scores that will place them in Class "B" for the next tournament.

Lulu Stalker shot a score that will place her in Class "A" for the next tournament.

Regardless of what score you shoot, you may not shoot in a lower class.

Many of the archers have not sent in their four 28 target scores used to figure the handicap in Class "A". This applies to new groups in general. As soon as they have sent me sufficient scores they will be given a handicap.

HANDICAPS

Elmer Bedwell	210	Robert Hoover	110	June Franklin	80
Earl Grubbs	200	Emery Watts	110	Bessie Stephenson	70
William Horr	180	Alfonso Gonzales	100	Mary Calvert	60
Jim Murphy	160	E. Woodward	80	Margaret Quayle	60
Roy Hoff	160	Fred Gadberry	80	Babe Bitzenberger	50
Bernie Ahman	150	K. Jones	70	Ruth Davis	50
John Yount	150	Merle Hathaway	-10	Eva Bedwell	-30

June, 1941   YE SYLVAN ARCHER   15

Irving Davis 130   Delmer Pletcher .. -10   Gene Bacon, Mrs. -90
George Calvert 130   Roland Quayle .... -40

The above handicaps are for 56 targets.

The Mid-Western Archery Association arranged for Friday for a full day's tournament of field archers. The equipment of the Michigan Archers Association was used. Fred Bear was in charge.

Be sure to read the account of the field tournament held by the club at Columbus, Ohio.

Be sure to indicate whether or not the person is a man or woman.

60 archers shot in the first mail tournament — 75 in this one.

Letter Box

Arrow Suggestions

Fresno, Calif.
5-24-41.

Dear Mr. Davis:

The purpose of this note is to pass on some information that might be of interest to some of our archer friends who like to hunt small game.

It is prompted by reading Donald M. Cole's article, "The Proof of the Pudding," to be found in "Ye Sylvan Archer" of May, 1941.

While Howard Hill, Bob Faas, Johnny Garret, Frank De Wolf, Ernie Antle and I were hunting with bow and arrows in the Caribou district of British Columbia, and on an island east of Seymour Narrows, along the Inside Passage to Alaska, we were offered many shots at grouse.

We were using blunts on these birds. Our shafts were fitted tightly into .38 caliber revolver shell cases, from which the cap had been removed. A number 28 or 9/64" hole was drilled through where the cap had been, and a 6x¾" round head brass screw was screwed into the tip end of the shaft. This made what we thought was a very satisfactory arrow, as we were able to bag all the grouse we could use. But we were sick when we thought of the number that got away, not through faulty shooting, but through the inability of the arrow to STOP the game.

To those who might be skeptical, would you consider it poor shooting if, upon driving a blunt up to the feathers through a grouse, the bird would "take off" and glide down the side of a mountain, sometimes catching the protruding arrow on the trunk or branches of a tree, to land in the almost impenetrable underbrush?

Before going North the following year, I had some washers made of duralium, 9/16" in diameter and 1/16" in thickness. The round head wood screw was removed, and put through the number 28 hole in the washer, then replaced in the end of the shaft.

Evidently the grouse did not receive sufficient SHOCK from the first blunt, as the penetration was more than ample. On the second trip, for every grouse I hit with the IMPROVED BLUNT, it was "curtains."

The "Frontal Area" was greatly increased and the shocking power, in proportion. The slight overhang of the washer (1/16") does not prevent its being a good brush arrow, as was satisfactorily proven.

There is no question in my mind about archers being glad to learn of ways of improving their tackle, so I am attempting to do my part to contribute to the success and pleasure of my fellow archers.

Hoping that some others try, and have good luck with this improved blunt (I believe it to be worth a try, at least), I am,

Yours ar-cheerily,
H. F. Woodley.

Blunts from the Old Stump

(Continued from page 3)

DON'T forget the NAA tournament at Portland. We are planning to attend this tournament and will be happy to renew old acquaintances and meet in person our many new field archer friends. We'll be seeing you at Portland.

SUBSCRIBERS PLEASE NOTICE

A cross appearing in this space means that your subscription has expired and we would appreciate your prompt renewal so that your name may be kept on our mailing list.

CLASSIFIED ADVERTISING

RATES for Classified Advertising 5 cents per word per issue. Count initials and numbers as words. Minimum charge is 50 cents.

RELICS AND CURIOS

INDIAN RELICS, Beadwork, Coins, Curios, Books, Minerals, Weapons. Old West Photos. Catalog, 5c. Genuine African Bow, $3.75. Ancient flint arrowheads, perfect, 6c each—Indian Museum, Osborne, Kansas.

BOOKS AND MAGAZINES

The AMERICAN ARCHER, a national quarterly, $1.00 per year, 521 Fifth Ave., New York City.

"ARCHERY TACKLE, HOW TO MAKE AND HOW TO USE IT," by Adolph Shane. Bound in cloth and illustrated with more than fifty drawings and photographs. Information for making archery tackle and instructions for shooting. Price is $1.75. Send orders to Ye Sylvan Archer, 505 North 11th street, Corvallis, Oregon.

Write us for your needs in Archery books. Ye Sylvan Archer.

HANDBOOK—How to Make and Use Bows and Arrows—90 Pages well illustrated (with catalog) 35c.

CATALOG—100 pictures—color spread—Instruction Folder. 10c.

CATALOG alone 5c. Stamps or Coin.

L·E·STEMMLER· QUEENS VILLAGE·N·Y·

The Flat Bow—70 pages of Archery information for 50 cents, well illustrated. *Ye Sylvan Archer*, 505 N. 11th St., Corvallis, Oregon.

NEW LOCATION :—
3109 Burnet Ave.
Cincinnati, Ohio

E. BUD PIERSON
Bud & Charlie

VIKING ARCHERY

1874 Market Street

San Francisco, Calif.

PORT ORFORD CEDAR ARROW SHAFTS
(Cypressa Lawsonia)

Specials. P.O. Cedar Shafts, 1/4 to 11/32":

Parallel, per 100 .... $4.00

Tapered or barreled, 100 .. $4.50

Extra Select. Units segregated, per 100 .... $5.00

Douglas Fir, 100 .... $3.00, $3.50

Douglas Fir, Extra Select, per 100 .... $4.00

Full line finished tackle. Raw Materials. Write for price lists. Special rates to dealers and clubs.

PORT ORFORD ARCHERY SUPPLY CO.
C. F. Douglas, Mgr.
Box 137   Port Orford, Oregon

Please mention Ye Sylvan Archer when writing advertisers.

WIN WITH BEN PEARSON ARROWS

Beautiful and accurate to the Nth degree but win their real laurels on the range. Arrows made as arrows should be—and at prices you can afford to pay. Send for catalogue.

BEN PEARSON, INC. — PINE BLUFF, ARK.

CHANDLER
Universal Broadheads

The Broadhead that costs less than a big rifle bullet, from 5c to 8-1/3c each. The inexpensive Broadhead for hunting.

Also Universal Broadhead Kits, with complete material for making one doz., good Broadhead Arrows.

Also Hunting, Fishing and roving Points.

FREE CATALOGUE

T. B. CHANDLER

11819 4th Ave., Compton, Calif.

B-80   FISH HEAD   B-1

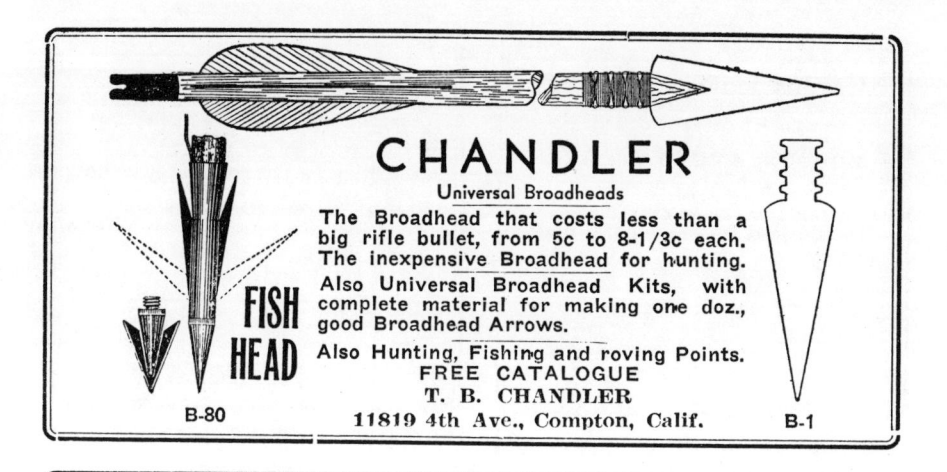

APPROVED NFAA FIELD TARGET FACES

Printed in black and white on heavy, double thickness corrugated board. In sets containing sizes necessary for a 14-target course and including extras of the smaller sizes that shoot out fastest.

$2.25 per set, f.o.b. Detroit — Order two sets for a 28-target course

BEAR ARCHERY CO.
2611 W. Philadelphia Ave., Detroit, Michigan

G

"THE MARK OF DISTINCTION IN ARCHERY TACKLE

Fine Yew Target and Hunting Bows, Plain or Backed with Rawhide. Lemonwood Bows with Rawhide Backs.

College and School Equipment

Target, Hunting and Roving Arrows

Price List on Request

Wholesale — Retail

EARL GRUBBS
5518 W. Adams

Los Angeles, : California

Arcadian Life Magazine
Stories of the Ozarks

Pioneer History - Folklore

Pastoral Living

$1.00 a Year; 25c a Copy

Display Adv. $1.50 per inch Classified, 3c a word. Three insertions for the price of two.

O. E. RAYBURN, Editor
Dept. 15

616 S. Benton St
Cape Girardeau, Mo.
P. O. Box 200
Caddo Gap, Arkansas

Please mention Ye Sylvan Archer when writing advertisers.

Ye Sylvan Archer—$1.00 per year

Cassius Hayward Styles

BOWYER AND FLETCHER

—Tackle that has stood the test—

28 Vicente Place

BERKELEY, CALIFORNIA

ARCHERY SUPPLIES
at prices everyone can afford to pay.
YEW WOOD STAVES
at .... $2.00 and $3.00
P. O. CEDAR DOWELS
per 100 .... $2.75
FINE YEW WOOD BOWS
any weight and length
to 6 feet .... $6.50 to $12.50
Send money with order.
Monte Vista Archery Co.
Rt. 1, Box 149, Tacoma, Wash.

Archery Raw Materials

WM. A. JOY

9708 So. Hoover Street
LOS ANGELES, CALIF.

---

70 pages of Archery information for 50 cents, well illustrated. Ye Sylvan Archer, 505 N. 11th St., Corvallis, Oregon.

Ye Sylvan Archer—$1.00 per year.

NEW! ROVING GLOVE!

KM-25—A professional type glove, not recommended for use with bows pulling under 40 pounds. Each $2.50

SPECIFICATIONS: Finger stalls are made of two thicknesses of leather, with top leather of genuine heavy cordovan. Between the outer and inner thicknesses, a durable turkey quill is inserted. This prevents deep string indentations and a sloppy release. With turkey quill finger stalls, a clean snap release is always assured—a most important consideration for maximum accuracy. An indispensable glove when heavy equipment is used. Glove custom made to your hand sketch, or dress glove size.

KM-22—Without quill, but with two thicknesses of leather $1.75

KING ★ MOORE

7011 N. Figueroa St.
LOS ANGELES, CALIF.

Write today for **FREE CATALOG** — FREE

Ye Sylvan Archer

July, 1941

Vol. 13, No. 3

Ye Sylvan Archer

Official Publication of the National Field Archery Association

Vol. 13　　　July, 1941　　　No. 3

Published the fifteenth of each month
for archers by archers
505 North 11th Street, Corvallis, Oregon

J. E. DAVIS .... Editor
RUSSELL JONES .... Business Manager
Subscription Price .... $1.00 Per Year
Foreign Subscription .... $1.25 Per Year
Single Copies .... 10 Cents

Advertising Rates on Application

TABLE OF CONTENTS

	Page
THE BATTLE OF KLAMATH MARSH 　By James C. Stovall, Eugene, Ore.	1
BLUNTS FROM THE OLD STUMP	3
OSAGE — THE BOW FOR ROVING 　By Paul J. Sampson	5
NFAA BULLETIN 　By John L. Yount	6
PACIFIC NORTHWEST SHOOT	7
PASADENA FIELD ARCHERS	7
OREGON STATE TOURNAMENT	7
EDITORIAL	8
LETTER BOX	9
BROWN COUNTY OPEN 　By Mrs. G. F. Martin	9
FIELD ARCHERS OF SO. CALIF. 　By Elmer Bedwell, Secretary	10
PATERSON LONG BOWMAN	10
WILL HISTORY REPEAT ITSELF? 　By Geo. Brommers	11
JUNE NFAA TOURNAMENT REPORT 　By Karl Palmatier	12

The Battle of Klamath Marsh

By James C. Stovall, Special War Correspondent to Ye Sylvan Archer

Eugene, Ore., July 2, 1941. (Special War Bulletin). Hints had been received from authoritative sources for some days that the summertime enemy of all archers of the realm, the ground squirrels, had been mobilizing in large numbers in the upper Klamath Marsh section of Eastern Oregon.

We archers had piously maintained a strict neutrality throughout the early part of the season, but when we received communiques from such sources as the official organ and the high indignant himself, we decided to delete the "non" from our belligerent and become non-neutral. "The Brain" mobilized Paul Smith and myself for fifth calling duty.

On June 15 last, Paul and I received our forged passports and full field equipment as tourists entering enemy territory, with orders to reconnoiter any possible fields of battle, soften up the enemy and then feel out his strength. As early as noon on that day we encountered seven long-axis mule deer who were going away from there. We held a conference and decided it was best to leave these to other secret agents. Our second contact was with two disgustingly neutral ground hogs whom we observed to strengthen their positions by a strategic retreat.

We crossed the frontier at exactly one-sixty-one Klamath Marsh Time, without showing our passports, and found the enemy to be fully mobilized over an area of nearly fifty square miles. They were sitting about their pill boxes and earthworks in large numbers, while numerous dispatch carriers scurried from one stronghold to another, conversing in a sharp whistle-like code which we couldn't find in the international code book. The enemy had very few oldsters in view, only the class of '41, which had been called up but a few weeks back. (As a matter of record, they are about the size of your forefinger, or almost.)

We had been especially trained in course number A-73 at the ground school of secret agents for the purpose of estimating the strength of the enemy, and as near as we could figure there were about 10,000 non-Aryan ground squirrels per square mile. Actually as many as five full divisions could be seen from the frontier alone. Had we known the real strength of the enemy in the interior we would not have ventured as far as we did without strong support.

Paul and I sized up the situation and decided that we had best disguise ourselves as archers and work from within, which we did. We advanced rapidly towards the interior, fighting every inch of the way for three solid hours until our fingers, arms and shoulders were in need of medical attention. We discovered that the enemy had developed the art of camouflage to a high degree so that only eyes and ears were visible under distances of twenty feet but beyond that more and more of the big burly torsos could be seen. They had perfected a new technique of defense which practically stopped the inertia of our initial momentum. The enemy would stand before their strongholds in such nonchalant attitudes as to appear to be eating, or just thumbing their noses at us; but when we loosed an arrow at them all a well-aimed shaft would strike was where they had been. They would disappear at the flash of the bow and as soon as the arrow struck they would reappear to smell the arrow, and were ever ready to repeat the performance as long as we had arrows. We soon evolved a nice bit of strategy, which was this—"if you miss him fifteen times straight, pick up your arrows and shoot at his neighbor."

We were led into a neatly prepared trap in the moister section of the marsh and found that the enemy was not without adequate air power, although it did not operate far from its base. We were subjected to a terrific blitz of twin-motored, dive-bombing, poison-injecting mosquitoes.

We retreated in rout until we brought up our anti-aircraft killing lotion, which is very effective if you can put it on the mosquito. We were subjected to nuisance raids from time to time until we moved back to the frontier.

We each destroyed two burly officers of the enemy high command, and returned to report our activities to the war council in Eugene. We followed the true axiom of all good fifth columnists, "we passed the buck, shot the bull, and made six copies." The war council decided after a couple of minutes serious deliberation that we could stand the oppression no longer. We must act. It was decided that we had best send out a pantser* division to be followed by all-out warfare.

Knowing the strength and numbers of the enemy, we were certain that the pantser division would be under fire both day and night; so Russell "Trigger Mortis" Jones was chosen— and we couldn't have chosen better. His asthma wouldn't let him sleep nights and his hay fever would keep him awake days; so all he would have to do was engage the enemy.

On the evening of June 27, Russ contacted the enemy and accounted for four, plus a ground hog and a muskrat. The following day was a long and tiresome one for our pantser division but, though tired as he was and often without ammunition, our flag was flying valiantly over one hundred and forty strongholds by nightfall. All enemy communiques to the contrary are nuts.

On June 29, our full force, with the exception of John Davis and Ned Myers, who were diverted to Alsea to put down an uprising of maliciously objecting jack rabbits to the new order, were on hand with complete supply trains and photographic divisions. We engaged the enemy in the wake of Trigger Mortis immediately, first as skirmishers, then in advancing columns and mass attacks, and finally laid siege to the more obstinate strongholds. By noon the enemy resistance was not yet broken, but the field tan of their uniforms could still be seen by the thousands, still occupying strongholds, carrying dispatches and forever using that baffling code of theirs. We fought our way back to the supply depot to obtain food, more ammunition, and to put tape over blistered hands and fingers as well as some few chins which were becoming raw from continued scarifying by ragged finger tabs. The supply division came in for some criticism in that it had no right arm and shoulder liniment on hand. This was duly reported to headquarters. It is known to all that our forces shot constantly, except while gathering arrows, for the duration, and most of us had been foolish enough to use heavy hunting tackle.

If anything, the enemy was out in greater force during the afternoon than before, but by the end of the day Trigger Mortis had accounted for another eighty-seven of the enemy. (Once during the afternoon when one of the enemy protested the fatal treatment, a whole division stood at attention, and Russ accounted for nine in nine consecutive shots.) Herbert Jones accounted for eighteen, and he refrained from shooting when they sat on his arrows; Clare Hamlin for twenty-three, and we know he counted all but the six for Daisy Hamlin; George Golden for twenty-seven by not letting the enemy know he was out of arrows; Sid Claypool for ten by startling them with words in their own language; Billy Armstrong who had to give up at that number, for six; Paul Smith for fifteen and two mosquitoes with a broadhead; Howard Dixon for twenty-eight and fragments of his beard are all over the marsh; Howard Null for nine which he won with words of friendship; Phil Gilmore for twelve, with a squirrel and a broken string on the last shot of the day; and I worried twenty to death. The official communique says our valiant army, though out-numbered, blistered and bone weary, accounted for a total of four hundred and five for the duration of the engagement, and that ain't no lie.

Just before the dust of battle cleared for the day an Indian came up on horseback, accosted Trigger Mortis, and said that if we really wanted some squirrels to come up to his ranch where the gun hunters hadn't been shooting at them to make them so wild.

---

*The handwriting of our noted war correspondent isn't too legible, so we are wondering if this word should not have ended 'sy' instead of 'tser.' —Editor's note.

A. J. Michelson, president of the NFAA, is taking a five months auto cruise through the Northwest, including the NAA tournament in his itinerary.

Blunts from the Old Stump

The Legal Committee, consisting of A. J. Michelson, John Yount and Paris B. Stockdale, has drafted the NFAA permanent Constitution into final form. The Constitution is now being submitted to the various states for ratification. Under the Constitution, a state with twenty-five NFAA members is entitled to representation on the Board of Field Governors. The following states have more than twenty-five members: California, Michigan, Washington, Oregon, Ohio, New Mexico, New Jersey, Pennsylvania, and Arizona. Many more states lack just a few more members to entitle them to representation on the Board of Field Governors. All field archers of your state should support the NFAA. Why not get those few extra members your state needs to fully participate and have a voice in all national NFAA affairs? We have members in practically all of the states. Our membership is growing rapidly. It should not be long before every state will be represented on the Board of Field Governors of the NFAA.

The Art Young Big Game Award Committee, consisting of Dr. Paul Klopsteg, Erle Stanley Gardner, and Forrest Nagler, has submitted its report on the requirements for the Big Game Award. This award is given NFAA members successful in bagging big game with the bow and arrow. The Committee's report has been splendidly prepared and shows a great deal of thought and work. It will meet with the unanimous approval of all field archers. The full report will be published in next month's Ye Sylvan Archer. The Big Game pin is a coveted award, and it would be just too bad if you bag your big game and miss this award because you are not an NFAA member.

The San Diego, California, Club will be heard from as a real live field archery club. Their course is in Balboa Park, about ten minutes from the heart of the city. At a regular monthly shoot held there in June, archers attended from as far as 250 miles, which shows that this club has "something on the ball," and that field archery is not a passing fancy when it can draw archers from that distance to attend an ordinary monthly shoot.

Delmar Pletcher won the championship medal at the Southern California shoot at San Diego. His brother, Erwin Pletcher, a lieutenant in the Army, won the Northern California tournament at Oakland. Their high scores on their own course at Bakersfield evidently were no accidents. They shoot just as well on a strange course.

We have a new member from Hawaii, Lieut. F. D. Latta, stationed at the U. S. Submarine Base. He has recently written of some of his bow hunting experiences. We hope he will soon have one for the Archer.

Is the Secretary's face red! He has been corresponding with "Buddy" Feathers, assuming that "Buddy" was a younger brother of Dawson Feathers, formerly secretary of the Northern California Field Archers' Association, who is in South America on a scientific expedition. It now develops that "Buddy" Feathers is Mrs. Dawson Feathers. We can sympathize with Palmatier when he squawks about the use of nicknames on score cards.

A large number of our Canadian brothers are joining the NFAA. A. Wyttenbach of Toronto, tells us they have been holding field shoots on a temporary course each fall, with an attendance of about fifty. They are now planning on a permanent twenty-eight target course to be shot all the year around.

Northern California field archers held their annual election. The new officers are: Tom Farnsworth, President (Albany Club); Jack Peters, Vice-President (Albany Club); Mrs. Dawson Feathers, Secretary-Treasurer (Sequoia Club). Farnsworth is the head of the Albany Recreation Department for the City of Albany, which is in Berkeley County.

H. C. MacQuarrie, 3400 Fruitvale Avenue, Oakland, California, is gradually collecting his film on field archery. If you have good 16 mm. film that can be used, and which you are willing to donate to the good of the cause, write to Mac.

We see E. Hill Turnock of Wilkinsburg, Pennsylvania, is still shooting his usual high scores. On June 8, 1941, he shot 181-192-176-185, or a total of 734 for 56 targets. This reads more like a club score, rather than an individual score. Good form is as necessary in field shooting as in target shooting. If a good consistent field form of shooting is developed, it will be reflected in greater accuracy in your field shooting and hunting.

We are glad to welcome new members from Meridian, Mississippi. Archers in Mississippi interested in forming a State Field Association can contact Luther Littleton, Route No. 5, Meridian, Mississippi.

It is a pleasure to find that the New York Field Archers are at last organizing. Wm. L. Young, 96 Wabash Avenue, Rochester, New York, is chairman of the summer schedule committee of the Rochester Archery Club. The Sherrill Archery Club, Jos. A. Sweeney, Secretary, 175 W. Seneca Street, Sherrill, New York, is also planning on an NFAA field course. New York is a great hunting state. Come on, you field archers of New York; let's get organized!

You really don't appreciate how badly field archery needs publicity and organizing until you find that Pontiac, Michigan, (forty miles from Flint) field archers have to write to California for information on the NFAA. You can bet we are giving them a glad hand, and inviting them to shoot the Flint Bowmen course, one of the finest and sportiest courses in the country.

One of the most enthusiastic field archers and efficient organizers of field archers is Jean C. Tritten, 232 South Francis Street, Dallas, Texas. Tritten was formerly of New Mexico, and took an active part in organizing field archery in that state. On July 5 and 6, Tritten and other field archers met with the Texas Archery Association to organize field archery in that state. We can soon look for Texas to take a leading part in promoting National Field Archery.

Fall is not far off, when the game seasons will be opening in most states, and bow and arrow hunters will be sharpening their broadheads and fletching their small game arrows. There are thousands of new converts to the bow who are anxious to learn of the most efficient kinds of hunting tackle and tested hunting methods. If you have interesting knowledge and experience to contribute to bow and arrow hunting, now is the time to do it, before the hunting season opens. Write Ye Sylvan Archer.

Field archers should be proud to wear the NFAA felt emblem. In doing so, you are publicizing our national organization. If you do not have yours, you can get them from the Secretary for 25c each.

Progressive state target associations are getting more and more field conscious, which is as it should be. M. E. Foster, President of the Oklahoma State Archery Association, writes: "The State Archery Tournament is to be held in Bartlesville, Oklahoma, next year, and in order to have a tournament which will attract all of the archers in the state, we plan to include, for the first time, field archery as well as the regular target rounds, clout and flight. Neither the Bartlesville Archery Club, which will be the host, nor the State Association belongs to the National Field Association, but this is a defect which can be remedied." To attract and hold all archers, field archery is a necessary part of every state archery program. Some archers shoot target only—others shoot only field—but many like both. If your local or state organization is to progress and expand, you cannot afford to neglect field archery.

By the time this reaches you, we will be well on our way to the National Target Tournament at Portland. We expect to go by way of the Black Hills and Yellowstone, doing a lot of sightseeing and trout fishing on the way. We are making a leisurely trip, and expect to be able to warm up the bow at the various stops on the way West. We field archers attending the tournament at Portland are going to get together while there. Kore Duryee, George Brommers, and Dr. Hewitt have been appointed as the NFAA Field Archers Committee at this tournament. They will make all necessary arrangements to steer the field archers and corral them for a get-together. Announcements will be made at the National as to when and where the field archers will gather. You know there is no law against your shooting your hunting bow and blunts at the National Target Tournament, without points of aim or sights, if you

(Continued on page 15)

Osage -- The Bow for Roving

By Paul J. Sampson, Union Bridge. Md.

Bows are like boats, there is no possibility of finding every advantage in one product. The perfect bow is a matter of balanced compromises. Each type of wood has its strong points and its weak points as well. In selecting a bow, consideration must be given to the type of shooting to be done and to local conditions. I find an unreasoned prejudice against osage on the part of many archers, and am convinced that many shooters are passing up a good thing because of lack of experience. This discussion of osage as a bow wood is an attempt to share my experiences with those who have had little opportunity to make their own tests.

The died-in-the-wool yew man will disagree with much I have to say, but so be it.

It has long been recognized that osage is in a class by itself for hunting bows. It can be made in shorter lengths, which is a distinct advantage, and unfortunate experiences with yew in cold weather has convinced me that when the temperature is down about freezing, which is usually the case in hunting weather, osage is the wood. I have never had an osage bow break yet because of cold weather (this is not saying, of course, that it cannot happen), but I will never forget the heart-rending explosion of my first yew when it divided itself into a dozen pieces. Since then, when winter comes I hang my yew bows up until spring. Also, it is generally conceded that osage will stand greater bending strains, hence is more durable at heavier draws.

But for roving and target shooting there are many archers who dismiss osage as unsuitable. Here I beg to differ. It is contended, first, that yew has a superior cast. I think a great mistake is made in making blanket assertions concerning any bow wood. I have seen some yew bows shoot harder than some osage bows and I have also seen some osage bows shoot harder than some yew bows. Incidentally, the longest shot I have ever made in my life with a standard target arrow was made with a lemonwood hunting bow. So what? It is impossible to ascribe superior cast to one type of wood or another, as the cast of a particular bow depends entirely upon the quality of the wood and the workmanship. I will make this statement, which I consider conservative—out of a thousand mine-run staves of both kinds of wood, the cast of the osage bows will equal that of the yew, workmanship being equal. If I am wrong, I would like someone to prove it.

But there is another angle to this cast business that I believe favors osage. That is the matter of temperature. Under moderate weather conditions yew is good but when the thermometer goes up and the atmosphere gets thick, then look out, brother. The other day at a tournament in Washington, D. C., my forty pound yew went down to thirty-four pounds and refused to snatch the arrows out of my hand. I switched to a forty-eight pound osage which dropped but very little in the course of shooting, under most unfavorable atmospheric conditions, and again got in the groove. Temperature and atmosphere do affect osage somewhat, but not nearly so much as yew, and who knows several days ahead of time what the conditions will be at the tournament you have been waiting for all winter. It is a comfort to know that the bow to be shot will resemble itself at least approximately under varying conditions.

Most experienced shooters will admit what has been said thus far but will outlaw osage on this one single count, harshness. But even here there is something to be said. I will readily admit that osage does not shoot as soft as yew, but I believe that this point is over stressed. One reason for this is the fact that many osage bows are not properly made. I miscued on one not long ago, and it kicks like a Missouri mule. But I have made several dozen that were not at all objectionable. Unfortunately, a properly designed osage bow is not the handsomest thing in the world. It should be made to bend

(Continued on page 15)

NFAA Bulletin

OFFICERS

President—A. J. Michelson
610 F. P. Flint Bldg., Flint, Mich.

Vice-President—Paris B. Stockdale,
Geology Dept., OSU, Columbus, Ohio.

Secretary-Treasurer—John L. Yount,
Box 383, Redlands, California.

EXECUTIVE COMMITTEE

Western—H. C. MacQuarrie,
3400 Fruitvale Ave., Oakland, Calif.

Mid-Western—Fred Bear,
2611 W. Philadelphia, Detroit, Mich.

Eastern—T. C. Davidson,
53 Mountain Ave., Springfield, N. J.

By John L. Yount

APPEAL TO CLUB SECRETARIES

When you hold a tournament, please remember that we want to hear about it. Yours may be a new club in this field game and your course a cow pasture borrowed for the day, but we still want to know about that tournament—and all about it.

We want this information for the files of the NFAA and we want it for Ye Sylvan Archer. While there may be months when there will not be space for a full account of all tournaments, there will be space for a summary, and Mike can use a lot of the interesting sidelights in his column, "Blunts from the Old Stump."

Report your tournament as a sports event; don't make it look like a stock market report. Tell us what kind of a day it was, whether the course is permanent or laid out for a single tournament, whether it is a 14 or 28 target affair, hilly or level, and what has been done to make it a sporty and interesting course.

The results are necessary. You can't report a tournament without them, BUT tell us about the shooting. Surely there was a favorite; if he got beat, tell us about it. Make it a human interest story. Men go to pieces or shoot over their heads. Tell us who did which and what his alibi was.

To sum the whole thing up, we want the statistics on your tournament, and we want a whole lot more. Please do the best you can for us.

TO THE HUNTERS

We need a complete record of the hunting activities of our members, and must have your help to get it. If you are planning a trip, plan to keep a record of it, and then mail that record in just as soon as possible. It may make an interesting story for some issue of the Archer, as well as be of value to our records.

We want to know how many hunt, where they hunt, what they hunt, the amount of game seen, the number of shots obtained, whether or not any game was taken, and an estimate of the amount of game that could have been taken had you used a gun on the same trip. In short, we want to know all the answers.

We need this information, for, whether you know it or not, there are still plenty of states where such organizations as the Humane Society look upon a bowman as something slightly lower than a snake, and it is going to take a lot of evidence to change their attitude.

Be sure that all members of your hunting party are members of the NFAA and eligible for the Big Game pin, if big game is what you are after.

Pacific Northwest Shoot

The fifteenth annual tournament of the Pacific Northwest Archery Association was held at Seattle on July 12 and 13.

Damon Howatt of Yakima, Washington, was first with a total of 2122 for the York and double American rounds. De Witt Hawkins and Pat Chambers, both of Portland, were second and third, respectively.

Belvia Carter of Tacoma, won the women's championship with a score of 1885 for the double National and double Columbia. Vivian Chambers was second, and Harriette Warnick was third.

Billy Boak of Bordeaux, Washington, took the junior boys' championship, Larry Daniel and Dean Gibson placing in second and third positions.

Dorothy Axtelle of Tacoma, beat Muriel Reichart of Corvallis, Oregon, by 5 points for the junior girls' championship, each shooting a perfect at the same end.

Men flight shooters will be startled to learn that for the first time to our knowledge in tournament competition a woman, Glendolene Vinyard, Canby, Oregon, outshot all the men in the flight event, and by over 20 yards. Don McFarland of Portland, won the men's flight, and Billy Boak the junior flight.

Spokane won the men's team shoot and the Portland women's team was high. Pat Chambers took the men's clout and Harriette Warnick the women's.

The next tournament will be held in Portland, with the following officers in charge: President, Glendolene Vinyard; Vice-Presidents, DeWitt Hawkins of Portland, and Harold Meyer of Spokane; and Secretary-Treasurer, Kore T. Duryee of Seattle.

Pasadena Field Archers

The annual meeting was held in our new club building amid turkey and fixin's, and settled by the steam roller that put the following good men in office: Keith Olsen, President; Henry Bitzenburger, Vice-President and Business Manager; S. F. Foster, Secretary-Treasurer; and Roland (Porky) Quayle, Target Captain. On the Board of Managers are Bob King, Victor Jenson, H. M. Hoyte, and Geo. F. Miles.

Henry Bitzenburger (and Babe), our retiring Secretary, spoke well of the finances; also reported many new members during the year, with a paid up membership of 163.

There are no scores to report this time, as the "C" class men did not beat the "A" class men this meet.

Pat Chambers was a visitor some time back, as was Harold A. Titcomb, Esq. The latch string is out, and we hope that more of our nearby and out-of-town friends will pull it.

—(Not written by the Secretary, but by a hired ghost writer.)

Oregon State Tournament

The fifteenth annual tournament of the Oregon State Archery Association was held at Cottage Grove, July 4, 5 and 6.

In the NFAA round Glendolene Vinyard rather showed up the men by shooting 180, while L. L. Daily's 166 was the best the men could do. Miss Vinyard also won the women's archery-golf contest with a 36 for 9 holes, while Gene Warnick scored 59 for 18 holes in the men's division. Clout winners were: men, Pat Chambers; women, Harriette Warnick; boys, Edgar Hunter; girls, Janice Jamison.

Flight winners: men, H. Prouty, 425 yards, 6½ feet; women. Glen Vinyard, 402 yards 1-2/3 feet (a new state record); boys, Edgar Hunter, 315 yards 2-5/6 feet; girls, Janice Jamison, 265 yards 2¾ feet.

De Witt Hawkins won the men's championship with 2076 for the York and double American rounds. Mrs. Ann Halseth of Heppner, won the women's championship, scoring 1416 in the single National and double Columbia rounds. This is the first time any of the state trophies have gone to Eastern Oregon, Mrs. Halseth having come about 300 miles to attend the tournament.

Miss Muriel Reichart of Corvallis, and Robert Nixon of Forest Grove, are this year's junior champions.

Forest Grove was selected for next year's tournament, which will be held July 3, 4 and 5, 1942. Officers elected were as follows: President, Ted Hunter, Sheridan; Vice-Presidents, LeRoy Smith, Cornelius, Forest Lemley, Cottage Grove, J. E. Halseth, Heppner; Secretary-Treasurer, V. D. McCauley, Corvallis.

Editorial

Oregon Archery-Golf Rules

We have been asked to publish in this issue the rules used by the Sylvan Archery Golf Club of Portland, as these rules will be used at the National tournament. Lack of space makes it impossible to publish the entire set of rules, but we give herewith the important ones, especially regarding equipment.

Only one bow for each player is permitted, except if the bow or string breaks a substitution may be made; bows not to be equipped with any kind of sights or aiming devices.

Any number and length arrows may be used but they must be standard bullet tipped or parallel pile point arrows, not larger than .30 calibre—blunt, barbed and/or broadhead arrows not allowed.

The practice of predetermining the length of the draw required for specific distances by markings on the arrow and/or bow or measuring distances to be shot other than by calculation is not permitted.

The targets are elevated approximately two inches from the ground. Should this height become less than one inch, players must correct before shooting.

A full draw is not required at any time.

Players may shoot at the targets from the spot where the arrow lies from the drive or approach shots. No player will be required to shoot at the targets from an arbitrary distance.

On tournament days no preliminary activity on the course will be permitted prior to the completion of competitive playing.

Tournament play shall be by foursome wherever possible, and not less than twosomes, each player keeping

(Continued on page 15)

Nelson Grumley of Michigan, with deer killed with bow and arrow in 1938. (Cut through courtesy of Fred Bear).

Letter Box

From New Zealand

16th June '41,
Oamaru, New Zealand.

Editor, Ye Sylvan Archer.
Dear Sir:

This magazine just about fills the bill for us N. Z. archers, as the majority of us are field archers and hunters, and if it hadn't been for the War placing restrictions on money orders and such, I'm sure that you would have had quite a number of subscribers by now.

I was very interested to see that the NFAA had decided to make your magazine the Official Organ for their side of the archery argument, as this will help to put the field archers in the running for a bit of recognition that is well overdue them, especially for the swell advertising that some of your archer hunters have given to archery.

I'm not in the position to talk archery to you, as I am but a pup at the game, but if you could just find time to drop me a couple of lines I would be very pleased.

Thanking you, I am,
Yours sincerely,
Ian L. McVinnie.

Brown County Open
By Mrs. G. F. Martin

Seventy persons attended the outdoor steak fry and singfest held May 30 in Brown County State Park, Indiana, prior to the Brown County Open tournament there May 31 and June 1. The group gathered on Greenhorn Creek at the archers' shelter built by the Indiana Conservation department. Several outdoor ovens surround the building which served as living quarters for eleven shooters during the meet. It is a stone and timber structure with tables and benches, lockers for tackle, bow-hanging pegs, and an indoor fireplace.

One hundred and twenty-eight shot in the meet, representing forty-seven cities in six states. Ninety attended the chicken dinner and entertainment the evening of May 31 in the Abe Martin Lodge. The Chicagoites who sponsored the meet really gave out with the merry-making. With E. S. Richter as chief brewer they blended efficient range management with plenty of laughs during the 'tween the rounds times.

Mildred Miller from Milwaukee, Wisconsin, went home with the women's championship cup. R. V. Bradley, Morton, Illinois, won the men's championship trophy. Bob Andersen, Chicago, annexed the intermediate boys' title; Verdelle Kreuger, Western Springs, Illinois, the junior girls', and Don Hoover, Dundas, Illinois, the junior boys'.

In the men's division Marvin Schmidt, Chicago, was second; Al Thorwarth, Belleview, Kentucky, was third; Robert Simmons, Chicago, was fourth; Lowell Stouder, Moline, Illinois, fifth; Dick Hughes, Evansville, sixth; Basil McCartney, Anderson, Indiana, seventh; Jack Wendling, Columbus, Indiana, eighth; Carl Joseph, Milwaukee, Wisconsin, ninth; and John Thompson, Terre Haute, Indiana, tenth.

Renette Yanke, Chicago, placed second for the women; Mrs. Olga Yanke, third; Alta Benedict, South Gate, Kentucky, fourth; and Ruth Thorwarth, Belleview, Kentucky, was fifth.

Those who shot six-golds ends were Ruth Thorwarth, Edith Radtke, Hazel Crest, Illinois, and Roy Brandes, Dayton, Ohio.

Renette Yanke shot 36 hits for 298 to win the women's clout event. Bill Conger, Milwaukee, scored 36-248 to to take first place in the men's division. Allen Cammack, Louisville, Kentucky, was high scorer for the junior boys with 34-210. Bob Andersen led the intermediates, and Verdelle Kreuger the junior girls.

In the flight event the Hills from Dayton retained their 1940 titles. Curt shot 416 yards and Millie shot 351 yards for a new meet record. Bancroft Henderson, Evansville, shot farthest for the intermediates, Don Hoover for the junior boys, and Verdelle Kreuger for the junior girls.

Don Seal, Mt. Vernon, Indiana, shot the highest scores among the instinctive shooters, a 68-290 York and a 75-411 American.

Because of rain at noon June 1, the meet was terminated before the usual number of rounds had been shot.

"Gurgles from the Little Brown Jug," the official tournament newspaper, edited by "Doc" Baldwin of Chicago, missed a good story by not getting out a post meeting issue. The villagers in Nashville, near the park, reported Sunday night that there wasn't a loaf of store bread or a frying size chicken to be had within a radius of eighteen miles, which proves that, next to shooting, archers like to eat. So for next year's meet May 30 and 31 the villagers are planning to serve double portions to all people with sunburns right at the start, instead of waiting for the guests to request another half-dozen or so biscuits with strawberry preserves, etc.

FIELD ARCHERS OF SOUTHERN CALIFORNIA

By Elmer Bedwell, Secretary

A large attendance of archers were present for the regular FAASC bi-monthly tournament held at San Diego, the Old Mission Archery Club being the host club for the first time. We hope to see more of them. Clubs from all over the Southland were represented from as far north as Bakersfield.

The San Diego Club has been doing a lot of work, and now has a complete 28 target standard course, with plenty of hazards, and it is interesting to shoot. This time of year the shade trees they have are appreciated, especially by the inland clubs.

As an example of enthusiastic archers, we have Dr. Delmer Pletcher, who, with his family and his brother and family, made a round trip of 500 miles for one day's shooting, and at least twenty-five other archers made 250 mile round trip drives, a long day, all tired, but having a good time.

Dr. Pletcher had some compensation for his trip in the fact that he took home the Championship Medal.

The high scores for the day were well distributed among the clubs, and were: Men's Championship Class — M. D. Hathaway, Malibu, gold bar, score 533; Irving Davis, Redlands, silver bar, score 361.

Ladies' Championship Class—Eva Bedwell, Redlands, gold bar, score 297; Ruth Hathaway, Malibu, silver bar, score 293.

General Division, Men — Dr. Delmer Pletcher, Bakersfield, Championship Medal, score 513; Robert Hoover, San Diego, red ribbon, score 483; Jess Quayle, Pasadena, white ribbon, score 482.

General Division, Ladies' —Margaret King, Redlands, Championship Medal, score 264; Minerva Gandy, Malibu, red ribbon, score 233; Carmelita Swarts, San Diego, white ribbon, score 129.

There were seventy registered archers for the tournament, and thirty-three were registered for the Third National Mail Tournament.

Paterson Long Bowman

The Paterson (New Jersey) Long Bowman, in conjunction with the Passaic County (New Jersey) Park Commission, will sponsor an open Field Shoot at Garret Mountain Reservation, Paterson, New Jersey, September 14, starting at ten A. M.

The morning shoot will be over a 28-target course at the Overlook Meadow.

The afternoon event will be a timed shoot. This popular round of 6 ends of 6 arrows, each end to be shot within 45 seconds, will be held on the lawn of Lambert's Castle.

There will be three prizes for men and three for the women. The morning and afternoon scores will be combined to determine the winners.

Entries should be sent to Miss Clara Amanda King, 154 North 3rd Street, Paterson, New Jersey. Kindly include your address and club affiliation. The entry fee for the shoot is fifty (50c) cents, payable on the day of the shoot.

Louis C. Smith, secretary of the NAA, has announced that three members of the Board of Governors are to be elected at the annual business meeting of the NAA to be held in Portland on August 7. Members whose terms expire are W. M. Folberth, Cleveland, Ohio; Capt. C. H. Styles, Berkeley, California; and E. Hill Turnock, Wilkinsburg, Pennsylvania. Each NAA member has the privilege of submitting the name of the person of his choice for Board member from his region.

Clare and Daisy Hamlin of Eugene are preparing and directing an archery pageant for the evening of August 6, at the National.

Will History Repeat Itself

By George Brommers

(This painstakingly accurate report, recently unearthed, was written in 1935, after the National Tournament in Los Angeles.)

"DOGHOUSE POLITICS"

"I want your advice," says Dr. Klopsteg. "I am supposed to bring the next tournament back to Chicago. As I see it, the chance is mighty slim. Michigan has done too much hard work, and — I hate to admit it — has just about earned it. We got under way too late, that's all."

"Never say die," I counsel. "If Mr. Farley knows his bermudas and comes to see me, Mr. Roosevelt is re-elected right now. I will see that you get the tournament, don't you worry." Dr. Klopsteg was my house guest, and when I go to bat for a friend . . . . .

"How will you go about it?" asks the practical Paul.

"Don't know, yet," I admit, "but you may consider the thing in the bag. We might send some telegrams, calling the Battle Creekers out of town just before the business meeting. Or stall a flivver outside the hall. Any normal Michigander will want to stop and tinker with it, and if we cut the right wires —"

"Kind of crude, don't you think?" argues Paul.

"Nothing's too crude in politics," I point out, "but we might use a little more finesse. For instance, the president of the Board of Health and two police captains are members of our Art Young Club. If they will do their duty we can have Palmatier quarantined for hydrophobia, and the Michigan rooters pinched on general principles. Don't give up the ship."

"Count me out," says Paul. "You politicians work too fast for me. You will be as popular as a skunk under the bed. It is your funeral from now on, I will buy the flowers."

I ran into unsuspected difficulties. The Board of Health let out a loud squawk to the effect that hydrophobia — even in a visitor — was unthinkable in hygienic L. A. Nor did I fare any better with the cops. They would take care of public enemies like Joe Cosner, but that was as far as they would go.

There was no reason, but there was some kind of excuse for the stand-offishness of the cops. There was the match of pistol against bow and arrow that I had arranged. It seems that at 100 yards the same pistol that registered only bullseyes at 50 yards, began to scatter, while the bow occasionally did not scatter. Then, too, there was the unfortunate and accidental switching of target pistols with — to the cops — a little embarrassing results. The minds of the police were not wholly free from unjust suspicions.

It wasn't, quoth Capt. Murray bitterly, that there was enough evidence to hang anybody. But he did know to a moral certainty that there were double-crossing and framing going on in his district, and that between these sordid elements and visitors from Michigan, his was a benevolent neutrality in favor of the visitors, if not an actual state of non-belligerency.

You can't down a good politician. I got out some statistics showing that two out of every three Michiganders died of typhoid, if some other disease didn't get them first. I quoted speed laws and the number of arrests of tourists. Lovingly I dwelt on the summer heat and on mosquitoes as big as a Douglas air liner. Feelingly I referred to the Model T, its rattles and its repair bills. On the shooting line I did some sly sniping at the Palmatier goat.

Well, even I can't win every time. Paul claims to this day that the thirteen votes we did get must have come from members I didn't contact. But that's gratitude for you.

(Now, if there are campaign managers wanted for any more lost causes, take the matter up with me personally at Portland.)

Special doe licenses for Grant County will be issued to 3000 hunters in Oregon this season. The Archery Reserve is included in the area in which does may be killed.

June NFAA Tournament Report

By Karl E. Palmatier

CLASS "A"—MEN

	Actual 28 Target Score	Actual 28 Target Score	Actual 56 Target Score	Handicap Score
Delmer Pletcher, Bakersfield, Calif.	89-351	72-280	161-631	621
K. L. Jones, Bakersfield, Calif.	70-272	73-268	143-540	610
Robert Hoover, San Diego, Calif.	62-248	61-235	123-483	593
Kore Duryee, Seattle, Wash.	51-189	62-233	113-422	582
Emery Watts, Los Angeles, Calif.	60-238	58-224	118-462	572
Irl Stamps, Seattle, Wash.	67-265	62-248	129-513	563
Fred Badberry, Bakersfield, Calif.	60-230	64-245	124-475	555
Elmer Bedwell, San Bernardino, Cal.	51-185	41-151	92-336	546
Jim Murphy, Bakersfield, Calif.	53-211	47-163	100-374	534
Merle Hathaway, Los Angeles, Calif.	58-222	77-311	135-533	523
John Yount, Redlands, Calif.	51-185	50-184	101-369	519
Earl Grubbs, Los Angeles, Calif.	46-172	40-142	86-314	514
William Horr, San Diego, Calif.	43-159	44-162	87-321	501
Irving Davis, Bryn Mawr, Calif.	47-179	48-182	95-361	491
E. J. Woodward, Redlands, Calif.	56-220	49-179	105-399	479
Alfonso Gonzales, Bakersfield, Calif.	46-172	46-174	92-346	446
George Calvert, Flint, Mich.	40-150	42-159	82-309	439
E. Hill Turnock, Wilkinsburg, Pa.	92-374	89-361	181-735	
Leo Cornell, Oakland, Calif.	65-255	62-227	127-482	
Jack Young, Oakland, Calif.	66-234	59-229	125-463	
Perzy High, Los Angeles, Calif.	68-248	54-202	122-450	
John Willard, Hollywood, Calif.	52-190	52-204	104-394	
Jack Peters, Oakland, Calif.	49-197	42-191	91-388	
E. J. Flesher, Pittsburgh Club, Pa.	53-191	54-194	107-385	
Harry Ussack, Pittsburgh Club, Pa.	36-142	59-215	95-357	
Don Lumley, San Diego, Calif.	43-157	54-198	97-355	
Robert King, Los Angeles, Calif.	48-174	49-179	97-353	
C. W. Seastrom, West Hollywood, Cal.	44-168	47-163	91-331	

CLASS "A"—LADIES

Mary Calvert, Flint, Mich.	51-189	40-152	91-341	401
Bertha Hoffmeyer, Flint, Mich.	43-161	43-151	86-312	392
Lulu Stalker, Flint, Mich.	41-151	32-126	73-277	387
Bessie M. Stephenson, Flint, Mich.	41-176	36-140	77-316	386
June Franklin, San Bernardino, Cal.	32-116	34-128	66-244	324
Ruth Davis, Bryn Mawr, Calif.	35-127	34-126	69-253	303
Eva Bedwell, San Bernardino, Cal.	39-147	38-150	77-297	267
Mrs. C. J. Code, Pittsburgh Club, Pa.	36-142	36-140	72-282	
Margaret King, Redlands, Calif.	35-135	35-129	70-264	
Minerva Gandy, Los Angeles, Calif.	32-110	33-123	65-233	

CLASS "B"—MEN

	28 Target Score	28 Target Score	Total
Ken Moore, Los Angeles, Calif.	51-199	52-212	103-411
Franklin Jones, Everett, Wash.	42-160	47-176	89-336
B. Granger, Flint, Mich.	43-161	45-159	88-320
Lewis Richardson, Flint, Mich.	47-191	32-122	79-313
William Smith, Flint, Mich.	51-187	34-126	85-313
Albert Biordi, Los Angeles, Calif.	39-145	45-163	84-308
Russell Berry, San Diego, Calif.	44-158	35-143	79-301
Frank Eicholtz, San Diego, Calif.	44-160	37-129	81-289

	28 Target Score	28 Target Score	Total
L. D. Markham, Durand, Mich.	43-163	34-120	77-283
Harvey Franklin, San Ber'd'o, Cal.	42-152	36-126	78-278
Tracy Stalker, Flint, Mich.	39-145	37-131	76-276
W. M. Scheffler, Pittsburg, Pa.			74-276
Carl Seastrom, West Hollywood, Cal.	32-122	37-151	79-273
Fred Drake, Pittsburgh Club, Pa.			69-271
Bert Wallis, Seattle, Wash.	34-120	38-144	72-264
S. Leo Sipe, Los Angeles, Calif.	20-120	33-127	53-247
Bennett Gandy, Los Angeles, Calif.	33-123	31-115	64-238
Angus Bruce, Redlands, Calif.	29-105	21-71	50-176

CLASS "C"—MEN

Fred Brockhoff, Seattle, Wash.	36-134	37-135	73-269
Paul Ludwig, Los Angeles, Calif.	32-120	33-123	65-243
Con Caldwell, Seattle, Wash.	31-123	31-111	62-234
Karl Palmatier, Kalamazoo, Mich.	34-120	33-107	67-227
Ralph O'Roark, Pittsburg, Pa.			42-193
W. Harmon, Langley, Wash.	23-83	31-109	54-192
A. J. Michelson, Flint, Mich.	29-103	23-89	52-192
Orville Smith, San Diego, Calif.	22-78	30-108	52-186
Joe Monroe, Redlands, Calif.	29-101	23-85	52-186
Paul Hougham, San Diego, Calif.	24-80	26-100	50-180
Jimmy Ratcliff, Detroit, Mich.	25-89	25-87	50-176
W. B. Blackmore, Marysville, Wash.	17-67	22-86	39-153
William Irvin, Seattle, Wash.	16-56	21-83	37-139
Ed Tweeddale, Everett, Wash.	20-70	17-65	37-135
Ed W. Tweeddale, Everett, Wash.	16-58	20-68	36-126
Charles Frieburg, Pittsburgh, Pa.			34-120
G. E. Nevergold, Pittsburgh, Pa.			31-115
Roy Norton, Everett, Wash.	16-58	14-52	30-110
T. Petersen, Pittsburgh, Pa.			32-104
Robert Blackmore, Marysville, Wash.	12-46	14-56	26-102
Dean Tweeddale, Everett, Wash.	9-37	16-62	25-99
Ben Bredimus, Seattle, Wash.	13-43	11-39	24-82
Robert Thacker, Everett, Wash.	5-15	16-64	21-79
R. Polis, Pittsburgh, Pa.			20-72
H. Nevergold, Pittsburgh, Pa.			16-56
B. Stangle, Bellingham, Wash.	12-44		
J. Purvis, Pittsburgh, Pa.			12-40

CLASS "B"—LADIES

Ruth Hathaway, Los Angeles, Calif.	38-144	41-149	79-293
Kay Ratcliff, Highland Park, Mich.	26-92	32-116	58-208
Phyllis Diehl, Flint, Mich.	25-99	23-85	48-184
Ina Woolnough, Trenton, Mich.	25-83	21-71	46-154
Blanche Wallis, Seattle, Wash.	13-49	21-75	34-124
Mercella Kuntz, Pittsburgh, Pa.			31-121

CLASS "C" LADIES

Mrs. Valeria Irvin, Seattle, Wash.	10-32	16-60	26-92
Bessalee Jones, Everett, Wash.	11-39	6-18	17-57
Mrs. Ralph O'Roark, Pittsburgh, Pa.			10-30

The archers from the Pittsburgh Club did not send in the scores for each 28 targets (in Classes "B" and "C"), so only the total could be reported.

The following archers reported scores that will put them in class "A" for the next mail tournament, in each case sufficient 28 target scores having been reported to figure the handicap:

Ken Moore   Franklin Jones   Ruth Hathaway   Kay Ratcliff

HANDICAPS FOR NEXT TOURNAMENT (LADIES)

Gene Bacon	-90	Lulu Stalker	90	Bessie Stephenson	50
Eva Bedwell	-20	June Franklin	80	Babe Bitzenberger	50
Kay Ratcliff	140	Bertha Hoffmeyer	60	Mrs. Code	40
Ruth Hathaway	100	Margaret Quayle	60	Mary Calvert	30
Margaret King	90	Ruth Davis	50		

HANDICAPS FOR NEXT TOURNAMENT (MEN)

E. Turnock	-140	R. Hoff	160	E. Bedwell	100
D. Pletcher	-40	R. King	160	R. Hoover	90
R. Quayle	-40	J. Murphy	150	P. High	90
M. Hathaway	-10	J. Yount	150	E. Woodward	90
E. Grubbs	210	B. Ahman	150	L. Cornell	80
L. Hoffmeyer	210	I. Davis	140	J. Young	80
E. J. Flesher	200	G. Calvert	140	F. Gadberry	80
F. Jones	190	K. Duryee	140	K. Jones	40
C. W. Seastrom	190	J. Peters	110	I. Stamps	40
W. Horr	190	A. Gonzales	110	P. Chambers	20
K. Moore	170	E. Watts	100		

If you are reported as a class "A" archer and no handicap is given above it is because you have not sent in four 28 target scores. If you have shot in one tournament that will take care of two of them. When you send in your next tournament score you may include two 28 target practice scores that are recognized by the secretary of your club. Be sure to indicate which are the practice scores.

You will note that the Third Mail Tournament shows a substantial increase in the number participating. As the number increases there is more work for the secretary. In this report I have reported the figures exactly as they were turned in, with the exception of a very few cases where the error was great. Check your score and see if you have an even number of hits for an even number for score. An odd number for hits means an odd number for score. Did you make an error?

The secretary did not receive a single set of score cards before the end of the month. Any delay on your part will hold up the report of the tournament. The report of each tournament should be in Ye Sylvan Archer for the following month. Try to get your reports in a little earlier.

Sunday, July 6, was given over to field archery at the Mid-Western held at Cincinnati, Ohio. Fifty-eight archers entered. A report of this meet will be sent to Ye Sylvan Archer. The Mid-Western now covers sixteen states.

Mr. and Mrs. Grumley, J. Scott and R. DeForest have sent in their NFAA memberships since the last report. These have been sent to John Yount, P. O. Box 383, Redlands, California.

The archers of Indiana are now starting a program of field archery. Several of them have attended Michigan meets to get an idea of how to conduct a meet.

The complaint most often made to the secretary is that it takes too long to get the archers under way at a meet. Assign the archers to a target the same as in target archery. When the whistle blows all start to shoot. They will all finish at about the same time. In this way 28 targets may be shot by all archers in two hours easily.

Osage—the Bow for Roving
(Continued from page 5)

clear to the handles with a very sharp handle dip. A long, gradual, rounded, unbending midsection such as is used on lemonwood and some yew bows will not work with osage. It necessitates a longer bow which means a larger mass of wood to be zipped, and the shock is not so evenly distributed. If an osage bow is made to bend clear to the handles, hence shortened as much as possible with not more than a half-inch of thickness in the bending section, then it is amazing how sweet it will shoot. Of course, this description will entirely eliminate the old style stacked bow, which is not adaptable to osage. My experience has been that a properly designed osage bow will shoot as soft as lemonwood and that is all that one can reasonably ask. Also here again the weather speaks. Take your yew bow out when the temperature is below fifty (if you are not afraid it will burst) and see if it shoots with the same ease that it did at the last Fourth of July tournament. It will not.

Our discussion thus far leads us to this conclusion. Osage is superior in durability, equal in cast, and inferior in smoothness. Yew is inferior in durability, equal in cast, superior in smoothness. Osage is more consistent under varying weather conditions. Yew is generally better looking. So if you are a yew man you will probably stick to yew, if you are an osage fancier you will stay with osage, and if you are a beginner, well, your five dollar lemonwood will suit you fine until you make up your mind. I do believe, however, that osage is the ideal wood for roving and hunting, and that it deserves more consideration from the target shooter than it has received.

Archery-Golf Rules
(Continued from page 8)

score for himself and all other players, the scores being read aloud before teeing off at the next tee.

The four players of each class with the lowest scores for 18 targets must play an additional 18 targets, remaining in their respective classes and competing for their respective trophies. Those with the lowest score for the second 18 targets shall be declared winners of the tournament and trophies awarded accordingly.

If the final play-off results in a tied score or scores, the winner shall be determined by playing additional targets in match play for each target until the tie is broken.

Blunts from the Old Stump
(Continued from page 4)

want to. We attend the tournament for good fellowship and fun, and not for the medals that we expect to win. Be sure and look us up. You will probably find us on about target Z-4. We urge all field archers who can possibly attend to come to Portland. We'll be seein' you.

The Klamath County (Oregon) Izaak Walton League is sponsoring a sport show at Klamath Falls on September 4, 5 and 6, at which archery will be featured in exhibitions and competitive shooting. Mr. L. G. Rose tells us there are many archers in the Klamath Falls area but most are field archers and very few are interested in target archery.

Oregon archers are reminded that the annual Oregon Pope-Young tournament will be held at the Williams Ranch in the Archery Reserve on September 18 and 19, the two days preceding the opening of the deer season.

Our cover photo this month is by Chester Stevenson of Eugene.

Paul H. Gordon
Author of "The New Archery"
Producing
Tackle — Materials
Latest and Finest for Field
or Range
Write for Free Catalog
Beacon Hill Craftsmen
Beacon, N. Y.

BACK NUMBERS
YE SYLVAN ARCHER
Volumes I to V Inclusive
$1.00 Per Volume
B. G. THOMPSON
R. F. D. 1, Corvallis, Oregon

SUBSCRIBERS PLEASE NOTICE

A cross appearing in this space means that your subscription has expired and we would appreciate your prompt renewal so that your name may be kept on our mailing list.

CLASSIFIED ADVERTISING

RATES for Classified Advertising 5 cents per word per issue. Count initials and numbers as words. Minimum charge is 50 cents.

RELICS AND CURIOS

INDIAN RELICS, Beadwork, Coins, Curios, Books, Minerals, Weapons. Old West Photos. Catalog, 5c. Genuine African Bow, $3.75. Ancient flint arrowheads, perfect, 6c each—Indian Museum, Osborne, Kansas.

BOOKS AND MAGAZINES

The AMERICAN ARCHER, a national quarterly, $1.00 per year, 521 Fifth Ave., New York City.

"ARCHERY TACKLE, HOW TO MAKE AND HOW TO USE IT," by Adolph Shane. Bound in cloth and illustrated with more than fifty drawings and photographs. Information for making archery tackle and instructions for shooting. Price is $1.75. Send orders to Ye Sylvan Archer, 505 North 11th street, Corvallis, Oregon.

HANDBOOK—How to Make and Use Bows and Arrows—90 Pages well illustrated (with catalog) 35c.

CATALOG—100 pictures—color spread—Instruction Folder. 10c.

CATALOG alone 5c. Stamps or Coin.

L. E. STEMMLER · QUEENS VILLAGE · N·Y·

The Flat Bow—70 pages of Archery information for 50 cents, well illustrated. *Ye Sylvan Archer*, 505 N. 11th St., Corvallis, Oregon.

E. BUD PIERSON
Bowyer — Fletcher
Tournament Tackle, Sinew, Glue, Raw Materials.
Custom Made Tackle
3109 Burnet Ave. — Cincinnati, Ohio

VIKING ARCHERY
1874 Market Street
San Francisco, Calif.

PORT ORFORD CEDAR ARROW SHAFTS
(Cypressa Lawsonia)

Specials. P.O. Cedar Shafts, 1/4 to 11/32":

Parallel, per 100 .... $4.00
Tapered or barreled, 100 .. $4.50
Extra Select. Units segregated, per 100 .... $5.00
Douglas Fir, 100 .... $3.00, $3.50
Douglas Fir, Extra Select, per 100 .... $4.00

Full line finished tackle. Raw Materials. Write for price lists. Special rates to dealers and clubs.

PORT ORFORD ARCHERY SUPPLY CO.
C. F. Douglas, Mgr.
Box 137   Port Orford, Oregon

HI THERE, FIELD ARCHERS—TAKE A LOOK AT THIS!
Write for full information

A special introductory offer. Complete set of 14 official "Arro-Mat" field targets and faces for only $29.75.

BEN PEARSON
INCORPORATED
Bows and Arrows of Excellence
PINE BLUFF, ARK.

This offer limited to full sets only. Your club can now enjoy the field round on official targets at a new low cost.

CHANDLER
Universal Broadheads

The Broadhead that costs less than a big rifle bullet, from 5c to 8-1/3c each. The inexpensive Broadhead for hunting.

Also Universal Broadhead Kits, with complete material for making one doz., good Broadhead Arrows.

FISH HEAD Also Hunting, Fishing and roving Points.
FREE CATALOGUE
T. B. CHANDLER
11819 4th Ave., Compton, Calif.

B-80   B-1

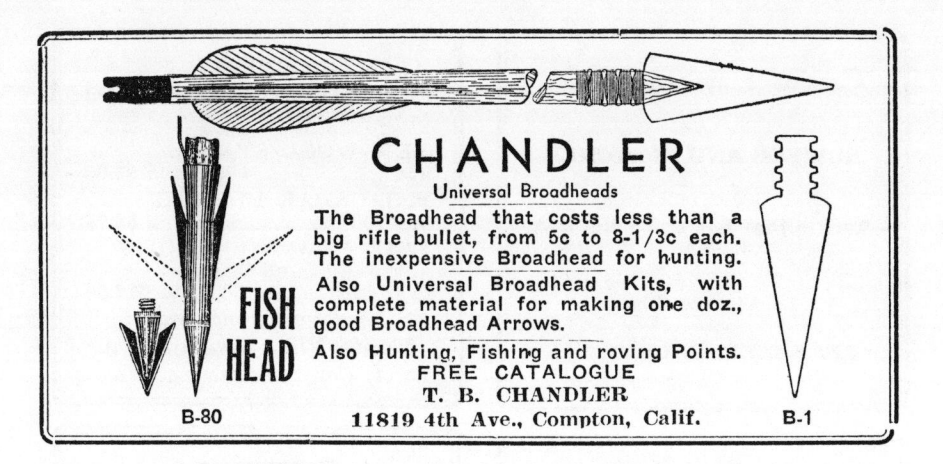

APPROVED NFAA FIELD TARGET FACES

Printed in black and white on heavy, double thickness corrugated board. In sets containing sizes necessary for a 14-target course and including extras of the smaller sizes that shoot out fastest.

$2.25 per set, f.o.b. Detroit — Order two sets for a 28-target course

BEAR ARCHERY CO.
2611 W. Philadelphia Ave., Detroit, Michigan

Ⓖ

"THE MARK OF DISTINCTION IN ARCHERY TACKLE
Fine Yew Target and Hunting Bows, Plain or Backed with Rawhide. Lemonwood Bows with Rawhide Backs.
College and School Equipment Target, Hunting and Roving Arrows
Price List on Request
Wholesale — Retail
EARL GRUBBS
5518 W. Adams
Los Angeles, : California

Arcadian Life Magazine
Stories of the Ozarks

Pioneer History - Folklore
Pastoral Living

$1.00 a Year; 25c a Copy

Display Adv. $1.50 per inch Classified, 3c a word. Three insertions for the price of two.

O. E. RAYBURN, Editor
Dept. 15
616 S. Benton St
Cape Girardeau, Mo.
P. O. Box 200
Caddo Gap, Arkansas

Please mention Ye Sylvan Archer when writing advertisers.

Ye Sylvan Archer—$1.00 per year

Cassius Hayward Styles

BOWYER AND FLETCHER

—Tackle that has stood the test—

28 Vicente Place

BERKELEY, CALIFORNIA

ARCHERY SUPPLIES
at prices everyone can afford to pay.
YEW WOOD STAVES
at .... $2.00 and $3.00
P. O. CEDAR DOWELS
per 100 .... $2.75
FINE YEW WOOD BOWS
any weight and length
to 6 feet .... $6.50 to $12.50
Send money with order.
Monte Vista Archery Co.
Rt. 1, Box 149, Tacoma, Wash.

Archery
Raw Materials

WM. A. JOY

9708 So. Hoover Street
LOS ANGELES, CALIF.

---

70 pages of Archery information for 50 cents, well illustrated. Ye Sylvan Archer, 505 N. 11th St., Corvallis, Oregon.

Ye Sylvan Archer—$1.00 per year.

NEW! ROVING GLOVE!

KM-25—A professional type glove, not recommended for use with bows pulling under 40 pounds. Each $2.50

SPECIFICATIONS: Finger stalls are made of two thicknesses of leather, with top leather of genuine heavy cordovan. Between the outer and inner thicknesses, a durable turkey quill is inserted. This prevents deep string indentations and a sloppy release. With turkey quill finger stalls, a clean snap release is always assured— a most important consideration for maximum accuracy. An indispensable glove when heavy equipment is used. Glove custom made to your hand sketch, or dress glove size.

KM-22—Without quill, but with two thicknesses of leather $1.75

KING ★ MOORE

7011 N. Figueroa St.
LOS ANGELES, CALIF.

Write today for **FREE CATALOG**

Ye Sylvan Archer

August, 1941

Vol. 13, No. 4

Ye Sylvan Archer

*Official Publication of the
National Field Archery Association*

Vol. 13   August, 1941   No. 4

Published the fifteenth of each month
for archers by archers
505 North 11th Street, Corvallis, Oregon

J. E. DAVIS .... Editor

Subscription Price .... $1.00 Per Year

Foreign Subscription $1.25

Single Copies .... 10 Cents

Advertising Rates on Application

TABLE OF CONTENTS

	Page
THE SIXTY-FIRST NATIONAL	1
BLUNTS FROM THE OLD STUMP	3
OREGON POPE-YOUNG FIELD TOURNAMENT	4
NFAA BULLETIN By John L. Yount	5
THE WASHINGTON ARCHERY RESERVE	6
LETTER BOX	7
EDITORIAL	8
SH! DON'T SCARE THE GAME By Natalie Reichart	9
KEASEY AT THE BAT By the Doghouse Editor	10
ARROW TIP POISON	10
JULY NFAA TOURNAMENT REPORT By Karl E. Palmatier	11
ARCHERY IN ANCIENT BATTLE	13
NEW MICHIGAN CLUB By James M. Redfield	14

The Sixty-first National

While in every National Archery Association annual tournament for the last ten years many new records have been established, the 61st annual tournament, held at Portland, Oregon, August 4-9, was unique in that new records were made in every one of the championship events.

Here is the list:

Single Columbia Round:
Old—72-582, Ann Weber (1940).
New—72-584, Ree Dillinger.

Double Columbia Round:
Old—144-1148, Ann Weber (1940).
New—144-1148, Ree Dillinger.

Single National Round:
Old—71-513, Ann Weber (1940).
New—72-522, Mildred Miller.

Double National Round:
Old—143-979, Ann Weber (1940).
New—144-1010, Mildred Miller.

Single York Round:
Old—134-826, Pat Chambers (1939).
New—141-827, Larry Hughes.

Double York Round:
Old—262-1614, R. Hoogerhyde (1940).
New—279-1637, Larry Hughes.

Single American Round:
Old—90-626, R. Hoogerhyde (1940).
New—90-744, Larry Hughes.

Double American Round:
Old—180-1428, R. Hoogerhyde (1940)
New—180-1464, Larry Hughes.

Jr. Girls, Single Columbia Round:
Old—72-516, Mary Thompson (1940).
New—72-516, Dorothy Axtelle.

Jr. Girls, Double Columbia Round:
Old—144-1006, Mary Thompson ('40).
New—144-1022, Dorothy Axtelle.

Boys, Single Jr. American Round:
Old—90-698, Sonny Johns (1938).
New—90-720, Paul Cowin.

Boys, Double Jr. American Round:
Old—180-1370, Sonny Johns (1938).
New—180-1426, Billy West.

The women's championship events ended like the stories of baseball games being won by a home run in the last half of the ninth inning with two out and two strikes on the batter. Ree Dillinger, Summit, New Jersey, shot a perfect on the last end of the championship events to win the championship by one point, totaling 2098, over Mildred Miller of Milwaukee, Wisconsin. Belvia Carter of Tacoma, Washington, was third with 1985. Vivian Chambers, Portland, Oregon, fourth with 1918; Gladys Hammer, Los Angeles, California, fifth, 1840.

Larry Hughes, Burbank, California, was not only unbeatable in his record-smashing drive for the men's championship, but was unapproachable. He led his nearest opponent, Willard Bacon, Redondo Beach, California, by 248 points, 3101 to 2853. G. Wayne Thompson, Richmond, California, scored 2832 points; Carl Strang, Dearborn, Michigan, 2757; Leslie Berg, San Francisco, California, 2715; Damon Howatt, Yakima, Washington, 2597; DeWitt Hawkins, Portland, Oregon, 2594; Pat Chambers, Portland, Oregon, 2502; Maynard L. Parker, Los Angeles, California, 2413; Eugene Warnick, Portland, Oregon, 2315.

Mildred Miller gained three points for tournament total by leading Ree Dillinger 1309 to 1306 in the double American round, but this event did not count in championship totals. Gladys Hammer won the 120 yard women's clout with a score of 36-230; Margaret Thompson was second with 34-198, and Frances Styles third with 32-184. Harriet Warnick took the 140 yard clout with 34-224 points, Mary Marquis scoring 34-188, and Gene Bacon 33-181.

Willard Bacon captured the men's clout with 36-240, with Wayne Thompson scoring 35-225, and Earl P. Clark 35-224. Dean Gibson took the junior clout, scoring 35-229, to 35-225 for Dixon Rich, and 34-206 for Dan Davis. Myrtle Webb won the girls' clout with 29-123.

Dorothy Axtelle of Tacoma, Washington, is the new girls' champion, with a total of 3276 points. Muriel Reichart, Corvallis, Oregon, was second with 2434 points. Betty Griesel of Portland, Oregon, had 1625, and Myrtle Webb, Glenwood, Oregon, 1545.

Nine boys from six states faced the targets, with Billy West of Joplin, Missouri, taking the championship with a total of 4088 points in a double American and four junior American rounds. The total of Paul Cowin of Bethlehem, Pennsylvania, was 3914; Fred Folberth, Cleveland, Ohio, 3762; Dan Davis, Columbia, South Carolina, 3583; Billy Boak, Bordeau, Washington, 3167; Robert Nixon, Forest Grove, Oregon, 2953.

The women's team trophy went to the Elysian Archers of Los Angeles, who defeated the Portland Archery Club 380-2456 to 370-2176. The Elysian men's team also won with 382-2526, in competition with the Greenwood Archers of Berkeley, California, with 375-2299, and the Chicago Grant Park Archery Club with 366-2226.

Results of the flight shoot were as follows:

LADIES

Class 1—Bows up to 35 pounds:
1. Mrs. Bitzenberger, 303 yds. 10 in.
2. Glen Vinyard, 295 yds. 2 ft.
3. Mrs. M. B. Davis, 230 yds. 2 ft.

Class 2—Bows up to 50 pounds:
1. Mrs. Bitzenberger, 336 yds. 2 ft.
2. Glen Vinyard, 314 yds. 8 in.
3. Mrs. Clara Prouty, 287 yds. 2 ft.

Class 3—Bows all weights:
1. Glen Vinyard, 396 yds. 2 ft. 9 in.*
2. Mrs. Bitzenberger, 361 yds. 26 in.
*New record.

MEN

Class 1—Bows up to 50 pounds:
1. Homer Prouty, 385 yds. 2 ft. 10 in.
2. Herb Henderson, 382 yds. 2 ft. 3 in.
3. L. L. Daily, 361 yds. 1 ft.

Class 2—Bows up to 65 pounds:
1. Homer Prouty, 430 yds. 1 ft.
2. Morton Mendels, 417 yds. 2 ft. 8 in.
3. M. B. Davis, 391 yds. 2 ft. 2 in.

Class 3—Bows up to 80 pounds:
1. H. Henderson, 478 yds. 2 ft.
2. M. Mendels, 440 yds. 2 ft.
3. H. Prouty, 439 yds. 2 ft. 6 in.

Class 4—Bows all weights:
1. H. Henderson, 483 yds. 2 in.
2. M. Mendels, 460 yds. 1 ft. 10 in.
3. R. W. Denton, 453 yds. 11 in.

GIRLS

1. Betty McFarlane, 251 yds.
2. Muriel Reichart, 219 yds. 25 in.
3. Betty Greisel, 200 yds. 2 ft. 8 in.

BOYS

1. Billy West, 331 yds. 2 ft.
2. Billy Boak, 320 yds. 1 ft.
3. Dixon Rich, 268 yds. 2 ft. 1 in.

FREE STYLE

1. Glen Vinyard, 423 yds.
2. M. B. Davis, 403 yds. 2 ft.

The report of the field events will be found in "Blunts from the Old Stump."

Total attendance for the tournament was about one hundred and sixty, about twenty states being represented. Harold Titcomb of Farmington, Maine, came the greatest distance to participate.

The next National tournament will be held in Columbus, Ohio.

Mrs. Paul H. Gordon informs us that Mr. Gordon has been ill over a month and is still under the doctor's care, with orders to take things easy for awhile. Mr. Gordon's illness was the result of overwork in getting out some large orders for army camp archery equipment.

Willard Bacon (left), Larry Hughes (right), runner-up and champion. (Photo by Harry Walyn)

Blunts from the Old Stump

We are writing this in Seattle—after attending the NAA Tournament at Portland. Elsewhere you will find a detailed report of the tournament—of how many National archery records were broken. We were pleased to see Larry Hughes of Burbank, California, one of the foremost archers of all time, win the National Championship honors with his double York of 279-1637 and double American of 180-1464. Larry is a friendly, unassuming chap and will make a popular champ. Ree Dillinger of Summit, New Jersey, is the new women's champion with a score of 2098, nosing out Mildred Miller of Milwaukee, Wisconsin, by only one point. Ree came in from behind with a six golds on her last end to win the championship. We were naturally pulling for our homestate boy, Carl Strang, on the English York,—much more difficult than the American York. Carl won with a 135-839 (a new NAA record) to beat Larry Hughes' 141-827.

The NAA tournament was not the largest held, in numbers, but there were plenty of outstanding archers to make it one of the finest tournaments ever held.

There were probably more combination field and target archers than strictly target archers at the National. Some of the prominent field archers attending were: Wm. G. Williams of Portland, Oregon, President of the NAA; Dr. Geo. A. Cathey, Portland, field captain at the tournament; Wm. M. Folberth of Cleveland, and Kore T. Duryee of Seattle, of the Board of Governors of the NAA; Dr. H. H. Hewitt of Portland, and many others.

On Wednesday, August 6, the field archers had a get-together. A general discussion on field archery was held, and Kore Duryee showed some beautiful colored slides of his various bow hunting trips.

Kore T. Duryee was honored by being awarded the J. Maurice Thompson Medal of Honor. This medal is awarded annually to the person in the United States who has rendered the most outstanding service to archery. Kore for years has given unselfishly of his time and effort in teaching and promoting archery—both target and field. Kore, without question, has more friends than any other archer in the United States. It was an honor for us to meet and know him personally.

Dr. H. H. Hewitt of Portland, was in charge of the Field Events at the National. A 14-target NFAA field course was laid out on the Reed College campus. 28 targets were shot on Friday afternoon, August 8. The field event was won by Larry Hughes with a score of 72-308. The other top field scores were: Willard Bacon, Redondo Beach, California, 76-288; Wayne Thompson, Richmond, California, 67-277; Dr. Delmar Pletcher, Bakersfield, California, 72-276; Pat Chambers, Portland, Oregon, 64-250. Delmar used his hunting bow and roving arrows and did pretty well against target tackle. Pletcher, John Willard and several other field archers used their hunting tackle during the entire NAA tournament.

Babe Bitzenberger of Los Angeles, won the field round in the women's class with a score of 84-175. The others were Glen Vinyard, Canby, Oregon, 41-153; Gene Bacon, Redondo Beach, California, 39-149; Evelyne Pletcher, Bakersfield, California, 27-103; Edna Howatt, Yakima, Washington, 20-64.

The Oregon Pope-Young round, shot Saturday, August 9, with only one arrow at each of 36 targets, was won by Dr. Delmar Pletcher with 18 hits. This round is shot with broadheads, but *blunts* were used at the National. This is an interesting round and will be more fully described soon in Ye Sylvan Archer. This round will appeal to many field archers.

Sixty-eight archers—fifty-five men and thirteen women—shot the NFAA Field Round. This was a good turnout when you consider that the total NAA attendance was one hundred and sixty-three.

Mr. Williams, Dr. Cathey, Dr. Hewitt, Kore Duryee, Gene Warnick, and the various committees working with them are to be complimented on their splendid efforts in making the stay of the field archers most enjoyable. We wish to thank Henry Cummings and the Board of Governors of the

NAA for their thoughtfulness and consideration in providing field events at a National target tournament. There will be no better evidence of the good will of the NAA toward the NFAA than providing an opportunity for field archers all over the country to personally compete in field events until such time as the NFAA can provide its own National Field Tournament. Even dyed-in-the-wool field archers who never shoot target must recognize and acknowledge the splendid sportsmanship of target archers in giving us an opportunity to shoot our field round at their national target tournament. It is this mutual consideration of the other fellow's game that assures good will, respect and cooperation between target and field archers, and builds up the grand old sport of Archery.

It would have done your heart good to see even Dr. Elmer shoot the field round. This was the first time he had shot the official NFAA field round. If the Father of Modern Archery is interested enough to try the field round, the target archer who has never tried it may realize he is not getting over fifty per cent out of his archery hobby and recreation.

At the field archers' meeting at the NAA, the discussion developed on the necessity for more information to educate the public in the effectiveness and humaneness of the bow and arrow as a hunting weapon, particularly the need for securing the good will and cooperation of humane societies, who in the past have been so antagonistic in many states when archers have sought better hunting conditions and privileges. Field archers of Oregon strongly urge the elimination of the barbs on broadheads, on the ground that in minor wounds the head would have a better chance to work out without serious injury to the animal. This suggestion merits serious consideration and study. In Michigan, we have practically eliminated the use of the barbed arrow because the barbs are forever hooking on the brush. Our Michigan field archers all write their names and addresses on all hunting arrows. We voluntarily do this because we found that this, more than anything else, has gained us the respect and good will of the gun hunters. They know that any hunter who writes his name on his missile is not going to be a law violator, and is pretty careful what he shoots at.

Our trip through the West has been especially pleasant. Everywhere we found people most courteous and friendly. The Oregon people, especially, outdid themselves in making the stay of the archers most comfortable and enjoyable. We will cherish the memory of many happy hours spent in the West.

FIELD MEET AND DEER HUNT OF OREGON PYFA

Oregon field archers have a unique opportunity for a wonderful vacation from September 18 and beyond, when the sixth Pope-Young Field Archers state tournament will be held on the A-Bar-L Ranch in the Archery Reserve on the two days preceding the opening of the deer season.

Those who have never visited the Lee Williams A-Bar-L Ranch can not realize the beauty and grandeur of the site or the hospitality of the Williams family. Just try to imagine a valley of several hundred acres of irrigated meadow land surrounded by rugged pine-clad mountains. Just try to imagine the rambling ranch house with its big fireplace and other comforts. Just try to imagine a place where deer can be seen any day from the ranch house. But do not leave too much to the imagination. Come to Canyon Creek for the Pope-Young tournament and the deer hunt.

On the afternoon of the 18th, the NFAA round will be shot. Target arrows or blunts will be used for this event but broadheads will be used for all other events. On September 19 the events will be the battle clout at 180 yards, the wand shoot at 100 yards, and the Pope-Young round consisting of thirty-six arrows at thirty-six animal targets at unknown distances. These events will determine the championship. Arrows must weigh at least one ounce avoirdupois, with $7/8$ inch or wider steel blades. The same bow must be used in all events except in case of breakage. There are no weight requirements for women and juniors.

September 20 the deer season opens and there will be plenty of opportunity to kill a deer—if you can hit them.

(Continued on page 13)

NFAA Bulletin

OFFICERS

President—A. J. Michelson
610 F. P. Flint Bldg., Flint, Mich.

Vice-President—Paris B. Stockdale,
Geology Dept., OSU, Columbus, Ohio.

Secretary-Treasurer—John L. Yount,
Box 383, Redlands, California.

EXECUTIVE COMMITTEE

Western—H. C. MacQuarrie.
3400 Fruitvale Ave., Oakland, Calif.

Mid-Western—Fred Bear,
2611 W. Philadelphia, Detroit, Mich.

Eastern—T. C. Davidson,
53 Mountain Ave., Springfield, N. J.

By John L. Yount

PRELIMINARY REPORT - ART YOUNG AWARD COMMITTEE

Accompanying this report is a statement of principles and procedures together with an application form, the adoption of which by the NFAA is hereby recommended by this committee.

The committee further recommends that the Art Young big game pin be small and unobtrusive, so that it may be freely worn without being excessively conspicuous; and that each award include a felt or leather emblem of larger size which may be fastened to quiver, shooting jacket or tackle box.

It is further recommended that claims for awards be considered for big game secured after January 1, 1941, only. (This latter does not affect those already given).

Committee on Awards:
Erle Stanley Gardner
Forrest Nagler
Paul E. Klopsteg, Ch'm'n.

Art Young Big Game Pin

PURPOSE:
The purpose of the Art Young Big Game Pin is to promote interest in hunting with the bow and arrow, to encourage good sportsmanship, and to give recognition by the organized field archers to their members who obtain big game with the bow.

DEFINITION OF "BIG GAME:"
Any of the larger game animals difficult to shoot with bow and arrow, specifically: moose, elk, caribou, deer, antelope, goat, sheep, leopard, cougar, panther, lynx, wolf, coyote, wild hog, javelina, bear, but not including the young of these animals.

ELIGIBILITY:
Eligibility for the Art Young Award is limited to members of the NFAA at the time the award is claimed; but no claim will be entertained by the committe on awards unless it is made within three months of the hunt in which the game was secured. Any one person will be entitled to one award only, but there shall be no geographical restrictions either as to residence of the claimant or to location in which the game was secured.

CLAIM OF AWARD:
Any member of the NFAA claiming the Art Young Big Game Pin will apply to the secretary for an application blank, supply the information and evidence called for, and mail it to the secretary. The secretary will forward applications to the chairman of the committe on awards.

COMMITTEE REPORTS:
The committee shall report on its work at the end of each association year. In the report shall be included the names of those who have received the Art Young Award, and there may be included the names of hunters who though not qualifying for the
(Continued on page 8)

The Washington Archery Reserve

The Washington State Field Archers Association, I. M. Stamps, president, is again inviting out-of-state archers as well as Washington archers to hunt this fall in the Mad Lake Reserve. The reserve covers about thirty square miles, and is composed of little and big meadows with plenty of cover but little underbrush. The main valley is from 5000 to 6000 feet in elevation, with ridges on the east and west sides rising from 1000 to 1500 feet higher. There are three little lakes with good fishing. Mad River ranch is in the heart of the reserve, where horses are available for packing out deer.

How to Get There

In driving from Seattle, go over Stevens Pass to Coles Corner where you turn left for Lake Wenatchee. Just before you reach the lake turn right. After crossing the Wenatchee River turn left on the Chiwawa River road to Deep Creek, then right till you come to the top of the ridge. Here, where the road makes a sharp reverse curve, is Maverick Peak and the beginning of the Archers Hunting Reserve. This is an elevation of 4300 feet. You can start hunting from here going north. Less than a quarter of a mile from here on the Mad River trail there are good camp sites along the river. Six miles in over a beautiful trail up Mad River is Mad River Ranch, and on this six miles of trail you only climb 1200 feet. There are beautiful campsites all over the whole valley.

For those wishing to go up the Entiat River road there is a good forest camp near Three Creek, and there are two trails from there going up into the reserve. One trail goes to Klone Peak and the other is Three Creek trail, which is the north boundary of the reserve. They are steep.

If you come over Stevens Pass you can get information from Cole's Store and Service Station where you leave the highway for Lake Wenatchee. They also have cabins, food supplies, and serve meals.

Mad River Ranch Accommodations

If enough archers send in reservations, Al Constans will open up Mad River Ranch for the hunting season at the following rates:

Per week—including meals, bedding and bringing in your duffel, $25.00.

Per day—including meals and bedding, $4.00. This rate means that you can hunt in from the car, stay overnight, have three meals and bedding furnished you and hunt back to your car for only $4.00.

Packing Charges

Man and his horse is $5.00, and $1.50 for each additional horse per day. You can figure on each horse carrying 150 to 200 pounds, depending upon the bulk. It is well to have each box or roll weighed and marked thereon. Egg crates and similar divided boxes are fine for pack horses.

Make all reservations with deposits with: Al Constans, 1616 East Howell, Seattle, Washington, phone Ea 6061.. Mad River Ranch will only accommodate about fifteen people so get yours in by the 15th of September. After October 1, Al Constans' address will be Mad River Ranch, Leavenworth, Washington. You can phone Mad River Ranch through Stiliko Ranger Station by Entiat, Washington. Riding horses available for an additional charge of 51.50 per day.

Remember this is about 6000 feet elevation, so bring plenty of wool clothes. You may have a foot of snow and the temperature may go down to twenty degrees above at night. Hunting season is October 5 to 27, inclusive. Grouse is October 5 and 6 only. License for Washington citizen is $3.00 plus 50 cents for Big Game Seal — Out-of-state, $25.00.

Dr. Robert P. Elmer of Wayne, Pennsylvania, took his first trip west of St. Louis to attend the National at Portland. It was a real treat to the western archers to have the opportunity to meet the genial doctor who has done so much to promote Archery in the United States, especially by the publication of his authoritative book "Archery." Too few modern archers appreciate the debt we owe to those older archers who so long kept alive the spark that burst into flame a decade or so ago, fanned to a great degree by Dr. Elmer's book.

Letter Box

Archery Hunting Hints

Toronto, July 28, 1941.
Ye Sylvan Archer,
Gentlemen:

Apropos of the impending hunting season and particularly because it may serve as a reminder to our hunters that success in hunting depends more on perpetual alertness than anything else, I would suggest that you copy from Mr. Roy Case's letter, dated December 16, 1940, the bracketed portion, which reads as follows:

"Well, I got the shot at a big deer that I have been waiting for for 10 years—and was, of course, wholly unprepared and muffed it. I had been sitting on a runway all afternoon on the last day of the season. At 10 minutes of 4 I decided it was no use—might as well go home. Got up off my stump, laid my bow and arrow against a tree and leaning myself against the tree I was trying to locate some of the gang with my binoculars. Just then I heard a slight noise behind me (I had turned my back on the runway). Yes, there he was standing 15 yards away. I went for my bow—buck started, I whistled as I fumbled the arrow on the string, buck stops—but as I raise and draw he starts—fast. I lead (too much) and shoot and hear a sickening crack as the arrow strikes his skull. He runs away and I can see the arrow sticking out both sides of his head. I rounded up the gang and we looked for him, but it was soon dark and no luck. I stayed over and looked next morning, but it rained all night and was still raining, so gave it up after a couple of hours.

"Some 1170 archers got 5 bucks this year, one less than last year, when it was 600 plus and 6 bucks."

This is a particularly valuable reminder, since Mr. Case is probably as experienced at big game hunting as any of our archers and, as I have previously commented, is one of the best field shots I have ever seen in action.

It is a good thing to remind oneself that game is never found when and where a white man expects it. The Indian is far superior, in this respect, because for centuries his life has depended on that knowledge.

Yours very truly,
F. Nagler.

Vocabulary Suggestions

Dear Sir:

What the roving game really needs is a good five cent word bearing the same relationship to each target as "tee" does to each hole in golf; in other words, something easy meaning shooting position. Imagine anyone trying to write a play by play description of a Field Meet. Shooting position is a bit heavy for repeated use.

The writer brought this up when shooting at a Michigan Field Meet, and Fred Bear suggested that we find a word or make one. During the discussion, these offerings were made:

The Loose: a noun to signify the place where you loose.

The Stand: ditto where you stand.

X: x always marks the spot.

Spee: coined from the initials S.P.

We are wondering if anyone else has an idea on the subject. You might run a contest—each entrant to accompany his suggestion with a new NFAA member or reasonable facsimile. What do you think about it?

Sincerely yours,
Lulu Stalker.

J. E. Cooter, formerly of Salem, Oregon, now has charge of the Federal Reemployment Service for the eleven western states, with headquarters in San Francisco. Mr. Cooter has moved his family to San Mateo, California.

Bowstrings will twang at the Indian encampment on the Oregon coast in September as tribesmen from various parts of the state compete with the weapons of their ancestors.

The Wisconsin Archer, published quarterly by Clarence Rhubesky, Wauwatosa, Wisconsin, contains much interesting material for archers. It is the official publication of the Wisconsin Archery Association.

Editorial

It was with considerable trepidation that we attended our first National tournament. It is one thing to "bawl out" some husky archer at long distance through the columns of Ye Sylvan Archer and quite another matter to meet him face to face. And then there are those who have failed to get their magazines on time, those whose letters haven't been answered promptly, and those who have suffered from other misdemeanors for which the editor has on sundry occasions been indicted. But we find that archers are either forgetful or forgiving, and the time we found it possible to be on the shooting line or at the "commons" was pleasantly spent. It was a great pleasure to meet Dr. Elmer, but suspecting that the doctor was taking his archery rather seriously, we kept at a repectful distance while he was shooting. We didn't meet many of the archers on the number one target because it is just impossible to keep the editorial "bazoo" closed, and we do not have the Brommers indifference to being kicked off the field. It hardly seems possible that a woman could do it, but Mrs. Carl Strang hid behind a bench on the number one target for two hours without saying a word. She said it was worth it to watch the champions shoot. Women are doing a lot of things these days that we never expected of them. Who would have thought a woman could beat the men in free style flight? Well, Glen Vinyard did it.

One of the greatest treats of the week was meeting "Mike," the so-efficient president of NFAA. We thought we had something planned for Mike, but Michiganders, we believe, are a suspicious lot, and what chance has a mere editor trying to frame a lawyer! Just wait, Mike, we have a smart lawyer friend, and your time is coming.

We had more opportunity to visit with "Cash" Styles on account of the fact that he wasn't "among the first ten," as he usually is. Styles pulled one worthy of Literary Digest's "Picturesque Speech and Patter." He said his wife said of him that "he was just bursting with self-control."

We cannot take space to mention all the old and new friends we met, but down on the last target was a man we cannot pass up. Any winner of the "Elmer Wooden Spoon" is a celebrity. Any man who can shoot through the entire tournament, coming from over a thousand miles, and make the lowest complete score has qualities which make him worth knowing. Such a man is Dr. H. W. Smiley of Indio, California, and we shall never forget our visit with him on Saturday evening.

Just about the most worthwhile trophy of the tournament was the good sportsmanship trophy won by T. B. Brotherton, Los Angeles.

The Wisconsin archery hunters have secured the "buck or doe" concession from their game commission, that is, they can shoot at *all* game during their deer season. Archers can appreciate that this will not be a great drain on the deer population, but it is usually hard to make game commissioners see it that way.

NFAA BULLETIN

(Continued from page 5)
award, are thought worthy of honorable mention.

Mail Tournament Rules

We have had it brought to our attention that there is some question as to the necessity of turning in a certain score when that score is very poor and the archer is certain that he or she is capable of shooting a much more presentable one.

The answer is that this is tournament shooting and under the same rules that would apply were we shooting on the same course instead of by mail. Your chance for a better score comes next month.

Once you declare your intention of shooting your official round, the score must be turned in. Further, no score shall be considered as official unless before shooting the first target you have openly announced your intention of turning the score in as your official score for the month.

Sh! Don't Scare the Game

By Natalie Reichart

With a finger to his lips demanding quiet from the group following him, Kore stepped gingerly toward the small rise ahead. A fleeting smile of satisfaction and warning on his face, he dropped to one knee, and almost immediately came the twang of the bowstring, speeding his arrow toward the target dimly seen through the woods beyond us. A characteristic "c-r-k-k" sounded as the arrow found its mark. The sound mingled with the archer's shout of triumph and his companions' approval, as the leader of our party added another to the regular menagerie of animals which had this day felt the prick of his well-directed shaft. What a lucky day! So far there had been a rabbit, a hawk, a squirrel, an owl, a snake, an antelope and now a kangeroo! No one else had had such luck.

Half tripping through the underbrush in our haste to verify his hit, our small party rushed to the spot where the arrow had appeared to penetrate its mark.

"No hit," said Larry.

"How do you figure?" questioned Kore belligerently. "Why you can see where it went in right here. It went right on through and came out here along the ground. I killed him, I tell you, I want ten points!"

"Ten points, nothing......" from Larry. "You didn't touch him; went right under."

"Why I heard it hit—we all did," insisted Kore.

Then grudgingly from Larry: "Well—maybe you ticked the lower edge here—I'll allow five points. That mark on the body is an old hit . . . ."

Catch on? This was not really a group of doughty hunters of the hinterlands, but a group of Seattle archers trying out their skill in their own very special "game preserve" just outside of the city. Sponsored by the Seattle Archers, a local club, whose members of both sexes range from national figures in the field of archery to novices who are drawing their first bow, this unusual range has been established to give opportunity for the practice of hunting skills. The "animals" are "prowling" about in the State Park at 165th Street and 15th Avenue, northeast; and the trails open, now and then, on groups of Boy Scouts intent on their study of nature or woodsmanship, or perhaps groups of horsemen making their way over the riding trails which lead over hills and through the trees.

Thirty-eight animals, all different—count 'em—fierce or friendly, realistic and imaginary, are painted on corrugated cardboard targets and placed at points which test the skill of the unsuspecting archer. Here is a wild Indian runing out in the open about fifty yards away. Take accurate aim or, instead of a "dead" Indian you will be minus an arrow which has skittered under the deceptive underbrush round about. Over there is a picture which is a cross between a pelican and a stork, and it is so involved in the trees about thirty-five yards away that you are more apt to take the bark off of one of the saplings than to hit the "pelistork" in a vital spot.

After a short climb to the top of a hill, three targets may be seen about a hundred yards away on the opposite hill. The first is near the base of the slope, the second about half way up, the third near the top. Think of it as a hunting situation, with an animal first sighted at the base of the hill, running toward the top, giving you time for three shots at it. Out come the broadheads this time—and pray that we can find them if we don't hit the target. Up till now we have been taking two shots at each target with blunts, an arrow made like a hunting arrow but with a bullet jacket slipped on over the end to give it a strong blunt end. For each shot that actually touches the animal we score ten points; if we come close enough to hit the target but not the animal we are given five.

I soon learned that it was part of the game to have to persuade your fellow hunters that you really made a successful hit. Every point has to be fought for twice—once when the arrow is shot, and again when it is

(Continued on page 13)

Keasey at the Bat

By the Doghouse Editor

Once more I have seen two champions pitted against each other. The first time was six years ago in Los Angeles.

This time the contest wasn't quite so spirited. Gilman was too busy telling about the big ones that got away, and offering photographic evidence of the smaller ones that didn't. Also, turn about is fair play.

I reminded the principals of their first contest, and showed them some notes I had taken at that time. Both Gilman and Larry agreed that it was probably as truthful an account as any other I had written, which is high praise, indeed. Here it is:

"The row of the century is over. Battling Gilman, the Oregon Mastodon, met Kid Larry, the White Hope of Glendale, and the mighty Gil brought home the Hughes scalp to the tune of 56 points. Follows an account of the fracas by rounds:

"Round 1—Principals square off, Larry leading with a left for the Keasey smeller. Gil blocks, and aims a kick for the Hughes shins. The Oregonian heaves a loaded spittoon at our champion, and Larry counters with an aromatic dead cat. They clinch, Larry getting a well earned mouthful of Gil's left ear, as Gil plants a powerful knee in the Glendalian stomach. Referee Yount separates them with a fire hose. Larry's round.

"Round 2—Larry breaks a baseball bat over the Keasey conk. Gil misses a blunt at the Hughes kitchen. Larry gathers a handful of mane as the Oregon mauler butts him under the chin. Gil hits Larry with an arrow case. Larry jabs Gil in the stomach with a bow end. They clinch, and roll on the ground swapping lies, paying no attention to the gong. Referee throws a tear gas bomb, being unable to decide which is the bigger prevaricator. Gil's round.

"Round 3—Keasey feints with a broad axe and scores with a punch to the snout. Larry jabs with a ground quiver, follows it up with a pail of lye. Gil springs one of Cosner's cartoons on Larry. Larry faints for a count of three. He gets up with a glassy stare, claiming a foul. Referee rules Joe is an Act of God, and to go on fighting. At the sound of the bell the referee calls a cop to sit on the pair. Keasey's round.

"Round 4—The Glendale Terror claims the bout on a technical knockout when Gil stoops to pick up a whiskey bottle Larry has thrown at him. Referee rules for Keasey, as the bottle is empty. Larry blames the Four Horsemen for its being empty, and he is probably right. Not that it does him any good. Larry is weakening fast and is down for a count of eight when Gil crowns him with a park bench. Both parties have previously been searched for concealed broadheads. At the gong neither contestant has the strength to get up. Referee raises Gil's left foot in token of victory, but all he gets is a kick in the slats. Referee Yount resigns right there."

This is the end of my notes. If any slight inaccuracies have crept in it could be due to the fact that I had previously been kicked off the field for coaching the ladies, and therefore had to watch the bout some distance away.

Arrow Tip Poison

The secret of the deadly poison used by the South American Indians of the Amazon on their arrow tips—a touch of which means instant death—has been discovered, it is claimed, by a Brazilian chemist, Dr. P. E. B. Carneiro.

He has been awarded a prize of £200 in recognition of his achievement, says a Reuter Rio de Janeiro message.

Although the poison has been known to civilisation for hundreds of years, this is said to be the first time that the actual composition has been definitely ascertained.

Curare, or curara, is produced from Strychnos and other plants. It is made by the South American Indians by boiling various barks and leaves and straining and evaporating the liquid until it forms a thick solid paste suitable for smearing on their arrow tips.—Archery News, England.

August, 1941   YE SYLVAN ARCHER   11

July NFAA Tournament Report

By Karl E. Palmatier

	Actual 28 Target Score	Actual 28 Target Score	Actual 56 Target Score	Handicap Score
CLASS "A"—MEN				
Alfonso Gonzales, Bakersfield, Calif.	69-287	69-277	138-564	674
Fred Gadberry, Bakersfield, Calif.	76-308	72-267	148-575	655
Roy Hoff, Los Angeles, Calif.	57-219	65-243	122-402	622
Earl Grubbs, Los Angeles, Calif.	58-196	52-194	110-390	600
Leo Hoffmeyer, Flint, Mich.	54-210	48-180	102-390	600
Delmer Pletcher, Bakersfield, Calif.	77-307	84-330	161-637	597
K. L. Jones, Bakersfield, Calif.	67-267	66-274	133-541	581
Leo Cornell, Oakland, Calif.	59-245	61-239	120-484	564
Jim Murphy, Bakersfield, Calif.	56-224	50-188	106-412	562
Irving Davis, Bryn Mawr, Calif.	54-208	56-202	110-410	560
Jack Peters, Oakland, Calif.	59-210	60-239	119-449	559
Elmer Bedwell, San Bernardino, Cal.	43-161	54-196	97-357	557
C. W. Seastrom, West Hollywood, Cal.	45-161	53-193	98-354	544
Merle Hathaway, Los Angeles, Calif.	72-270	73-279	145-549	539
John Yount, Redlands, Calif.	50-194	51-187	101-381	531
E. Hill Turnock, Wilkinsburg, Pa.	87-343	81-327	168-670	530
Jack Young, Oakland, Calif.	58-227	56-216	114-443	523
Don Lumley, San Diego, Calif.	51-187	55-215	106-402	522
William Horr, San Diego, Calif.	35-131	46-174	81-305	495
George Calvert, Flint, Mich.	41-149	40-160	81-309	449
Phil Conrad, Long Beach, Calif.	83-341	86-338	169-679	
Trueman Farnsworth, Albany, Calif.	77-289	70-316	147-605	
William Oho, , Calif.	58-220	53-197	111-417	
M. E. Spansel, Berkeley, Calif.	52-201	54-197	106-398	
Joe Brooks, San Leandro, Calif.	61-214	42-150	103-564	
Al Eggers, Ingraham, Pa.	48-191	43-153	91-344	
Alex Gilliland, Bellevue, Pa.	50-172	46-164	96-336	
CLASS "A"—LADIES				
Mrs. C. J. Code, Crafton, Pa.	55-197	61-233	116-430	470
Ruth Hathaway, Los Angeles, Calif.	45-175	48-174	93-349	449
Lulu Stalker, Flint, Mich.	41-155	46-166	87-321	411
Bessie M. Stephenson, Flint, Mich.	47-169	48-174	95-343	393
Kay Ratcliff, Highland Park, Mich.	37-139	31-107	68-246	386
Daisey Olsen, Royal Oak, Mich.	45-169	55-199	82-304	359
June Franklin, San Bernardino, Cal.	34-122	41-157	75-279	359
Ruth Davis, Bryn Mawr, Calif.	37-131	48-160	85-291	341
Eva Bedwell, San Bernardino, Cal.	56-222	53-197	109-319	299
Mary Calvert, Flint, Mich.	36-134	34-130	70-264	294
Minerva Gandy, Los Angeles, Calif.	22-78	25-91	47-169	

	28 Target Score	28 Target Score	Total
CLASS "B"—MEN			
Russell Berry, San Diego, Calif.	47-173	52-196	99-369
Harvey Franklin, San Ber'd'o, Cal.	44-160	56-200	100-360
S. Leo Sipe, Los Angeles, Calif.	38-146	49-177	87-323
W. M. Scheffler, Pittsburg, Pa.	42-158	41-153	83-311
Gene Holston, San Diego, Calif.	39-153	41-157	80-310
Bennett Gandy, Los Angeles, Calif.	39-145	45-159	84-304
Carl Seastrom, West Hollywood, Cal.	45-154	41-147	86-301
Bennie Sells, , Calif.	45-165	34-128	79-293
Tracy Stalker, Flint, Mich.	38-138	41-155	79-293

12   YE SYLVAN ARCHER   August, 1941

	28 Target Score	28 Target Score	Total
Harry Eckels, , Calif.	40-156	32-126	72-282
William Smith, Flint, Mich.	39-147	37-135	76-282
LeRoy Stephenson, Flint, Mich.	37-137	33-124	70-261
Charles Frieburg, Etna, Pa.	33-123	35-130	68-253
Ralph Edwards, , Calif.	42-146	23-87	65-233
J. B. Loop, Bellevue, Pa.	25-89	37-139	62-228
Paul Ludwig, Los Angeles, Calif.	31-111	33-117	64-228
Karl Palmatier, Kalamazoo, Mich.	28-96	27-103	55-199
L. J. Markham, Durand, Mich.	26-84	29-99	55-183

CLASS "C"—MEN

W. C. Woolnough, Trenton, Mich.	42-164	39-139	81-301
Jimmy Ratcliff, Detroit, Mich.	34-118	30-106	64-224
Ralph O'Roark, Pittsburg, Pa.	18-64	27-93	45-157

CLASS "B"—LADIES

Ina Woolnough, Trenton, Mich.	24-94	36-138	60-232
Frieda Hoff, Los Angeles, Calif.	25-99	34-126	59-225
Mercella Kuntz, Etna, Pa.	24-88	35-119	59-207
Phyllis Diehl, Flint, Mich.	25-97	27-93	52-190
Irene Wierzbicki, Flint, Mich.	18-64	23-87	41-151
Mrs. A. Eggers, Ingraham, Pa.	12-42	22-82	34-124

CLASS "C" LADIES

Betty Richardson, Flint, Mich.	12-44	8-29	20-73
Mrs. Ralph O'Roark, Pittsburgh, Pa.	10-38	7-27	17-65

HANDICAPS FOR NEXT TOURNAMENT (MEN)

E. Turnock	-130	R. King	160	F. Gadberry	30
D. Pletcher	-50	B. Ahman	150	P. Chambers	20
R. Quayle	-40	J. Yount	150	A. Gilliland	
K. Jones	-30	J. Murphy	140	A. Eggers	
P. Conrad	-30	K. Duryee	140	J. Brooks	
M. Hathaway	-10	M. Spansel	130	W. Oho	
S. Sipe	230	I. Davis	130	T. Farnsworth	
E. Flesher	200	R. Hoff	120	H. Ussack	
W. Horr	190	D. Lumley	120	J. Scott	
E. Bedwell	190	J. Peters	100	C. Ratcliff	
F. Jones	190	E. Watts	100	J. Willard	
H. Franklin	190	P. High	90	W. Bacon	
L. Hoffmeyer	180	E. Woodward	90	V. Jones	
W. Seastrom	180	R. Hoover	90	P. Cozad	
G. Calvert	170	J. Young	90	P. Stockdale	
E. Grubbs	170	L. Cornell	70	L. Carter	
R. Berry	170	A. Gonzales	50		
K. Moore	170	I. Stamps	40		

HANDICAPS FOR NEXT TOURNAMENT (LADIES)

Gene Bacon	-90	June Franklin	70	Daisey Olsen	50
Eva Bedwell	-20	Margaret Quayle	60	Babe Bitzenberger	50
Minerva Gandy	130	Bertha Hoffmeyer	60	Bessie Stephenson	30
Kay Ratcliff	110	Lulu Stalker	60	Mrs. Curtis	
Margaret King	90	Mary Calvert	50		
Ruth Hathaway	70	Ruth Davis	50		

Only those scores actually shot with other archers in competition for a mail tournament should be reported. Secretaries are to check this point carefully. Any regular tournament score is all right.

Those names without a handicap have not sent in four twenty-target scores so that a handicap could be figured.

Sixty-seven archers shot in this tournament. This should be the poorest one, because of the time of year.

Fall—the season for field archery—will start next month. Everybody get set for a record meet.

REPORT OF THE FIELD TOURNAMENT AT THE MID-WESTERN
Cincinnati, Ohio

MEN:
Craig Clarke, Angela, Ind.—129-495
Hal Burris, Detroit, Mich.— 108-416
Ben Johnson, St. Louis, Mo.— 97-397
Bob Rothfuss, Bellevue, Ky.—101-375

LADIES:
Elsie Johnson,, St. Louis, Mo.—83-299
Ruth Thorwarth, Bellevue, Ky.-67-259
Alta Benedict, Newport, Ky.—58-204

SH! DON'T SCARE GAME
(Continued from page 9)

retrieved, for many times it went completely through leaving a mark often difficult to distinguish from old wounds. Many times it depends on whether you can talk faster or louder than your companions to make your demands for your score stick.

And it wasn't always the men who were carrying off the scoring honors. Jane was in fine form and part of the time it was nip and tuck between Jane and Kore, with first one and then the other ahead. Here was a "stump" shot—a seat-high stump to sit on comfortably while making a difficult shot through the trees, and Jane finds herself in scoring lead; a kneeling shot follows and two well directed hits shift the lead to Kore; and so it goes through the day.

An hour and a half or more are consumed in going around the course, the longer limit not specified since the arrows sometimes are as elusive as the well known golf ball. Rain and coldish weather are no barrier to the enjoyment of this sport which does not require the fine concentration and steady aim of the brand of archery which is practiced at Seattle's other important outdoor archery playfield, the target range at Montlake Park.

PYFA MEET AND HUNT
(Continued from page 4)

Out-of-state archers are cordially invited to attend the tournament and hunt with the Oregon archers. Out-of-state archers are not eligible for championship awards, but special prizes are being provided for them, a beautiful plaque on a yewwood base having been donated for first place. Out-of-state hunting license fee is $15.00.

The Oregon reserve contains many square miles, extending back into the high elevations of the Strawberry Mountains, where the big bucks hold sway. The A-Bar-L Ranch is a "dude ranch" and pack and riding horses are available. The reserve is well traversed with trails and is well watered by clear mountain streams. The East Fork and Canyon Creek offer opportunities for archers who enjoy fishing.

There will be a convenient camp ground with plenty of pure water. Cabins are available just off the reserve.

The reserve can be reached from the John Day-Burns highway—from Burns on the south and John Day on the north.

For further particulars write
    J. E. Davis, Sec'y. PYFA,
    505 N. 11th Street,
    Corvallis, Oregon.

Archery IN Ancient Battle

The battle of Hastings was the decisive victory of heavy cavalry over infantry, and this overwhelming predominance of the cavalry arm lasted until the coming of the long bow tipped the scale again in favour of the infantryman. Both sides used archers at Hastings, but they were armed with the old short bow, of high trajectory and low power, the arrows from which were incapable of penetrating the armour of a mounted knight. The short bow was never considered a weapon of great value and is unmentioned in the Assize of Arms of Henry II in 1181. In that century the crossbow, of great stopping power, but clumsy and slow in use, was the favoured weapon.

The first hint we get of the rise of the long bow is from Geraldus Cambrensis, an ecclesiastic and historian writing at the close of the twelfth century, who praises the "stiff, large and strong bows of the men of Gwent" and tells us that the Normans would never have conquered Ireland without their Welsh archers. So the famed English long bow was really a Welsh weapon. The bow had come sufficiently into favour in England to be mentioned in the Assize of Arms in 1252 and Edward I, in his Welsh and Scotch wars, perceived the tactical possibilities of the new weapon in breaking up the charges of heavy cavalry and the solid bodies of pipemen which had for long been the principal features of the field of battle. In the next century the long bow, with its amazing accuracy, low trajectory, long range, rapidity of fire and great power of penetration, gave the English infantry a superiority over all other arms which lasted a full hundred years.

Crecy, Poictiers and Agincourt were the triumphs of the English bowmen. In fortification, the use of loopholes for the discharge of missiles did not become at all general until the early thirteenth century and neither the short bow with its high trajectory nor the clumsy, slow-firing crossbow, were very suitable for use from high battlements. When such loopholes first appear they were obviously designed for the crossbow; there is an excellent example in Hilton Castle, and it was not until after the introduction of the long bow, an admirable weapon for the defence, that we find any great importance being attached to the volume of small-arm fire from the fortifications. In the Edwardian castle the long bow came fully into its own: Carnarvon, with its wall galleries, its loops designed for simultaneous use by three archers, and its elaborated battlements, shows to perfection the influence of the new weapon in the art of fortification.

Note—The length of the long bow was usually equal to the height of the Archer: it was drawn back to the shoulder and discharged an arrow a cloth-yard in length. The "self-bow" (*i.e.* one made from one piece of wood as distinct from "backed" when it is made of two or more strips glued together) was almost always fashioned from yew. The effective range was fully 250 yards.

The slits seen in eleventh and twelfth century keeps and towers were usually only for the admittance of light and air.

Jazerine (Jesseraunt)—Small plates of steel attached to some strong flexible material, worn as light armour by archers. Brigandine was used for a similar purpose but the metal plates were worn inside the material; sometimes known as "mascled armour," the best historical example is depicted in the Bayeux Tapestry.

—J. L. Illingworth in Archery News, England.

New Michigan Club
By James M. Redfield

A group of archery enthusiasts met August 14, at the home of Mr. and Mrs. William Trupiano, West Mansion Street, Marshall, Michigan, and organized the Marshall Archery Club.

Officers were chosen as follows: President, Mrs. William Trupiano; Vice-President, Willis Acevedo; Secretary-Treasurer, Patricia Waite; Councellors, James M. Redfield, Lyle Hulbert, and Junior Hazel, student instructor in archery at University of Mississippi.

Charter members are Mr. and Mrs. Trupiano, Mr. and Mrs. Redfield, Mr. and Mrs. Hulbert, Miss Bessie Kiefer, Willis A. Acevedo, Miss Patricia Waite, and Miss Emily Ann Trupiano.

Necessary equipment has been ordered and will arrive the latter part of August, after which target practice will start immediately.

A letter was read from the vice-chairman of the Athletic Field Board of Control granting the club permission to use the Municipal Athletic Field for target practice, providing the equipment is removed after each session. It was suggested by the board that the football field be used in the evening when the baseball and softball games are in progress on other parts of the field.

While Marshall has had individual archery enthusiasts in the past, this is the first organized effort to promote the sport in this vicinity.

J. C. Burke reports the organization of a new archery club at Lewiston, Idaho.

Paul H. Gordon
Author of "The New Archery"
Producing
Tackle — Materials
Latest and Finest for Field or Range
Write for Free Catalog
Beacon Hill Craftsmen
Beacon, N. Y.

**BACK NUMBERS
YE SYLVAN ARCHER**
Volumes I to V Inclusive
$1.00 Per Volume
B. G. THOMPSON
R. F. D. 1, Corvallis, Oregon

E. BUD PIERSON
Bowyer — Fletcher
Tournament Tackle, Sinew, Glue, Raw Materials.
Custom Made Tackle
3109 Burnet Ave. — Cincinnati, Ohio

SUBSCRIBERS PLEASE NOTICE

A cross appearing in this space means that your subscription has expired and we would appreciate your prompt renewal so that your name may be kept on our mailing list.

CLASSIFIED ADVERTISING

RATES for Classified Advertising 5 cents per word per issue. Count initials and numbers as words. Minimum charge is 50 cents.

RELICS AND CURIOS

INDIAN RELICS, Beadwork, Coins, Curios, Books, Minerals, Weapons. Old West Photos. Catalog, 5c. Genuine African Bow, $3.75. Ancient flint arrowheads, perfect, 6c each—Indian Museum, Osborne, Kansas.

BOOKS AND MAGAZINES

"ARCHERY TACKLE, HOW TO MAKE AND HOW TO USE IT." by Adolph Shane. Bound in cloth and illustrated with more than fifty drawings and photographs. Information for making archery tackle and instructions for shooting. Price is $1.75. Send orders to Ye Sylvan Archer, 505 North 11th street, Corvallis, Oregon.

VIKING ARCHERY

1874 Market Street

San Francisco, Calif.

BROADHEAD ARROWS

Meeting the requirements for the Pope-Young Field Tournament. Chandler Universal Blades and Fiber Inset Nocks. *State weight of bow.*

Set of 8, for Men—
28 inch $3.75

For Women—26 inch $3.50

V. D. McCauley
505 N. 11th   Corvallis, Ore.

The AMERICAN ARCHER, a national quarterly, $1.00 per year, 521 Fifth Ave., New York City.

—FINE ARCHERY EQUIPMENT—

Archery Raw Materials

WM. A. JOY

9708 So. Hoover Street
LOS ANGELES, CALIF.

ARCHERY SUPPLIES
at prices everyone can afford to pay.
YEW WOOD STAVES
at .... $2.00 and $3.00
P. O. CEDAR DOWELS
per 100 .... $2.75
FINE YEW WOOD BOWS
any weight and length
to 6 feet .... $6.50 to $12.50
Send money with order.
Monte Vista Archery Co.
Rt. 1, Box 149, Tacoma, Wash.

AIR SEASONED QUALITY YEW WOOD and PORT ORFORD CEDAR

Yew wood when green is stored in a dark ventilated shed the 1st year. 2nd year it is moved to this open shed. Next step is working it into billet form, and placing it in racks from 2 to 3 years to finish seasoning.

W. A. COCHRAN
Rt. 2, Eugene, Oregon

HANDBOOK—How to Make and Use Bows and Arrows—90 Pages well illustrated (with catalog) 35c.

CATALOG—100 pictures—color spread—Instruction Folder. 10c.

CATALOG alone 5c. Stamps or Coin.

L·E·STEMMLER· QUEENS VILLAGE· N·Y·

The Flat Bow—70 pages of Archery information for 50 cents, well illustrated. *Ye Sylvan Archer*, 505 N. 11th St., Corvallis, Oregon.

HI THERE, FIELD ARCHERS—TAKE A LOOK AT THIS!
Write for full information

A special introductory offer. Complete set of 14 official "Arro-Mat" field targets and faces for only $29.75.

BEN PEARSON
INCORPORATED
Bows and Arrows of Excellence
PINE BLUFF, ARK.

This offer limited to full sets only. Your club can now enjoy the field round on official targets at a new low cost.

CHANDLER
Universal Broadheads

The Broadhead that costs less than a big rifle bullet, from 5c to 8-1/3c each. The inexpensive Broadhead for hunting.
Also Universal Broadhead Kits, with complete material for making one doz. good Broadhead Arrows.
Also Hunting, Fishing and roving Points.
FREE CATALOGUE
T. B. CHANDLER
11819 4th Ave., Compton, Calif.

FISH HEAD

B-80   B-1

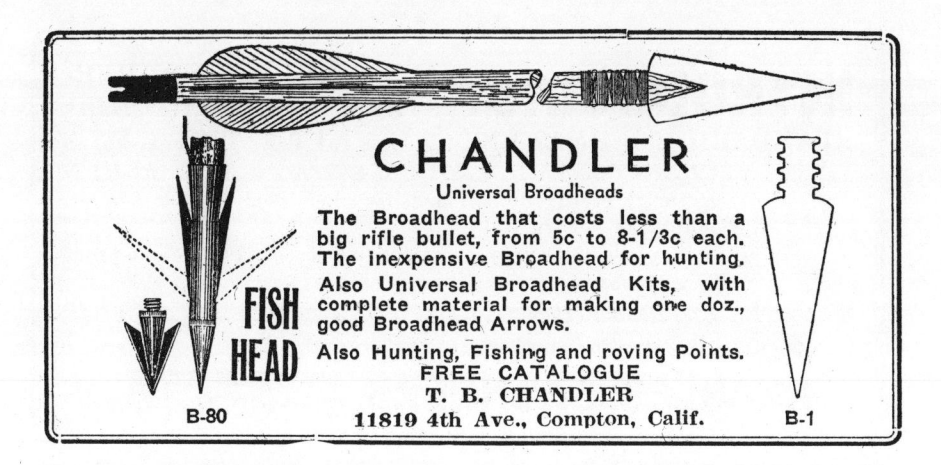

APPROVED NFAA FIELD TARGET FACES

Printed in black and white on heavy, double thickness corrugated board. In sets containing sizes necessary for a 14-target course and including extras of the smaller sizes that shoot out fastest.

$2.25 per set, f.o.b. Detroit — Order two sets for a 28-target course

BEAR ARCHERY CO.
2611 W. Philadelphia Ave., Detroit, Michigan

G
"THE MARK OF DISTINCTION IN ARCHERY TACKLE"
Fine Yew Target and Hunting Bows, Plain or Backed with Rawhide. Lemonwood Bows with Rawhide Backs.
College and School Equipment
Target, Hunting and Roving Arrows
Price List on Request
Wholesale — Retail
EARL GRUBBS
5518 W. Adams
Los Angeles,   :   California

Arcadian Life Magazine
Stories of the Ozarks

Pioneer History - Folklore
Pastoral Living

$1.00 a Year; 25c a Copy

Display Adv. $1.50 per inch
Classified, 3c a word. Three insertions for the price of two.

O. E. RAYBURN, Editor
Dept. 15

616 S. Benton St
Cape Girardeau, Mo.
P. O. Box 200
Caddo Gap, Arkansas

Please mention Ye Sylvan Archer when writing advertisers.

Ye Sylvan Archer—$1.00 per year

INTRODUCING: MACHINE - WOUND, RYE-STRAW, HAND-STITCHED, STANDARD TOURNAMENT QUALITY TARGETS

MACHINE CONTROL PRODUCES STRONGER TARGETS:
With accurately graduated density which compensates for additional wear toward Gold.
With compact midsections; somewhat looser, bounce-out-proof striking surfaces.

GREATER SATISFACTION OVER A LONGER PERIOD OF TIME
Write for further description and prices

CHARLES SAUNDERS 3030 POLK STREET CHICAGO, ILLINOIS

"SWITCH" TO KING-MOORE HUNTING AND ROVING EQUIPMENT

KM-77—MEN'S LARGE SIZE HUNTING AND ROVING QUIVER
Made of genuine water-Leather, with large outside zipper pocket ideal for extra equipment. Ample room for 2 dozen broadheads. An outstanding value at **$4.95**

NEW SHOOTING GLOVE FOR ROVING AND HUNTING, WITH "TURKEY QUILL"
KM-25 — A professional type glove to be used only with bows pulling over 40 pounds. "Turkey quill" insert prevents deep string indentations which assures a perfect release. Genuine Cordovan Leather **$2.50**

When ordering be sure to send outline of hand or glove size.

KM-77

Patronize your dealer — if he cannot supply you send check or money order to

KING ★ MOORE
7011 NORTH FIGUEROA STREET
LOS ANGELES — CALIFORNIA

Cassius Hayward Styles

BOWYER AND FLETCHER

—Tackle that has stood the test—

28 Vicente Place

BERKELEY, CALIFORNIA

PORT ORFORD CEDAR ARROW SHAFTS
(Cypressa Lawsonia)

Specials. P.O. Cedar Shafts, 1/4 to 11/32":
Parallel, per 100 .... $4.00
Tapered or barreled, 100 .. $4.50
Extra Select. Units segregated, per 100 .... $5.00
Douglas Fir, 100 .... $3.00, $3.50
Douglas Fir, Extra Select, per 100 .... $4.00

Full line finished tackle.
Raw Materials.
Write for price lists. Special rates to dealers and clubs.

PORT ORFORD ARCHERY SUPPLY CO.
C. F. Douglas, Mgr.
Box 137   Port Orford, Oregon

Ye Sylvan Archer

September, 1941

Vol. 13, No. 5

Ye Sylvan Archer

Official Publication of the National Field Archery Association

Vol. 13   September, 1941   No. 5

Published the fifteenth of each month
for archers by archers
505 North 11th Street, Corvallis, Oregon

J. E. DAVIS .... Editor

Subscription Price .... $1.00 Per Year
Foreign Subscription $1.25
Single Copies .... 10 Cents
Advertising Rates on Application

TABLE OF CONTENTS

	Page
QUIET DAY AT TEMECULA By Ben Hibbs	1
BLUNTS FROM THE OLD STUMP	3
NFAA BULLETIN	5
EDITORIAL	6
LETTER BOX	7
FIELD ARCHERS OF SOUTHERN CALIFORNIA By Roy Hoff	7
THE WOES OF THE HEAD COACH By the Doghouse Editor	8
THE FLINT BOWMEN	8
CALIFORNIA STATE TOURNAMENT	11

Quiet Day at Temecula

By Ben Hibbs, Editor of Country Gentleman

(Reprinted by special permission from the Country Gentleman, copyright 1941, by The Curtis Publishing Company.)

"Now," said Erle Gardner, "you need a good rest." It was evening, and I had just arrived at his ranch in the lonely, mysterious desert country some sixty miles south of San Bernardino, California. He elaborated the diagnosis: "You've had a tough trip, what with traveling all over the map and interviewing mobs of people. There's no doggoned sense in a man pushing himself so hard. Editors don't know how to live anyway. Tomorrow we'll just loaf around the ranch and take it easy."

So the next morning at 5:30 o'clock there was a vigorous knocking at the door of the guest cottage. "It's such a swell day," Erle explained, "that I thought you might like to climb a mountain before breakfast." So we scaled the ridge which rises precipitously behind the ranchhouse, following an ancient Indian trail, and were back down by the time coffee and eggs were on the table. The shank of the morning we devoted to archery, Erle's favorite sport, and that afternoon we took a four-mile hike around the ranch. Returning, we came upon a great live oak with low-spreading branches, which Erle felt we should climb just to see if our muscles were still youthful. So we climbed the tree. This left just time enough before the evening meal to work up an appetite by flinging a hundred or so arrows at a target.

Supper over, we sat on the front steps watching the jagged desert mountains turn from lavender to purple in the twilight, and Erle discoursed eloquently on the virtues of the quiet life. People these days, he said, are just plain silly—never satisfied unless they are doing something or going somewhere.

So as soon as it was dark we went over to a near-by hill where Gardner has an excellent little telescope, worked for a half hour getting it adjusted and studied the stars until midnight. Then we adjourned to his study to look at the amazing collection of curios which he has brought home from the far corners of the earth. At 1 A.M.—because I had had a hard trip—Erle solicitously sent me to bed. He would take a turn around the ranch buildings to get a breath of air and then work an hour or so on the revision of a story before hitting the hay. After a loafing day, he explained, he needed a bit of activity to get him in the mood for sleep.

Erle Stanley Gardner was born in Massachusetts fifty-two years ago, but didn't stay there long. His father was a mining engineer, and Erle spent his early years moving from one

Erle Stanley Gardner, whose favorite sport is archery

mining camp to another through the West and Alaska. At seventeen he went to work in a law office and was admitted to the bar when he was twenty-one. Eventually he became one of the ablest trial lawyers on the Pacific Coast. He handled chiefly criminal cases. "I liked courtroom work," says this devotee of the quiet life, "because there was always an opportunity for a battle."

As an attorney he acquired so much fascinating material about crime that it seemed a shame not to put it down on paper. He began writing thrillers and mysteries and achieved such success that presently he turned his practice over to his law partners and devoted all his time to writing. He has produced millions of words of fiction for the magazines and is a favorite of mystery fans everywhere. A round two dozen of his books have been published by William Morrow & Company. Several of his stories are in the White House library.

Gardner is perhaps best known as

the author of the Perry Mason mysteries, but his newer "D. A." series—with Douglas Selby, the district attorney of Madison City, as the central character—is rapidly acquiring an equally loyal following. Gardner created Doug Selby for Country Gentleman several years ago, in answer to our earnest plea for a murder mystery that was different. We were frankly tired of mystery stories in which the characters were mere pieces of a puzzle, and in which the action usually took place in a swank apartment, a country estate or on board a yacht. We wanted a story in a small-town setting such as we all know, and with ordinary but vividly portrayed people as the characters. So well did Gardner fill the order that our new Selby story, The D. A. Cooks a Goose, beginning in this issue (September, 1941), is our fourth in this series. The D. A. mysteries have never appeared anywhere but in Country Gentleman and in books.

Erle Gardner travels widely, and many of his stories have been written on shipboard, in China, in auto trailers—wherever his love of the quiet life takes him. A few years ago he bought the ranch where he now lives, near the tiny village of Temecula. The chief crop is fiction, but for fun he has a couple of tractors, some burros, and an indefinite number of dogs. (One of the dogs nipped me enthusiastically on the ankle while I was at the ranch, but Gardner explained this lapse of conduct by saying the dear little fellow apparently had overheard and taken too seriously some of his remarks about editors.)

Once he starts a story, Gardner can't rest until the first draft is down on paper. He pours the story into dictaphones so rapidly that it takes two secretaries to transcribe it. While thus involved he eats one meal a day, sleeps maybe four or five hours out of the twenty-four and works the rest of the time. The rough draft having been completed, he takes three deep breaths, spreads the copy out on a desk approximately the size of a haymow floor and carefully revises. With the story on its way to market, he knocks off in earnest and proceeds to enjoy the quiet life by going to Mexico, where he hunts crocodiles, wild boars and other mild little creatures, with bow and arrow. Or perhaps he takes a packtrain trip into the desert, or drives over to New Orleans or Florida for a day or so.

Now and then he comes East to see editors and his publisher, but he always cuts his stay short because he has just thought up a new story that needs writing. The quiet, pastoral life of the rancho and those uneventful eighteen-hour days call him home.

FIELD ARCHERS OF SOUTHERN CALIFORNIA
By Roy Hoff

The regularly scheduled shoot of Field Archers of Southern California was held August 24 on the range of the Malibu Mountain Archery Club. The attendance was somewhat under par with only about fifty members in attendance. The opening of deer season and many members on vacation probably affected the attendance.

By lunch time it was evident that unless there were some unexpected form reversals the Malibu members were going to walk away with the lion's share of the prizes. Merle Hathaway in the championship division was in with a card well over 300, as was Phil Conrad in the general division.

The ladies were doing quite all right themselves. By evening a good many red faces were noted among the he-men shooters, especially certain husbands.

The now famous feud of Grubbs vs. Yount reached a climax on the short four-position eleventh. Up to this point, on the last 14, Yount was coasting along with 14 points to the good—then the fireworks started. Score on target 11: Grubbs, 18; Yount, 0. Here's the payoff—to assuage the pang of defeat, Yount accused his worthy opponent of deliberately, and with malice aforthought, buying him one too many bottles of beer at lunch time to get him dizzy; then to employ professional hecklers, just to ruin his score.

Mr. and Mrs. Ben Pearson, of Pinebluff, Arkansas, were guests of the club for the day. Both enjoyed themselves and were highly complimentary of the sportsmen of Southern California and the fine course at Malibu.

At the Board of Governors meeting it was decided to hold the next shoot

(Continued on page 7)

Blunts from the Old Stump

In most states the target seasons are now over and archers all over the country are turning their thoughts to field shooting and hunting. If you are one of those archers who has not shot the field round, or participated in the NFAA mail matches, it is not too late to shoot in these monthly mail matches. These tournaments continue throughout September, October, November and December. Awards are made every month. There is nothing better to sharpen your eye and coordinate your muscles for your fall and winter hunting than practice on the NFAA field course. If your club has no course, why not build one? If you have a field course, why not participate in the mail tournaments—just for fun? You can find genuine pleasure in shooting in the mail tournaments, even if you don't expect to win top awards. Pick out some archers in other states shooting around your own scores and then go out and beat them. You will get a lot of personal satisfaction from your own improvement and achievement.

Archery is indebted to the showmanship of archers like Howard Hill, Walt and Ken Wilhelm, Russ Hoogerhyde, and others, who present spectacular and daring bow and arrow acts to the public. They have aroused much public curiosity and some genuine interest in archery. But that kind of publicity is not enough, for it has a tendency to create the impression that archery is for the super-man, and not the ordinary, average person, who is looking for a hobby or recreation. Archery needs the kind of publicity which every person who shots a bow and arrow can pass on to his interested friends—that the pleasures of the bow are within the physical capacities of every man and woman, and that they can learn to shoot and enjoy the bow without any special difficulty.

The Southern California field archers are publicizing field archery in its proper light as a gentleman's and gentlewoman's sport. Roy Hoff, President of the Southern California Field Archers, has arranged for the distribution of 60,000 maps of various recreational areas in California, which along with other advertising carries the following ad: "Archery, unexcelled sportsmanship, offering competition and adventure. Hunt with the bow and arrow! For particulars write Roy Hoff, Southern California Field Archers, 2414 Garth Avenue, Los Angeles, California." Roy Hoff is also Chairman of the National Publicity Committee of the NFAA. The NFAA does not wish to high pressure anybody into archery, but we do desire and will strive to publicize field archery so that anyone interested can be advised where he can get information on field archery, local clubs, hunting equipment, shooting technique, and places to hunt and hunting conditions.

I. M. Stamps of Seattle, is the new president of the Washington Field Archers. The Tacoma field archers have just completed a new field course. The Everett, Washington, archers have an NFAA field course. The Bellingham, Washington, archers are just organizing and constructing their field course. They are called the "Quiver Club." R. F. Hollingsworth, 106 W. Holly Street, is their president.

West Virginia field archers interested in organizing, please contact Mr. Carl Keefer, 11 Mount Wood Road, Wheeling, West Virginia.

Target clubs which have not yet provided field activities for their members can profit from the experience of the Fort Wayne Archery Club of Indiana. They write: "Until this year we have been strictly target archers, although a few individuals would go roving or hunting, but never as a club project. This year we scheduled one NAA all day target meet, two combination NAA target and field meets, and one all day field archery meet. To date we have held the first three meets as scheduled. The largest attendance was in the combination meets, and very favorable comments were made regarding the field part, which very definitely was the outstanding feature of the meets."

A 28-target field course has been established at Enid, Oklahoma. Oklahoma archers who want to shoot the course or organize can contact C. Balbin, care of Oxford Hotel, Enid, Oklahoma.

Flagstaff, Arizona, field archers are organizing. They are in some of the finest hunting territory in the West. Northern Arizona field archers can contact Ed. B. Drew at Flagstaff. They are anxious to organize a strong association to get earlier seasons and reservations for bow and arrow hunters.

Missouri field archers, attention! The St. Louis club is holding a big field tournament on October 25-26, with plenty of prizes and fun. We urge all field archers in Missouri and near-by states to attend this tournament for a swell time. You target archers who have never shot a field round—come out and try the field round. Find a new thrill and enthusiasm.

Kore T. Duryee of Seattle, Don Cole, and others, left September 5th for a month's hunting trip in East British Columbia, Canada. They are going to try for a grizzly with the bow. We wish them the best of luck. We will get the details of the trip later in Kore's article in "Ye Sylvan Archer," or in his obituary—(But, save your flowers—they tell us Kore can run 100 yards in nothing flat.)

Wisconsin is very fortunate in having its game laws and hunting conditions regulated by a game commission. In most states the game laws are fixed by the state legislature. In states like Wisconsin, where archery hunting conditions are controlled by a friendly game commission, the problems of bow and arrow hunters are comparatively simple. But in those states where laws must be passed by legislators who know nothing of bow and arrow hunting and whose votes are apt to be influenced by political expediencies, the archers have a serious problem on their hands. In the latter states, and where game commissions are indifferent, the need for education and publicity is apparent if bow and arrow hunters are to secure the recognition and privileges that their type of hunting merits. That is why strong state associations are needed, and the assistance of the NFAA, with its information and statistics on bow and arrow hunting in other states is of value to local archers in securing favorable legislation.

Through the NFAA you get the benefit of the experience of field archers in other states to assist you with your problems.

Wisconsin will have a month of advance deer season for bow and arrow hunters. They will be permitted to shoot one deer, buck or doe, and the non-residence license fee for archers has been reduced from $50.00 to $5.00. In Michigan the one-buck law is still in force, but a doe may be shot on a camp permit issued to four or more hunters. Michigan will have a two-week advance hunting season for bow and arrow deer hunting, from November 1-14, inclusive. The license fee for non-resident bow and arrow hunters has been reduced from $25.00 to $5.00.

Bow and arrow hunters in Illinois, Minnesota, Indiana, Ohio and other states desiring to take advantage of these reduced non-residence hunting fees will undoubtedly flock into Wisconsin and Michigan this fall.

At the Texas Archery Association annual tournament a permanent Constitution was adopted, in which it was provided that all field events should be shot in accordance with NFAA rules. Archie Gassman, 1434 West Lywood, San Antonio, is the new president. Archie is a seasoned bow and arrow hunter. Field archery is in for a big increase in Texas under such able leadership. The San Antonio archers have secured a lease on some 5,000 acres in the nationally known Kerville deer hunting area.

The letter of appreciation which the Secretary received from Alfonso Gonzales, of Bakersfield, California, after winning the Class A medal for July, is very gratifying, and justifies the handicap system. Gonzales has shot a bow and arrow for only a year, but he loves it, and worked hard to improve his shooting. His medal was well earned and just recognition for his achievement. Class A consistent high scorers have all been good sportsmen enough to applaud these deserving awards to those whose improved shooting has brought them to the top.

Two qualifications are necessary for membership in the National Field Archery Association — good moral character and good sportsmanship. Applications for membership may be secured from the Secretary, which

(Continued on page 9)

NFAA Bulletin

OFFICERS

President—A. J. Michelson
610 F. P. Flint Bldg., Flint, Mich.

Vice-President—Paris B. Stockdale,
Geology Dept., OSU, Columbus, Ohio.

Secretary-Treasurer—John L. Yount,
Box 383, Redlands, California.

EXECUTIVE COMMITTEE

Western—H C. MacQuarrie.
3400 Fruitvale Ave., Oakland, Calif.

Mid-Western—Fred Bear,
2611 W. Philadelphia, Detroit, Mich.

Eastern—T. C. Davidson,
53 Mountain Ave., Springfield, N. J.

By John L. Yount

Have you an archer friend who takes a bit of pride in the fact that he doesn't belong to any organization? If you have, show him the following—it may help convince him of the error of his ways:

To the Field Archer who is not a member of the National Field Archery Association—

The National Field Archery Association is your organization. Its dues are low enough so that any who can afford a set of arrows and the cheapest lemonwood bow can afford to belong. Yet we have set out to prove to the world that field archery need not be a cheap little sport, and I use that word in its broadest sense. In our opinion, a sport is made cheap not by its cost but by the attitude of those who participate.

Do you and your archery friends "let Bill do it?" Too many do and when Bill doesn't or can't get it done do you crab? Probably.— It is always the man who doesn't vote that knocks the government.

Say you are crabbing because the archers of your state have failed in their efforts to get an advanced season. Let's see what you did to help.

You left the publicity up to the archery showman. This helped convince the public that archery hunting was a stunt and not a sport. The work you left to some three or four, who probably couldn't afford the time but had enough love and respect for the game to do what little they could without support.

The matter of money was left to Providence. Stamps and decent stationery cost money.

Now, wouldn't you feel better if you had done your share and knew that no part of this defeat could be laid at your door?

It is true that some states are lucky. At the head of these is Wisconsin, where the Fish and Game Commission has full authority and has shown itself to be broadminded. Others, also where the control was in the hands of the commission, have made considerable headway, but where it is a matter of legislation concessions are usually gained by catching the legislature in a frivolous mood, making a huge joke of the whole thing, and with some wise cracks about Robin Hood and cupid get a bill through.

The NFAA can't do the actual job in your state. That is up to your State Association, BUT it can lay the ground work by making its library of statistics available to all. By fall we expect to have complete records and keep them up-to-date. Your state will also benefit from our publicity campaign, which is just now getting under way, and from our many other activities all designed to gain the respect of the public and give our sport some of the prestige it deserves.

(Continued on page 10)

YE SYLVAN ARCHER September, 1941

Editorial

"Cheerily blow the bugle horn
In the cool green woods of morn;
Loose the hounds and let them go,
Wax the cord and bend the bow."
—From The Witchery of Archery.

While modern hunters are deprived of the thrilling bay of the hounds and there is no need for the blowing of the bugle horn we can still wax the cord and bend the bow. And, during the next two months, thousands of archers will be stealing out through the cool, or cold, green woods in search of that greatest of trophies, the antlers of a noble stag killed by the power of a good strong arm as it looses a shaft from man's most primitive weapon of the chase. Few will know the thrill of the successful hunter but each year conditions are being made better for the archers and more should be successful this year than ever before. Ye Sylvan Archer wishes the best of luck to all flingers of the feathered shafts.

Tournament Report Late

The report of the August NFAA mail tournament did not reach us in time for insertion in this issue but will be included in the October issue with the September report. This month it was a case of getting YSA out on time or not going deer hunting, so we are getting out on time and not waiting for Mr. Palmatier's report. We hope that the October issue will be bigger and better with reports of many successful hunts.

Prof. Stockdale Moves

Ohio archers are regretting the loss from their state of Prof. Paris B. Stockdale who has resigned his position with the University of Ohio and has accepted a position with the University of Tennessee. At this distance we see benefit to archery in the move as Tennessee seems to need some of the fine promotional work that Prof. Stockdale is so capable of doing and has carried on so successfully in Ohio. Archery in Ohio has plenty of good boosters who will carry on.

POME

A young squirrel, watching archers,
His mother's eyes did meet;
"Yes, my dear, they are," she said,
"But not the kind we eat!"
—Adapted from a radio gag bearing no relation to the ancient and honorable game.

Jean C. Trittin is now located in Salt Lake City at 122 E. So. Temple St. Salt Lake City archers please take notice of the arrival of a noted and enthusiastic archer.

One of the greatest pleasures of the National tournament was meeting "Uncle Hat" Titcomb of Farmington, Maine. Mr. Titcomb came all the way from Maine to Portland to attend the tournament and in spite of the long tiring trip showed a persistency in shooting in all events that made many a younger man wonder how some of the older archers can "take it." Mr. Titcomb wears some interesting medals won at English tournaments during the several years he spent in the British Isles.

What the fragments of Sapphic song and the Homeric epics are to the literature of today, the bow is to the weapons of today. The Sapphic songs were the natural music of love; the Homeric epics were the natural outpourings of a great self-sufficient soul surcharged with the inspiration of heroism. So the bow was the natural weapon of the simple, perfect physical manhood represented in the idea of Apollo, who, with drawn bow, was the symbol of such manhood displayed in its highest powers and graces.—The Witchery of Archery.

The Hillbilly

The Hillbilly is a little of the bulldog and the roast beef of England, the humor, pride and canniness of Scotland, the romance of Ireland, and the hickory, mountain dew and sow belly of the Ozarks. He is the true American. — Alice Gregory, in Arcadian Life.

Letter Box

TOO MANY DEER

Dear Mr. Davis:

There is a place in Colorado that every field archer should know about. It is the Eilson Twin Buttes Ranch, located on Douglas Creek, right on the Eastern border of Utah.

There is a two hundred acre alfalfa field on the ranch that is literally covered with deer tracks. The alfalfa is cut close, but not by the owners of the ranch. The deer performed that task for them—gratis.

"I figure," said Mr. Eilson sadly, "that I am feeding fifteen hundred head of deer. I have had to move my cattle out because I have no winter feed."

"Won't the state help you?" I ask.

"I will show you some correspondence," says the owner of the devastated tract. He did. The state evidently thought that Mr. Eilson was trying to put something over on them. For one who had settled the ranch thirty years ago it made poor reading. There was nothing that could be done about it, evidently.

"What am I going to do?" Mr. Eilson asked me. "I am not going to be run off the place by any thrice condemned deer, I know that much. I won't kill what I can't eat, so that's out. Can you suggest something?"

I could suggest something, and that was an archer's game preserve. I saw some Denver archers about it. The first result of it was that the state investigated the damage, and the game commission authorized four miles of electric fence, which saves the alfalfa. But the deer are still there, hungrier than ever.

Last year I made another trip over to the ranch in the deer season. A few rifle hunters were around, and I interested the Eilson boys in hunting with bow and arrow. That's another story, however.

Now the boys are anxious to get some archers to hunt their range, and they have promised that if I can get them as many archers as there have been gun hunters there — between twenty and thirty — that they will close the range to rifle hunters altogether. There is a chance for us to obtain the use of 6000 acres of the finest hunting country in America.

There are cabins, camp sites, water, horses, not to mention some of the finest boys who ever hunted.

I promised the Eilsons to do everything within my power to acquaint the archers of the country with the opportunity. Will interested parties please contact either the Eilson Brothers, Twin Buttes Ranch, Rangely, Colorado, direct, or you may write to me for further information.

Sincerely,
W. A. Joy,
Los Angeles, Calif.

FIELD ARCHERS OF SOUTHERN CALIFORNIA

(Continued from page 2)

on the range of the Redlands club on the fourth Sunday in October.

The day's winners and their respective club and scores follow:

MEN—Championship Class—

Gold Bar — Merle D. Hathaway, Malibu, 626.

Silver Bar—Willard Bacon, Pasadena, 619.

MEN—General Division—

Championship medal — Phil Conrad, Malibu, 649.

Red ribbon—Emery Watts, Malibu, 605.

White ribbon—Perzy High, Malibu, 521.

LADIES—Championship Class—

Gold Bar—Gene Bacon, Pasadena, 397.

Silver Bar—Ruth Hathaway, Malibu, 376.

LADIES—General Division—

Championship medal—Babe Bitzenberger, Pasadena, 305.

Red ribbon—Minerva Gandy, Malibu, 271.

White ribbon—Freda Hoff, Malibu, 240.

If all the archers who are planning to attend the Oregon Pope-Young Field Tournament really get there this year's tournament should be the biggest and best. And why shouldn't it be—in the heart of the Archery Reserve on the beautiful A-Bar-L ranch?

The Woes of the Head Coach

By the Doghouse Editor

In every sport that I know of, archery alone excepted, the coach is a gent of standing and influence. Football coaches, for instance, are widely publicized, interviewed over the radio, and so forth. In archery the best coach in the world, meaning myself, considers himself lucky to escape with his life at a national tournament. Ignominously do I get myself ejected from every field.

No, I take that back, not from every field. The field archers wouldn't know how to act if they weren't properly coached and heckled at every turn. And even among target archers there is one glowing exception, and that is the Los Angeles club. There they know a good coach, and value him.

In contrast we have the Elysian club, also of Los Angeles. The Elysian is a very low type of an organization, where a coach is ejected even before he opens his mouth.

I am getting tired of violence applied bodily, as well as of dark looks and intemperate language from the very ones I am trying to help.

Take Portland, for instance. There Gladys Hammer begged me with tears in her eyes to stand behind her and advise her. I was no sooner stationed properly before Natalie Reichart was upon me like a thunder cloud.

"None of that this time," she says. "I know all about you." Being a lady she does not enforce her commands with her pedal extremities, but she grabs me by the arm, and gives it a good pinch as she finally lets go of me. And there the day was spoiled both for Gladys and the rest of the girls. How could I help it?

Sadly I make my way to the men's targets, where I am received with shouts of acclaim by Hughes, Strang, Bacon and Thompson. If there was any strain at that target I never noticed it. Each of them was ragging the other as he stepped up to shoot. Having about run out of insults they opened up on me. I defended myself manfully, and long will I remember that quartet for the genuinely good time they had while the championship was being decided.

And there is old Eagle-Eye, Dr. Cathey, bearing down like a destroyer on a submarine. Suspiciously he squats down beside me on the bench, while the boys keep cackling away. I am on my very best behavior, as I apologize for the racket Larry is making. There is nothing George can do about it, though you can see his mind is not at ease. He still harbors unjust suspicions.

Getting tired of not hearing my own voice I walk over to one of the cops, whom I engage in guarded conversation. I speak very low, as Eagle-Eye is not over twenty feet away, but the cop does not speak low.

"Sh-h-h," hisses the field captain. "Get the hell out of here,—both of you!" Yes, he includes me in the invitation. Was that cop's face red? I forget the injury to my feelings. I have been kicked off the grounds by a cop several times, but never before with one. And now I am blamed for framing one of Portland's finest.

The crying injustice of the whole thing oppresses me. Just why should I always be singled out when somebody on the field lets out a yap? Walt Wilhelm, Ted Rand, and now a cop; they all have done me wrong. If this keeps up I will have to take in future tournaments in full armor, and if I do, I hope somebody will break his damn number fourteens on the back plate.

P.S. The doghouse provided for me in Portland had barely enough space to hold Mike Michelson and John Davis. The coon hunters had to be chained outside. I hope it rains.

The Flint Bowmen

When the average Michigan archer hears about a Flint Bowmen invitational Field Meet, he feels comparatively certain about two things; first, there will be a good crowd (our friends surely are loyal), and second, it will rain! We fooled them August 24, however, and after three consecutive rainy meets, we drew a beautiful day, and sixty-four archers, more than half of them out-of-towners, gathered to enjoy it with us.

The range was in company condition and 'twas a jolly group that gathered around the picnic tables during the noon intermission. There being no water supply at our course, we initiated our new drinking fountain. Purchasing a twenty gallon garbage can (new!), we had a faucet soldered on. Filled with ice and water, and augmented with a goodly supply of paper cups, the thirsty were taken care of all day.

Though this was an open tournament, as a side issue the crowns of the city champions were at stake. Last year, when our first championship meet was held, supposedly traveling trophies were awarded. As a surprise element at this meet the defending champions, both of whom were defeated, were presented with their trophies "for keeps," the club policy having been changed. Mrs. Lulu Stalker was defeated by Mrs. Bessie Stephenson, while George Hamaker bowed to George Calvert.

An innovation introduced at a meet last year has proven so popular as to become practically a "must." A member makes up miniature stumps, colored brown with a burning pen, about 1" in height, mounted on irregular slabs of osage, approximately 3"x 4". Into each stump has been shot (?) a single arrow, 3" long, faithfully fletched with feathers from a sparrow wing, and crested in color, a replica of the National Field Archery Association's emblem. These have been used as incidental prizes, sometimes for most center shots, sometimes for most perfects and once for high novice scores. Sunday they were given for the most center shots, and Chuck Ratcliff, Highland Park, collected twelve, three on one target, to win his stump. Mrs. Stephenson led the ladies with six center shots.

For men's and ladies' low score, another such stump was given—a good sportsmanship trophy—and while no one would try for low, it eased the pain a little to take home one of these coveted trophies.

Following is a tabulation of the results of the day's shoot. Awards were made in three classes for both men and ladies, medals being given for first place and ribbons for the first three places in each class. Classes in the Flint Bowmen meets, due to the large number of beginners, are determined by dividing the entire number of entrants three ways, giving more people a chance. We like it.

Class A Men—
J. P. Scott, Detroit 479
Geo. Calvert, Flint 387
Carlos Barfield, Detroit 386
Class B Men—
Larry Mytinger, Fenton 291
Laurel Markham, Durand 289
Walter Weick, Detroit 273
Class C Men—
Ed Harris, Corunna 229
Elsworth Allen, Grand Blanc 223
Jim Hendrickson, Detroit 217
Class A Ladies—
Bessie Stephenson, Flint 348
Mary Calvert, Flint 295
Lulu Stalker, Flint 295
Class B Ladies—
Ina Woolnough, Trenton 175
Marie Bear, Detroit 173
Marie Grumley, Atlas 165
Class C Ladies—
Irene Wierzbicki, Flint 134
Pauline Harris, Corunna 105
Phyllis Diehl, Flint 82
Juniors—
Walter Knoblock, Jr., Flint 176
Jack Ratcliff, Highland Park 81

Blunts from the Old Stump

(Continued from page 4)

contain a signed pledge to support the constitutional purposes of the NFAA, which are:

"To encourage the use of the bow in the hunting of all legal game birds and animals, and to protect, improve and increase the privileges of bow and arrow hunters.

"To promote various types of bow and arrow field games, and adopt and enforce uniform rules, regulations, conditions and methods for playing the same.

"To cooperate with the Federal and State governments, and sportsmen and conservation organizations, in the propagation and conservation of game and its natural habitat, the forests and fields.

"To conduct a continuous educational program designed to acquaint the public with the bow and its uses as a practical and humane weapon, suitable, under proper regulations, for the hunting of all game animals and birds on the American Continents."

The applicant also agrees: "I further promise to abide by all the game laws of any state in which I hunt and to conduct myself as a gentleman and sportsman at all times when in the field."

Violations of game laws is made much easier by the use of the bow, and for this reason our fraternity must be zealously on its guard to preserve the honor of our noble sport, and be ready to frown upon and if necessary to prosecute any unlawful use of the bow in game hunting. The bow and arrow hunter has the reputation of being a sportsman of the first water. Let us keep it that way.

We are going to have to coin some new words for use in field archery. Mrs. Stalker asks for a name for "shooting position." How about "post?" What shall we name the NFAA field round? We don't like the word "target" either in field shooting. Send your suggestions to the Secretary. The lucky winners will be awarded with an arrow to match the one he has that never misses.

The Secretary is anxious to establish a newspaper clipping service for field archery. Will club Secretaries undertake to clip all news articles on field archery, tournaments, hunting stories, comments (good and bad), state bow hunting regulations, etc., and mail to the Secretary? This will provide the NFAA with much-needed material for national publicity and information. We would appreciate all archers hunting in groups to keep accurate records of their hunts — time and place hunted, game seen and shot at, distances of shots, animals shot, or wounded and lost, kind of bows and arrows used, where game hit, and distance traveled after hit; and also other information of interest or value. Send data to the Secretary for compilation and publication.

NFAA BULLETIN

(Continued from page 5)

For a brief outline of NFAA activities read the enclosed membership application. This is all work that can best, and much of it only can be done by a national organization, yet upon the success of this program, in large part, rests the future of field archery.

The foregoing may have given you the impression that ours is purely an idealistic organization with little of immediate and personal value to offer its members. Instead, the NFAA, despite its low dues, offers more to the individual than nearly any other sports organization.

For the hunter we have the Art Young Big Game Award. We don't think you will ever feel quite the same again if you are successful in your hunt this fall but neglect first to join the NFAA.

For the competitive field archer we have the mail tournaments with classes for all. These tournaments have proved very popular. Then in the not too distant future we expect to have a real National Field Tournament.

For all members there is "Ye Sylvan Archer," a first class field archery magazine that will grow better as our membership increases. We have included it in each membership, even though to do so necessitated raising the dues from fifty cents to one dollar, not because we are selling magazines, but because if we are to work together we must have some means of contact, and the magazine with the NFAA news section offers the most economical and satisfactory method. As a special inducement to those with Scotch blood, we might mention that the subscription price of this magazine alone is $1.00, or the same as an NFAA membership combined with the magazine.

There is a time honored tradition that the field archer is a sort of lone wolf that can't be organized, even for his own good. Won't you help us give this the lie?

Sincerely yours,
National Field Archery Association

National Field Archery Association
MEMBERSHIP APPLICATION

I believe in the NFAA and in the things for which it stands.

PURPOSE
(As Set Forth in the Constitution))

To encourage the use of the bow in the hunting of all legal game birds and animals, and to protect, improve and increase the privileges of bow and arrow hunters.

To promote various types of bow and arrow field games, and adopt and enforce uniform rules, regulations, conditions and methods for playing the same.

To cooperate with the Federal and

State governments, and sportsmen and conservation organizations, in the propagation and conservation of game and its natural habitat, the forests and fields.

To conduct a continuous educational program designed to acquaint the public with the bow and its uses as a practical and humane weapon, suitable under proper regulations, for the hunting of all game animals and birds on the American Continents.

In submitting my name for membership I agree to do my fair share in the fostering of this program.

I further promise to abide by all the game laws of any state in which I hunt and to conduct myself as a gentleman and a sportsman at all times when in the field.

California State Tournament

The eighth Annual Championship Tournament of the California State Archery Association was held at Santa Barbara on August 30-31. Bee Hodgson won the ladies' championship with a total score of 992 for National and Columbia. Gene Bacon was second and Margaret Thompson was third. Larry Hughes, national champion, scored 870 in the York and 756 in the American for a total of 1626 to take the men's championship. A. Mericourt followed with 1557 and Willard Bacon with 1540. Henry Elder won the Junior event with 1193 for double junior American.

SUBSCRIBERS PLEASE NOTICE

A cross appearing in this space means that your subscription has expired and we would appreciate your prompt renewal so that your name may be kept on our mailing list.

CLASSIFIED ADVERTISING

RATES for Classified Advertising 5 cents per word per issue. Count initials and numbers as words. Minimum charge is 50 cents.

BOOKS AND MAGAZINES

The Flat Bow—70 pages of Archery information for 50 cents, well illustrated. *Ye Sylvan Archer, 505 N. 11th St., Corvallis, Oregon.*

"ARCHERY TACKLE, HOW TO MAKE AND HOW TO USE IT." by Adolph Shane. Bound in cloth and illustrated with more than fifty drawings and photographs. Information for making archery tackle and instructions for shooting. Price is $1.75. Send orders to Ye Sylvan Archer, 505 North 11th street, Corvallis, Oregon.

GET YOUR SET NOW—26 beautiful and perfect Archery Stamps from 5 different countries for only $3.59. A Free one year subscription is given with each order. First 6 American Archer back issues for $1. The American Archer, national quarterly, at $1 per year. THE AMERICAN ARCHER, 521 5th Ave., New York City.

RELICS AND CURIOS

INDIAN RELICS, Beadwork, Coins, Curios, Books, Minerals, Weapons. Old West Photos. Catalog, 5c. Genuine African Bow, $3.75. Ancient flint arrowheads, perfect, 6c each—Indian Museum, Osborne, Kansas.

Ye Sylvan Archer—$1.00 per year

70 pages of Archery information for 50 cents, well illustrated. Ye Sylvan Archer, 505 N. 11th St., Corvallis, Oregon.

BACK NUMBERS
YE SYLVAN ARCHER
Volumes I to V Inclusive
$1.00 Per Volume
B. G. THOMPSON
R. F. D. 1, Corvallis, Oregon

Please mention Ye Sylvan Archer when writing advertisers.

The AMERICAN ARCHER, a national quarterly, $1.00 per year, 521 Fifth Ave., New York City.

Archery Raw Materials

WM. A. JOY

9708 So. Hoover Street
LOS ANGELES, CALIF.

YEW WOOD STAVES
at .... $2.00 and $3.00
P. O. CEDAR SHAFTS
.... Doz., 40c; 100, $3.00
Try our new PLASTIC NOCK. It's just a little different and cheaper. The best nock on the market. Doz., 20c; 100, $1.50; 500, $5.00; 1000, $8.50. Five colors, 3 sizes.
Send money with order.
Monte Vista Archery Co.
Rt. 1, Box 149, Tacoma, Wash.

HANDBOOK—How to Make and Use Bows and Arrows—90 Pages well illustrated (with catalog) 35c.

CATALOG—100 pictures—color spread—Instruction Folder. 10c.

CATALOG alone 5c. Stamps or Coin.

L·E·STEMMLER· QUEENS VILLAGE·N·Y·

BROADHEAD ARROWS

Meeting the requirements for the Pope-Young Field Tournament. Chandler Universal Blades and Fiber Inset Nocks. *State weight of bow.*

Set of 8, for Men—
  28 inch $3.75
For Women—26 inch $3.50

V. D. McCauley
505 N. 11th   Corvallis, Ore.

VIKING ARCHERY

1874 Market Street

San Francisco, Calif.

E. BUD PIERSON
Bowyer — Fletcher
Tournament Tackle, Sinew, Glue, Raw Materials.
Custom Made Tackle
3109 Burnet Ave. — Cincinnati, Ohio

Paul H. Gordon
Author of "The New Archery"
Producing
Tackle — Materials
Latest and Finest for Field or Range
Write for Free Catalog
Beacon Hill Craftsmen
Beacon, N. Y.

Please mention Ye Sylvan Archer when writing advertisers.

HI THERE, FIELD ARCHERS—TAKE A LOOK AT THIS!
Write for full information

A special introductory offer. Complete set of 14 official "Arro-Mat" field targets and faces for only $29.75.

Ben Pearson
INCORPORATED
Bows and Arrows of Excellence
PINE BLUFF, ARK.

This offer limited to full sets only. Your club can now enjoy the field round on official targets at a new low cost.

CHANDLER
Universal Broadheads

The Broadhead that costs less than a big rifle bullet, from 5c to 8-1/3c each. The inexpensive Broadhead for hunting.

Also Universal Broadhead Kits, with complete material for making one doz. good Broadhead Arrows.

Also Hunting, Fishing and roving Points.

FREE CATALOGUE

T. B. CHANDLER
11819 4th Ave., Compton, Calif.

FISH HEAD
B-80
B-1

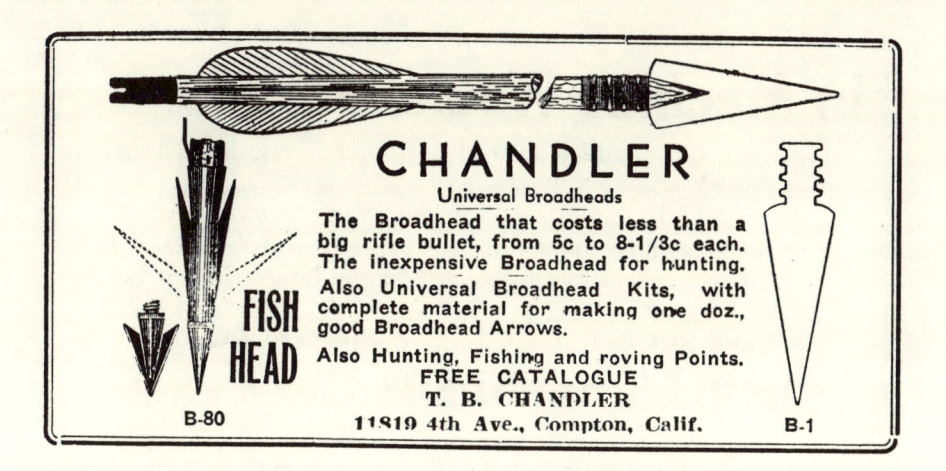

APPROVED NFAA FIELD TARGET FACES

Printed in black and white on heavy, double thickness corrugated board. In sets containing sizes necessary for a 14-target course and including extras of the smaller sizes that shoot out fastest.

$2.25 per set, f.o.b. Detroit — Order two sets for a 28-target course

BEAR ARCHERY CO.
2611 W. Philadelphia Ave., Detroit, Michigan

G
"THE MARK OF DISTINCTION IN ARCHERY TACKLE
Fine Yew Target and Hunting Bows, Plain or Backed with Rawhide. Lemonwood Bows with Rawhide Backs.
College and School Equipment
Target, Hunting and Roving Arrows
Price List on Request
Wholesale — Retail
EARL GRUBBS
5518 W. Adams
Los Angeles : California

Arcadian Life Magazine
Stories of the Ozarks

Pioneer History - Folklore
Pastoral Living

$1.00 a Year; 25c a Copy

Display Adv. $1.50 per inch Classified, 3c a word. Three insertions for the price of two.

O. E. RAYBURN, Editor
Dept. 15

616 S. Benton St
Cape Girardeau, Mo.
P. O. Box 200
Caddo Gap, Arkansas

Please mention Ye Sylvan Archer when writing advertisers.

Ye Sylvan Archer—$1.00 per year

In Machine-Wound Targets

Every coil is pulled into place under a regulated tension adjusted to give maximum wear.

Allowance is made for additional wear toward center.

The natural resilience of the rye straw is retained and becomes a participating factor in the longer life of Saunders' targets.

Hand Stitched   **Standard Quality**

CHARLES SAUNDERS
3030 POLK STREET
CHICAGO, ILLINOIS

"SWITCH" TO KING-MOORE HUNTING AND ROVING EQUIPMENT

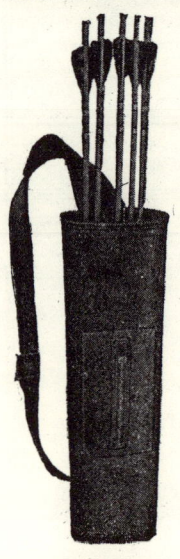

KM-77—MEN'S LARGE SIZE HUNTING AND ROVING QUIVER
Made of genuine water-Leather, with large outside zipper pocket ideal for extra equipment. Ample room for 2 dozen broadheads. An outstanding value at **$4.95**

NEW SHOOTING GLOVE FOR ROVING AND HUNTING, WITH "TURKEY QUILL"
KM-25 — A professional type glove to be used only with bows pulling over 40 pounds. "Turkey quill" insert prevents deep string indentations which assures a perfect release. Genuine Cordovan Leather **$2.50**

When ordering be sure to send outline of hand or glove size.

KM-77

Patronize your dealer — if he cannot supply you send check or money order to

KING ★ MOORE
7011 NORTH FIGUEROA STREET
LOS ANGELES — CALIFORNIA

Cassius Hayward Styles

BOWYER AND FLETCHER

—Tackle that has stood the test—

28 Vicente Place

BERKELEY, CALIFORNIA

PORT ORFORD CEDAR ARROW SHAFTS
(Cypressa Lawsonia)

Specials. P.O. Cedar Shafts, 1/4 to 11/32":
Parallel, per 100 .... $4.00
Tapered or barreled, 100 .. $4.50
Extra Select. Units segregated, per 100 .... $5.00
Douglas Fir, 100 .... $3.00, $3.50
Douglas Fir, Extra Select, per 100 .... $4.00

Full line finished tackle. Raw Materials.
Write for price lists. Special rates to dealers and clubs.

PORT ORFORD ARCHERY SUPPLY CO.
C. F. Douglas, Mgr.
Box 137   Port Orford, Oregon

Ye Sylvan Archer

October, 1941

Vol. 13, No. 6

Ye
Sylvan Archer

*Official Publication of the
National Field Archery Association*

Vol. 13   October, 1941   No. 6

Published the fifteenth of each month
for archers by archers
505 North 11th Street, Corvallis, Oregon

J. E. DAVIS .... Editor

Subscription Price .... $1.00 Per Year

Foreign Subscription $1.25

Single Copies .... 10 Cents

Advertising Rates on Application

TABLE OF CONTENTS

                                                    Page

WE WENT HUNTING
    By Morgan Jones 1

MICHIGAN FIELD TOURNAMENT 2

NEWARK ROVERS SHOOT
    By C. B. Young 2

BLUNTS FROM THE OLD STUMP 3

NFAA BULLETIN
    By John L. Yount 5

EDITORIAL 6

NEW MEXICO GETS FINE RESERVE
    By Leon H. Mudgett 7

LETTER BOX 8

FIFTH NFAA TOURNAMENT REPORT
    By Karl E. Palmatier 11

SIXTH NFAA TOURNAMENT REPORT
    By Karl E. Palmatier 13

OREGON POPE-YOUNG FIELD
    TOURNAMENT 15

We Went Hunting

By Morgan Jones, in Australasian Archer

Two utility cars, each carrying six persons and their gear, went on a hunting trip to Nebo. Out of these, only George Theodore, Allan Wilson and myself used bows; the rest used guns. The first car left at 12 noon, Saturday; the other about 2 P.M.; and they passed us in the first car, about a mile from where we were camped. We reckon they flew, but they say not.

We arrived at our destination at 7:30 and got tea ready as quickly as we could. Eating it occupied us for about an hour—the country air sure gives one an appetite.

After tea we rigged up a tent fly and got our beds ready, and sleep followed very soon afterwards.

We were up again at 5:30 Sunday morning and out came the weapons to hunt pigs along the creek. Parties of three and four went in different directions.

Our party, consisting of George, Allan, Noel Nielson, Walter Hayward and myself, went up the creek towards the mouth, and although we followed fresh pig trails for a couple of miles we never came in contact with them.

Later on George and I parted from the other three and struck away from the creek and saw two large birds in the distance.

We crawled on hands and knees for about a hundred yards and, when within about 80 yards of them a herd of cattle grazing near by started a miniature stampede, and with them went our birds, so we had a three mile walk back to camp.

On arrival there we learned we were not the only ones who returned empty handed. Although the other three we had gone up the creek with saw a couple of turkeys they could not get within bow-shot.

The rest of the day was spent in walking miles and miles for nothing. We found out later that the heavy rains we have had have sent most of the game to higher country.

Monday morning turned out cloudy and rain threatened. We had breakfast, and packed up all our gear, and set out for the Brigalow, which grows about 10 miles farther west from our camp.

On the way, with the three bowmen, Noel, Sid and Noel's father, who was driving in the rear car, we had a little engine trouble and had to stop for a few minutes, and when we caught up to the other car it had stopped and one of their gunmen was creeping up on two kangaroos about 200 yards distant.

Taking careful aim, he got one and the other jumped away a few yards, so, reloading his gun, he let it have it. He knocked it down but it was up in an instant, with we three bowmen and Noel in pursuit, but the grass being waist-high, the going was tough and we were soon left far behind, so we returned to the cars, where the kill had been skinned (a beautiful skin, too). I have it curing to make a hunting quiver out of it.

Eventually we reached the Brigalow and there was miles of it, too; but before cutting some we decided to have a hunt around; so, splitting up into two's and three's, we went into the forest of Brigalow.

George and I went together and were soon in the thick of it. We came on to a bunch of wallabies, and I don't know who got the biggest surprise; but, anyway, we got a shot each, which went wide of its mark.

Creeping further along we came to two lots and parted in chase of them, but they were too good for us.

That was the last I saw of George until I got back to the car a couple of hours later, for I got well and truly lost, and only for running into one of the party who knew the country around there I might have still been there.

Setting off in a direction which I thought was taking us away from the cars, we later came to a fence, and following this for a while we came to a gate which we had passed through earlier in the morning, and I knew where I was then, and it did not take long to get back to the cars.

On arrival there I found all the Brigalow cut and loaded on the cars. I wasn't sorry, for my legs were like lumps of lead.

Next stop was creek a few miles further on where we had dinner, after which we started for home at 1 p.m. We had plenty of stops on the way to shoot at kangaroos and pigeons. Sid hit a kangaroo, but only wounded him, not seriously and away it went before another shot could be fired.

About 40 miles from home we ran into the rain which had been·threatening all day. Then about 23 miles from home our car was bogged to the running boards and had to be pulled out by the other car.

We arrived home at 9 p.m., and so ends our hunting trip; we lost a few arrows—got no game—enough Brigalow to make about 25 bows—and memories of a wonderful trip.

Michigan Field Tournament

Well over one hundred archers gathered in a field six miles north of Owosso to determine Field Champions for the state, closing the summer's program of tournaments. Archers from all over the state were there, the outlying posts being Muskegon and Buchanan. Rain fell at intervals throughout the day, and it grew increasingly colder, but the meet progressed according to schedule. Following are the scores:

Class A Men—Instinctive—
1. John P. Scott, Detroit 479
2. Nels Grumley, Atlas 411
3. Earl Eurick, Lansing 376
4. Larry Mytinger, Fenton 365
5. Jack Skanes, Detroit 355

Class B Men—Instinctive—
1. Max Goldman, Ann Arbor 350
2. Frank Litchfield, Flint 325
3. George Calvert, Flint 322
4. Ralph Councilman, Detroit 309
5. T. L. Stalker, Flint 308

Class C Men—Instinctive—
1. Woodrow Harris, Corunna 238
2. Fred Hall, Buchanan 202
3. Glen Ebert, Flint 192
4. Frank Lubis, Royal Oak 191
5. John Law, Owosso 191

Class A Men—Free Style—
1. Vaughn Blanchard, Howell 456
2. Don Hootman, East Lansing .. 410

Class B Men—Free Style—
1. Frank Ash, Detroit 262
2. Wayne Bernard, Howell ....
3. George Higgins, Detroit ....

Junior Girls—
1st place—Susan Law, Owosso.

Junior Boys—
1. Pat Law, Owosso.
2. Wally Knoblock, Flint.
3. Gordon Ash, Detroit.

Ladies' Class A—Instinctive—
1. Daisy Olson, Royal Oak 349
2. Bertha Hoffmeyer, Flint 276
3. Shirley Richey, Royal Oak 250
4. Bessie Stephenson, Flint 242
5. Lulu Stalker, Flint 235

Ladies' Class B—Instinctive—
1. Muriel MacIntyre, Roy. Oak .. 173
2. Ina Woolnough, Trenton 160
3. Donna Diehl, Flint 154
4. Jean Small, Trenton 146
5. Eva Sawyer, Owosso 122

Ladies' Free Style—
1. Edith Hastings, Muskegon 276
2. Carrie Sherman, Eaton Rapids 123
3. Mary Law, Owosso 104

In accordance with the custom established some time ago, the Conservation Department has reserved deer license No. 1 for the first place man, instinctive division; J. P. Scott in this instance. License No. 2 goes to first place man, free style; this year, Vaughn Blanchard of Howell. License No. 3 goes to the first place woman; Mrs. Daisy Olson of Royal Oak, whose score in this tournament tops the record score for women of the state by 46 points.

Newark Rovers Shoot

By C. B. Young

On Sunday, October 5, 1941, the fourth annual Newark Rover of the Longbow Archery Club was held at the Y.M.C.A. Camp north of Newark, Ohio.

After three days of rain before the shoot, Sunday turned out to be a fine day. One hundred and thirty-five attended the shoot and there probably would have been even more if previous weather had not dampened the spirits of some who had planned to attend.

There was a thirty target course laid out over the camp in two sections. The group shot half the course, then ate and shot the rest in the afternoon. The targets were animal targets and scoring zones were laid out on them. They were announced to be all Ohio animals but some of the archers who shot the course had their doubts of the truth of this.

Following are the winners, there (Continued on page 6)

Blunts from the Old Stump

We were a little previous in announcing a non-resident bow license of $5.00 for deer hunting in Michigan this year. The law was passed, but does not become effective until ninety days after the Legislature adjourns. The Legislature is in session, which means that the law cannot become effective for deer hunting in Michigan this year. The license will be $25.00 for non-residents this year, and $5.00 next year. We trust that no one has been inconvenienced. We were too late to correct the error for last month's "Ye Sylvan Archer," but made the correction in "The American Bowman Review."

After many years of effort the New Mexico field archers have at last been successful in securing an archery reserve for deer hunting. On August 30, the State Game Commission assigned the Sandia Refuge, about ten miles from Albuquerque, most of which has been closed for thirty years, to hunting with the bow and arrow exclusively, from November 1 to 9, inclusive. The Refuge contains forty-five square miles, and has an estimated deer population of 2,000. 300 permits will be issued to archers only. Non-resident archers may secure licenses for $25.00 by writing Mr. Barker, State Game and Fish Department, Santa Fe, New Mexico. Further information may be secured from Walter Bellman, Secretary New Mexico FAA, 109 South 14th Street, Albuquerque, New Mexico. The Game Commission is anxious to reduce the herd by at least 200. Bows must be not less than 50 pounds in weight. There should be splendid hunting in this virgin, protected territory for all archers who can possibly make it.

We urge all bow hunters to write their name, city and state on their hunting arrows. When you meet gun hunters who want to discuss your equipment with you, call their attention to this. It will increase the good will and respect of gun hunters toward bow hunters, and help maintain bow hunting on the high plane of law-abiding sportsmanship which it has earned, and deserves.

The Bastille has at last fallen! ! !

Arizona, the last state to hold out against recognizing the bow as a legitimate hunting weapon, has seen the light! ! ! After twelve years of effort, the field archers of Arizona have persuaded the Game Commission to legalize the bow in the hunting of birds and game, wherever hunting is permitted. Bows must be 50 lb., and broadheads one inch in width. Archers must secure permits from the game warden. This success was achieved through the good will and recommendation of the State Game Warden, K. C. Kartchner of Phoenix. Mr. Kartchner read a sheaf of letters to the Commission that he had received from other states on his own initiative, and the Game Commission capitulated. The NFAA, not only on behalf of the Arizona archers, but archers everywhere, expresses to Mr. Kartchner their sincerest appreciation and gratitude for his splendid efforts.

On September 29, the Michigan Archery Association held its state field championship tournament at Owosso, Michigan. The weather man promised rain, and made good. The tournament was delayed for an hour and a half, but finally got under way. Fifty-six targets were shot between showers. 101 field archers shot the tournament. All but twelve shot instinctively. The Michigan instinctive class prohibits even the use of one mark on the bow. The new Michigan field champion is John P. Scott of Detroit, with a score of 479. The ladies' champion is Daisy Olson of Royal Oak, with a score of 349. The free style winner was J. Vaughn Blanchard of Howell, with a score of 456. Again the instinctive champion outshot the best free style archer. By arrangement with the Michigan Conservation Department, the first three bow and arrow deer hunting licenses are reserved for these champions. No. 1 goes to the field champion, No. 2 to the free style champion, and No. 3 goes to the ladies' champion. These bow licenses are coveted prizes.

We are pleased to announce that A. J. Michelson, President, Dr. Paris Stockdale, Vice-President, and John

Yount, Secretary, representing the NFAA—and Henry S. C. Cummings, Chairman, Louis Smith, Secretary, and Karl Palmatier, representing the NAA, will act as a Contact Committee between the two associations, for the purpose of preserving and promoting good will, harmony, and cooperation between the NFAA and the NAA, and working together on national problems involving the interests of archery in general. The two associations will continue to expand in their respective fields, and pull together on all matters of mutual interest.

There has been a tremendous increase in archery during the past five years. We must keep the ball a-rolling. We cannot permit archery to suffer any war-time lag. In national emergencies when nerves are on edge, the need for good, wholesome recreation increases. We take the liberty of quoting from a letter recently written by Erle Stanley Gardner to Dr. Paul Klopsteg:

"In this international emergency when concededly a war of nerves is an integral part of the weapons which are being turned against us, I think it is a splendid time to take time out to realize the importance of archery as a national defense measure. Nerve tension distorts perspective. It is quite possible that after a few years when we look back on this crisis and come to realize how much bluff and nerves played a part in the making of history, we will realize that our sport programs were as vital to national defense as munitions."

On October 3, 4, and 5, the field archers of Southern California staged a deer hunt at Rock Creek, California, in the High Sierras. More than 30 archers took part in the hunt, including Roy Hoff of Los Angeles, Dr. Delmar Pletcher of Bakersfield, John Willard of Hollywood, Dr. C. W. Hoff of San Bernardino, Max Stemple, Earl Mace, Albert Biordi and Bennett Gandy. For the benefit of local sportsmen an archery demonstration was staged at Tony's Place, at Rock Creek, to show accuracy in shooting, and the penetration of the broadheads. To demonstrate penetration a 30-30 calibre rifle bullet was fired into a bag of sand, and the bullet sifted out. Then a broadhead was shot clear through the bag of sand. This was an impressive demonstration. We will get the details of the hunt in a later issue.

Keep your broadheads sharp. We figure a dull broadhead decreases your bow efficiency by ten pounds. If you do any practice shooting be sure and sharpen them up, if you expect to use the same arrows on game.

Most of the shots we have had in deer hunting, under forty yards, have been kneeling shots. What do you think of having some such shots in our field round? We would like to hear more from our field archers on your ideas for improving our game and our organization.

We are going to stick our neck out on field shooting technique. We have had the opportunity to study the shooting technique of some of the foremost target and field shots from coast to coast and learn why they get that way. It is because they have developed a good, consistent shooting technique. Snap shooting is quite prevalent among many field archers. We have some first class shots who are snap shooters, but their accuracy has been developed by years of shooting, and plenty of it. Most snap shooters are that way because they are shooting a heavier bow than they should shoot. The result is that improvement is slow. We believe a field archer needs a good, consistent form to become an accurate shot— more so, in fact, than the target archer does, because he has no point of aim or sights. For the beginner or novice, and old timers, too (who are not so set that they cannot change), we recommend a full draw to a definite anchor point, with a definite pause (the length of hold is immaterial) before release, to insure steadiness, and a follow through with both arms after release. A good steady bow hand before and *after* release means the difference between hits and misses. If you develop good form for your still shots, we will guarantee you can out-snap the snap shooters on the running shots, when quick shooting is necessary.

The Big Mid-West Field Event! ! The Saint Louis Archery Club Pow-Wow, Bar-B-Q, and Field Shoot, is in Forest Park, Saint Louis, Missouri,

(Continued on page 7)

NFAA Bulletin

OFFICERS

President—A. J. Michelson
610 F. P. Flint Bldg., Flint, Mich.

Vice-President—Paris B. Stockdale,
Geology Dept., OSU, Columbus, Ohio.

Secretary-Treasurer—John L. Yount,
Box 383, Redlands, California.

EXECUTIVE COMMITTEE

Western—H C. MacQuarrie,
3400 Fruitvale Ave., Oakland, Calif.

Mid-Western—Fred Bear,
2611 W. Philadelphia, Detroit, Mich.

Eastern—T. C. Davidson,
53 Mountain Ave., Springfield, N. J.

By John L. Yount

Once again let me remind you that we are depending on you for a full report of that hunting trip, together with all the local archery hunting news, how many hunted, what they got, etc.

We want a complete record of archery hunting and don't have any other way of getting it. As has been explained before, this information will be available to any who need it and should be of inestimable value to the archers of those states now having difficulties with their state legislatures.

Please don't think that because you didn't get your deer that there is nothing to report. We would like to know whether you had any shots or even saw deer and, if so, would they have been good rifle shots. Give us all the dope and above all don't forget to report the dark side of the picture, if there is one. Do you know of any wounded animals that got away? There are bound to be a few, and it is best that we know of them first and be ready to spike any ridiculous stories such as are apt to be started by some one with an anti-archer complex. Yes, there are such people!

This brings us up to the matter of the clipping service mentioned in the last issue.

Please send us all field archery clippings whether of tournaments or hunting feats. These clippings may be sent to Roy Hoff, Chairman of Publicity, 2414 Garth Ave., Los Angeles, Calif., or myself.

Don't hesitate about sending clippings in because they may duplicate those sent in by someone else. He may feel the same way about it, and we really want those clippings.

* * * *

Our records are very incomplete in so far as the names and addresses of club officials are concerned. Will the secretaries of all clubs interested in field archery be so kind as to send me their names and addresses and the name of their club. In case the secretary of your local club is not a member of the NFAA will you, who are, please call this request to his or her attention?

* * * *

Highlights in the Month's Field Activities

Some of us thought we had our troubles. We didn't have an advance season and we didn't have a reserve, but compared with the archers of Arizona ours was a bed of roses. They couldn't hunt at all, except in one small section where they had to compete with the rifle boys. It was a sort of reserve with reverse English. Now this is all changed and the Arizona archer has been given the same rights as any other hunter, the right

(Continued on page 6)

Editorial

We had notices from a number of New Mexico and Arizona archers regarding the opening of the entire state of Arizona to archery hunting, and the opening of the refuge in the Sandia Mountains of New Mexico to bow and arrow hunting. We are sorry we go to press too late to give proper publicity for this season's hunting.

A good proof of the popularity of field archery is the fact that 135 archers competed in the Newark, Ohio, Rover Shoot of the Long Bow Archery Club—nearly as many as competed in the National Archery Tournament.

Cover photo is by Chester Stevenson, Eugene, Oregon.

NFAA BULLETIN
(Continued from page 5)

to hunt during the regular season, in any open territory in the state.

For you fellows who can get off for a few days during the first two weeks of November, we highly recommend a trip to New Mexico.

They have just been given a three by fifteen mile reserve in the Sandia Mountains east of Albuquerque. This area has been a game preserve for thirty years and has an estimated deer population of 2000. With a license that allows either a buck or doe to be taken, there should be some real sport for those who can get there.

For further information write Joe Robb, 322 Harvard Avenue, Albuquerque, New Mexico.

* * * *

Secretarial Troubles

A lot of fellows keep writing in asking where they can find the nearest field club, or some such question. Now, this is as it should be and we hope they keep right on rolling in, but it is quite a job looking up the answers so we thought we would simplify matters by geting a big map and sticking it full of pins just like the big business men do. All went well until we came to New Jersey, where we were surprised to find the field archers scattered through 24 towns and cities. Some of these towns were a little hard to find on our map and so before we got more than half of the pins in place we had received over thirty new members from there. I am not sure, but I think we are losing ground and will have to call in reserves in this pin sticking campaign.

This New Jersey bunch held their first field tournament at Teanock, New Jersey, this past month, and for comparative beginners turned in some mighty fine scores. The tournament was won by Mr. W. H. Jackson of Newark, with a score of 212 for 28 targets. Second place went to Harry Podles of Irvington, with a score of 198; third to Wm. Sidden of Millington, whose score was 191.

The winning lady was Mrs. Dorothy Jackson of Newark, with a score of 125. Second and third places went to Mrs. Alfreda Hewitt of Englewood, and Mrs. R. Hait of Whippany.

NEWARK ROVERS SHOOT
(Continued from page 2)

being two classes for men and women:

Women's Instinctive—
1. Mrs. Kearns, Dayton.
2. Irene Lewis, Columbus.
3. Clara Kennedy, Newark.

Women's Sight—
1. Doris Schenk, Newark.
2. Beth McCoy, Columbus.
3. Millie Cozad, Columbus.

Men's Instinctive—
1. Clive Schneider, Columbus.
2. Harry Kuntz, Newark.
3. W. T. Burgess, Mt. Vernon.

Men's Sight—
1. Phil Cozad, Columbus.
2. Bob Hahn, Columbus.
3. E. D. McNabb, Columbus.

Juniors—One Class—
1. David Deithweilor, Finlay.
2. Douglass Bradburry, Chillocothe.
3. Don Schaller, Newark.

Prizes and trophies were awarded to the winners and those who had the (good or bad) luck to come in on the tail end of the scores.

Everyone seemed to have a good time and the committee is already laying plans for the fifth annual, to be held the first Sunday in October, 1942.

New Mexico Gets Fine Reserve

By Leon H. Mudgett, Albuquerque, New Mexico

The New Mexico Field Archers Association invites archers who would like to have an Art Young Big Game Pin to hunt in their state.

An area for archers has been opened in the Sandia Mountain refuge from Nov. 1 to 9, inclusive. This area has been closed to hunting for about thirty years; the deer are beginning to destroy the forest and some of them must be taken out. Being a recreational area for Albuquerque, a town of fifty thousand, these deer are accustomed to seeing people and are not very wild, in fact there are many which will come up to you for an apple or a head of lettuce.

The Forest Service estimates that there are two thousand deer in this refuge, which is roughly six by fifteen miles square. In this area almost any kind of hunting country may be found. Heavily timbered areas with glades, brushy sections or steep rocky canyons. There are many springs and one nice little stream. There are good camping places everywhere, but Albuquerque is only a few miles, and you can stay in a good hotel or camp ground and drive out each day for the hunt.

There will be three hundred permits issued to archers, allowing them one buck or one doe—either one, but not both. No firearms of any kind will be allowed, There is no cost for the permit, but you must have a big game license before the permit will be issued. The non-resident big game license is $25.25. Apply to State Game Warden, Santa Fe, New Mexico, for license and permit.

The minimum bow weight will be fifty pounds at your draw. The arrows must be barbless broadheads with a minimum width of one inch and a minimum length of one and one-half inches. Your first initial and name must be on each of your arrows. To do this, sand the varnish off where you want your name. Print your name with a pencil and varnish over.

You must check in and out of the hunting area. Checking stations will be conveniently located.

There are mountain sheep, bear and wild turkeys in this area, but they are protected and will not be included on your permit.

Here is a prediction. There will be more Art Young Big Game Pins awarded New Mexico archers for deer than will be awarded in any other state.

We hope to have one hundred New Mexico archers hunt this area.

BLUNTS FROM STUMP

(Continued from page 4)

on October 25 and 26. Don't miss this if you can possibly go.

The Montana Archery Association has added field archery to its activities. Mr. W. E. Korpi of 24 Granite Street, Butte, Montana, is the secretary. Field archers around Butte are building a field course and expect to shoot regularly, and also enter the NFAA monthly mail matches. They are active with their Legislature to secure advance seasons and reserves for bow hunting. The NFAA will render all possible advice and assistance in their efforts to secure better hunting conditions for their bowmen.

As a result of continuous publicity, we are constantly finding new archers in our city who did not know that there is an archery club in their community. Every club should have a club reporter whose job it is to publicize all club news. Get your local newspapers to publish reports and stories of your club activities. Have your local sporting goods dealers who handle archery tackle, tell interested people where your club is located, and where you can be contacted. Flint, Michigan, gets A.P. service on national archery news because local archers have demanded that their local papers carry it. You can do the same in your community. The NFAA is arranging for national publicity on field archery, but you won't get it, unless you request your local papers to carry national archery news through the Associated Press or other national news services. Archery is no longer a minor sport. Let us tell the world about it.

Letter Box

Rah! For Arizona!

Dear Davis:

Just a line to tell you that the Arizona archers are all rolling around this morning in a beastly state of insobriety. We are ordinarily sober enough at times but in this instance the shock was too much for us. Even Haywire Moore, of target fame, and a teetotaler was last seen full of coca cola and burping loudly.

All day yesterday I was with the State Game Commission in the hope that I could get an area set aside for archery hunting. After four hours of routine matter, my proposition was introduced. Imagine my surprise when the Game Warden himself read letters he had gotten from other states with regard to the matter and recommended that the bow be used here. With a Santy Claus look on their faces the commission members agreed with him and one of them suggested that they might as well open the whole state for hunting everything. "Whoops!" Let's turn 'em loose and let 'em get fun," says the other two. "Fine! It is so ordered." "Now, let's make this permanent, or until rescinded, so that we won't be bothered any more. Cosner has been here every meeting for ten years and I am tired of looking at that ignorant puss of his and that dumb hopeful look in his eyes." Unquote. "We agree emphatically," says the other two. I was too happy to get mad. Otherwise I might have tied a fist onto something and begun swinging it about.

As the matter stands we now have the following rulings:

All game birds and animals and all predators may be taken with bow and arrow. Migratory game may be taken subject to U. S. game rulings.

Archers may hunt in any legal area in the state.

The bow must be fifty pounds and the broadhead must be an inch in width. This applies to big game only.

Any arrow may be used for small game birds and animals.

All archers must have a special permit from the game warden, which is free.

Archers must have the usual hunting license in addition to the permit.

The game department cordially invites all out-of-state archers to come here and hunt at any time.

Arizona was the last state to come through and, believe me, we are happy. Now if we can keep our house clean we are ready to have fun.

A. J. Cosner,
Rt. 10, Box 1327,
Phoenix, Arizona.

(Editor's Note: In the last paragraph Joe says, "Fevenssake don't print this letter. It's awful. Literarily, it stinks," but as it tells the story more graphically than if we tried to make a "literary gem" of it, we are printing same *verboten*, or should we say *verbatim?*)

From New Zealand

Dunedin, New Zealand,
September 8, 1941.

Dear Mr. Davis:

Your kind action in sending Ye Sylvan Archer will always be remembered and appreciated, and I hope that the emergency conditions will not last much longer, and that we archers in N. Z. will be free to import archery gear and materials from the States, which in all sincerity we regard as the home of modern archery.

The Dunedin Archery Club has only been in existence for two years now, and the main interest is in target archery, but there is a small number who are beginning to realise that by using archery in hunting it is possible to have more thrill.

For my part, although archery in general first attracted me, yet it is the hunting and the design and manufacture of gear that has been the outcome of that first interest. I have hopes that we will eventually have an organisation similar to your NFAA, if not actually associated with that body.

In this country we are very limited in our supply of archery materials, and for the most part, have to rely on the imports of American hickory, Douglas fir and spruce—the latter at the equivalent of a dollar a foot. Of the timbers available locally we have hopes that Kowhai *(Edwardsia microphylla)* might prove satisfactory for bows, but as there are no stocks of the dry timber it is necessary to obtain it in the green state and wait the seasoning period. As for arrow woods, it is to be feared that none of our timbers will qualify for the target class but two of the beeches—the silver and the red—which seem to have the same characteristics as your northern birch have proved satisfactory for hunting shafts.

I understand Nick Ryan sent you a dowel of N. Z. kauri *(Agathis australis)* and one of white pine *(Podocarpus dacrydiodis)* which he then had hopes would prove satisfactory. Unfortunately this was not so — we often got better wood in American packing cases—and he is now using American spruce for his target shafts though he is getting them cut on a dowelling machine which tears the fibers rather excessively.

I had hoped to tell you of a hunting trip that I proposed to Ian McVinnie to try out the bow and arrow on wild pigs, but as you might care to hear of it in slightly longer form than time permits in this letter, I will write again soon.

There is one request I would really like to make and that is if you have a spare photo of yourself I would be very pleased if you could let me have it. Our only contact with you people can be by letter and so a photo makes a greater bond.

Ian tells me he forestalled me and sent a print of what my wife refers to as the Headless Horror, but what I affectionately term "Pic-a-bac, or Bringing Home the Bacon," which Ian and I believe to be the first pig in N. Z. to be shot with b & a.

Trusting I will hear from you again,
Sincerely yours,
Eric Strang.

Good Hunting "Down Under"

Oamaru, N. Z.,
August 27, 1941.
Dear Mr. Davis:

I was tickled pink to get your letter and the programme this morning, and wish to thank you for sending the Y.S.A. I really do look forward to getting them each month. The enclosed photos are all I have just now, and may not be just what you want, but in future I will keep anything interesting for you. I carry a camera with me on all my hunts and occasionally get something good. Wild pigs are the only big stuff killed in N. Z. with the bow and arrow, so far, but I have tried three times for wallabies without success; my luck was a bit bad. However, there are moose, wapiti, red deer, German grey deer, fallow deer, chamois, thar, wild goats, wild sheep, wild cattle, hares, opossum, and plenty of rabbits, to say nothing of game birds of many kinds, and big game fishing. So with any sort of luck, we Enzed's should be able to contribute a little of interest to Archery in the future.

Of course, the world affairs at the moment don't help very much, and I expect to be in Camp before very long. I may be able to pick up something interesting in my future travels abroad, but anyway any letters you care to send to the above address will always get me sooner or later, and no matter where I am it will be a pleasure to receive and answer them.

Our bows are all made from hickory, imported from the U.S.A. The staves are meant for making ski's and most of it is reddish in colour.

Les Rutherford is justly proud of wild pig killed with bow and arrow.

The bows follow the string badly, and the only way I can get decent results from mine is to leave it unstrung until the last minute before shooting. We have a timber here called Kowhai, pronounced go-high, that has possibilities. It grows very slowly, is close-grained, with a fairly decided difference between heart and sap. The general colour is yellowish grey heart-wood, yellow sap. I have shot from two of these bows, one made entirely from sap. The cast was very smooth, the bow only following the string slightly. The other bow had sap and heart but the owner tried to make a long bow from a flat bow stave, and then didn't worry about the grain—even so it is very superior to hickory—or the kind we get, anyway. I haven't been able to get any seasoned Kowhai as yet, but when I do I will send you a bow stave. By-the-way, the customs here told me it was O.K. to send or receive bow staves duty free, provided it wasn't in any way worked, otherwise the duty is about 80 per cent. For arrows I use Oregon Pine (Douglas Fir) which is imported from your country, but now we aren't allowed to buy it—builders only. We have a beech here that is good, but I won't send you any, as Eric Strang said he would, so I'll just make sure he does.

There are some beautiful big sharks about a hen's run from where I live and, Boy, wouldn't I like a crack at them. I shoot fish and eels with ordinary fish arrows, but I think the sharks wouldn't appreciate the joke if I used the small prongs on them. The Society for the Prevention of Cruelty to Animals are after me for shooting pigs with bow and arrow, and are making a fairly decent smell, too. I think I will be able to convince them that it is O.K. though, as I have Saxton Pope's "Hunting with the Bow and Arrow" to show them. The enclosed poem was in the Christchurch "Press." I hope you like it. If suitable for publishing in the "Archer" I don't think there is any law against doing so. It's about me, anyway, so I guess that makes it square.

This must be all for now, so thanking you again,

Yours sincerely,
Ian C. McVinnie.

TOXOPHILITE

By Whim-Wham

Whether the shooting of wild pigs with bows and arrows constitutes cruelty is being considered by the Sociey for the Prevention of Cruelty to Animals. . . . It has been alleged that hunting wild pigs with bows and arrows has taken place in North Otago.—News item.

I shot an arrow into the Air—
It struck the Wild Pig in his Lair.
Poor Beast! He would have thought it Fun
If I had used a Tommy-gun,
Or had he known — Ah, no such Luck—
The Luxury of being stuck!
Oh hapless Hog, ill-fated Swine,
What murderous Marksmanship was mine
That pierc'd you in a vital Part
With cruel anachronistic Dart!
These Fingers that the Bowstring drew,
To drive the fatal Arrow through,
More mercifully might have sped
A well-aimed Bullet through your Head.
The barbarous Scythian did not know
A handier weapon than the Bow,
He fought and slaughtered, none the less,
With some conspicuous Success;
The Parthian used it quite a Lot
When loosing off his famous Shot;
While British Bowmanship wrote Pages
Of History in the Middle Ages.
But those were crude and brutish Ways
Of Sport and Warfare! Better Days
Have tamed our Hunting Instinct, till
We're much more careful how we kill.
Yes, even Pigs deserve in Death
The latest Kind of latest Breath . . .
Oh spare the Wild Pig and his Farrow
The Horrors of the Bow and Arrow!

We have just received a letter, enclosing subscription to Ye Sylvan Archer, from E. Rivera de Hostos of Vega Alta, Puerto Rico. He says he became interested in archery when an archer from the States gave a demonstration at the San Juan Skeet and Gun Club. He immediately ordered an archery outfit and is now ready to practice. We are pleased that he selected Ye Sylvan Archer to keep him informed regarding archery events.

Fifth NFAA Tournament Report

By Karl E. Palmatier, Mail Tournament Secretary

	Actual 28 Target Score	Actual 28 Target Score	Actual 56 Target Score	Handicap Score
CLASS "A"—MEN				
Emery Watts, Los Angeles, Calif.	72-292	81-313	153-605	705
Jack Peters, Oakland, Calif.	67-249	74-280	141-529	629
Robert King, Los Angeles, Calif.	65-245	56-222	121-467	627
Phil Conrad, Long Beach, Calif.	92-342	79-307	171-649	619
Merle Hathaway, Los Angeles, Calif.	73-295	83-331	156-626	616
Perzy High, Los Angeles, Calif.	67-269	66-252	133-521	611
Harvey Franklin, San Ber'd'o, Cal.	56-208	57-213	113-421	611
C. W. Seastrom, West Hollywood, Cal.	54-212	53-203	107-415	595
Alfonso Gonzales, Bakersfield, Calif.	75-301	65-239	140-540	590
Elmer Bedwell, San Bernardino, Cal.	52-198	52-196	104-394	584
Delmer Pletcher, Bakersfield, Calif.	75-325	78-308	153-633	583
Jack Young, Oakland, Calif.	61-235	64-258	125-493	583
Fred Gadberry, Bakersfield, Calif.	78-282	66-256	144-538	568
S. Leo Sipe, Los Angeles, Calif.	40-146	48-182	88-328	558
George Calvert, Flint, Mich.	54-204	47-183	101-387	557
Kenneth Jones, Bakersfield, Calif.	57-221	77-305	134-526	556
Earl Grubbs, Los Angeles, Calif.	50-178	56-208	106-386	556
Leo Hoffmeyer, Flint, Mich.	48-178	53-193	101-371	551
Fred Bear, Detroit, Mich.	55-193	49-179	104-372	542
Charles Ratcliff, Highland Pk, Mich.	49-191	37-141	86-332	542
John Yount, Redlands, Calif.	57-215	46-174	103-389	539
Roy Hoff, Los Angeles, Calif.	49-183	49-179	98-362	482
E. J. Woodward, Redlands, Calif.	49-189	45-191	94-380	470
Leo Cornell, Oakland, Calif.	42-160	52-202	94-362	432
Kore Duryee, Seattle, Wash.	35-137	38-146	73-283	423
Bernie Ahman, Bryn Mawr, Calif.	37-133	35-131	72-264	414
Franklin Jones, Everett, Wash.	20-84	31-119	53-203	393
Willard Bacon, Redondo Beach, Calif.	76-298	79-321	155-619	
Joe Brooks, San Leandro, Calif.	45-167	53-189	98-356	
William Otto, Los Angeles, Calif.	45-171	45-183	90-354	
Bernard Granger, Flint, Mich.	48-188	43-165	91-353	
CLASS "A"—LADIES				
Ruth Hathaway, Los Angeles, Calif.	56-206	46-170	102-376	426
Minerva Gandy, Los Angeles, Calif.	33-121	40-150	73-271	401
Bessie Stephenson, Flint, Mich.	47-167	47-181	94-348	378
Freida Hoff, Los Angeles, Calif.	36-130	31-113	67-243	373
Lulu Stalker, Flint, Mich.	35-133	42-162	77-295	355
Ruth Davis, Bryn Mawr, Calif.	44-154	40-150	84-304	354
Marv Calvert, Flint, Mich.	44-160	35-135	79-295	345
Bertha Hoffmeyer, Flint, Mich.	44-150	36-130	80-280	340
Ina Woolnough, Trenton, Mich.	28-94	21-81	49-175	325
June Franklin, San Bernardino, Cal.	37-133	32-110	69-243	313
Gene Bacon, Redondo Beach, Calif.	63-221	48-176	111-397	307
Eva Bedwell, San Bernardino, Calif.	46-164	48-178	94-342	302
Margaret King, Redlands, Calif.	21-83	24-90	45-173	263
CORRECTION—				
Fourth Mail Tournament				
Mrs. C. J. Code, Crafton, Pa.	55-197	61-233	116-430	470
Ruth Hathaway, Los Angeles, Calif.	45-175	48-174	93-349	449
Lulu Stalker, Flint, Mich.	41-155	46-166	87-321	411
Eva Bedwell, San Bernardino, Cal.	56-222	53-197	109-419	399
Bessie M. Stephenson, Flint, Mich.	47-169	48-174	95-343	393

CLASS "B"—MEN

	28 Target Score	28 Target Score	Total
Albert Biordi, Los Angeles, Calif.	57-219	66-236	123-455
Carl Seastrom, West Hollywood, Cal.	50-194	52-186	102-380
Meryl Graham, Flint, Mich.	46-172	49-187	95-359
T. B. Chandler, Compton, Calif.	45-163	38-144	83-307
L. J. Markham, Durand, Mich.	38-140	39-149	77-289
Bennett Gandy, Los Angeles, Calif.	38-138	40-146	78-284
George Miles, Los Angeles, Calif.	36-130	39-145	75-275
Tracy Stalker, Flint, Mich.	36-140	37-131	73-271
Max Goldman, Ann Arbor, Mich.	34-124	40-146	74-270
Fred Brockhoff, Seattle, Wash.	34-122	38-140	72-262
S. F. Foster, Los Angeles, Calif.	32-112	37-141	69-253
LeRoy Stephenson, Flint, Mich.	34-126	29-117	63-243
Jimmy Ratcliff, Detroit, Mich.	34-124	32-116	66-240
Fred Brockway, Tacoma, Wash.	36-116	27-101	63-217
Angus Bruce, Redlands, Calif.	26-100	25-97	51-197
Bill Wallis, Seattle, Wash.	21-73	21-73	42-146
Bert Wallis, Seattle, Wash.	10-34	24-94	34-128
Harvey Strandwold, Shelton, Wash.	24-94		

CLASS "C"—MEN

S. L. Michael, Tacoma, Wash.	22-86	28-96	50-182
George Clark, Tacoma, Wash.	20-74	27-95	47-169
Harold Abig, Seattle, Wash.	18-66	21-79	39-145
William Irvin, Seattle, Wash.	19-69	12-38	31-107
Robert Schmid, Tacoma, Wash.	17-63	14-44	31-107
William Meiras, Tacoma, Wash.	21-85		
Ben Bredimus, Seattle, Wash.	11-41	7-29	18-70
George Ulleberg, Tacoma, Wash.	9-39		

CLASS "B"—LADIES

Irene Wierzbicki, Flint, Mich.	16-56	20-78	36-134
Blanche Wallis, Seattle, Wash.	3-9	12-42	15-51

CLASS "C" LADIES

Valeria Irvin, Seattle, Wash.	8-28	6-22	14-150

The following persons will be in Class "A" next time:

    Albert Biordi   Carl Seastrom   Meryl Graham

HANDICAPS FOR NEXT TOURNAMENT (MEN)

E. Turnock	-130	R. Berry	170	R. King	120
D. Pletcher	-60	E. Grubbs	170	D. Lumley	120
P. Conrad	-60	E. Bedwell	170	E. Woodward	100
R. Quayle	-40	J. Brooks	160	R. Hoover	90
M. Hathaway	-40	B. Ahman	160	L. Cornell	80
W. Bacon	-30	F. Bear	160	J. Young	70
M. Graham	220	H. Franklin	160	J. Scott	60
S. Sipe	220	W. Seastrom	150	P. High	60
C. Ratcliff	200	G. Calvert	150	J. Peters	60
F. Jones	200	J. Yount	150	A. Gonzales	40
C. Seastrom	200	K. Duryee	150	I. Stamps	40
E. Flesher	200	A. Biordi	150	E. Watts	30
B. Granger	190	R. Hoff	140	F. Gadberry	30
W. Horr	190	J. Murphy	140	K. Jones	30
L. Hoffmeyer	180	M. Spansel	130	P. Chambers	20
K. Moore	170	I. Davis	130		

HANDICAPS FOR NEXT TOURNAMENT (LADIES)

Mrs. Bacon -80	Margaret King 100	Babe Bitzenberger 50
Eva Bedwell -30	Minerva Gandy 100	Daisey Olsen 50
Mrs. Code -20	June Franklin 80	Ruth Davis 40
Ina Woolnough 160	Bertha Hoffmeyer 70	Mary Calvert 40
Frieda Hoff 110	Margaret Quayle 60	Ruth Hathaway 30
Kay Ratcliff 110	Lulu Stalker 60	Bessie Stephenson 20

Is Bert Wallis and Bert Wallace the same person?
Is Bill Wallis and Bill Wallace the same person?
Is William Otto and William Oho the same person?
Jack Peters—did you intend to inclose the target fees with the score cards?
To determine the national champions the actual scores are used. To qualify an archer must have competed in at least four tournaments while he was a paid up member of the NFAA. If an archer has shot in more than four tournaments the four highest scores will be used to figure the average. There will be tournaments for September, October, November, and December. You still have time to get in on the championship standing.
Pennsylvania — Ohio — Texas — Missouri — Oregon — Arizona — and Wisconsin — where are your score cards?

Sixth NFAA Tournament Report

By Karl E. Palmatier, Mail Tournament Secretary

CLASS "A"—MEN	Actual 28 Target Score	Actual 28 Target Score	Actual 56 Target Score	Handicap Score
Phil Conrad, Long Beach, Calif.	93-363	87-349	180-712	652
C. W. Seastrom, W. Hollywood, Calif.	62-258	64-238	126-496	646
S. Leo Sipe, Los Angeles, Calif.	52-196	59-229	111-425	645
Alfonso Gonzales, Bakersfield, Calif.	73-275	78-306	151-581	621
Fred Gadberry, Bakersfield, Calif.	68-281	76-290	144-571	601
Carl Seastrom, W. Hollywood, Calif.	52-184	58-214	110-398	598
Leo Hoffmeyer, Flint, Mich.	55-207	54-210	109-417	597
Kenneth Jones, Bakersfield, Calif.	70-260	76-302	146-562	592
Ken Moore, Los Angeles, Calif.	55-218	52-198	107-416	586
Fred Bear, Detroit, Mich.	57-209	50-204	107-413	573
Willard Bacon, Fontana, Calif.	72-282	84-318	156-600	570
Delmer Pletcher, Bakersfield, Calif.	82-329	78-298	160-627	567
Perzy High, Los Angeles, Calif.	63-241	71-265	134-506	566
Robert King, Los Angeles, Calif.	60-228	59-211	119-439	559
Emery Watts, Los Angeles, Calif.	74-260	69-268	143-528	558
Roy Hoff, Los Angeles, Calif.	58-218	48-192	106-410	550
Jim Murphy, Bakersfield, Calif.	61-221	51-189	112-410	550
John Scott, Detroit, Mich.	60-228	64-244	122-472	542
Earl Grubbs, Los Angeles, Calif.	48-178	49-177	97-355	525
E. Hill Turnock, Wilkensburg, Pa.	86-342	82-318	168-660	520
Irving Davis, Bryn Mawr, Calif.	53-203	48-186	101-389	519
Bernie Ahman, Bryn Mawr, Calif.	42-162	45-169	87-331	491
William Otto, Los Angeles, Calif.	45-157	51-189	96-346	486
M. E. Spansel, Berkeley, Calif.	49-183	44-168	93-351	481
Leo Cornell, Oakland, Calif.	41-147	49-195	90-342	422
E. J. Flesher, Pittsburgh, Pa.	27-103	30-106	57-209	409
John Yount, Redlands, Calif.	44-154	20-82	64-246	396
Jack Peters, Oakland, Calif.	40-142	51-171	91-313	373
Joe Brooks, San Leandro, Calif.	37-133	37-145	74-278	338
Tom Farnsworth, Albany, Calif.	62-244	63-233	125-477	
John Willard, Hollywood, Calif.	50-184	58-208	108-392	
Al Eggers, Ingraham, Pa.	41-155	52-190	93-345	

14   YE SYLVAN ARCHER   October, 1941

	28 Target Score	28 Target Score	56 Target Score	Handicap Score
CLASS "B"—MEN				
Bennett Gandy, Los Angeles, Calif.	55-211	50-184	105-395	
Fred Drake, Pittsburgh, Pa.	53-203	52-190	105-393	
Paul Ludwig, Los Angeles, Calif.	41-153	49-187	90-340	
William Smith, Flint, Mich.	41-147	48-182	89-329	
Tracy Stalker, Flint, Mich.	38-148	39-147	77-295	
Charles Frieburg, Etna, Pa.	35-127	43-155	78-282	
Wm. Scheffler, Bradford Woods, Pa.	40-138	28-108	68-246	
L. J. Markham, Durand, Mich.	39-139	31-105	70-244	
W. C. Woolnough, Trenton, Mich.	30-124	29-101	63-225	
Jimmy Ratcliff, Detroit, Mich.	29-105	25-97	54-202	
Karl Palmatier, Kalamazoo, Mich.	25-85	28-94	53-179	
J. B. Loop, Bellevue, Pa.	20-76	28-98	48-174	
CLASS "C"—MEN				
Kilbourne Anderson, Trenton, Mich.	39-139	31-115	70-254	
A. J. Michelson, Flint, Mich.	33-121	24-82	57-203	
CLASS "A"—LADIES				
Lulu Stalker, Flint, Mich.	46-162	43-163	89-325	385
Bessie Stephenson, Flint, Mich.	44-166	48-186	92-352	372
Eva Bedwell, San Bernardino, Calif.	52-188	59-213	111-401	371
Gene Bacon, Fontana, Calif.	57-229	52-198	109-427	347
Frieda Hoff, Los Angeles, Calif.	25-91	40-140	65-231	341
Bertha Hoffmeyer, Flint, Mich.	38-136	34-134	72-270	340
Mrs. C. Code, Crafton, Pa.	45-159	46-172	91-331	331
Ruth Davis, Bryn Mawr, Calif.	37-141	31-115	68-256	296
Margaret King, Redlands, Calif.	29-99	28-96	57-195	295
Minerva Gandy, Los Angeles, Calif.	28-96	21-79	49-175	275
Mercella Kuntz, Etna, Pa.	21-69	23-85	44-154	264
CLASS "B"—LADIES				
Jean Small, Trenton, Mich.	19-65	21-81	40-146	

HANDICAPS FOR THE NEXT TOURNAMENT

E. Turnock ....-120	J. Yount 160	P. Chambers 20
P. Conrad ....-100	J. Willard 130	K. Jones 10
D. Pletcher .... -60	A. Biordi 150	A. Gonzales 10
W. Bacon .... -40	K. Duryee 150	F. Gadberry 10
M. Hathaway .... -40	G. Calvert 150	Mrs. G. Bacon .... -80
R. Quayle .... -40	L. Hoffmeyer 150	Eva Bedwell .... -40
P. Ludwig 240	W. Otto 150	Mrs. C. Code ....
M. Graham 220	M. E. Spansel 140	Mercella Kuntz 170
E. J. Flesher 210	I. Davis 140	Ina Woolnough 160
W. Smith 210	K. Moore 140	Minerva Gandy ... 120
C. Ratcliff 200	F. Bear 140	Frieda Hoff 110
F. Jones 200	J. Murphy 130	Margaret King 110
F. Drake 200	R. Hoff 130	Kay Ratcliff 110
W. Horr 190	D. Lumley 120	June Franklin 80
B. Granger 190	R. King 120	Bertha Hoffmeyer 70
B. Gandy 190	W. Seastrom 110	Margaret Quayle .. 60
C. Seastrom 180	E. J. Woodward 100	Ruth Davis 50
A. Eggers 180	R. Hoover 90	Daisey Olsen 50
S. L. Sipe 170	L. Cornell 90	Babe Bitzenberger 50
E. Grubbs 170	J. Peters 80	Lulu Stalker 40
B. Ahman 170	Jack Yount 70	Mary Calvert 40
R. Berry 170	J. Scott 70	Ruth Hathaway 30
E. Bedwell 170	P. High 60	Bessie Stephenson 10
J. Brooks 170	I. Stamps 40	
H. Franklin 160	E. Watts 40	

Is Bert Wallis and Bert Wallace the same person? No report received.

The following need to shoot in one more tournament to qualify for the championship standing average. Try to get in at least one more score.

Franklin Jones	William Horr	E. J. Flesher	Meryl Graham
Wilard Bacon	Joe Brooks	William Otto	M. E. Spansel
Ken Moore	Robert Hoover	Irl Stamps	Kay Ratcliff
Joe Monroe	A. J. Michelson	Valeria Irvin	William Irvin
Charles Frieburg	William Scheffler	W. C. Woolnough	Bill Wallis
Fred Brockway	Fred Brockhoff	L. C. Stephenson	Irene Wierzbicki

OREGON POPE-YOUNG FIELD TOURNAMENT

The annual tournament of the Pope Young Field Archers of Oregon was held on the A-Bar-L ranch, Canyon City, September 18th and 19th. This is the first time an archery tournament has been held in Eastern Oregon, and it gave the many Eastern Oregon archers a chance to participate. Almost 60 archers registered with target fees.

Dr. Geo. A. Cathey of Portland, and Howard Dixon of Eugene, tied for first place. J. W. Cudd of Ontario was third and Van E. Robertson of Portland was fourth.

Miss Natalie Reichart, Professor of Physical Education, Oregon State College, won first in the Women's division, with Mrs. Mabel Tatro of Portland, and Ethel Davis of Corvallis, taking second and third. Norman Thompson of Corvallis won the junior division.

The mountain setting of the A-Bar-L ranch made the tournament very much a success and the archers intend to hold an informal shoot preceding the hunting season each year to get used to the altitude, atmosphere and natural hazards encountered in hunting.

CLASSIFIED ADVERTISING

RATES for Classified Advertising 5 cents per word per issue. Count initials and numbers as words. Minimum charge is 50 cents.

BOOKS AND MAGAZINES

The Flat Bow—70 pages of Archery information for 50 cents, well illustrated. Ye Sylvan Archer, 505 N. 11*th* St., *Corvallis, Oregon.*

GET YOUR SET NOW—26 beautiful and perfect Archery Stamps from 5 different countries for only $3.59. A Free one year subscription is given with each order. First 6 American Archer back issues for $1. The American Archer, national quarterly, at $1 per year. THE AMERICAN ARCHER, 521 5th Ave., New York City.

RELICS AND CURIOS

INDIAN RELICS, Beadwork, Coins, Curios, Books, Minerals, Weapons. Old West Photos. Catalog, 5c. Genuine African Bow, $3.75. Ancient flint arrowheads, perfect, 6c each—Indian Museum, Osborne, Kansas.

SUBSCRIBERS PLEASE NOTICE

A cross appearing in this space means that your subscription has expired and we would appreciate your prompt renewal so that your name may be kept on our mailing list.

Ye Sylvan Archer—$1.00 per year

Please mention Ye Sylvan Archer when writing advertisers.

---

70 pages of Archery information for 50 cents, well illustrated. Ye Sylvan Archer, 505 N. 11th St., Corvallis, Oregon.

PORT ORFORD CEDAR ARROW SHAFTS
(Cypressa Lawsonia)

Specials. P.O. Cedar Shafts, 1/4 to 11/32":

Parallel, per 100 .... $4.00
Tapered or barreled, 100 .. $4.50
Extra Select. Units segregated, per 100 .... $5.00
Douglas Fir, 100 .... $3.00, $3.50
Douglas Fir, Extra Select, per 100 .... $4.00

Full line finished tackle. Raw Materials. Write for price lists. Special rates to dealers and clubs.

PORT ORFORD ARCHERY SUPPLY CO.
C. F. Douglas, Mgr.
Box 137   Port Orford, Oregon

Paul H. Gordon
Author of "The New Archery"
Producing
Tackle — Materials
Latest and Finest for Field or Range
Write for Free Catalog
Beacon Hill Craftsmen
Beacon, N. Y.

Please mention Ye Sylvan Archer when writing advertisers.

HANDBOOK—How to Make and Use Bows and Arrows—90 Pages well illustrated (with catalog) 35c.

CATALOG—100 pictures—color spread—Instruction Folder. 10c.

CATALOG alone 5c. Stamps or Coin.

L·E·STEMMLER·QUEENS VILLAGE·N·Y·

E. BUD PIERSON
Bowyer — Fletcher
Tournament Tackle, Sinew, Glue, Raw Materials.
Custom Made Tackle
3109 Burnet Ave. — Cincinnati, Ohio

VIKING ARCHERY
1874 Market Street
San Francisco, Calif.

BROADHEAD ARROWS
Meeting the requirements for the Pope-Young Field Tournament. Chandler Universal Blades and Fiber Inset Nocks. *State weight of bow.*

Set of 8, for Men—
   28 inch $3.75
For Women—26 inch $3.50

V. D. McCauley
505 N. 11th   Corvallis, Ore.

Archery Raw Materials

WM. A. JOY

9708 So. Hoover Street
LOS ANGELES, CALIF.

HI THERE, FIELD ARCHERS—TAKE A LOOK AT THIS!
Write for full information

A special introductory offer. Complete set of 14 official "Arro-Mat" field targets and faces for only $29.75.

BEN PEARSON
INCORPORATED
Bows and Arrows of Excellence
PINE BLUFF, ARK.

This offer limited to full sets only. Your club can now enjoy the field round on official targets at a new low cost.

CHANDLER
Universal Broadheads

The Broadhead that costs less than a big rifle bullet, from 5c to 8-1/3c each. The inexpensive Broadhead for hunting.

Also Universal Broadhead Kits, with complete material for making one doz., good Broadhead Arrows.

Also Hunting, Fishing and roving Points.
FREE CATALOGUE
T. B. CHANDLER
11819 4th Ave., Compton, Calif.

B-80   B-1
FISH HEAD

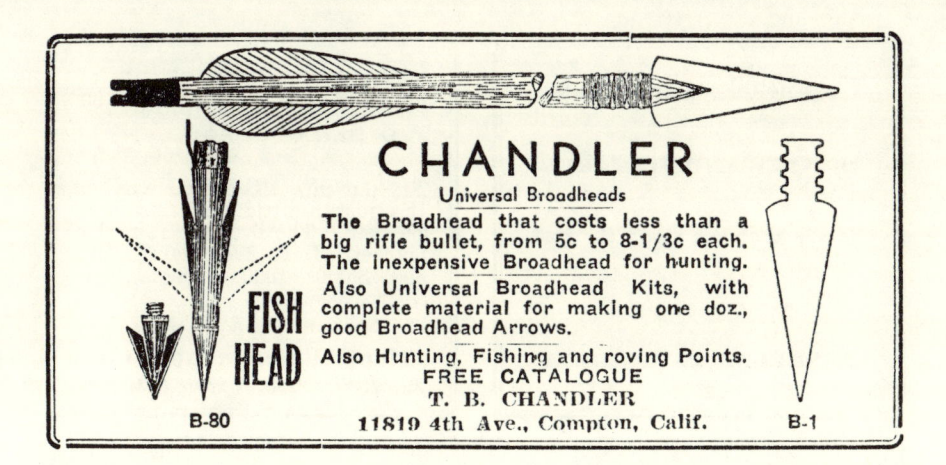

APPROVED NFAA FIELD TARGET FACES

Printed in black and white on heavy, double thickness corrugated board. In sets containing sizes necessary for a 14-target course and including extras of the smaller sizes that shoot out fastest.

$2.25 per set, f.o.b. Detroit — Order two sets for a 28-target course

BEAR ARCHERY CO.
2611 W. Philadelphia Ave., Detroit, Michigan

Ⓖ

"THE MARK OF DISTINCTION IN ARCHERY TACKLE"
Fine Yew Target and Hunting Bows, Plain or Backed with Rawhide. Lemonwood Bows with Rawhide Backs.
College and School Equipment
Target, Hunting and Roving Arrows
Price List on Request
Wholesale — Retail
EARL GRUBBS
5518 W. Adams
Los Angeles, : California

Arcadian Life Magazine
Stories of the Ozarks

Pioneer History - Folklore
Pastoral Living

$1.00 a Year; 25c a Copy

Display Adv. $1.50 per inch Classified, 3c a word. Three insertions for the price of two.

O. E. RAYBURN, Editor
Dept. 15

616 S. Benton St
Cape Girardeau, Mo.
P. O. Box 200
Caddo Gap, Arkansas

Please mention Ye Sylvan Archer when writing advertisers.

Ye Sylvan Archer—$1.00 per year

Cassius Hayward Styles

BOWYER AND FLETCHER

—Tackle that has stood the test—

28 Vicente Place

BERKELEY, CALIFORNIA

YEW WOOD STAVES
at .... $2.00 and $3.00
P. O. CEDAR SHAFTS
.... Doz., 40c; 100, $3.00
Try our new PLASTIC NOCK. It's just a little different and cheaper. The best nock on the market. Doz., 20c; 100, $1.50; 500, $5.00; 1000, $8.50. Five colors, 3 sizes.
Send money with order.

Monte Vista Archery Co.
Rt. 1, Box 149, Tacoma, Wash.

In Machine-Wound Targets

Every coil is pulled into place under a regulated tension adjusted to give maximum wear.

Allowance is made for additional wear toward center.

The natural resilience of the rye straw is retained and becomes a participating factor in the longer life of Saunders' targets.

Hand Stitched   Standard Quality

CHARLES SAUNDERS   3030 POLK STREET
                       CHICAGO, ILLINOIS

SWITCH TO KING-MOORE'S
NEW ROVING GLOVE!

KM-25—A professional type glove, not recommended for use with bows pulling under 40 pounds. Each $2.50
SPECIFICATIONS: Finger stalls are made of two thicknesses of leather, with top leather of genuine heavy cordovan. Between the outer and inner thicknesses, a durable turkey quill is inserted. This prevents deep string indentations and a sloppy release. With turkey quill finger stalls, a clean snap release is always assured—a most important consideration for maximum accuracy. An indispensable glove when heavy equipment is used. Glove custom made to your hand sketch, or dress glove size.

KM-22—Without quill, but with two thicknesses of leather $1.75
SEE YOUR DEALER — If he cannot supply you send remittance direct to

KING ★ MOORE
LEATHER GOODS COMPANY

7011 N. Figueroa St.
LOS ANGELES, CALIF.

Write today for **FREE CATALOG**

Ye Sylvan Archer

November, 1941

Vol. 13, No. 7

Ye Sylvan Archer

Official Publication of the National Field Archery Association

Vol. 13   November, 1941   No. 7

Published the fifteenth of each month
for archers by archers
505 North 11th Street, Corvallis, Oregon

J. E. DAVIS .... Editor

Subscription Price .... $1.00 Per Year
Foreign Subscription $1.25
Single Copies .... 10 Cents
Advertising Rates on Application

TABLE OF CONTENTS

                                                      Page

NAGLER SHOOTS THE BULL
   By Roy Case 1
BLUNTS FROM THE OLD STUMP 3
PSST! WHAT WAS THAT? 4
NEW WOOD TREATMENT 4
NFAA BULLETIN
   By John L. Yount 5
EDITORIAL 6
MAKING A BOW CASE
   By B. G. Thompson 6
FIELD ARCHERY IN MISSOURI
VALLEY
   By Emmet B. Johnson 7
7TH NFAA TOURNAMENT REPORT
   By Karl E. Palmatier 8
THE BOYS IN THE LOWER
BRACKETS
   By the Doghouse Editor 10
CALIFORNIA ARCHERS GIVE
DEMONSTRATION
   By Roy Hoff 11
WISCONSIN DEER SEASON
   By Roy Case 12

Nagler Shoots the Bull

By Roy Case, Racine, Wisconsin

Nagler got his Ontario moose on October 10, and made a beautifully placed shot to do it. Nag and I had flown from Kenova in to Unexpected Lake on October 7, so you see he didn't waste much time.

That morning, our old friend and guide, Alfred, and I headed west in one canoe while Nag and the Indian boy, Andy, headed for the mouth of the river. They were going fishing, they said!

Before we were a scant half-mile from the camp I got a shot at a cow moose with a blunt arrow. A miss, as she was watching us and ran when I pulled the blunt from the quiver. A moose will often stand, even if downwind, if there is no sudden motion to set him off. Some forty-five minutes or so later we were paddling around a small rocky, island-like point. No game there. We could look right across, for there were few trees and hardly any brush.

No game? A bull got up out of his sunny bed and stood gazing dumbly at us. Dumb? Yes, that's the word, but not too dumb if it is arrows you are shooting. Alfred silently swung the canoe toward him, for I'm left handed and he was on our left. He was facing almost directly toward us. No position for a bow shot. I rose from my seat in the canoe and *threw* up my bow. And that was my mistake. It should have been a slow, imperceptible movement, for he was off in a hurry and my arrow clattered on the rocks.

Then we made our second mistake. We landed to find the arrow and look around—and saw the bull dash off into the brush on the mainland, a bare seventy-five yards away. If we had only rounded the point and been ready, I should have had a second shot.

The arrow doesn't scare them much, for witness Nagler's experience. When we pushed toward camp that afternoon Nag was just landing, and his canoe was full of moose head, dressed out hind quarters, and two tired and bloody but happy hunters.

At about the same time I was missing my moose, Nag was having his fun. They heard the moose before they saw him; then at twenty-five yards there he was, facing them. It was a small head, and that darn fool Nagler decided to try for a picture instead of shooting, and reached for his camera. Andy nearly fainted as he hesitated, but felt better as Nag drew his bow and shot as the moose ran along the shore. A close miss at perhaps fifty yards.

The bull stopped back of some low bushes and a few silent strokes put the hunters into position for a broadside shot. Andy grabbed the bushes to steady the canoe. Nagler slowly rose, and took careful aim with the lower line of his half-inch adhesive tape sight. The arrow cleared the brush and landed in the ribs. Mr. Bull wheeled into the brush. The boys landed and quietly looked for blood, found it, and re-

Nagler and about 100 pounds of moose quarter

turned as quietly to the canoe. Andy thought he heard a death cough as they paddled silently across the river to land and hunt partridges, to keep their minds off what they hoped was transpiring in the brush not so far away.

An hour passed; they could wait no longer, and were soon on the trail again. More blood—a goodly trail—and there he was, a victim of man's first ballistic weapon!

Now the work began. Ontario law requires that two hind quarters of the animal be shipped with the trophy head. This is to prevent the waste of meat, so common to rifle trophy hunters. But Nag and Andy did a better job. The whole animal was skinned and dressed. Andy's stepfather from the island camp was happy to get the meat to dry for winter use and for his sled dogs. The arrow had punctured both lungs, and a solid hunk of clotted blood attested to the efficiency of a lung shot with an arrow. I paced the distance the bull ran before crashing at 113 paces.

The next day Nag saw another bull swim the river at about the same spot. Alfred and I were following, having hunted a bay on the way. Nag pulled into the weeds and waited for us. We pushed ahead, but Mr. Bull hadn't waited. This was the last moose we saw.

We made two side trips from the cabin, camping overnight, the four of us under my little two-man canoe tent. Wonderful nights, with the northern lights to watch as the fire died away and a horned owl gave his disturbing cry, more disturbing than the distant howl of a lone wolf!

The second trip was to bring us nearer the scene of a moose killing by Simon, Andy's stepfather, made the morning we landed on our lake. It was discovered that a bear was working on the remains. Nag made a blind, easy to reach from the canoe, and we visited it at dawn and late in the evening but the wind was always in favor of the bear. He had been there each time but was gone when we arrived. He carried the head away into the woods but we found it and took it back to the cabin, where the horns were removed and nailed over the door. The hide of Nagler's moose was nailed to the south side of the cabin. He stretched it so tight that the arrow slit rounded like a bullet hole. On the smooth logs of the inside back wall are scribbled the names of the bow hunters who have used the cabin, and the facts of the killing of the first moose. I suppose some fisherman or roving

(Continued on page 6)

Andy displays Nagler's trophy

Blunts from the Old Stump

We are writing this at our deer camp at Lake St. Helen, Michigan, where twenty-five Michigan and Ohio archers are located. From Ohio are Bill Folberth of Cleveland, Chuck Young of Newark, Dick Schroeder of Rocky River, Howdy Harding of Cleveland, Fred Schrenk of Newark, Ole Oelschlager of Cleveland, and Clarence Jones of Cleveland. Detroit archers here are Fred Bear, Nels Gumley, Leo Lange, Frank and Gordon Ash, Carl Strang, Barney Grenier, Mr. and Mrs. W. J. McIntyre, Mr. and Mrs. Sherril Richey, Mr. and Mrs. Fred Leach. From Flint are Mr. and Mrs. Tracy Stalker, Mr. and Mrs. Geo. Calvert, C. N. MacGillivray, Russell De Forest, A. J. Michelson; and Fred Kibbe of Coldwater, Max Goldman of Ann Arbor. From St. Helen are Lester Lawn, Bert Jones, Evert Jones, Ed Baker, Dell Bader and Carl Beers.

Most of the archers at St. Helens have had some shooting. To date (November 6) two bucks have been hung up. Lester Lawn shot the first one, a hundred-twenty-five pound spike horn. Ole Oelschlager shot a hundred-fifty pound, seven point buck. Lawn's buck was hit forward through the lungs and it traveled about forty yards. Ole's was shot through the liver and went about 400 yards. Two more bucks were hit tonight by Nels Gumley and Tracy Stalker which we hope to recover in the morning. This is a good average for our bowmen, when you consider that the average is one buck to 100 archers. First buck in Michigan was shot by Pat Smith of Rochester, a six point, 175-pounder. Fred Wesendorf of Saginaw, Michigan, shot a 200-pound black bear. It looks like Michigan bowmen are going to have a banner hunting season.

Don't feel too badly if you miss your running shots. A running buck, going places, is a pretty hard target to hit. One of our foremost field archers and also one of the leading national target shots missed a running buck at 12 and 22 yards respectively. The importance of sharp broadheads was demonstrated on Les Lawn's shot. On a hurried shot he drew an arrow from his quiver that had been shot into sand. He used a 65-pound bow that ordinarily would have shot an arrow clear through the buck. The dull arrow went through the ribs and lungs and stopped in the ribs on the other side. Keep your broadheads sharp!

We haven't the results on the Wisconsin hunt. Fred Bear of Detroit, shot a 180-pound six point buck near Manitowish. Nelson Hoffman of Painsville, Ohio, shot his first buck in Wisconsin this season, although he had previously shot two black bear with the bow. We have reports of two other bucks shot in Wisconsin, but we do not have the totals.

We take off our hats to Wausaukee, Wisconsin, for planning a wonderful reception for the hunting archers. The archers were to arrive on a special Pullman car. Three hundred townspeople met the train; the high school band was on hand; the judge, state representative, division conservation officer and other prominent citizens were there with speeches of welcome. When the train stopped one lone archer got off—Fred Kibbe of Coldwater, Michigan. The publicity man had made all the arrangements except contacting the archers. Wausaukee was disappointed, but decided to go ahead with the celebration, anyway. Fred Kibbe led the parade—band, townspeople, and all—to the reception dinner. Welcome speeches were given as scheduled and everyone had a good time. Kibbe was king for a day. We regret the crossed wires, but extend the archers' thanks to Wausaukee for the fine intentions. Next time we hope we can get together.

The Michigan legislature played "in again, out again, Finnegan" with the non-resident bow license fee. At the last minute, the legislature gave immediate effect to the $5.00 non-resident license fee. The attorney-general said it wasn't legal, but the Conservation Commission said, "Oh, yeah?" and put it into effect. Sorry we couldn't get word out in time to all non-resident archers. But get all set for the deer hunt next year in Michigan and Wisconsin. The non-resident fee will be $5.00 in each state.

There is nothing like practice on the NFAA field round to get you in shape to really connect with that buck next year. Don't forget your NFAA membership, if you want the Art Young Big Game award.

We have some new members for the "Buck Missers Club." You can't belong unless you miss a standing shot at less than thirty yards.

We have an interesting letter from Damon Howatt of Yakima, Washington, on his deer hunt. He also mentions that he has shot some 200 rabbits with the bow. He states that he finds the best points for rabbits to be a half inch concave disc soldered to a short length of brass tubing for a ferrule. He says, "When a rabbit is shot with this point, he stays put, and no fooling."

Henry I. Collignon, Bert Jorgensen, Ralph Pagent and Clay Woods of Chicago, Illinois, hunted the early part of October at Clam Lake in Ashland county, Wisconsin. They didn't connect but had some shooting and a swell time. Bill Duncan, Dr. Baldwin, Geo. Nichols, Luke Marble, Bill Labersky, and Mrs. Labersky hunted deer at Fishtrap, Wisconsin.

Who said there were no field archers in Ohio? On October 5, at a roving meet at Newark, they had a turnout of 135. At Columbus on October 19, 160 field archers shot. On October 26 at Dayton, 341 attended. You are all invited into Michigan and Wisconsin next year to try your luck on deer.

On October 26, the California Field Tournament was shot at Fresno, California. Eighty-three archers from all over the state attended— over 60 drove 200 miles each way. This shows real enthusiasm for field archery. Remarkable scores were recorded on a field course brand new to all participating. Conrad, shooting instinctively, shot a 711. Second score was 691. At least six shot over 600. This is remarkable shooting, and shows that instinctive shooting can be developed to a high degree of accuracy by good shooting technique.

Congratulations to Forrest Nagler on that 1200 pound moose he bagged in Canada. We ought to have a good story for Ye Sylvan Archer on that one.

The first week of our hunt is over, with another week left. Chuck Young is going to give us a story of the hunt in Ye Sylvan Archer. It will be interesting and entertaining, we assure you.

Psst! What Was That?

We were siting around the fire at the deer camp after a long hard day in the woods. Major issues were being brought up by this archer or that, and being settled by everybody until we came to that much-discussed, never-settled question: "We went today where the bucks were yesterday, but where were they today?" A stalemate was declared and then one of the top-flights spoke up:

"I had a peculiar experience today," he said, and we all hung on his words. "I was walking along a few rods north of the refuge when I heard a most unusual sound. It wasn't a cry—it wasn't a chirp—it wasn't a squeak—it was rather a combination of all these with a dash of the eerie thrown in. I stopped. It seemed to be at my left and just in front of me. I eased over that way. It stopped. I waited several minutes. Absolute silence. I gave it up and went back to my hunting. Again I heard it— this time slightly more piercing and insistent! It seemed behind me—close behind—practically on the ground at my left. I stopped short and turned quickly around! . . . . You know, I never did find out what that darn noise was!"   —Anonymous.

New Wood Treatment

"In the newest miracle at the Laboratory, ordinary wood is soaked in a solution of urea, an inexpensive chemical. It is then heated to 212 degrees. Thereupon the wood can be bent, twisted, compressed, and molded. When it is again bone-dry and thoroughly cooled, it is as strong as mild steel." This is how the beefwood is treated that is placed on the tips of flight arrows. It also accounts for the footing being so small and still able to stand the shock.

— K. E. Palmatier.

The annual dinner and election of the Pittsburgh Archery Club was held October 25.

NFAA Bulletin

OFFICERS

President—A. J. Michelson
  610 F. P. Flint Bldg., Flint, Mich.

Vice-President—Paris B. Stockdale,
  Geology Dept., OSU, Columbus, Ohio.

Secretary-Treasurer—John L. Yount,
  Box 383, Redlands, California.

EXECUTIVE COMMITTEE

Western—H. C. MacQuarrie,
  3400 Fruitvale Ave., Oakland, Calif.

Mid-Western—Fred Bear,
  2611 W. Philadelphia, Detroit, Mich.

Eastern—T. C. Davidson,
  53 Mountain Ave., Springfield, N. J.

By John L. Yount

Will all you NFAA members please have a look at your membership cards and make sure that you are still in good standing. In a new organization such as ours there is so much for a secretary to do besides the routine secretarial duties that we sometimes get quite a ways behind. That "we" isn't just a figure of speech, for if the wife didn't take over the treasurer's job I don't know just how far behind I would be. Even so, we are behind in our delinquent notices, so you will be doing yourself and your association a service by giving your membership card a little study and then acting accordingly. Thank you.

* * * *

A Field Archery Handbook

A book that would give you carefully gathered, authentic information on practically every subject of interest to a field archer — don't you wish you had such a book? Well, you can and will have it, for the executive committee of the NFAA has decided that with your help we shall compile and print just such a book. We expect to complete the job shortly after the first of the year.

To make certain that this book is complete we are asking you for suggestions. Is there information that you would like that is not covered in the departments listed below, or have you any ideas about the makeup of any of these departments?

The following are the principal subjects to be covered in this book: Constitution, by-laws; rules for roving, archery golf, battle clout, and other field games; detailed information on laying out courses; tournament procedure; "Big Game Award" rules; award winners, mail tournament winners, and the championship standings for '41; hunting laws of all states and Canada, as they affect archery; recommended tackle for different kinds of game; and shooting technique written by the year's leading field shots. We also expect to have our program for '42 ready by then and include it; also the locations and dates of as many major tournaments as possible, and the names and addresses of the state association officers of the states sponsoring them. We have asked for this latter information before, and the response has been not too gratifying. Now that we have a deadline to make, won't you please rush the information along.

* * * *

Applications for **Big Game Awards** have been received from the follow-
(Continued on **page 6**)

Editorial

Forrest Nagler suggests that, "as most of the antagonism to bow and arrow hunting is sponsored by the S.P.C.A., might it not be well to advocate, in the pages of our magazines, the desirability of having some well-informed archer contact the officials of that society in each community and give them the real facts of the case? I do not know whether it would be a hopeless task, but if we could show that our objectives are the same and that we should not have inflicted on our conservation efforts the stigma that they place on trapping, rifle hunting and killing in general, perhaps we would not be under as great pressure from them as we have been in the past."

A very good suggestion, and one that should be considered by each individual archery club.

Apparently Fred Kibbe's first edition of his book, "What I Know About Deer Hunting," proved so popular that he was forced to publish a second edition, for the new and up-to-date 1941-42 edition is off the press. It will, we believe, be sent free to those who write for it. Mr. Kibbe's address is Coldwater, Michigan. A worthwhile companion volume to Kibbe's masterpiece would be a tome by George Brommers on "What I Know About Coon Hunting."

We are informed that Elmer Bedwell, who has served so efficiently as secretary of the Field Archers Association of Southern California, has resigned. However, the job is still in excellent hands in the election of Mrs. Dorothy Ahman of Bryn Mawr, California, to whom correspondence regarding the association should be directed.

Nagler Shoots the Bull
(Continued from page 2)

hunter, finding the cabin and reading our message, will look at that rounded hole in the hide and say, "An arrow? Oh, yuh!"

But I know how it was done—just six years of planning and trying. I'll do it myself, maybe, for I've still three years to go.

A headline, "Bowman Bags 1200 Pound Elk," attracted our eager attention, but our interest lagged when we read on — "Floyd Bowman of the Oakville community brought home a huge elk from Eastern Oregon."

J. B. Hollingsworth of the Bellingham (Washington) Archery Club, which name was selected instead of "Quiver Club," as previously stated, writes us that the club has a field course nearly completed. Several of the members of the club have been deer hunting.

Making a Bow Case
By B. G. Thompson

A cheap, substantial, water-resisting bow case is made from a pasteboard tube which comes in each roll of linoleum. Your furniture dealer will probably give you one.

These tubes are approximately four and one-half inches in diameter and six feet long. The tube is covered with ordinary friction tape. Two of Mr. Woolworth's twenty cent rolls are sufficient to cover a tube. A coffee can, also covered with the friction tape, makes a good cover. The bottom is cut from a soft piece of pine and nailed in before the tube is covered with the tape.

A half-inch leather strap is riveted to the side of the tube, run through a guide on the end of the cover and into a buckle riveted on the opposite side of the tube.

Such a case is strong, light in weight, and will hold four or five bows.

NFAA Bulletin
(Continued from page 5)

ing. They will receive their awards just as soon as the committee has checked the applications.

Fred Bear, Detroit, Mich.—Buck.
Forrest Nagler, Toronto, Canada—Moose.
Joe Cosner, Phoenix, Ariz.—Javalina.
Tom Imler Jr., Phoenix, Ariz.—Javalina.
L. G. Vergana, Albuquerque, N. M.—Bear.
Ronald Power, Waterloo, Iowa—Buck.
Jerry W. Hill, Boise, Idaho—Buck.

Field Archery in Missouri Valley

By Emmet B. Johnson

It wasn't a large crowd and it wasn't the weather that made the First Annual St. Louis Open Field Tourney a success on October 25-26. The fact that it was the first all-field shoot in this section of the country, plus the fact that everything was run off so smoothly, plus a lot of good fellowship and sportsmanship, made it an outstanding first effort to bring field archery to the fore in this area.

Fifty archers attended the two day shoot; the majority were local archers in the St. Louis vicinity. We were a bit disappointed in the poor out-of-state attendance, but that didn't in any way dampen the grand time everyone had.

The tourney started off at 2 P.M. on Saturday with a Turkey Shoot, originated to take the same place as the wand shoot in targets. Twelve arrows were shot at eighty yards and twelve at sixty. The targets were life-size painted turkeys. Hits on the turkeys scored one point. Ben Johnson of St. Louis won the event with nine hits. Jim Cooper of North Vernon, Indiana, was tied, with eight hits, with John Ellet of St. Louis. In the shoot-off, Cooper scored five hits out of six arrows at sixty yards, to Ellet's two.

At 3 P.M. we had the Art Young round. Two sets of targets were set up to speed up the shooting. This event was won by Les Shaffer of St. Louis, with nineteen hits out of 36. Jim Cooper again tied with Dick Hughes of Evansville, Indiana, with sixteen hits each. In the shoot-off, Cooper had two hits to Hughes' one.

The final event for Saturday was the Running Deer. This was a life-sized outline of a young buck, suspended and pulled on a cable over a thirty yard course. Each archer had two rounds of as many arrows as he could loose during the running. The fast shots got off as many as four arrows before the deer stopped. Vital hits scored five, semi-vital hits scored three, and just flesh wounds scored one. Jim Cooper and Don Seal, both of North Vernon, Indiana, tied for first with 28 points. Mrs. Edna Peters of St. Louis, was third with 27 points. In the shoot-off, Cooper again won, with 8 points to Seal's 5.

The Running Deer concluded Saturday's shooting, but the big event of the tourney and the thing that most archers will remember was the big bonfire and Bar-B-Q and song fest held on the picnic grounds of Forest Park. After a delicious rib barbeque, the archers and friends gave forth in song for hours, gathered around a huge open bonfire. Singing at times was even good, and at all times it was loud. Enough field archers brought guitars, fiddles and banjos to give the singing plenty of rhythm. Roy McQuitty was number one fiddler, with Mr. and Mrs. Bill Hunter, Earl Hoyt, Pete Peters, and Lee Fox coming in on the downbeat. The party broke up as the fire burned low and everyone retired with dreams of the NFAA round to be shot on Sunday.

The double NFAA round was shot on Sunday over a tricky course. The morning round saw a high sidewind that gave all archers trouble on the long shots. Natural hazards of trees and brush gave everyone trouble on the short shots. On the results of the morning shooting, all archers were classified into A, B and C. Beginning at one that afternoon the archers and the weather started to perform. Despite the constant drizzle and intermittent showers, all archers finished, very wet and weary. You might say, not a feather was standing.

The last event was the Clay Bird shoot, six arrows at twenty yards at clay pigeons swinging through a four-foot arc. Earl Hoyt came through with two dead pigeons to take the event.

At the conclusion of this final event the trophies were awarded. A mounted gold turkey was the main award for the Turkey Shoot. A standing bear was awarded for the Art Young round. A porcelain mounted deer was awarded for the
(Continued on page 9)

7th NFAA Tournament Report

By Karl E. Palmatier, Mail Tournament Secretary

CLASS "A"—MEN

	Actual 28 Target Score	Actual 28 Target Score	Actual 56 Target Score	Handicap Score
Robert King, Los Angeles, Calif.	73-271	70-279	143-550	670
William Otto, Los Angeles, Calif.	56-218	67-255	123-473	623
Emery Watts, Los Angeles, Calif.	76-294	73-283	149-577	617
M. E. Spansel, Berkeley, Calif.	68-262	53-203	121-465	605
Phil Conrad, Long Beach, Calif.	88-356	89-347	177-703	603
Perzy High, Los Angeles, Calif.	72-277	62-254	134-531	591
S. Leo Sipe, Los Angeles, Calif.	52-188	59-219	111-407	577
Delmer Pletcher, Bakersfield, Calif.	77-293	83-346	165-639	570
Don Lumley, San Diego, Calif.	56-212	64-238	120-450	570
Carl Seastrom, W. Hollywood, Calif.	52-194	51-195	103-389	569
Joe Brooks, San Leandro, Calif.	56-209	50-180	106-389	559
Ken Moore, Los Angeles, Calif.	52-300	59-215	111-415	555
Merle Hathaway, Los Angeles, Calif.	74-287	75-293	149-580	540
Russell Berry, San Diego, Calif.	52-206	43-161	95-367	537
Bennett Gandy, Los Angeles, Calif.	43-161	50-186	93-347	537
John Yount, Redlands, Calif.	50-186	52-190	102-376	536
Alfonso Gonzales, Bakersfield, Calif.	62-240	77-275	139-515	525
C. W. Seastrom, W. Hollywood, Calif.	54-202	56-212	110-414	524
E. J. Woodward, Redlands, Calif.	53-199	53-197	106-396	496
Fred Gadberry, Bakersfield, Calif.	56-208	72-276	128-484	494
Kenneth Jones, Bakersfield, Calif.	71-246	64-226	135-472	482
Jack Peters, Oakland, Calif.	52-194	56-212	108-402	482
Trueman Farnsworth, Albany, Calif.	73-289	74-277	147-566	
Tom Farnsworth, Albany, Calif.	65-249	74-284	139-533	
John Willard, Hollywood, Calif.	53-187			
H. H. Miller, San Diego, Calif.	42-156	48-168	90-324	

CLASS "B"—MEN

W. C. Woolnough, Trenton, Mich.	42-158	37-135	79-293	
Tracy Stalker, Flint, Mich.	45-159	34-128	79-287	
Harry Eckels, , Calif.	43-167	30-112	73-279	
Gene Holston, San Diego, Calif.	26-92	31-121	57-213	
Jimmy Ratcliff, Detroit, Mich.	28-98	30-108	58-206	

CLASS "A"—LADIES

Ruth Hathaway, Los Angeles, Calif.	55-189	61-217	116-406	436
Margaret King, Redlands, Calif.	37-137	39-143	76-280	390
Minerva Gandy, Los Angeles, Calif.	37-137	35-123	72-260	380
Ina Woolnough, Trenton, Calif.	26-90	26-90	52-180	340
Ruth Davis, Bryn Mawr, Calif.	29-109	40-136	69-245	295

The secretary reported that the second score for J. Willard would be sent in as soon as he could get it.

HANDICAPS FOR NEXT TOURNAMENT (MEN)

E. Turnock	-60	E. Bedwell	170	W. Otto	110
P. Conrad	-110	B. Ahman	170	M. Spansel	110
D. Pletcher	-60	R. Berry	170	D. Lumley	110
W. Bacon	-40	C. Seastrom	170	E. Woodward	110
R. Quayle	-40	H. Franklin	160	R. Hoover	90
T. Farnsworth	-40	J. Brooks	160	L. Cornell	90
M. Hathaway	-30	J. Yount	160	J. Peters	90
P. Ludwig	240	S. Sipe	160	J. Young	70
M. Graham	220	L. Hoffmeyer	150	J. Scott	70
E. Flesher	210	G. Calvert	150	R. King	60
W. Smith	210	K. Duryee	150	P. High	40
C. Ratcliff	200	A. Biordi	150	I. Stamps	40

F. Jones 200	K. Moore 140	F. Gadberry 40
F. Drake 200	I. Davis 140	T. Farnsworth 40
B. Gandy 200	F. Bear 140	P. Chambers 20
W. Horr 190	R. Hoff 130	K. Jones 20
B. Granger 190	J. Murphy 130	A. Gonzales 20
A. Eggers 180	C. W. Seastrom 130	E. Watts 10
E. Grubbs 170	J. Willard 130	

HANDICAPS FOR NEXT TOURNAMENT (LADIES)

Gene Bacon .... -80	Kay Ratcliff 110	Daisey Olsen 50
Eva Bedwell .... -40	Minerva Gandy 90	B. Bitzenberger 50
Ruth Hathaway .... -10	June Franklin 80	Mary Calvert 40
Mrs. Code 0	Margaret King 80	Lulu Stalker 40
Mercella Kuntz 170	B. Hoffmeyer 70	B. Stephenson 10
Ina Woolnough 150	Ruth Davis 60	
Frieda Hoff 110	M. Quayle 60	

FIELD ARCHERY IN MISSOURI VALLEY

(Continued from page 7)

Running Deer. A mounted pigeon was awarded for the Clay Bird shoot.

The NFAA awards were beautiful Indian archers and mounted deer horns for Class A. Class B and C awards were polished fox horns.

The winners of NFAA awards were as follows:

	Morning Round	Afternoon Round	Double Round
CLASS "A"—MEN			
First — Ben Johnson	43-173	49-197	92-370
Second — Earl Hoyt Jr.	50-188	50-178	100-366
Third — Don Seal	41-153	51-187	92-340
CLASS "B"—MEN			
First — John Ellet	36-132	37-145	73-277
Second — Dick Hughes	36-122	36-128	72-250
Third — R. L. Freer	25-85	38-146	63-231
CLASS "C"—MEN			
First — Harry Weber	20-68	28-96	48-164
Second — Roy McQuitty	21-75	23-83	44-158
Third — Frank Fox	16-56	25-87	41-143
CLASS "A"—LADIES			
First — Elsie Johnson	24-84	23-87	47-171
Second — Ruth Pierson	20-78	22-84	42-162
Third — Clara Hoyt	18-66	16-56	34-122
CLASS "B"—LADIES			
First — Marjorie McQuitty	9-35	22-78	31-113
Second — Edna Peters	12-40	19-71	31-111
Third — Edna Taylor	17-63	12-44	29-107
CLASS "C" LADIES			
First — Mrs. Billy Sparks	8-30	9-33	17-63
Second — Kay Schrick	5-15	11-41	16-56
Third — Ruth Hanstein	3-11	3-13	6-25
JUNIORS			
First — Rudy Lusch	23-81	27-105	50-186
Second — Jimmy McQuitty	20-78	30-100	50-178
Third — Gilbert Meir	15-51	24-90	29-141

The above scores are far from tops, but considering this was the first time the double NFAA round has been shot in actual competition, and considering the bad wind and rain, we feel we are under way to a good start for 1942. Next year's tourney will probably be held a lot earlier in the season to give the Michigan and Wisconsin field archers a chance to come down without conflicting with their hunting season. Reserve a weekend during the last of September or first of October, 1942, for the second St. Louis Open Field Tourney.

We're going to plan a bigger and better tourney for you in '42.

The Boys in the Lower Brackets

By the Doghouse Editor

This great organization saw its birth at Yermo, California, in the summer of 1935. All of you have read the official accounts by Mr. Gardner; how he, Erle, strove mightily, but finally met defeat at the hands of Sasha Siemel, who shot an even lower score than did the defeated champion.

All this is history, and official history, at that. Who is to doubt Erle's account, released through Ye Sylvan Archer? Sasha Siemel was the new Basement Champion, and Sasha Siemel was unanimously elected the new president. Red ribbons, the insignia of the Lower Brackets, sprouted all over the country, and at our tournaments the underdog came into his own.

The official and determining round took place in the afternoon, and the results were more or less as given—mostly less. Of course, you wouldn't expect a fiction writer to be too literal. Nothing was said about the warming up round in the forenoon. There the defending champion more than held his ground and demonstrated once more the great powers that had made him undisputed holder of all low-down records.

It all started because Erle, "Kid Erle, the Ventura Underweight," to use his ring name, insisted on defending his title as the rottenest archer in the universe, instead of allowing it to go by default. The Lord knows he held it long enough, and most of the time by sufferance. Also, the title covered quite a lot of territory, and in this case it led to international complications.

It was not to be expected that Bigfoot Sasha, the Pride of Matto Grosso, should have allowed Kid Erle to get away with it forever. Sasha, too, has a reputation. His technique is to aim an arrow at a cat's heart in order to hit it on the nose. It works splendidly, the cat loses its naturally sweet and lovable disposition, and Sasha gets in some dirty work with a spear. Or he aims at a tiger's head and hits its tail, with about the same laudable results.

So when the Kid begins to paw the earth and bellow forth his challenge to all and sundry, what can Sasha do? He challenges the champion, and the bout is on. But first comes the practice match.

A target is set up and Walt Wilhelm is selected for referee. Having known the champ for some time, he drives his car between the defender and himself. Cautiously Walt peers over the top.

"You can't beat six misses out of six shots," instructs Walt. "That's a perfect score." He blows his whistle. The champ steps up and unlimbers.

The first arrow was a fair miss by eight yards. Just about what Erle had expected, and he feels all his old-time confidence. He will show these young upstarts something. He does.

The second arrow is even better—it misses by eleven yards and four inches. Unfortunately, John Yount hasn't realized the power of the champion and looks kind of doubtful when he finds a flat tire on his car resulting from the shot.

The third arrow takes the hat off Ken Wilhelm. Well, Erle will pay for a new hat—Ken knows that—but he isn't too sure just how far the champ would go towards paying for a new conk in case the arrow had struck lower. There wasn't a heck of a lot of trade-in value in the old conk, and well Ken knows it.

The fourth one is a common or garden miss without any trimmings, but the fifth one is something to remember, because Erle is getting tired of conventional shooting and aims his arrow straight up in the air and lets go. It lands in one of Walt's eastside pants pockets.

Fair enough, you say, and a fine catch. Walt won't agree with you.

He will be an upright man and eat his meals standing for weeks to come. Ken takes his brother's place as referee, but you can see that his heart isn't in it.

Erle offers to shoot the fifth arrow over, but both Ken and Sasha enter a prompt waiver. Let sleeping dogs lie and shot arrows stand.

Sasha and the referee get behind the champion for the sixth and final loose. They shouldn't have, and they know it now, because while the arrow flew harmlessly enough through a window in Ken's garage, the bow leaves the champ's hands about the same time and flies over backward. One end of it draws blood from Ken's smeller and the other end twists around to give Sasha a rabbit punch in the neck.

"Madre de Mil Diablos," yells Sasha, giving the Portuguese equivalent to our "hell's bells." "I will have to shoot you in the afternoon, but truly, Senhor, you are magnificent. You are so rotten you are good, if I may be allowed to say so."

Erle feels flattered, as well he may. Domestic fame has been his for a long time, but here is foreign recognition, and by a brother craftsman.

"Thank you, Senhor Big-foot," he replies and extends his hand. "When you and I go tiger hunting you will find me right by your side."

A thoughtful look comes into Sasha's face—Erle will be a real protection in the jungle, but just to whom he can't quite make out. And then a slow diplomat's smile breaks out over the Tiger-man's map.

"You are far too valuable, Senhor Kid," he insists, "to waste your talents on the purely mechanical art of cat killing. You carry the camera and write the story."

And what a story that will be, when and if —

CALIFORNIA ARCHERS GIVE DEMONSTRATION
By Roy Hoff

Last month a group of archers from Southern California staged an archery demonstration at Rock Creek, California. The event was held in this mountain resort to promote interest in the sport and to better acquaint sportsmen with the capabilities of the bow and arrow as a hunting weapon.

Tiny Munson, a lad of some 326 pounds, opened the program with a comedy number. After being appropriately introduced by the master of ceremonies, Tiny stepped on to the stage with his head high and his chest out, and took careful aim at a balloon some 15 inches in diameter and 25 yards distant. The first shot was a clean miss, as were the second and third shots. After each miss Tiny was prompted to move a little closer to the target. To eliminate any possibility of further misses, Merle Hathaway came to the rescue, holding a huge funnel in front of the balloon. The fourth shot, being guided by the funnel, finally broke the balloon.

In defense of Tiny's reputation as an archer, it must be explained that all the misses had been prearranged to get the audience in the right frame of mind.

"This exhibition," to quote the announcer, "is non-professional, the intent of which is not to show individual brilliancy by shooting buttons off of somebody's vest, but that the bow and arrow is within the physical capacity of everyone, and that a good degree of accuracy can be attained by all."

The next number consisted of five men shooting alternately at 5-inch balloons at 20 yards.

Number 3 on the program was the same as number 2, only with a different set of five men. The best record in these events was by Phil Conrad, with six consecutive broken balloons.

Number 4 was a 5-position match, with Phil Conrad and Emery Watts shooting five arrows at 3-inch black dots, one arrow in each position, standing, kneeling, sitting, prone and lying on their backs.

The rest of the program was devoted to shooting at playing card aces, arranged four to a row per man, and shooting blunts through a pine board. A deer silhouette was shot at from forty yards.

The high light of the program was when a .30-.30 rifle was fired into a sack of sand and then a few broadheads. For the benefit of the audience, the sack was brought up for inspection. The broadheads had penetrated completely through the sack, while the rifle bullets were retrieved with approximately four inches penetration.

About one hundred people attended the event, and from the generous applause, it would seem that it was a success.

Wisconsin Deer Season
By Roy Case, Racine, Wisconsin

The Wisconsin bow and arrow season for deer closed November 2. The official reports are not in yet but I hear that there were about 2000 permits issued to hunt with the bow and some 17 bucks were killed. Of these 17 bucks, 6 were killed by non-resident hunters who took advantage of our $5.00 non-resident bow and arrow license. It seems that the out-of-staters kinda wiped up the Wisconsin boys.

Fred Bear of Detroit was one of the lucky ones. Fred hunted up in my neck of the woods, but I was in Canada at the time. I found a note from him in my cabin woodshed when I got up there some weeks later. The note was written on a Bear Archery catalogue. The Wisconsin boys say Fred is a damn good shot and knows a bit about what to do when hunting deer with the bow besides advertising Bear tackle.

Fred's buck was one of the several "paid for" by the Wisconsin Bowhunters Association. Fred has also received the "Bow-hunters' gold pin." Be it known that the Wisconsin Bowhunters Association agrees to pay $10.00 to the owners of any land upon which a legal bow and arrow buck is killed by a member of the WBH. The effect upon posting and the general attitude toward the bowhunter is already noticeable. As the news gets around about the $10.00 handouts we look for even more satisfactory results. It behooves the bow and arrow hunter to become a member of the association for without the card or button some land owners won't let you hunt. Membership is only one dollar. A diamond is added to a member's gold pin when he kills his second legal buck. Howard Thrapp, our secretary-treasurer for '41, got his second buck this season and is the first and only Wisconsin bowhunter to have this honor, and he now sports his diamond pin. Howard did a wonderful job as secretary-treasurer. We wanted him to carry on for another year, but he reluctantly begged off.

The annual meeting was scheduled for a week before the season started but was actually held a week after the season, November 8-9, at the Dell View Hotel near Wisconsin Dells. Roy Luhman was re-elected president and Keith Hill, 1342 Porter Ave., Beloit, was elected secretary-treasurer. Howard Thrapp was voted a life membership to show our appreciation for his fine work as secretary-treasurer. The board of governors was increased from 5 to 6 and Larry Whiffen chosen as the additional member.

Sunday morning the members in hunting regalia shot at the writer's bounding buck, Oscar. Oscar was pulled at about 20 m.p.h. behind my car and didn't suffer as many wounds as one might suppose. Dick Wilke, who got his buck in 1940, was the winner. Dick and I each hit it 2 out of 3 times. In the shoot-off, Dick made a fine shot close to the heart and I missed. Keith Hill won the hunting tackle flight shoot. Otto Wilke was the star tin can buster when we tried out Erickson's "Target Tosser." We hardly got started on this, however, when we had to quit for the big feed.

HE'S YOURS WITH A BEN PEARSON BROADHEAD

Port Orford Cedar Broadhead Arrows — Matched within 15 grains. No great variation in spine. Plastic nocks. 5 1-2 in. hunting feathers. Choice of 3 sizes. Spined to match bow, any length. Dozen $6.00

Port Orford Cedar Blunts and Roving Arrows—Same fletching and specifications as broadheads. Blunt steel points or parallel steel pyles. Dozen $4.50 Birch at same prices.

SEE YOUR DEALER TODAY
or write for
Free Illustrated Catalogue

BEN PEARSON
INCORPORATED
PINE BLUFF ARKANSAS

PINE BLUFF, ARK.

GET YOUR SET NOW—26 beautiful and perfect Archery Stamps from 5 different countries for only $3.59. A Free one year subscription is given with each order. First 6 American Archer back issues for $1. The American Archer, national quarterly, at $1 per year. THE AMERICAN ARCHER, 521 5th Ave., New York City.

A cross appearing in this space means that your subscription has expired and we would appreciate your prompt renewal so that your name may be kept on our mailing list.

E. BUD PIERSON
Bowyer — Fletcher
Tournament Tackle, Sinew, Glue, Raw Materials.
Custom Made Tackle
3109 Burnet Ave. — Cincinnati, Ohio

PORT ORFORD CEDAR ARROW SHAFTS
(Cypressa Lawsonia)

Specials. P.O. Cedar Shafts, 1/4 to 11/32":
Parallel, per 100 .... $4.00
Tapered or barreled, 100 .. $4.50
Extra Select. Units segregated, per 100 .... $5.00
Douglas Fir, 100 .... $3.00, $3.50
Douglas Fir, Extra Select, per 100 .... $4.00

Full line finished tackle. Raw Materials. Write for price lists. Special rates to dealers and clubs.

PORT ORFORD ARCHERY SUPPLY CO.
C. F. Douglas, Mgr.
Box 137   Port Orford, Oregon

Cassius Hayward Styles

BOWYER AND FLETCHER

—Tackle that has stood the test—

28 Vicente Place

BERKELEY, CALIFORNIA

Paul H. Gordon
Author of "The New Archery"
Producing
Tackle — Materials
Latest and Finest for Field or Range
Write for Free Catalog
Beacon Hill Craftsmen
Beacon, N. Y.

YEW WOOD STAVES
at .... $2.00 and $3.00
P. O. CEDAR SHAFTS
.... Doz., 40c; 100, $3.00

Try our new PLASTIC NOCK. It's just a little different and cheaper. The best nock on the market. Doz., 20c; 100, $1.50; 500, $5.00; 1000, $8.50. Five colors, 3 sizes.
Send money with order.
Monte Vista Archery Co.
Rt. 1, Box 149, Tacoma, Wash.

KING ★ MOORE
LEATHER GOODS COMPANY

7011 N. Figueroa St.
LOS ANGELES, CALIF.

Write today for **FREE CATALOG**

CHANDLER
Universal Broadheads

The Broadhead that costs less than a big rifle bullet, from 5c to 8-1/3c each. The inexpensive Broadhead for hunting.

Also Universal Broadhead Kits, with complete material for making one doz., good Broadhead Arrows.

FISH HEAD Also Hunting, Fishing and roving Points.
FREE CATALOGUE
T. B. CHANDLER
11819 4th Ave., Compton, Calif.

B-80   B-1

APPROVED NFAA FIELD TARGET FACES

Printed in black and white on heavy, double thickness corrugated board. In sets containing sizes necessary for a 14-target course and including extras of the smaller sizes that shoot out fastest.

$2.25 per set, f.o.b. Detroit — Order two sets for a 28-target course

BEAR ARCHERY CO.
2611 W. Philadelphia Ave., Detroit, Michigan

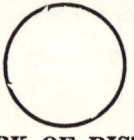

"THE MARK OF DISTINCTION IN ARCHERY TACKLE"
Fine Yew Target and Hunting Bows, Plain or Backed with Rawhide. Lemonwood Bows with Rawhide Backs.
College and School Equipment
Target, Hunting and Roving Arrows
Price List on Request
Wholesale — Retail
EARL GRUBBS
5518 W. Adams
Los Angeles, : California

The Flat Bow—70 pages of Archery information for 50 cents, well illustrated. Ye Sylvan Archer, 505 N. 11th St., Corvallis, Oregon.

VIKING ARCHERY
1874 Market Street
San Francisco, Calif.

HANDBOOK—How to Make and Use Bows and Arrows—90 Pages well illustrated (with catalog) 35c.
CATALOG—100 pictures—color spread—Instruction Folder. 10c.
CATALOG alone 5c. Stamps or Coin.
L. E. STEMMLER · QUEENS VILLAGE · N·Y·

Please mention Ye Sylvan Archer when writing advertisers.

Ye Sylvan Archer

Christmas Greetings

December, 1941   Vol. 13, No. 8

Ye Sylvan Archer

Official Publication of the National Field Archery Association

Vol. 13   December, 1941   No. 8

Published the fifteenth of each month
for archers by archers
505 North 11th Street, Corvallis, Oregon

J. E. DAVIS .... Editor

Subscription Price .... $1.00 Per Year
Foreign Subscription $1.25
Single Copies .... 10 Cents
Advertising Rates on Application

TABLE OF CONTENTS

	Page
OHIO ARCHER GOES DEER HUNTING By C. B. "Chuck" Young	1
BLUNTS FROM THE OLD STUMP By the President	5
CAN'T GET 'EM IF YOU CAN'T SEE 'EM By Roy Hoff	7
EDITORIAL	8
NFAA BULLETIN By John Yount	9
DEFENSE STAMPS AS PRIZES	9
CALIFORNIA FIELD TOURNAMENT By Peter C. Ting	10
8TH NFAA TOURNAMENT REPORT By Karl E. Palmatier	12
SOUTHERN CALIFORNIA TOURNAMENT By Roy Hoff	14

Ohio Archer Goes Deer Hunting

By C. B. "Chuck" Young, Newark, Ohio

During the course of this hunt I write about, "Mike" Michelson, President of the National Field Archery Assn., asked me to write an account of the hunt. Now Mike has agreed to accept any responsibility for anything that may arise from this article. And so anyone who has any kicks to render, write Mike—don't jump me.

On the 4th of July at the Midwestern tournament at Cincinnati, Ohio, I received an invitation from Fred Bear to hunt deer in Michigan with him and his party.

I wasn't sure at the time, because I could hunt my buck in Pennsylvania for 15 bucks, against Michigan's 25. But Fred said he would make up the difference in the good time I would have, and so I finally told him that I would appear on the date and at the place he specified.

Two weeks previous to the time I was supposed to be there the State of Michigan generously reduced the nonresident archers' bow and arrow license fee to 5 bucks. I sent in my 5 and received license number 2.

Fred wrote and said to meet the party at the St. Helen's Club, St. Helen, Michigan, on Friday, October 31, so that I would be all set for the opening day, November 1.

Well, that took care of everything, except for the fact that my tackle wasn't ready. Now I make my own tackle and that is the last thing I ever get ready. On Friday afternoon on the day I was supposed to arrive in St. Helen, I finished my arrows. At 7:45 I left Newark, Ohio, with 400 and some odd miles to go. I arrived at St. Helen's Club (after getting lost about a half dozen times on the way up) about 5:00 a.m. the morning of the first, just in time for breakfast. I was met by a bunch of archers who were all pepped up to be out on a runway somewhere before daylight.

That old "Siwash," Bill Folberth, was there and he wanted to know how long it was going to take me to get my clothes changed and ready to travel. Well, I wolfed down some breakfast, grabbed a bag from my car that I had packed my hunting clothes in, registered, and found that I had been assigned to room 1, with Carl Oelschleger from Cleveland, for a roommate.

Carl was generous enough to wait a total of 5 minutes while I changed clothes. I found I had packed my hunting socks in another bag which I had left in the car, and had to wait till I got to the hunting grounds to finish dressing.

Carl and I went in my car. I was pilot; Carl, the navigator. When he said turn, I turned. We finally got to the picked spot and I finished my dressing. Folberth, Harding and Schroder from Cleveland, and Jones and Schenk from Newark, who had come up the day before, along with Oelschleger, made up the party that I hunted with the first day.

They told me where to go and what to do. I don't think that they intended to run me into the swamp that first day, as they weren't any more familiar with the country than I was. But I did get into it and got wet up to my ——. Felt kind of bad about it, but before I got back home I had become used to it, as this wasn't the first time I had been wet that far up. And part of the time I believe it was with malice aforethought that I was sent into some of those swamps.

Hunted all day that day, only seeing a few tails. Came in that night and finished meeting the gang. I won't attempt to tell all who were there, as there were about twenty-five there over the first weekend.

I didn't want to admit that 36 hours without any sleep meant anything to me, so sat around in the lobby and spread some of that barnyard stuff with some of the gang. Finally, that dashing, debonair archer and tackle maker of Coldwater, Michigan, Mr. Fred Kibbe, self-styled "World's foremost conservationist," came in and invited me to come with him to the beer garden. Still keeping up that he-man disguise, I accepted, and I guess it was around 2 a.m. that they put me to bed. I didn't know anything, much, from some time before that until about four the next afternoon — one day's hunting lost.

Monday I got back to hunting. Was awakened at 5 a.m. by that cry of "Daylight in the swamp." They did have it well timed, for by rushing dressing and eating breakfast, and then driving about ten miles, you arrived at your hunting grounds at daylight.

Monday's hunting brought little or no results until Carl and I decided to see whether we couldn't find some better location than the one we were in.

We took a ride in the car, hunting for runways and found many deer on our drive. It was along late in the afternoon and deer were coming out of the swamps to feed. Saw in round numbers perhaps 30 deer that evening, and found what we thought was a better location.

We headed back for the clubhouse, Carl, as before, doing the navigating. We came to a place that I thought we should turn, but Carl said, "No." So, like a good pilot should, who doesn't argue with his navigator, I kept straight on. Boy, oh, boy! What a navigator! The road he directed me on was under construction and sometimes the front end was ahead, and sometimes the rear of the car was in front. No chance to stop and turn around, and as it had rained for three days, that just wasn't a road any more. We finally made it and arrived at the clubhouse after driving some 15 extra miles.

On Tuesday morning, Ole and I pulled up at a spot that we had previously agreed upon. He took one side of the road, and I the other. We were supposed to meet back at the car at 10 a.m., for we were to make a drive in the afternoon.

I took off up through the woods and working straight back from the road, I intended on making a circle that would bring me back at the car on time. About 9:30, after seeing a few tails, I flushed a nice rack of horns. Didn't get a shot at it, though—about 60 yards through the brush. I decided to head straight back for the car, as it was about time I was arriving there. I laid my course by the compass and started, running head first into a swamp, a bog and a few other things. Finally found a fence and followed it out to a road, not the one the car was on, but another. And after about two miles of walking, arrived back at the spot at 1 p.m. Carl was ready to shoot me. We started for the clubhouse and met the gang going out for the drive, turned around and went with them.

They assigned me to one end of the drive because I had on rubber hunting boots. Told me to work down along the edge of the swamp until I came to the lake, and then work along the edge of the lake until I met the rest of the gang. I believe this was one of the occasions that they tried to get rid of me, for all I needed to follow the directions given me was a bathing suit and a canoe.

Arriving at the spot where we were supposed to meet, I met one archer, Barney Grenier, who had traveled the same kind of a course I had. We moved out on dry land, drained our boots, and went back where we had left our cars.

The rest of the gang were conspicuous by their absence. Did find Bill Folberth there, who told us the drive was over. It had netted one buck, which had evaded the arrows of Fred Bear, Carl Strang, and Carl Oelschleger. After trying to lose Folberth and Grenier, and deciding I was lost myself, thought I had better call it a day.

Got back to the clubhouse and cleaned up a little. As it was rather early I thought that maybe by taking the camera out in the car I might be able to get some pictures of deer. I gathered up my camera and started out. On the way through the lobby I discovered Lester Lawn, of the local St. Helen's Archery Club, busily engaged in reading the funny section of a Sunday paper. He told me that Kibbe had left that afternoon for home, and he had decided to rest up. After much coaxing I persuaded him to come with me, after he had cast one last longing look at the funnies. He got his bow and arrow and we departed.

I had the camera strapped around my neck and was all set to take pictures. After driving quite a distance without seeing anything, we spotted one up ahead, which proved to be a buck with a nice set of horns. Gone was all of Lester's reluctance for hunting. Out of the car he piled, with his bow and a couple of arrows. I was to drive on down the road with the car, which was supposed to hold the deer's attention, while he slipped up on it. As I passed the deer I saw he was paying no attention to me but was watching Les. I stopped the car behind some bushes, untangled myself from my camera, got the bow from the back of the car, strung it up and grabbed some arrows. Just started to slip around from behind the bush between me and the deer when Les let out a war whoop. He had discovered that the deer was watching him and had let drive at 140 yards, sticking his arrow into the back of the buck.

After a couple of jumps the deer got rid of the arrow, which, when we found it, had blood up the shaft about two inches. The arrow must have struck a rib high up. Lester's broadheads were duller than a hoe, as he had been shooting them into a sandbank that afternoon, and hadn't sharpened them.

We loaded back into the car and started on. We decided on coming back the next morning and look for the deer, although Les didn't believe he was fatally injured. We didn't find him the next day, so hope he recovered.

I gathered up my camera again and we started on. We saw another buck ahead but he left the country in a hurry, allowing no shots, either with camera or bow. We saw still another one ahead but didn't get a shot at him, either. I had an awful time trying to get untangled from the camera and getting my bow when we saw bucks, as we hadn't expected to see bucks so close to the road—usually does, but no bucks.

We drove along a way and I spotted another one off to the side of the road about 20 yards. Stopped the car to get a good look and decided that it wasn't a legal buck. Started to drive on when I happened to remember I had started out to take pictures. We backed up, starting to get out the camera, when Les decided it was a legal deer, and piled out of the car. He let drive with an arrow from the road, striking the buck high in the lung, and it only traveled about 40 yards before it dropped.

Les rough dressed it, and we found there was no place on my car to lay it, and neither of us had anything to use for tying it on, so we laid it across the hood with its belly toward the windshield. Each of us grabbed a leg—and that is how we brought in first blood for the group. It was a short spike, but over the required three inches.

The gang all congratulated Les on his kill. He has been shooting less than a year. By the way, the St. Helen's Archery Club has seven members from a population of seventy. I know a lot of clubs which would be glad to have ten per cent of the population in their archery clubs.

Tuesday night I got into a poker game with Russ Carter, who manages the club. Nelson Grumley, bow maker for Fred Bear, also played for a short while, contributing along with me; and last, but not least, Leo Lane, attorney from Detroit. I have seen a lot of the present day comedians, but never have I seen his equal. It was all I could do to stay on my chair during that poker game. The other three divided up the dollars and dimes that Fred and I lost between us.

Leo is also an expert at camouflage. He and Bill Folberth combined their talents and came forth with a new traveling blind. You cut two evergreen trees. Tie one on the top and one on the bottom of your bow—then cut a little hole to shoot through and there you have it. They guarantee that anyone can walk up on a buck, to within 5 yards without him ever getting suspicious. They excepted Fred Kibbe, as Leo says he makes too much noise anywhere. Leo also parted with this bit of advice: "Don't lead a deer running broadside to you. Let the son-of-a-gun find his own way!"

Leo also made a good driver when we drove for deer. He could take care of the same amount of space as two ordinary men, and if allowed to roll could take care of as much as three. He drove three deer past me on one of the drives, but he picked the wrong kind of deer; they didn't have horns.

On Wednesday, Oelschleger got a 7-point buck. He was hunting with Harding and Schroder at the time (the "Dick" Schroder who designed the NFAA emblem). Dick had become disgusted with the runway he had been watching and asked "Ole" to trade with him. At 7 a.m. "Ole" shot his buck off Dick's runway. (Was Dick's face red!)

Harding also pulled a good one. He was hunting down in one of the swamps when he heard something growl. He left right now! Someone else started down into the place he was just vacating and he told them not to go in there as there was a bear in there. We all had a good laugh that night as the gang told it on him. But after some of the shooting I did later, I think that from now on I am going to leave, too, when I hear something growl at me.

On Wednesday evening I had one of my two good shots, a snap shot at 50 yards went over his short ribs about six inches. I felt pretty good, for any time I come close it is good shooting for me. Les and I were hunting bear after Tuesday, as he already had his buck. He took me through all the swamps in that locality, I believe. We didn't find any trace of bear, although some of the boys claimed they had found tracks on Saturday and Sunday, following quite a snow we had Friday night.

On Friday evening, Kibbe came back and brought his wife. Marie Bear and Mrs. Grumley also came in with a lot of other archers who came in for a weekend's hunting, since they hunt on Sunday in Michigan.

Kibbe left special word that he was to be called on Saturday morning, as he wanted to go out with the gang. He had regained his hunting enthusiasm after sticking a blue-crested arrow into a buck's antlers down in another county while he had been gone from us—thereby almost losing his title of the world's foremost conservationist. Kibbe retired early, and awakened upon hearing a commotion out in the hall. He got out of bed and opened his door to see what was going on. He found two archers in the hall, dressed ready for the woods. Fred wanted to know what was going on and they told him it was time to pile out. He went back and dressed, and going downstairs, found the place in darkness, with the clock showing that it was 2 a.m. He was discovered, and is now being accused of watching a runway in the middle of the night. The two archers who had disturbed Kibbe were just getting in from town.

On Saturday, Max Goldwin, who shoots good scores on the field round in Michigan, was having quite a heated argument on the merits of light and heavy hunting arrows. It was finally decided to have a practical illustration, using Lester's deer for the purpose. Max stood 10 yards from where the deer was hanging, and shooting the light arrow, missed two shots. He then moved up to 20 feet, where the first arrow shaved the deer's belly and the second one sank in, projecting out the opposite side of the deer about 4 inches. He took a heavy arrow, shooting it from the same bow, and buried it to the feathers. Both arrows struck the deer in practically the same spot, neither one touching a bone; thereby proving that he can shoot a heavy arrow better than a light one, or something like that.

Max now wants the Michigan conservation department to paint targets on all bucks for next year so that he will have something to shoot at (that he can hit). Maybe Max really had an excuse for poor shooting, because just before coming hunting his wife presented him with a new boy. I have forgotten the weight, but Max says it is a new archer.

Saturday afternoon I hunted by myself, and didn't see anything until I started back for the clubhouse in the evening. I came upon a big doe standing in the middle of the road, not seeming to want me to get past. I rummaged around in the back seat of the car, hunting the camera. I finally came up with it just as she walked off the road. No picture.

Driving down the road about 100 yards I saw a nice rack of horns, standing not so far off the road.

Boy! This is my chance! I had planned to leave Saturday night for home, and this would just make it right—getting big buck just before leaving. I could see the head of this one hanging on the wall at home. It really was a pretty sight.

The buck was contentedly grazing, not paying any attention to me. I stopped the car, leaving it right in the middle of the road, took the bow and one arrow and started to stalk him. There were a few small poplars between me and him. I picked out a nice aisle and waited for him to cross it, which he did at about 40 yards. I got down on one knee, took great

(Continued on page 13)

Blunts from the Old Stump

By the President

America is at war! Many of our field archers are in active service. Many others soon will be. Others are engaged in home defense work. The war will affect all of us, but we will all do our full part to win the war. There is no need to urge field archers to do their full share. We will do all in our humble power to serve our country. What of archery during the present emergency? There should be no let-down in archery—if anything it should and will be more active than ever before. During times of stress and high nervous tension the need for good, wholesome recreation increases. When you return from your office or shop tired and worn out, with nerves on edge, what recreation offers a better opportunity for an outlet of stored up nervous energy and stimulating sluggish blood than archery? Archery gives you an opportunity to stretch your muscles, expand your lungs, and divert your thoughts from world troubles. Archery must and will play its wartime part in providing much needed relaxation and recreation. Let's keep the ball a-rolling. Soldiers in training camps need recreation. The NFAA and NAA are now investigating the possibilities of introducing archery into the recreation programs of training camps. An effort is being made to provide funds for this purpose through the USO and other camp recreational organizations. If archery can be introduced into the recreational facilities of army camps, there will be a need for supervision and instruction by local archery associations. Will archery associations near army camps volunteer their services for these purposes? Please write the Secretary.

Field archers in the service are still keeping up their NFAA memberships. Arthur Jones of Albuquerque, stationed at Camp Claiborne, Louisiana, sent in his membership renewal with this comment, "I find it inconvenient to practice my archery here in the army, but with the added inducement of 'Ye Sylvan Archer' I belive it will pay me to keep up my membership. The copies of the magazine which I have read have been very interesting." If you are in the service, or expect to be, we know that you will want to keep up your contact with your fellow archers.

The NFAA is compiling and will publish shortly after the first of the year the first authoritative American book on field archery. It will be pocket size, about 100 pages long, and will contain the following subjects:

I. Aims and Aspirations of the NFAA—by A. J. Michelson, President.

2. Constitution and By-Laws of the NFAA.

3. Rules for tournament play on all field games sponsored by NFAA.

4. The Art Young Big Game Award, and regulations governing the award—by Dr. Paul Klopsteg.

5. Compilation of the game laws of all the States, as well as the Provinces of Canada, regulating bow and arrow hunting.

6. Field champions of 1941 and winners of the monthly NFAA mail shoots, with scores.

7. Big game award winners of 1941, with short descriptive data on the hunts.

8. How to lay out a field course.

9. How to conduct a field tournament.

10. Article on the playing of archery-golf.

11 The technique of field shooting, by one of the leading field archers of America.

12. Field and Hunting Tackle—by Forrest Nagler.

13. Hints on Big Game Hunting with the Bow—by one of the foremost American big game hunters.

14. How to organize a field club, with model constitutions.

15. The National Field Archery Association Program for 1942.

16. The NAA—by H. S. C. Cummings.

17. Why all field archers should belong to the NFAA—by the President.

18. The book will contain many cuts of field courses, leading field archers, big game hunts, etc.

This year book will be a ready reference manual for the expert as well as the novice. If the response from advertisers is satisfactory, we expect to distribute them free of charge or at a nominal cost to our members. All field archers should send in their memberships at once, in order to be sure to get this book. Archery tackle manufacturers and dealers can secure advertising rates from the Secretary.

Applications for the Art Young Big Game Award are pouring in. Jerry Hill of Boise, Idaho, shot a big three-year old, two-point buck at 40 yards. The arrow passed through both hips. The buck traveled about 300 yards. Jerry writes, "We were hunting in a veritable archer's paradise. Deer were very plentiful and not at all wary. During six days of hunting, we saw not less than 100 deer, loosed, I should say, 50 arrows at deer at ranges varying from 30 yards to 125 yards. We hit five deer, killing three." His hunting companion, Carroll Smith, shot a 250-pound buck with 13 points.

Dr. L. G. Vergara of Albuquerque, New Mexico, shot a two-year-old brown bear in Chama County, New Mexico. One arrow from an 80-pound bow at 40 yards did the trick. Dr. Vergara says, "As a physician and surgeon, it is my conviction that bows and arrows do a better and more humane killing than bullets, provided the archer has enough experience so as to convey the maximum destructive power in his arrows. Wild snap shots without sense of direction are out of the question. Pope and Young were accurate shooters—the foundation of their success."

Ontario archers didn't do so badly during this past season. We have all heard of Nagler's moose. Now we hear from A. Wyttenbach and R. J. Mitchele of Toronto, Canada. With one arrow apiece, Mitchele bagged a seven-point buck and Wyttenbach downed a ten-pointer. Wyttenbach also writes, "We have made considerable progress in archery since I wrote to you last. At a recent Field Archery tournament, we started an organization called 'Hunting and Field Archers of Ontario,' and succeeded in signing up twenty-six members on the first day. The intention is to embrace all the archers in the Province of Ontario that are not now affiliated with any organization or club." The officers elected are: Honorary President, Forrest Nagler; President, Arnold Wyttenbach; Vice-President, K. W. Bash; Secretary-Treasurer, R. J. Mitchele; and a Field Committee of six members, four men and two ladies, and a Hunting Committee of four members were also elected."

Ken Glackin, Roy Hilton, Ronald Power, and Jack Donath, all of Iowa, hunted along the Trempealeau River in Buffalo County of Western Wisconsin. Power shot an 8-point, 200-pound buck at about 50 feet with a 52-pound osage bow. The shot was a direct front shot, the arrow entering the chest cavity. The buck traveled about 200 yards after the hit.

Jean Tritten, southern Representative on the Executive Board, now located in Salt Lake City, Utah, writes, "The Utah archers were successful in obtaining a bow and arrow reserve for this year in Wasatch Mountains, fifteen miles east of Salt Lake City . . . . Mr. Carl Weise donated his mountain cabin to the archers . . . . . Approximately fifteen men and one woman, my wife, used the cabin during the season. Twenty-seven archery licenses good for antlerless deer or bucks were sold for the area. Three deer were hit, none were brought into camp. I saw in the neighborhood of two hundred deer during the week. . . . . . In a short time the Utah Archery Association will hold a business meeting and banquet. We will endeavor to organize field archery at that time." Jean is one of our most active field archers and organizers. Utah is very fortunate to count Jean as one of its members. Field archery is in for a big increase in Utah.

We have had several requests for Art Young Big Game Awards from non-members. We regret that this coveted prize can be awarded only to members of the NFAA.

The NFAA is compiling information received from the game commissions of the various states and also the provinces of Canada on bow and arrow hunting laws and regulations. Much interesting information has been received. We thought that Arizona was the last state to legalize bow and arrow hunting. However, we find that in Florida game may be hunted with

(Continued on page 15)

Can't Get 'Em If You Can't See 'Em

By Roy Hoff

Thirty Southern California Archers to Stalk Game with Bow and Arrow!

Headlines in Los Angeles Times of recent date, that conjure up a mental picture of red-blooded sportsmen roaming through the woods in quest of elusive bucks, disdaining the idea of using a rifle, but giving their game a chance by hunting with a bow and arrow. What a feather in one's cap to be able to bag a deer with this type of weapon!

But they didn't get any!

So what? Everybody had a good time, with but few actually disappointed. We knew before we started that there were two strikes against us and if we brought back one buck we would have more than our share, according to past performances. But we came pretty close to knocking over a couple of beauties. IF - -

But let's start at the beginning. The hunt was the result of weeks of planning and preparation, with one thought in mind, that some time California nimrods may enjoy the privileges of an archery reserve. To gain that end the sport must have publicity and make friends with all sportsmen, whether they be rifle hunters or fishermen. Also the 1001 skeptics must be convinced that a bow and arrow is humane and capable of killing a deer.

On Friday evening, October 3, seven car loads of archers left Los Angeles for Tom's Place at Rock Creek, in Mono County of the High Sierras. Stopping at Mojave and Bishop en route, to gas up and have something to eat, delayed the caravan until it was 12:45 a.m. before we reached our destination, having traveled some 325 miles.

No one needed prompting to go to bed, as we had to be up at 4:30 a.m., with breakfast at 5:00, then a 15-mile jaunt to the cabin of Emmett Hayden, who was to be our guide.

At the Hayden cabin we found Mr. H. downing the last of a plate of scrambled eggs and bacon. Within a few minutes he was leading us over the windingest wood-roads, which were never meant for an automobile and over which it seemed impossible to travel without losing at least one fender. After about thirty minutes of skooting around windfalls and thru a maze of pine trees, our guide stopped at a sheer drop and announced we had reached the end of the line.

All archers piled out nearly simultaneously, stringing up their bows and taking a few warm-up shots at stumps and what not, all eager to get on with the hunt. Right here one of the boys, Max Stempel, had the rather unpleasant experience of having both limbs of his yew bow blow up on his second warm-up shot. Another bow was procured and away we went, fanning out into groups of two and three. All hunters had agreed to meet back at the starting point to report any evidences of game found.

Around ten o'clock the archers began to appear back at the starting point. All had about the same report to make: Plenty of fresh tracks but no game sighted—not even a doe. One of the last ones to return was Earl Mace, with a more startling report. Said Earl: "I sure hate to say it, but there is a 3-point buck running loose down the canyon with my broadhead sticking in his neck. When I saw him he was partly concealed by some pine trees, only his head and neck exposed, looking directly at me. When I 'drawed' down on him I just knew I wouldn't miss. I loosed the shaft and at the instant the arrow took flight he turned to dart into the trees. I saw the broadhead hit high up on the back of the neck, midway between the shoulders and horns."

Upon questioning, Earl admitted he had tried to track the buck but lost his trail in the pine needles.

A fine kettle of fish! A buck at large with an arrow sticking into him, the one thing that none of us wanted to see.

The whole gang immediately hiked down to the spot where the buck was last seen and took up the trail. We tracked him for perhaps a half mile

(Continued on page 8)

Editorial

SEASON'S BEST

We wish to make this a personal message to each of our archery friends in lieu of a greeting card at this time. The war already has darkened many a home, and the 1941 Christmas will not be a boisterously happy event. However, the true spirit of Christmas should not be forgotten, and the Christmas star should still lead the way to "Peace on earth; good will to men." Again we extend to all the season's greetings and hope that Christmas time may bring an inner joy that will help to carry us over the rough road that is inevitably ahead.

IF YOU CAN'T SEE 'EM
(Continued from page 7)

and found the bloody arrow near a big log where the deer had apparently stopped and brushed it out. We soon gave up the chase as all indications pointed to the fact the buck was not hurt much.

Upon examination of the arrow it was found the point was badly turned, and from the angle at which the shaft was loosed, it was evident that the point had merely creased the hide, probably traveling just below the skin to the base of the skull and lodging against the root of the horns. The latter accounts for the curl of the point. Had the arrow been an inch or two lower the buck would probably have dropped in his tracks.

During all the excitement, with everybody intent on following the buck tracks, we had strayed quite a distance from the cars with most everyone having a different idea of which way was back. Indeed, it was not until we had tramped for over two hours did we find the cars. The country all looks alike with the only view out being straight up.

The next day we decided to split up into smaller groups and go in different directions. Some were to hunt the high country around Inyo Crater Lakes, others to hunt in the neighborhood of Sherwin Lakes, while the rest would work the flat country along Laurel and Rock Creeks.

That evening the boys came in with about the same reports as the day before—a good many does sighted, but very few, if any, bucks. The most favorable report came from the group that hunted the lower elevations. Fifteen or twenty deer were jumped in sage brush, where they had bedded down. Two of the boys, Leo Sipe and Bennett Gandy, actually got shots at bucks.

Benny tells this story: "I was approaching a fairly deep sage brush covered canyon when I heard a rifle shot some distance up the canyon. I hurried over to the edge so I could see the canyon floor, thinking the rifleman might scare something down my way. Sure enough there was a three or four pointer racing down the canyon like the mill tails of h—. I drew back and loosed a shaft at a likely spot about 75 yards down hill and about 30 or 40 feet in front of Mr. Buck. For the next few seconds it was a race to see which would get there first, the deer or the arrow. Well, it was practically a dead heat. I led him perfectly, but just a little too much elevation. Leo took a shot at him as the deer passed below him but also missed."

Alas, just a couple of arrows lost and no meat on the table.

Many of you old timers will say we didn't go about it right. I for one am inclined to agree. The only way to hunt with a bow is to find a nice comfortable spot near a likely game crossing and sit there until the game comes to you. It is practically impossible to walk quietly enough to keep from frightening the deer.

NFAA Bulletin

OFFICERS

President—A. J. Michelson
610 F. P. Flint Bldg., Flint, Mich.

Vice-President—Paris B. Stockdale,
Univ. of Tenn., Knoxville, Tenn.

Secretary-Treasurer—John L. Yount,
Box 383, Redlands, California.

EXECUTIVE COMMITTEE

Western—H. C. MacQuarrie.
3400 Fruitvale Ave., Oakland, Calif.

Mid-Western—Fred Bear,
2611 W. Philadelphia, Detroit, Mich.

Eastern—T. C. Davidson,
53 Mountain Ave., Springfield, N. J.

By John L. Yount

Once again, how about those clippings? After my last request a number were sent in but lately you seem to have forgotten that the matter was ever brought up. It may be that my failure to acknowledge most of those sent in is the reason for this. If so, please remember there are hundreds of you and only one of me. If there is a question in your letter I try to answer it, but others I sometimes have to file without answering. I firmly believe the secretary should be supplied with a snappy blonde stenographer.

Another subject that we want to mention again is letters from the unsuccessful hunters. Big game applications accompanied by letters are still rolling in and there will be a full report on them next month; but this covers only one side of the picture. We want more letters from you boys who didn't make good. Quite often more can be learned from the fellows who came back empty handed than from the fellow with the game. The latter is apt to have his head too high in the clouds for a really accurate report of conditions.

We expect to have several new announcements ready for next month. Among them a "Twenty pin" award, somewhat like the target archers' perfect end pin. In the meantime we are going back to work on the handbook. The more we get done on this the better we think it is going to be. The fellows who have agreed to do the writing are real authorities on their subjects.

Defense Stamps as Prizes

Editor Ye Sylvan Archer:

It may be of interest to your readers to know that the Malibu Archery Club has adopted a resolution to dispense with the customary awarding of medals and trophies as prizes for their regular tournaments. The resolution provides that in the future, Defense Savings Stamps will be awarded in lieu of medals and trophies.

I believe our club has established a precedent in sporting circles that if mentioned in your columns would encourage other clubs to follow suit.

The names of the winners for this month's tournament follow:

Men—Leo Sipe, 1st; "Tiny" Munson, 2nd; Bill Otto, 3rd; Vincent Ruh, 4th.

Ladies—Frieda Hoff, 1st; Frankie Watts, 2nd; and Minerva Gandy, 3rd.

ROY HOFF,
President, Malibu Archery Club.

California Field Tournament

By Peter C. Ting, Berkeley, California

The California Field Archers held their second annual championship tournament on Sunday, October 26, at Fresno, California. All agree it was a great success, lasting from early Saturday eve 'til late Sunday night. The actual shooting was done between 8:30 A.M. and 5:00 P.M. Sunday — the rest of the time being devoted to what good fellows usually do when they get together.

This year's tournament was sponsored by the Northern California Field Archers Association, which is headed by President Tom L. Farnsworth. His committee, consisting of Jack Peters and M. E. Spansel, worked closely with John Yount of Redlands, and made plans to hold the tournament at Fresno, due to its central location in the state. Mr. Warren Moody of Fresno, with the help of other local archers, offered to lay out the course. A well arranged official course was laid out over comparatively level ground adjoining the Pine Lake Lodge four miles north of Fresno, on Highway 99. Although most of the California field archers prefer a course arranged over hilly country, with most of the shots up or down hill or across canyons, the arrangement of the Fresno course is excellent for large tournaments where a hundred or more archers, both men and women, must shoot around 56 targets in one day. There are good motel, banquet, and other facilities at the Pine Lake Lodge, where most of the participants stayed. The annual banquet and business meeting was held at 9:00 P. M. Saturday, so that those leaving San Francisco or Los Angeles Saturday afternoon could be on hand. There were fifty-eight present for the banquet, which was very good, considering the fact that it was raining that week-end over most of the state. (Sunny California!) As if requested by the field archers, Fresno was actually about the only city in the state to escape rain on Sunday. Tom Farnsworth acted as toastmaster, and amused the gathering by relating a recent dream of his in which Harold MacQuarrie was the leading man.

"Harold," according to Tom, "was teaching his art of salesmanship to a huge convention of archery dealers when someone in the back row broke up the party by announcing that John Yount, as secretary of the National Field Archery Association, was the all-time champion of archery salesmen (and Santa Claus to tackle makers) by his selling over three million dollars worth of memberships to the NFAA."

Numerous other after dinner speakers waxed fluently with inspired tongues, received in the little room adjoining the banquet hall. Jack Peters set forth the rules of the tournament, which were those of the NFAA, and Norton Lapkin, President of the San Francisco Archers, explained the "Twenty" pins donated by the Viking Archery Shop of San Francisco. This pin, first adopted by the San Francisco Archers, is awarded at the NCFAA shoots to any archer making four consecutive bulls-eyes (a perfect end) on any 18 or 24-inch target. Mr. Lapkin announced that should the NFAA care to adopt the "Twenty" pin as an official award, the dies of the pin would be presented to the association.

Harold MacQuarrie gave the report of the nominating committee and the following men were unanimously elected as the 1942 officers of the California State Field Archers Association: President, L. B. Garner, 345 Brown Street, Fresno; Northern Vice-President, M. E. Spansel, 1707 Grove Street, Berkeley; Southern Vice-President, Emery Watts, 551 W. Adams, Los Angeles; Secretary-Treasurer, J. W. Canfield, Santa Ana and Arthur Street, Fresno.

A committee on archery legislation was also appointed. California needs game reserves badly for its many bow and arrow hunters and it is hoped that these men from different parts of the state will through various ways facilitate the passing of such a bill. The committee members are as folows: John Yount, Box 383, Redlands; Harold MacQuarrie, 3400 Fruitvale Avenue, Oakland; Norton

Lapkin, 647 Masonic Avenue, San Francisco; Delmer Pletcher, 631 Magnolia Street, Bakersfield.

Eighty-three registered for the shoot, and to give you some idea of the competition, 45 out of the 66 men participating shot NFAA class "A" scores, and 7 of the 17 women also shot class "A". The Malibu Mountain Field Archers swept the field by winning all events except the novelty shoot. Phil Conrad shot the remarkable score of 711 to win the men's division. Minerva Gandy and Ruth Hathaway, both of Malibu, tied for first with 342, and were given duplicate awards of gold medals. However, they shot the tie off over a three target course and Minerva Gandy won by a margin of two points. Minerva was also first in the ladies' battle clout. Carl Seastrom, also from the Malibu club, won the junior division with the score of 327, which is a class "A" score, even in the men's division. Bill Holmes of the Sequoia Field Archers, of Oakland, placed second in the men's division with the excellent score of 691, just twenty points behind Phil Conrad. Dawson Feathers of the Sequoia club placed third with 643. Dawson also won the battle clout, which was the novelty event. Peggy Smith of Fresno was second in the ladies' division with 271, and Maxine Olson of Albany was third with a score of 263.

Mrs. Buddie Feathers and Mrs. Audrey Grubbs did a fine job of conducting the registration, and also helped with the awards. The Southern California group furnished the medals and the Northern California association furnished most of the merchandise prizes. The trophies awarded to the winners of the battle clout in both the men's and ladies' divisions are perpetual. As previously stated, the rules of the tournament were those used in the NFAA mail shoots except that no handicap was used and entrants did not shoot according to classification. Except in the junior division and battle clout, medals were awarded to the first three places. Fourth place winners were given a choice of the prizes. The rest of the merchandise prizes were awarded on a percentage basis, which was determined by dropping down to 90 per cent of the top score, then to 80 per cent of the top score, and so on. Prizes were donated by King-Moore Leather Goods Co., Earl Grubbs, Potter & MacQuarrie, Trueman's Archery Shop, Viking Archery Shop, Granat Brothers, and perhaps by numerous other archery dealers which were not called to the attention of the writer.

A more complete and detailed list of winners and runner-ups is as follows:

"Twenty" Pins (Perfect End)
Tom Lee .... San Francisco
Bill Holmes .... Sequoia Field Archers
Delmer Pletcher .... Bakersfield
C. W. Seastrom .... Malibu
Bill Holmes .... Sequoia

Battle Clout—Men
Dawson Feathers .... Sequoia

Battle Clout—Ladies
Minerva Gandy .... Malibu

Junior Division
Carl Seastrom, Malibu 327
Horace White, Fresno 265
Jack Garner, Fresno 181

Ladies' Division
Minerva Gandy, Malibu 342
Ruth Hathaway, Malibu 342
Peggy Smith, Fresno 271
Maxine Olson, Albany 263
Edith Smith, Albany 247
Ruth Davis, Malibu 245
Lillian Rice, Albany 211
Evelyn Pletcher, Bakersfield 186
Amanda Ting, Albany 178
Cecelia Stever, San Francisco 178

Men's Division
Phil Conrad, Malibu 711
Bill Holmes, Sequoia 691
Dawson Feathers, Sequoia 643
Delmer Pletcher, Bakersfield 622
M. D. Hathaway, Malibu 607
T. L. Farnsworth, Albany 594
Emery Watts, Los Angeles 579
Bob King, Los Angeles 554
M. E. Spansel, Albany 536
M. Anderson, Fresno 526
A. Smalley, Stockton 514
Bill Stever, San Francisco 514
Trueman Farnsworth, Albany 509
A. Gonzales, Bakersfield 470
Perzy High, Malibu 459
S. L. Sipe, Malibu 459
Fred Woodley, Fresno 450
Warren Moody, Fresno 444
C. S. Seastrom, Malibu 443
Marvin Compton, San Francisco 438
Peter C. Ting, Albany 435
Jack Young, Sequoia 429
B. Y. Smith, Albany 423
J. Renell Smith, Fresno 418
Harold MacQuarrie, Sequoia 412

8th NFAA Tournament Report

By Karl E. Palmatier, Mail Tournament Secretary

	Actual 28 Target Score	Actual 28 Target Score	Actual 56 Target Score	Handicap Score
CLASS "A"—MEN				
Delmer Pletcher, Bakersfield, Calif.	86-354	86-344	172-698	638
Ken Moore, Los Angeles, Calif.	63-241	66-254	129-495	635
S. Leo Sipe, Los Angeles, Calif.	62-242	52-206	114-448	608
Roy Hoff, Los Angeles, Calif.	65-245	59-221	124-466	596
Phil Conrad, Long Beach, Calif.	89-355	90-350	179-705	595
Carl Seastrom, W. Hollywood, Calif.	57-207	56-208	113-425	595
E. J. Woodward, Redlands, Calif.	58-220	65-255	123-475	585
Merle Hathaway, Los Angeles, Calif.	78-306	76-306	154-612	582
Perzy High, Los Angeles, Calif.	65-259	76-282	141-541	581
John Willard, Hollywood, Calif.	58-221	58-220	116-441	571
Alfonso Gonzales, Bakersfield, Calif.	70-272	69-283	139-555	570
Bennett Gandy, Los Angeles, Calif.	50-190	48-176	98-366	566
Willard Bacon, Fontana, Calif.	72-278	73-305	145-583	543
Kore Duryee, Seattle, Wash.	47-179	56-214	103-393	543
C. W. Seastrom, W. Hollywood, Calif.	55-217	47-181	102-398	528
Emery Watts, Los Angeles, Calif.	68-266	62-250	130-516	526
Fred Gadberry, Bakersfield, Calif.	66-252	64-234	130-486	526
Russell Berry, San Diego, Calif.	46-180	46-176	92-356	526
Kenneth Jones, Bakersfield, Calif.	66-272	59-233	125-505	525
Paul Ludwig, Los Angeles, Calif.	38-140	40-144	78-284	524
Earl Grubbs, Los Angeles, Calif.	50-182	43-168	93-350	520
Robert King, Los Angeles, Calif.	65-249	50-194	115-443	503
John Yount, Redlands, Calif.	38-140	44-164	82-304	464
Irl Stamps, Seattle, Wash.	52-192	56-218	108-410	450
Franklin Jones, Everett, Wash.	30-104	33-133	63-237	437
William Otto, Los Angeles, Calif.	38-138	48-180	86-318	428
William Horr, San Diego, Calif.	37-125	29-101	66-226	416
Walt Wilhelm, San Bernardino, Calif.	52-192	54-208	106-400	
Elmer Bedwell, San Bernardino, Cal.	39-139			
CLASS "B"—MEN				
W. C. Woolnough, Trenton, Mich.	34-108	50-197	84-305	
Tiny Munson, Los Angeles, Calif.	35-127	47-173	82-300	
Bert Wallis, Seattle, Wash.	34-126	42-158	76-284	
E. L. Holston, San diego, Calif.	28-88	33-125	61-213	
Angus Bruce, Redlands, Calif.	30-114	20-70	50-184	
Fred Brockhoff, Seattle, Wash.	42-140			
CLASS "C"—MEN				
Joe Monroe, Redlands, Calif.	29-103	39-147	68-250	
Harold Lusk, Seattle, Wash.	25-95	31-113	56-208	
W. B. Blackmore, Marysville, Wash.	27-93	22-82	49-175	
W. Harmon, Langley, Wash.	24-98	17-59	41-157	
Miland Elott, Seattle, Wash.	12-40	32-110	44-150	
William Irvin, Seattle, Wash.	22-76	22-74	44-150	
C. D. Cole, Seattle, Wash.	14-52	27-97	41-149	
Ed Tweeddale, Everett, Wash.	18-68	17-59	35-127	
Robert Blackmore, Marysville, Wash.	18-58	12-46	30-104	
CLASS "A"—LADIES				
Minerva Gandy, Los Angeles, Calif.	47-177	47-179	94-356	446
Ruth Davis, Bryn Mawr, Calif.	42-156	41-157	83-313	373
Frieda Hoff, Los Angeles, Calif.	35-128	30-112	65-240	350

December, 1941   YE SYLVAN ARCHER   13

	28 Target Score	28 Target Score	56 Target Score	Handicap Score
CLASS "A"—LADIES (Cont.)				
Gene Bacon, Fontana, Calif.	51-185	63-237	114-422	342
Eva Bedwell, San Bernardino, Calif.	46-170	51-183	97-353	313
Margaret King, Redlands, Calif.	33-117	29-109	62-226	306
Ruth Hathaway, Los Angeles, Calif.	39-137	45-155	84-292	282
CLASS "B"—LADIES				
Ann Lusk, Seattle, Wash.	16-56	27-99	43-155	
Blanche Wallis, Seattle, Wash.	8-26	10-32	18-58	
CLASS "C" LADIES				
Jane Duncan, Seattle, Wash.	9-31	11-39	20-70	
Valeria Irvin, Seattle, Wash.	5-19			

Harold Lusk and Joe Monroe will be in Class "B" for the next report.

HANDICAPS FOR THE NEXT TOURNAMENT

The following archers who shot in this tournament will have the following handicaps for the last tournament.

Gene Bacon -90	Franklin Jones 210	John Willard 120
Eva Bedwell -30	William Horr 200	Roy Hoff 100
Margaret King 100	Elmer Bedwell 180	Ken Moore 90
Frieda Hoff 100	Bennett Gandy 180	Robert King 80
Minerva Gandy 50	John Yount 170	E. J. Woodward 80
Ruth Davis 40	Earl Grubbs 170	Irl Stamps 50
Ruth Hathaway 10	Russell Berry 170	Fred Gadberry 40
Phil Conrad -120	Carl Seastrom 140	Perzy High 30
Delmer Pletcher -100	Kore Duryee 140	Kenneth Jones 20
Merle Hathaway -50	S. Leo Sipe 130	Emery Watts 20
Willard Bacon -40	William Otto 130	Alfonso Gonzales 00
Paul Ludwig 270	C. W. Seastrom 120	

At the present time there are 67 men and 21 women in Class "A," 41 men and 7 women in Class "B," and 39 men and 7 women in Class "C." 182 archers have participated in tournaments to date.

Ruth Davis of Bryn Mawr, California, John Yount of Redlands, California, and four archers from Bakersfield, California, Delmer Pletcher, Alfonso Gonzales, Kenneth Jones and Fred Gadberry, have shot in every meet to date. Such loyalty to their sport merits the praise of all archers.

Your mail tournament secretary must soon make a report to the officers of the NFAA. Each officer receives a copy of each report, but they will want to know what the archers wish to do. Will each of you who are interested in the mail tournaments, the work we have attempted to do—get the field archery round under way, and to educate the archers to the plan of the field layout and the rules—write your suggestions to me? We can increase our interest by knowing what will please you more. I know that the Christmas holiday season is at hand. I also know that we have but one more report. We must make our plans early in 1942. Please take a little time to drop me a line for my report.

A Merry Christmas and a Happy New Year to you all.

OHIO ARCHER HUNTS DEER

(Continued from page 4)
pains and turned one loose — and hit every * '/ £"? ! *? !* poplar between me and him. That arrow rattled down through there like an elephant going through a standing cornfield.

The deer took off like a shot, ran about 20 yards, stopped, turned and laughed at me, and trotted off for the swamp.

"How did I feel?" Wait till you miss one like that and you'll know. If I had shot in the opposite direction

I would have come twice as close.

I went back to the car, threw in the bow, took some shots where they would do the most good at a time like that, and headed for the clubhouse, looking neither to the right or to the left — I was afraid a buck would come out and attack me.

I stopped for some more shots before arriving at the clubhouse somewhat the worse for wear, or something. Most of the gang had beat me in and were eating venison. Les had had his deer butchered and we ate it Saturday night for dinner. I took some pictures of the gang eating which, surprisingly enough, turned out not so bad, considering the shape I was in. After eating I proceeded to finish the job I had started before dinner, and someone finally put me to bed. I partially recovered Sunday, and took off for home.

Now, "Mike" in his monthly column, "Blunts from the Old Stump," will probably give a statistical report of this hunt, so you can get details there. Up to the time I left, there were two deer killed in our group. Several others were reported killed in other parts of the state. Two hunters, hunting somewhere near us, were reported to have one buck. Neither were experienced archers. One had a bow made from green osage by his son in a manual training class, while the other had a bow of hickory, made from two pick handles. Boy, I am really rooting for him!

I want to give plenty of thanks to the Carters, who managed the place where we stayed. They really did treat us royally — and to Fred Bear for inviting me up, for I surely had a swell time. Those fellows in Michigan are surely a swell bunch of archers.

Final score: Saw about 300 deer, 25 to 35 bucks — two shots — two misses — no deer (oh, dear!) — one good time.

A wish: That I might gain the same philosophy that our President, "Mike" Michelson, has gained, for a man can't hunt deer for sixteen years without getting one, and not have found something better in the meantime. To all outward appearances he still maintains the same enthusiasm for hunting that he had initially.

Southern California Tournament
By Roy Hoff

Harking back to the year 1740 or thereabouts, when Jolly Rogers feasted in Sherwood Forest, after the day's hunt, was the setting and atmosphere of a novel banquet staged by the Redlands Archery Club Saturday night, November 22, as a prelude to the regular field tournament of Southern California Field Archers.

The dinner announcements aroused a good deal of curiosity and speculation, stating that all were to bring their hunting knives. When the 40 guests were seated around the banquet table, it was evident that those who failed to bring their knives would have to eat with their fingers, as the table was bare of dishes, knives or forks. The menu consisted of excellent beef stew, hot buttered beets, mustard greens, French bread and butter, served on large thin flapjacks, in lieu of plates. For drinks a barrel of burgundy wine, in the center of the table, was tapped from time to time. After the dinner the remainder of the evening was devoted to dancing and boasting of what good scores could be expected the following day.

Next day the weather was perfect, but why so many consistently low scores were turned in still remains a mystery. Not one score of 600 was recorded, in fact about all of the 50 or more archers shot around 100 points below par.

Perhaps some felt there was too much wine and dine the night before. This was not the case of Phil Conrad, who was one of those unable to attend the banquet, yet shot only 570 after turning in three previous consecutive tournament scores of over 700. Maybe it was the humidity—or something.

At the Board of Governors meeting it was decided to hold the next tournament at San Diego on the fourth Sunday in January.

A new Tyro class will be noted in the following list of scores, which elicited a great deal of favorable comment. This new classification was started with the thought towards giving those in the lower brackets a chance to win something.

The scores, with the name of the shooter and affiliated club, follow:
Championship Class—Men:
 Gold Bar—Willard Bacon
  (Pasadena) 583

Silver Bar—Phil Conrad (Malibu) 570
General Division—Men:
 Championship Medal—Ken Moore (Pasadena) 495
 Red Ribbon—E. J. Woodward (Redlands) 475
 White Ribbon—Emory Watts (Malibu) 464
Tyro Division—Men:
 First—R. C. King (Pasadena) .. 443
 Second—Victor Jensen (San Diego) 388
 Third—Roy Hoff (Malibu) 379
Championship Class—Women:
 Gold Bar—Gene Bacon (Pasadena) 422
 Silver Bar—Eva Bedwell (Redlands) 353
General Division—Women:
 Championship Medal—Minerva Gandy (Malibu) 307
 Red Ribbon—Little Glenn Curtis (Redlands) 254
 White Ribbon—Margaret King (Pasadena) 226
Tyro Division—Women:
 First—Frankie Watts (Malibu) 215
 Second—Amanda Conrad (Malibu) 104
 Third—Marilynn Monroe (Redlands) 91

BLUNTS FROM OLD STUMP

(Continued from page 6)

shot gun only, and that the bow is not recognized as a legal hunting weapon. Bow and arrow hunting is also illegal in North and South Dakota. Field archers in those states had better get busy. The compiled reports, with comments, will be published shortly, and copies will be furnished the game commissions of the various states and provinces. Fourteen states provide special seasons or areas for bow and arrow hunting. Game commissions of sixteen states are opposed to giving archers special seasons or areas. Eighteen states are noncommittal or are willing to be shown. British Columbia and Ontario have under consideration the granting of special areas or seasons for bow and arrow hunters. A little organized effort on the part of local archers can get them favorable hunting conditions. These statistics which your game commission will receive from the NFAA will open their eyes, and will be a tremendous stimulant to favorable action on your reasonable requests for better bow and arrow hunting conditions in your state.

Ivan F. Hutchens, Agent Burlington Transportation Company, Rapid City, South Dakota, is anxious to start a field club in that section of the state. Will South Dakota field archers please contact him?

The Rochester Archers of Rochester, New York, held their first field meet with an attendance of fifty-three. W. L. Young is Chairman of activities, and an increased field archery program is planned for next year.

The Framingham Archers of Massachusetts held their field meet on October 26. E. B. Kallander, President of the club, says, "All agree that this field archery course has a great deal of natural appeal. In my opinion, it is a better all-around test than the target shooting because, not only does it demand a good hold and release, but close estimate of distance. Then, too, the terrain is far more interesting."

The Paterson Long Bowmen of New Jersey held a field meet at the Garret Mountain Reserve. The NFAA field round was shot in the morning and the Pope-Young round was shot in the afternoon, all on animal targets. Forty-three archers representing nine clubs participated. Ralph W. King, publicity chairman, says, "The comments heard on the field were very favorable. The only adverse comments were that we were not going to have another shoot in the very near future." On the method of making the animal targets, he says, "While it might seem quite a task to draw pictures the right size and proportion for the different size targets, in fact it is rather easy. We gathered our pictures from children's painting books and traced or drew them on transparent paper. The drawings were then placed in a projector and thrown on a wall. The projector was moved forward and back until the picture would take the target. The target was then traced on the material with charcoal. It was painted in black paint."

The Executive Committee is considering establishing an award of a "perfect" button to be awarded to our members who make four "5's" on either the 16 or the 24-inch faces at NFAA recognized tournaments. This will be similar to the "6 golds" pin awarded by the NAA, although perhaps a little harder to make. In addition to the Big Game Award, the Executive Committee is considering the issuing of felt emblems about one and one-half inches square with the insignia of a bear, deer, or other big game that the archer has shot, which emblem he may wear on his field clothes or quiver. In recognition of the number of years in field shooting, we are also considering the issuance of small felt broadhead arrows in colors to indicate the number of years devoted to our sport. This will be an inspiration to novices, and some recognition to the old timers like ourselves, who just don't seem to be there when the medals are passed around. Official announcements will be made later.

We have received some unfavorable comment on newspaper pictures of big game with the arrows showing in the carcass. While location of hit and penetration are of interest to bow hunters from the statistical standpoint, the sight and thought of cold steel does offend the esthetic senses of many individuals. Could we not tell the story of the hunt by showing the hunter with his bow and quiver of arrows beside his game, and thus avoid some unfavorable comment and criticism of our sport?

We are gaining much knowledge on the effectiveness of the broadhead as a lethal weapon. A hit in the body cavity is almost certain to cause death although the animal may or may not be recovered, due to the distance traveled after being hit, and the difficulty of tracking. A hit well forward through the lungs results in quick death. With a hit in the rear part of the lungs or a paunch shot, the animal may travel many hundreds of yards and as much as a mile. Shots in the front or hind quarters are not fatal unless large blood vessels are severed, resulting in severe internal hemorrhage. We must recognize the fact that every hit with the arrow is not fatal. Wounded animals will be left in the woods from arrows as well as from rifle bullets or shot gun slugs, but an arrow wound has a reasonable chance to heal without the crippling effects of shattered bones caused by rifle bullets. Those who hunt with the bow should make every effort to improve their shooting accuracy. It will increase their chances of getting game, as well as reduce the number of wounded and unrecoverable animals. Practice on the official field round is what every bow hunter needs, as it simulates as nearly as possible shooting under actual hunting conditions. Very shortly the NFAA will publish detailed instructions on the technique of field shooting that has developed so many good field shots on the West Coast.

Please check expiration dates on your membership cards. Please send in your renewals without waiting for a delinquent notice. It will save the Secretary extra work and postage. Urge your field archer friends to let you send their dollars for membership and the year's subscription to "Ye Sylvan Archer." The NFAA membership makes a nice Xmas gift, too. There will be many interesting developments in field archery this coming year. Don't miss out on the Big Game Award, the NFAA year book, instructive articles on field shooting technique and equipment, hunting hints and stories, and many others.

The NFAA and Executive Committee extends to the field archers of America its season's greetings and appreciation for the past successful year of this association which you have made possible. With your continued cooperation we will look forward to a bigger and finer organization during the coming year.

SUBSCRIBERS PLEASE NOTICE

A cross appearing in this space means that your subscription has expired and we would appreciate your prompt renewal so that your name may be kept on our mailing list.

Paul H. Gordon
Author of "The New Archery"
Producing
Tackle — Materials
Latest and Finest for Field or Range
Write for Free Catalog
Beacon Hill Craftsmen
Beacon, N. Y.

Cassius Hayward Styles

BOWYER AND FLETCHER

—Tackle that has stood the test—

28 Vicente Place

BERKELEY, CALIFORNIA

PORT ORFORD CEDAR ARROW SHAFTS
(Cypressa Lawsonia)

Specials. P.O. Cedar Shafts, 1/4 to 11/32":
Parallel, per 100 .... $4.00
Tapered or barreled, 100 .. $4.50
Extra Select. Units segregated, per 100 .... $5.00
Douglas Fir, 100 .... $3.00, $3.50
Douglas Fir, Extra Select, per 100 .... $4.00

Full line finished tackle.
Raw Materials.
Write for price lists. Special rates to dealers and clubs.

PORT ORFORD ARCHERY SUPPLY CO.
C. F. Douglas, Mgr.
Box 137   Port Orford, Oregon

YEW WOOD STAVES
at .... $2.00 and $3.00
P. O. CEDAR SHAFTS
.... Doz., 40c; 100, $3.00
Try our new PLASTIC NOCK. It's just a little different and cheaper. The best nock on the market. Doz., 20c; 100, $1.50; 500, $5.00; 1000, $8.50. Five colors, 3 sizes.

Send money with order.

Monte Vista Archery Co.
Rt. 1, Box 149, Tacoma, Wash.

E. BUD PIERSON
Bowyer — Fletcher

Tournament Tackle, Sinew, Glue, Raw Materials.
Custom Made Tackle
3109 Burnet Ave. — Cincinnati, Ohio

HE'S YOURS WITH A BEN PEARSON BROADHEAD

Port Orford Cedar Broadhead Arrows — Matched within 15 grains. No great variation in spine. Plastic nocks. 5 1-2 in. hunting feathers. Choice of 3 sizes. Spined to match bow, any length. Dozen $6.00
Port Orford Cedar Blunts and Roving Arrows—Same fletching and specifications as broadheads. Blunt steel points or parallel steel pyles. Dozen $4.50
Birch at same prices.

SEE YOUR DEALER TODAY
or write for
Free Illustrated Catalogue

BEN PEARSON
INCORPORATED
PINE BLUFF, ARKANSAS

PINE BLUFF, ARK.

KING ★ MOORE
LEATHER GOODS COMPANY

7011 N. Figueroa St.
LOS ANGELES, CALIF.

Write today for **FREE CATALOG**

CHANDLER
Universal Broadheads

The Broadhead that costs less than a big rifle bullet, from 5c to 8-1/3c each. The inexpensive Broadhead for hunting.

Also Universal Broadhead Kits, with complete material for making one doz., good Broadhead Arrows.

Also Hunting, Fishing and roving Points.
FREE CATALOGUE
T. B. CHANDLER
11819 4th Ave., Compton, Calif.

FISH HEAD

B-80　　　　B-1

APPROVED NFAA FIELD TARGET FACES

Printed in black and white on heavy, double thickness corrugated board. In sets containing sizes necessary for a 14-target course and including extras of the smaller sizes that shoot out fastest.

$2.25 per set, f.o.b. Detroit — Order two sets for a 28-target course

BEAR ARCHERY CO.
2611 W. Philadelphia Ave., Detroit, Michigan

The Flat Bow—70 pages of Archery information for 50 cents, well illustrated. *Ye Sylvan Archer, 505 N. 11th St., Corvallis, Oregon.*

G
"THE MARK OF DISTINCTION IN ARCHERY TACKLE

Fine Yew Target and Hunting Bows, Plain or Backed with Rawhide. Lemonwood Bows with Rawhide Backs.
College and School Equipment
Target, Hunting and Roving Arrows
Price List on Request
Wholesale — Retail
EARL GRUBBS
5518 W. Adams
Los Angeles, : California

VIKING ARCHERY
1874 Market Street
San Francisco, Calif.

BOWS · ARROWS · MATERIALS

HANDBOOK—How to Make and Use Bows and Arrows—90 Pages well illustrated (with catalog) 35c.

CATALOG—100 pictures—color spread—Instruction Folder. 10c.

CATALOG alone 5c. Stamps or Coin.

L. E. STEMMLER · QUEENS VILLAGE · N.Y.

Please mention Ye Sylvan Archer when writing advertisers.